THE PORTABLE JOHN ADAMS

JOHN ADAMS, the successor to George Washington and the second president of the United States, came as close as any American political leader to fulfilling Plato's wish to see a philosopher in power. Having entered Harvard College at age fifteen, Adams studied Latin and Greek and classical political philosophy as well as science and religion. Years before the Declaration of Independence, Adams made the case for America's breaking away from England. In addition to carrying on a rich correspondence with his wife, Abigail, Adams wrote numerous texts defending the American system of government against its European critics. His thoughts express a prescient postmodern awareness that power will remain a presence even with the advent of democracy and that the purpose of government is to provide the mechanism to control it. He was also prescient in his sociopsychological understanding of human nature and its irrational passions. These insights aided him as a diplomat in Paris negotiating the Treaty of 1783, which ended the war with England.

JOHN PATRICK DIGGINS is Distinguished Professor of History at the Graduate Center, City University of New York. He is the author of *John Adams,* in a new series on the American presidents, edited by Arthur Schlesinger, Jr. He has taught at the University of California, Irvine, Princeton University, Cambridge University, and the Sorbonne. Among his recent books are *On Hallowed Ground: Abraham Lincoln and the Foundation of American History, Max Weber: Politics and the Spirit of Tragedy, The Promise of Pragmatism, The Lost Soul of American Politics,* and the forthcoming *Desire Under Democracy: Eugene O'Neill's America.*

The Portable John Adams

Edited with an introduction by
JOHN PATRICK DIGGINS

PENGUIN BOOKS

PENGUIN BOOKS

Published by the Penguin Group

Penguin Group (USA) Inc., 375 Hudson Street, New York, New York 10014, U.S.A.

Penguin Group (Canada), 90 Eglinton Avenue East, Suite 700, Toronto,
Ontario, Canada M4P 2Y3 (a division of Pearson Penguin Canada Inc.)

Penguin Books Ltd, 80 Strand, London WC2R 0RL, England

Penguin Ireland, 25 St Stephen's Green, Dublin 2, Ireland (a division of Penguin Books Ltd)

Penguin Group (Australia), 250 Camberwell Road, Camberwell,
Victoria 3124, Australia (a division of Pearson Australia Group Pty Ltd)

Penguin Books India Pvt Ltd, 11 Community Centre, Panchsheel Park,
New Delhi – 110 017, India

Penguin Group (NZ), 67 Apollo Drive, Rosedale, North Shore 0632, New Zealand
(a division of Pearson New Zealand Ltd)

Penguin Books (South Africa) (Pty) Ltd, 24 Sturdee Avenue,
Rosebank, Johannesburg 2196, South Africa

Penguin Books Ltd, Registered Offices:
80 Strand, London WC2R 0RL, England

First published in Penguin Books 2004

3   5   7   9   10   8   6   4

Copyright © Penguin Group (USA) Inc., 2004
All rights reserved.

LIBRARY OF CONGRESS CATALOGING-IN-PUBLICATION DATA
Adams, John 1735–1826.
The portable John Adams / edited by John Patrick Diggins.
p.   cm.
Includes bibliographical references (p.   )
ISBN 978-0-14-243778-0
1. Adams, John, 1735–1826—Political and social views.   2. United States—Politics and government—
1775–1783.   3. United States—Politics and government—1783–1865.   4. Adams, John, 1735–1826—
Diaries.   5. Adams, John, 1735–1826—Correspondence.   I. Diggins, John P.   II. Title.
E302.A262 2004
973.4'4'092—dc22   2003065564

Printed in the United States of America
Set in Adobe Sabon

Contents

Introduction

The men who create power make an indispensable contribution to the nation's greatness, but the men who question power make a contribution just as indispensable, especially when that questioning is disinterested, for they determine whether we use power or power uses us.

—President John F. Kennedy, 1963

Power must be opposed to power, force to force, strength to strength, interest to interest, as well as reason to reason, eloquence to eloquence, and passion to passion.

—John Adams, 1787

A PRESIDENT OF THE PEN

John Adams, the successor to George Washington and the second president of the United States, was the one chief executive in American history whose reflections are more important than his actions and whose philosophical writings are more significant than his political accomplishments. A political philosopher steeped in the classics, he was a president of the pen, one who regarded writing as tantamount to thinking. "A pen is certainly an excellent instrument to fix a man's attention and to inflame his ambition," he observed. So voluminous were his writings, often composed at the pitch of passion, that he once exclaimed: "My hand is impatient of the pen and longs to throw it down."

Adams's friends, colleagues, and political opponents could

count on long letters, some written during a storm on the high seas crossing the Atlantic on his way to a diplomatic post. Easily provoked, Adams usually wrote in response to the published ideas of another author. The slightest observation by Thomas Jefferson brought forth a flow of arguments and counter-thoughts from Adams, and from French criticisms of America's constitutional system, state and national, came a four-volume treatise defending it. Mercy Otis Warren, his old friend, and an even closer friend to his wife, Abigail, couldn't believe that the former president would explode in numerous letters to her in response to the few comments about him in her history of the American Revolution. The sustained "rancor" of Adams's letters exhausted Warren, who wondered what could possibly have led him to erupt so angrily.

The explanation is simple. Like so many others, Warren completely misunderstood what Adams was analyzing and proposing in his formal texts in political philosophy, controversial writings published before he became president. Jefferson and the French critics also misunderstood Adams, and so do some contemporary historians and readers. Adams stood accused of being a closet monarchist, an elitist who had allowed himself to be seduced by the trappings of royalty. Jefferson believed Adams had been thus seduced after the Revolution, when he served in London as minister to the Court of St. James's and met King George III and supposedly fell under the spell of "kingly authority."

But years earlier, after the American Revolution had started, Jefferson could hardly doubt Adams's passionate commitment to republicanism and opposition to monarchism. At the Continental Congress in the summer of 1776, members debated if America should declare itself separate from England. Jefferson, who had little talent for oratory, could never forget Adams standing up to make a speech. He started with "deep conceptions and nervous style," moving forward with "the force of his arguments and the boldness of his patriotism," taking to the floor as "the colossus of independence," giving such "power of thought and expression which moved the members from their seats."

But that occasion was the one instance in Adams's vast political career when he chose to refrain from writing. The subject at hand, on July 2, 1776, was the drafting of the Declaration of Independence:

Jefferson proposed to me to make the draught. I said, "I will not."

"You should do it."

"Oh! no."

"Why will you not? You ought to do it."

"I will not."

"Why?"

"Reasons enough."

"What can be your reasons?"

"Reason first—you are a Virginian, and a Virginian ought to appear at the head of this business. Reason second—I am obnoxious, suspected, unpopular. You are very much otherwise. Reason third—you can write ten times better than I can."

It is interesting to speculate what the Declaration of Independence would be like had Adams composed it. No doubt it would be a more legalistic document with Adams citing English political philosophers to make the case against England on its own constitutional grounds. If government is based upon an original social contract, freely entered into by the people, then the colonies have the right to withdraw once government passes legislation violating their wishes and hence is no longer based on the consent of the governed. Adams could well have used the expression "life, liberty, and the pursuit of happiness," but might he have added that to be happy, one must be free and then possibly made some reference toward slavery, of which he was critical? No doubt southern members of the Congress would have opposed any such reference, but Adams was not one to compromise. In Adams's version there might not have been any mention of nature's "self-evident" truths or the idea that "all men are created equal." While he saw human abilities and talents distributed too diversely to believe in natural equality, he did believe in the inalienable right of all people to equality

before the law and in the eyes of God. In today's political culture, the Constitution's provision for the "equal protection of
the laws" has helped to forge civil rights, the women's movement, and other contemporary causes. What Jefferson meant
by "created equal" was the idea, derived from the philosopher
John Locke, that in the state of nature all people are born equal
in that no one is authorized by nature or God to dominate others. But the Declaration by itself could only announce the principles of liberty and equality. It took the U.S. Constitution,
which Adams defended, to realize and protect such principles.

Jefferson was chosen to write the Declaration because of
his reputation for unsurpassed felicity in dealing with popular
ideas. The preamble of the Declaration is a statement of beauty,
but then the document trails off into a series of complaints and
grievances and begins to read like a text in victimology, as
though the colonists' quarrel were with the king instead of Parliament. That the colonists were about to be taxed concerned
Adams less than being told, in effect, to pay up and shut up.
Long before the Declaration, Adams had already given Americans the reasons why they had a right to speak up and be lis-
tened to. No doubt Jefferson was a better writer than Adams,
but the question remains: Was not Adams the better thinker?

The political philosophy that John Adams expounded, in a series of penetrating ideas about liberty, power, virtue, reason,
and human motivation, directly relates to his mind and tem-
perament and to his political career. He believed deeply in liberty and saw himself acting virtuously as he dedicated his life to
the public good. Yet as much as he craved recognition and distinction, and projected such desires onto all humanity, and as
much as he himself was moved by "the spur of fame," such
passionate objectives eluded the second president of the United
States. Even on inauguration day, March 4, 1797, he still felt
himself to be under the shadow of the outgoing president,
George Washington. No one doubted Adams's integrity, and he
was often called Honest John Adams, but fame and glory went
to the general who had led the country to victory. During the
inauguration all eyes were on the tall, imposing Washington,

while the audience almost forgot about the little man who was about to be sworn in. Adams wrote to his Abigail about the incident: "He [Washington] seemed to enjoy a triumph over me. Methought I heard him say: 'Ay, I am fairly out, and you are fairly in! See which one of us will be the happiest!'"

Two words commonly used to describe John Adams are "lovable" and "impossible." His contemporaries, and many scholars today, find in him a rare character, almost transparent in his candidness and forthrightness. He is perhaps the one president who cannot be called a politician with a cunning for politics, once defined by Abraham Lincoln as "this incessant human wriggle and struggle for office, which is a way to live without work." Historians regard Lincoln as America's greatest president, but it is curious that he never gave a speech or wrote an essay calling upon young Americans to enter politics as a noble vocation. A half century after Lincoln, Theodore Roosevelt would so call upon Americans, especially college graduates, the one group he believed he could count on to take politics away from the politicians. A century earlier, in Adams's era, "politik" was a term of opprobrium, and American leaders generally regarded themselves as statesmen or elected representatives of the people. Adams was, and still is, revered for his integrity and his occasional self-doubt and humility. But he also frustrates those who wish he had behaved less stubbornly and conducted himself more pragmatically as president. If he had done so, the young Republic might have been able to relax a bit and enjoy what Thomas Jefferson immortalized as the "pursuit of happiness," while Adams himself might have enjoyed a few minutes of fame. But unlike the Virginian Jefferson, Adams hailed from New England and its Calvinist legacy. He was perhaps the first and last Puritan in American politics, one who believed in duty, responsibility, and the striving for moral excellence.

JOHN, ABIGAIL, JOHN QUINCY

John Adams was born on October 30, 1735, the fourth generation of the first Adams settler, Henry, of yeoman stock from
a manor in Somerset County, England. A third-generation de-
scendant of Henry's, John Adams, Sr., had married Susanna
Boylston of a family prominent in science and medicine. It was
a marriage that combined different gene traits. The Boylstons
had culture and learning, while the senior Adams was a small
farmer and the village cobbler in Braintree (later named Quincy),
Massachusetts. Their son was to join the erudition on his
mother's side of the family with his father's humble notions of
equality and fairness.

At the age of fifteen, Adams entered Harvard at a time when
the college ranked students according to social standing; he
was fourteenth in a class of twenty-four. As indicated in the se-
lections from his diary, Adams's college years were unfocused
and restless; he was a conscience-struck Puritan who found he
could seldom buckle down to hard study. Many classes consisted in copying word for word what was said by the professors or conveyed in texts. Appropriate recitation rather than
critical inquiry seemed to be the way to success. But in later life
Adams would manage both, as he copied at length passages
from political philosophers and then subjected their ideas to his
severe scrutiny.

Adams graduated from Harvard in 1755 and taught school
at Worcester while making up his mind to become either a minister or a lawyer. He lost interest in the former occupation the
more he thought about the pessimistic doctrines of Calvinism
and the hindrances facing clergy who sought to teach with an
open mind. He decided to study law, and in 1758 he was presented for admission to the Boston bar. He would handle routine legal cases while taking an interest in local civic issues,
such as rowdy town taverns, for which he advocated strict licens-
ing. For Adams good laws would be the answer to bad morals.
But the practice of law put Adams in touch with those who
lived on its fringes, and he warned himself against *la dolce vita*:

Let virtue address me: "Which, dear youth, will you prefer, a life of effeminacy, indolence and obscurity, or a life of industry, temperance and honor? Take my advice; rise and mount your horse by the morning's dawn, and shake away, amidst the great and beautiful scenes of nature that appear at that time of day, all the crudities that are left in your stomach, and all the obstructions that are left in your brains. Then return to your studies, and bend your whole soul to the institutes of the law and the reports of cases that have been adjudged by the rules in the institutes; let no trifling diversion, or amusement, or company, decoy you from your book; that is, let no girl, no gun, no cards, no flutes, no violin, no dress, no tobacco, no laziness. . . .

(By the way, laziness, languor, inattention are my bane. I am too happy to rise early and make a fire; and when my fire is made, at ten o'clock my passion for knowledge, fame, fortune, for any good, is too languid to make me apply with spirit to my books, and by reason of my inattention, my mind is liable to be called off from law by a girl, a pipe, a poem, a love-letter, a Spectator, a play, &c. &c.)

A young woman did win out. In 1764 Adams married Abigail Smith, the daughter of the prominent Reverend William and Elizabeth Quincy Smith of Weymouth. It was perhaps the happiest and most fulfilling of all the presidential marriages, lasting more than a half century and producing four children; one, John Quincy Adams, became the sixth president. Although one of the sons drank himself to death, the two surviving boys and a girl, Abigail, nicknamed Nabby, produced a bevy of grandchildren that the former president enjoyed in later life. Abigail was bright, witty, an accomplished letter writer, the wife of one president and the mother of another, although she passed away years before her son took office in 1825. The correspondence between Abigail and John testifies to a relationship rich in personal affection and intellectual stimulation. Her moments of humor and gaiety often rescued Adams from his darker moods.

While General Washington led America to victory in the Revolution, Adams, an astute, hardworking diplomat, made the war financially and diplomatically possible by securing loans and recognition in Europe. After the war he was the first American to be presented at the Court of St. James's. During the many years Adams served abroad or in the nation's capital as vice president and president, wife Abigail often remained in Quincy for budgetary or health reasons; the two kept in touch through a rich correspondence. Abigail died in 1818, and Adams survived her by eight years, living to see his son sworn into office as president.

John Adams and son John Quincy had one thing in common. They were the only presidents of the founding generation to serve just a single term in office, and each made a better name in history either before and after serving as president, or perhaps both before and after. Before entering the White House, the son drafted the Monroe Doctrine, one of the most significant documents in American foreign policy, which established the Western Hemisphere as America's sphere of interest. Historians regard John Quincy Adams as the greatest secretary of state in American history. After serving as president, he became active in the struggle against slavery as a congressman from Massachusetts, fighting against the gag rule, which forbade bringing up the subject of slavery, and defending escaped African slaves in the *Amistad* case in 1841.

Similarly, the father made his name primarily in his prepresidential years when he wrote texts defending the American cause of liberty against the British colonial system and again when he served on a diplomatic mission to France, where he, Ben Franklin, and John Jay drafted the Paris Treaty of 1783, which ended the Revolutionary War on terms favorable to America. John Adams also wrote his controversial texts on political philosophy when just elected vice president in 1788.

The first situation confronting Adams as president in 1797 was France, a country that by then had had its own revolution and was looking to America to support it as France had once supported America during its ordeal with England. But Adams's Federalist party saw the American and French revolutions as distinct, and the treaty once made between the two countries was now regarded as abrogated, since America had been allied with a monarchist regime that no longer existed. The delicate subject of relations with France and the meaning and significance of the French Revolution divided America down the middle, separating the northern-based Federalists from the Virginian Republicans. During Adams's four years in office America was in an undeclared war with France on the high seas, called the Quasi War. Both England and France, who were at war with each other, seized American ships and impressed sailors. As president Adams authorized the development of the American navy, which outfought the French in numerous encounters in the West Indies and elsewhere. Notwithstanding the afterglow of the eighteenth-century Enlightenment, often called the Age of Reason, Adams knew that in international relations the faculty of reason would be less impressive than the force of cannon power.

Aside from the naval skirmishes with the French Navy, Adams's presidency was noneventful, with the exception of the controversial Alien and Sedition Acts, passed in 1798. In part this infamous body of legislation, which prohibited certain expressions of political opinion as libelous and threatened to export aliens for seditious activities, grew out of a heated political climate of the late 1790s that involved embittered newspaper wars and scores of French and Irish immigrants whose loyalties were with the French Revolution and the Jeffersonian Republicans. A few of the more incendiary journalists spent a short time in jail, but for the most part Adams's heart was not in the acts, which went unenforced and were rescinded when he left office in 1800. In his early writings at the time of the Revolution and later in his defense of the Constitution, Adams remained an ardent defender of free speech and freedom of the press. Still, his view of human nature could be skeptical enough to render him cautious about absolute, unrestrained freedom, whether of opinion or action. "Philosophers, theologians, legislatures, politicians, and moralists," Adams judged, "will find the regulation of the press is the most difficult, dangerous, and important problem they will have to solve." At the heart of Adams's political philosophy inheres a perplexing question: If democracy is defined as self-government, can the self be trusted to govern itself? With Adams there appears almost to be two answers, yes and no, depending on the era in which his thoughts were expressed.

During the struggle against England in the early 1770s, John Adams appeared as a young rebel on the radical left, resisting illegitimate power and defending the right of revolution and the possibility of self-government. In the late 1780s, during the development of the new U.S. Constitution and the outbreak of the French Revolution shortly afterward, Adams appeared as an older man on the conservative right, more concerned about defending property rights and valuing social order and less convinced of the prospect of self-government without checks. Over a period of time the thinker who espoused the imperative of liberty became the thinker who advocated the necessity of control. One thinks of the adage "Those who are not radical while young have no heart; those who are not conservative when old have no head." Yet with Adams the shifting thoughts had little to do with different ages as much as with the different situations he had to face. Revolution called for one form of thinking; the Constitution another. That Adams could advocate the right of revolution and then proceed to ask Americans to obey the new national government made it seem that he had betrayed the Spirit of '76.

CONSISTENCY AND CHANGE

Yet to dramatize the various Adamses thinking differently in different circumstances obscures the consistency of his political philosophy. For in some respects there was as much continuity as change in his thinking. The first essays he wrote, at the age of twenty-eight, dealt with the emotions of revenge and self-delusion. In his early years as a schoolteacher, before he studied law, Adams had been curious about motivation—that is, the causes of human conduct, what in the eighteenth century were called the springs of action. He wondered what it is that moves people to act, why they do so, and if their own explanations can be regarded as reliable. Might not language be used to justify behavior rather than explain it? Endowed with the right to free speech as we are, it may be that speaking enables us to hide our thoughts as much as to express them. Recall that Jefferson asked Adams for his "reasons" in choosing not to write the Declaration, and Adams replied with three. But are reasons causes? Such questions, more in the nature of psychology, remained with Adams when he later turned to studying political philosophy. In the Enlightenment's Age of Reason, did human beings really reason or did they rationalize and so deceive themselves? That question remains as important today as it was in the eighteenth century, and Adams was one of the first thinkers to probe its depths.

Adams's thinking did indeed change, though it was not a matter of his growing a few years older or finding himself reasoning in changing circumstances. Actually, America disappointed Adams. At the time of the Declaration of Independence, Adams wrote Abigail convinced that the fulfillment of its ideals depended on the behavior of the colonists during the War for Independence, "the times that try man's soul," as Thomas Paine put it. Adams hoped that the Revolution would demonstrate the character and moral qualities of the American people. Facing England, the greatest military power in the world, America had the opportunity to prove itself on the field of battle in nothing less than a test of virtue.

The Revolution turned out to be a long war, from 1775 to 1783, and before Washington's encouraging military victories, America suffered several defeats. According to Adams, only one-third of Americans fully supported the Revolution, one-third opposed it, and one-third remained indifferent. During the war there were some desertions from the army, and a few merchants traded with the enemy. Although those who fought did so with honor and courage, Adams would have found it hard to say what Winston Churchill said of the British people standing up to Nazi Germany in 1940: "This was our finest hour."

If the American Revolution brought out the best in many people, it also brought out the worst in some. Adams's disillusionment expressed itself in a scene he recalled after the Declaration of Independence had been proclaimed. Near his house he encountered on the road a "horse jockey," a town deadbeat, in debt and in trouble with the authorities:

> He was always in the Law, and has been sued in many actions, at almost every court. As soon as he saw me, he came up to me, and his first Salutation to me was "Oh! Mr. Adams what great things have you and your colleagues done for us! We can never be grateful enough for you. There are no Courts of Justice now in this Province, and I hope there never will be another!" . . . Is this the Object for which I have been contending? said I to myself, for I rode along without any answer to this Wretch. Are these the Sentiments of such a People? And how many of them are there in the Country? Half the Nation for what I know: for half the Nation are debtors if not more, and these have been in all Countries the Sentiments of debtors. If the Power of the Country should get into such hands, and there is great danger that it will, to what purpose have we sacrificed our Time, health and every Thing else? Surely we must guard against this Spirit and these Principles or we shall repent of all our Conduct. However the good Sense and Integrity of the Majority of the great Body of the People, came into my thoughts for my relief, and the last resources was after all in a good Providence. How much reason there was for these melancholy reflections, the subsequent times have too fully shewn.

Typically, Adams remained ambivalent about the character of people upon whom a republican government depends. After the Revolution the "day of the debtor" did take place in Massachusetts, Rhode Island, and elsewhere, and Shay's Rebellion suggested the stirring of class warfare as people took over state legislatures and began issuing cheap currency and passing laws against mortgage foreclosures. At the time of the Constitution, in 1787–1788, Adams, even though in England, had further reasons for "melancholy reflections."

In the readings collected in this volume there could well appear to be three John Adamses: the cautious optimist of the prerevolutionary years, 1765–1778; the profound skeptic of the constitutional era, 1787–1790; and the rather grumpy, ruminating, sardonic wise man of his later postpresidential years, 1810–1826. Adams proceeded from revolutionary idealism to constitutional pessimism, then to the cynicism of a former leader and statesman who once had had high hopes for America only to become bitterly disappointed with the ways of the country's politics. Convinced that American politics lacked all conviction, that seeking and holding office required little more than scheming and manipulation, Adams foresaw government's coming to depend upon appearance rather than on wisdom. In a letter to his grandsons in 1811, he wrote that he would rather see them "worthy shoemakers than secretary of states or treasury acquired by libels in newspapers." Adams was referring to former secretary of state Jefferson and former treasury secretary Alexander Hamilton, both of whom had used the press to libel him as an allegedly incompetent and distrustful president. Adams's most important thoughts and reflections were expressed both before he was president and afterward, the former in several volumes of writings, the latter in a body of rich correspondence. To proceed through Adams's political ideas, we can begin with what may seem to be a simple question: Whence springs authority?

CHRISTIANITY AND CLASSICAL REPUBLICANISM

Throughout history political philosophers have addressed that question. They seek to know what makes social order possible and what bestows legitimacy on a given regime. Often philosophers could be divided between different orientations, called the Ancients and the Moderns, one group looking to the past, the other to the present and future. Which perspective did Adams look to in order to find the basis of authority in America?

One traditional source of authority was the two thousand years of Christianity. Much of Christian religion involved the idea of original sin, salvation of the soul, the Bible and the teachings of Jesus, weakness of the will and temptations of the flesh, and, often overlooked today, suspicion of wealth. Adams was far from prudish about sex, and he saw wealth and prosperity as inevitable. He believed the Bible contained important moral truths, such as "Love thy neighbor," and he valued whatever sources emphasized duties as well as rights. But institutionalized Christianity, with its dogmatic creeds, obedient priests, false miracles, authoritarian councils, and other repressive tendencies, had little appeal for him. One of his earliest writings was *A Dissertation on Canon and Feudal Law,* in which he attempted to show the colonists why they were fortunate to have escaped both doctrines. One referred to the rule of the church; the other to the rule of the state. Neither endowed people with rights, and thus, Adams advised, such laws should be left to the Middle Ages, where they belonged. Adams was proud to point out that the Puritans had broken away from both feudal and canon teachings with all their inequalities and commands of obedience. He quoted Jean-Jacques Rousseau's description of feudal law as "that most iniquitous and absurd form of government by which human nature was so shamefully degraded." Along with the later philosopher Friedrich Nietzsche, Adams came close to claiming that ancient Christianity represented a "slave morality" that had people believing that as long as they remained poor, they were sure of entering the gates of heaven—after they had been fed to the lions. But Adams knew Americans were going to become rich, and religion, while worthwhile, could not be counted upon to direct the citizen toward the good, true, and virtuous.

A second historical source of authority was classical republicanism, which had its origins in the philosophy of Aristotle, was fructified in the writings of Machiavelli, and then found expression in certain aspects of the eighteenth-century Enlightenment. Republicanism has recently enjoyed a revival in scholarship in intellectual history and political philosophy. Whereas Christianity was a theology of submission, republicanism was a philosophy of assertion. It emphasized the importance of the civic virtues, active participatory involvement in public life, fear of ease and corruption, and a periodic return to the "first principles" on which a republic was founded. Republicanism did share one idea with Christianity, a distrust of wealth and of the rise of commerce and trade. Christianity taught that an excess of money deflects the true spiritual purposes of life, while republicanism taught that wealth renders a political regime decadent and unable to avoid its inevitable decline and fall.

Karl Marx was eight years old when John Adams died in 1826, but within a short time the German philosopher offered a third way out of commerce and its corruptions. If Christianity kept people responsible by instilling worry about the state of their souls, and republicanism had citizens worrying about the health of the body politic, Marxism taught the masses that there was nothing to worry about at all. The stages of economic development will bring forth the end of "prehistory" and issue in a world free of private property, competition, and selfish striving. Marx chided a Western world haunted by the "specter of communism," and he confidently assumed that the rise of class consciousness would rid the world of capitalism. But Adams, who saw how "emulation" would frustrate class consciousness, also saw that the specter haunting the world was commercialism and its "gangrene of greed," and he presaged some of our postmodern thinkers by grasping that there would be no challenge to capitalism (a term that did not exist in his era), no dialectical negation of the existing order, no stage beyond modern liberalism. This, Adams could well have said of bourgeois society, is as good as it gets.

Today in China the impulse of capitalism has sprung forth from the institution of communism, and the wealthy classes are not content with enjoying their ability to buy and consume. Instead they must do so conspicuously and display their riches before a camera. "To get rich," exhorted the Communist leader Deng Xiaoping, "is glorious." In the world we find ourselves in today, communism can no more extirpate egotism than could Christianity or classical republicanism. Two centuries ago John Adams warned us of this human predicament.

THE FRENCH REVOLUTION

Adams's warnings took place in the context of the French Revolution, or even preceded it, since in some respects he predicted the disastrous outcome of the Revolution before it broke out in the summer of 1789. In the United States the leading champions of the French Revolution were Thomas Paine and Thomas Jefferson. Earlier, at the time of the American Revolution, the two had joined Adams in common cause against England. With impressive erudition, Adams had defended America in his treatise *Novanglus* (the name is Latin for "New England"). The series of essays, published in a newspaper in 1774–1775, aimed to deny the loyalist argument that the authority of the British Parliament extended to the colonies in the same way it extended to Ireland and Wales. On the contrary, Adams argued, the American territory had not been conquered by England but had been discovered and settled by the colonists, with the permission of the king. Moreover, when subjects departed from the royal realm, they carried with them "all the rights of nature," the rights with which people are born and from which they cannot be alienated. At the Revolution, Adams, Paine, and Jefferson had stood together, upholding the rights of the colonists against the intrusions of government.

But a decade after the American Revolution, Adams began writing treatises in defense of government and the necessity of its controlling mechanisms. He argued for the importance of a strong executive branch, which some colonists feared as the "foetus of monarchy," and for an upper-house Senate, which suggested the rule of aristocracy. When Paine published his *The Rights of Man* (1791) in enthusiastic support of the French Revolution, Jefferson wrote him a comment and sent it along with his copy of the book to a Philadelphia printer. The letter came out as a preface encouraging Americans to read Paine's book as an answer "to the political heresies which had of late sprung up among us." Most Americans knew Jefferson had Vice President Adams in mind. Toward the end of the 1790s Jefferson and the newly organized Republican party aimed to drive the president and his Federalist party out of office in the election of 1800. Adams was accused of being a monarchist manqué who was raising his son to take his place as the next president; America was on the road to inherited royalty.

During the French Revolution, Jefferson and Paine seemed to want to see the world rid of all government. Whereas Adams had always looked to a constitution to control power, Jefferson and Paine were hardly bothered by the French getting along without one as Paris moved on to the Terror and the guillotine. Paine tried to save the lives of the French king and queen, but Jefferson approved of their execution as an "absolute necessity." Adams insisted that the French Revolution bore no resemblance to the American; Jefferson believed that the future of freedom depended upon the success of the Revolution in France. "Rather than it should have failed, I would have seen half the earth desolated," declared Jefferson.

The French Revolution highlighted the difference between Adams and his critics on the left. Adams believed that sovereignty would remain a source of tyranny if it continued to be concentrated in one body, as it had been under monarchy. Paine and Jefferson believed that sovereignty inhered in the will of the majority. Adams's opponents had little patience with the kind of "mixed" government he advocated, in which different social strata would be represented in different branches of government and the chambers of the legislature, all to be balanced against one another. Paine and Jefferson, like the French radicals, believed that the purpose of revolution was to abolish the differences that divided people so that democracy could express its true unanimity.

To support the French Revolution, Jefferson felt compelled to defeat Adams and rescue America from a monarchist future directed by a leader under the spell of the "harlot of England." In the eyes of Jefferson, and of French thinkers Condorcet and Turgot, Adams had condemned his political future by writing two texts, the three-volume *A Defence of the Constitutions of the United States of America,* published in 1787–1788, and *Discourses on Davila,* published in 1790, just prior to Adams's becoming vice president. The French critics could hardly be-

lieve that a new republic would continue the political structures of old England, with an upper and a lower house in the
legislature, a strong executive, and power divided among the
branches of government rather than concentrated in a national
assembly that would represent the "general will" of all the people. The French looked more kindly on Ben Franklin's proposal
for the Pennsylvania constitution that would have a unicameral
legislature and more possibilities for direct democracy. Like Jefferson and Paine, the French were convinced that if their own
revolution adopted Adams's scheme, the old aristocratic order
would remain in power. Condorcet, a former friend of Adams's,
insisted that America was trying to tell France what to do without realizing that the French, unlike the Americans, had to declare their rights before they possessed them. In truth, America
never really had a revolution, for on this side of the Atlantic all
classes fought on the same side to preserve their rights, and there
was no aristocracy to oppose the forces of change. But France
had to rid itself of older political structures to make way for
the regeneration of society, and what made possible the hope of
regeneration was the powerful promise of reason. Indeed the
French looked to the American Revolution itself as the triumph
of wisdom over "prejudice, dogma, and superstition," and the
successful outcome of the struggle had paved the way "for liberty,
virtue and reason."

Adams may have agreed about liberty, but he was not altogether sure that the American Revolution met the test of reason
and virtue. The skeptical Adams had many more doubts that
set him apart from the exponents of the radical Enlightenment.
We might call the following issues Adams's ten theses of the
Counterenlightenment.

TEN THESES OF THE
COUNTERENLIGHTENMENT

1. The Role of Reason

Many thinkers of the Enlightenment, especially Condorcet, Rousseau, and Thomas Paine, assumed that the universe was inherently rational and that humanity's ability to think rationally would enable the mind to understand nature and its laws. Adams could share certain of these assumptions, and he looked to "lawgivers and philosophers to enlighten the people's understanding, and improve their morals, by good and general education." But he also agreed with the Scottish philosopher David Hume that more often than not the mind is "the slave to passion," and thus he doubted that the authority of political institutions could rely upon the rational nature of the citizenry. In the *Defence* he drew upon Plato's *Republic* to sketch the degeneration of various polities from the ideal republic to timocracy, oligarchy, democracy, and tyranny. Classical thinkers seldom thought of politics in religious terms, but Adams reminded readers that the presence of sin stood in the way of the possibility of reason:

> If Socrates and Plato, Cicero and Seneca, Hutchinson and Butler are to be credited, reason is rightfully supreme in man, and therefore it would be most suitable to the reason of mankind to have no civil or political government at all. The moral government of God, and his vicegerent Conscience, ought to be sufficient to restrain men to obedience to justice and benevolence, at all times and in all places; we must therefore descend from the dignity of our nature, when we think of civil government at all. But the nature of mankind is one thing, and the reason of mankind another; and the first has the same relation to the last as the whole to a part: the passions and appetites are parts of human nature as well as reason and the moral sense. In the institution of government, it must be remembered, that although reason ought to govern individuals, it certainly never did since the Fall, and never

will till the Millennium; and human nature must be taken as it is, as it has been, and will be.

2. The Promise of Virtue

Closely related to the Enlightenment's claims for reason was the promise of virtue that had been inherited from classical antiquity. In the *Defence* Adams scrutinized all the meanings of virtue: the Roman ideals of courage and manliness, the ancient principles of prudence, temperance, and fortitude, and even the Christian concept, "so much more sublime," observed Adams, of Jonathan Edwards's Calvinist ethic of "universal benevolence." The one concept of virtue that troubled Adams was Montesquieu's notion that the individual could undergo "a renouncement of the self" for the sake of the public good. "If the absence of avarice is necessary to republican virtue," Adams wrote of the history of all republics, "can you find any age or country in which republican virtue has existed?" Adams drew on two sources, Christian pessimism and Scottish skepticism. "To expect self-denial from men, when they have a majority in their favour, and consequently power to gratify themselves, is to believe all history and universal experience; it is to disbelieve Revelation and the Word of God, which informs us [that] the heart is deceitful above all things, and desperately wicked." Uneasy with the philosopher's atheism, Adams was "not often satisfied with the opinions of Hume, but in this he seems well founded, that all projects of government founded on the supposition of expectation or extraordinary degrees of virtue are evidently chimerical."

3. Liberty as Power

Two decades after its publication, Adams's *Defence* provoked the Virginian John Taylor into writing *An Inquiry into the Principles and Policy of the Government of the United States*. Taylor asked how it was possible to insist, as did Adams, that the American Constitution as a mechanistic system was "virtuous" while the people living under it were "vicious." Moreover, how could a system so preoccupied with controlling power sustain liberty? During the revolutionary era it was widely believed that liberty meant that one lived independently of another's will and that power was that which was determined by forces external to the will. The *Federalist* authors, the architects of the Constitution, had also to reconcile what was thought to be the incompatibility of liberty and power. Adams followed them in identifying liberty as power—that is, the capacity to have effect and make things happen. "The definition of liberty," wrote Adams, "is a self-determining power in the intellectual agent." But if liberty makes possible the power to act and choose, could not evil as well as good be chosen? Liberty as power and efficacy must be subordinated to law, insisted Adams, who found dangerous the French assumption that humankind's attachment to liberty as a natural right was so deep a commitment that it would never be abused or alienated.

4. Liberty and Property

In the eighteenth century it was commonly assumed that liberty and property were synonymous and that power followed property. No one, not even severe critics of the Constitution, not even Tom Paine, who was to become a hero to later generations of radicals, questioned the conventional premise that property provided the foundation of liberty. But during the French Revolution, Gracchus Babeuf anticipated Karl Marx's communism in calling for the abolition of property, and Gabriel Bonnet de Mably, once a friend of Adams's, claimed that the desire for wealth arose from the "envy" and "avarice" born in situations of scarcity and inequality.

In the *Federalist* the protection of property is regarded as the "first object of government." But neither Alexander Hamilton nor James Madison provided a philosophical rationale for the institution. Nor did Jefferson, who substituted *happiness* for *property* in the Declaration. In the liberal, Lockean tradition, it was assumed that property arose from man's adding value to natural objects by means of his own labor, and because labor was the essential means of preserving life, man had a natural right to the products of his work. Of American political philosophers, only Abraham Lincoln espoused a labor theory of value. Adams did not partake of the Lockean tradition. On the contrary, he seems closer to the Scottish tradition that saw property as a social convention that deserved protection in the name of social order. Bonnet de Mably may have been right to say that the masses envy the possessions of others, but that is all the more reason to keep "the idle from usurping the industrious" and bringing about a state of debauchery and anarchy. "Indolence is the natural character of man, to such a degree that nothing but the necessities of hunger, thirst, and other wants equally pressing, can stimulate him to action, until education is introduced in civilized societies, and the strongest motives of ambition to excel in arts, trade, and professions are established in the minds of most men. Until this emulation is introduced, the lazy savage holds property in too little estimation to give himself trouble for the preservation or acquisition of it."

Amazingly, Adams did not see in colonial society what later came to be called the Protestant Ethic, the determination to work hard and acquire property and wealth as a means of pleasing God and attaining the salvation of the soul. Moreover, even though he saw how emulation would tie classes together as the lower strata imitated the upper, he foresaw America as a distinct class society.

5. The Inevitability of Classes

French critics of the American constitutions, of both the states and the national government, wondered why all the controlling mechanisms were necessary. America had no class systems, no aristocracy, no peasantry, no proletariat, no socialists trying to radicalize the Revolution or royalists trying to stage a counter-revolution and restore the old order. Adams, however, did believe America had, or would have, distinct class strata resembling the social orders of Europe. Not that immigrants would bring with them such clear class categories that had ridden Europe with class conflict. On the contrary, conflict had less to do with class structures than with deeper human emotions and anxieties—for example, competitive rivalry, the fear of being shunned, and the yearning for distinction—which meant that society would never attain unanimity but only degrees of differences and variations of styles of life. "We are told that our friends in the National Assembly of France," said Adams, "have abolished all distinctions. But do not be deceived, my dear countrymen. Impossibilities cannot be performed. Have they leveled all fortunes and equally divided all property? Have they made all men equal and women equally elegant, wise, and beautiful? . . . Have they blotted out all memories, the names, places of abode, and illustrious actions of their ancestors?"

Adams's critics insisted that class distinctions were artificial and had no basis in nature, particularly in the open, natural landscape of America. But Adams asked his critics to take a good look around and see if names, residences, reputations, positions of prestige, and other objects of envy and emulation were not pervasive in all societies and cultures. Prejudice and favoritism were natural traits, just as friends preferred each other to strangers and families stuck together. In fact, Adams's analysis presaged by centuries what today's social scientists call "social capital," that is, having connections, interacting with others, networking, support systems, and other resources enabling one to make contact and get ahead. Adams put it this way in a letter to John Taylor:

Here, sir, I will appeal to yourself. A young man appears. You ask of the bystanders who he is? The answer is, "I do not know." "No matter; let him go." Another appears,—"Who is he?" The answer is, "The son of A. B." "I do not know A. B." A third appears,—"Who is this?" "The son of C. D." "C. D.! my friend! He has been dead these fifty years; but I love his memory, and should be glad to be acquainted with any of his posterity. Please to walk in, sir, and favor me with your company for a few weeks or months; you will be always welcome to my house, and will always oblige me with your company."

6. Commerce and Corruption

The French Enlightenment, to the extent it followed Rousseau, regarded civic virtue as incompatible with commerce and saw as the mission of classical republicanism the unswerving resistance to the coming of bourgeois society, an idea put into practice in Robespierre's Reign of Terror in the name of virtue, when all luxury was despised in favor of simplicity. But Adams drew upon thinkers of the Scottish Enlightenment, who were less interested in showing how political virtue was to be sustained than in explaining how wealth was created and liberty preserved in an emergent market economy. David Hume and Adam Smith saw self-interest as a healthy motive of human action. The pursuit of wealth, rather than corrupting character, emancipated man from natural scarcity and thereby enlarged the possibility of human freedom.

In the *Defence* Adams followed the Scots but went beyond them in suggesting that the decline and fall of Rome were due not to the economic preoccupation of its citizens but to the poorly constructed political system with which they had to live. The lesson of Rome "may lead us to doubt the universality of the doctrine, that commerce corrupts manners." Adams believed with Hume that the austere Spartan state distorted man's natural drives and thereby smothered the lifeblood of liberty. But Adams was uneasy with the consequences of commerce as he recognized that democracy fed the appetite for affluence. In the "late war," he noted of the Revolution, Americans delighted in the influx of huge amounts of money and, "without the least degree of prudence, foresight, consideration, or measure, rushed headlong into a greater degree of luxury than ought to have crept in in a hundred years." Conventional wisdom saw luxury as the indulgence of the aristocratic classes, but Adams observed that "a free people are the most addicted to luxury of any." Although he saw the advent of the wealth of society as progressive, he also feared that a "mania for money" would become a nation's obsession to the neglect of more ennobling conduct. Here Adams differed from Jefferson, whose aristocratic tastes compelled him to spend himself into debt, and from Alexander Hamilton, who believed that the "rich, well-born, and able" would be so satisfied with what they had that they could be counted upon to serve the public good. With the legacy of Puritanism in his veins, Adams was troubled by the gaudy spectacle of luxury, but he saw no way of turning back the clock as he questioned the classical assumption that a properly constructed political system could restrain such behavior. "But what has poverty to do with the form of government? If mankind must be voluntarily poor in order to be free, it is too late in the age of the world to preach liberty."

7. Society and the Spectatorial

Although formally a political philosopher, Adams tried to teach us to look to society to learn about human behavior. His writings represent what might be called the sociological turn in political theory. For all his emphasis on the structure of government, it was the tendencies and traits of society and culture that concerned him as well. Here his thoughts anticipate certain of our contemporary French thinkers such as René Girard, Pierre Bourdieu, and Gilles Deleuze, as well as America's own Thorstein Veblen. Their concerns are also the will to power, the agency of desire, the craving for distinction, the tendencies to status rivalry, envy, emulation, conspicuous consumption, all of which reaffirm Adams's conviction that everything turns on "the attention of the public," "the eyes of the spectator," and the "language of signs."

Adams's *Discourses on Davila* criticizes Western thought for regarding humankind as a "political animal," in Aristotle's expression, when he or she is really a social creature. The text cites Shakespeare to suggest how the play of power is caught up with the performance in society. Not only *Troilus and Cressida* but many other of Shakespeare's political plays deal with the inevitability of class distinction and the ineluctability of power as life becomes a delicate balance of forces. "Take but Degree away; untune that string / And hark! what discord follows!" Shakespeare affirmed what Adams suspected: Human behavior remains the same whether characters live under a monarchy or in a republic.

Shakespeare also affirmed what Adams learned from Adam Smith: Human relations turned on what was observed rather than what was known; what you see is what you get. Centuries earlier Machiavelli anticipated this spectatorial turn wherein the visual replaced any vestige of the intellectual. "Men on the whole judge more with their eyes," wrote Machiavelli. Adams drew on Smith's *Theory of Moral Sentiments* (1759) to discover how sympathy enabled people to be concerned with others to the extent that the imagination empathized with their suffering. Adams was less concerned with benevolence and altruism than with the ways the self was constructed as a social phenomenon and how politics would be determined by public opinion that was itself shaped by visual images, as it certainly is now in our era of presidential television debates.

Adams's sensitivity to the spectatorial dimension of politics is as prescient as it is original. In the older Christian outlook, anything involving the spirit could not be seen, and thus one must trust "the Word." Even during the Enlightenment the printed page was regarded as more reliable than seeing and gazing, which befitted art and the theater, whereas politics remained a matter of pen and tongue, exercises that required reflections of the mind. In *Discourses on Davila,* however, we are in the world that Shakespeare put on the stage, what our contemporary theorists call the society of the spectacle. In such a world "attractions command the notice and attention of the public," Adams observed; "they draw the eyes of spectators." Although Adams was a president of the pen, he anticipated that modern politics would be about visual performance and images, and when people watch and respond rather than read and reflect, the eye would replace the mind as seeing becomes believing.

8. Language and Its Deconstruction

Another way in which Adams turned out to be prescient lay in his grasp of the complexities and duplicities of language, particularly political language. Traditionally it was assumed that language was a transparent medium that grasped reality as it really was, unmediated and undistorted. In this respect the mind had the capacity to mirror nature and to penetrate to the truth of things. Some modern scholars, who have doubts about language's capacity to reveal the truth, still believe that language constitutes the discourse through which politics expresses itself. A few even go so far as to claim that in politics what cannot be said cannot be thought.

Centuries ago Adams turned such assumptions upside down. In the *Defence* he devoted considerable space to Machiavelli, and while he praised the Italian for putting the study of politics on a more realistic, scientific basis, he also proceeded to "deconstruct" his texts. He did so by showing that the language Machiavelli used was mainly rhetoric with little basis in reality—that is, more persuasion than proof by an author who gives us metaphors when we ask for evidence. Machiavelli sought to flatter the citizens of Florence by telling them that they were not to blame for the situation in which they found themselves, one of endless bloody civil wars; instead they were victims of the vicissitudes of misfortune and the "iniquity of the times." To make the people feel good about themselves, Machiavelli tried to convince them that the causes of their troubles lay elsewhere than in their own hearts and souls. "It is very provoking to read these continual imputations to fortune, made by Machiavel, of events which he knew very well were the effects of secret intrigue," wrote Adams of Machiavelli's rhetorical strategy. The Italian philosopher "would have been much better advised" had he "imputed all these evils to their true cause, an imperfect and unbalanced constitution of government." Machiavelli was deceiving himself as well as Italy's citizens with his "pious exhortations" of patriotism and virtue. "One is . . . astonished at the reflection of Machiavelli,—'Such was the spirit of patriotism amongst them in those days that they cheerfully gave up their private interests for the public good,'—when every page of his history shows that the public good was sacrificed every day by all parties to their private interest, friendships, and enmities." Long interested in the riddle of motivation, Adams questioned if we can understand why people do what they do on the basis of the language they use and the reasons they provide. To demonstrate how language can contradict itself, and to show how it functions to conceal more than it reveals, are to deconstruct it.

9. The Primacy of the Executive

Not only did Adams's keen sensitivity to the ways of society and the misuses of language make him amazingly prescient, but he was also the only one of the American founders who saw that the presidency would become America's most important political institution. Alexander Hamilton did call for "energy in the executive," but he looked to the wealthy classes to guide the government, whereas Adams remained skeptical of all elites. During Adams's era, and for centuries earlier, political philosophers gave little attention to the possibility of an executive office in a republic. Rome had its tribunes, but they rarely rose above factional squabble, and those who wrote about the decline and fall of Rome mistook the causes for the effect. "The Romans charged the ruin of their commonwealth to luxury," wrote Adams; "they might have charged it to the want of a balance in their constitution."

By *balance* Adams meant a strong, independent executive who would mediate between democracy and aristocracy, between the struggling many and the fortunate few. Rather than advocating the rule of aristocracy and the importance of monarchy, as his critics charged, Adams looked to the role of the state to control domination from above, and he ridiculed royalty with its claim of a "divine right" to rule. Both the classical republicanism of Machiavelli and the radical Jacobinism of the French Revolution assumed that an independent executive branch of government was unnecessary. Machiavelli thought that the rich and educated, the *prominenti e cognoscenti*, could be assimilated with the plebs and other elements in the doge. The French, seeing the executive office as containing the tyranny of monarchy, believed that all power should be invested in a national assembly. Adams, however, could not bring himself to believe that power is capable of controlling itself, for it is always in motion, always augmenting and asserting itself, forever moving to exclude, control, and dominate others. Whereas classical republican philosophy and the French Revolution believed that power is rendered safe to the extent that it is in the hands of a unified people dedicated to the public good, Adams insisted that it is the nature of politics that people quarrel and fall out into factions; hence politics presupposes opposition, and power requires countervailing forces to control it.

In modern American history it was the two Roosevelts, Theodore and Franklin D., who best represented Adams's ideal of a president. Both disdained, as did he, the "malefactors of wealth," and both used the executive office as an instrument of justice. Both departed, as did he, from the classical republican assumption, also known as the Whig theory of politics, that in all circumstances the legislature is the supreme branch of government. Adams believed as well that it is only in the singular executive office that one can expect responsibility, the one place, as the feisty Harry Truman put it, "where the buck stops."

10. The Human Condition

The amazing prescience of John Adams may be further appreciated if we consider what scholars have only recently begun to write about: the parallels between the Counterenlightenment of the eighteenth century and the postmodernism of the late twentieth century, between two schools of thought separated by two centuries yet sharing a critique of the Age of Reason. Postmodernists criticize the rational Enlightenment of France for its faith in progress, its belief in unanimity at the cost of diversity, and its assumption that the advent of knowledge would constitute an answer to the threat of power. Most postmodernists, flowering in France or in America's universities, especially in English departments, are unaware of the writings of John Adams, unaware too that through those writings America had its own Counterenlightenment, which drew not upon French thinkers but upon those of the Scottish Enlightenment.

Thus Adams is close to our contemporary postmodernists, sharing their skepticism about progress, seeing diversity as not only inevitable but desirable, and doubting that the rise of knowledge itself suffices to deal with the riddles of power. On the contrary, knowledge may only exacerbate the capacity to do wrong as talent is more abused than used. "Does not the increase of knowledge in any man increase his emulation, and the diffusion of knowledge among men increase their rivalries?"

Adams's sense of the limitations of knowledge, his awareness that reason itself cannot help people reason themselves out of what they have not reasoned into, his conviction that the ego is slave to its passions—all such "melancholy reflections" bring him readily into the contemporary world of Freud, existentialism, and postmodernism. It is "the human condition," to use Hannah Arendt's phrase, in which the mind is out of joint with the world, the self divided into a spray of desires, and the will determined by forces beyond itself. Jean-Jacques Rousseau declared: "Man was born free; and everywhere he is in chains." Adams's reply to the philosophe starts from an opposite premise and arrives at a different conclusion: Man was born alienated, and everywhere he is in society. Whereas Rousseau believed that government could be dispensed with once society returned to the harmony of nature and its happy contentments, Adams believed government was indispensable, since it was society itself that expressed nature's conflicting tendencies and its restless discontents. "It is weakness rather than wickedness which renders men unfit to be trusted with unlimited power. The passions are all unlimited; nature has left them so; [if] they could be bounded, they would be extinct."

Adams's sense of alienation lies in his insight that humankind is not born with an innate self but instead develops it out of social interaction; hence the self is produced rather than found, a social construction instead of the essence of one's being. Thus even to try to "know thyself" compels people to look to others for approbation. So great is the "desire for the attention, consideration, and congratulations of mankind" that human beings even go against their own self-interests to attain it. "To be wholly overlooked, and to know it, are intolerable. Instances of this are not uncommon. When a wretch could no longer attract the notice of a man, woman, or child, he must be respectable in the eyes of his dog. 'Who will love me then?' was the pathetic reply of one, who starved himself to feed his mastiff, to a charitable passenger, who advised him to kill or sell the animal. In this *who will love me then?* there is the key to the human heart; to the history of human life and manners; and to the rise and fall of empires."

Although the American Republic was born with the Declaration of Independence, John Adams would not be surprised to discover how dependent and interdependent and even submissive America and the American people have become. His insights into the social determinants of human behavior—the utter neediness to have the attention of others and, at the same time, to be preoccupied with the self—presage the thoughts of contemporary thinkers: Thorstein Veblen, who saw the need for recognition's displaying itself in "conspicuous consumption"; David Reisman, who saw the American character sunk in an "other-directed" conformity; Sigmund Freud, who saw one's emotions predetermined by family conditions; Jean-Paul Sartre, who saw the individual surrendering to the "gaze of the other"; Christopher Lasch, who saw Americans gazing upon themselves in a "culture of narcissism"; and even Arthur Miller, whose Willy Loman, in *Death of a Salesman,* desperately identifies success with being "well liked." Adams anticipated all such tendencies in *Discourses on Davila.* "A desire to be observed, considered, esteemed, praised, beloved, and admired by his fellows, is one of the earliest, as well as keenest dispositions discovered in the heart of man."

In theory, America values individualism and self-reliance, but as Adams predicted, the institutions of government and the economy would involve the politician and the salesman; one needs the voter, the other the buyer, and both become as dependent upon the people as people are on each other. Adams held the mirror up to his beloved country. Born free, America is everywhere in chains, its people driven by desires that induce the subject to seek the recognition of others. What Adams called "emulation," and what the modern sociologist called "other-directedness," Tocqueville called the "sweet despotism" of democracy.

John Adams has been one of America's most neglected political philosophers and social theorists. In a country of smiling optimism, his skepticism has rendered him politically incorrect. Yet reading his vast array of rich thoughts enables us to understand not only his times but ours as well. If Adams tells us what we would prefer not to know about ourselves, that is all the more reason to ponder it.

BIBLIOGRAPHICAL SUGGESTIONS

The book that did more than any other to bring Adams to the attention of the public is David McCullough's spectacular best-selling *John Adams* (New York: Simon & Schuster, 2001). It is an engaging narrative of Adams's life and times. Joseph J. Ellis's *Passionate Sage: The Character and Legacy of John Adams* (New York: Norton, 1994) deals astutely with Adams's political thought, particularly his differences with Jefferson, as well as his presidential and postpresidential careers. An earlier book that is out of print, but can be found in used-book stores and possibly over the Internet, is Page Smith's two-volume *John Adams* (New York: Doubleday, 1976). It is a finely detailed study that tells us everything we want to know about John Adams and Abigail and their friends and antagonists. For a comprehensive study of Adams as a political thinker, see C. Bradley Thompson, *John Adams and the Spirit of Liberty* (Lawrence: University Press of Kansas, 1998). More slender but still valuable studies are Peter Shaw, *The Character of John Adams* (New York: Norton, 1977), and John Howe, *The Changing Political Thought of John Adams* (Princeton: Princeton University Press, 1966). An old but still remarkable study of Adams's dialogues with the Parisian philosophes is Zoltán Haraszti, *John Adams and the Prophets of Progress* (Cambridge: Harvard University Press, 1952).

Thanks to David McCullough's widely read book, John

Adams is now known as the president America almost forgot. Curiously, in historiography, America's greatest intellectual historian, Professor Perry Miller of Harvard University, paid no attention to Adams as he took his studies from the Puritans to the Transcendentalists and, for some reason, barely stopped to consider the political founding of the country. But one of Miller's many brilliant students, Henry F. May, wrote with discernment on Adams in *The American Enlightenment* (New York: Oxford, 1976). The reason Adams was marginalized in American political philosophy was the hegemony of liberalism, evidenced in Vernon L. Parrington's three-volume *Main Currents in American Thought* (New York: Harcourt, 1927–1930). The Parringtonian view, which saw Jefferson, Andrew Jackson, and Walt Whitman as the true Americans, and Adams, Alexander Hamilton, and Nathaniel Hawthorne as brooding subversives, became the paradigm in American history textbooks throughout the first half of the twentieth century. Supposedly Jeffersonianism involved high ideals while its antagonists dealt with sordid realities. For a critique of this dubious dualism, see Lionel Trilling, *The Liberal Imagination* (New York: Vintage, 1950). Another valuable corrective to the liberal bias is the discussion of Adams in Russell Kirk, *The Conservative Mind* (Chicago: Gateway, 1953). If there need be a countervoice to the one presented in the introduction above, see Merrill Peterson, *Adams and Jefferson: A Revolutionary Dialogue* (New York: Oxford, 1975), which is more sympathetic to Jefferson and more critical of Adams.

But the real rebuttal to Adams, even if inadvertently, is Alexis de Tocqueville's great book, *Democracy in America,* a two-volume work published in France in the 1830s and rarely well known in America until the post–World War II years. Although Tocqueville did not address Adams specifically, he did question the theory of the American founding and suggested, in contradiction to Adams, that it is society, not government, that explains America. Adams believed that the rationality of the "machinery of government" was absolutely necessary to control the passions and irrationalities of a conflict-ridden society. But Tocqueville questioned the basic political apparatus of

America. "I have always considered what is called a mixed government to be a chimera." Had America really had the conflicting social strata that had to be controlled by political means, it would have had a short, unhappy life, for in a society based on "contrary principles, either a revolution breaks out or that society breaks up." Adams failed to see the consensual nature of America's social order, and he looked to institutions to deal with conflict, whereas Tocqueville demonstrated that Americans shared values of property, liberty, opportunity, and individual natural rights. Adams feared America might go the way of all flesh and follow Europe's corrupting social conflicts; Tocqueville saw America as having made a profound break with the Old World. Tocqueville's perspective came to be known as American exceptionalism.

But was America exceptional? Tocqueville believed that the troubles that had afflicted the Old World, especially the corruptions of politics and commerce, would not trouble the New. But John Adams's great-grandson Henry Adams tried to tell readers there was plenty to be troubled about and that America's fate was tied up with that of Europe and the Old World of power politics. Writing in the post–Civil War era, Adams saw corruption everywhere and virtue nowhere, except perhaps in his two novels, *Democracy* and *Esther,* in which the female protagonists stand for morality and truth against the compromises of politics and religion. Adams was not even sure that the Constitution his ancestor had so proudly expounded and defended was a success, since it had failed to prevent the Civil War. See his *Education of Henry Adams.* For the ambiguous legacy of John Adams, see John Patrick Diggins, *The Lost Soul of American Politics: Virtue, Self-Interests, and the Foundations of Liberalism* (New York: Basic, 1985), and *John Adams* (New York: Henry Holt, 2003).

I

DIARY AND AUTOBIOGRAPHY[1]

W. H. Auden once made the remark that talking to others is rhetoric, while speaking to oneself is poetry. Adams's diary and autobiography were written by one who was in a conversation with himself, and if the writings are not quite poetry, they do illuminate the abiding concerns of his mind, his theological speculations, and his infinite curiosities about nature as well as human society. Adams's descriptions of the crossing of the Atlantic and his activities as a diplomat in France and Holland make for good reading, not to mention his gibes at Ben Franklin. To accompany Adams is to see the world as he saw it in the late eighteenth century.

DIARY

[1756. FEBRUARY] 15. Sunday. Staid at home reading the Independent Whig.*

Very often shepherds that are hired to take care of their masters' sheep go about their own concerns and leave the flock to the care of their dog. So bishops, who are appointed to oversee

---

*By Thomas Gordon, the Translator of Tacitus and author of Cato's Letters. His works have passed into oblivion, but at this period they were much read on account of their free and independent spirit. The Tacitus and Cato's Letters are placed by the side of Sidney and Locke and Bacon, in a special bequest of Josiah Quincy, Jun., to his son in his last will. *"Memoir,"* &c., p. 350.

the flock of Christ, take the fees themselves but leave the drudgery to their dogs, that is, curates and understrappers.

16. Monday. We have the most moderate winter that ever was known in this country. For a long time together we have had serene and temperate weather, and all the roads perfectly settled and smooth like summer.

The Church of Rome has made it an article of faith that no man can be saved out of their church, and all other religious sects approach to this dreadful opinion in proportion to their ignorance, and the influence of ignorant or wicked priests.

Still reading the Independent Whig.

Oh! that I could wear out of my mind every mean and base affectation; conquer my natural pride and self-conceit; expect no more deference from my fellows than I deserve; acquire that meekness and humility which are the sure mark and characters of a great and generous soul; subdue every unworthy passion, and treat all men as I wish to be treated by all. How happy should I then be in the favor and good will of all honest men and the sure prospect of a happy immortality!

18. Wednesday. Spent an hour in the beginning of the evening at Major Gardiner's, where it was thought that the design of Christianity was not to make men good riddle-solvers, or good mystery-mongers, but good men, good magistrates, and good subjects, good husbands and good wives, good parents and good children, good masters and good servants. The following questions may be answered some time or other, namely,—Where do we find a precept in the Gospel requiring Ecclesiastical Synods? Convocations? Councils? Decrees? Creeds? Confessions? . . .

19. Thursday. No man is entirely free from weakness and imperfection in this life. Men of the most exalted genius and active minds are generally most perfect slaves to the love of fame. They sometimes descend to as mean tricks and artifices in pursuit of honor or reputation as the miser descends to in pursuit of gold. The greatest men have been the most envious, malicious, and revengeful. The miser toils by night and day, fasts and watches, till he emaciates his body to fatten his purse and increase his coffers. The ambitious man rolls and tumbles in his bed, a stranger to refreshing sleep and repose, through anxiety

about a preferment he has in view. The philosopher sweats and labors at his book, and ruminates in his closet, till his bearded and grim countenance exhibits the effigies of pale want and care and death, in quest of hard words, solemn nonsense, and ridiculous grimace. The gay gentleman rambles over half the globe, buys one thing and steals another, murders one man and disables another, and gets his own limbs and head broke for a few transitory flashes of happiness. Is this perfection, or downright madness and distraction?

20. Friday. Symptoms of snow. . . .

21. Saturday. Snow about ankle deep. I find, by repeated experiment and observation in my school, that human nature is more easily wrought upon and governed by promises, and encouragement, and praise, than by punishment, and threatening, and blame. But we must be cautious and sparing of our praise, lest it become too familiar and cheap, and so, contemptible; corporal as well as disgraceful punishments depress the spirits, but commendation enlivens and stimulates them to a noble ardor and emulation.

22. Sunday. Suppose a nation in some distant region should take the Bible for their only law-book, and every member should regulate his conduct by the precepts there exhibited! Every member would be obliged, in conscience, to temperance and frugality and industry; to justice and kindness and charity towards his fellow men; and to piety, love, and reverence, towards Almighty God. In this commonwealth, no man would impair his health by gluttony, drunkenness, or lust; no man would sacrifice his most precious time to cards or any other trifling and mean amusement; no man would steal, or lie, or in any way defraud his neighbor, but would live in peace and good will with all men; no man would blaspheme his Maker or profane his worship; but a rational and manly, a sincere and unaffected piety and devotion would reign in all hearts. What a Utopia; what a Paradise would this region be! . . .

24. Tuesday. We are told that Demosthenes transcribed the history of Thucydides eight times, in order to imbibe and familiarize himself with the elegance and strength of his style. . . .

27. Friday. All day in high health and spirits. . . . That comet

which appeared in 1682 is expected again this year; and we have intelligence that it has been seen about ten days since, near midnight, in the east. I find myself very much inclined to an unreasonable absence of mind, and to a morose and unsociable disposition; let it therefore be my constant endeavor to reform these great faults.

28. Saturday. Attended Mrs. Brown's funeral. Let this and every other instance of human frailty and mortality prompt me to endeavor after a temper of mind fit to undergo this great change.

1756. March 1. Monday. Wrote out Bolingbroke's Reflections on Exile.

2. Tuesday. Began this afternoon my third quarter.* The great and Almighty author of nature, who at first established those rules which regulate the world, can as easily suspend those laws whenever his providence sees sufficient reason for such suspension. This can be no objection, then, to the miracles of Jesus Christ. Although some very thoughtful and contemplative men among the heathen attained a strong persuasion of the great principles of religion, yet the far greater number, having little time for speculation, gradually sunk into the grossest opinions and the grossest practices. These, therefore, could not be made to embrace the true religion till their attention was roused by some astonishing and miraculous appearances. The reasoning of philosophers, having nothing surprising in them, could not overcome the force of prejudice, custom, passion, and bigotry. But when wise and virtuous men, commissioned from heaven, by miracles awakened men's attention to their reasonings, the force of truth made its way with ease to their minds.

3. Wednesday. Natural philosophy is the art of deducing the general laws and properties of material substances from a series of analogous observations. The manner of reasoning in this

---

*[Three months after this, (during the second quarter,) the Selectmen procured lodgings for me at Dr. Nahum Willard's. This physician had a large practice, a good reputation for skill, and a pretty library. Here were Dr. Cheyne's works, Sydenham, and others, and Van Swieten's Commentaries on Boerhaave. I read a good deal in these books and entertained many thoughts of becoming a physician and a surgeon.]

art is not strictly demonstrative, and, by consequence, the knowledge hence acquired is not absolutely scientific, because the facts that we reason upon are perceived by sense, and not by the internal action of the mind contemplating its ideas. But these facts being presumed true in the form of axioms, subsequent reasonings about them may be in the strictest sense scientific. This art informs us in what manner bodies will influence us and each other in given circumstances, and so teaches us to avoid the noxious, and embrace the beneficial qualities of matter. By this art, too, many curious engines have been constructed to facilitate business, to avert impending calamities, and to procure desired advantages. . . .

7. Sunday. . . . Honesty, sincerity, and openness I esteem essential marks of a good mind. I am, therefore, of opinion that men ought, (after they have examined with unbiased judgments every system of religion, and chosen one system, on their own authority, for themselves,) to avow their opinions and defend them with boldness.

12. Friday. Laid a pair of gloves with Mrs. Willard* that she would not see me chew tobacco this month.

14. Sunday. . . . Spent the evening very sociably at Mr. Putnam's. Several observations concerning Mr. Franklin,† of Philadelphia, a prodigious genius, cultivated with prodigious industry.

15. Monday. I sometimes in my sprightly moments consider myself, in my great chair at school, as some dictator at the head of a commonwealth. In this little state I can discover all the great geniuses, all the surprising actions and revolutions of the great world, in miniature. I have several renowned generals but three feet high, and several deep projecting politicians in petticoats. I have others catching and dissecting flies, accumulating remarkable pebbles, cockle shells, &c., with as ardent curiosity

---

*[The family of the Willards of Lancaster were often at Worcester, and I formed an acquaintance with them, especially Abel Willard, who had been one year with me at College, and had studied the law under Mr. Pratt in Boston. With him I lived in friendship.]

†Benjamin Franklin, whose growing reputation in Europe, on account of his experiments in electricity, was coming back to increase his reputation at home.

as any virtuoso in the Royal Society. Some rattle and thunder out A, B, C, with as much fire and impetuosity as Alexander fought, and very often sit down and cry as heartily upon being outspelt, as Cæsar did, when at Alexander's sepulchre he recollected that the Macedonian hero had conquered the world before his age. At one table sits Mr. Insipid, foppling* and fluttering, spinning his whirligig, or playing with his fingers, as gaily and wittily as any Frenchified coxcomb brandishes his cane or rattles his snuff-box. At another, sits the polemical divine, plodding and wrangling in his mind about "Adam's fall, in which we sinned all," as his Primer has it. In short, my little school, like the great world, is made up of kings, politicians, divines, L.D.'s, fops, buffoons, fiddlers, sycophants, fools, coxcombs, chimney sweepers, and every other character drawn in history, or seen in the world. Is it not, then, the highest pleasure, my friend, to preside in this little world, to bestow the proper applause upon virtuous and generous actions, to blame and punish every vicious and contracted trick, to wear out of the tender mind every thing that is mean and little, and fire the new-born soul with a noble ardor and emulation? The world affords no greater pleasure. Let others waste their bloom of life at the card or billiard table among rakes and fools, and when their minds are sufficiently fretted with losses, and inflamed by wine, ramble through the streets assaulting innocent people, breaking windows, or debauching young girls. I envy not their exalted happiness. I had rather sit in school and consider which of my pupils will turn out in his future life a hero, and which a rake, which a philosopher, and which a parasite, than change breasts with them, though possessed of twenty laced waistcoats and a thousand pounds a year. Methinks I hear you say, This is odd talk for John Adams! I'll tell you, then, the occasion of it. About four months since, a poor girl in this neighborhood, walking by the meeting-house upon some occasion in the evening, met a fine gentleman with laced hat and waistcoat, and a sword, who solicited her to turn aside with him into the horse stable. The girl relucted a little, upon which he gave her

---

*There is no such English word, but its meaning is clear enough.

three guineas, and wished he might be damned if he did not have her in three months. Into the horse stable they went. The three guineas proved three farthings, and the girl proved with child, without a friend upon earth that will own her, or knowing the father of her three-farthing bastard.

17. Wednesday. . . . I took my faith on trust from Dr. Mayhew,[2] and added, that he believed the doctrine of the satisfaction of Jesus Christ to be essential to Christianity, and that he would not believe this satisfaction unless he believed the Divinity of Christ. Mr. Balch was there too, and observed, that he would not be a Christian if he did not believe the mysteries of the gospel; that he could bear with an Arminian,[3] but when, with Dr. Mayhew, they denied the Divinity and satisfaction of Jesus Christ, he had no more to do with them; that he knew not what to make of Dr. Mayhew's two discourses upon the expected dissolution of all things. They gave him an idea of a cart whose wheels wanted greasing; it rumbled on in a hoarse, rough manner; there was a good deal of ingenious talk in them, but it was thrown together in a jumbled, confused order. He believed the Doctor wrote them in a great panic. He added further that Arminians, however stiffly they maintain their opinions in health, always, he takes notice, retract when they come to die, and choose to die Calvinists. Set out for Braintree, and arrived about sunset. . . .

[May] 3. Monday. . . . The love of fame naturally betrays a man into several weaknesses and fopperies that tend very much to diminish his reputation, and so defeat itself. Vanity, I am sensible, is my cardinal vice and cardinal folly; and I am in continual danger, when in company, of being led an *ignis fatuus* chase by it, without the strictest caution and watchfulness over myself.

4. Tuesday. Let any man, suppose of the most improved understanding, look upon a watch when the parts are separated. Let him examine every wheel and spring separately by itself. Yet, if the use and application of these springs and wheels is not explained to him, he will not be able to judge of the use and advantage of particular parts; much less will he be able if he has only one wheel. In like manner we, who see but a few cogs in

one wheel of the great machine of the universe, can make no right judgment of particular phenomena in nature.

7. Friday. Spent the evening and supped at Mr. Maccarty's. A man's observing the flux of the tide to-day, renders it credible that the same phenomenon may be observed to-morrow. In the same manner, our experience that the Author of nature has annexed pain to vice, and pleasure to virtue, in general, I mean, renders it credible that the same, or a like disposition of things, may take place hereafter. Our observing that the state of minority was designed to be an education for mature life, and that our good or ill success, in a mature life, depends upon our good or ill improvement of our advantages in minority, renders it credible that this life was designed to be an education for a future one; and that our happiness or misery, in a future life, will be allotted us according as our characters shall be virtuous or vicious. For God governs his great kingdom, the world, by very general laws. We cannot, indeed, observe many instances of these laws, but wherever we see any particular disposition of things, we may strongly presume that there are other dispositions of things, in other systems of nature, analogous and of a piece with this. . . .

9. Sunday. Since last Sunday I have wrote a few pages of the Spectator; read the last part of Butler's Analogy; wrote out the tract upon Personal Identity, and that upon the Nature of Virtue. A poor week's work!

11. Tuesday. The first day of Court. Nature and truth, or rather truth and right are invariably the same in all times and in all places; and reason, pure unbiased reason, perceives them alike in all times and in all places. But passion, prejudice, interest, custom, and fancy, are infinitely precarious; if, therefore, we suffer our understandings to be blinded or perverted by any of these, the chance is that of millions to one, that we shall embrace errors. And hence arises that endless variety of opinions entertained by mankind. The weather and the season are, beyond expression, delightful; the fields are covered with a bright and lively verdure; the trees are all in bloom, and the atmosphere is filled with a ravishing fragrance; the air is soft and yielding; and the setting sun sprinkled his departing rays over

the face of nature, and enlivened all the landscapes around me; the trees put forth their leaves, and the birds fill the spray.

12. Wednesday. Rambled about all day, gaping and gazing.

14. Friday. Drank tea at the Colonel's. Not one new idea this week.

15. Saturday. A lovely day; soft vernal showers. Exercise invigorates and enlivens all the faculties of body and of mind; it arouses our animal spirits, it disperses melancholy; it spreads a gladness and satisfaction over our minds, and qualifies us for every sort of business, and every sort of pleasure.

16. Sunday. The week past was court week. I was interrupted by company, and the noisy bustle of the public occasion, so that I have neither read nor wrote any thing worth mentioning. . . .

17. Monday. The elephant and the lion, when their strength is directed and applied by man, can exert a prodigious force. But their strength, great and surprising as it is, can produce no great effects when applied by no higher ingenuity than their own. But man, although the powers of his body are but small and contemptible, by the exercise of his reason can invent engines and instruments, to take advantage of the powers in nature, and accomplish the most astonishing designs. He can rear the valley into a lofty mountain, and reduce the mountain to a humble vale. He can rend the rocks and level the proudest trees; at his pleasure the forest is cleared, and palaces rise; when he pleases the soaring eagle is precipitated to earth, and the light-footed roe is stopped in his career. He can cultivate and assist nature in her own productions, by pruning the trees and manuring the land. He makes the former produce larger and fairer fruit; and the latter to bring forth better and greater plenty of grain. He can form a communication between remotest regions for the benefit of trade and commerce, over the yielding and fluctuating element of water. The telescope has settled the regions of heaven, and the microscope has brought up to view innumerable millions of animals that escape the observation of our naked sight.

23. Sunday. Heard Mr. Maccarty. He is particularly fond of the following expressions: carnal, ungodly persons; sensuality

and voluptuousness; walking with God, unregeneracy, rebellion against God; believers; all things come alike to all; there is one event to the righteous and to the wicked; shut out of the presence of God; solid, substantial, and permanent joys; joys springing up in the soul; the shines of God's countenance.

When we consider the vast and incomprehensible extent of the material universe, those myriads of fixed stars that emerge out of the remote regions of space to our view by glasses,—and the finer our glasses the more of these systems we discover;—when we consider that space is absolutely infinite and boundless, that the power of the Deity is strictly omnipotent, and his goodness without limitation, who can come to a stop in his thoughts and say, hither does the universe extend and no further?

"Nothing can proceed from nothing." But something can proceed from something, and thus the Deity produced this vast and beautiful frame of the universe out of nothing; that is, He had no preexistent matter to work upon, or to change from a chaos into a world. But He produced a world into being by his Almighty fiat, perhaps, in a manner analogous to the production of resolutions in our minds. . . .

24. Monday. Had the projectile force in the planets been greater than it is, they would not describe circles, but very eccentrical ellipses round the sun; and then the inhabitants would be tormented, yea, destroyed, and the planets left barren and uninhabitable wastes, by extreme vicissitudes of heat and cold. It was many million times as likely that some other degree of velocity would have been lighted on, as that the present would, if chance had the disposal of it; and any other degree would have absolutely destroyed all animal and sensitive, if not vegetable, inhabitants. *Ergo,* an intelligent and benevolent mind had the disposal and determination of these things.

28. Friday. If we examine critically the little prospect that lies around us, at one view we behold an almost infinite variety of substances over our heads. The sun blazes in divine effulgence; the clouds, tinged with various colors by the refracted sunbeams, exhibit most beautiful appearances in the atmosphere. The cultivated plains and meadows are attired in a delightful verdure, and variegated with the gay enamel of flowers and

roses; on one hand we see an extensive forest, a whole kingdom of vegetables of the noblest kind; upon the hills we discern flocks of grazing cattle; and on the other hand a city rises up to view, with its spires among the clouds. All these, and many more objects encounter our eyes in the prospect of our horizon, perhaps two or three miles in diameter. Now every animal that we see in this prospect, men and beasts, is endued with a most curiously organized body. They consist of bones, and blood, and muscles, and nerves, and ligaments, and tendons, and chyle, and a million other things, all exactly fitted for the purposes of life, and motion, and action. Every plant has almost as complex and curious a structure as animals; and the minutest twig is supported and supplied with juices and life, by organs and filaments proper to draw this nutrition of the earth. It would be endless to consider, minutely, every substance or species of substances that falls under our eyes in this one prospect. Now let us for a minute consider how many million such prospects there are upon this single planet, all of which contain as great, and some a much greater variety of animals and vegetables. When we have been sufficiently astonished at this incomprehensible multitude of substances, let us rise in our thoughts, and consider how many planets, and satellites, and comets, there are in this one solar system, each of which has as many such prospects upon its surface as our earth. Such a view as this may suffice to show us our ignorance; but if we rise still higher in our thoughts, and consider that stupendous army of fixed stars that is hung up in the immense space, as so many suns, each placed in the centre of his respective system, and diffusing his enlivening and invigorating influences to his whole choir of planets, comets, and satellites; and that each of this unnumbered multitude has as much superficies, and as many prospects, as our earth, we find ourselves lost and swallowed up in this incomprehensible, (I had almost said) infinite magnificence of nature. Our imaginations, after a few faint efforts, sink down into a profound admiration of what they cannot comprehend. God, whose almighty fiat first produced this amazing universe, had the whole plan in view from all eternity; intimately and perfectly knew the nature and all the properties of all these his creatures. He looked forward through all duration, and perfectly knew all the effects, all the events and revolutions that could possibly and would actually take place throughout eternity.

29. Saturday. . . .

What is the proper business of mankind in this life? We come into the world naked, and destitute of all the conveniences and necessaries of life; and if we were not provided for and nourished by our parents, or others, should inevitably perish as soon as born; we increase in strength of body and mind, by slow and insensible degrees; one third of our time is consumed in sleep, and three sevenths of the remainder is spent in procuring a mere animal sustenance; and if we live to the age of threescore and ten, and then sit down to make an estimate in our minds of the happiness we have enjoyed, and the misery we have suffered, we shall find, I am apt to think, that the overbalance of happiness is quite inconsiderable. We shall find that we have been, through the greatest part of our lives, pursuing shadows, and empty but glittering phantoms, rather than substances. We shall find that we have applied our whole vigor, all our faculties, in the pursuit of honor, or wealth, or learning, or some other such delusive trifle, instead of the real and everlasting excellencies of piety and virtue. Habits of contemplating the Deity and his transcendent excellencies, and correspondent habits of complacency in, and dependence upon him; habits of reverence and gratitude to God, and habits of love and compassion to our fellow men; and habits of temperance, recollection, and self-government, will afford us a real and substantial pleasure. We may then exult in a consciousness of the favor of God, and the prospect of everlasting felicity.

30. Sunday. Heard Mr. Maccarty. "You, who are sinners, are in continual danger of being swallowed up quick, and borne away by the mighty torrent of God's wrath and justice. It is now, as it were, restrained and banked up by his goodness. But he will, by and by, unless repentance prevent, let it out in full fury upon you." . . .

31. Monday. When we see or feel any body, we discern nothing but bulk and extension. We can change this extension into

a great variety of shapes and figures, and, by applying our senses to it, can get ideas of those different figures; but can do nothing more than change the figure. If we pulverize glass or salt, the original constituent matter remains the same, only we have altered the contexture of its parts. Large loads and heaps of matter, as mountains and rocks, lie obstinate, inactive, and motionless, and eternally will remain so, unless moved by some force extrinsic to themselves. Dissolve the cohesion, and reduce these mountains to their primogenial atoms; these atoms are as dull and senseless as they were when combined into the shape of a mountain. In short, matter has no consciousness of its own existence, has no power of its own, no active power I mean, but is wholly passive; nor can thought be ever produced by any modification of it. To say that God can superadd to matter a capacity of thought, is palpable nonsense and contradiction. Such a capacity is inconsistent with the most essential properties of matter.

June 1. Tuesday. The reasoning of mathematicians is founded on certain and infallible principles. Every word they use conveys a determinate idea, and by accurate definitions they excite the same ideas in the mind of the reader that were in the mind of the writer. When they have defined the terms they intend to make use of, they premise a few axioms, or self-evident principles, that every man must assent to as soon as proposed. They then take for granted certain postulates, that no one can deny them, such as, that a right line may be drawn from one given point to another; and from these plain simple principles they have raised most astonishing speculations, and proved the extent of the human mind to be more spacious and capable than any other science.

2. Wednesday. When we come into the world, our minds are destitute of all sorts of ideas. Our senses inform us of various qualities in the substances around us; as we grow up our acquaintance with things enlarges and spreads; colors are painted in our minds through our eyes; all the various modulations of sounds enter by our ears; fragrance and fœtor are perceived by the smell; extension and bulk by the touch. These ideas that enter, simple and uncompounded, through our senses, are called

simple ideas, because they are absolutely one and indivisible. Thus, the whiteness of snow cannot be divided or separated into two or more whitenesses. The same may be said of all other colors. It is, indeed, in our power to mix or compound colors into new and more beautiful appearances than any that are to be found in nature; so we can combine various sounds into one melodious tune; in short, we can modify and dispose the simple ideas of sensation into whatever shape we please. But these ideas can enter our minds no other way but through the senses. A man born blind will never gain one idea of light or color. One born deaf will never get an idea of sound.

5. Saturday. Dreamed away the afternoon.

14. Monday. He is not a wise man, and is unfit to fill any important station in society, that has left one passion in his soul unsubdued. The love of glory will make a General sacrifice the interest of his nation to his own fame. Avarice exposes some to corruption, and all to a thousand meannesses and villainies destructive to society. Love has deposed lawful kings, and aggrandized unlawful, ill deserving courtiers. Envy is more studious of eclipsing the lustre of other men by indirect stratagems, than of brightening its own lustre by great and meritorious actions. These passions should be bound fast, and brought under the yoke. Untamed, they are lawless bulls; they roar and bluster, defy all control, and sometimes murder their proper owner. But, properly inured to obedience, they take their places under the yoke without noise, and labor vigorously in their master's service. From a sense of the government of God, and a regard to the laws established by his providence, should all our actions for ourselves or for other men primarily originate; and this master passion in a good man's soul, like the larger fishes of prey, will swallow up and destroy all the rest.

15. Tuesday. Consider for one minute the changes produced in this country within the space of two hundred years. Then the whole continent was one continued dismal wilderness, the haunt of wolves and bears and more savage men. Now the forests are removed, the land covered with fields of corn, orchards bending with fruit, and the magnificent habitations of rational and civilized people. Then, our rivers flowed through

gloomy deserts and offensive swamps. Now, the same rivers glide smoothly on, through rich countries fraught with every delightful object, and through meadows painted with the most beautiful scenery of nature and of art. The narrow huts of the Indians have been removed, and in their room have arisen fair and lofty edifices, large and well compacted cities. . . .

[July] 31. Saturday. The nature and essence of the material world is not less concealed from our knowledge than the nature and essence of God. We see ourselves surrounded on all sides with a vast expanse of heavens, and we feel ourselves astonished at the grandeur, the blazing pomp of those stars with which it is adorned. The birds fly over our heads and our fellow animals labor and sport around us; the trees wave and murmur in the winds; the clouds float and shine on high; the surging billows rise in the sea, and ships break through the tempest; here rises a spacious city, and yonder is spread out an extensive plain. These objects are so common and familiar that we think ourselves fully acquainted with them; but these are only effects and properties; the substance from whence they flow is hid from us in impenetrable obscurity.

God is said to be self-existent, and that therefore he must have existed from eternity, and throughout immensity. God exists by an absolute necessity in his own nature; that is, it implies a contradiction to suppose him not to exist. To ask what this necessity is, is as if you should ask what the necessity of the equality between twice two and four is; twice two are necessarily in their own nature equal to four, not only here, but in every point of space; not only now, but in every point of duration. In the same manner God necessarily exists, not only here, but throughout unlimited space; not only now, but throughout all duration, past and future. We observe in the animate and in the inanimate creation a surprising diversity and a surprising uniformity. Of inanimate substances there is a great variety, from the pebble in the streets quite up to the vegetables in the forest; of animals there is no less a variety of species, from the animalcula, that escape our naked sight, quite through the intermediate kinds up to elephants, horses, men. Yet, notwithstanding this variety, there is, from the highest species of animals upon this globe, which is generally thought to be man, a regular and uniform subordination of one tribe to another, down to the apparently insignificant animalcules in pepper water; and the same subordination continues quite through the vegetable kingdom. And it is worth observing that each species regularly and uniformly preserve all their essential and peculiar properties without partaking of the peculiar properties of others. We do not see chickens hatched with fins to swim; nor fishes spawned with wings to fly; we do not see a colt foaled with claws like a bird, nor man with the clothing or armor which his reason renders him capable of procuring for himself. Every species has its distinguishing properties, and every individual that is born has all those properties without any of the distinguishing properties of another species. What now can preserve this prodigious variety of species and this inflexible uniformity among the individuals but the continual and vigilant providence of God? . . .

[August] 7. Saturday. All this past week my designs have been interrupted by the troubles and confusion of the house. I shall be able to resume the thread of my studies, I hope, now. Wrote pretty industriously in Bolingbroke. I have never looked attentively into my own breast; I have never considered (as I ought) the surprising faculties and operations of the mind. Our minds are capable of receiving an infinite variety of ideas from those numerous material objects with which we are surrounded; and the vigorous impressions which we receive from these, our minds are capable of retaining, compounding, and arranging into all the varieties of picture and of figure; our minds are able to retain distinct comprehensions of an infinite multitude of things, without the least labor or fatigue. By curiously inquiring into the situation, fruits, produce, manufactures, &c., of our own, and by travelling into or reading about other countries, we can gain distinct ideas of almost every thing upon this earth, at present; and by looking into history we can settle in our minds a clear and a comprehensive view of this earth at its creation; of its various changes and revolutions; of its various catastrophes; of its progressive cultivation, sudden depopulation, and gradual repeopling; of the growth of several kingdoms and empires; of their wealth and commerce, wars and politics; of the characters of their principal leading men; of their grandeur and power; of their virtues and vices; and of their insensible decays at first, and of their swift destruction at last. In fine, we can attend the earth from its nativity through all the various turns of fortune; through all its successive changes; through all the events that happen on its surface; and through all the successive generations of mankind to the final conflagration, when the whole earth, with all its appendages, shall be consumed and dissolved by the furious element of fire. And after our minds are furnished with this ample store of ideas, far from feeling burdened or overloaded, our thoughts are more free, and active, and clear than before, and we are capable of diffusing our acquaintance with things much further; we are not satiated with knowledge; our curiosity is only improved and increased; our thoughts rove beyond the visible diurnal sphere; they range through the heavens and lose themselves amidst a labyrinth of worlds; and, not contented with what is, they run forward into futurity, and search for new employment there. Here, they can never stop; the wide, the boundless prospect lies before them; here alone they find objects adequate to their desires.

I know not by what fatality it happens, but I seem to have a necessity upon me of trifling away my time. Have not read fifty lines in Virgil this week; have wrote very little.

12. Thursday. Friday. I know not what became of these days.

14. Saturday. I seem to have lost sight of the object that I resolved to pursue. Dreams and slumbers, sloth and negligence, will be the ruin of my schemes. However, I seem to be awake now; why can't I keep awake? I have wrote Scripture pretty industriously this morning. Why am I so unreasonable as to expect happiness, and a solid, undisturbed contentment, amidst all the disorders and the continual rotations of worldly affairs? Stability is nowhere to be found in that part of the universe that lies within our observation; the natural and the moral world are continually changing; the planets, with all their appendages, strike out their amazing circles round the sun; upon the earth one day is serene and clear, no cloud intercepts the kind influ-

ences of the sun, and all nature seems to flourish and look gay;
but these delightful scenes soon vanish, and are succeeded by
the gloom and darkness of the night; and, before the morning
appears, the clouds gather, the winds rise, lightnings glare, and
thunders bellow through the vast of heaven. Man is sometimes
flushed with joy, and transported with the full fury of sensual
pleasure, and the next hour lies groaning under the bitter pangs
of disappointment and adverse fortune. Thus, God has told us
by the general constitution of the world, by the nature of all
terrestrial enjoyments, and by the constitution of our own bodies, that this world was not designed for a lasting and a happy
state, but rather for a state of moral discipline; that we might
have a fair opportunity and continual incitement to labor after
a cheerful resignation to all the events of Providence, after
habits of virtue, self-government, and piety; and this temper of
mind is in our power to acquire, and this alone can secure us
against all the adversities of fortune, against all the malice of
men, against all the operations of nature. A world in flames,
and a whole system tumbling in ruins to the centre, have nothing terrifying in them to a man whose security is builded on the
adamantine basis of good conscience and confirmed piety. If I
could but conform my life and conversation to my speculations,
I should be happy. . . .

[1759.] March 14. Reputation ought to be the perpetual subject of my thoughts, and aim of my behavior. How shall I gain
a reputation? how shall I spread an opinion of myself as a
lawyer of distinguished genius, learning, and virtue? Shall I
make frequent visits in the neighborhood, and converse famil-
iarly with men, women, and children, in their own style, on the
common tittletattle of the town and the ordinary concerns of
a family, and so take every fair opportunity of showing my
knowledge in the law? But this will require much thought and
time, and a very particular knowledge of the province law and
common matters, of which I know much less than I do of the
Roman law. Shall I endeavor to renew my acquaintance with
those young gentlemen in Boston who were at college with me,
and to extend my acquaintance among merchants, shopkeepers, tradesmen, &c., and mingle with the crowd upon Change,

and traipse the town-house floor with one and another, in order to get a character in town? But this, too, will be a lingering method and will require more art, and address, and patience, too, than I am master of. Shall I, by making remarks and proposing questions to the lawyers at the bar, endeavor to get a great character for understanding and learning with them? But this is slow and tedious, and will be ineffectual; for envy, jealousy, and self-interest, will not suffer them to give a young fellow a free, generous character, especially me. Neither of these projects will bear examination, will avail. Shall I look out for a cause to speak to, and exert all the soul and all the body I own, to cut a flash, strike amazement, to catch the vulgar; in short, shall I walk a lingering, heavy pace, or shall I take one bold determined leap into the midst of fame, cash, and business? That is the question;—a bold push, a resolute attempt, a determined enterprise, or a slow, silent, imperceptible creeping; shall I creep or fly?

I feel vexed, fretted, chafed; the thought of no business mortifies, stings me. But let me banish these fears; let me assume a fortitude, a greatness of mind. . . .

[1760.] Few things, I believe, have deviated so far from the first design of their institution, are so fruitful of destructive evils, or so needful of a speedy regulation, as licensed houses. The accommodation of strangers, and, perhaps, of town inhabitants on public occasions, are the only warrantable intentions of a tavern; and the supply of the neighborhood with necessary liquors in small quantities,* and at the cheapest rates, are the only excusable designs of a retailer; and that these purposes may be effected, it is necessary that both should be selected from the most virtuous and wealthy people, who will accept the trust, and so few of each should be erected that the profits may enable them to make the best provision at a moderate price. But at the present day, such houses are become the eternal haunt of loose, disorderly people of the same town, which renders them offensive and unfit for the entertainment of a traveller of the

---

* "To be consumed at home," written and erased.

least delicacy; and it seems that poverty and distressed circumstances are become the strongest arguments to procure an approbation; and for these assigned reasons, such multitudes have
been lately licensed that none can afford to make provision for
any but the tippling, nasty, vicious crew that most frequent them.
The consequences of these abuses are obvious. Young people
are tempted to waste their time and money, and to acquire habits of intemperance and idleness, that we often see reduce many
to beggary and vice, and lead some of them, at last, to prisons
and the gallows. The reputation of our county is ruined among
strangers, who are apt to infer the character of a place from
that of the taverns and the people they see there. But the worst
effect of all, and which ought to make every man who has the
least sense of his privileges tremble, these houses are become in
many places the nurseries of our legislators. An artful man, who
has neither sense nor sentiment, may by gaining a little sway
among the rabble of a town, multiply taverns and dram shops,
and thereby secure the votes of taverner and retailer, and of all;
and the multiplication of taverns will make many who may be
induced by flip and rum to vote for any man whatever. I dare
not presume to point out any method to suppress or restrain
these increasing evils, but I think for these reasons, it would be
well worth the attention of our legislature to confine the number
of, and retrieve the character of licensed houses, lest that impiety
and profaneness, that abandoned intemperance and prodigality,
that impudence and brawling temper, which these abominable
nurseries daily propagate, should arise at length to a degree of
strength that even the legislature will not be able to control. . . .

1764. [Here it may be proper to recollect something which
makes an article of great importance in the life of every man. I
was of an amorous disposition, and, very early, from ten or
eleven years of age, was very fond of the society of females. I
had my favorites among the young women, and spent many of
my evenings in their company; and this disposition, although
controlled for seven years after my entrance into college, returned and engaged me too much till I was married.

I shall draw no characters, nor give any enumeration of my
youthful flames. It would be considered as no compliment to the

dead or the living. This, I will say;—they were all modest and virtuous girls, and always maintained their character through life. No virgin or matron ever had cause to blush at the sight of me, or to regret her acquaintance with me. No father, brother, son, or friend, ever had cause of grief or resentment for any intercourse between me and any daughter, sister, mother, or any other relation of the female sex. These reflections, to me consolatory beyond all expression, I am able to make with truth and sincerity; and I presume I am indebted for this blessing to my education. This has been rendered the more precious to me, as I have seen enough of the effects of a different practice. Corroding reflections through life are the never failing consequence of illicit amours in old as well as in new countries. The happiness of life depends more upon innocence in this respect, than upon all the philosophy of Epicurus or of Zeno without it.

I passed the summer of 1764 in attending courts and pursuing my studies, with some amusement on my little farm, to which I was frequently making additions, until the fall, when, on the 25th of October, I was married to Miss Smith,[4] second daughter of the Rev. William Smith, minister of Weymouth, granddaughter of the Honorable John Quincy of Braintree, a connection which has been the source of all my felicity, although a sense of duty, which forced me away from her and my children for so many years, produced all the griefs of my heart, and all that I esteem real afflictions in life.] . . .

[1773.] December 17. Last night, three cargoes of Bohea tea were emptied into the sea. This morning a man-of-war sails. This is the most magnificent movement of all.* There is a dignity, a majesty, a sublimity, in this last effort of the patriots, that I greatly admire. The people should never rise without doing something to be remembered, something notable and striking. This destruction of the tea is so bold, so daring, so firm, intrepid and inflexible, and it must have so important consequences, and so lasting, that I cannot but consider it as an

---

*In the general correspondence, will be found a letter of this date directed to General James Warren, of Plymouth, showing some degree of acquaintance with this movement.

epocha in history. This, however, is but an attack upon property. Another similar exertion of popular power may produce the destruction of lives Many persons wish that as many dead carcasses were floating in the harbor, as there are chests of tea. A much less number of lives, however, would remove the causes of all our calamities. . . .

AUTOBIOGRAPHY

1777. November. When I asked leave of [the Continental—ED.] Congress to make a visit to my constituents and my family in November, 1777, it was my intention to decline the next election, and return to my practice at the bar. I had been four years in Congress, had left my accounts in a very loose condition, my debtors were failing, the paper money was depreciating; I was daily losing the fruits of seventeen years' industry; my family was living on my past acquisitions, which were very moderate, for no man ever did so much business for so little profit; my children were growing up without my care in their education, and all my emoluments as a member of Congress, for four years, had not been sufficient to pay a laboring man upon my farm. Some of my friends, who had more compassion for me and my family than others, suggested to me what I knew very well before, that I was losing a fortune every year by my absence. Young gentlemen who had been clerks in my office, and others whom I had left in that character in other offices, were growing rich; for the prize causes, and other controversies had made the profession of a barrister more lucrative than it ever had been before. I thought, therefore, that four years' drudgery, and a sacrifice of every thing, were sufficient for my share of absence from home, and that another might take my place. Upon my arrival at my home in Braintree, I soon found that my old clients had not forgotten me, and that new ones had heard enough of me to be ambitious of engaging me in suits which were depending. I had applications from all quarters in the most important disputes. Among others, Col. Elisha Doane applied to me to go to Portsmouth, in New Hampshire, upon the case of a large ship and cargo, which had been seized, and was to be tried in the court of admiralty, before Judge Brackett.

At the trial of the cause at Portsmouth, and while I was speaking in it, Mr. Langdon came in from Philadelphia, and leaning over the bar, whispered to me, that Mr. Deane was recalled, and I was appointed to go to France. As I could scarcely believe the news to be true, and suspected Langdon to be sporting with me, it did not disconcert me. As I had never solicited such an appointment, not intimated to any one the smallest inclination for it, the news was altogether unexpected. The only hint I ever had of such a design in Congress was this. After I had mounted my horse for my journey home, Mr. Gerry, at Yorktown, came out of the house of Mr. Roberdeau, where we lodged together, and said to me, between him and me, that I must go to France; that Mr. Deane's conduct had been so intolerably bad as to disgrace himself and his country, and that Congress had no other way of retrieving the dishonor but by recalling him. I answered that, as to recalling Mr. Deane, Congress would do as they thought fit, but I entreated him that neither Mr. Gerry nor any one else would think of me for a successor, for I was altogether unqualified for it. Supposing it only a sudden thought of Mr. Gerry, and that when he should consider it a moment he would relinquish it, I know not that I recollected it again, till Mr. Langdon brought it to remembrance. At Portsmouth, Captain Landais was introduced to me as then lately arrived from France, who gave me an account of his voyage with Bougainville round the world, and other particulars of his life. Upon my return to Braintree, I found to my infinite anxiety, that Mr. Langdon's intelligence was too well founded. Large packets from Congress, containing a new commission to Franklin, Lee, and me, as plenipotentiaries to the King of France, with our instructions and other papers had been left at my house, and waited my arrival. A letter from the President of Congress informed me of my appointment, and that the navy board in Boston was ordered to fit out the frigate Boston as soon as possible, to carry me to France. It should have been observed before, that in announcing to me the intelligence of my appointment, Langdon neither expressed congratulation nor regret, but I soon afterwards had evidence enough that he lamented Mr. Deane's recall, for he had already formed lucrative connections in France, by Mr. Deane's recommendation, particularly with Mr. Le Ray de Chaumont, who had shipped merchandise to him to sell upon commission, an account of which, rendered to Chaumont by Langdon, was shown to me by the former, at Passy, in 1779, in which almost the whole capital was sunk by the depreciation of paper money.

When the despatches from Congress were read, the first question was, whether I should accept the commission, or return it to Congress. The dangers of the seas, and the sufferings of a winter passage, although I had no experience of either, had little weight with me. The British men-of-war were a more serious consideration. The news of my appointment, I had no doubt, were known in Rhode Island, where a part of the British navy and army then lay, as soon as they were to me, and transmitted to England as soon as possible. I had every reason to expect that ships would be ordered from Rhode Island and from Halifax to intercept the Boston, and that intelligence would be secretly sent them, as accurately as possible, of the time when she was to sail. For there always have been and still are spies in America, as well as in France, England, and other countries. The consequence of a capture would be a lodging in Newgate. For the spirit of contempt, as well as indignation and vindictive rage, with which the British government had to that time conducted both the controversy and the war, forbade me to hope for the honor of an apartment in the Tower as a state prisoner. As their Act of Parliament would authorize them to try me in England for treason, and proceed to execution too, I had no doubt they would go to the extent of their power, and practise upon me all the cruelties of their punishment of treason. My family, consisting of a dearly beloved wife and four young children, excited sentiments of tenderness, which a father and a lover only can conceive, and which no language can express; and my want of qualifications for the office was by no means forgotten.

On the other hand, my country was in deep distress and in great danger. Her dearest interests would be involved in the relations she might form with foreign nations. My own plan of these relations had been deliberately formed and fully communicated to Congress nearly two years before. The confidence of my country was committed to me without my solicitation. My wife, who had always encouraged and animated me in all antecedent dangers and perplexities, did not fail me on this occasion. But she discovered an inclination to bear me company, with all our children. This proposal, however, she was soon convinced, was too hazardous and imprudent.

It was an opinion, generally prevailing in Boston, that the fisheries were lost forever. Mr. Isaac Smith, who had been more largely concerned in the cod-fishery than any man, excepting Mr. Hooper and Mr. Lee of Marblehead, had spoken to me on the subject, and said that whatever should be the termination of the war, he knew we should never be allowed to fish again upon the Banks. My practice as a barrister, in the counties of Essex, Plymouth, and Barnstable, had introduced me to more knowledge, both of the cod and whale fisheries, and of their importance, both to the commerce and naval power of this country, than any other man possessed who would be sent abroad if I refused; and this consideration had no small weight in producing my determination.

After much agitation of mind, and a thousand reveries unnecessary to be detailed, I resolved to devote my family and my life to the cause, accepted the appointment, and made preparation for the voyage. A longer time than I expected was required to fit and man the frigate. The news of my appointment was whispered about, and General Knox came up to dine with me at Braintree. The design of his visit was, as I soon perceived, to sound me in relation to General Washington. He asked me what my opinion of him was. I answered, with the utmost frankness, that I thought him a perfectly honest man, with an amiable and excellent heart, and the most important character at that time among us; for he was the centre of our Union. He asked the question, he said, because, as I was going to Europe, it was of importance that the General's character should be supported in other countries. I replied, that he might be perfectly at his ease on the subject, for he might depend upon it, that, both from principle and affection, public and private, I should do my ut-

most to support his character, at all times and in all places, unless something should happen very greatly to alter my opinion
of him; and this I have done from that time to this. I mention
this incident, because that insolent blasphemer of things sacred,
and transcendent libeller of all that is good, Tom Paine, has
more than once asserted in print that I was one of a faction, in
the fall of the year 1777, against General Washington.

I was almost out of patience waiting for the frigate till the
thirteenth day of February, 1778.

DIARY

1778. February 13. Friday. Captain Samuel Tucker, commander of the frigate Boston, met me at Mr. Norton Quincy's,
where we dined, and after dinner I sent my baggage, and
walked myself with Captain Tucker, Mr. Griffin, a midship-
man, and my eldest son, John Quincy Adams, between ten and
eleven years of age, down to the Moon Head, where lay the
Boston's barge. The wind was very high, and the sea very
rough; but, by means of a quantity of hay in the bottom of the
boat, and good watch-coats, with which we were covered, we
arrived on board the Boston, about five o'clock, tolerably
warm and dry. On board I found Mr. Vernon, a son of Mr. Vernon of the navy board, a little son of Mr. Deane of Wethers-
field, between eleven and twelve years of age, and Mr. Nicholas
Noel, a French gentleman, surgeon of the ship, who seems to
be a well-bred man. Dr. Noel showed me a book which was
new to me. The title translated is, "The Elements of the English
Tongue, developed in a new, easy, and concise Manner, in
which the Pronunciation is taught by an Asemblage of Letters,
which form similar Sounds in French." . . .

14. Saturday. A very fine morning; the wind at north-west. At
daybreak, orders were given for the ship to unmoor. My lodging
was a cot, with a double mattress, a good bolster, my own
sheets, and blankets enough; my little son with me. We lay very
comfortably, and slept well. A violent gale of wind in the night.

15. Sunday. This morning, weighed the last anchor, and

came under sail, before breakfast. A fine wind and a pleasant sun, but a sharp, cold air. Thus I bid farewell to my native shore. Arrived and anchored in the harbor of Marblehead about noon. Major Reed, Captain Gatchell, father-in-law of Captain Tucker, came on board, and a Captain Stephens, who came to make me a present of a single pistol. [He made many apologies for giving me but one. He had no more. He had lately presented to Mr. Hancock a beautiful pair, and this was all he had left. I understood they had been taken from the English, in one of the prize ships.]

16. Monday. Another storm for our mortification; the wind at north-east, and the snow so thick that the captain thinks he cannot go to sea. Our excursion to this place was unfortunate, because it is almost impossible to keep the men on board; mothers, wives, sisters, come on board, and beg for leave for their sons, husbands, and brothers, to go on shore for one hour, &c.; so that it is hard for the commander to resist their importunity. I am anxious at these delays; we shall never have another wind so good as we have lost. Congress and the navy-board will be surprised at these delays, and yet there is no fault that I know of. The commander of the ship is active and vigilant, and does all in his power, but he wants men.* He has very few seamen indeed. All is as yet chaos on board. His men are not disciplined; the marines are not. The men are not exercised to the guns; they hardly know the ropes.

My son is treated very complaisantly by Dr. Noel, and by a captain and lieutenant of artillery, who are on board, all French gentlemen. They are very assiduous in teaching him French. The Doctor, Monsieur Noel, is a genteel, well-bred man, and has received somewhere a good education. He has wounds on his forehead and on his hands, which he says he received, last war,

---

* "Seeing no probability of going to sea, I gave two midshipmen, two mates, and the purser, liberty to go on shore. At two, P.M., the wind got round to the northward. I ordered preparation for sea, fired several signal guns, for my officers on shore to come on board, but without effect. I was obliged to go myself and get them on board, not without a great deal of trouble." *Extract from the Log Book.*

in the light-horse service. The name of the captain of artillery is
Parison, and that of the lieutenant is Bégard.

Since my embarkation, Master Jesse Deane delivered me a
letter from his uncle Barnabas Deane, dated 10th February, rec-
ommending to my particular care and attention the bearer, the
only child of his brother, Silas Deane, Esq., now in France,
making no doubt, as the letter adds, "that I shall take the same
care of a child in his situation, which I would wish to have
done to a child of my own, in the like circumstances. It is needless to mention his youth and helplessness, also how much he
will be exposed to bad company, and to contract bad habits,
without some friendly monitor to caution and keep him from
associating with the common hands on board."

About the same time, another letter was delivered to me
from William Vernon, Esq., of the Continental Navy Board,
dated February 9, in these words: "I presume it is unnecessary
to say one word, in order to impress your mind with the anxiety a parent is under in the education of a son, more especially
when not under his immediate inspection, and at three thousand miles distance. Your parental affection fixes this principle.
Therefore I have only to beg the favor of you, sir, to place my
son in such a situation, and with such a gentleman as you
would choose for one of yours, whom you would wish to accomplish for a merchant. If such a house could be found, either
at Bordeaux or Nantes, of Protestant principles, of general and
extensive business, I rather think one of those cities the best.
Yet, if it should be your opinion that some other place might be
more advantageous to place him at, or that he can be employed
by any of the States' agents, with a good prospect of improving
himself in such manner that he may hereafter be useful to society, and in particular to these American States, my views are
fully answered. I have only one observation more to make,
namely, in respect to the economy of this matter, which I am
persuaded will engage your attention, as the small fortune that
remains with me I would wish to appropriate for the education
of my son, which I know must be husbanded; yet I can't think
of being rigidly parsimonious, nor must I be very lavish, lest my
money should not hold out.

"I imagine a gratuity of one hundred pounds sterling may be given to a merchant of eminence to take him for two or three years, and, perhaps, his yearly board paid for. I shall be entirely satisfied, in whatsoever may seem best for you to do, and ever shall have a grateful remembrance of your unmerited favors. And sincerely hope, in future, to have it in my power to make compensation. I wish you health, and the utmost happiness, and am, with the greatest regards, &c."

Thus I find myself invested with the unexpected trust of a kind of guardianship of two promising young gentlemen, besides my own son. This benevolent office is peculiarly agreeable to my temper. Few things have ever given me greater pleasure than the tuition of youth to the bar, and the advancement of merit.

[I was soon relieved from the principal care of it, however, for Mr. Vernon chose to remain at Bordeaux; and Mr. Deane, by the advice of Dr. Franklin, was put to Le Cœur's *pension,* at Passy, with my son, J.Q.A., and his grandson, Benjamin Franklin Bache, since that time, famous enough as the editor and proprietor of the Aurora.]

17. Tuesday. I set a lesson to my son, in Chambaud's French Grammar, and asked the favor of Dr. Noel to show him the precise, critical pronunciation of all the French words, syllables, and letters, which the Doctor very politely did, and Mr. John is getting his lessons accordingly, very much pleased.

The weather is fair, and the wind right, and we are again weighing anchor in order to put to sea.

Captain Diamond and Captain Inlaker came on board and breakfasted; two prisoners taken with Manly in the Hancock, and lately escaped from Halifax. Our captain is an able seaman, and a brave, active, vigilant officer, but I believe he has no great erudition. His library consists of Dychè's English Dictionary, Charlevoix's Paraguay, The Rights of the Christian Church Asserted *vs.* The Romish and other Priests who claim an Independent Power over it, the second volume of Chubb's Posthumous Works, one volume of the History of Charles Horton, Esq., and one volume of the Delicate Embarrassments, a novel. I shall, at some other time, take more notice of some of these books.

18. Wednesday. Last night, about sunset, we sailed out of Marblehead harbor, and have had a fine wind from that time to this, twenty-four hours. The constant rolling and rocking of the ship, last night, made us all sick. Half the sailors were so. My young gentlemen, Jesse and Johnny, were taken about twelve o'clock last night, and have been very sea-sick ever since. I was seized with it myself this forenoon. My servant, Joseph Stevens, and the captain's Will, have both been very bad.

19. Thursday. Arose at four o'clock. The wind and weather still fair. The ship rolls less than yesterday, and I have neither felt nor heard any thing of sea sickness last night, nor this morning. Monsieur Parison, one of General Du Coudray's captains, dined with us yesterday, and made me a present of a bottle of a nice French dram, a civility which I must repay. He seems a civil and sensible man.

The *mal de mer* seems to be merely the effect of agitation. The smoke, and smell of sea-coal, the smell of stagnant, putrid water, the smell of the ship where the sailors lie, or any other offensive smell, will increase the qualminess, but do not occasion it.

Captain Parison says, that the roads from Nantes to Paris are very good, no mountains, no hills, no rocks, all as smooth as the ship's deck, and a very fine country; but the roads from Bordeaux to Paris are bad and mountainous.

In the morning we discovered three sail of vessels ahead; we went near enough to discover them to be frigates, and then put away. We soon lost sight of two of them; but the third chased us the whole day; sometimes we gained upon her, and sometimes she upon us.*

* "At 6, A.M., saw three large ships bearing east, standing to the northward. I mistrusted they were cruising for me. I hauled my wind to the southward; found they did chase me. I consulted my officers whether it was not best to give them chase. We agreed in opinion. Wore ship to the north, and gave them chase one hour. I then discovered one of the ships to be as large as myself; the other a twenty gun ship; the third out of sight almost. A man at the mast head cried out, 'A ship on our weather-quarter;' the other two under our lee, and I under small sail. I then consulted the Honorable John Adams and my officers what was best to do, not knowing the best of my ship's sailing. They, one and all, consented to stand to the southward from them. The two that were under my lee were before me, and stood after me. I then wore, and at meridian, the

20. Friday. In the morning nothing to be seen, but soon after, another sail discovered ahead, which is supposed to be the same.*

[When the night approached, the wind died away, and we were left rolling and pitching in a calm, with our guns all out, our courses all drawn up, and every way prepared for battle; the officers and men appeared in good spirits, and Captain Tucker said his orders were to carry me to France, and to take any prizes that might fall in his way; he thought it his duty, therefore, to avoid fighting, especially with an unequal force, if he could, but if he could not avoid an engagement, he would give them something that should make them remember him. I said, and did all in my power, to encourage the officers and men to fight them to the last extremity. My motives were more urgent than theirs; for it will easily be believed that it would have been more eligible for me to be killed on board the Boston, or sunk to the bottom in her, than to be taken prisoner. I sat in the cabin, at the windows in the stern, and saw the enemy gaining upon us very fast, she appearing to have a breeze of wind, while we had none. Our powder, cartridges, and balls, were placed by the guns, and every thing ready to begin the action. Although it was calm on the surface of the sea, where we lay, the heavens had been gradually overspread with black clouds, and the wind began to spring up. Our ship began to move. The night came on, and it was soon dark. We lost sight of our enemy, who did not appear to me very ardent to overtake us. But the wind increased to a hurricane.]

---

small ship out of sight, the other at three leagues to leeward." *Log Book.* 19 February.

*"Ship still in chase, but being poorly manned, dare not attack her. For this, and sundry other reasons at 6, P.M., lost sight of the chase. Hauled my wind. The next morning saw the same ship ahead, standing to the southward and westward. I could not weather her on that tack. After running three hours to the westward, the wind favoring me, I then hove in stays, and came to windward of the ship, about four miles. Was satisfied it was the same ship; she tacked, and continued chasing me all day, but I rather gain upon her." *Log Book.* 20 February.

21. Saturday; 22. Sunday; and 23. Monday; exhibited such scenes as were new to me. We lost sight of our enemy, it is true, but we found ourselves in the Gulf stream, in the midst of an *épouvantable orage;* the wind north-east, then north, and then north-west.

It would be fruitless to attempt a description of what I saw, heard, and felt, during these three days and nights. To describe the ocean, the waves, the winds; the ship, her motions, rollings, wringings, and agonies; the sailors, their countenances, language, and behavior, is impossible. No man could keep upon his legs, and nothing could be kept in its place; an universal wreck of every thing in all parts of the ship, chests, casks, bottles, &c. No place or person was dry. On one of these nights, a thunderbolt struck three men upon deck, and wounded one of them a little, by a scorch upon his shoulder; it also struck our maintop-mast.*

Wednesday, 25. Tuesday, 24. Tuesday we spied a sail and gave her chase. We overhauled her, and, upon firing a gun to leeward and hoisting American colors, she fired a friendly gun, and hoisted the French colors of the Province of Normandy; she lay to for us, and we were coming about to speak to her, when the wind sprung up afresh of a sudden, and carried away our maintop-mast. We have been employed ever since in getting a new one, repairing the sails and rigging, much damaged in the late storm, and in cleaning the ship and putting her in order. From the 36th to the 39th degrees of latitude, are called the squally latitudes, and we have found them to answer their character. I should have been pleased to have kept a minute

---

* "21. Still chased by the ship. At 4 P.M. variable winds, and calm; at 7 P.M. sprung up a small breeze to the westward; run E.S.E. till 10 P.M. Heavy thunder and sharp lightning. At midnight the ship was struck by lightning at the mainmast and topmast, and wounded twenty-three men, and struck down three. Although we were in the greatest danger, received but little damage. Lost sight of the ship. Heavy and hard gales; we scudding."

"22. Heavy gales and head sea. One thing and another continually giving way on board the ship. Lay by under mainsail. Down top gallant yards; at 4 P.M. carried away slings and chains of mizzen yards; at 4 A.M. somewhat moderate; made sail, and began to repair the rigging." *Log Book.*

journal of all that passed, in the late chases and turbulent weather; but I was so wet, and every thing and place was so wet, every table and chair was so wrecked, that it was impossible to touch a pen, or paper.

It is a great satisfaction to me, however, to recollect that I was myself perfectly calm, during the whole. I found, by the opinion of the people aboard, and of the captain himself, that we were in danger, and of this I was certain also, from my own observation; but I thought myself in the way of my duty, and I did not repent of my voyage. I confess I often regretted that I had brought my son. I was not so clear that it was my duty to expose him as myself, but I had been led to it by the child's inclination, and by the advice of all my friends. Mr. Johnny's behavior gave me a satisfaction that I cannot express; fully sensible of our danger, he was constantly endeavoring to bear it with a manly patience, very attentive to me, and his thoughts constantly running in a serious strain.

26. Thursday. I have made many observations, in the late bad weather, some of which I do not think it prudent to put in writing. A few I will set down. 1st. I have seen the inexpressible inconvenience of having so small a space between decks, as there is in the Boston. As the main deck was almost constantly under water, the sea rolling in and out of the ports and scuppers, we were obliged to keep the hatchways down, whereby the air became so hot and so dry in the 'tween-decks, that, for my own part, I could not breathe or live there; yet the water would pour down, whenever a hatchway was opened, so that all was afloat. 2d. The Boston is over-metalled; her number of guns, and the weight of their metal, is too great for her tonnage; she has five twelve-pounders, and nineteen nines. We were obliged to sail, day and night during a chase, with the guns out, in order to be ready, and this exposed us to certain inconvenience, and great danger; they made the ship labor and roll, so as to oblige us to keep the chain pumps, as well as the hand pumps, almost constantly going; besides, they wring and twist the ship in such a manner as to endanger the starting of a butt, but still more to endanger the masts and rigging. 3d. The ship is furnished with no pistols, which she

ought to be, with at least as many as there are officers, because there is nothing but the dread of a pistol will keep many of the men to their quarters in time of action. 4th. This ship is not furnished with good glasses, which appear to me of very great consequence. Our ships ought to be furnished with the best glasses that art affords; their expense would be saved a thousand ways. 5th. There is the same general inattention, I find, to economy, in the navy, that there is in the army. 6th. There is the same general relaxation of order and discipline. 7th. There is the same inattention to the cleanliness of the ship, and the persons and health of the sailors, as there is at land to the cleanliness of the camp, and the health, and cleanliness of the soldiers. 8th. The practice of profane cursing and swearing, so silly as well as detestable, prevails in a most abominable degree. It is indulged and connived at by officers, and practised, too, in such a manner, that there is no kind of check against it. And I take upon me to say, that order of every kind will be lax as long as this is so much the case.

This morning, Captain Tucker made me a present of Charlevoix's History of Paraguay. Yesterday, Doctor Noel put into my hand a pocket volume, entitled "Le Géographe manuel, contenant la Description de tous les Pays du Monde, leurs Qualités, leur Climat, le Caractère de leurs Habitans, leur Villes Capitales, avec leur Distances de Paris, et des Routes qui y menent tant par Terre que par Mer; &c. &c. Par M. l'Abbé Expilly, de la Société royale des Sciences et Belles-Lettres de Nancy."

These manuals come out annually, and are to be had in any of the great towns in France.

27. Friday. A calm. As soft and warm as summer. A species of black fish, which our officers call bonitos, appeared about the ship.

One source of the disorders in this ship, is the irregularity of meals. There ought to be a well digested system for eating, drinking, and sleeping. At six, all hands should be called up; at eight, all hands should breakfast; at one, all hands should dine; at eight again, all hands should sup. It ought to be penal for the cook to fail of having his victuals ready punctually. This would be for the health, comfort, and spirits of the men, and would greatly promote the business of the ship.

I am constantly giving hints to the captain concerning order, economy, and regularity, and he seems to be sensible of the necessity of them, and exerts himself to introduce them. He has cleared out the 'tween decks, ordered up the hammocks to be aired, and ordered up the sick, such as could bear it, upon deck for sweet air. This ship would have bred the plague or the jail fever, if there had not been great exertions, since the storm, to wash, sweep, air, and purify clothes, cots, cabins, hammocks, and all other things, places, and persons. The captain, yesterday, went down into the cockpit and ordered up everybody from that sink of devastation and putrefaction; ordered up the hammocks, &c. This was in pursuance of the advice I gave him in the morning: "If you intend to have any reputation for economy, discipline, or any thing that is good, look to your cockpit."

Yesterday, the captain brought in a curiosity which he had drawn up over the side in a bucket of water, which the sailors call a Portuguese man-of-war, and to-day I have seen many of them sailing by the ship. They have some appearances of life and sensibility. They spread a curious sail, and are wafted along very briskly. They have something like guts hanging down, which are said to be in a degree poisonous to human flesh. The hulk is like blue glass. I pierced it with the sharp point of my penknife, and found it empty. The air came out, and the thing shrunk up almost to nothing.

28. Saturday. Last night and this day we have enjoyed a fine easy breeze; the ship has had no motion but directly forward. I slept as quietly and as soundly as in my own bed at home. Doctor Noel gave me a phial of *Balsamum Fioravanti*, for an inflammation in my eyes, which seems to be very good for them. It is very much compounded; it is very subtle and penetrating. Pour a few drops into the palms of your hands, rub it over the palm and the fingers, and then hold the insides of your hands before your eyes, and the steam which evaporates enters the eyes, and works them clear. This balsam derives its name from its author.

The ship is now in very good order, cleaned out between decks, on the main deck, in the cabin and quarter decks. The masts, yards, sails, and rigging are well repaired. The captain has just now sent written orders to the steward of the ship, to make weekly returns to him of the state of provisions, and to be very frugal of provisions and candles, which appeared to be very necessary, as near one half of the ship's stores of candles are expended.

This is Saturday night; a fortnight yesterday since I took leave of my family. What scenes have I beheld since! What anxiety have my friends on shore suffered on my account, during the north-east storm which they must have had at land!

What is this gulf stream? What is the course of it? from what point, and to what point does it flow? how broad is it? how far distant is it from the continent of America? What is the longitude and latitude of it?

March 1. Sunday. Discovered that our mainmast was sprung in two places; one beneath the main deck, where if the mast had wholly failed in the late storm, it must have torn up the main deck, and the ship must have foundered. This is one among many instances, in which it has already appeared that our safety has not depended on ourselves.

A fine wind all day and night. Somewhat sea-sick. The ship was very quiet and still, no disturbance, little noise. I hope for the future we shall carry less sail, especially of nights, and at all times when we are not in chase.

2. Monday. A fair wind still, and a pleasant morning. The color of the water, which is green, not blue, as it has been for many days past, the appearance of large flocks of gulls and various other birds, convinced the knowing ones to-day, that we were not far from the Grand Bank of Newfoundland. The captain, however, thinks it thirty-five leagues to the north-west of us.

Our mast was yesterday repaired with two large fishes, as they call them; that is, large oaken planks, cut for the purpose, and put on. It seems now as firm as ever. The sailors are very superstitious. They say the ship has been so unfortunate that they really believe there is some woman on board. Women are the unluckiest creatures in the world at sea, &c.

This evening the wind is very fresh, and the ship sails at a great rate. We are out of the reach, I hope, of the gulf stream and British cruisers, two evils which I have great aversion to.

3. Tuesday. Our wind continued brisk and fresh all the last night and this morning.

Our course is about north-east. Showers in the night and this morning. The flock of gulls still pursuing us. This morning, Mr. Parison breakfasted with us. Our captain in gay spirits, chattering in French, Spanish, Portuguese, German, Dutch, Greek, and boasting that he could speak some words in every language. He told us he had ordered two more fishes upon the mainmast, to cover the flaws above deck. The captain, lieutenants, master, mates, and midshipmen, are now making their calculations to discover their longitude, but I conjecture they will be very wild.

The life I lead is a dull scene to me; no business, no pleasure, no study. Our little world is all wet and damp. There is nothing I can eat or drink without nauseating. We have no spirits for conversation, nor any thing to converse about. We see nothing but sky, clouds, and sea, and then sea, clouds, and sky.

I have often heard of learning a language, as French or English, on the passage, but I believe very little of any thing was ever learned on a passage. There must be more health and better accommodations.

My young friend, Mr. Vernon, has never had the least qualm of the sea-sickness since we came aboard. I have advised him to begin the study of the French tongue methodically by reading the grammar through. He has begun it accordingly, and we shall see his patience and perseverance.

4. Wednesday. Fair weather, but an adverse wind from the north-east, which obliges us to go to the southward of the south-east, which is out of our course.

[Our general intention was to make for Nantes, one of the most commercial cities of France, which I was very anxious to see, not only on account of its wealth and antiquity, and the connection of its merchants with those of Bilbao, but also as the scene of the edict of Nantes proclaimed by Henry IV. in 1590, so much to the honor and interest of humanity, and revoked by Louis XIV. in 1685, so much to its disgrace and injury.]

5. Thursday. This morning we have the pleasantest prospect we have yet seen; a fine easy breeze from the southward, which gives us an opportunity of keeping our true course, a soft, clear, warm air, a fair sun, no sea. We have a great number of sails

spread, and we go at the rate of nine knots, yet the ship has no perceptible motion, and makes no noise.

My little son is very proud of his knowledge of all the sails, and last night the captain put him to learn the mariner's compass. Oh, that we might make prize to-day of an English vessel, lately from London, with all the newspapers and Magazines on board, that we might obtain the latest intelligence, and discover the plan of operations for the ensuing campaign!

Whenever I arrive at any port in Europe, whether in Spain or France, my first inquiry should be concerning the designs of the enemy. What force they mean to send to America? where they are to obtain men? what is the state of the British nation? what the state of parties? what the state of finances and of stocks? Then the state of Europe, particularly France and Spain. What the real designs of those courts? What the condition of their finances? what the state of their armies, but especially, of their fleets? what number of ships they have fitted for the sea? what their names, number of men and guns, weight of metal, &c., where they lie, &c. The probability or improbability of a war, and the causes and reasons for and against each supposition. The supplies of clothing, arms, &c., gone to America during the past winter. The state of American credit in France. What remittances have been made from America in tobacco, rice, indigo, or any other articles?

We are now supposed to be nearly in the latitude of Cape Finistere, so that we have only to sail an easterly course.

"Finistère, Finis Terræ; c'est le cap le plus occidental, non seulement de la Galice et de l'Espagne, mais même de l'Europe; ce qui fait que les Anciens qui ne connoissoient rien au dela, lui ont donné son nom, qui signifie l'Extrêmité de la Terre, ou le bout du monde. Il y a une Ville de même nom."[5]

This day, we have enjoyed the clearest horizon, the softest weather, the best wind, and the smoothest sea, that we have seen since we came on board. All sails are spread, and we have gone ten knots, upon an average, the whole day.

6. Friday. The wind continued in the same point, about south, all night; and the ship has gone nine knots upon an average. This is great favor.

I am now reading the Amphitryon of Molière, which is his sixth volume. Rêvai-je? do I dream? have I dreamed? I have been in a dream? J' ai rêvé? I have been in a dream. It is in the Preterit.

We shall pass to the northward of the Western Islands, and are now supposed to be as near them as we shall be. They all belong to Portugal.

7. Saturday. The same prosperous wind, and the same beautiful weather continue. We proceed in our course, at the rate of about two hundred miles in twenty-four hours. We have passed all the dangers of the American coast. Those of the Bay of Biscay remain. God grant us a happy passage through them all.

Yesterday, the ship was all in an uproar with laughter. The boatswain's mate asked one of his superior officers, if they might have a frolic. The answer was, yes. Jerry accordingly, with the old sailors, proposed to build a galley, and all the raw hands, to the number of twenty or thirty, were taken in, and suffered themselves to be tied together by their legs. When, all of a sudden, Jerry and his knowing ones were found handing buckets of water over the sides and pouring them upon the poor dupes, until they were wet to the skin. The behavior of the gulled, their passions, and speeches, and actions, were diverting enough. So much for Jerry's fun. This frolic, I suppose, according to the sailors' reasoning, is to conjure up a prize.

This morning the captain ordered all hands upon deck, and took an account of the number of souls on board, which amounted to one hundred and seventy-two; then he ordered the articles of war to be read to them. After which he ordered all hands upon the forecastle, and then all hands upon the quarter deck, in order to try experiments, for determining whether any difference was made in the ship's sailing, by the weight of the men being forward or abaft.

Then all hands were ordered to their quarters, to exercise them at the guns. Mr. Barron gave the word of command; and they spent an hour, perhaps, in the exercise, at which they seemed tolerably expert. Then the captain ordered a dance upon the main deck, and all hands, negroes, boys, and men, were obliged to dance. After this, the old sailors set on foot another frolic, called

the miller, or the mill. I will not spend time to describe this odd
scene. But it ended in a very high frolic, in which almost all the
men were powdered over with flour, and wet again to the skin.
Whether these whimsical diversions are indulged in order to
make the men wash themselves, and shift their clothes, and to
wash away vermin, I don't know. But there is not in them the
least ray of elegance, very little wit, and a humor of the coarsest
kind. It is not superior to negro and Indian dances.

8. Sunday. The same wind and weather continues, and we go
at seven and half and eight knots. We are supposed to be past
the Western Islands.

Mr. Barron, our first lieutenant, appears to me to be an excellent officer. Very diligent and attentive to his duty. Very
thoughtful and considerate about the safety of the ship, and
about order, economy, and regularity among the officers and
men. He has great experience at sea; has used the trade to London, Lisbon, Africa, West Indies, Southern States, &c.

This morning, the captain ordered all hands upon quarter-
deck to prayers. The captain's clerk, Mr. William Cooper, had
prepared a composition of his own, which was a very decent
and comprehensive prayer, which he delivered in a grave and
proper manner. The officers and men all attended in clean clothes,
and behaved very soberly.

The weather has been cloudy all day. Towards night it became rainy and windy, and now the ship rolls a little in the old
fashion. We are about two thousand miles from Boston.

The late storm showed the beauty of Boileau's description
d'une Tempête. [As it was the first morsel of French verse, except Molière, which I ever attempted to understand, it may be
inserted here.]

> Comme l'on voit les flots, soulevés par l'orage,
> Fondre sur un vaisseau qui s'oppose a leur rage.
> Le vent avec fureur dans les voiles frémit,
> La mer blanchit d'écume, et l'air au loin gémit.
> Le matelot troublé, que son art abandonne,
> Croit voir dans chaque flot la mort qui l'environne.[6]
>
> *Trad. de Longin.*

9. Monday. Last night the wind shifted to the north-west, and blew fresh. It is now still fairer for us than before. The weather is fine, and we go on our voyage at a great rate. Some officers think we shall reach our port by Thursday night; others, by Saturday night. But these make no account of chases and cruises, and make no allowance for the variability of the winds.

14. Saturday. I have omitted inserting the occurrences of this week, on account of the hurry and confusion we have been in. Tuesday we spied a sail,* and gave her chase, we soon came up with her; but as we had borne directly down upon her, she had not seen our broadside, and knew not our force. She was a letter of marque, with fourteen guns, eight nines, and six sixes. She fired upon us, and one of her shot went through our mizzen yard. I happened to be upon the quarter deck, and in the direction from the ship to the yard, so that the ball went directly over my head. We, upon this, turned our broadside, which the instant she saw, she struck. Captain Tucker very prudently ordered his officers not to fire.†

---

* "Saw a ship to the south-east standing to the westward. Asked the favor of the Hon. John Adams to chase, which was immediately granted. Made sail and gave chase. At 3 P.M. came up with the chase, gave her a gun and she returned me three, one shot of which carried away my mizzen yard. She immediately struck. Out boat. Got the prisoners on board. She proved the ship Martha from London, bound to New York. I ordered a prize-master on board, intending to send her to France, but on consulting Mr. Adams, he thought most advisable to send her to America." *Log-book.*

†It must be to this occasion, being the only one upon which a shot was fired by an enemy, that Mr. Sprague, in his *Eulogy of Adams and Jefferson,* refers, in the following anecdote. He doubtless had it from Tucker in his latest days, when a sailor's stories commonly lose nothing in the telling.

"Discovering an enemy's ship, neither Commodore Tucker nor Mr. Adams could resist the temptation to engage, although against the dictates of prudent duty. Tucker, however, stipulated that Mr. Adams should remain in the lower part of the ship, as a place of safety. But no sooner had the battle commenced, than he was seen on deck, with a musket in his hands, fighting as a common marine. The Commodore peremptorily ordered him below; but called instantly away, it was not until considerable time had elapsed, that he discovered this public minister still at his post, intently engaged in firing upon the enemy. Advancing, he exclaimed, 'Why are you here, sir? I am commanded by the Continental Congress to carry you in safety to Europe, and I will do it;' and, seizing him in his arms, forcibly carried him from the scene of danger."

The prize is the ship Martha, Captain McIntosh, from London to New York, loaded with a cargo of great value. The captain told me that seventy thousand pounds sterling was insured upon her at Lloyd's, and that she was worth eighty thousand. The captain is very much of a gentleman. There are two gentlemen with him, passengers, the one Mr. R. Gault, the other, Mr. Wallace of New York. Two young Jews were on board. That, and the next day, was spent in despatching the prize, under the command of the third lieutenant, Mr. Welch, to Boston.* After that, we fell in chase of another vessel, and overtaking her, found her to be a French snow, from Bordeaux to Miquelon. We then saw another vessel, chased, and came up with her, which proved to be a French brig, from Marseilles to Nantes. This last cost us very dear. Mr. Barron, our first lieutenant, attempting to fire a gun as a signal to the brig, the gun burst, and tore the right leg of this excellent officer in pieces, so that the doctor was obliged to amputate it, just below the knee. I was present at this affecting scene, and held Mr. Barron in my arms, while the doctor put on the tourniquet and cut off the limb. Mr. Barron bore it with great fortitude and magnanimity; thought he should die, and frequently entreated me to take care of his family. He had an helpless family, he said, and begged that I would take care of his children. I cannot but think the fall of this officer a great loss to the United States. His prudence, his moderation, his attention, his zeal, were qualities much wanted in our navy. He is by birth a Virginian.

[He said he had a mother, a wife and children who were dependent on him, and in indigent circumstances. I promised him that as soon as I could write to America, I would recommend his family to the care of the public, as well as of individuals. I recollect to have done something of this, but the scenes of dis-

---

* "After finding the papers necessary and giving Mr. Adams time to pack them, I consulted him about sending one of my lieutenants to command her, as she was a commissioned ship and in the King's service, mounting sixteen nine and six pound cannon; her cargo insured at £72,000 in London. At 3 P.M. I sent her by Mr. Welch, my third lieutenant, by the consent of the Hon. J. Adams, with fourteen good men and four prisoners for Boston or any port adjacent." Log-Book.

traction in which I was soon involved, I fear prevented me from doing so much as I ought to have done; and I feel it to this hour to be one of the omissions which I ought to regret.]*

19. Thursday. I have scarcely been able to stand or sit, without holding fast with both my hands upon some lashed table, some lashed gun, the side or beams of the ship, or some other fixed object, such has been the perpetual motion of the ship, arising from violent gales, and a heavy sea. In the course of the last five days, we have seen a great number of vessels, two of which, at least, if not four, were supposed to be cruisers. But here we are, at liberty as yet. The wind has been directly against us, but this morning has veered, and we now steer, at least our head lies by the compass, south-east. Who knows but Providence has favored us by the last gale, as it seemed to do by the first? By the last gale we have already escaped cruisers, as we did by the first, and possibly this violent gale from the south-east may have driven all the cruisers from the coast of Spain, and the southerly part of the Bay of Biscay, and by this means have opened a clear passage for us to Bordeaux. This is possible, and so is the contrary; God knows.

20. Friday. Yester afternoon, the weather cleared up, and the wind came about very fair. We had a great run last night. This morning, spied a sail under our leeward bow, chased, and soon came up with her, a snow from Amsterdam to Demerara and Essequibo.

I made inquiry to-day of our prisoner, Captain McIntosh, concerning the Trinity House. He says it is the richest corporation in the kingdom; that Lord Sandwich is an elder brother of it; that any master of a vessel may be made a younger brother of it, if he will; that there are many thousands of younger brothers; that this house gives permission to every vessel to take out or to take in ballast, and that a few pence, 6d. perhaps, per ton, are paid them for such license; that they have the care of all light-houses, &c.

---

*17. "Tuesday. At 2 P.M. discovered two large ships under courses, in full chase of me. When they came within about a half mile, made one a two-decker; the other, I could not tell what she was. I then set my mainsail, and left them." *Log-Book.*

My principal motive for omitting to keep a regular and particular journal, has been the danger of falling into the hands of my enemies, and an apprehension that I should not have an opportunity of destroying these papers in such a case. We have now so fine a wind, that a very few days will determine whether we shall meet any capital disaster, or arrive safe at port.

21. Saturday. Five weeks yesterday since my embarkation. This morning, a heavy wind and high sea. We go east, south-east.

27. Friday. On Wednesday evening Mr. Barron died, and yesterday was committed to the deep, from the quarter-deck. He was put into a chest, and ten or twelve twelve pounds shot put in with him, and then nailed up. The fragment of the gun which destroyed him was lashed on the chest, and the whole launched overboard through one of the ports, in presence of all the ship's crew, after the burial service had been read by Mr. Cooper.

In the course of the last week we have had some of the worst winds that we have felt yet.

Monday last we made the land upon the coast of Spain.

Tuesday, we run into the Bay of Saint Antonio. Four or five boats, with fifteen or sixteen men in each, came to us, out of which we took a pilot.

Upon sight of the Spanish shore, which I viewed as minutely as possible through the glasses, I had a great curiosity to go on shore; there was a fine verdure near the sea, although the mountains were covered with snow. I saw one convent; but we did not come in sight of the town. The moment we were about turning the point of the Rock to go into the harbor, a sail appeared; we put out to see who she was; found her a Spanish brig, and after this, upon repeated efforts, found it impracticable to get into the harbor. In the night the wind caught us suddenly at north-west, and we were obliged to make all the sail we could and put to sea; we steered our course for Bordeaux. Yesterday was a calm, the little wind there was directly against us. This morning the wind is a little better. We are supposed to be within thirty leagues of Bordeaux River.

28. Saturday. Last night, and this morning, we were in the thoroughfare of all the ships from Bordeaux; we had always a great number in sight. By observations, to-day, our latitude is

forty-six degrees three minutes, north, about seven minutes south of the middle of the Isle of Ré; we are, therefore, about twenty leagues from the Tower of Cordouan. We have no wind; and nothing can be more tedious and disagreeable to me than this idle life.

Last evening we had two little incidents which were disagreeable: one was, the French barber, attempting to go below contrary to orders, the sentinel cut off his great toe with his cutlass, which raised at first a little ill blood in the French people who are on board, but, on inquiry, finding the fellow deserved it, they acquiesced. The other unpleasant incident was, that one of our prisoners of war, a little more elevated than usual, grew out of temper, and was very passionate with Mr. Vernon, and afterwards with Captain Palmes; but it has all subsided.

[Our English prisoners, though in general they behaved very well, were sometimes out of humor, and had made some invidious remarks upon our officers and men and their awkward conduct of the ship; and, especially on the evening of St. Patrick's day, when many of them, who had declared they would get drunk, and, I suppose, had been as good as their word, were overheard to wish to meet a British man-of-war, and hinted that we could not stand an engagement of half an hour with a British vessel of half our force, &c.]

Mr. McIntosh is of North Britain, and appears to be very decided against America in this contest; and his passions are so engaged that they easily enkindle.

Mr. Gault is an Irish gentleman, and as decided against America, in her claim of independence at least, as the other; Mr. Wallace is more reserved, cautious, silent, and secret.

Jealousies arise among our men, that the prisoners are plotting with some of our profligate people. But I believe this jealousy is groundless.

All day yesterday, and all the forenoon of this day, we have been looking out for land; about four o'clock we found it. The Isles of Ré and Oléron, between which two is the entrance into the harbor of Rochelle, which is about half way between Bordeaux and Nantes. The land is extremely flat and low. We see the Tower. The water is shoal, twenty or thirty fathoms, the bottom, sand; the reverse of the Spanish coast on the other side of the Bay of Biscay.

This afternoon a clock calm, and Mr. Goss played upon his fiddle the whole afternoon, and the sailors danced, which seemed to have a very happy effect upon their spirits and good humor. Numbers of small birds, from the shore, came along today; some of them, fatigued, alighted on our rigging, yards, &c., and one of them we caught, a little lark he was called. These birds lose the shore, and get lost, and then they fly until they are so fatigued that the instant they alight upon a ship they drop to sleep.

29. Sunday. Becalmed all last night. This morning a vast number of sails in sight; St. Martin's and Oléron in sight; many towers and windmills; land very low and level. A pilot boat, with two sails and four men, came on board, and the pilot instantly undertook to pilot us to Bordeaux. He says this ship may go up quite to the city, if she drew twenty feet of water, at high water. We are now sailing very agreeably towards our port.

The pilot says war is declared, last Wednesday, and that the pavilions* were hoisted yesterday at every port and lighthouse. *Quære.*

There is a civil Frenchman on board whose name I never asked until to-day. His name is Quillau, Fourrier des Logis de M. Le Comte D'Artois. He was not of M. Du Coudray's corps.

The French gentlemen on board can scarcely understand our new pilot. He speaks Gascon, the dialect of Bordeaux, they say, which is not good French.

This day six weeks, we sailed from Nantasket road. How many dangers, distresses, and hair-breadth escapes have we seen! [There was one, however, which has been omitted. One evening when we were approaching the French coast, I was sitting in the cabin, when Captain McIntosh, our prisoner, came down to me, and addressed me with great solemnity. "Mr. Adams, this ship will be captured by my countrymen in less than half an hour. Two large British men-of-war are bearing directly down upon us, and are just by. You will hear from them, I warrant you, in six minutes. Let me take the liberty to say to

---

*The French term for flags.

you that I feel for you more than for any one else. I have always liked you since I came on board, and have always ascribed to you, chiefly, the good treatment I have received, as well as my people; and you may depend upon it, all the good service I can render you with my countrymen, shall be done with pleasure."

I saw by his countenance, gestures, air, language, and every thing, that he believed what he said; that he most heartily rejoiced in his own prospect of deliverance, and that he heartily pitied me. I smiled, however, at his offers of kind offices to me, knowing full well, that his prayers and tears would be as unavailing as my own, if he should be generous and I weak enough to employ them with British officers, ministers, judges, or king, in the then circumstances of things and temper of the Britons. I made him a bow, expressive of my sense of his politeness, but said nothing. Determined to see my danger, before I would be intimidated at it, I took my hat, and marched up to the quarter-deck. I had before heard an uncommon trampling upon deck, and perceived signs of some alarm and confusion, but when upon deck I saw the two ships indeed. They both appeared larger than our frigate, and were already within musket-shot of us. The air was clear, and the moon very bright. We could see every thing, even the men on board. We all expected every moment to be hailed, and, possibly, saluted with a broadside. But the two ships passed by us, without speaking a word, and I stood upon deck till they had got so far off as to remove all apprehensions of danger from them. Whether they were two American frigates, which had been about that time in France, we never knew. We had no inclination to inquire about their business or destination, and were very happy that they discovered so little curiosity about ours.]*

A Story.—Garrick had a relation convicted of a capital of-

---

*The log-book fixes this upon the fifteenth of March, as appears from the following entry:

"At 8 p.m. saw two ships on my starboard bow, standing to the westward. I crossed them about half a mile under their lee. Discovering them to be British ships, one a two-decker, the other a frigate, I then bore away from them, by order of Hon. John Adams. One of the gentleman passengers informed me, they were boarded the day before I took them, by three men-of-war boats; that there were six two-deckers and frigates in company. At 9 a.m. lost sight of them."

fence. He waited on His Majesty, to beg a pardon. The King asked what was the crime? He has only taken a *cup too much,* says Garrick, may it please your Majesty. Is that all? said the King, let him be pardoned. *Gault.*

A Story.—A Frenchman, in London, advertised an infallible remedy against fleas. The ladies all flocked to purchase the powder; but after they had bought it, one of them asked for directions to use it. "Madam," says the Frenchman, "you must catch the flea, and squeeze him between your fingers until he gape, then you must put a little of this powder in his mouth, and I will be responsible he will never bite you again." "But," says the lady, "when I have him between my fingers, why may I not rub him to death?" "O, Madam, dat will do just as well den." *Tucker.*

We have been becalmed all day in sight of Oléron. The village of St. Denis was in sight, and multitudes of windmills and sand hills all along the shore. Multitudes of vessels in sight, French, Spanish, Dutch vessels, and English smugglers. I feel a curiosity to visit this Island of Oléron, so famous in antiquity for her sea laws; at least, I take this to be the place.

30. Monday. This morning, at 5, the officer came down and told the captain that a lofty ship was close by us, and had fired two heavy guns; all hands called; she proved to be a heavy loaded snow. The weather cloudy, but no wind. Still, except a small swell. The Tower of Cordouan, or in other words Bordeaux light-house, in sight, over our larboard bow. The captain is now cleaning ship, and removing his warlike appearances.

This day has been hitherto fortunate and happy. Our pilot has brought us safely into the river, and we have run up with wind and tide as far as Pauillac, where we have anchored for the night, and have taken in another pilot. This forenoon a fisherman came alongside, with hakes, skates, and gurnards; we bought a few and had a high regale.

This river is very beautiful on both sides; the plantations are very pleasant, on the south especially; we saw, all along, horses, oxen, cows, and great flocks of sheep grazing, the husbandmen ploughing, &c., and the women, half a dozen in a drove, with their hoes. The churches, convents, gentlemen's seats, and the villages appear very magnificent.

This river seldom swells with freshes; for the rural improvements, and even the fishermen's houses, are brought quite down to the water's edge. The water in the river is very foul to all appearance, looking all the way like a mud puddle. The tide sets in five knots. We outrun every thing in sailing up the river. The buildings, public and private, are of stone; and a great number of beautiful groves appear between the grand seats and best plantations; a great number of vessels lay in the river.

The pleasure resulting from the sight of land, cattle, houses, &c., after so long, so tedious and dangerous a voyage, is very great. It gives me a pleasing melancholy to see this country; an honor which a few months ago I never expected to arrive at. Europe, the great theatre of arts, sciences, commerce, war! am I at last permitted to visit thy territories? May the design of my voyage be answered!

31. Tuesday. Lying in the River of Bordeaux, near Pauillac— a twenty-four gun ship close by us, under French colors, bound to St. Domingue.

A dark misty morning. My first inquiry should be, who is Agent for the United States of America at Bordeaux, at Blaye, &c.; who are the principal merchants on this river concerned in the American trade? What vessels, French or American, have sailed, or are about sailing for America? What their cargoes, and for what ports? Whether on account of the United States, of any particular State, or of private merchants, French or American?

This morning the captain and a passenger came on board the Boston, from the Julie, a large ship bound to St. Domingue, to make us a visit. They invited us on board to dine. Captain Palmes, Master Jesse and Johnny, and myself, went. We found half a dozen genteel persons on board, and found a pretty ship, an elegant cabin, and every accommodation. The white stone plates were laid, and a clean napkin placed in each, and a cut of fine bread. The cloth, plates, servants, every thing was as clean as in any gentleman's house. The first dish was a fine French soup, which I confess I liked very much. Then a dish of boiled meat. Then the lights of a calf, dressed one way and the liver another. Then roasted mutton, then fricasseed mutton, a fine salad, and something very like asparagus, but not it. The bread was very fine, and it was baked on board. We had prunes, almonds, and the most delicate raisins I ever saw. Dutch cheese, then a dish of coffee, then a French cordial; and wine and water, excellent claret with our dinner. None of us understood French, none of them English; so that Doctor Noel stood interpreter. While at dinner we saw a pinnace go on board the Boston with several, half a dozen, genteel people on board. On the quarter deck I was struck with the hens, capons and cocks, in their coops, the largest I ever saw. After a genteel entertainment, Mr. Griffin, one of our petty officers, came with the pinnace and Captain Tucker's compliments, desiring to see me. We took leave and returned, where we found very genteel company, consisting of the captain of another ship bound to Martinique, and several King's officers bound out. One was the Commandant. Capt. Palmes was sent forward to Blaye in the pinnace, to the officer at the Castle, in order to produce our commission and procure an entry and pass to Bordeaux. Palmes came back full of the compliments of the broker* to the captain and to me. I shall not repeat the compliments sent to me, but he earnestly requested that Capt. Tucker would salute the fort with thirteen guns, &c., which the captain did.† All the gentlemen we have seen to-day agree that Doctor Franklin has been received by the King in great pomp, and that a treaty is concluded, and they all expect war every moment.

This is a most beautiful river. The villages and country seats appear upon each side all the way. We have got up this afternoon within three leagues of the town.

April 1. Wednesday. This morning Mr. J. C. Champagne, négociant et courtier de marine, at Blaye, came on board to make a visit and pay his compliments. He says, that of the first growths of wines in the Province of Guienne there are four sorts, Chateau-Margaux, Haut-brion, Lafitte, and Latour.

This morning I took leave of the ship and went up to town with my son and servant, Mr. Vernon, Mr. Jesse, and Doctor

---

*Probably Mr. Champagne, mentioned the next day.
†"At 2 P.M. came to sail up the river to town. Saluted a small town called Blaye, with the Independent salute." *Log-Book.*

Noel, in the pinnace.* When we came up to the town we had the luck to see Mr. McCreery and Major Frazer on the shore. Mr. McCreery came on board our boat, and conducted us up to his lodgings. Mr. Pringle was there. We dined there in the fashion of the country; we had fish and beans, and salad, and claret, champagne, and mountain wine. After dinner, Mr. Bond-field, who is agent here, invited me to take a walk, which we did, to his lodgings, where we drank tea; then we walked about the town, and to see the new comédie; after this we went to the opera, where the scenery, the dancing, the music, afforded to me a very cheerful, sprightly amusement, having never seen any thing of the kind before. [Our American theatres had not then existed even in contemplation.] After this we returned to Mr. McCreery's lodgings, where we supped.

2. Thursday. Walked round the town, to see the Chamber and Council of Commerce, the Parliament which was sitting, where we heard the council. Then we went round to the ship-yards, &c. Made many visits. Dined at the Hotel d'Angleterre. Visited the custom-house, the post-office; visited the comman-dant of the chateau Trompette, a work of Vauban's. Visited the Premier President of the Parliament of Bordeaux.

[Here I met a reception that was not only polite and respect-ful, but really tender and seemingly affectionate. He asked per-mission to embrace me a la françoise. He said he had long felt for me an affection resembling that of a brother. He had pitied me, and trembled for me, and was cordially rejoiced to see me. He could not avoid sympathizing with every sincere friend of liberty in the world. He knew that I had gone through many dangers and sufferings in the cause of liberty, and he had felt for me in them all. "He had reason," he said, "to feel for the sufferers in the cause of Liberty, because he had suffered many years in that cause himself. He had been banished for coöperating with Mr. Malesherbes, and the other courts and parliaments of the kingdom, in the time of Louis XV. in their remonstrances

* "I sent the pinnace to town with the Hon. John Adams, son, and the two gen-tlemen passengers; likewise the cutter with the French gentlemen passengers. At 1 P.M. came within one mile of the town. A number of gentlemen and ladies came on board, who seemed much pleased with the ship." Log-Book.

against the arbitrary conduct and pernicious edicts of the court, &c. &c." Mr. Bondfield had to interpret all this effusion of compliments; and I thought it never would come to an end. But it did; and I concluded, upon the whole, there was a form of sincerity in it, decorated and almost suffocated with French compliments.] . . .

4. Saturday. About 10 o'clock we commenced our journey to Paris, and went about fifty miles.

[During my delay at Bordeaux, Mr. McCreery informed me, in confidence, that he had lately come from Paris, where he had been sorry to perceive a dryness between the American Ministers, Franklin, Deane, and Lee. Mr. McCreery was very cautious and prudent, but he gave me fully to understand that the animosity was very rancorous, and had divided all the Americans, and all the French people connected with Americans or American affairs, into parties very bitter against each other. This information gave me much disquietude, as it opened a prospect of perplexities to me that I supposed must be very disagreeable. Mr. Lee, Mr. Izard, Dr. Bancroft, and others whom Mr. McCreery named, were entire strangers to me but by reputation. With Dr. Franklin I had served one year and more in Congress. Mr. Williams I had known in Boston. The French gentlemen were altogether unknown to me. I determined to be cautious and impartial, knowing, however, very well, the difficulty and the danger of acting an honest and upright part in all such situations.]

5. Sunday. Proceeded on our journey more than one hundred miles. . . .

8. Wednesday. Rode through Orleans, &c., and arrived at Paris about 9 o'clock. For thirty miles or more the road is paved, and the scenes extremely beautiful.

At Paris we went to several hotels, which were full, particularly the Hotel d'Artois, and the Hotel Bayonne. Then we were advised to the Hotel de Valois, where we found entertainment; but we could not have it without taking all the chambers upon the floor, which were four in number, very elegant and richly furnished, at the small price of two crowns and a half a day, without any thing to eat or drink; we send for victuals to the cooks. I took the apartments only for two or three days.

At our arrival last night at a certain barrier, we were stopped and searched, and paid the duties for about twenty-five bottles of wine, which we had left of the generous present of Mr. Delap, at Bordeaux.

My little son has sustained this long journey of near five hundred miles, at the rate of a hundred miles a day, with the utmost firmness, as he did our fatiguing and dangerous voyage.

Immediately on our arrival we were called upon for our names, as we were at Mrs. Rives's, at Bordeaux.

We passed the bridge last night over the Seine, and passed through the Louvre. The streets were crowded with carriages with livery servants.

9. Thursday. This morning the bells and carriages and various cries in the street make noise enough; yet the city was very still last night, towards the morning. L'hôtel de Valois, Rue de Richelieu, is the name of the house and street where I now am. Went to Passy, in a coach, with Dr. Noel and my son. Dr. Franklin presented to me the compliments of M. Turgot, lately comptroller of the finances, and his invitation to dine with him. Went with Dr. Franklin and Mr. Lee, and dined in company with the Duchess d'Enville, the mother of the Duke de la Rochefoucauld, and twenty of the great people of France.

[I thought it odd that the first lady I should dine with in France should happen to be the widow of our great enemy, who commanded a kind of armada against us, within my memory; but I was not the less pleased with her conversation for that. She appeared to be venerable for her years, and several of her observations at table, full, as I thought, of bold, masculine, and original sense, were translated to me.]

It is in vain to attempt a description of the magnificence of the house, gardens, library, furniture, or the entertainment of the table. Mr. Turgot has the appearance of a grave, sensible, and amiable man.

[I was very particularly examined by the company through my colleagues and interpreters, Franklin and Lee, concerning American affairs. I should have been much better pleased to be permitted to remain less conspicuous; but I gave to all their in-

quiries the most concise and clear answer I could, and came off
for the first time, I thought, well enough.]

Came home and supped with Dr. Franklin on cheese and beer.

10. Friday. Dined at Monsieur Brillon's, with many ladies and
gentlemen. Madame Brillon is a beauty and a great mistress of
music, as are her two little daughters. The dinner was luxury, as
usual;—a cake was brought in with three flags flying; on one,
Pride subdued; on another, Hæc Dies in quâ fit Congressus, exul-
temus et potemus in eâ. Supped in the evening at Mr. Chaumont's.

[Dr. Franklin had shown me the apartments and furniture
left by Mr. Deane, which were every way more elegant than I
desired, and comfortable and convenient as I could wish. Although Mr. Deane, in addition to these, had a house, furniture,
and equipage, in Paris, I determined to put my country to no
further expense on my account, but to take my lodgings under
the same roof with Dr. Franklin, and to use no other equipage
than his, if I could avoid it. This house was called the Basse
cour de Monsieur Le Ray de Chaumont, which was, to be sure,
not a title of great dignity for the mansion of ambassadors,
though they were no more than American ambassadors. Nevertheless, it had been nothing less than the famous Hotel de
Valentinois, with a motto on the door, "Se sta bene, non si
muove," which I thought a good rule for my conduct.

The first moment Dr. Franklin and I happened to be alone, he
began to complain to me of the coolness, as he very coolly called
it, between the American ministers. He said there had been disputes between Mr. Deane and Mr. Lee; that Mr. Lee was a man
of an anxious, uneasy temper, which made it disagreeable to do
business with him; that he seemed to be one of those men, of
whom he had known many in his day, who went on through life
quarrelling with one person or another till they commonly
ended with the loss of their reason. He said, Mr. Izard was there
too, and joined in close friendship with Mr. Lee; that Mr. Izard
was a man of violent and ungoverned passions; that each of
these had a number of Americans about him, who were always
exciting disputes, and propagating stories that made the service
very disagreeable; that Mr. Izard, who, as I knew, had been appointed a minister to the Grand Duke of Tuscany, instead of go-

ing to Italy, remained with his lady and children at Paris; and instead of minding his own business, and having nothing else to do, he spent his time in consultations with Mr. Lee, and in interfering with the business of the commission to this court; that they had made strong objections to the treaty, and opposed several articles of it; that neither Mr. Lee nor Mr. Izard was liked by the French; that Mr. William Lee, his brother, who had been appointed to the court of Vienna, had been lingering in Germany; that he called upon the ministers at Paris for considerable sums of money, and by his connection with Lee and Izard and their party, increased the uneasiness, &c. &c. &c.

I heard all this with inward grief and external patience and composure. I only answered that I was personally much a stranger to Mr. Izard and both the Lees; that I was extremely sorry to hear of any misunderstanding among the Americans, and especially among the public ministers; that it would not become me to take any part in them; that I ought to think of nothing in such a case but truth and justice, and the means of harmonizing and composing all parties.

When Mr. Lee arrived at my lodgings one morning, it was proposed that a letter should be written to Mr. Dumas, at the Hague, to inform him of my arrival; and my colleagues proposed that I should write it. I thought it an awkward thing for me to write an account of myself, and asked Dr. Franklin to write it, after we should have considered and agreed upon what should be written; which I thought the more proper, as he was the only one of us who had been acquainted with Mr. Dumas. Accordingly, on the 10th of April, the letter was produced, in these words, which I insert at full length, because it was the only public letter, I believe, which he wrote while I was with him in that commission.*]

*Here follow two letters to Mr. Dumas, one of them covering the draught of a letter to the Grand Pensionary of Holland, which, having been since printed in the *Diplomatic Correspondence of the American Revolution*, vol. i, pp. 376–378, are now omitted. In the copy book of the commission, for 1778, left in Mr. Adams's hands, almost all the letters appear to have been drawn up by him. The two above-mentioned are noted as having been drawn by Dr. Franklin, and a few others are in the handwriting of Mr. Lee.

In the evening, two gentlemen came in and advised me to go to Versailles to-morrow. One of them was the secretary to the late ambassador in London, the Count de Noailles.

[This gentleman informed me that the Count de Vergennes had expressed to him his surprise that I had not been to Court. They had been informed by the police of my arrival in Paris, and had accidentally heard of my dining in company at one place and another; but when any question was asked them concerning me, they could give no answer. He supposed I was waiting to get me a French coat, but he should be glad to see me in my American coat.]

11. Saturday. Went to Versailles, with Dr. Franklin and Mr. Lee. Waited on the Count de Vergennes, the secretary of foreign affairs; was politely received. He hoped I should stay long enough to learn French perfectly; assured me that every thing should be done to make France agreeable to me; hoped the treaty would be agreeable, and the alliance lasting. I told him I thought the treaty liberal and generous, and doubted not of its speedy ratification. I communicated to him the resolutions of Congress respecting the suspension of Burgoyne's embarkation, which he read through and pronounced *fort bonnes*. I was then conducted to the Count Maurepas, the prime minister; was introduced by Dr. Franklin as his new colleague, and politely received.

[This gentleman, often called the King's Mentor, was near fourscore years of age, with a fresh, rosy countenance, and apparently in better health and greater vigor than Dr. Franklin himself. He had been dismissed from office and exiled to his lands by Louis XV. in 1749, and in his retirement, if not before, had obtained the reputation of a patriot, for which reason he had been recalled to court by Louis XVI. and placed at the head of affairs.]

The Palace of Versailles was then shown to me, and I happened to be present when the king passed through, to council. His Majesty, seeing my colleagues, graciously smiled and passed on. The galleries and royal apartments, and the king's bedchamber, were shown to me. The magnificence of these scenes is immense; the statues, the paintings, the every thing, is sublime.

We then returned; went into the city, and dined with the

Count, where was the Count de Noailles, his secretary, and twenty or thirty others, of the grandees of France.

After dinner we went in the coach to see the royal Hospital of Invalids, the chapel of which is immensely grand, in marble and paintings and statuary. After this, we went to the École Militaire, went into the chapel and into the hall of council, &c. Here we saw the statues of the great Condé, Turenne, Luxembourg, and Saxe. Returned and drank tea at Madame Brillon's, who lent me the Voyage Pittoresque de Paris, and entertained me again with her music and her agreeable conversation.

12. Sunday. The attention to me which has been shown, from my first landing in France, at Bordeaux, by the people in authority, of all ranks, and by the principal merchants, and since my arrival in Paris, by the ministers of state and others of the first consideration, has been very remarkable, and bodes well to our country. It shows in what estimation the new alliance with America is held.

On Friday last I had the honor of a visit from a number of American gentlemen. Mr. James Jay, of New York, brother of the Chief Justice, Mr. Johnson, brother of the Governor of Maryland, Mr. ———, Mr. Amiel, Mr. Livingston, from Jamaica, Mr. Austin, from Boston, Dr. Bancroft, Mr. R. Izard. I must return the visits of these gentlemen.

This day I had the honor to dine with the Prince de Tingry, Duc de Beaumont, of the illustrious house of Montmorency. The Duke and Duchess of . . . . .

[By this time I began to catch the sense, now and then, of the conversation in society, but very imperfectly. A conversation between the Prince de Tingry and my colleagues I understood so well as to perceive that he was haranguing upon toleration and liberty of conscience. With an air of great condescension and self-complacency for his great liberality, he vouchsafed to acknowledge, that although he should ardently desire the conversion of all Protestants to the Catholic religion, yet he would not persecute them, &c.]

Edisti satis, lusisti satis, atque bibisti;
Tempus est abire tibi;[7]

written under the picture of Sir Robert Walpole. Some one made an amendment of bribisti instead of bibisti.

13. Monday. This morning, the Duchess d'Ayen and Mad. la Marquise de Lafayette came to visit me and inquire after the Marquis.

Went to Versailles; was introduced to the levee of M. de Sartine, the minister;—a vast number of gentlemen were attending in one room after another, and we found the minister at last entrenched as deep as we had formerly seen the Count Maurepas. The minister politely received us, and showed us into his cabinet, where were all the books and papers of his office. After he had finished the business of his levee, he came into the cabinet to us, and asked whether I spoke French, and whether I understood French? The answer was, un peu, and, si on parle lentement ou doucement. He then made an apology to each of us separately, in the name of his lady, for her absence, being gone into Paris to see a sick relation. After this, we were conducted down to dinner, which was as splendid as usual; all elegance and magnificence. A large company; four ladies only. During dinner time many gentlemen came in, and walked the room, and leaned over the chairs of the ladies and gentlemen, and conversed with them while at table. After dinner, the company all arose as usual, went into another room, where a great additional number of gentlemen came in. After some time, we came off, and went to make a visit to Madame Maurepas, the lady of the prime minister, but she was out, and we left a card.

[Count de Lauraguais, who had conducted us to her apartments, wrote our card for us in the porter's book. "Messrs. Franklin, Lee, et Adams, pour avoir l'honneur de voir Madame de Maurepas." This, I believe, was the only time that I saw De Lauraguais. He spoke our language so well, and seemed to have so much information, that I wished for more acquaintance with him; but finding that he was not a favorite at court, and especially with those ministers who had the principal management of our American affairs, and hearing from Dr. Franklin and Dr. Bancroft that Mr. Lee and Mr. Izard had given offence by too much familiarity with him, I declined any farther inquiry concerning him; and I never heard that those gentlemen had any intercourse with him after that time.]*

We then went to the office of the secretary of M. de Vergennes, and delivered him a copy of my commission; then went and made a visit to Madame Vergennes, who had her levee, and returned to Passy. . . .

16. Jeudi. Doctor Franklin is reported to speak French very well, but I find, upon attending to him, that he does not speak it grammatically, and, indeed, upon inquiring, he confesses that he is wholly inattentive to the grammar. His pronunciation, too, upon which the French gentlemen and ladies compliment him, and which he seems to think is pretty well, I am sure is very far from being exact.

Indeed, Dr. Franklin's knowledge of French, at least his faculty of speaking it, may be said to have begun with his embassy to this court. He told me that when he was in France before, Sir John Pringle was with him, and did all his conversation for him, as interpreter, and that he understood and spoke French with great difficulty, until he came here last, although he read it.

Dined at M. La Ferté's. The magnificence of the house, garden, and furniture, is astonishing. Saw here a History of the Revolution in Russia, in the year 1762. This family are fond of paintings. They have a variety of exquisite pieces, particularly, a Storm and a Calm.

17. Vendredi. . . .

[On this week all the theatres of Paris are shut up, and the performers forbidden to play. By this decree, whether of the Church or State, or both, all the fashionable people of Paris and its environs are deprived of their daily amusements, and lose their ordinary topics of conversation; the consequence of which is that they are *si ennuyés* that they cannot live. To avoid this direful calamity, they have invented this new spectacle, and

*Mr. Deane's character of this gentleman is to be found in the first volume of the *Diplomatic Correspondence of the Revolution*, p. 150, a work in which much information respecting the action of all the persons here mentioned can be obtained. Of De Lauraguais, the wit, the spendthrift, and the roué, many traces are visible in the *Correspondance Littéraire de Grimm et Diderot*, vol. iii. pp. 297–302, vol. viii. and elsewhere.

have made it fashionable for every person who owns a carriage
of any kind that rolls upon wheels, and all those who can hire
one, to go out of town and march their horses slowly along one
side of the great road to the end of it; then they come about,
and return on the other side, and in this manner the carriages
are rolling all day. It was asserted on that day that there was
not a pair of wheels left in the city.

For some years, certain persons of equivocal reputation were
observed to appear in unusual splendor in these processions,
and the scandal increased from year to year, till one of the most
notorious females in Paris appeared in the most costly and
splendid equipage in the whole row;—six of the finest horses in
the kingdom; the most costly coach that could be built; more
numerous servants and richer liveries than any of the nobility
or princes; her own dress in proportion. It was generally agreed
to be the finest show that had ever been exhibited. This was so
audacious an insult to all modest women, and indeed to the national morality and religion, that the Queen, to her honor, sent
an order that if she should ever appear again, anywhere, in that
equipage, she should find herself in Bicêtre the next morning.*
Yet even this was a modest fancy in comparison with the palace
of Bellevue. This was another symptom of the pure, virtuous
manners, which I was simple enough to think would not ac-
cord with our American republican institutions. To be sure, it
had never yet entered into my thoughts that any rational being
would ever think of demolishing the monarchy and erecting a
republic in France.]

18. Samedi. . . .

[Mr. Franklin, who at the age of seventy odd had neither lost
his love of beauty nor his taste for it, called Mademoiselle de
Passy his favorite, and his flame, and his love, which flattered
the family, and did not displease the young lady. After the Mar-

---

*This happened in 1775. It ought in justice to be added that, even then, the in-
dividual was driven off the ground by the public indignation. Perhaps the supposed insult to the Queen had as much to do with it, however, as the cause of
morals. The anecdote is told in that curious repertory of Parisian manners and
opinions, during the reign of Louis XVI., the *Correspondance Secrète* of
Bachaumont, vol. i. p. 314.

quis had demanded Mademoiselle for a wife, and obtained her, Madame de Chaumont, who was a wit, the first time she saw Franklin, cried out, "Hélas! tous les conducteurs de Monsieur Franklin n'ont pas empêché le tonnerre de tomber sur Mademoiselle de Passy."[8]

A year or two after this, in conversation with M. de Marbois, Boulainvilliers happened to be mentioned, and Marbois said he had a most detestable character. "But," said I, "he has married a daughter to a man of great character?" "Ay," says Marbois, "I suppose you will say, what signifies character in France, when the worst cannot hinder a man from marrying his daughter to a Marquis de Tonnerre?"]

19. Dimanche. [From my first arrival in France, I had employed every moment of my time, when business and company would permit, in the study of the French language. I had not engaged any master, and determined to engage none. I thought he would break in upon my hours, in the necessary division of my time between business and study and visits, and might often embarrass me. I had other reasons, too, but none were sufficient to justify me. It was an egregious error, and I have seen cause enough to regret it. Instead of a master, I determined to obtain the best advice of those who were masters of the language, and purchase the books in which it was taught upon principle. Two abbés, De Chalut and Arnoux, the former a brother of the farmer-general of that name, and himself a knight of Malta, as well as of the order of St. Louis, and both of them learned men, came early to visit me. They had a house in the city, and another in the country at Passy, in our neighborhood, where they resided in summer. Whether they were spies of the court, or not, I know not, but I should have no objection to such spies, for they were always my friends, always instructive and agreeable in conversation. They were upon so good terms, however, with the courtiers, that if they had seen any thing in my conduct, or heard any thing in my conversation, that was dangerous or very exceptionable, I doubt not they would have thought it their duty to give information of it. They were totally destitute of the English language; but by one means and another they found a way of making me understand them, and sometimes by calling an in-

terpreter, and sometimes by gibbering something like French, I made them understand me.] . . .

20. Lundi. My son has been with me since Saturday. The *Concert Spirituel* is in the Royal Garden, where was an infinite number of gentlemen and ladies walking. Dined with the Duchess d'Enville, at her house, with her daughter and granddaughter, dukes, abbots, &c. &c. &c. [Among whom was M. Condorcet, a philosopher, with a face as pale, or rather as white, as a sheet of paper, I suppose from hard study. The Duchess d'Enville and her son, the great friends of Monsieur Turgot, were said to have great influence with the Royal Academy of Sciences, to make members at pleasure, and the *secrétaire perpétuel,* M. d'Alembert, was said to have been of their creation, as was M. Condorcet afterwards. His gratitude, a few years after this, will be recorded in history. This family was beloved in France, and had a reputation for patriotism, that is, of such a kind of patriotism as was allowed to exist and be esteemed in that kingdom, where no man, as Montesquieu says, must esteem himself or his country too much.] . . .

21. Mardi. . . .

It is with much grief and concern that I have learned, from my first landing in France, the disputes between the Americans in this kingdom; the animosities between Mr. Deane and Mr. Lee; between Dr. Franklin and Mr. Lee; between Mr. Izard and Dr. Franklin; between Dr. Bancroft and Mr. Lee; between Mr. Carmichael and all. It is a rope of sand. I am at present wholly untainted with these prejudices, and will endeavor to keep myself so. Parties and divisions among the Americans here must have disagreeable, if not pernicious, effects. Mr. Deane seems to have made himself agreeable here to persons of importance and influence, and is gone home in such splendor, that I fear there will be altercations in America about him. Dr. Franklin, Mr. Deane, and Dr. Bancroft, are friends. The Lees and Mr. Izard are friends. Sir James Jay insinuated that Mr. Deane had been at least as attentive to his own interest, in dabbling in the English funds and in trade, and in fitting out privateers, as to the public; and said he would give Mr. Deane fifty thousand pounds for his fortune, and said that Dr. Bancroft too had made a fortune. Mr. McCreery insinuated to me that the Lees were selfish, and that this was a family misfortune. What shall I say? What shall I think? It is said that Mr. Lee has not the confidence of the ministry, nor of the persons of influence here; that he is suspected of too much affection for England, . . . ; that he has given offence by an unhappy disposition, and by indiscreet speeches before servants and others, concerning the French nation and government—despising and cursing them. I am sorry for these things, but it is no part of my business to quarrel with anybody without cause; it is no part of my duty to differ with one party or another, or to give offence to anybody; but I must do my duty to the public, let it give offence to whom it will.

The public business has never been methodically conducted. There never was, before I came, a minute book, a letter book, or an account book; and it is not possible to obtain a clear idea of our affairs.

Mr. Deane lived expensively, and seems not to have had much order in his business, public or private; but he was active, diligent, subtle, and successful, having accomplished the great purpose of his mission to advantage. Mr. Gérard is his friend; and I find that Dr. Bancroft has the confidence of persons about the ministry, particularly of the late secretary to the ambassador to Great Britain.

[In this place, it is necessary to introduce a few portraits of characters, that the subsequent narrative may be better understood.

Dr. Franklin, one of my colleagues, is so generally known that I shall not attempt a sketch of his character at present. That he was a great genius, a great wit, a great humorist, a great satirist, and a great politician, is certain. That he was a great philosopher, a great moralist, and a great statesman, is more questionable.

Mr. Arthur Lee, my other colleague, was a native of Virginia. His father had been long a counsellor under the Crown, and some time commander-in-chief of the Colony and ancient dominion of Virginia. He left several sons, Thomas, Richard Henry, William, Francis Lightfoot, and Arthur, with all of whom, except Thomas, I have been intimately acquainted. Their father had given them all excellent classical educations, and they were all virtuous men. Arthur had studied and practised physic, but not finding it agreeable to his genius, he took chambers in the temple in England, and was there admitted to practise as a barrister, and being protected by several gentlemen of rank among the opposition, was coming fast into importance. Animated with great zeal in the cause of his native country, he took a decided part in her favor, and became a writer of some celebrity by his Junius Americanus and other publications. Being known in America as a zealous advocate of our cause, the two Houses of the Legislature of Massachusetts Bay appointed him provisionally their agent to the court of Great Britain, in case of the death, absence, or disability of Dr. Franklin, in which capacity he corresponded with some of the members of that assembly, particularly with Mr. Samuel Adams, and with the assembly itself, transmitting from time to time information of utility and importance. After a Congress was called in 1774-5 and 6, he continued to transmit to us some of the best and most authentic intelligence which we received from England. In 1776, when the election of ministers to the court of France was brought forward, and after I had declined the nomination, and Mr. Jefferson had refused the election and appointment sent him by Congress, Mr. Arthur Lee was elected in his place. He came immediately over to Paris, and joined his colleagues in commission. His manners were polite, his reading extensive, his attention to business was punctual, and his integrity without reproach.

Mr. Ralph Izard was a native of South Carolina. His grandfather or great-grandfather was one of Mr. Locke's landgraves, and had transmitted to his posterity an ample landed estate. Mr. Izard had his education, I believe, at Westminster or Eton School, certainly at the University of Cambridge, in England. When he came to the possession of his fortune, he married Miss De Lancey, a daughter of Chief Justice De Lancey, who was so long at the head of the party in New York, in opposition to the Livingstons, a lady of great beauty and fine accomplishments, as well as perfect purity of conduct and character through life. This accomplished pair had a curiosity to travel. They went to Europe, and passed through Italy, Germany, Holland, and I know not how many other countries. When the American war commenced, they were in England, and Mr. Izard, embracing the cause of his country with all the warmth of his character, passed with his family over to France, on his way to America. Congress had been advised, by persons who knew no better, to send a minister to the Emperor, and to the Grand Duke of Tuscany, because they were brothers to the Queen of France. In this measure there was less attention to the political interests and views of princes, than to the ties of blood and family connections. Congress, however, adopted the measure, and Mr. Izard was nominated by Mr. Arthur Middleton, in the name of South Carolina, and highly recommended for his integrity, good sense, and information. The members from New York, and other States, supported the nomination and concurred in all the particulars of his character. Mr. Izard was accordingly appointed, and when he arrived in Paris, he found his commission to the Grand Duke. With a high sense of honor and great benevolence of heart as well as integrity of principle, Mr. Izard had a warmth of temper and sometimes a violence of passions, that were very inconvenient to him and his friends, and not a little dangerous to his enemies.

Dr. Edward Bancroft was a native of Massachusetts Bay, in the town of Suffield. He had been a school-boy under Mr. Silas Deane, when he was a schoolmaster, whether in any town of the Massachusetts or Connecticut, I do not recollect. After some education, he had been bound an apprentice to a trade; but being discontented, ran away and went to sea, carrying with him some property of his master. After some years of adventures, the history of which I have not heard, he had acquired property enough to return to his native town, make his apologies to his master, pay him honorably all his demands, and then he went to sea again.

The next information I have of him is, that he was in England, and had published his Essay towards a Natural History of Guiana, which I have in a handsome volume, presented me with his own hand; and it is a work, considering the advantages of the author, of great merit. He wrote also in England the History of Sir Charles Wentworth, a novel, which no doubt was recommended to many readers, and procured a considerably better sale, by the plentiful abuse and vilification of Christianity, which he had taken care to insert into it. He had also been in the intimacy and confidence of Dr. Franklin, who had recommended him to the editors and proprietors of the Monthly Review, in which his standing share was to review all publications relative to America. This information I had from Dr. Franklin himself. I understood this very well, as I thought—to wit, that Bancroft was the ostensible reviewer, but that Franklin was always consulted before the publication. Bancroft was a meddler in the stocks as well as reviews, and frequently went into the alley, and into the deepest and darkest retirements and recesses of the brokers and jobbers, Jews as well as Christians, and found amusement as well, perhaps, as profit, by listening to all the news and anecdotes, true or false, that were there whispered or more boldly pronounced. This information I had from his own mouth. When Mr. Deane arrived in France, whether he wrote to Bancroft, or Bancroft to him, I know not, but they somehow or other sympathized with each other so well, that Bancroft went over to Paris, and became a confidential associate with his old friends, Franklin and Deane. Bancroft had a clear head and a good pen. He wrote some things relative to the connection between France and America, with the assistance of Franklin and Deane, as I presume, which were translated into French, by M. Turgot, or the Duke de la Rochefoucauld, I forget which, and printed in a publication called, Affaires de l'Angleterre et de l'Amérique, and which were very well done. After the peace he obtained a patent in France for the exclusive importation of the bark of the yellow oak for the dyers, and then he went to England and procured a similar patent there, by both of which together he is said to have realized an income of eight hundred a year.

Another character ought to be introduced here; although he had gone to America before my arrival at Passy, and I never had an opportunity of seeing him. A letter or two may have passed between him and me, when he was Chargé des Affaires at Madrid; but no misunderstanding ever occurred between us, and I never received, to my knowledge, any injury or offence from him. He was a native of Maryland, of Scotch extraction; wherever he may have had his education, he was in England or Scotland when the Revolution commenced, and in this year, 1778, came over to Paris, and, as I was informed, commenced an opposition to all the commissioners, Franklin, Deane, and Lee, and indeed to all who had any authority in American affairs, and was very clamorous. Mr. Deane and Dr. Franklin and Dr. Bancroft, however, a little before or after his departure, found means to appease him in some degree; and, after his arrival in America, he was chosen one of the delegates, from Maryland, in Congress, where in a year or two he got an appointment as Secretary of Legation and Chargé des Affaires to Mr. Jay, when, in 1779, he was appointed minister to the court of Spain. Here he remained for many years, and finally died.* He had talents and education, but was considered, by the soundest men who knew him, as too much of an adventurer. What was his moral character, and what his conduct in Spain, I shall leave to Mr. Jay; but he was represented to me as having contributed much to the animosities and exasperations among the Americans at Paris and Passy. There were great divisions in Spain among the Americans, and Mr. Jay had as much trouble with his own family, Mr. Carmichael, Mr. Brockholst Livingston, and Mr. Littlepage, as I had at Paris. I shall leave this scene to be opened by the memorials of the actors in it, if any such should ever see the light.

I have now given a faint sketch of the French and American personages who had been concerned in our affairs, at and before the time of my arrival.

I may have said before, that public business had never been methodically conducted. There never was, before I came, a minute-book, a letter-book, or an account-book; or, if there had been, Mr. Deane and Dr. Franklin had concealed them from Mr. Lee, and they were now nowhere to be found. It was utterly impossible to acquire any clear idea of our affairs. I was now determined to procure some blank books, and to apply

---

*William Carmichael. Mr. Sparks says that he returned to America. *Dipl. Corresp. of the Rev.* vol. ix. p. 4.

myself with diligence to business, in which Mr. Lee cordially joined me. To this end it was necessary to alter the course of my life. Invitations were sent to Dr. Franklin and me, every day in the week, to dine in some great or small company. I determined, on my part, to decline as many as I could of these, and attend to my studies of French, and the examination and execution of that public business which suffered for want of our attention every day. An invitation came from the Duke of Brancas to dine with him at his seat. I determined to send an apology; and on—] . . .

27. Monday. Dined with M. Boulainvilliers, at his house in Passy, with generals and bishops, and ladies, &c. In the evening went to the French comedy, and happened to be placed in the first box, very near to the celebrated Voltaire, who attended the performance of his own *Alzire*. Between the acts, the audience called out Voltaire, and clapped and applauded him the whole time. The old poet arose, and bowed respectfully to the audience. He has yet much fire in his eyes, and vigor in his countenance, although very old.* After the tragedy, they acted *Le Tuteur*, a comedy, or a farce of one act. This theatre does not exceed that at Bordeaux.

[I had not been a month as yet in France, nor three weeks in Passy, but I had seized every moment that I could save from business, company, or sleep, to acquire the language. I took with me the book to the theatre, and compared it, line for line, and word for word, with the pronunciation of the actors and actresses, and in this way I found I could understand them very well. Thinking this to be the best course I could take, to become familiar with the language, and its correct pronunciation, I determined to frequent the theatres as often as possible. Accordingly, I went as often as I could, and found a great advantage in it, as well as an agreeable entertainment. But as Dr. Franklin had almost daily occasion for the carriage, and I was determined the public should not be put to the expense of another for me, I could not go so often as I wished. Another proj-

---

*He was eighty-four. His death took place on the thirtieth of the succeeding month.

ect occurred to me, to familiarize the language, which was to keep a journal in French. This was accordingly attempted, and continued for a few days, but I found it took up too much time, and what was more decisive, I was afraid to keep any journal at all, for I had reason to believe that the house was full of spies, some of whom were among my own servants; and if my Journal should fall into the hands of the police full of free re- marks, as it must be to be of any value, it might do more injury to my country, than mischief to me.] . . .

29. Wednesday. . . .

After dinner we went to the Academy of Sciences, and heard M. d'Alembert, as perpetual secretary, pronounce eulogies on several of their members, lately deceased. Voltaire and Franklin were both present, and there presently arose a general cry that M. Voltaire and M. Franklin should be introduced to each other. This was done, and they bowed and spoke to each other. This was no satisfaction; there must be something more. Nei- ther of our philosophers seemed to divine what was wished or expected; they, however, took each other by the hand. But this was not enough; the clamor continued, until the explanation came out. "Il faut s' embrasser, à la Françoise." The two aged ac- tors upon this great theatre of philosophy and frivolity then em- braced each other, by hugging one another in their arms, and kissing each other's cheeks, and then the tumult subsided. And the cry immediately spread through the whole kingdom, and, I suppose, over all Europe. "Qu'il etait charmant de voir em- brasser Solon et Sophocle!"*[9] . . .

[1778. May] 21.Thursday. [. . . There is one subject which lies heavily on my mind, and that is the expense of the com- missioners. You have three commissioners at this Court, each of whom lives at an expense of at least three thousand pounds sterling a year, I fear at a greater expense. Few men in this world are capable of living at a less expense than I am; but I find the other gentlemen have expended from three to four thousand a year each, and one of them from five to six. And by

*This anecdote is told in the Life of Voltaire, by Condorcet. Œuvres Com- plètes, vol. c. p. 161.

all the inquiries I have been able to make, I cannot find any article of expense which can be retrenched.

"The truth is, in my humble opinion, our system is wrong in many particulars.

"1. In having three commissioners at this Court. One in the character of envoy is enough. At present, each of the three is considered in the character of a public minister plenipotentiary, which lays him under an absolute necessity of living up to this character, whereas one alone would be obliged to incur no greater expense, and would be quite sufficient for all the business of a public minister.

"2. In leaving the salaries of these ministers at an uncertainty. You will never be able to obtain a satisfactory account of the public moneys while this system continues; it is a temptation to live at too great an expense, and gentlemen will feel an aversion to demanding a rigorous account.

"3. In blending the business of a public minister with that of a commercial agent. The business of various departments is by this means so blended, and the public and private expenses so confounded with each other, that I am sure no satisfaction can ever be given to the public of the disposition of their interests, and I am very confident that jealousies and suspicions will hereafter arise against the characters of gentlemen who may, perhaps, have acted with perfect integrity, and the fairest intentions for the public good.

"My idea is this;—separate the offices of public ministers from those of commercial agents; recall, or send to some other Court, all the public ministers but one at this Court; determine with precision the sum that shall be allowed to the remaining one for his expenses, for his salary, and for his time, risk, trouble, &c.; and when this is done, see that he receives no more than his allowance. The inconveniences arising from the multiplicity of ministers and the complication of business are infinite."

This letter was received by Mr. Adams in due season, and by him communicated to Mr. Richard Henry Lee and others. Mr. Lee wrote me immediately that he had seen it, and was entirely of my opinion. It was communicated to so many members of

Congress, that it produced the revolution which followed; my friends, and the friends of Mr. Arthur Lee, uniting with those of Dr. Franklin, Mr. Deane, and Mr. Izard, in introducing the new plan.

The representation in my letter of the expenses of the commissioners, related only to the state of things before my arrival. My expenses were very trifling. I had no house rent to pay separate from Dr. Franklin. I kept no carriage, and used none but that of Dr. Franklin, and that only when he had no use for it. I had very little company more than Dr. Franklin would have had if I had not been there. But, before my arrival, Mr. Deane had his house and furniture and establishment of servants, as well as his carriage, in Paris, and another establishment for his apartments in the country at Passy, and another carriage and set of horses and servants. Mr. Lee had a house, furniture, and carriage, and organization of servants, at Chaillot. Dr. Franklin had his in the Basse-cour de Monsieur Le Ray de Chaumont, at what rent, I never could discover; but, from the magnificence of the place, it was universally suspected to be enormously high. Making the best estimate I could, from the representations that were made to me, I wrote as I then believed. But, after a longer residence, more experience, and further inquiry, I was convinced that I had admitted much exaggeration into the account. Nevertheless, the expenses of Mr. Deane never have been known, and never, I presume, can be known.*

I had taken pains to persuade my colleagues to take a house in Paris, and have but one establishment for us all. Mr. Lee, whose opinion was that we ought to live in Paris, readily con-

---

*Mr. Deane never succeeded in throwing much light upon his mode of doing business in France. But his personal expenses have been ascertained by the banker's accounts, whose charges to the three members of the first commission, during the period from December, 1776, to March, 1778, stood thus:

		livres.		
To Dr. Franklin,		65,956	3	13.
"Silas Deane,		113,004	12	13.
"Arthur Lee, including two journeys,		68,846	2	16.

Diplomatic Correspondence of the Revolution, vol. ii. p. 159.

sented, but Dr. Franklin refused. I proposed that Mr. Lee should take apartments with us at Passy, and there was room enough for us all; and I offered to resign my apartments to him, and take others which were not so convenient; but he refused to live together, unless it were in Paris, where the Americans in general, and the French too, seemed to think we ought to live. All my proposals were therefore abortive.

Before I wrote the letter to Mr. Adams, I had many things to consider. What would be the consequence if my plan should be adopted? Dr. Franklin's reputation was so high in America, in the court and nation of France, and all over Europe, that he would undoubtedly, as he ought, be left alone at the Court of Versailles. Mr. Lee held two commissions, one to the Court of France, and one to the Court of Spain. If that to the Court of Versailles should be annulled, the other, to the Court of Madrid, would remain in force. It would, therefore, make little odds to him. I had but one, and that to the Court of Versailles. If this were annulled, what would become of me? There was but one country to which I thought it possible Congress would send a minister at that time, and that was Holland. But there was no hope that Holland would then receive a minister, and I thought Congress ought not to send one there as yet. I thought, therefore, that there was no alternative for me, but to return to America; and I very deliberately determined, that I had rather run the gauntlet again through all the British men-of-war in the Bay of Biscay, the British Channel, and the Gulf Stream, with all their storms and calms, than remain where I was, under a system and in circumstances so ruinous to the American cause. I expected, however, that Congress would make some provision for my return, by giving me orders to receive money enough for my expenses, and give me a passage in a frigate, if any one should be in France. In this last expectation alone I was disappointed.] . . .

[1778.] June 2. Tuesday. Went to Versailles, and found it deserted, the Court being gone to Marly. We went to Marly; met the Comte de Vergennes, and did some business; then went to Mr. De Sartine's and dined with him. His lady was at home, and dined with the company. The Prince de Montbarey dined there. Went with Madame de Sartine to the Count d'Aranda's, the Spanish Ambassador's Coffee, as they call it, where he gives ice cream and cakes to all the world. Marly is the most curious and beautiful place I have yet seen. The water-works here, which convey such a great body of water from the Seine to Versailles, and through the gardens at Marly, are very magnificent. The Royal Palace is handsome; the gardens before it are grand. There are six pavilions on each side of the garden, that is, six houses, for the use of the king's ministers, while the royal family is at Marly, which is only for three weeks. There is nothing prettier than the play of the fountains in the garden. I saw a rainbow in all its glory in one of them. The shades, the walks, the trees, are the most charming that I have seen.

[We had not time to visit Luciennes, the elegant retreat for devotion, penitence, and mortification, of Madame du Barry; and, indeed, I had been in such a reverie in the morning, in passing Bellevue, that I was not averse to postpone the sight of another object of the same kind to a future opportunity.

On the road from Paris, and from Passy to Versailles, beyond the river Seine, and not far from St. Cloud, but on the opposite side of the way, stood a palace of uncommon beauty in its architecture, situated on one of the finest elevations in the neighborhood of the river, commanding a prospect as rich and variegated, as it was vast and sublime. In a few of the first times that I went to Versailles, I had other things to occupy my attention; but, after I had passed through my ceremonies, and began to feel myself more at ease, I asked some questions about this place, and was informed that it was called Bellevue, and was the residence of the King's aunts, Adelaide and Victoire, two of the surviving daughters of Louis XV. This palace had been built, and this establishment made, by that monarch, for Madame de Pompadour, whom he visited here for twenty years, leaving a worthy woman, his virtuous queen, alone at Versailles, from whom he had sworn an eternal separation. I cannot describe the feelings, nor relate half the reflections, which this object and history excited. Here were made judges and counsellors, magistrates of all sorts, nobles and knights of every order, generals and admirals, ambassadors and other foreign ministers, bishops, archbishops, cardinals, and popes. Hither were directed all eyes that wished and sought for employment, promotion, and every species of court favor. Here Voltaire and Richelieu, and a thousand others of their stamp, obtained royal favor and commissions. Travellers, of all ranks and characters, from all parts of Europe, were continually passing from Paris to Versailles, and spreading the fame of this house, its inhabitants and visitors, and their commerce, infamous in every point of view, civil, political, moral, and religious, all over the world. The attention of all France had been turned to Bellevue more than to Paris or Versailles. Here *lettres de cachet,* the highest trust and most dangerous instrument of arbitrary power in France, were publicly sold to any persons who would pay for them, for any, the vilest purposes of private malice, envy, jealousy, revenge, or cruelty. Here licenses were sold to private smugglers, to contravene the king's own laws, and defraud the public revenue. Here were sold dukedoms and peerages, and even the cordon bleu of the knights of the Holy Ghost. Here still lived the daughters of the last king, and the aunts of the present. Instead of wondering that the licentiousness of women was so common and so public in France, I was astonished that there should be any modesty or purity remaining in the kingdom, as there certainly was, though it was rare. Could there be any morality left among such a people, where such examples were set up to the view of the whole nation? Yes. There was a sort of morality. There was a great deal of humanity, and what appeared to me real benevolence. Even their politeness was benevolence. There was a great deal of charity and tenderness for the poor. There were many other qualities that I could not distinguish from virtues. This very monarch had in him the milk of human kindness, and, with all his open, undisguised vices, was very superstitious. Whenever he met the host, he would descend from his coach, and down upon his knees in the dust, or even in the mud, and compel all his courtiers to follow his example. Such are the inconsistencies in the human character!

From all that I had read of history and government, of human life and manners, I had drawn this conclusion, that the manners of women were the most infallible barometer to ascertain the degree of morality and virtue in a nation. All that I have since read, and all the observations I have made in different nations, have confirmed me in this opinion. The manners of women are the surest criterion by which to determine whether a republican government is practicable in a nation or not. The Jews, the Greeks, the Romans, the Dutch, all lost their public spirit, their republican principles and habits, and their republican forms of government, when they lost the modesty and domestic virtues of their women.

What havoc, said I to myself, would these manners make in America! Our governors, our judges, our senators or representatives, and even our ministers, would be appointed by harlots, for money; and their judgments, decrees, and decisions, be sold to repay themselves, or, perhaps, to procure the smiles of profligate females.

The foundations of national morality must be laid in private families. In vain are schools, academies, and universities, instituted, if loose principles and licentious habits are impressed upon children in their earliest years. The mothers are the earliest and most important instructors of youth. The vices and examples of the parents cannot be concealed from the children. How is it possible that children can have any just sense of the sacred obligations of morality or religion, if, from their earliest infancy, they learn that their mothers live in habitual infidelity to their fathers, and their fathers in as constant infidelity to their mothers? Besides, the catholic doctrine is, that the contract of marriage is not only a civil and moral engagement, but a sacrament; one of the most solemn vows and oaths of religious devotion. Can they then believe religion, and morality too, any thing more than a veil, a cloak, a hypocritical pretext, for political purposes of decency and conveniency?]

7. Sunday. Went to Versailles, in company with Mr. Lee, Mr. Izard and his lady, Mr. Lloyd and his lady, and Mr. François. Saw the grand procession of the Knights *du Saint-Esprit,* or *du cordon bleu.* At nine o'clock at night, went to the *grand couvert,* and saw the king, queen, and royal family, at supper; had

a fine seat and situation close by the royal family, and had a distinct, and full view, of the royal pair.

[Our objects were to see the ceremonies of the knights, and, in the evening, the public supper of the royal family. The kneelings, the bows, and courtesies of the knights, the dresses and decorations, the king seated on his throne, his investiture of a new created knight with the badges and ornaments of the order, and his majesty's profound and reverential bow before the altar as he retired, were novelties and curiosities to me, but surprised me much less than the patience and perseverance with which they all kneeled, for two hours together, upon the hard marble of which the floor of the chapel was made. The distinction of the blue ribbon was very dearly purchased at the price of enduring this painful operation four times in a year. The Count de Vergennes confessed to me that he was almost dead with the pain of it. And the only insinuation I ever heard, that the King was in any degree touched by the philosophy of the age, was, that he never discovered so much impatience, under any of the occurrences of his life, as in going through those tedious ceremonies of religion, to which so many hours of his life were condemned by the catholic church.

The queen was attended by her ladies to the gallery opposite to the altar, placed in the centre of the seat, and there left alone by the other ladies, who all retired. She was an object too sublime and beautiful for my dull pen to describe. I leave this enterprise to Mr. Burke.[10] But, in his description, there is more of the orator than of the philosopher. Her dress was every thing that art and wealth could make it. One of the maids of honor told me she had diamonds upon her person to the value of eighteen millions of livres; and I always thought her majesty much beholden to her dress. Mr. Burke saw her probably but once. I have seen her fifty times perhaps, and in all the varieties of her dresses. She had a fine complexion, indicating perfect health, and was a handsome woman in her face and figure. But I have seen beauties much superior, both in countenance and form, in France, England, and America.

After the ceremonies of this institution are over, there is a collection for the poor; and that this closing scene may be as elegant as any of the former, a young lady of some of the first families in France is appointed to present the box to the knights. Her dress must be as rich and elegant, in proportion, as the queen's, and her air, motions, and curtsies, must have as much dignity and grace as those of the knights. It was a curious entertainment to observe the easy air, the graceful bow, and the conscious dignity of the knight, in presenting his contribution; and the corresponding ease, grace, and dignity of the lady, in receiving it, were not less charming. Every muscle, nerve, and fibre, of both, seemed perfectly disciplined to perform its functions. The elevation of the arm, the bend of the elbow, and every finger in the hand of the knight, in putting his louis d'ors into the box, appeared to be perfectly studied, because it was perfectly natural. How much devotion there was in all this I know not, but it was a consummate school to teach the rising generation the perfection of the French air, and external politeness and good breeding. I have seen nothing to be compared to it in any other country. The House of Lords in England I thought the most likely to rival this. But seven years afterwards, when I had seen that assembly on two extraordinary occasions, the first, the introduction of the Prince of Wales to his seat in Parliament, and the second, the trial of Warren Hastings, I concluded the peers of Great Britain were too intent on the great interests of the nation, to be very solicitous about the charms of the exterior exhibition of a spectacle. The procession of the peers, and the reverences they made to the throne, in conformity to the usage of their ancestors, as they passed to their seats in Westminster Hall, were decent and graceful enough.

At nine o'clock we went and saw the king, queen, and royal family, at the *grand couvert*. Whether M. François, a gentleman who undertook upon this occasion to conduct us, had contrived a plot to gratify the curiosity of the spectators, or whether the royal family had a fancy to see the raw American at their leisure, or whether they were willing to gratify him with a convenient seat, in which he might see all the royal family, and all the splendors of the place, I know not; but the scheme could not have been carried into execution, certainly, without the orders of the king. I was selected, and summoned

indeed, from all my company, and ordered to a seat close beside the royal family. The seats on both sides of the hall,
arranged like the seats in a theatre, were all full of ladies of the
first rank and fashion in the kingdom, and there was no room
or place for me but in the midst of them. It was not easy to
make room for one more person. However, room was made,
and I was situated between two ladies, with rows and ranks of
ladies above and below me, and on the right hand and on the
left, and ladies only. My dress was a decent French dress, becoming of the station I held, but not to be compared with the
gold, and diamonds, and embroidery, about me. I could neither
speak, nor understand the language in a manner to support a
conversation, but I had soon the satisfaction to find it was a
silent meeting, and that nobody spoke a word, but the royal
family, to each other, and they said very little. The eyes of all
the assembly were turned upon me, and I felt sufficiently humble and mortified, for I was not a proper object for the criticisms of such a company. I found myself gazed at, as we in
America used to gaze at the sachems who came to make
speeches to us in Congress, but I thought it very hard if I could
not command as much power of face as one of the chiefs of the
Six Nations, and, therefore, determined that I would assume a
cheerful countenance, enjoy the scene around me, and observe
it as coolly as an astronomer contemplates the stars. Inscriptions of *Fructus Belli* were seen on the ceiling and all about the
walls of the room, among paintings of the trophies of war,
probably done by the order of Louis XIV. who confessed, in his
dying hour, as his successor and exemplar Napoleon will probably do, that he had been too fond of war. The king was the
royal carver for himself and all his family. His majesty ate like
a king, and made a royal supper of solid beef, and other things
in proportion. The queen took a large spoonful of soup, and
displayed her fine person and graceful manners, in alternately
looking at the company in various parts of the hall, and order-
ing several kinds of seasoning to be brought to her, by which
she fitted her supper to her taste. When this was accomplished,
her majesty exhibited to the admiring spectators, the magnificent spectacle of a great queen swallowing her royal supper in

a single spoonful all at once. This was all performed like perfect clock work; not a feature of her face, nor a motion of any part of her person, especially her arm and her hand, could be criticized as out of order. A little, and but a little, conversation seemed to pass among the royal personages of both sexes, but in so low a voice, that nothing could be understood by any of the audience.

The officers about the king's person brought him many letters and papers, from time to time, while he was at table. He looked at these. Some of them he read, or seemed to read, and returned them to the same officers who brought them, or some others.

These ceremonies may be condemned by philosophy, and ridiculed by comedy, with great reason. Yet the common sense of mankind has never adopted the rigid decrees of the former, nor ever sincerely laughed with the latter. Nor has the religion of nations, in any age, approved of the dogmas or the satires. On the contrary, it has always overborne them all, and carried its inventions of such exhibitions to a degree of sublimity and pathos, which has frequently transported the greatest infidels out of themselves. Something of the kind every government and every religion has, and must have; and the business and duty of lawgivers and philosophers is to endeavor to prevent them from being carried too far.] . . .

1779.

February 2. Tuesday. Last Tuesday I dined in company with the Abbé Raynal and M. Gébelin, and asked them to dine with me on the then next Sunday. Accordingly the day before yesterday they both came.

Monsieur Raynal is the most eloquent man I ever heard speak in French; his voice is sharp and clear, but pleasant; he talks a great deal, and is very entertaining. M. Gébelin is much less addicted to talking. He is silent, soft, and still; his mind always upon a stretch.

4. Thursday. Breakfasted with the Abbé Raynal at his house, at his particular invitation, with a large company of gentlemen

and ladies. The Abbé is more than sixty, seems worn with studies, but he has spirit, wit, eloquence, and fire enough.

5. Friday. The Duke de la Rochefoucauld, M. Turgot, Abbés Rochon, and De la Roche, dined here.

8. Monday. In conversation with Dr. Franklin, in the morning, I gave him my opinion of Mr. Deane's Address to the people of America with great freedom and perhaps with too much warmth. I told him that it was one of the most wicked and abominable productions that ever sprang from a human heart; that there was no safety in integrity against such a man; that I should wait upon the Count de Vergennes and the other ministers, and see in what light they considered this conduct of Mr. Deane; that if they and their representatives in America were determined to countenance and support by their influence such men and measures in America, it was no matter how soon the alliance was broke; that no evil could be greater, nor any government worse, than the toleration of such conduct. No one was present but the Doctor and his grandson.

In the evening I told Dr. Bancroft, to the same effect, that the address appeared to me in a very atrocious light; that however difficult Mr. Lee's temper might be, in my opinion he was an honest man, and had the utmost fidelity towards the United States; that such a contempt of Congress, committed in the city where they sit, and the publication of such accusations in the face of the universe, so false and groundless as the most heinous of them appeared to me, these accusations attempted to be colored by such frivolous tittle-tattle, such accusations made too by a man who had been in high trust, against two others, who were still so,—appeared to me evidence of such a complication of vile passions, of vanity, arrogance, and presumption, of malice, envy, and revenge, and at the same time of such wickedness, indiscretion, and folly, as ought to unite every honest and wise man against him; that there appeared to me no alternative left but the ruin of Mr. Deane or the ruin of his country; that he appeared to me in the light of a wild boar, that ought to be hunted down for the benefit of mankind; that I would start fair with him, Dr. Bancroft, and give him notice that I had hitherto been loth to give up Mr. Deane, but that this measure of his appeared to me to be so decisive against him, that I had given him up to Satan to be buffeted.

In all this it is easy to see there is too much declamation; but the substantial meaning of it is such as appears to me exactly true, and such as I will abide by, unless future evidence, which I don't expect, should convince me of any error in it.

9. Tuesday. Abbé C.

> "Terruit Hispanos, Ruiter, qui terruit Anglos
> Ter ruit in Gallos, territus ipse ruit."[11]

> "Cum fueris Romæ, Romano vivito more;
> Si fueris alibi, vivito sicut ibi."[12]

Any thing to divert melancholy and to soothe an aching heart. The uncandor, the prejudices, the rage, among several persons here, make me sick as death.

Virtue is not always amiable. Integrity is sometimes ruined by prejudices and by passions. There are two men in the world who are men of honor and integrity, I believe, but whose prejudices and violent tempers would raise quarrels in the Elysian fields, if not in Heaven. On the other hand, there is another, whose love of ease and dissipation will prevent any thorough reformation of any thing, and his silence and reserve render it very difficult to do any thing with him. One of the others, whom I have allowed to be honest, has such a bitter, such a sour, in him, and so few of the nice feelings, that God knows what will be the consequence to himself and to others. Besides, he has as much cunning and as much secrecy.

Called at M. Garnier's; he not at home. At Mr. Grand's; he and his son began about the Address,*—bien faché, &c. I said, coolly, that I was astonished at the publication of it, without sending it to Congress; that I believed Mr. Lee a man of in-

---

*The Address of Silas Deane to the people of America, in November, 1778, already alluded to in the preceding page, which first published to the world the extent of the differences that had taken place, and which deeply agitated the parties in Congress and in the country. It is almost needless to say that Mr. Arthur Lee, Mr. Izard, and Dr. Franklin, are the persons referred to.

tegrity, and that all suggestions of improper correspondences in England were groundless; that my brother Lee was not of the sweetest disposition, perhaps, but he was honest; that virtue was not always amiable. M. Grand replied, Il est soupçonneux, il n'a du confiance en personne, il croit que tout le monde est— I can't remember the precise word. I believe this is a just observation. He has confidence in nobody; he believes all men selfish, and no man honest or sincere. This I fear is his creed, from what I have heard him say. I have often, in conversation, disputed with him on this point; however, I never was so nearly in his situation before. There is no man here that I dare trust at present. They are all too much heated with passions and prejudices and party disputes. Some are too violent, others too jealous, others too cool and too reserved at all times, and at the same time, every day, betraying symptoms of a rancor quite as deep. The wisdom of Solomon, the meekness of Moses, and the patience of Job, all united in one character, would not be sufficient to qualify a man to act in the situation in which I am at present; and I have scarcely a spice of either of these virtues.

On Dr. Franklin the eyes of all Europe are fixed, as the most important character in American affairs, in Europe: neither Lee nor myself are looked upon of much consequence. The attention of the Court seems most to Franklin, and no wonder: his long and great reputation, to which Lee's and mine are in their infancy, are enough to account for this; his age and real character render it impossible for him to search every thing to the bottom; and Lee, with his privy council, is evermore contriving: the results of their contrivances render many measures more difficult.

11. Thursday. When I arrived in France, the French nation had a great many questions to settle. The first was, Whether I was the famous Adams? Le fameux Adams? Ah, le fameux Adams. In order to speculate a little upon this subject, the pamphlet entitled "Common Sense," had been printed in the "Affaires de l'Angleterre et de l'Amérique," and expressly ascribed to Mr. Adams, the celebrated member of Congress—le célèbre membre du Congrès. It must be further known, that although the pamphlet, Common Sense, was received in France and in

all Europe with rapture, yet there were certain parts of it that they did not choose to publish in France. The reasons of this any man may guess. Common Sense undertakes to prove that monarchy is unlawful by the Old Testament. They therefore gave the substance of it, as they said; and, paying many compliments to Mr. Adams, his sense and rich imagination, they were obliged to ascribe some parts to republican zeal. When I arrived at Bordeaux, all that I could say or do would not convince anybody but that I was the fameux Adams. "C'est un homme célèbre. Votre nom est bien connu ici." My answer was, It is another gentleman, whose name of Adams you have heard; it is Mr. Samuel Adams, who was excepted from pardon by General Gage's proclamation. "Oh non, Monsieur, c'est votre modestie."[13]

But when I arrived at Paris, I found a very different style. I found great pains taken, much more than the question was worth, to settle the point that I was not the famous Adams. There was a dread of a sensation; sensations at Paris are important things. I soon found, too, that it was effectually settled in the English newspapers that I was not the famous Adams. Nobody went so far in France or England as to say that I was the infamous Adams. I make no scruple to say that I believe both parties, for parties there were, joined in declaring that I was not the famous Adams. I certainly joined both sides in this, in declaring that I was not the famous Adams, because this was the truth.

It being settled that he was not the famous Adams, the consequence was plain; he was some man that nobody had ever heard of before, and therefore a man of no consequence—a cipher. And I am inclined to think that all parties, both in France and England,—Whigs and Tories in England, the friends of Franklin, Deane, and Lee, in France,—differing in many other things, agreed in this, that I was not the famous Adams.

Seeing all this, and saying nothing,—for what could a man say?—seeing also that there were two parties formed among the Americans, as fixed in their aversion to each other as both were to Great Britain, if I had affected the character of a fool, in order to find out the truth and to do good by-and-by, I should have had the example of a Brutus for my justification; but I did not affect this character. I behaved with as much prudence and civility and industry as I could; but still it was a settled point at Paris and in the English newspapers that I was not the famous Adams; and therefore the consequence was settled, absolutely and unalterably, that I was a man of whom nobody had ever heard before,—a perfect cipher; a man who did not understand a word of French; awkward in his figure, awkward in his dress; no abilities; a perfect bigot and fanatic.

It is my indispensable duty to tell the Count de Vergennes that I think one great cause of this horrid address of Mr. Deane, is Mr. Franklin's certificate in his favor that he is an able and faithful negotiator, and that Mr. Franklin was deceived in this; that Mr. Franklin's knowledge actually in America, for a great many years, has not been long; that he was upright in this, but deceived; that there are such certain and infallible proofs of vanity, presumption, ambition, avarice, and folly, in Mr. Deane, as render him very unworthy of confidence, and therefore that Dr. Franklin has been deceived.

12. Friday. My mind has been in such a state, since the appearance of Mr. Deane's Address to the People, as it never was before. I confess it appeared to me like a dissolution of the constitution. It should be remembered that it first appeared from London in the English papers; then in the Courier de l'Europe; and we had not received the proceedings of Congress upon it. A few days later, Dr. Franklin received from Nantes some Philadelphia papers, in which were the pieces signed Senex and Common Sense, and the account of the election of the new President, Mr. Jay. When it was known that Congress had not censured Mr. Deane for appealing to the people, it was looked upon as the most dangerous proof that had ever appeared of the weakness of government, and it was thought by some that the confederation was wholly lost. I confess it appeared terrible to me indeed; it appeared to me that it would wholly lose us the confidence of the French Court. I did not see how they could ever trust any of us again; that it would have the worst effects upon Spain, Holland, and in England, besides endangering a civil war in America. In the agony of my heart I expressed myself to one gentleman, Dr.

Bancroft, with perhaps too much warmth. But this day Dr. Winship arrived here from Brest, and soon afterwards the aide-de-camp du Marquis de Lafayette, with despatches from Congress, by which it appears that Dr. Franklin is sole plenipotentiary, and of consequence that I am displaced: The greatest relief to my mind that I have ever found since the appearance of the address. Now business may be done by Dr. Franklin alone; before, it seemed as if nothing could be done.

13. Saturday. There is no such thing as human wisdom; all is the providence of God. Perhaps few men have guessed more exactly than I have been allowed to do upon several occasions; but at this time, which is the first, I declare, of my whole life, I am utterly at a loss to foresee consequences.

March 3. Wednesday. Went to Versailles, in order to take leave of the ministry. Had a long conversation with the Count de Vergennes in French, which I found I could talk as fast as I pleased. . . .

22. Thursday. Yesterday morning embarked at Nantes with Mr. Hill, the first lieutenant, and Mr. Park, who is captain of marines, and my son. We stopped and dined at Port-Launay. After dinner crossed over to Pélerine, where we went to the house of a Mr. Carmichael, a Scotchman, who lives by salting beef and making bacon for the navigation of this river. This man, I suppose, was a Jacobite, who fled in 1745. We reached no farther than Paimbeuf, where we went ashore, and slept at a tavern.

This day we arrived safe on board the Alliance, and sent off to the cartel ship all the British prisoners. Thus, by my excursion to Lorient and Brest, I have accomplished successfully the expedition of the frigate, and the exchange of the prisoners; and have happily joined the ship, and got my son and baggage on board. The frigate lies at St.-Nazaire, where are several French vessels of war, but none so large as the Alliance.

My idea of the beauty, the wealth, and convenience of Nantes and Paimbeuf, and indeed of the country on both sides of the river, is much heightened, since my return from Brest, having taken a more leisurely view of it. I thought it my duty to come down, although the weather was disagreeable, and the

wind contrary and very strong, because I found the British prisoners had not been discharged from the frigate, and could not
be, until an order went down, and because I feared that other
business would be neglected, and my not being ready alleged as
an excuse for it. But I was obliged to leave Joseph Stevens sick
of the measles at the tavern. This was a painful circumstance to
me, although I took all the precautions in my power, by speaking to Mr. Schweighauser, Mr. Dobrée, Captain Landais, and
Dr. Winship, to look to him, and engaged a careful woman to
nurse him. I hope he will be well in a few days. He must have
taken the infection at Brest, where he imprudently exposed
himself, I fear, on shore. The distemper, it seems, is prevalent in
this kingdom, at present; the Queen of France is said to be ill
of it.

I have now had an opportunity of seeing Bordeaux, Nantes,
Lorient, and Brest, and the intermediate countries. I could wish
to have seen Rochefort and Rochelle. At Brest, I visited the commandant, whose name I have forgot, the Count d'Orvilliers,
who is the marine General, and Monsieur de la Porte, who is
the Intendant of the Marine. At Lorient, I did not visit the intendant nor commandant; nor at Nantes.

The zeal, the ardor, the enthusiasm, the rage, for the new
American connection, I find, is much damped among the merchants, since the loss of so many of their East and West India
ships. The adventurers to America have lost so many ships, and
have received so small returns for those which went safe, that
they are discouraged; and I cannot learn that any expeditions
are formed or forming for our country. But all their chagrin
cannot prevent the Court from continuing the war. The existence of French commerce and marine both, are at stake; they
are wholly undone without American independence.

The pleasure of returning home is very great. But I confess it
is a mortification to leave France. I have just acquired enough
of the language to understand a conversation, as it runs at a
table, at dinner or at supper, and to conduct all my affairs myself, in making journeys through the country, with the post-
masters, postilions, tavern-keepers, &c. &c. I can go to a shop
and examine the goods, and understand all the prattle of the

shop-keeper, or I can sit down with a gentleman who will have a little patience to speak a little more distinctly than common, and to wait a little longer for my sentences than common, and maintain a conversation pretty well. In travelling, the best way is to dine and sup at the taverns with the company, *avec les autres,* as they express it. You meet here a vast variety of company, which is decent, and after a few *coups de vin,* their tongues run very fast, and you learn more of the language, the manners, the customs, laws, politics, arts, &c. in this way, perhaps, than in any other. You should preserve your dignity, talk little, listen much, not be very familiar with any in particular, for there are sharpers, gamblers, quack-doctors, strolling comedians, in short, people of all characters, assembled at these dinners and suppers, and, without caution, you may be taken into parties of pleasure and diversion which will cost you very dear.

Were I to come to France again, I would wait on the intendant, commandant, mayor, &c. of every place. I would dine and sup at the taverns with the company. I would go to the *palais,* and hear the causes; and to the Comédie, and hear the plays; and that as constantly as possible. I would go to church whenever I could hear a sermon. These are the ways to learn the language; and if to these are added a diligent study of their grammars, and a constant use of their best dictionaries, and reading of their best authors, a man, in one year, may become a great master of it. After all, if a man's character would admit of it, there is much of the language to be learned at the shops. The female shop-keepers are the most chatty in the world. They are very complaisant, talk a great deal, speak pretty good French, and are very entertaining. I took a walk this morning to the back part of the little town of Paimbeuf, and found behind it a pleasant country prospect, with one beautiful country seat of a gentleman in sight.

25. Sunday. Fair weather again. My time has been employed since I have been on board, in writing answers to my letters from Paris, Bordeaux, Passy, &c. and in assisting my son to translate into English, which he does in writing, Cicero's first Philippic against Catiline, which we have gone more than half through. He is also translating into English the French Preface

of the Abbé d'Olivet, to his translation of the Philippics of
Demosthenes and the Catilinaries of Cicero. Are these classical
amusements becoming my situation? Are not courts, camps,
politics, and war, more proper for me? No; certainly, classical
amusements are the best I can obtain on board ship, and here I
cannot do any thing or contrive any thing for the public.

A boat came on board to-day with a custom-house officer, to
examine and give an *acquit*—a caution for a chest of tea which
is on board, belonging to somebody, I know not whom. I have
been here so long, that I find the cabin to be rather a trite *séjour*.
It is dull to be here alone. Tully's Offices and Orations are an
agreeable amusement; but *toujours Tully* is as bad as *toujours
Perdreaux*, and infinitely worse than *toujours "sa femme,"* al-
luding to the anecdote of Henry IV. which I was told by the
Abbé Raynal.

26. Monday. Spent the morning in translating with my son
the *Carmen Seculare* and the notes.

There is a feebleness and a languor in my nature. My mind
and body both partake of this weakness. By my physical constitution I am but an ordinary man. The times alone have destined me to fame; and even these have not been able to give me
much. When I look in the glass, my eye, my forehead, my brow,
my cheeks, my lips, all betray this relaxation. Yet some great
events, some cutting expressions, some mean hypocrisies, have,
at times, thrown this assemblage of sloth, sleep, and littleness
into rage a little like a lion. Yet it is not like the lion; there is extravagance and distraction in it that still betray the same weakness. . . .

[May] 13. Thursday. Went on shore, and dined with Captain
Jones at the *Epée Royale;* M. Amiel, Mr. Dick, Dr. Brooks, officers of the Poor Richard, Captain Cazneau, Captain Young, Mr.
Ingraham, Mr. Blodgett, Mr. Glover, Mr. Conant, Messrs. Moy-
lans, Mr. Mease, Mr. Nesbit, Mr. Cummings, and Mr. Taylor,
made the company, with Captain Landais, myself, and my son.
An elegant dinner we had, and all very agreeable. No very instructive conversation; but we practised the old American custom of drinking to each other, which I confess is always
agreeable to me. Some hints about language, and glances about

women, produced this observation;—that there were two ways of learning French commonly recommended,—take a mistress, and go to the comedy. Dr. Brooks, (in high good humor): "Pray, sir, which in your opinion is the best?" Answer, in as good humor: "Perhaps both would teach it soonest; to be sure, sooner than either. But," continued I, assuming my gravity, "the language is nowhere better spoken than at the comédie. The pulpit, the bar, the Academy of Sciences, and the faculty of medicine,—none of them speak so accurately as the French Comédie."

After dinner, walked out with Captains Jones and Landais, to see Jones's marines, dressed in the English uniform, red and white; a number of very active and clever sergeants and corporals are employed to teach them the exercise, and manœuvres and marches, &c.; after which, Jones came on board our ship. This is the most ambitious and intriguing officer in the American navy. Jones has art and secrecy, and aspires very high. You see the character of the man in his uniform, and that of his officers and marines, variant from the uniforms established by Congress,—golden button-holes for himself, two epaulettes,—marines in red and white, instead of green. Eccentricities and irregularities are to be expected from him. They are in his character, they are visible in his eyes. His voice is soft and still and small; his eye has keenness and wildness and softness in it.*

14. Friday. On board all day, ill of a cold. Many gentlemen came on board to visit me. A Dr. Brooks, surgeon to the Poor Richard, drank tea with me. He seems to be well acquainted with philosophical experiments. I led him to talk upon this subject. He had much to say about phlogiston, fixed air, gas, &c.; about absolute and sensible heat, experiments with the thermometer, to show the absolute and sensible heat in water, air, blood, &c.

Finding he had ideas of these things, I led him to talk of the ascent of vapors in the atmosphere, and I found he had considered this subject. He mentioned a natural history of North and South Carolina, by Catesby, in four volumes, folio, with stamps

---

*Mr. Cooper's character of John Paul Jones, though favorable, seems to be summed up with impartiality. *History*, vol. i. p. 209, note.

of all the plants and animals; price twenty-five guineas. He mentioned a Dr. Erving, and a Dr. Black of Glasgow, as great philosophers, whose hints Priestley had taken. This Dr. Brooks is a gentleman of family, whose father has a great fortune and good character in Virginia.* Mr. Dick, captain of marines on board of Jones, is also of good family and handsome fortune in Virginia. Mr. Gimat came on board to visit me, aide-de-camp of the Marquis de la Fayette.

15. Saturday. Went on shore, and dined with Captain Jones at the mess at *L'Epée Royale,* Mr. Hill, Captain Cazneau, Captain Young, Mr. Dick, Dr. Brooks, and Mr. Gourlade, &c. and another aide-de-camp of the Marquis. Gourlade married a Scotch lady. Captain Jones this morning showed me a letter from Lieutenant Browne, desiring, or rather apologizing for leaving the ship, because of the word, *first,* in Mr. Amiel's commission. I said I thought Mr. Browne could not serve under Mr. Amiel; it would be, in a manner, giving up the claims of many lieutenants, whose commissions were dated between his and Mr. Amiel's, as well as his own, and would expose him to censure; that the word, *first,* was agreed to be inserted by the commissioners, because we expected that either we or Captain Jones would fill up the commissions to the other lieutenants of that ship, and it was intended to give him an assurance that he should be the first on board that ship. It was not so well considered as it ought to have been, to be sure, but could not now be helped. That, however, the word, *first,* was void; it could not supersede the date of any former commission. M. Amiel was so urgent to have it in, that it was agreed to, perhaps too inconsiderately.

After dinner, took a walk out of town; returned, and went to view the two churches, the least of which has some fine paintings,—St. Joseph, St. Joachim, the Virgin feeling the babe leap in her womb at the sight of Elizabeth, and many others; some handsome marble pillars, and two fine statues in plaster of Paris.

---

*In the roll of the ship he is entered as Laurence Brooks, of New Hampshire. Most of the persons here mentioned are more or less noticed in the *Life and Character of J. P. Jones,* by John Henry Sherburne.

In the evening, Captain Landais chagrined,—suspecting plots among his officers against him,—had written to Dr. Franklin, relating things to him, &c. &c. Mr. Blodgett came in, and said he had one chest in the ward-room, which the officers had ordered him to take away; but as he had but one, and they so many, he ventured to wait for the captain's orders; that the officers were now about to treat him better, conscious that they could not treat him worse. To-day they invited him to dine in the ward-room; but he begged Mr. Degge not to invite him; they had d——d him, and he could not dine there, yet did not love to refuse,—he begged off. Such is the danger of favoritism in the government of a ship, as well as of a state! I have had the pleasure to restore this ship to peace and harmony, and am persuaded it would have continued; but when I leave here, I see plainly all will become unhappy again. There is such a mixture of ductility and obstinacy in the government of her, as will not keep her together. A tender heart and an obstinate will sometimes go together. . . .

[June] 18. Friday. This morning, The Monsieur, a French privateer, which sailed out from Lorient as we went into it in the Alliance, came in with four English prizes, having made six this cruise. She and her prizes saluted the Sensible, and their salutes were returned. Received a card from Mr. Williams third, apologizing for the Three Friends,—that the pilot refused to take charge of her until the morning. I asked a gentleman how he slept. "Very badly, dans la Sainte Barbe." "Il faut chercher ce mot là," said I, "dans le Dictionnaire de la Marine." He ran and brought it, and found *la Sainte Barbe* to be the gun-room. "Connoissez vous l'étymologie, Monsieur?" said he. "Que non?" said I. Sainte Barbe is the tutelary saint of the *canonniers*,— gunners. Each trade has its patron. The shoemakers have Saint Crispin, &c.; and the gunners Sainte Barbe. The Sainte Barbe, therefore, is the gun-room, or the *salle d'armes*,—place of arms. There are nine persons who sleep in the Sainte Barbe. The *serruriers* have chosen Saint Cloud for their patron. M. Marbois discovered an inclination to-day to slide into conversation with me. I fell down the stream with him as easily as possible. He thought the alliance beneficial to both countries, and hoped it would last for ever. I agreed that the alliance was useful to both, and hoped it would last. I could not foresee any thing that should interrupt the friendship. Yes, recollecting myself, I could foresee several things that might interrupt it. "Ay! what were they?" I said it was possible a king of France might arise, who, being a wicked man, might make attempts to corrupt the Americans. A king of France hereafter might have a mistress that might mislead him, or a bad minister. I said I could foresee another thing that might endanger our confederation. "What was that?" The Court of France, I said, might, or their ambassadors or consuls might, attach themselves to individuals or parties in America, so as to endanger our Union. He caught at this with great avidity, and said it was a great principle not to join with any party. It was the King's determination and the Chevalier's, not to throw the weight of the French Court into the scale of any individual or party. He said he believed, or was afraid, it had been done; but it was disapproved by the King, and would not be done again. He said that the Chevalier and himself would have the favor of the greatest part,—the generality of the honest people in France,—although there would be individuals against them. He said he hoped the United States would not think of becoming conquerors. I said it was impossible they should for many ages; it would be madness in them to think of conquering foreign countries, while they had an immense territory near them uncultivated; that if any one State should have a fancy for going abroad, it would be in the interest of all the rest, and their duty, to hinder her. He seemed to be pleased with this. He said we would explain ourselves wholly on the passage. I said, with all my heart; for I had no secrets. All this conversation was in French; but he understood me very well, and I him. He said M. Gérard was a man of wit, and had an advantage of them in understanding the language very well, and speaking it easily. I said, I believed not much. I had heard it affirmed by some that M. Gérard spoke English perfectly; but by others very indifferently; that it was often affirmed that Mr. Franklin spoke French as fluently and elegantly as a courtier at Versailles; but every man that knew, and spoke sincerely, agreed that he spoke it very ill. Persons spoke of these things according to their affections. He said it was flattery,—that *he* would not flatter,—it was true that both Mr. F. and I spoke French badly. A cutter and a lugger hove in sight about noon, and dogged about all the afternoon. M. Marbois began with me again this afternoon,—inquired who was Dr. Bancroft? who Dr. Berkenhout? &c. &c.

18. Friday. The orders are to breakfast at ten, dine at five, and sup at ten.

19. Saturday. The two privateers which were in sight yesterday, are so still, with two others. Our Captain at length laid to, hoisted his colors, and fired a gun as a challenge. One of them hoisted English colors, and fired a gun, which I suppose was accepting the challenge. Our Captain gave her two broadsides, for the sake of exercising his men; and some of his balls went beyond her, some before, and some behind her; I cannot say that any one hit; but there were two which went so well, that it is possible they might. It is certain they were frightened; for, upon our wearing to give her chase, all four of them were about in an instant, and ran. But, at evening, there were several others in sight.

20. Sunday. Two privateers have been in sight all this day; one advanced, and fired several guns, in order to make us hoist our colors; but Captain Chavagnes would not do them that honor; they are afraid to come near; but this it is, every day we have a number in sight, so that there is no chance for a vessel to pass without convoy. Our Captain, M. Chavagnes, has a cross of St. Louis, and one of his midshipmen has a cross of St. Louis; his second has none. He is a youth of eighteen or nineteen, an *enseigne du vaisseau,* and very able for his years. He has a fine countenance.

The Chevalier de la Luzerne and M. Marbois are in raptures with my son. They get him to teach them the language. I found this morning the Ambassador seated on the cushion in our state-room, M. Marbois in his cot, at his left hand, and my son stretched out in his, at his right. The Ambassador reading out loud, in Blackstone's Discourse at his entrance on his Professorship of the Common Law at the University, and my son correcting the pronunciation of every word and syllable and letter.

The Ambassador said he was astonished at my son's knowledge; that he was a master of his own language, like a professor. M. Marbois said, your son teaches us more than you; he has *point de grâce, point d'éloges*. He shows us no mercy, and makes us no compliments. We must have Mr. John.

This evening had a little conversation with the Chevalier upon our American affairs and characters,—Mr. Samuel Adams, Mr. Dickinson, Mr. Jay,—and upon American eloquence in Congress and assemblies, as well as in writing. He admired our eloquence. I said that our eloquence was not corrected. It was the time of Ennius with us. That Mr. Dickinson and Mr. Jay had eloquence; but it was not so chaste, nor pure, nor nervous, as that of Mr. Samuel Adams. That this last had written some things that would be admired more than any thing that has been written in America in the dispute. He inquired after Mr. Dickinson, and the reason why he disappeared. I explained, as well as I could in French, the inconsistency of the Farmer's Letters, and his perseverance in that inconsistency in Congress, Mr. Dickinson's opposition to the Declaration of Independency. I ventured, as modestly as I could, to let him know that I had the honor to be the principal disputant in Congress against Mr. Dickinson upon that great question; that Mr. Dickinson had the eloquence, the learning, and the ingenuity, on his side of the question; but that I had the hearts of the Americans on mine; and, therefore, my side of the question prevailed. That Mr. Dickinson had a good heart, and an amiable character; but that his opposition to the independency had lost him the confidence of the people, who suspected him of timidity and avarice, and that his opposition sprung from those passions; but that he had since turned out with the militia against the British troops, and, I doubted not, might in time regain the confidence of the people. I said that Mr. Jay was a man of wit, well-informed, a good speaker, and an elegant writer. The Chevalier said, perhaps he will not be President when we arrive; he accepted only for a short time. I said I should not be sorry to hear of his resignation, because I did not much esteem the means by which he was advanced to the chair; it appearing to me that he came in by the efforts of a faction, at that moment dominant by means of an influence which I was afraid to mention; that I did not care to say what I thought of it.

We fell into a great deal of other conversation this evening, upon literature and eloquence, ancient and modern,— Demosthenes, Cicero, the poets, historians, philosophers, the English, Bacon, Newton, Milton, &c. He said Milton was very ancient. I said, No; in the reign of Charles and the protectorship of Cromwell, and the reign of Charles II. He thought it was much more ancient. I said there were three epochs in the English history, celebrated for great men,—the reign of Elizabeth, the reign of Charles I. and the interregnum, and the reign of Queen Anne. The Chevalier said Lord Bolingbroke was a great man. I said, Yes; and the greatest orator that England ever produced. M. Marbois, upon this, said it would be easy in France to produce an orator equal to Bolingbroke. I asked, Who? Jean Jacques? No, Malesherbes. Malesherbes's orations might be placed on a footing with Demosthenes and Cicero. . . .

20 [actually 22]. Tuesday. We have had a fine wind ever since we came out of Lorient; but it blows fresher to-day than ever; yet we go but about five knots, because, being obliged to wait for the Three Friends and the Foudroyant, which sail slow, we cannot carry sail. With all our sails we might now go eleven knots. This is mercantile politics, in getting the Chevalier's baggage on board those ships.

M. Marbois, with whom I fell into conversation this afternoon very easily upon deck, said a great many things that deserve notice. He said that Mr. Franklin had a great many friends among the *gens de lettres* in France, who make a great impression in France; that he had *beaucoup d'agrément, beaucoup de charlatanerie;* that he has wit, but that he is not a statesman. That he might be recalled at this moment, and, in that case, that his opinion was, he would not return to America, but would stay in Paris. That he heard many of the honest people in France lament that I left France, particularly the Count —— and the Marquis de ——; that I might possibly return to France, or to some other part of Europe; that the Court of France would have confidence in any gentleman that Congress should have confidence in; that there ought to be a *chargé*

des affaires, or a secretary, and a successor pointed out, in case
of the death of Dr. Franklin.

M. Marbois said some were of opinion, that as I was not recalled, I ought to have staid until I was. I told him that if Congress had directed me to return, I would have returned; if they
had directed me to stay until further orders, I should have
staid. But, as they reduced me to a private citizen, I had no
other duties but those of a private citizen to fulfil, which were
to go home as soon as possible, and take care of my family. Mr.
Franklin advised me to take a journey to Geneva; my own inclinations would have led me to Holland; but I thought my
honor concerned to return directly home. He said I was right.

In the evening I fell into chat with the Chevalier. He asked
me about Gouverneur Morris. I said it was his Christian name;
that he was not governor. The Chevalier said he had heard of
him as an able man. I said he was a young man, chosen into
Congress since I left it; that I had sat some years with his elder
brother in Congress; that Gouverneur was a man of wit, and
made pretty verses; but of a character *très léger.* That the cause
of America had not been sustained by such characters as that of
Gouverneur Morris, or his colleague, Mr. Jay, who also was a
young man about thirty, and not quite so solid as his predecessor, Mr. Laurens, upon whose resignation in the sudden heat
Mr. Jay was chosen.* That Mr. Laurens had a great landed fortune, free from debt; that he had long experience in public life,

---

*It is scarcely necessary to say that the writer subsequently changed his senti-
ments respecting Mr. Jay, whose political character took a bolder development
after his departure from Congress, on his mission to Spain. In the violent disputes of that body respecting Silas Deane's conduct, Mr. Jay had taken a very
active part in his favor; and the resignation of Mr. Laurens, as President, as
well as his election to that post, had turned upon the question of hearing
Deane's charges against Mr. Lee, in the form in which he chose to present
them. All these circumstances contributed to raise expectations in the French
and Spanish agents, at Philadelphia, which secured their cooperation in promoting his nomination as minister to Spain. But in this they were completely
disappointed by Mr. Jay's later, which, like his earlier conduct, was prompted
only by his conscientious convictions. He outlived his confidence in Mr. Silas
Deane. *Gordon's History,* vol. iii. p. 218; *Life of J. Jay,* by his son, W. Jay,
vol. i. p. 99, 129.

and an amiable character for honor and probity; that he is between fifty and sixty years of age.

23. Wednesday. This forenoon, fell strangely, yet very easily, into conversation with M. Marbois. I went up to him. "M. Marbois," said I, "how many persons have you in your train, and that of the Chevalier, who speak the German language?" "Only my servant," said he, "besides the Chevalier and myself." "It will be a great advantage to you," said I, "in America, especially in Pennsylvania, to be able to speak German. There is a great body of Germans in Pennsylvania and Maryland. There is a vast proportion of the city of Philadelphia of this nation, who have three churches in it, two of which, one Lutheran, the other Calvinist, are the largest and most elegant churches in the city, frequented by the most numerous congregations, where the worship is all in the German language." "Is there not one Catholic?" said M. Marbois. "Not a German church," said I. "There is a Roman Catholic church in Philadelphia, a very decent building, frequented by a respectable congregation, consisting partly of Germans, partly of French, and partly of Irish." "All religions are tolerated in America," said M. Marbois; "and the ambassadors have in all courts a right to a chapel in their own way; but Mr. Franklin never had any." "No," said I, laughing, "because Mr. Franklin had no"—I was going to say what I did not say, and will not say here. I stopped short, and laughed. "No," said M. Marbois; "Mr. Franklin adores only great Nature, which has interested a great many people of both sexes in his favor." "Yes," said I, laughing, "all the atheists, deists, and libertines, as well as the philosophers and ladies, are in his train,—another Voltaire, and thence—" "Yes," said M. Marbois, "he is celebrated as the great philosopher and the great legislator of America." "He is," said I, "a great philosopher, but as a legislator of America he has done very little. It is universally believed in France, England, and all Europe, that his electric wand has accomplished all this revolution. But nothing is more groundless. He has done very little. It is believed that he made all the American constitutions and their confederation; but he made neither. He did not even make the constitution of Penn-

sylvania, bad as it is. The bill of rights is taken almost verbatim
from that of Virginia, which was made and published two or
three months before that of Philadelphia was begun; it was
made by Mr. Mason, as that of Pennsylvania was by Timothy
Matlack, James Cannon, and Thomas Young, and Thomas
Paine. Mr. Sherman, of Connecticut, and Dr. Franklin made an
essay towards a confederation about the same time. Mr. Sherman's was best liked, but very little was finally adopted from either, and the real confederation was not made until a year after
Mr. Franklin left America, and but a few days before I left Congress." "Who," said the Chevalier, "made the Declaration of
Independence?" "Mr. Jefferson, of Virginia," said I, "was the
draughtsman. The committee consisted of Mr. Jefferson, Mr.
Franklin, Mr. Harrison,* Mr. R. and myself; and we appointed
Jefferson a sub-committee to draw it up."

I said that Mr. Franklin had great merit as a philosopher. His
discoveries in electricity were very grand, and he certainly was
a great genius, and had great merit in our American affairs. But
he had no title to the "legislator of America." M. Marbois said
he had wit and irony; but these were not the faculties of statesmen. His Essay upon the true means of bringing a great Empire
to be a small one, was very pretty. I said he had wrote many
things which had great merit, and infinite wit and ingenuity.
His Bonhomme Richard was a very ingenious thing, which had
been so much celebrated in France, gone through so many editions, and been recommended by curates and bishops to so
many parishes and dioceses.

M. Marbois asked, are natural children admitted in America
to all privileges like children born in wedlock? I answered,
They are not admitted to the rights of inheritance; but their fathers may give them estates by testament, and they are not excluded from other advantages. "In France," said M. Marbois,
"they are not admitted into the army nor any office in government." I said, they were not excluded from commissions in the

---

*A singular slip of the memory. Mr. Sherman and Mr. R. R. Livingston were
of the committee, and Mr. Harrison was not.

army, navy, or state, but they were always attended with a mark of disgrace. M. Marbois said this, no doubt, in allusion to Mr. F.'s natural son, and natural son of a natural son. I let myself thus freely into this conversation, being led on naturally by the Chevalier and M. Marbois on purpose, because I am sure it cannot be my duty, nor the interest of my country, that I should conceal any of my sentiments of this man, at the same time that I do justice to his merits. It would be worse than folly to conceal my opinion of his great faults.

24. Thursday. M. Marbois told a story of an ecclesiastic, who pronounced a funeral oration on Marshal Saxe. He compared him to Alcides, who balanced long whether he should follow the path of virtue or of sloth, and at last chose the former. But Saxe, after balancing long, did better by determining to follow both, that is, pleasure and virtue.

This evening I went into our state-room, where I found M. Marbois alone. "M. Marbois," said I, "what books are the best to give a stranger an idea of the laws and government of France?" "I shall surprise you, sir," said M. Marbois, "and I shall make you laugh; but there is no other but the Almanach Royal." "You say this," said I, laughing, "on purpose to make me laugh." "No," says he, "there is no *droit public* in France. There are different customs and prerogatives in different provinces. But if you wish I should talk with you more seriously, there are several books in which there are some good notions upon this subject. There are four volumes, by Boulainvilliers, of observations sur l'Ancien Gouvernement de France, and four volumes more, by the Abbé de Fleury, on the same subject." He ran over a great deal more concerning the *salique law,* and the *capitula regum Francorum,* &c. which I will be more particular with him about another time. I mentioned Domat. He said it was excellent on the civil law, but had little on the *droit public.* "How happened it," said I, "M. Marbois, that I never saw you at Paris?" "You have," said he. "Ay, where?" said I; "I don't remember it." "I dined with you," said he, "at the Count Sarsfield's." I said there was a great deal of company, but that I had never seen any one of them before; they were all strangers; but

I remember the Count told me they were all men of letters. "There were four ladies," said M. Marbois, "the handsomest of whom was the Countess de la Luzerne, the wife of the Count de la Luzerne. The Count himself was there, who is the eldest brother of the Chevalier de la Luzerne. There was another lady there, who is not handsome, and was never married. She is a sister." "She was the lady who sat at my left hand at table," said I, "and was very sociable. I was charmed with her understanding, although I thought she was not handsome. There was a gentleman there, who asked me if the Mahometan religion was tolerated in America. I understood he had been in Constantinople, as ambassador, or secretary to some embassy. And there was a bishop there, who came in after dinner." "Yes," said he, "he is the bishop of Langres; another brother of the Chevalier de la Luzerne." "I fell," said I, "unaccountably, into a dispute with that bishop. He sat down by me, and fell into conversation about the English, and their conduct in America. In the course of the conversation, I said it was the misfortune of the English, that there was no consistent character among those in opposition to the Court; no man who would adhere to his principles. The two Howes were in opposition to the ministry and the American measures, but when the honor and emoluments of command were offered them, they accepted to serve under that Ministry, and in support of those measures; even Keppell, who refused to serve against America, was induced to serve against France, who were only supporting the Americans. The Bishop said it was the will of the King that must control public officers. I said, an officer should beg to be excused or resign, rather than serve against his conscience. He said the king's will must govern. I said it was a doctrine I could not understand. There was a gentleman present who attended to our conversation in silence till this, when he said, laughing, 'C'est une doctrine ecclésiastique, Monseigneur L'Evêque.'" "This bishop," said M. Marbois, "is no slave; he is a man of free sentiments; he is *duc et pair*. There are three bishops who are dukes and peers, and three others who are counts and peers, who are always present at the consecration of our kings. The Bishop of Langres is one. The Dukes of Normandy and of Burgundy used

to be present, but as there are not any at present, Monsieur and
the Count d'Artois represented them at the consecration of the
present King, about four years ago. The origin of the custom is
not known." "The Chevalier de la Luzerne," said I, "is of a
high family." "Yes," said M. Marbois, "he is of an ancient family, who have formerly had in it cardinals and maréchals of
France, but not lately. They are now likely to regain their splendor, for the three brothers are all very well at Court."

28. Monday. We have been favored in our voyage, hitherto,
beyond my utmost expectations. We have enjoyed a succession
of favorable winds and weather from the time of our leaving
Lorient to this moment.

The discipline on board this ship is a constant subject of
speculation to me. I have seen no punishments inflicted, no
blows struck, nor heard scarcely an angry word spoken from
the captain to any of his officers, or from any of the officers to
the men. They live together in greater intimacy and familiarity
than any family I ever saw. The *gaillard,* or quarter-deck, seems
to be as open to the foremast men as the captain. Captain, all
other officers, the ambassador, his train, common sailors, and
domestic servants, are all walking upon deck, and sitting round
upon seats on it, upon a footing of perfect equality, that is not
seen in one of our country town meetings in America. I never
saw so much equality and levelling in any society whatever.
Strange contrast to a British, or even an American frigate. . . .

July 2. Friday. Walking this afternoon with M. Marbois
upon the quarter-deck, I said frankly to him, that I had expected M. Garnier would have been sent to America; that I had
observed some things in the conduct of B. and C. which made
me conjecture and believe that they were planning to have M.
Garnier succeed M. Gérard; that there was a great intimacy between B. and M. Garnier. "Between ourselves," said M. Marbois, "I believe that was a reason why he did not go. M.
Garnier is a man of spirit, and has a great deal of merit; in England he did us good service, and he speaks English very well,
and understands affairs very well; but in this affair of his going
out upon this embassy, I cannot reconcile his conduct with a
man of spirit." I said I had had the pleasure of some acquain-

tance with M. Garnier; that he did me the honor to visit me several times, and I had several long conversations with him alone; that I was much pleased with his knowledge of our affairs from the beginning, and with his manners; but I thought him too much connected and attached to a particular circle, particularly to B., to whom he seemed to me to have a blind attachment. "There is reason to believe," said M. Marbois, "that Dr. Franklin is not too much pleased with the appointment of the Chevalier. What is the reason of the attachment of Dr. Franklin to B.?"* "Because B. is devoted to Mr. D. and because he is the only American at Paris who loves him; all the Americans but him are, at present, very bitter against Franklin; he would probably be very glad to get his grandson secretary, but as I fancy he must think him too young to obtain the appointment, he will join with Mr. D. in endeavoring to get B. D. I know, from authentic information, is endeavoring to get B. appointed; that B. was so irregular and eccentric a character, and his conduct in American affairs had been such, that I confessed I had an entire distrust of him; that, at present, he and M. C.† had in a manner the direction of American affairs; that Congress might as well appoint M. C. their ambassador, but that he had not the brains for the management of such affairs." M. Marbois said, "In fact, he had the management, but it was altogether improper; that the King would never suffer any of his subjects to represent foreign courts at his," &c. The Chevalier came up and said, as our Court would take it amiss if an American minister should meddle in the cabals or intrigues at Versailles, so the United States should resent a French minister's taking a part in any disputes among them; that there was no need of policy between France and the United States; they need only understand one another—*rien que s'entendre*. I said, that in my youth I had often heard of the address and intrigues of the French Court, but I could sincerely say, I had found more

---

*Probably Dr. Bancroft, a sketch of whom is given [on pages 65–66—ED.].
†Le Ray de Chaumont.

intrigue and *finesse* among my own countrymen at Paris, than among the French. . . .

17. Saturday. Three days past we have sounded for the Grand Bank, but have not found it. By the reckonings of all the officers we ought to be now ten leagues upon the Bank.

It is surprising to me that we have not seen more fish; a few whales, a few porpoises, and two sharks are all we have seen. The two sharks we caught with a shark-hook and a bit of pork for a bait; we cut up the first, and threw overboard his head and entrails, all of which the other, who was playing after the ship, snatched at with infinite greediness, and swallowed down in an instant; after we had taken him, we opened him, and found the head and entrails of his companion in him.

M. Marbois is indefatigable; as soon as he is up, he reads the Correspondence of M. Gérard for some hours. The Minister it seems has furnished them with a copy of all M. Gérard's Letters, which appear to be voluminous. After this, he reads aloud to M. Carré, M. Otto, M. Restif, or M. Forest, one of Congreve's or Garrick's plays; then he writes some hours.

He is unwilling to let me see Gérard's letters, or what he writes. . . .

[August] 10. Friday. Supped and slept at my lodgings. Breakfasted on Spanish chocolate, which answers the fame it has acquired in the world. Everybody congratulates us on our safe arrival at this place. The leak in the Sensible increases since she has been at anchor; and everybody thinks we have been in great danger.

13. Monday. Yesterday I walked about the town; but there is nothing to be seen excepting two churches, and the arsenals, dry docks, fortifications, and ships of war.

The inconvenience of this harbor is, the entrance is so narrow that there is no possibility of going out but when the wind is one way, that is, southeast, or thereabouts.

The three French ships of the line here are,—the Triomphant, the Souverain, and the Jason; the first of eighty guns, the second seventy-four, the third sixty-four.

M. le Comte de Sade is the Chief d'Escadre or General; M. le

Chevalier de Gras Préville is the Capitaine de Pavillon; M. le Chevalier de Glandevès is Captain of the Souverain; M. de la Marthonie commands the Jason.

14. Tuesday. Walked to the barracks and dry docks, to show them to Charles. The stone of which these works are made is about as good as Braintree south-common stone. Went into the Church of St. Julien, which is magnificent; numbers of *dévots* upon their knees. This afternoon we cross the water to go to Corunna.

We have lodged en la Calle de la Madalena, junto coca, en casa de Pepala Botoneca. The chief magistrate of this town is the *Corregidor.* Last evening, and the evening before, I spent in conversation with the Consul, on the law of nations and the writers on that law, particularly on the titles in those authors concerning ambassadors and consuls. He mentioned several on the rights and duties of ambassadors and consuls, and some on the etiquette and formalities and ceremonies. I asked him many questions. He told me that the office of consul was regulated by an ordinance of the King; but that some nations had entered into particular stipulations with the King; that the consuls of different nations were differently treated by the same nation; that as Consul of France he had always claimed the privileges of the most favored nation; that he inquired what privileges were enjoyed by the consuls of England, Italy, Germany, &c. &c.; that there is for the province of Galice a sovereign court of justice, which has both civil and criminal jurisdiction; that it is without appeal in all criminal cases, but in some civil cases an appeal lies to the Council; that there is not time for an application for pardon, for they execute forthwith; that hanging is the capital punishment; they burn sometimes, but it is after death; that there was lately a sentence for parricide; the law required that the criminal should be headed up in a hogshead with an adder, a toad, a dog, a cat, &c. and cast into the sea; that he looked at it, and found that they had printed those animals on the hogshead, and that the dead body was put into the cask; that the ancient law of the Visigoths is still in use, with the institutes, codes, *novelles,* &c. of Justinian, the current law and *ordonnances* of the King; that he will procure for me a passport from the General or Governor of the Province, who resides at Corunna, which will secure me all sorts of facilities as I ride the country; but whether through the kingdom, or only through the province of Galice, I don't know.

I have not seen a chariot, coach, phaëton, chaise, or sulky, since I have been in the place. Very few horses, and those small, poor, and shabby. Mules and asses are numerous, but small. There is no hay in this country; the horses, &c. eat straw,— wheat straw. The bread, the cabbages, the cauliflowers, apples, pears, &c. are good; the beef, pork, poultry, &c. are good; the fish are good,—excellent eels, sardines, and other fish, and tolerable oysters, but not like ours.

There has been no frost yet. The verdure in the gardens and fields is fresh. The weather is so warm that the inhabitants have no fires nor fireplaces but in their kitchens; they tell us we shall have no colder weather before May, which is the coldest month in the year. Men and women and children are seen in the streets with bare feet and legs, standing on the cold stones in the mud, by the hour together. The inhabitants of both sexes have black hair and dark complexions, with fine black eyes; men and women have long hair ramillied down to their waists, and even sometimes to their knees. There is little appearance of commerce or industry, except about the King's docks and yards and works. Yet the town has some symptoms of growth and prosperity; many new houses are building of stone, which comes from the rocky mountains round about, of which there are many. There are few goods in the shops, little show in their market or in their exchange. There is a pleasant walk a little out of town, between the Exchange and the barracks. There are but two taverns in this town. Captain Chavagnes and his officers are lodged in one, at six livres each per day; the other is kept by a native of America, who speaks English and French, as well as Spanish, and is an obliging man. Here we could have lodged at a dollar a day each; but we were obliged to give one hundred and twenty-nine dollars for six days, besides the barber, and a multitude of other little expenses, and besides being kept constantly unhappy by an uneasy landlady.

Finding that I must reside some weeks in Spain, either wait-

ing for a frigate, or travelling through the kingdom, I determined to acquire the language, to which purpose I went to a
bookseller, and purchased Sobrino's Dictionary, in three volumes in quarto, and the Grammatica Castellana, which is an
excellent Spanish grammar in their own tongue, and also a
Latin grammar in Spanish, after which, Monsieur de Gras
made me a present of a very handsome grammar of the Spanish tongue in French, by Sobrino. By the help of these books,
the children and gentlemen are learning the language very fast.
To a man who understands Latin it is very easy. I flatter myself
that in a month I should be able to read it very well, and to
make myself understood, as well as understand the Spaniards.
The Consul, and Mr. Linde, an Irish gentleman, a master of a
mathematical academy here, say that the Spanish nation in
general have been of opinion that the revolution in America
was of bad example to the Spanish Colonies, and dangerous to
the interests of Spain, as the United States, if they should become ambitious, and be seized with the spirit of conquest,
might aim at Mexico and Peru. The Consul mentioned Raynal's opinion, that it was not for the interest of the powers of
Europe, that America should be independent. I told the Irish
gentleman that Americans hated war; that agriculture and
commerce were their objects, and it would be their interest, as
much as that of the Dutch, to keep peace with all the world,
until their country should be filled with population, which
could not be in many centuries; that war, and the spirit of conquest, was the most diametrically opposite to their interests, as
they would divert their attention, wealth, industry, activity, &c.
from a certain source of prosperity, and even grandeur and
glory, to an uncertain one, nay, to one that it is certain they
could never make any advantage of; that the government of
Spain over their colonies had been such, that she never could
attempt to introduce such fundamental innovations as those by
which England had provoked and compelled hers to revolt,
and the Spanish constitution was such as could extinguish the
first sparks of discontent, and quell the first risings of the
people; that it was amazing to me, that a writer so well informed as Raynal, could ever give an opinion that it was not

for the interest of the powers of Europe that America should be independent, when it was so easy to demonstrate that it was for the interest of every one except England. They could lose nothing by it, but certainly would every one gain something, many a great deal. It would be a pretty work to show how France, Spain, Holland, Germany, Russia, Sweden, Denmark, would gain; it would be easy to show it. . . .

22. Wednesday. Drank tea at Signor Lagoanere's. Saw the ladies drink chocolate in the Spanish fashion. A servant brought in a salver, with a number of tumblers of clean, clear glass, full of cold water, and a plate of cakes, which were light pieces of sugar. Each lady took a tumbler of water and a piece of sugar, dipped her sugar in her tumbler of water, eat the one, and drank the other. The servant then brought in another salver, of cups of hot chocolate. Each lady took a cup and drank it, and then cakes and bread and butter were served; then each lady took another cup of cold water, and here ended the repast. The ladies were Señora Lagoanere, and the lady of the Commandant of Artillery, the Consul's sister, and another. The Administrator of the King's Tobacco, the French Consul, and another gentleman, with Mr. Dana, Mr. Thaxter, and myself, made the company.

Three Spanish ships of the line and two French frigates came into this harbor this afternoon. A packet arrived here yesterday from Havana. The Administrator gave me a map of Gibraltar, and the Spanish ships about it by sea, and lines by land.

Orders of Ecclesiastics.—Dominicans, Franciscans, Augustines, only, at Corunna. Nuns of Ste. Barbe, Capuchins.

24. Friday. Dined on board the Belle Poule with the officers of the Galatea and the Belle Poule.

25. Saturday. Christmas. Went to the Palace at eleven o'clock to take my leave of his Excellency. Mr. O'Hara, the Governor of the town, went with me. The General repeated a thousand obliging things which he had said to me when I first saw him and dined with him.

26. Sunday. At half after two we mounted our carriages and mules, and rode four leagues to Betanzos, the ancient capital of the kingdom of Galicia, and the place where the archives are still kept. We saw the building, a long, square, stone building,

without any roof, opposite the church. There are in this place two churches and two convents. The last league of the road was very bad, mountainous, and rocky to such a degree as to be very dangerous. Mr. Lagoanere did us the honor to bear us company to this place. It would appear romantic to describe the house, the beds, and the people.

27. Monday. Travelled from Betanzos to Castillano. The roads still mountainous and rocky. We broke one of our axle-trees, early in the day, which prevented us from going more than four leagues in the whole.

The house where we lodge is of stone, two stories high. We entered into the kitchen,—no floor but the ground, and no carpet but straw, trodden into mire by men, hogs, horses, mules, &c. In the middle of the kitchen was a mound, a little raised with earth and stone, upon which was a fire, with pots, kettles, skillets, &c. of the fashion of the country, about it. There was no chimney. The smoke ascended, and found no other passage than through two holes drilled through the tiles of the roof, not perpendicularly over the fire, but at angles of about forty-five degrees. On one side was a flue oven, very large, black, smoky, and sooty; on the opposite side of the fire was a cabin filled with straw, where I suppose the *patron della casa,* that is, the master of the house, his wife, and four children, all pigged in together. On the same floor with the kitchen was the stable; there was a door which parted the kitchen and stable, but this was always open, and the floor of the stable was covered with miry straw like the kitchen. I went into the stable, and saw it filled on both sides with mules belonging to us and several other travellers, who were obliged to put up by the rain.

The smoke filled every part of the kitchen, stable, and other parts of the house as thick as possible, so that it was very difficult to see or breathe. There was a flight of steps of stone, from the kitchen floor up into a chamber, covered with mud and straw; on the left hand, as you ascended the stairs, was a stage built up about half way from the kitchen floor to the chamber floor; on this stage was a bed of straw on which lay a fatting hog. Around the kitchen fire were arranged the man, woman, four children, all the travellers, servants, muleteers, &c. The

chamber had a large quantity of Indian corn in ears, hanging
over head upon sticks and pieces of slit work—perhaps an hundred bushels; in one corner was a large bin full of rape seed or
colza; on the other side, another bin full of oats. In another
part of the chamber lay a bushel or two of chestnuts, two
frames for beds, straw beds upon them, a table in the middle.
The floor had never been washed nor swept for an hundred
years; smoke, soot, dirt everywhere; two windows in the chamber, that is, port-holes, without any glass; wooden doors to
open and shut before the windows. Yet, amidst all these horrors, I slept better than I have done before since my arrival in
Spain. . . .

[1782. October] 2. Wednesday. . . .

It is the fashion among the Dutch, to arrange all the company by putting a card with the name of each gentleman and
lady upon the napkins in the plate; this I never saw practised in
France; indeed, they attend but to one person in France; the feast
is made in honor of one person; that is the ton. Mr. Visscher,
being told by the Count that he and I were to dine to-morrow
with General Van der Dussen, appeared surprised, and said that
the General, although he had dined with me and rode with me
on horseback, would not have dared to have invited me, if he
had not met me at M. Boreel's.

I saw the other day Joachimi Hoppii Commentatio Succincta
ad Institutiones Justinianas, at Mr. Luzac's.

Mr. Gyzelaer informed me, that the Committee for examining the administration of the Marine, were to-morrow to announce their authority to the Prince. I told him he must make a
harangue in order to give dignity and solemnity to his commission. He said it was a delicate thing to make a speech upon the
occasion. This I agreed.

I gave the gentlemen an account of the practice of the Provincial Congress of Massachusetts, when they first formed their
army. Dr. Warren, their President, made a harangue in the form
of a charge, in the presence of the Assembly, to every officer,
upon the delivery of his commission; and he never failed to
make the officer, as well as all the Assembly, shudder upon
those occasions. Count Sarsfield appeared struck and affected

with this anecdote. I dare say he has it in his journal. Count
Sarsfield told me the news of the destruction of the Spanish
floating batteries, by the English red hot bullets. He seemed
much affected. Said all Europe would laugh at them, and that
they deserved it for attempting a thing so evidently impossible.
No governments, says he, but monarchies, are subject to this
kind of misfortunes from absurdity. In France, a Madame Pompadour, or Du Barry, may ruin a kingdom. In Spain, an absurd
priest, the father confessor of a superstitious king, may so far
gain his confidence by working upon his conscience and superstitious fears, as to lead him into such foolish councils. How
much mischief, says I, has Spain done in this just cause! . . .

9. Saturday. . . .

I went out to Passy to dine with Mr. Franklin, who had been
to Versailles, and presented his memorial and the papers ac-
companying it. The Count said he would have the papers translated, to lay them before the King; but the affair would meet
with many difficulties. Franklin brought the same message to
me from the Court, and said he believed it would be taken
kindly if I went. I told both the Marquis and the Doctor that I
would go to-morrow morning.

10. Sunday. Accordingly, at eight this morning I went and
waited on the Comte. He asked me how we went on with the
English. I told them we divided upon two points,—the Tories
and Penobscot; two ostensible points; for it was impossible to
believe that my Lord Shelburne or the nation cared much about
such points. I took out of my pocket and showed him the
record of Governor Pownal's solemn act of burying a leaden
plate with this inscription:

"May 23. 1759. Province of Massachusetts Bay. Penobscot,
dominions of Great Britain. Possession confirmed by Thomas
Pownal, Governor."

This was planted on the east side of the river of Penobscot,
three miles above marine navigation. I showed him also all the
other records,—the laying out of Mount Desert, Machias, and
all the other towns to the east of the river Penobscot; and told
him that the grant of Nova Scotia by James I. to Sir William
Alexander, bounded it on the river St. Croix; and that I was

possessed of the authorities of four of the greatest governors the King of England ever had,—Shirley, Pownal, Bernard, and Hutchinson, in favor of our claim,—and of learned writings of Shirley and Hutchinson in support of it. The Comte said that Mr. Fitzherbert told him they wanted it for the masts; but the Comte said that Canada had an immense quantity. I told him I thought there were few masts there, but that I fancied it was not masts, but tories that again made the difficulty; some of them claimed lands in that territory, and others hoped for grants there. The Comte said it was not astonishing that the British Ministry should insist upon compensation to them, for that all the precedents were in favor of it; that there had been no example of an affair like this, terminated by a treaty, without reëstablishing those who had adhered to the old government in all their possessions. I begged his pardon in this, and said that in Ireland at least there had been a multitude of confiscations without restitution. Here we ran into some conversation concerning Ireland, &c.

Mr. Rayneval, who was present, talked about the national honor and the obligation they were under to support their adherents. Here I thought I might indulge a little more latitude of expression than I had done with Oswald and Strachey; and I answered, if the nation thought itself bound in honor to compensate these people, it might easily do it, for it cost the nation more money to carry on this war one month, than it would cost it to compensate them all; but I could not comprehend this doctrine of national honor; those people, by their misrepresentations, had deceived the nation who had followed the impulsion of their devouring ambition until it had brought an indelible stain on the British name, and almost irretrievable ruin on the nation; and now that very nation was thought to be bound in honor to compensate its dishonorers and destroyers. Rayneval said it was very true.

The Comte invited me to dine. I accepted. When I came, I found the Marquis de Lafayette in conference with him. When they came out, the Marquis took me aside, and told me he had been talking with the Comte upon the affair of money; he had represented to him Mr. Morris's arguments, and the things I had said to him as from himself, &c.; that he feared the arts of the English; that our army would disband, and our governments relax, &c.; that the Comte feared many difficulties; that France had expended two hundred and fifty millions in this war, and that he talked of allowing six millions, and my going to Holland with the scheme I had projected, and having the King's warranty, &c. to get the rest; that he had already spoken to some of M. de Fleury's friends, and intended to speak to him, &c.

We went up to dinner. I went up with the Comte alone. He showed me into the room where were the ladies and the company. I singled out the Countess, and went up to her to make her my compliments. The Countess and all the ladies rose up; I made my respects to them all, and turned round and bowed to the rest of the company. The Count, who came in after me, made his bows to the ladies, and to the Countess last. When he came to her, he turned round and called out, "Monsieur Adams, venez ici, voilà la Comtesse de Vergennes." A nobleman in company said, "Mr. Adams has already made his court to Madame la Comtesse." I went up again, however, and spoke again to the Countess, and she to me. When dinner was served, the Comte led Madame de Montmorin, and left me to conduct the Countess, who gave me her hand with extraordinary condescension, and I conducted her to table. She made me sit next her on her right hand, and was remarkably attentive to me the whole time. The Comte, who sat opposite, was constantly calling out to me to know what I would eat, and to offer me *petits gateaux,* claret and madeira, &c. &c. In short, I was never treated with half the respect at Versailles in my life.

In the antechamber, before dinner, some French gentlemen came to me and said they had seen me two years ago; said that I had shown in Holland that the Americans understand negotiation as well as war. The compliments that have been made me since my arrival in France, upon my success in Holland, would be considered a curiosity if committed to writing. "Je vous félicite sur votre succès," is common to all. One adds, "Monsieur, ma foi, vous avez réussi bien merveilleusement. Vous avez fait reconnoître votre indépendance; vous avez fait un traité, et vous avez procuré de l'argent. Voilà un succès parfait." Another says, "Vous avez fait des merveilles en Hollande: vous avez culbuté le Stathouder et le parti Anglois; vous avez donné bien du mouvement, vous avez remué tout le monde." Another said, "Monsieur, vous êtes le Washington de la négociation."[14] This is the finishing stroke. It is impossible to exceed this. Compliments are the study of this people, and there is no other so ingenious at them.

11. Monday. Mr. Whitefoord, the Secretary of Mr. Oswald, came a second time, not having found me at home yesterday, when he left a card with a copy of Mr. Oswald's commission, attested by himself, (Mr. Oswald.) He delivered the copy, and said Mr. Oswald was ready to compare it to the original with me. I said, Mr. Oswald's attestation was sufficient, as he had already shown me his original. He sat down, and we fell into conversation about the weather, and the vapors and exhalations from Tartary, which had been brought here last spring by the winds, and given us all the influenza; thence, to French fashions, and the punctuality with which they insist upon people's wearing thin clothes in spring and fall, though the weather is ever so cold, &c. I said it was often carried to ridiculous lengths, but that it was at bottom an admirable policy, as it rendered all Europe tributary to the city of Paris for its manufactures. We fell soon into politics. I told him that there was something in the minds of the English and French which impelled them irresistibly to war every ten or fifteen years. He said the ensuing peace would, he believed, be a long one. I said it would, provided it was well made, and nothing left in it to give future discontents; but if any thing was done which the Americans should think hard and unjust, both the English and French would be continually blowing it up and inflaming the American minds with it, in order to make them join one side or the other in a future war. He might well think, that the French would be very glad to have the Americans join them in a future war. Suppose, for example, they should think the tories men of monarchical principles, or men of more ambition than principle, or men corrupted and of no principle, and should, therefore, think them more easily seduced to their purposes than

virtuous republicans, is it not easy to see the policy of a French minister in wishing them amnesty and compensation? Suppose a French minister foresees that the presence of the tories in America will keep up perpetually two parties,—a French party and an English party,—and that this will compel the patriotic and independent party to join the French party; is it not natural for him to wish them restored? Is it not easy to see that a French minister cannot wish to have the English and Americans perfectly agreed upon all points, before they themselves, the Spaniards and Dutch, are agreed too? Can they be sorry, then, to see us split upon such a point as the tories? What can be their motives to become the advocates of the tories?

The French minister at Philadelphia, has made some representations to Congress in favor of a compensation to the royalists, and the Count de Vergennes, no longer than yesterday, said much to me in their favor. The Comte probably knows that we are instructed against it, or rather, have not constitutional authority to do it; that we can only write about it to Congress, and they to the States, who may and probably will deliberate upon it eighteen months, before they all decide, and then every one of them will determine against it. In this way, there is an insuperable obstacle to any agreement between the English and Americans, even upon terms to be inserted in the general peace, before all are ready. It was the constant practice of the French, to have some of their subjects in London, during the conferences for peace, in order to propagate such sentiments there as they wished to prevail. I doubted not such were there now. Mr. Rayneval had been there. Mr. Gérard, I had heard, is there now, and probably others. They can easily persuade the tories to set up their demands, and tell them and the ministers that the King's dignity and nation's honor are compromised in it.

For my own part, I thought America had been long enough involved in the wars of Europe. She had been a foot-ball between contending nations from the beginning, and it was easy to foresee that France and England both would endeavor to involve us in their future wars. I thought it our interest and duty to avoid as much as possible, and to be completely independent, and have nothing to do, but in commerce, with either of them. That my thoughts had been from the beginning constantly employed to arrange all our European connections to this end, and that they would continue to be so employed, and I thought it so important to us, that if my poor labors, my little estate, or (smiling) sizy blood could effect it, it should be done. But I had many fears.

I said, the King of France might think it consistent with his station, to favor people who had contended for a crown, though it was the crown of his enemy. Whitefoord said, they seem to be, through the whole of this, fighting for reputation. I said, they had acquired it, and more, they had raised themselves high from a low estate by it, and they were our good friends and allies, and had conducted generously and nobly, and we should be just and grateful. But they might have political wishes, which we were not bound by treaty nor in justice or gratitude to favor, and these we ought to be cautious of. He agreed that they had raised themselves very suddenly and surprisingly by it. We had more conversation on the state of manners in France, England, Scotland, and in other parts of Europe, but I have not time to record this.

12. Tuesday. Dined with the Abbés Chalut and Arnoux; the Farmer-General and his daughter, Dr. Franklin and his grandson, Mr. Grand and his lady and niece, Mr. Ridley, and I, with one young French gentleman, made the company. The Farmer's daughter is about twelve years old, and is, I suppose, an *enfant trouvée*. He made her sing at table, and she bids fair to be an accomplished opera girl, though she has not a delicate ear. The compliment of "Monsieur, vous êtes le Washington de la négociation," was repeated to me by more than one person. I answered, "Monsieur, vous me faites le plus grand honneur, et le compliment le plus sublime possible." "Eh, Monsieur, en vérité, vous l'avez bien mérité." A few of these compliments would kill Franklin, if they should come to his ears. . . .

15. Friday. . . .

He [Richard Oswald, a Scottish merchant sent by England to Paris to discuss the peace terms with Adams and Franklin—ED.] said he had been reading Mr. Paine's Answer to the Abbé

Raynal, and had found there an excellent argument in favor of the tories. Mr. Paine says, "that before the battle of Lexington we were so blindly prejudiced in favor of the English, and so closely attached to them, that we went to war at any time and for any object, when they bid us." Now, this being habitual to the Americans, it was excusable in the tories to behave upon this occasion as all of us had ever done upon all others. He said, if he were a member of Congress, he would show a magnanimity upon this occasion, and would say to the refugees, take your property; we scorn to make any use of it in building up our system.

I replied, that we had no power, and Congress had no power, and, therefore, we must consider how it would be reasoned upon in the several legislatures of the separate States, if, after being sent by us to Congress, and by them to the several States, in the course of twelve or fifteen months, it should be there debated; you must carry on the war six or nine months certainly for this compensation, and consequently spend, in the prosecution of it, six or nine times the sum necessary to make the compensation; for, I presume, this war costs every month to Great Britain a larger sum than would be necessary to pay for the forfeited estates.

"How," said I, "will an independent man in one of our assemblies consider this? We will take a man who is no partisan of England or France, one who wishes to do justice to both and to all nations, but is the partisan only of his own." "Have you seen," says he, "a certain letter written to the Count de Vergennes, wherein Mr. Samuel Adams is treated pretty freely?" "Yes," says I, "and several other papers, in which Mr. John Adams has been treated so too; I don't know what you may have heard in England of Mr. S. Adams; you may have been taught to believe, for what I know, that he eats little children; but I assure you he is a man of humanity and candor, as well as integrity; and further, that he is devoted to the interest of his country, and, I believe, wishes never to be, after a peace, the partisan to France or England, but to do justice and all the good he can to both; I thank you for mentioning him, for I will make him my orator. What will he say when the question of amnesty and compensation to the tories comes before the Senate of Massachusetts, and when he is informed that England makes a point of it, and that France favors her? He will say, here are two old, sagacious courts, both endeavoring to sow the seeds of discord among us, each endeavoring to keep us in hot water, to keep up continual broils between an English party and a French party, in hopes of obliging the independent and patriotic party to lean to its side; England wishes them here and compensated, not merely to get rid of them and to save themselves the money, but to plant among us instruments of their own, to make divisions among us, and between us and France, to be continually crying down the religion, the government, the manners of France, and crying up the language, the fashions, the blood, &c. of England; England also means, by insisting on our compensating these worst of enemies, to obtain from us a tacit acknowledgment of the right of the war, an implicit acknowledgment that the tories have been justifiable, or at least excusable, and that we only, by a fortunate coincidence of events, have carried a wicked rebellion into a complete revolution. At the very time when Britain professes to desire peace, reconciliation, perpetual oblivion of all past unkindnesses, can she wish to send in among us a number of persons, whose very countenances will bring fresh to our remembrance the whole history of the rise and progress of the war, and of all its atrocities? Can she think it conciliatory, to oblige us to lay taxes upon those whose habitations have been consumed, to reward those who have burned them? upon those whose whole property has been stolen, to reward the thieves? upon those whose relations have been cruelly destroyed, to compensate the murderers? What can be the design of France, on the other hand, by espousing the cause of these men? Indeed, her motives may be guessed at. She may wish to keep up in our minds a terror of England, and a fresh remembrance of all we have suffered; or she may wish to prevent our ministers in Europe from agreeing with the British ministers, until she shall say, that she and Spain are satisfied in all points."

I entered largely with Mr. Oswald into the consideration of the influence this question would have upon the councils of the

British Cabinet and the debates in Parliament. The King and the old Ministry might think their personal reputations concerned, in supporting men who had gone such lengths, and suffered so much in their attachment to them. The King may say: "I have other dominions abroad,—Canada, Nova Scotia, Florida, the West India Islands, the East Indies, Ireland. It will be a bad example to abandon these men; others will lose their encouragement to adhere to my government." But the shortest answer to this is the best,—let the King, by a message, recommend it to Parliament to compensate them.

But how will my Lord Shelburne sustain the shock of opposition, when Mr. Fox and Mr. Burke shall demand a reason why the essential interests of the nation are sacrificed to the unreasonable demands of those very men who have done this great mischief to the empire, should these orators indulge themselves in philippics against the refugees, show their false representations, their outrageous cruelties, their innumerable demerits against the nation, and then attack the First Lord of the Treasury for continuing to spend the blood and treasure of the nation for their sakes? . . .

20. Wednesday. . . .

I thought it was now a crisis in which good will or ill will towards America would be carried very far in England; a time, perhaps, when the American Ministers may have more weight in turning the tide of sentiment, or influencing the changes of administration, than they ever had before, and, perhaps, than they would have again; that I thought it our duty, upon this occasion, to say every thing we could to the Englishmen here, in order that just sentiments might prevail in England at this moment; to countenance every man well-disposed, and to disabuse and undeceive everybody; to drive out of countenance and into infamy every narrow thought of cramping, stinting, impoverishing, or enfeebling us; to show that it is their only interest to show themselves our friends, to wear away, if possible, the memory of past unkindnesses; to strike with us now upon our own terms, because, though we had neither power nor inclination to make peace without our allies, yet the very report that we had got over all our difficulties, would naturally make all Europe expect peace, would tend to make Spain less exorbitant in her demands, and would make Holland more ardent for peace, and dispose France to be more serious in her importunities with Spain and Holland, and even render France herself easier, though I did not imagine she would be extravagant in her pretensions; to show them the ruinous tendency of the war if continued another year or two. Where would England be if the war continued two years longer? what the state of her finances? what her condition in the East and West Indies, in North America, Ireland, Scotland, and even in England? What hopes have they of saving themselves from a civil war? If our terms are not now accepted they will never again have such offers from America; they will never have so advantageous a line; never, their debts; never, so much for the tories, and, perhaps, a rigorous demand of compensation for the devastations they have committed.

Mr. Jay agreed with me in sentiment, and, indeed, they are the principles he has uniformly pursued through the whole negotiation before my arrival; I think they cannot be misunderstood or disapproved in Congress. There never was a blunder in politics more egregious than will be committed by the present ministry, if they attempt to save the honor of the old ministry and of the tories. Shelburne may be too weak to combat them; but the true policy would be to throw all the odium of the war, and all the blame of the dismemberment of the empire, upon the old ministers and the tories; to run them down, tarnish them with votes, inveigh against them in speeches and pamphlets, even strip them of the pensions, and make them both ridiculous, insignificant, and contemptible; in short, make them as wretched as their crimes deserve; never think of sending them to America. But Shelburne is not strong enough; the old party, with the King at their head, is too powerful and popular yet. I really pity these people, as little as they deserve it; for surely no men ever deserved worse of society. If Fox was in, and had weight enough, and should take this decided part, which is consistent enough with the tenor of his speeches, which have been constant philippics against the old ministry, and frequent sallies against the refugees, and should adopt a noble line of conduct towards America, grant her all she asks, do her honor, and promote her prosperity, he would disarm the hostile mind and soften the resentful heart, recover much of the affection of America, much of her commerce, and, perhaps, equal consideration and profit and power from her as ever; she would have no governor nor armies there, and no taxes; but she would have profit, reputation, and power. . . .

CORRESPONDENCE OF JOHN AND ABIGAIL ADAMS[1]

The remarkable correspondence between Abigail (née Smith) and John Adams is characterized by an openness of emotions, as though the letters were written from the heart as much as from the head. Theirs was a marriage of equals, born of romance and sustained by respect. The two likened their relationship to figures out of the classics, such as Diana, the goddess of love, and Lysander, her pursuer. Abigail took the pen name Portia, after the virtuous wife of the Roman leader Brutus. In our day, when communication is no longer even the telephone but e-mail, it is heartening to read the personal letters as almost an art form.

JA to AS

Octr. 4th. 1762

MISS ADORABLE

By the same Token that the Bearer hereof *satt up* with you last night I hereby order you to give him, as many Kisses, and as many Hours of your Company after 9 O'Clock as he shall please to Demand and charge them to my Account: This Order, or Requisition call it which you will is in Consideration of a similar order Upon Aurelia for the like favour, and I presume I have good Right to draw upon you for the Kisses as I have given two or three Millions at least, when one has been received, and of Consequence the Account between us is immensely in favour of yours,   JOHN ADAMS

JA to AS

Braintree Feby. 14th. 1763

DEAR MADAM

Accidents are often more Friendly to us, than our own Prudence.—I intended to have been at Weymouth Yesterday, but a storm prevented.—Cruel, Yet perhaps blessed storm!—Cruel for detaining me from so much friendly, social Company, and perhaps blessed to you, or me or both, for keeping me at *my Distance.* For every experimental Phylosopher knows, that the steel and the Magnet or the Glass and feather will not fly together with more Celerity, than somebody And somebody, when brought within the striking Distance—and, Itches, Aches, Agues, and Repentance might be the Consequences of a Contact in present Circumstances. Even the Divines pronounce casuistically, I hear, "unfit to be touched these three Weeks."

I mount this moment for that noisy, dirty Town of Boston, where Parade, Pomp, Nonsense, Frippery, Folly, Foppery, Luxury, Polliticks, and the soul-Confounding Wrangles of the Law will give me the Higher Relish for Spirit, Taste and Sense, at Weymouth, next Sunday.

My Duty, w[h]ere owing! My Love to Mr. Cranch And Lady, tell them I love them, I love them better than any Mortals who have no other Title to my Love than Friendship gives, and that I hope he is in perfect Health and she in all the Qualms that necessarily attend [*a beginning*] Pregnancy, and in all other Respects very happy.

Your—(all the rest is inexpressible)   JOHN ADAMS

AS to JA

Weymouth August th 11 1763

MY FRIEND

If I was sure your absence to day was occasioned, by what it generally is, either to wait upon Company, or promote some good work, I freely confess my Mind would be much more at ease than at present it is. Yet this uneasiness does not arise from any apprehension of Slight or neglect, but a fear least you are indisposed, for that you said should be your only hindrance.

Humanity obliges us to be affected with the distresses and Miserys of our fellow creatures. Friendship is a band yet stronger, which causes us to [fee]l with greater tenderness the afflictions of our Friends.

And there is a tye more binding than Humanity, and stronger than Friendship, which makes us anxious for the happiness and welfare of those to whom it binds us. It makes their Misfortunes, Sorrows and afflictions, our own. Unite these, and there is a threefold cord—by this cord I am not ashamed to own myself bound, nor do I [believe] that you are wholly free from it. Judg[e you then] for your Diana has she not this day [had sufficien]t cause for pain and anxiety of mind?

She bids me [tell] you that Seneca, for the sake of his Paulina was careful and tender of his health. The health and happiness of Seneca she says was not dearer to his Paulina, than that of Lysander to his Diana.

The Fabrick often wants repairing and if we neglect it the Deity will not long inhabit it, yet after all our care and solisitude to preserve it, it is a tottering Building, and often reminds us that it will finally fall.

Adieu may this find you in better health than I fear it will, and happy as your Diana wishes you.

Accept this hasty Scrawl warm from the Heart of Your Sincere   DIANA

JA to AS

Saturday morning Aug. 1763

MY DEAR DIANA

Germantown is at a great Distance from Weymouth Meeting-House, you know; The No. of Yards indeed is not so prodigious, but the Rowing and Walking that lyes between is a great Discouragement to a weary Traveller. Could my Horse have helped me to Weymouth, Braintree would not have held me, last Night.—I lay, in the well known Chamber, and dreamed, I saw a Lady, tripping it over the Hills, on Weymouth shore, and Spreading Light and Beauty and Glory, all around her. At first I thought it was Aurora, with her fair Complexion, her Crimson Blushes and her million Charms and Graces. But I soon found it was Diana, a Lady infinitely dearer to me and more charming.—Should Diana make her Appearance every morning instead of Aurora, I should not sleep as I do, but should be all awake and admiring by four, at latest.—You may be sure I was mortifyed when I found, I had only been dreaming. The Impression however of this dream awaked me thoroughly, and since I had lost my Diana, I enjoy'd the Opportunity of viewing and admiring Miss Aurora. She's a sweet Girl, upon my Word. Her breath is wholesome as the sweetly blowing Spices of Arabia, and therefore next to her fairer sister Diana, the Properest Physician, for your drooping   J. ADAMS

AS to JA

Weymouth Sepbr. th 12 1763

You was pleas'd to say that the receipt of a letter from your Diana always gave you pleasure. Whether this was designed for a complement, (a commodity I acknowledg that you very seldom deal in) or as a real truth, you best know. Yet if I was to judge of a certain persons Heart, by what upon the like occasion passess through a cabinet of my own, I should be apt to suspect it as a truth. And why may I not? when I have often been tempted to believe; that they were both cast in the same mould, only with this difference, that yours was made, with a harder mettle, and therefore is less liable to an impression. Whether they have both an eaquil quantity of Steel, I have not yet been able to discover, but do not imagine they are either of them deficient. Supposing only this difference, I do not see, why the same cause may not produce the same Effect in both, tho perhaps not eaquil in degree.

But after all, notwithstanding we are told that the giver is more blessed than the receiver I must confess that I am not of so generous a disposition, in this case, to give without wishing for a return.

Have you heard the News? that two Apparitions were seen one evening this week hovering about this house, which very much resembled you and a Cousin of yours. How it should ever enter into the head of an Apparition to assume a form like yours, I cannot devise. When I was told of it I could scarcly believe it, yet I could not declare the contrary, for I did not see it, and therefore had not that demonstration which generally convinces me, that you are not a Ghost.

The original design of this letter was to tell you, that I would next week be your fellow traveler provided I shall not be any encumberance to you, for I have too much pride to be a clog to any body. You are to determine that point. For your—
A. SMITH . . .

JA to AS

Saturday Evening Eight O'Clock
[7 April 1764]

MY DEAR DIANA

For many Years past, I have not felt more serenely than I do this Evening. My Head is clear, and my Heart is at ease. Business of every Kind, I have banished from my Thoughts. My Room is prepared for a Seven Days' Retirement, and my Plan is digested for 4 to 5 Weeks. My Brother retreats with me, to our preparatory Hospital, and is determined to keep me Company, through the Small Pox. Your Unkle, by his agreable Account of the Dr. and your Brother, their Strength, their Spirits, and their happy Prospects, but especially, by the Favour he left me from you, has contributed very much to the Felicity of my present Frame of Mind. For, I assure you Sincerely, that, (as Nothing which I before expected from the Distemper gave me more Concern, than the Thought of a six Weeks Separation from my Diana) my Departure from your House this Morning made an Impression upon me that was severely painfull. I thought I left you, in Tears and Anxiety—And was very glad to hear by your Letter, that your Fears were abated. For my own Part, I believe no Man ever undertook to prepare himself for the Small Pox, with fewer [. . .] than I have at present. I have considered thoughrououghly, the Diet and Medicine prescribed me, and am fully satisfyed that no durable Evil can result from Either, and any other Fear from the small Pox or it's Appurtenances, in the modern Way of Inoculation I never had in my Life.—Thanks for my Balm. Present my Duty and Gratitude to Pappa for his kind offer of Tom. Next Fryday, for certain, with suitable Submission, We take our Departure for Boston. To Captn. Cunninghams We go—And I have not the least doubt of a pleasant 3 Weeks, notwithstanding the Distemper.—Dr. Savil has no Antimony—So I must beg your Care that John Jenks makes the Pills and sends them by the Bearer. I enclose the Drs. Directions. We shall want about 10 I suppose for my Brother and me. Other Things we have of Savil.

Good Night, my Dear, I'm a going to Bed!

AS to JA

Weymouth April 8. 1764

SIR

If our wishes could have conveyed you to us, you would not have been absent to Day. Mr. Cranch and my Sister have been here, where they hoped to have found you. We talk'd of you, they desire to be rememberd to you, and wish you well thro the Distemper. Mr. Cranch told me that the Deacon with his children design for Boston next Saturday and that they propose going by water—that the Deacon would have you go with them, but I would by no means advise you to go by water, for as you are under prepairation you will be much more exposed to take cold, the weather too is so uncertain that tho the morning may look promising, yet you know it is frequently very raw and cold in the afternoon. Besides if you should wait till then and Saturday should prove an unplasent Day, you will make it so much the longer before you get into Town. Suffer me therefore to injoin it upon you, not to consent to go by water, and that you have no need to do as Tom will wait upon you any day that you desire. Let me know wheather you took your vomit, whether you got your pills and whether you have begun Lent—how it suits you? I am very fearful that you will not when left to your own management follow your directions—but let her who tenderly cares for you both in Sickness and Health, intreet you to be careful of that Health upon which depends the happiness of Your   A Smith

JA to AS

Braintree Ap. 11th. 1764

My ever dear Diana

The Room which I thought would have been an Hospital or a Musæum, has really proved a Den of Thieves, and a scene of Money Changers. More Persons have been with me about Business, since I *shut up*, than a few, and many more than I was glad to see, for it is a sort of Business that I get nothing by, but Vanity and Vexation of Spirit. If my Imprisonment had been in Consequence of Bankruptcy, I should not have endured much more Mortification and Disquiet. I wish this Day was a Fast, as well as Tomorrow, that I might be sure of two Days Tranquility, before my Departure. I am not very impatient at present: Yet I wish I was at Boston. Am somewhat fearful of foul weather, on Fryday. If it should be, the very first fair Opportunity must be embracd.

Abstinence from all, but the cool and the soft, has hitherto agreed with me very well; and I have not once transgressed in a single Iota. The Medicine we have taken is far from being loathsome or painful or troublesome, as I own I expected. And if I could but enjoy my Retreat in silence and solitude, there would be nothing Wanting but Obliviscence of your Ladyship, to make me as Happy as a Monk in a Cloyster or an Hermit in his Cell. You will wonder, perhaps at my calling in Monks and Hermits, on this Occasion, and may doubt about the Happiness of their situations: Yet give me leave to tell you freely, the former of these are so tottally absorbed in Devotion and the latter in Meditation, and such an Appetite, such a Passion for their Respective Employments and Pleasures grows habitually up in their Minds, that no Mortals, (excepting him who hopes to be bound to your Ladyship in the soft Ligaments of Matrimony) has a better security for Happiness than they.

Hitherto I have written with the Air and in the style of Rattle and Frolick; but now I am about to shift to the sober and the Grave.—My Mamma is as easy and composed, and I think much more so than I expected. She sees We are determined, and that opposition would be not only fruitless, but vexatious, and has therefore brought herself to acquiesce, and to assist in preparing all Things, as conveniently and comfortably as she can. Heaven reward her for her kind Care, and her Labours of Love!

I long to come once more to Weymouth before I go to Boston. I could, well enough. I am as well as ever, and better too. Why should not I come? Shall I come and keep fast with you? Or will you come and see me? I should be glad to see you in this House, but there is another very near it, where I should rejoice much more to see you, and to live with you till we shall have lived enough to ourselves, to Glory, Virtue and Mankind, and till both of us shall be desirous of Translation to a wiser, fairer, better World.

I am, and till then, and forever after will be your Admirer and Friend and Lover.   JOHN ADAMS

JA to AS

Thurdsdy. 5. Oclock. [12 April] 1764

DR. DIANA

I have Thoughts of sending you a Nest of Letters like a nest of Basketts; tho I suspect the latter would be a more genteel and acceptable Present to a Lady. But in my present Circumstances I can much better afford the former than the latter. For, my own Discretion as well as the Prescriptions of the Faculty, prohibit any close Application of Mind to Books or Business—Amusement, Amusement is the only study that I follow. Now Letter-Writing is, to me, the most agreable Amusement (*I can find*): and Writing to you the most entertaining and Agreable of all Letter-Writing. So that a Nest of an hundred, would cost me Nothing at all.—What say you my Dear? Are you not much obliged to me, for making you the cheapest of all possible Presents?

Shall I continue to write you, so much, and so often after I get to Town? Shall I send you, an History of the whole Voyage? Shall I draw You the Characters of all, who visit me? Shall I describe to you all the Conversations I have? I am about to make my Appearance on a new Theatre, new to me. I have never been much conversant in scenes, where Drs., Nurses, Watchers, &c. to make the Principal Actors. It will be a Curiosity to me. Will it be so to you? I was always pleased to see human Nature in a Variety of shapes. And if I should be much alone, and feel in tolerable Spirits, it will be a Diversion to commit my Observations to Writing.

I believe I could furnish a Cabinet of Letters upon these subjects which would be exceeded in Curiosity, by nothing, but a sett describing the Characters, Diversions, Meals, Wit, Drollery, Jokes, Smutt, and Stories of the Guests at a Tavern in Plymouth where I lodge, when at that Court—which could be equalled by nothing excepting a minute History of Close stools and Chamber Potts, and of the Operation of Pills, Potions and Powders, in the Preparation for the small Pox.

Heaven forgive me for suffering my Imagination to straggle into a Region of Ideas so nauseous And abominable: and suffer me to return to my Project of writing you a Journal. You would have a great Variety of Characters—Lawyers, Physicians (no Divines I believe), a Number of Tradesmen, Country Colonells, Ladies, Girls, Nurses, Watchers, Children, Barbers &c. &c. &c. But among all These, there is but one whose Character I would give much to know better than I do at present. In a Word I am an old Fellow, and have seen so many Characters in my Day, that I am almost weary of Observing them.—Yet I doubt whether I understand human Nature or the World very well or not?

There is not much Satisfaction in the study of Mankind to a benevolent Mind. It is a new Moon, Nineteen Twentyeths of it opaque and unenlightened.

Intimacy with the most of People, will bring you acquainted with Vices and Errors, and Follies enough to make you despize them. Nay Intimacy with the most celebrated will very much diminish our Reverence and Admiration.

What say you now my dear shall I go on with my Design of Writing Characters?—Answer as you please, there is one Character, that whether I draw it on Paper or not, I cannot avoid thinking on every Hour, and considering sometimes together and sometimes asunder, the Excellencies and Defects in it. It is almost the only one that has encreased, for many Years together, in Proportion to Acquaintance and Intimacy, in the Esteem, Love and Admiration of your   JOHN ADAMS

AS to JA

Weymouth April 12. 1764

MY DEAREST FRIEND

Here am I all alone, in my Chamber, a mere Nun I assure you, after professing myself thus will it not be out of Character to confess that my thoughts are often employ'd about Lysander, "out of the abundance of the Heart, the mouth speaketh," and why Not the Mind thinketh.

Received the pacquet you so generously bestowed upon me. To say I Fasted after such an entertainment, would be wronging my Conscience and wounding Truth. How kind is it in you, thus by frequent tokens of remembrance to alleviate the pangs of absence, by this I am convinced that I am often in your Thoughts, which is a satisfaction to me, notwithstanding you tell me that you sometimes view the dark side of your Diana, and there no doubt you discover many Spots—which I rather wish were erased, than conceal'd from you. Do not judge by this, that your opinion is an indifferent thing to me, (were it so, I should look forward with a heavey Heart,) but it is far otherways, for I had rather stand fair there, and be thought well of by Lysander than by the greater part of the World besides. I would fain hope that those faults which you discover, proceed more, from a wrong Head, than a bad Heart. E'er long May I be connected with a Friend from whose Example I may form a more faultless conduct, and whose benevolent mind will lead him to pardon, what he cannot amend.

The Nest of Letters which you so undervalue, were to me a much more welcome present than a Nest of Baskets, tho every stran of those had been gold and silver. I do not estimate everything according to the price the world set upon it, but according to the value it is of to me, thus that which was cheapest to you I look upon as highly valuable.

You ask whether you shall send a History of the whole voyage, characters, visits, conversations &c. &c. It is the very thing that I designd this Evening to have requested of you, but you have prevented my asking, by kindly offering it. You will greatly oblige me by it, and it will be no small amusement to me in my State of Seperation. Among the many who will visit, I expect Arpasia will be one, I want her character drawn by your pen (Aurelia says she appears most agreable in her Letters). I know you are a critical observer, and your judgment of people generally plases me. Sometimes you know, I think you too severe, and that you do not make quite so many allowances as Humane Nature requires, but perhaps this may be oweing to my unacquainedness with the World. Your Business Naturly leads you to a nearer inspection of Mankind, and to see the corruptions of the Heart, which I believe you often find desperately wicked and deceitful.

Methinks I have abundance to say to you. What is next? O that I should have been extreemly glad to have seen you to Day. Last Fast Day, if you remember, we spent together, and why might we not this? Why I can tell you, we might, if we had been together, have been led into temptation. I don't mean to commit any Evil, unless setting up late, and thereby injuring our Health, may be called so. To that I could have submitted without much remorse of Conscience, that would have had but little weight with me, had you not bid me adieu, the last time I saw you. The reflexion of what I that forenoon endured, has been ever since sufficient to deter me from wishing to see you again, till you can come and go, as you formerly used to.

Betsy sends her Love to you, says she designd to have kissed you before you went away, but you made no advances, and she never haveing been guilty of such an action, knew not how to attempt it. Know you of any figure in the Mathematicks whereby you can convey one to her? Inclining lines that meet in the same center, will not that figure come as nigh as any?

What think you of the weather. We have had a very promissing afternoon, tho the forenoon threatned a Storm. I am in great hopes that Sol will not refuse his benign influence to-morrow.

To-Morrow you leave Braintree. My best wishes attend you. With Marcia I say

> "O Ye immortal powers! that guard the just
> Watch round his Head, and soften the Disease
> Banish all Sorrow from his Mind
> Becalm his Soul with pleasing thoughts
> And shew Mankind that virtue is your care."

Thus for Lysander prays his   A SMITH

PS Let me hear from you soon as possible, and as often. By sending your Letters to the Doctor believe you may get conveyance often. I rejoice to hear you feel so comfortable. Still be careful, good folks are scarce. My Mamma has just been up, and asks to whom I am writing. I answerd not very readily. Upon my hesitating—Send my Love say'd she to Mr. Adams, tell him he has my good wishes for his Safty. A good Night to you—my fire is out. Pray be so kind (as to deliver) or send if they dont visit you, these Letters as directed.

Fryday morning

What a Beautiful morning it is, I almost wish I was going with you.—Here [I] send the Books, papa prays [you] would be careful of them. I send you some tobacco to smoke your Letters over, tho I don't imagine you will use it all that way.—A pleasant ride to you. Breakfast calls your   A SMITH

JA to AS

[*Boston, 13 April 1764*]

MY DEAREST

We arrived at Captn. Cunninghams, about Twelve O'Clock and sent our Compliments to Dr. Perkins. The Courrier returned with Answer that the Dr. was determined to inoculate no more without a Preparation preevious to Inoculation. That We should have written to him and have received Directions from him, and Medicine, before We came into Town. I was surprized and chagrined. I wrote, instantly, a Letter to him, and informed him we had been under a Preparation of his prescribing, and that I presumed Dr. Tufts had informed him, that We depended on him, in Preference to any other Gentleman. The Dr. came, immediately with Dr. Warren, in a Chaise—And after an Apology, for his not Recollecting—(I am obliged to break off my Narration, in order to swallow a Porringer of Hasty Pudding and Milk. I have done my Dinner)—for not recollecting what Dr. Tufts had told him, Dr. Perkins demanded my left Arm and Dr. Warren my Brothers. They took their Launcetts and with their Points divided the skin for about a Quarter of an Inch and just suffering the Blood to appear, buried a Thread about [*half*] a Quarter of an Inch long in the Channell. A little Lint was then laid over the scratch and a Piece of a Ragg pressed on, and then a Bandage bound over all—my Coat and waistcoat put on, and I was bid to go where and do what I pleased. (Dont you think the Dr. has a good Deal of Confidence in my Discretion, thus to leave me to it?)

The Doctors have left us Pills red and black to take Night and Morning. But they looked very sagaciously and importantly at us, and ordered my Brother, larger Doses than me, on Account of the Difference in our Constitutions. Dr. Perkins is a short, thick sett, dark Complexioned, Yet pale Faced, Man, (Pale faced I say, which I was glad to see, because I have a great Regard for a Pale Face, in any Gentleman of Physick, Divinity or Laws. It indicates search and study). Gives himself the alert, chearful Air and Behaviour of a Physician, not forgetting the solemn, important and wise. Warren is a pretty, tall, Genteel, fair faced young Gentleman. Not quite so much Assurance in his Address, as Perkins, (perhaps because Perkins was present) Yet shewing fully that he knows the Utility thereof, and that he will soon, practice it in full Perfection.

The Doctors, having finished the Operation and left Us, their Directions and Medicines, took their Departure in infinite Haste, depend on't.

I have one Request to make, which is that you would be very careful in making Tom, Smoke all the Letters from me, very faithfully, before you, or any of the Family reads them. For, altho I shall never fail to smoke them myself before sealing, Yet I fear the Air of this House will be too much infected, soon, to be absolutely without Danger, and I would not you should take the Distemper, by Letter from me, for Millions. I write at a Desk far removed from any sick Room, and shall use all the Care I can, but too much cannot be used.

I have written thus far, and it is 45 Minutes Past one O Clock and no more.

My Love to all. My hearty Thanks to Mamma for her kind Wishes. My Regards as due to Pappa, and should request his Prayers, which are always becoming, and especially at such Times, when We are undertaking any Thing of Consequence as the small Pox, undoubtedly, tho, I have not the Least Apprehension att all of what is called Danger.

I am as ever Yr.   JOHN ADAMS

AS to JA

Thursday Eve.—Weymouth April th 19 1764
Why my good Man, thou has the curiosity of a Girl. Who could have believed that only a slight hint would have set thy imagination a gig in such a manner. And a fine encouragement

I have to unravel the Mistery as thou callest it. Nothing less truly than to be told Something to my disadvantage. What an excellent reward that will be? In what Court of justice did'st thou learn that equity? I thank thee Friend such knowledg as that is easy eno' to be obtained without paying for it. As to the insinuation, it doth not give me any uneasiness, for if it is any thing very bad, I know thou dost not believe it. I am not conscious of any harm that I have done, or wished to any Mortal. I bear no Malice to any Being. To my Enimies, (if any I have) I am willing to afford assistance; therefore towards Man, I maintain a Conscience void of offence.

Yet by this I mean not that I am faultless, but tell me what is the Reason that persons had rather acknowledg themselves guilty, than be accused by others. Is it because they are more tender of themselves, or because they meet with more favor from others, when they ingenuously confess. Let that be as it will there is something which makes it more agreeable to condemn ourselves than to be condemned by others.

But altho it is vastly disagreeable to be accused of faults, yet no person ought to be offended when such accusations are deliverd in the Spirit of Friendship.—I now call upon you to fullfill your promise, and tell me all my faults, both of omission and commission, and all the Evil you either know, or think of me, be to me a second conscience, nor put me off to a more convenient Season. There can be no time more proper than the present, it will be harder to erase them when habit has strengthened and confirmd them.

Do not think I triffle. These are really meant as words of Truth and Soberness—for the present good Night.

Fryday Morning April th 20

What does it signify, why may not I visit you a Days as well as Nights? I no sooner close my Eyes than some invisible Being, swift as the Alborack of Mahomet, bears me to you. I see you, but cannot make my self visible to you. That tortures me, but it is still worse when I do not come for I am then haunted by half a dozen ugly Sprights. One will catch me and leep into the Sea, an other will carry me up a precipice (like that which Edgar describes to Lear,) then toss me down, and were I not then light as the Gosemore I should shiver into atoms—an other will be pouring down my throat stuff worse than the witches Broth in Macbeth.—Where I shall be carried next I know not, but I had rather have the small pox by inoculation half a dozen times, than be sprighted about as I am. What say you can you give me any encouragement to come? By the time you receive this hope from experience you will be able to say that the distemper is but a triffle. Think you I would not endure a triffle for the pleasure of seeing Lysander, yes were it ten times that triffle I would.—But my own inclinations must not be followed—to Duty I sacrifice them. Yet O my Mamma forgive me if I say, you have forgot, or never knew—but hush.—And do you Lysander excuse me that something I promis'd you, since it was a Speach more undutifull than that which I Just now stop'd my self in—for the present good by.

Fryday Evening

I hope you smoke your Letters well, before you deliver them. Mamma is so fearful least I should catch the distemper, that she hardly ever thinks the Letters are sufficiently purified. Did you never rob a Birds nest? Do you remember how the poor Bird would fly round and round, fearful to come nigh, yet not know how to leave the place—just so they say I hover round Tom whilst he is smokeing my Letters.

But heigh day Mr. whats your name?—who taught you to threaten so vehemently "a Character besides that of critick, in which if I never did, I always hereafter shall fear you."

Thou canst not prove a villan, imposible. I therefore still insist upon it, that I neither do, nor can fear thee. For my part I know not that there is any pleasure in being feard, but if there is, I hope you will be so generous as to fear your Diana that she may at least be made sensible of the pleasure.

Mr. Ayers will bring you this Letter, and the *Bag*. Do no[t] repine—it is fill'd with Balm.

Here is Love, respects, regards, good wishes—a whole waggon load of them sent you from all the good folks in the Neighbourhood.

To morrow makes the 14th Day. How many more are to come? I dare not trust my self with the thought. Adieu. Let me hear from you by Mr. Ayers, and excuse this very bad writing, if you had mended my pen it would have been better, once more adieu. Gold and Silver have I none, but such as I have, give I unto thee—which is the affectionate Regard of Your   A SMITH

JA to AS

Boston April 26th. 1764

Many have been the particular Reasons against my Writing for several days past, but one general Reason has prevailed with me more than any other Thing, and that was, an Absolute Fear to send a Paper from this House, so much infected as it is, to any Person lyable to take the Distemper but especially to you. I am infected myself, and every Room in the House, has infected People in it, so that there is real Danger, in Writing.

However I will write now, and thank you for yours of Yesterday. Mr. Ayers told you the Truth. I was comfortable, and have never been otherwise. I believe, None of the Race of Adam, ever passed the small Pox, with fewer Pains, Achs, Qualms, or with less smart than I have done. I had no Pain in my Back, none in my side, none in my Head. None in my Bones or Limbs, no reching or vomiting or sickness. A short shivering Fit, and a succeeding hot glowing Fit, a Want of Appetite, and a general Languor, were all the symptoms that ushered into the World, all the small Pox, that I can boast of, which are about Eight or Ten, (for I have not yet counted them exactly) two of which only are in my Face, the rest scattered at Random over my Limbs and Body. They fill very finely and regularly, and I am as well, tho not so strong, as ever I was in my Life. My Appetite has returned, and is quick enough and I am returning gradually to my former Method of Living.

Very nearly the same may be said of my Brother excepting that he looks leaner than I, and that he had more sickness and Head Ach about the Time of the Eruption than I.

Such We have Reason to be thankful has been our Felicity.

And that of Deacon Palmers Children has been, nearly the same. But others in the same House have not been so happy—pretty high Fevers, and severe Pains, and a pretty Plentiful Eruption has been the Portion of Three at last of our Companions. I join with you sincerely in your Lamentation that you were not inoculated. I wish to God the Dr. would sett up an Hospital at Germantown, and inoculate you. I will come and nurse you, nay I will go with you to the Castle or to Point Shirley, or any where and attend you. You say rightly safety there is not, and I say, safety there never will be. And Parents must be lost in Avarice or Blindness, who restrain their Children.

I believe there will be Efforts to introduce Inoculation at Germantown, by Drs. Lord and Church.

However, be carefull of taking the Infection unawares. For all the Mountains of Peru or Mexico I would not, that this Letter or any other Instrument should convey the Infection to you at unawares.

I hope soon to see you, mean time write as often as possible to yrs.,   JOHN ADAMS

P.S. Dont conclude from any Thing I have written that I think Inoculation a light matter.—A long and total Abstinence from every Thing in Nature that has any Taste, Two heavy Vomits, one heavy Cathartick, four and twenty Mercurial and Antimonial Pills, and Three Weeks close Confinement to an House, are, according to my Estimation of Things, no small matters.—However, who would not chearfully submit to them rather than pass his whole Life in continual Fears, in subjection, under Bondage. . . .

AS to JA

Weymouth April 30. 1764

DEAR LYSANDER

Your Friendly Epistle reach'd me a fryday morning, it came like an Infernal Mesenger, thro fire and Brimstone, Yet it brought me tidings of great joy. With gratitude may this month be ever rememberd by Diana. You have been peculiarly favourd, and may be numberd with those who have had the distemper lightest. What would I give that I was as well thro it. I thank you for your offerd Service, but you know that I am not permitted to enjoy the benifit of it.

Yesterday the Dr. returnd to our no small Satisfaction. I think there is but one person upon Earth, the Sight of whom would have more rejoiced me. But "not Sight alone would please." It would therefore be adviseable to keep at an unseeable distance till any approach would not endanger.

I was yesterday at the Meeting of a Gentleman and his Lady. Cloathe[s] all shifted—no danger—and no fear. A how do ye, and a how do ye, was exchanged between them, a Smile, and a good naturd look. Upon my word I believe they were glad to see each other. A tender meeting. I was affected with it. And thought whether Lysander, under like circumstances could thus coldly meet his Diana, and whether Diana could with no more Emotion receive Lysander. What think you. I dare answer for a different meeting on her part were She under no restraint. When may that meeting be? Hear you have sent for your Horse, the Doctor tells me that you rode out a friday, do not venture abroad too soon, very bad winds for invalids tho I hear you stand it like an oak.—O by the way you have not told me that insinuation to my disadvantage which you promised me. Now methinks I see you criticizeing—What upon Earth is the Girl after. Where is the connexion between my standing the distemper like an oak, and an insinuation to her disadvantage?—Why I did not expect that a short sighted mortal would comprehend it, it was a Complex Idea if I may so express myself. And in my mind there was a great connexion. I will show you how it came about. "I did expect this purgation of Lysander would have set us on a level and have renderd him a Sociable creature, but Ill Luck, he stands it like an oak, and is as haughty as ever." Now mentioning one part of this Sentence, brought to mind the accusation of haughtiness, and your faults naturally lead me to think of my own. But here look yee. I have more than insinuations against you. "An intolerable forbidding expecting Silence, which lays such a restraint upon but moderate Modesty that tis imposible for a

Stranger to be tranquil in your presence." What say you to that charge? Deny it not, for by experience I know it to be true. Yes to this day I feel a greater restraint in your Company, than in that of allmost any other person on Earth, but thought I had reasons by myself to account for it, and knew not that others were affected in the same manner till a late complaint was enterd against you. Is there any thing austere in your countanance? Indeed I cannot recollect any thing. Yet when I have been most pained I have throughly studied it, but never could discover one trace of the severe. Must it not then be something in Behaviour, (ask Silvia, (not Arpasia for these are not her complaints) what it is) else why should not I feel as great restraint when I write. But to go on, "Why did he read Grandison, the very reverse in practice. Sir Charles call'd forth every one's excellencies, but never was a thought born in Lysanders presence." Unsociable Being, is an other charge. Bid a Lady hold her Tongue when she was tenderly inquireing after your wellfare, why that sounds like want of Breeding. It looks not like Lysander for it wears the face of ingratitude.—I expect you [to] clear up these matters, without being in the least saucy.

As to the charge of Haughtiness I am certain that is a mistake, for if I know any thing of Lysander, he has as little of that in his disposition, as he has of Ill nature. But for Saucyness no Mortal can match him, no not even His   DIANA

JA to AS

Boston May 7th. 1764

I promised you, Sometime agone, a Catalogue of your Faults, Imperfections, Defects, or whatever you please to call them. I feel at present, pretty much at Leisure, and in a very suitable Frame of Mind to perform my Promise. But I must caution you, before I proceed to recollect yourself, and instead of being vexed or fretted or thrown into a Passion, to resolve upon a Reformation—for this is my sincere Aim, in laying before you, this Picture of yourself.

In the first Place, then, give me leave to say, you have been extreamly negligent, in attending so little to Cards. You have very little Inclination, to that noble and elegant Diversion, and whenever you have taken an Hand you have held it but aukwardly and played it, with a very uncourtly, and indifferent, Air. Now I have Confidence enough in your good sense, to rely upon it, you will for the future endeavour to make a better Figure in this elegant and necessary Accomplishment.

Another Thing, which ought to be mentioned, and by all means amended, is, the Effect of a Country Life and Education, I mean, a certain Modesty, sensibility, Bashfulness, call it by which of these Names you will, that enkindles Blushes forsooth at every Violation of Decency, in Company, and lays a most insupportable Constraint on the freedom of Behaviour. Thanks to the late Refinements of modern manners, Hypocrisy, superstition, and Formality have lost all Reputation in the World and the utmost sublimation of Politeness and Gentility lies, in Ease, and Freedom, or in other Words in a natural Air and Behaviour, and in expressing a satisfaction at whatever is suggested and prompted by Nature, which the aforesaid Violations of Decency, most certainly are.

In the Third Place, you could never yet be prevail'd on to learn to sing. This I take very soberly to be an Imperfection of the most moment of any. An Ear for Musick would be a source of much Pleasure, and a Voice and skill, would be a private solitary Amusement, of great Value when no other could be had. You must have remarked an Example of this in Mrs. Cranch, who must in all probability have been deafened to Death with the Cries of her Betcy, if she had not drowned them in Musick of her own.

In the Fourth Place you very often hang your Head like a Bulrush. You do not sit, erected as you ought, by which Means, it happens that you appear too short for a Beauty, and the Company looses the sweet smiles of that Countenance and the bright sparkles of those Eyes.—This Fault is the Effect and Consequence of another, still more inexcusable in a Lady. I mean an Habit of Reading, Writing and Thinking. But both the

Cause and the Effect ought to be repented and amended as soon as possible.

Another Fault, which seems to have been obstinately persisted in, after frequent Remonstrances, Advices and Admonitions of your Friends, is that of sitting with the Leggs across. This ruins the figure and the Air, this injures the Health. And springs I fear from the former source vizt. too much Thinking.—These Things ought not to be!

A sixth Imperfection is that of Walking, with the Toes bending inward. This Imperfection is commonly called Parrot-toed, I think, I know not for what Reason. But it gives an Idea, the reverse of a bold and noble Air, the Reverse of the stately strutt, and the sublime Deportment.

Thus have I given a faithful Portraiture of all the Spotts, I have hitherto discerned in this Luminary. Have not regarded Order, but have painted them as they arose in my Memory. Near Three Weeks have I conned and studied for more, but more are not to be discovered. All the rest is bright and luminous.

Having finished the Picture I finish my Letter, lest while I am recounting Faults, I should commit the greatest in a Letter, that of tedious and excessive Length. There's a prettily turned Conclusion for You! from yr.   LYSANDER

AS to JA

Weymouth May. th 9 1764

Welcome, Welcome thrice welcome is Lysander to Braintree, but ten times more so would he be at Weymouth, whither you are affraid to come.—Once it was not so. May not I come and see you, at least look thro a window at you? Should you not be glad to see your Diana? I flatter myself you would.

Your Brother brought your Letter, tho he did not let me see him, deliverd it the Doctor from whom received it safe. I thank you for your Catalogue, but must confess I was so hardned as to read over most of my Faults with as much pleasure, as an other person would have read their perfections. And Lysander must excuse me if I still persist in some of them, at least till I am convinced that an alteration would contribute to his happiness. Especially may I avoid that Freedom of Behaviour which according to the plan given, consists in Voilations of Decency, and which would render me unfit to Herd even with the Brutes. And permit me to tell you Sir, nor disdain to be a learner, that there is such a thing as Modesty without either Hypocricy or Formality.

As to a neglect of Singing, that I acknowledg to be a Fault which if posible shall not be complaind of a second time, nor should you have had occasion for it now, if I had not a voice harsh as the screech of a peacock.

The Capotal fault should be rectified, tho not with any hopes of being lookd upon as a Beauty, to appear agreeable in the Eyes of Lysander, has been for Years past, and still is the height of my ambition.

The 5th fault, will endeavour to amend of it, but you know I think that a gentleman has no business to concern himself about the Leggs of a Lady, for my part I do not apprehend any bad effects from the practise, yet since you desire it, and that you may not for the future trouble Yourself so much about it, will reform.

The sixth and last can be cured only by a Dancing School.

But I must not write more. I borrow a hint from you, therefore will not add to my faults that of a tedious Letter—a fault I never yet had reason to complain of in you, for however long, they never were otherways than agreeable to your own   A SMITH

AA to JA

Braintree october 16 1774

MY MUCH LOVED FRIEND

I dare not express to you at 300 hundred miles distance how ardently I long for your return. I have some very miserly Wishes; and cannot consent to your spending one hour in Town till at least I have had you 12. The Idea plays about my Heart, unnerves my hand whilst I write, awakens all the tender sentiments that years have encreased and matured, and which when with me were every day dispensing to you. The whole

collected stock of . . . weeks absence knows not how to brook
any longer restraint, but will break forth and flow thro my pen.
May the like sensations enter thy breast, and (in spite of all the
weighty cares of State) Mingle themselves with those I wish to
communicate, for in giving them utterance I have felt more sincere pleasure than I have known since the 10 of August.—
Many have been the anxious hours I have spent since that
day—the threatning aspect of our publick affairs, the compli-
cated distress of this province, the Arduous and perplexed
Buisness in which you are engaged, have all conspired to agitate my bosom, with fears and apprehensions to which I have
heretofore been [a] stranger, and far from thinking the Scene
closed, it looks [as] tho the curtain was but just drawn and only
the first Scene of the infernal plot disclosed and whether the
end will be tragical Heaven alone knows. You cannot be, I
know, nor do I wish to see you an inactive Spectator, but if the
Sword be drawn I bid adieu to all domestick felicity, and look
forward to that Country where there is neither wars nor rumors of War in a firm belief that thro the mercy of its King we
shall both rejoice there together.

I greatly fear that the arm of treachery and voilence is lifted
over us as a Scourge and heavy punishment from heaven for
our numerous offences, and for the misimprovement of our
great advantages. If we expect to inherit the blessings of our
Fathers, we should return a little more to their primitive Simplicity of Manners, and not sink into inglorious ease. We have
too many high sounding words, and too few actions that cor-
respond with them. I have spent one Sabbeth in Town since you
left me. I saw no difference in respect to ornaments, &c. &c.
but in the Country you must look for that virtue, of which you
find but small Glimerings in the Metropolis. Indeed they have
not the advantages, nor the resolution to encourage our own
Manufactories which people in the country have. To the Mercantile part, tis considerd as throwing away their own Bread;
but they must retrench their expenses and be content with a
small share of gain for they will find but few who will wear
their Livery. As for me I will seek wool and flax and work will-

ingly with my Hands, and indeed their is occasion for all our industry and economy.

You mention the removal of our Books &c. from Boston. I believe they are safe there, and it would incommode the Gentlemen to remove them, as they would not then have a place to repair to for study. I suppose they would not chuse to be at the expence of bording out. Mr. Williams I believe keeps pretty much with his mother. Mr. Hills father had some thoughts of removing up to Braintree provided he could be accommodated with a house, which he finds very difficult.

Mr. Cranch's last determination was to tarry in Town unless any thing new takes place. His Friends in Town oppose his Removal so much that he is determined to stay. The opinion you have entertaind of General Gage is I believe just, indeed he professes to act only upon the Defensive. The People in the Co[untr]y begin to be very anxious for the congress to rise. They have no Idea of the Weighty Buisness you have to transact, and their Blood boils with indignation at the Hostile prepairations they are constant Witnesses of. Mr. Quincys so secret departure is Matter of various Specculation—some say he is deputed by the congress, others that he is gone to Holland, and the Tories says he is gone to be hanged.

I rejoice at the favourable account you give me of your Health; May it be continued to you. My Health is much better than it was last fall. Some folks say I grow very fat.—I venture to write most any thing in this Letter, because I know the care of the Bearer. He will be most sadly dissapointed if you should be broke up before he arrives, as he is very desirous of being introduced by you to a Number of Gentlemen of respectable characters. I almost envy him, that he should see you, before I can. . . .

Your Mother sends her Love to you, and all your family too numerous to name desire to be rememberd. You will receive Letters from two, who are as earnest to write to Pappa as if the welfare of a kingdom depended on it. If you can give any guess within a month let me know when you think of returning to Your most Affectionate   ABIGAIL ADAMS

JA to AA

[Philadelphia] June 17 [1775]

I can now inform you that the Congress have made Choice of the modest and virtuous, the amiable, generous and brave George Washington Esqr., to be the General of the American Army, and that he is to repair as soon as possible to the Camp before Boston. This Appointment will have a great Effect, in cementing and securing the Union of these Colonies.—The Continent is really in earnest in defending the Country. They have voted Ten Companies of Rifle Men to be sent from Pensylvania, Maryland and Virginia, to join the Army before Boston. These are an excellent Species of Light Infantry. They use a peculiar King of [. . . ca]ll'd a Rifle—it has circular or [. . .] Grooves within the Barrell, and carries a Ball, with great Exactness to great Distances. They are the most accurate Marksmen in the World.

I begin to hope We shall not sit all Summer.

I hope the People of our Province, will treat the General with all that Confidence and Affection, that Politeness and Respect, which is due to one of the most important Characters in the World. The Liberties of America, depend upon him, in a great Degree.

I have never been able to obtain from our Province, any regular and particular Intelligence since I left it. Kent, Swift, Tudor, Dr. Cooper, Dr. Winthrop, and others wrote me often, last Fall—not a Line from them this Time.

I have found this Congress like the last. When We first came together, I found a strong Jealousy of Us, from New England, and the Massachusetts in Particular. Suspicions were entertained of Designs of Independency—an American Republic—Presbyterian Principles—and twenty other Things. Our Sentiments were heard in Congress, with great Caution—and seemed to make but little Impression: but the longer We sat, the more clearly they saw the Necessity of pursuing vigorous Measures. It has been so now. Every Day We sit, the more We are convinced that the Designs against Us, are hostile and sanguinary, and that nothing but Fortitude, Vigour, and Perseverance can save Us.

But America is a great, unwieldy Body. Its Progress must be slow. It is like a large Fleet sailing under Convoy. The fleetest Sailors must wait for the dullest and slowest. Like a Coach and six—the swiftest Horses must be slackened and the slowest quickened, that all may keep an even Pace. . . .

AA to JA

Sunday June 18 1775

DEAREST FRIEND

The Day; perhaps the decisive Day is come on which the fate of America depends. My bursting Heart must find vent at my pen. I have just heard that our dear Friend Dr. Warren is no more but fell gloriously fighting for his Country—saying better to die honourably in the field than ignominiously hang upon the Gallows. Great is our Loss. He has distinguished himself in every engagement, by his courage and fortitude, by animating the Soldiers and leading them on by his own example. A particuliar account of these dreadful, but I hope Glorious Days will be transmitted you, no doubt in the exactest manner.

The race is not to the swift, nor the battle to the strong, but the God of Israel is he that giveth strength and power unto his people. Trust in him at all times, ye people pour out your hearts before him. God is a refuge for us.—Charlstown is laid in ashes. The Battle began upon our intrenchments upon Bunkers Hill, a Saturday morning about 3 o clock and has not ceased yet and tis now 3 o'clock Sabbeth afternoon.

Tis expected they will come out over the Neck to night, and a dreadful Battle must ensue. Almighty God cover the heads of our Country men, and be a shield to our Dear Friends. How [many ha]ve fallen we know not—the constant roar of a cannon is so [distre]ssing that we can not Eat, Drink or Sleep. May we be supported and sustain in the dreadful conflict. I shall tarry here till tis thought unsafe by my Friends, and then I have secured myself a retreat at your Brothers who has kindly offerd me part of his house. I cannot compose myself to write any further at present. I will add more as I hear further.

Tuesday afternoon [20 June]

. . . I wish I could contradict the report of the Doctors Death, but tis a lamentable Truth, and the tears of multitudes pay tribute to his memory. Those favorite lines [of] Collin continually sound in my Ears

> How sleep the Brave who sink to rest,
> By all their Countrys wishes blest?
> When Spring with dew'ey fingers cold
> Returns to deck their Hallowed mould
> She their shall dress a sweeter Sod
> Than fancys feet has ever trod.
> By fairy hands their knell is rung
> By forms unseen their Dirge is sung
> Their [There] Honour comes a pilgrim grey
> To Bless the turf that wraps their Clay
> And freedom shall a while repair
> To Dwell a weeping Hermit there.

. . . PORTIA

JA to AA

July 23 1775

MY DEAR

You have more than once in your Letters mentioned Dr. Franklin, and in one intimated a Desire that I should write you something concerning him.

Dr. Franklin has been very constant in his Attendance on Congress from the Beginning. His Conduct has been composed and grave and in the Opinion of many Gentlemen very reserved. He has not assumed any Thing, nor affected to take the lead; but has seemed to choose that the Congress should pursue their own Principles and sentiments and adopt their own Plans: Yet he has not been backward: has been very usefull, on many occasions, and discovered a Disposition entirely American. He does not hesitate at our boldest Measures, but rather seems to think us, too irresolute, and backward. He thinks us at present in an odd State, neither in Peace nor War, neither dependent nor independent. But he thinks that We shall soon assume a Character more decisive.

He thinks, that We have the Power of preserving ourselves, and that even if We should be driven to the disagreable Necessity of assuming a total Independency, and set up a separate state, We could maintain it. The People of England, have thought that the Opposition in America was wholly owing to Dr Franklin, and I suppose their scribblers will attribute the Temper, and Proceedings of this Congress to him: but there cannot be a greater Mistake. He has had but little share farther than to co operate and assist. He is however a great and good Man. I wish his Colleagues from this City were All like him, particularly one, whose Abilities and Virtues, formerly trumpeted so much in America, have been found wanting. . . .   JOHN ADAMS

JA to AA

Octr. 29. 1775

There is, in the human Breast, a social Affection, which extends to our whole Species. Faintly indeed; but in some degree. The Nation, Kingdom, or Community to which We belong is embraced by it more vigorously. It is stronger still towards the Province to which we belong, and in which We had our Birth. It is stronger and stronger, as We descend to the County, Town, Parish, Neighbourhood, and Family, which We call our own.— And here We find it often so powerfull as to become partial, to blind our Eyes, to darken our Understandings and pervert our Wills.

It is to this Infirmity, in my own Heart, that I must perhaps attribute that local Attachment, that partial Fondness, that overweening Prejudice in favour of New England, which I feel very often and which I fear sometimes, leads me to expose myself to just Ridicule.

New England has in many Respects the Advantage of every other Colony in America, and indeed of every other Part of the World, that I know any Thing of.

1. The People are purer English Blood, less mixed with Scotch, Irish, Dutch, French, Danish, Sweedish &c. than any other; and descended from Englishmen too who left Europe, in purer Times than the present and less tainted with Corruption than those they left behind them.

2. The Institutions in New England for the Support of Religion, Morals and Decency, exceed any other, obliging every Parish to have a Minister, and every Person to go to Meeting &c.

3. The public Institutions in New England for the Education of Youth, supporting Colledges at the public Expence and obliging Towns to maintain Grammar schools, is not equalled and never was in any Part of the World.

4. The Division of our Territory, that is our Counties into Townships, empowering Towns to assemble, choose officers, make Laws, mend roads, and twenty other Things, gives every Man an opportunity of shewing and improving that Education which he received at Colledge or at school, and makes Knowledge and Dexterity at public Business common.

5. Our Laws for the Distribution of Intestate Estates occasions a frequent Division of landed Property and prevents Monopolies, of Land.

But in opposition to these We have laboured under many Disadvantages. The exorbitant Prerogatives of our Governors &c. which would have overborn our Liberties, if it had not been opposed by the five preceding Particulars.

AA to JA

November 27 1775

Tis a fortnight to Night since I wrote you a line during which, I have been confined with the Jaundice, Rhumatism and a most voilent cold; I yesterday took a puke which has releived me, and I feel much better to day. Many, very many people who have had the dysentery, are now afflicted both with the Jaundice and Rhumatisim, some it has left in Hecticks, some in dropsies.

The great and incessant rains we have had this fall, (the like cannot be recollected) may have occasiond some of the present disorders. The Jaundice is very prevelant in the Camp. We have lately had a week of very cold weather, as cold as January, and a flight of snow, which I hope will purify the air of some of the noxious vapours. It has spoild many hundreds of Bushels of Apples, which were designd for cider, and which the great rains had prevented people from making up. Suppose we have lost 5 Barrels by it.

Col. Warren returnd last week to Plymouth, so that I shall not hear any thing from you till he goes back again which will not be till the last of [*next*] this month.[2]

He Damp'd my Spirits greatly by telling me that the Court had prolonged your Stay an other month. I was pleasing myself with the thoughts that you would soon be upon your return. Tis in vain to repine. I hope the publick will reap what I sacrifice.

I wish I knew what mighty things were fabricating. If a form of Goverment is to be established here what one will be assumed? Will it be left to our assemblies to chuse one? and will not many men have many minds? and shall we not run into Dissentions among ourselves?

I am more and more convinced that Man is a dangerous creature, and that power whether vested in many or a few is ever grasping, and like the grave cries give, give. The great fish swallow up the small, and he who is most strenuous for the Rights of the people, when vested with power, is as eager after the perogatives of Goverment. You tell me of degrees of perfection to which Humane Nature is capable of arriving, and I believe it, but at the same time lament that our admiration should arise from the scarcity of the instances.

The Building up a Great Empire, which was only hinted at by my correspondent may now I suppose be realized even by the unbelievers. Yet will not ten thousand Difficulties arise in the formation of it? The Reigns of Goverment have been so long slakned, that I fear the people will not quietly submit to those restraints which are necessary for the peace, and security, of the community; if we seperate from Brittain, what Code of Laws will be established. How shall we be governd so as to retain our Liberties? Can any goverment be free which is not administred by general stated Laws? Who shall frame these Laws? Who will give them force and energy? Tis true your Resolution[s] as a Body have heithertoo had the force of Laws. But will they continue to have?

When I consider these things and the prejudices of people in favour of Ancient customs and Regulations, I feel anxious for the fate of our Monarchy or Democracy or what ever is to take place. I soon get lost in a Labyrinth of perplexities, but whatever occurs, may justice and righteousness be the Stability of our times, and order arise out of confusion. Great difficulties may be surmounted, by patience and perseverance.

I believe I have tired you with politicks. . . .

AA to JA

                                                    B[raintre]e May 7 1776
How many are the solitary hours I spend, ruminating upon the past, and anticipating the future, whilst you overwhelmd with the cares of State, have but few moments you can devote to any individual. All domestick pleasures and injoyments are absorbed in the great and important duty you owe your Country "for our Country is as it were a secondary God, and the First and greatest parent. It is to be preferred to Parents, Wives, Children, Friends and all things the Gods only excepted. For if our Country perishes it is as imposible to save an Individual, as to preserve one of the fingers of a Mortified Hand." Thus do I

supress every wish, and silence every Murmer, acquiesceing in a painfull Seperation from the companion of my youth, and the Friend of my Heart.

I believe tis near ten days since I wrote you a line. I have not felt in a humour to entertain you. If I had taken up my pen perhaps some unbecomeing invective might have fallen from it; the Eyes of our Rulers have been closed and a Lethargy has seazd almost every Member. I fear a fatal Security has taken possession of them. Whilst the Building is on flame they tremble at the expence of water to quench it, in short two months has elapsed since the evacuation of Boston, and very little has been done in that time to secure it, or the Harbour from future invasion till the people are all in a flame; and no one among us that I have heard of even mentions expence, they think universally that there has been an amaizing neglect some where. Many have turnd out as volunteers to work upon Nodles Island, and many more would go upon Nantaskit if it was once set on foot. "Tis a Maxim of state That power and Liberty are like Heat and moisture; where they are well mixt every thing prospers, where they are single, they are destructive."

A Goverment of more Stability is much wanted in this colony, and they are ready to receive it from the Hands of the Congress, and since I have begun with Maxims of State I will add an other viz. that a people may let a king fall, yet still remain a people, but if a king let his people slip from him, he is no longer a king. And as this is most certainly our case, why not proclaim to the World in decisive terms your own importance?

Shall we not be dispiced by foreign powers for hesitateing so long at a word?

I can not say that I think you very generous to the Ladies, for whilst you are proclaiming peace and good will to Men, Emancipating all Nations, you insist upon retaining an absolute power over Wives. But you must remember that Arbitary power is like most other things which are very hard, very liable to be broken—and notwithstanding all your wise Laws and Maxims we have it in our power not only to free ourselves but to subdue our Masters, and without voilence throw both your natural and legal authority at our feet—

> "Charm by accepting, by submitting sway
> Yet have our Humour most when we obey."

I thank you for several Letters which I received since I wrote Last. They alleviate a tedious absence, and I long earnestly for a Saturday Evening, and experience a similar pleasure to that which I used to find in the return of my Friend upon that day after a weeks absence. The Idea of a year dissolves all my Phylosophy.

Our Little ones whom you so often recommend to my care and instruction shall not be deficient in virtue or probity if the precepts of a Mother have their desired Effect, but they would be doubly inforced could they be indulged with the example of a Father constantly before them; I often point them to their Sire

> "engaged in a corrupted State
> Wrestling with vice and faction."

JA to AA

May 17. 1776

I have this Morning heard Mr. Duffil upon the Signs of the Times. He run[s—ED.] a Parrallell between the Case of Israel and that of America, and between the Conduct of Pharaoh and that of George.

Jealousy that the Israelites would throw off the Government of Egypt made him issue his Edict that the Midwives should cast the Children into the River, and the other Edict that the Men should make a large Revenue of Brick without Straw. He concluded that the Course of Events, indicated strongly the Design of Providence that We should be seperated from G. Britain, &c.

Is it not a Saying of Moses, who am I, that I should go in and out before this great People? When I consider the great Events which are passed, and those greater which are rapidly advancing, and that I may have been instrumental of touching some

Springs, and turning some small Wheels, which have had and will have such Effects, I feel an Awe upon my Mind, which is not easily described.

G[reat] B[ritain] has at last driven America, to the last Step, a compleat Seperation from her, a total absolute Independence, not only of her Parliament but of her Crown, for such is the Amount of the Resolve of the 15th.

Confederation among ourselves, or Alliances with foreign Nations are not necessary, to a perfect Seperation from Britain. That is effected by extinguishing all Authority, under the Crown, Parliament and Nation as the Resolution for instituting Governments, has done, to all Intents and Purposes. Confederation will be necessary for our internal Concord, and Alliances may be so for our external Defence.

I have Reasons to believe that no Colony, which shall assume a Government under the People, will give it up. There is something very unnatural and odious in a Government 1000 Leagues off. An whole Government of our own Choice, managed by Persons whom We love, revere, and can confide in, has charms in it for which Men will fight. Two young Gentlemen from South Carolina, now in this City, who were in Charlestown when their new Constitution was promulgated, and when their new Governor and Council and Assembly walked out in Procession, attended by the Guards, Company of Cadetts, Light Horse &c., told me, that they were beheld by the People with Transports and Tears of Joy. The People gazed at them, with a Kind of Rapture. They both told me, that the Reflection that these were Gentlemen whom they all loved, esteemed and revered, Gentlemen of their own Choice, whom they could trust, and whom they could displace if any of them should behave amiss, affected them so that they could not help crying.

They say their People will never give up this Government. . . .

JA to AA

Philadelphia July 3. 1776

... Yesterday the greatest Question was decided, which ever was debated in America, and a greater perhaps, never was or will be decided among Men. A Resolution was passed without one dissenting Colony "that these united Colonies, are, and of right ought to be free and independent States, and as such, they have, and of Right ought to have full Power to make War, conclude Peace, establish Commerce, and to do all the other Acts and Things, which other States may rightfully do." You will see in a few days a Declaration setting forth the Causes, which have impell'd Us to this mighty Revolution, and the Reasons which will justify it, in the Sight of God and Man. A Plan of Confederation will be taken up in a few days.

When I look back to the Year 1761, and recollect the Argument concerning Writs of Assistance, in the Superior Court, which I have hitherto considered as the Commencement of the Controversy, between Great Britain and America, and run through the whole Period from that Time to this, and recollect the series of political Events, the Chain of Causes and Effects, I am surprized at the Suddenness, as well as Greatness of this Revolution. Britain has been fill'd with Folly, and America with Wisdom, at least this is my Judgment.—Time must determine. It is the Will of Heaven, that the two Countries should be sundered forever. It may be the Will of Heaven that America shall suffer Calamities still more wasting and Distresses yet more dreadfull. If this is to be the Case, it will have this good Effect, at least: it will inspire Us with many Virtues, which We have not, and correct many Errores, Follies, and Vices, which threaten to disturb, dishonour, and destroy Us.—The Furnace of Affliction produces Refinement, in States as well as Individuals. And the new Governments we are assuming, in every Part, will require a Purification from our Vices, and an Augmentation of our Virtues or they will be no Blessings. The People will have unbounded Power. And the People are extreamly addicted to Corruption and Venality, as well as the Great.—I am not without Apprehensions from this Quarter. But I must submit all my

Hopes and Fears, to an overruling Providence, in which, unfashionable as the Faith may be, I firmly believe.

JA to AA

Philadelphia July 3d. 1776

Had a Declaration of Independency been made seven Months ago, it would have been attended with many great and glorious Effects. . . . We might before this Hour, have formed Alliances with foreign States.—We should have mastered Quebec and been in Possession of Canada. . . . You will perhaps wonder, how such a Declaration would have influenced our Affairs, in Canada, but if I could write with Freedom I could easily convince you, that it would, and explain to you the manner how.— Many Gentlemen in high Stations and of great Influence have been duped, by the ministerial Bubble of Commissioners to treat. . . . And in real, sincere Expectation of this Event, which they so fondly wished, they have been slow and languid, in promoting Measures for the Reduction of that Province. Others there are in the Colonies who really wished that our Enterprise in Canada would be defeated, that the Colonies might be brought into Danger and Distress between two Fires, and be thus induced to submit. Others really wished to defeat the Expedition to Canada, lest the Conquest of it, should elevate the Minds of the People too much to hearken to those Terms of Reconciliation which they believed would be offered Us. These jarring Views, Wishes and Designs, occasioned an opposition to many salutary Measures, which were proposed for the Support of that Expedition, and caused Obstructions, Embarrassments and studied Delays, which have finally, lost Us the Province.

All these Causes however in Conjunction would not have disappointed Us, if it had not been for a Misfortune, which could not be foreseen, and perhaps could not have been prevented, I mean the Prevalence of the small Pox among our Troops. . . . This fatal Pestilence completed our Destruction.—It is a Frown of Providence upon Us, which We ought to lay to heart.

But on the other hand, the Delay of this Declaration to this

Time, has many great Advantages attending it.—The Hopes of
Reconciliation, which were fondly entertained by Multitudes
of honest and well meaning tho weak and mistaken People,
have been gradually and at last totally extinguished.—Time has
been given for the whole People, maturely to consider the great
Question of Independence and to ripen their Judgments, dissi-
pate their Fears, and allure their Hopes, by discussing it in
News Papers and Pamphletts, by debating it, in Assemblies,
Conventions, Committees of Safety and Inspection, in Town
and County Meetings, as well as in private Conversations, so
that the whole People in every Colony of the 13, have now
adopted it, as their own Act.—This will cement the Union, and
avoid those Heats and perhaps Convulsions which might have
been occasioned, by such a Declaration Six Months ago.

But the Day is past. The Second Day of July 1776, will be the
most memorable Epocha, in the History of America.—I am apt
to believe that it will be celebrated, by succeeding Generations,
as the great anniversary Festival. It ought to be commemo-
rated, as the Day of Deliverance by solemn Acts of Devotion to
God Almighty. It ought to be solemnized with Pomp and Parade, with Shews, Games, Sports, Guns, Bells, Bonfires and Il-
luminations from one End of this Continent to the other from
this Time forward forever more.

You will think me transported with Enthusiasm but I am
not.—I am well aware of the Toil and Blood and Treasure, that
it will cost Us to maintain this Declaration, and support and
defend these States.—Yet through all the Gloom I can see the
Rays of ravishing Light and Glory. I can see that the End is
more than worth all the Means. And that Posterity will tryumph
in that Days Transaction, even altho We should rue it, which I
trust in God We shall not.

AA to JA

                                            August 14 1776
I wrote to you to day by Mr. Smith but as I suppose this will
reach you sooner, I omitted mentioning any thing of my family
in it.

Nabby has enough of the small Pox for all the family beside. She is pretty well coverd, not a spot but what is so soar that she can neither walk sit stand or lay with any comfort. She is as patient as one can expect, but they are a very soar sort. If it was a disorder to which we could be subject more than once I would go as far as it was possible to avoid it. She is sweld a good deal. You will receive a perticuliar account before this reaches you of the uncommon manner in which the small Pox acts, it bafels the skill of the most Experience'd here. Billy Cranch is now out with about 40, and so well as not to be detaind at Home an hour for it. Charlly remains in the same state he did.

Your Letter of August 3 came by this days Post. I find it very conveniant to be so handy. I can receive a Letter at Night, sit down and reply to it, and send it of[f—ED.] in the morning.

You remark upon the deficiency of Education in your Countrymen. It never I believe was in a worse state, at least for many years. The Colledge is not in the state one could wish, the Schollars complain that their professer in Philosophy is taken of[f—ED.] by publick Buisness to their great detriment. In this Town I never saw so great a neglect of Education. The poorer sort of children are wholly neglected, and left to range the Streets without Schools, without Buisness, given up to all Evil. The Town is not as formerly divided into Wards. There is either too much Buisness left upon the hands of a few, or too little care to do it. We daily see the Necessity of a regular Government.—You speak of our Worthy Brother. I often lament it that a Man so peculiarly formed for the Education of youth, and so well qualified as he is in many Branches of Litrature, excelling in Philosiphy and the Mathematicks, should not be imployd in some publick Station. I know not the person who would make half so good a Successor to Dr. Winthrope. He has a peculiar easy manner of communicating his Ideas to Youth, and the Goodness of his Heart, and the purity of his morrals without an affected austerity must have a happy Effect upon the minds of Pupils.

If you complain of neglect of Education in sons, What shall I say with regard to daughters, who every day experience the want of it. With regard to the Education of my own children, I find myself soon out of my debth, and destitute and deficient in every part of Education.

I most sincerely wish that some more liberal plan be laid and executed for the Benefit of the rising Generation, and that our new constitution may be distinguished for Learning and Virtue. If we mean to have Heroes, Statesmen and Philosophers, we should have learned women. The world perhaps would laugh at me, and accuse me of vanity, But you I know have a mind too enlarged and liberal to disregard the Sentiment. If much depends as is allowed upon the early Education of youth and the first principals which are instilld take the deepest root, great benifit must arise from litirary accomplishments in women.

Excuse me my pen has run away with me. I have no thoughts of comeing to P[hiladelphi]a. The length of time I have [and] shall be detaind here would have prevented me, even if you had no thoughts of returning till December, but I live in daily Expectation of seeing you here. Your Health I think requires your immediate return. I expected Mr. Gerry would have set off before now, but he finds it perhaps very hard to leave his Mistress—I wont say harder than some do to leave their wives. Mr. Gerry stood very high in my Esteem—what is meat for one is not for an other—no accounting for fancy. She is a queer dame and leads people wild dances.

But hush—Post, dont betray your trust and loose my Letter.

Nabby is poorly this morning. The pock are near the turn, 6 or 7 hundred boils are no agreable feeling. You and I know not what a feeling it is. Miss Katy can tell. I had but 3 they were very clever and fill'd nicely. The Town instead of being clear of this distemper are now in the height of it, hundreds having it in the natural way through the deceitfulness of innoculation.

Adieu ever yours. Breakfast waits.   PORTIA

AA to JA

Braintree Sepbr. 20 1777 [i.e. 1776]

I sit down this Evening to write you, but I hardly know what to think about your going to N.Y.—The Story has been told so many times, and with circumstances so perticuliar that I with others have given some heed [to] it tho my not hearing any thing of it from you leaves me at a loss.

Yours of Sepbr. 4 came to hand last Night, our Worthy unkle is a constant attendant upon the Post office for me and brought it me.

Yours of Sepbr. 5 came to Night to B[raintre]e and was left as directed with the Cannister. Am sorry you gave yourself so much trouble about them. I got about half you sent me by Mr. Gerry. Am much obliged to you, and hope to have the pleasure of making the greater part of it for you. Your Letter damp't my Spirits; when I had no expectation of your return till December, I endeavourd to bring my mind to acquiess in the too painfull Situation, but I have now been in a state of Hopefull expectation. I have recond the days since Bass went away a hundred times over, and every Letter expected to find the day set for your return.

But now I fear it is far distant. I have frequently been told that the communication would be cut of[f—ED.] and that you would not be ever able to return. Sometimes I have been told so by those who really wish'd it might be so, with Malicious pleasure. Sometimes your timid folks have apprehended that it would be so. I wish any thing would bring you nearer. If there is really any danger I should think you would remove. Tis a plan your Enemies would rejoice to see accomplished, and will Effect if it lies in their power.

I am not apt to be intimidated you know. I have given as little heed to that and a thousand other Bug Bear reports as posible. I have slept as soundly since my return not withstanding all the Ghosts and hobgoblings, as ever I did in my life. Tis true I never close my Eyes at night till I have been to P[hiladelphi]a, and my first visit in the morning is there.

How unfealing are the world! They tell me they Heard you was dead with as little sensibility as a stock or a stone, and I have now got to be provoked by it, and can hardly help snubing the person who tells me so.

The Story of your being upon this conference at New york came in a Letter. . . . Many very many have been the conjectures of the Multitude upon it. Some have supposed the War concluded, the Nation setled, others an exchange of prisoners, others a reconsiliation with Brittain &c. &c.

I cannot consent to your tarrying much longer. I know your Health must greatly suffer from so constant application to Buisness and so little exercise. Besides I shall send you word by and by as Regulus'es steward did, that whilst you are engaged in the Senate your own domestick affairs require your presence at Home, and that your wife and children are in Danger of wanting Bread. If the Senate of America will take care of us, as the Senate of Rome did of the family of Regulus, you may serve them again, but unless you return what little property you possess will be lost. In the first place the House at Boston is going to ruin. When I was there I hired a Girl to clean it, it had a cart load of Dirt in it. I speak within Bounds. One of the chambers was used to keep poultry in, an other sea coal, and an other salt. You may conceive How it look'd. The House is so exceeding damp being shut up, that the floors are mildewd, the sealing falling down, and the paper mouldy and falling from the walls. I took care to have it often opened and aird whilst I tarried in Town. I put it into the best state I could.

In the next place, the Lighter of which you are or should be part owner is lying rotting at the wharf. One year more without any care and she is worth nothing. You have no Bill of Sale, no right to convey any part of her should any person appear to purchase her. The Pew I let, after having paid a tax for the repairs of the meeting House.

As to what is here under my more immediate inspection I do the best I can with it, but it will not at the high price Labour is, pay its way.

I know the weight of publick cares lye so heavey upon you that I have been loth to mention your own private ones.

The Best accounts we can collect from New York assure us that our Men fought valiantly. We are no ways dispiritted here, we possess a Spirit that will not be conquerd. If our Men are all drawn of and we should be attacked, you would find a Race of Amazons in America.

But I trust we shall yet tread down our Enemies.

I must intreat you to remember me often. I never think your Letters half long enough. I do not complain. I have no reason to, no one can boast of more Letters than Your   PORTIA

JA to AA

Philadelphia Octr. 11. 1776

I suppose your Ladyship has been in the Twitters, for some Time past, because you have not received a Letter by every Post, as you used to do.—But I am coming to make my Apology in Person. I, Yesterday asked and obtained Leave of Absence. It will take me till next Monday, to get ready, to finish off a few Remnants of public Business, and to put my private Affairs in proper Order. On the 14th. day of October, I shall get away, perhaps. But I dont expect to reach Home, in less than a fortnight, perhaps not in three Weeks, as I shall be obliged to make stops by the Way.

FROM JOHN ADAMS'
AUTOBIOGRAPHY

[May 27th 1778]

I found that the Business of our Commission would never be done, unless I did it. My two Colleagues would agree in nothing. The Life of Dr. Franklin was a Scene of continual discipation. I could never obtain the favour of his Company in a Morning before Breakfast which would have been the most convenient time to read over the Letters and papers, deliberate on their contents, and decide upon the Substance of the Answers. It was late when he breakfasted, and as soon as Breakfast was over, a crowd of Carriges came to his Levee or if you like the term better to his Lodgings, with all Sorts of People; some Phylosophers, Accademicians and Economists; some of his small tribe of humble friends in the litterary Way whom he employed to translate some of his ancient Compositions, such as his Bonhomme Richard and for what I know his Polly Baker &c.; but by far the greater part were Women and Children, come to have the honour to see the great Franklin, and to have the pleasure of telling Stories about his Simplicity, his bald head and scattering strait hairs, among their Acquaintances. These Visitors occupied all the time, commonly, till it was time to dress to go to Dinner. He was invited to dine abroad every day and never declined unless when We had invited Company to dine with Us. I was always invited with him, till I found it necessary to send Apologies, that I might have some time to study the french Language and do the Business of the mission. Mr. Franklin kept a horn book always in his Pockett in which he minuted all his invitations to dinner, and Mr. Lee said it was the only thing in which he was punctual. It was the Custom in France to dine between one and two O Clock: so that when the time came to dress, it was time for the Voiture to be ready to carry him to dinner. Mr. Lee came daily to my Appartment to attend to Business, but we could rarely obtain the Company of Dr. Franklin for a few minutes, and often when I had drawn the Papers and had them fairly copied for Signature, and Mr. Lee and I had signed them, I was frequently obliged to wait several days, before I could procure the Signature of Dr. Franklin to them. He went according to his Invitation to his Dinner and after that went sometimes to the Play, sometimes to the Philosophers but most commonly to visit those Ladies who were complaisant enough to depart from the custom of France so far as to procure Setts of Tea Geer as it is called and make Tea for him. Some of these Ladies I knew as Madam Hellvetius, Madam Brillon, Madam Chaumont, Madam Le Roy &c. and others whom I never knew and never enquired for. After Tea the Evening was spent, in hearing the Ladies sing and play upon their Piano Fortes and other instruments of Musick, and in various Games

as Cards, Chess, Backgammon, &c. &c. Mr. Franklin I believe
however never play'd at any Thing but Chess or Checquers. In
these Agreable and important Occupations and Amusements,
The Afternoon and Evening was spent, and he came home at
all hours from Nine to twelve O Clock at night. This Course of
Life contributed to his Pleasure and I believe to his health and
Longevity. He was now between Seventy and Eighty and I had
so much respect and compassion for his Age, that I should have
been happy to have done all the Business or rather all the
Drudgery, if I could have been favoured with a few moments in
a day to receive his Advice concerning the manner in which it
ought to be done. But this condescention was not attainable.
All that could be had was his Signature, after it was done, and
this it is true he very rarely refused though he sometimes delayed.

JA to AA

Passi[3] *June 3 1778*
MY DEAREST FRIEND
    On the 13 of Feb. I left you. It is now the 3d of June, and I
have not received a Line, nor heard a Word, directly nor indi-
rectly, concerning you since my departure. This is a Situation of
Mind, in which I never was before, and I assure you I feel a
great deal of Anxiety at it: yet I do not wonder at it, because I
suppose few Vessels have sailed from Boston since ours.
    I have shipped for you, the Articles you requested, and the
black Cloth for your Father, to whom present my most affectionate and dutiful Respects. C[aptain] Tucker, if he should not
be unlucky, will give you an Account of your Things.
    It would be endless to attempt a Description of this Country.
It is one great Garden. Nature and Art have conspired to render every Thing here delightful. Religion and Government, you
will say ought to be excepted.—With all my Heart.—But these
are no Afflictions to me, because I have well fixed it in my
Mind as a Principle, that every Nation has a Right to that Religion and Government, which it chooses, and as long as any

People please themselves in these great Points, I am determined they shall not displease me.

There is so much danger that my Letter may fall into malicious Hands, that I should not choose to be too free in my Observations upon the Customs and Manners of this People. But thus much I may say with Truth and without offence, that there is no People in the World, who take so much Pains to please, nor any whose Endeavours in this Way, have more success. Their Arts, Manners, Taste and Language are more respected in Europe than those of any other Nation. Luxury, dissipation, and Effeminacy, are pretty nearly at the same degree of Excess here, and in every other Part of Europe. The great Cardinal Virtue of Temperance, however, I believe flourishes here more than in any other Part of Europe.

My dear Country men! how shall I perswade you, to avoid the Plague of Europe? Luxury has as many and as bewitching Charms, on our Side of the Ocean as on this—and Luxury, wherever she goes, effaces from human Nature the Image of the Divinity. If I had Power I would forever banish and exclude from America, all Gold, silver, precious stones, Alabaster, Marble, Silk, Velvet and Lace.

Oh the Tyrant! the American Ladies would say! What!—Ay, my dear Girls, these Passions of yours, which are so easily allarmed, and others of my own sex which are exactly like them, have done and will do the Work of Tyrants in all Ages. Tyrants different from me, whose Power has banished, not Gold indeed, but other Things of greater Value, Wisdom, Virtue and Liberty. My Son and Servant are well. I am, with an Ardour that Words have not Power to express, yours,   JOHN ADAMS

AA to JA

June 30 [1778]

. . . I own I was mortified at so Short a Letter, but I quiet my Heart with thinking there are many more upon their passage to me. I have wrote Seven before this and some of them very long. Now I know you are Safe I wish myself with you. Whenever you entertain such a wish recollect that I would have willingly hazarded all dangers to have been your companion, but as that was not permitted you must console me in your absence by a Recital of all your adventures, tho methinks I would not have them in all respects too similar to those related of your venerable Colleigue, Whose Mentor like appearence, age and philosiphy must certainly lead the polite scientifick Ladies of France to suppose they are embraceing the God of Wisdom, in a Humane Form, but I who own that I never yet wish'd an Angle [angel—ED.] whom I loved a Man, shall be full as content if those divine Honours are omitted. The whole Heart of my Friend is in the Bosom of his partner, more than half a score of years has so riveted [it] there that the fabrick which contains it must crumble into Dust e'er the particles can be seperated. I can hear of the Brilliant accomplishment[s] of any of my Sex with pleasure and rejoice in that Liberality of Sentiment which acknowledges them. At the same time I regret the trifling narrow contracted Education of the Females of my own country. I have entertaind a superiour opinion of the accomplishments of the French Ladies ever since I read the Letters of Dr. Sherbear, who professes that he had rather take the opinion of an accomplished Lady in matters of polite writing than the first wits of Itally and should think himself safer with her approbation than of a long List of Literati, and he give[s] this reason for it that Women have in general more delicate Sensations than Men, what touches them is for the most part true in Nature, whereas men warpt by Education, judge amiss from previous prejudice and refering all things to the model of the ancients, condemn that by comparison where no true Similitud ought to be expected.

But in this country you need not be told how much female Education is neglected, nor how fashonable it has been to ridicule Female learning, tho I acknowled[ge] it my happiness to be connected with a person of a more generous mind and liberal Sentiments. I cannot forbear transcribing a few Generous Sentiments which I lately met with upon this Subject. If women says the writer[s—ED.] are to be esteemed our Enemies, methinks it is an Ignoble Cowardice thus to disarm them and not allow them the same weapons we use ourselves, but if they deserve the title of our Friends tis an inhumane Tyranny to debar them of privileges of ingenious Education which would also render their Friendship so much the more delightfull to themselves and us. Nature is seldom observed to be niggardly of her choisest Gifts to the Sex, their Senses are generally as quick as ours, their Reason as nervious, their judgment as mature and solid. Add but to these natural perfections the advantages of acquired learning what polite and charming creatures would they prove whilst their external Beauty does the office of a Crystal to the Lamp not shrowding but discloseing their Brighter intellects. Nor need we fear to loose our Empire over them by thus improveing their native abilities since where there is most Learning, Sence and knowledge there is always observed to be the most modesty and Rectitude of manners.

AA to JA

[Braintree, 12–23 November 1778]

I have taken up my pen again to relieve the anxiety of a Heart too susceptable for its own repose, nor can I help complaining to my Dearest Friend that his painfull absence is not as formerly alleiviated by the tender tokens of his Friendship, 3 very short Letters only have reachd my Hands during 9 months absence.

I cannot be so unjust to his affection as to suppose he has not wrote much oftener and more perticularly, but must sit down to the Score of misfortune that so few have reachd me.

I cannot charge myself with any deficiency in this perticular as I have never let an opportunity slip without writing to you since we parted, tho you make no mention of having received a line from me; if they are become of so little importance as not to be worth noticeing with your own Hand, be so kind as to direct your Secretary

I will not finish the sentence, my Heart denies the justice of the acqusation, nor does it believe your affection in the least diminished by distance or absence, but my Soul is wounded at a

Seperation from you, and my fortitude all dissolved in frailty and weakness. When I cast my *(Eye)* thoughts across the Atlantick and view the distance, the dangers and Hazards which you have already passd through, and to which you must probably be again exposed, e'er we shall meet, the Time of your absence unlimitted, all all conspire to cast a Gloom over my solitary hours, and bereave me of all domestick felicity. In vain do I strive to through of [throw off] in the company of my Friends some of the anxiety of my Heart, it increases in proportion to my endeavours to conceal it; the only alleiviation I know of would be a frequent intercourse by Letters unrestrained by the apprehension of their becomeing food for our Enemies. The affection I feel for my Friend is of the tenderest kind, matured by years, [sanctified?] by choise and approved by Heaven. Angles [Angels—ED.] can witness to its purity, what care I then for the Ridicule of Britains should this testimony of it fall into their Hands, nor can I endure that so much caution and circumspection on your part should deprive me of the only consolor of your absence—a consolation that our Enemies enjoy in a much higher degree than I do, Many of them having received 3 or 4 Letters from their Friend[s] in England to one that I have received from France.

Thus far I wrote more than ten day[s] ago, my mind as you will easily see far from tranquil, and my Heart so wounded by the Idea of inattention that the very Name of my Dearest Friend would draw tears from me. Forgive me for harbouring an Idea so unjust, to your affection. Were you not dearer to me than all this universe contains beside, I could not have sufferd as I have done, But your Letters of April 12, of June 3 and June 16 calmd my Soul to peace. I cannot discribe the Effect they had upon me, cheerfullness and tranquility took place of greif and anxiety. I placed them Next my Heart and soothed myself to rest with the tender assurances of a Heart all my own.

I was not a little mortified to find that the few Lin[e]s wrote by way of Holland were the only ones you had received from me, when I had wrote many sheets of paper long before that time and sent by so many different hands that I thought you must have heard often from me, *(and led me to suppose that many of your Letters to me must have shared the same fate)*.

But this circumstance will make me more cautious how I suffer such cruel Ideas to [haunt? hound?] me again. Tis the 23 of November now. Count Estaing has saild near a fortnight, Biron with 15 sail lay upon the watch for him, but a very terrible Storm prevented the Count from sailing, and shatterd Birons Fleet. 11 Sail only have arrived at Newport, the Somerset was lost upon Nantucket Shoals. I fed many of the prisoners upon their march to Boston. About 40 were drowned, the rest deliverd themselves as prisoners. The two other ships which are missing were supposed to be lost there, as the Hulks appear and a 50 gun ship which came out with Biron from England has not been heard of since. Thus they have made a fine voyage of watching dEstaing, lost 3 capital ships, never saw the French Fleet, returnd into port with one Ship dismasted and the rest much damaged.

Heaven continue to be propitious to our Friends and allies for whom I have contracted a most sincere regard. If chastity, temperance, industery, frugality, sobriety and purity of morals, added to politeness and complasance can entitle any people to Friendship and respect, the Behaviour of this whole Fleet whilst they lay in this harbour which was more than two months, demand from every unprejudiced person an acknowledgment of their merrit. If I ever had any national prejudices they are done away and I am ashamed to own I was ever possessd of so narrow a spirit—and I blush to find so many of my country men possessd with such low vulgar prejudices and capable of such mean reflections as I have heard thrown out against the Nation of our allies though the unblamable conduct of this Fleet left them not one personal reflexion to cast.

Let me Imitate and instill it into my children the Liberal Spirit of that great Man who declared he had no Local attachments. It is indifferent to me to say[s] he whether a man is rocked in his cradle on this Side of the Tweed, or on that, I seek for merrit whereever it is to be found. Detested be national reflexions, they are unjust.

JA to AA

Amsterdam March 22. 1782

MY DEAREST FRIEND

Your humble Servant has lately grown much into Fashion in this Country. Nobody scarcely of so much importance, as Mynheer Adams. Every City, and Province rings with De Heer Adams &c. &c. &c. and if I were to judge of things here as We do in other Countries, I should think I was going to be received, at the Hague in awfull Pomp in a few Weeks. But I never can foresee one hour what will happen.

I have had however, great Pleasure to see, that there is a national Attachment to America, in the Body of this nation that is well worth cultivating, for there are no Allies more faithfull than they, as has abundantly appeared by their long Suffering with England.

Our Friends at Petersbourg are well. Pray God Charles may be with you.

I cant conceive what the English will do. They are in a strange Position at present. They cannot do much against America. But I hope, America will take their remaining Armies Prisoners in N.Y. and Charlestown. We must not relax, but pursue our Advantages.

The Proceedings of Rotterdam, will shew you, in the inclosed Paper, the Substance of what all the great Cities in this Republick are doing. Let Mr. Cranch translate it, and print it in the News papers. It is good News. You will have an Abundance of more, which will shew you, that We have not been idle here, but have sown Seeds for a plentifull Harvest. Some Folks will think your Husband, a Negotiator, but it is not he, it is General Washington at York Town who did the substance of the Work, the form only belongs to me.

Oh When shall I see my dearest Friend.—All in good Time. My dear blue Hills, ye are the most sublime object in my Imagination. At your reverend Foot, will I spend my old Age, if any, in a calm philosophical Retrospect upon the turbulent scænes of Politicks and War. I shall recollect Amsterdam, Leyden and the Hague with more Emotion than Philadelphia or Paris.

Adieu Adieu.

AA to JA

April 10th. 1782

MY DEAREST FRIEND

How great was my joy to see the well known Signature of my Friend after a Melancholy Solicitude of many months in which my hopes and fears alternately preponderated.

It was January when Charles arrived. By him I expected Letters, but found not a line; instead of which the heavy tidings of your illness reachd me. I then found my Friends had been no strangers of what they carefully conceald from me. Your Letter to Charles dated in November was the only consolation I had; by that I found that the most dangerous period of your illness was pass'd, and that you considerd yourself as recovering tho feeble. My anxiety and apprehensions from that day untill your Letters arrived, which was near 3 months, conspired to render me unhappy. Capt. Trowbridge in the Fire Brand arrived with your favours of October and December and in some measure dispeld the Gloom which hung heavy at my heart. How did it leap for joy to find I was not the misirable Being I sometimes feared I was. I felt that Gratitude to Heaven which great deliverences both demand and inspire. I will not distrust the providential Care of the supreem disposer of events, from whose Hand I have so frequently received distinguished favours. Such I call the preservation of my dear Friend and children from the uncertain Element upon which they have frequently embarked; their preservation from the hands of their enimies I have reason to consider in the same view, especially when I reflect upon the cruel and inhumane treatment experienced by a Gentleman of Mr. Laurences age and respectable character.

The restoration of my dearest Friend from so dangerous a Sickness, demands all my gratitude, whilst I fail not to supplicate Heaven for the continuance of a Life upon which my temporal happiness rests, and deprived of which my own existance would become a burden. Often has the Question which you say staggerd your philosophy occurred to me, nor have I felt so misirable upon account of my own personal Situation, when I considerd that according to the common course of Nature, more than half my days were allready passt, as for those in whom our days are renewed. Their hopes and prospects would vanish, their best prospects, those of Education, would be greatly diminished—but I will not anticipate those miseries which I would shun. Hope is my best Friend and kindest comforter; she assures me that the pure unabated affection, which neither time or absence can allay or abate, shall e'er long be crowned with the completion of its fondest wishes, in the safe return of the beloved object; the age of romance has long ago past, but the affection of almost Infant years has matured and strengthend untill it has become a vital principle, nor has the world any thing to bestow which could in the smallest degree compensate for the loss. Desire and Sorrow were denounced upon our Sex; as a punishment for the transgression of Eve. I have sometimes thought that we are formed to experience more exquisite Sensations than is the Lot of your Sex. More tender and susceptable by Nature of those impression[s] which create happiness or misiry, we Suffer and enjoy in a higher degree. I never wonderd at the philosopher who thanked the Gods that he was created a Man rather than a Woman.

I cannot say, but that I was dissapointed when I found that your return to your native land was a still distant Idea. I think your Situation cannot be so dissagreable as I feared it was, yet that dreadfull climate is my terror.—You mortify me indeed when you talk of sending Charles to Colledge, who it is not probable will be fit under three or four years. Surely my dear Friend fleeting as time is I cannot reconcile myself to the Idea of living in this cruel State of Seperation for [4?] or even three years to come. Eight years have already past, since you could call yourself an Inhabitant of this State. I shall assume the Signature of Penelope, for my dear Ulysses has already been a wanderer from me near half the term of years that, that Hero was encountering Neptune, Calipso, the Circes and Syrens. In the poetical Language of Penelope I shall address you

> "Oh! haste to me! A Little longer Stay
> Will ev'ry grace, each fancy'd charm decay:
> Increasing cares, and times resistless rage
> Will waste my bloom, and wither it to age."

You will ask me I suppose what is become of my patriotick virtue? It is that which most ardently calls for your return. I greatly fear that the climate in which you now reside will prove fatal to your Life, whilst your Life and usefullness might be many years of Service to your Country in a more Healthy climate. If the Essentials of her political system are safe, as I would fain hope they are, yet the impositions and injuries, to which she is hourly liable, and daily suffering, call for the exertions of her wisest and ablest citizens. You know by many years experience what it is to struggle with difficulties—with wickedness in high places—from thence you are led to covet a private Station as the post of Honour, but should such an Idea generally prevail, who would be left to stem the torrent?

Should we at this day possess those invaluable Blessings transmitted us by our venerable Ancestors, if they had not inforced by their example, what they taught by their precepts?

> "While pride, oppression and injustice reign
> the World will still demand her Catos presence."

Why should I indulge an Idea, that whilst the active powers of my Friend remain, they will not be devoted to the Service of his country?

Can I believe that the Man who fears neither poverty or dangers, who sees not charms sufficient either in Riches, power or places to tempt him in the least to swerve from the purest Sentiments of Honour and Delicacy; will retire, unnoticed, Fameless to a Rustick cottage there by dint of Labour to earn his Bread. I need not much examination of my Heart to say I would not willing[ly] consent to it.

Have not Cincinnatus and Regulus been handed down to posterity, with immortal honour?

Without fortune it is more than probable we shall end our days, but let the well earned Fame of having Sacrificed those prospects, from a principal of universal Benevolence and good will to Man, descend as an inheritance to our ofspring. The Luxery of Foreign Nations may possibly infect them but they have not before them an example of it, so far as respects their domestick life. They are not Bred up with an Idea of possessing Hereditary Riches or Grandeur. Retired from the Capital, they see little of the extravagance or dissipation, which prevails there, and at the close of day, in lieu of the Card table, some usefull Book employs their leisure hours. These habits early fixed, and daily inculcated, will I hope render them usefull and ornamental Members of Society.—But we cannot see into futurity. . . .

JA to AA

The Hague May 14 1782

MY DEAREST FRIEND

On the Twelfth, I removed into this House which I have purchased for the United States of America. But, it will be my Residence but a little while.

I must go to you or you must come to me. I cannot live, in this horrid Solitude, which it is to me, amidst Courts, Camps and Crowds. If you were to come here, such is the Unsteadiness of the Foundation that very probably We should have to return home again in a Month or Six Weeks and the Atlantick is not so easily passed as Pens hill. I envy you, your Nabby, Charly and Tommy, and Mr. Dana his Johnny who are very well. A Child was never more weary of a Whistle, than I am of Embassies. The Embassy here however has done great Things. It has not merely tempted a natural Rival, and an imbittered, inveterate, hereditary Ennemy, to assist a little against G[reat] B[ritain] but it has torn from her Bosom, a constant faithfull Friend and Ally of an hundred Years duration.

It has not only prevailed with a Minister or an absolute

Court to fall in with the national Prejudice: but without Money, without Friends, and in Opposition to mean Intrigue it has carried its Cause, by the still small Voice of Reason, and Perswasion, tryumphantly against the uninterrupted Opposition of Family Connections, Court Influence, and Aristocratical Despotism.

It is not a Temple forming a Triple Alliance, with a Nation whose Ruling Family was animated as well as the whole Nation, at that time, with even more Zeal than De Witt in the same Cause.

But you will hear all this represented as a Thing of Course, and of little Consequence—easily done and not worth much.— Very well! Thank God it is done, and that is what I wanted.

Jealousy is as cruel as the Grave, and Envy as spightfull as Hell—and neither have any regard to Veracity or Honour.

AA to JA

October 8th 1782

MY DEAREST FRIEND

. . . I want to know all about my dear Friend—O! that I could add Companion. Permit me my Dearest Friend to renew that Companionship. My Heart sighs for it. I cannot O! I cannot be reconcild to living as I have done for 3 years past. I am searious. I could be importunate with you. May I? Will you let me try to soften, if I cannot wholy releave you, from your Burden of Cares and perplexities? Shall others for their pleasure hazard, what I cannot have courage to incounter from an affection pure as ever burned in a vestal Heart—Warm and permanent as that which glows in your own dear Bosom. I Hardly think of Enemies, of terrors and storms. But I resolve with myself—to do as you wish. If I can add to your Happiness, is it not my duty? If I can soften your Cares, is it not my duty? If I can by a tender attention and assiduity prolong your most valuable Life, is it not my duty? And shall I from Female apprehensions of storms of winds, forego all these Calls? Sacrifice them to my personal ease?

Alass I have not even that, for wakeing or sleeping I am ever with you. Yet if you do not consent so much is my Heart intent upon it, that your refusal must be couched in very soft terms, and you must pledge yourself to return speedily to me.

Yet my dear Sir when I can conquer the too soft sensibility of my Heart, I feel loth you should quit your station untill an Honorable peace is established, and you have added that to your other Labours. Tis no small Satisfaction to me that my country is like to profit so largely by my sacrifices.

I doubt not of your Numerous avocations. Yet when you can get time to write to your Friends here, it is of vast service to you. It sets tongues and pens at work. It informs the people of your attention to their Interests, and our negotiations are extolled and our Services are held up to view. I am unfortunate in not having in my possession a News paper to inclose, in which some person has done justice to your patience, to your perseverance, and held up as far as was prudent the difficulties you have had to encounter.

I hope you are releaved by my last Letters in some measure from your anxiety about our dear Friend and Brother Cranch. He is recoverd far beyond our expectations; he is for the first time this week attending Court. I am of opinion that his Lungs are affected, and am in terrors for him least he should have a relapse. He owes his Life the doctors say under providence, to the incessant, unwearied, indefatigable, watchfull care of his wife; who has almost sacrificed her own, to save his Life.—O! my dear Friend, how often is my Heart torn with the Idea, that I have it not in my power, let sickness or misfortune assail you thus to watch round your Bed and soften your repose.

To the Care of a gracious providence I commit you.

Your good Mother went from here this afternoon, and desires her kind Regards to you. Uncle Q[uinc]y sends his Love, is always attentive to hear from you. He applied to me a little while ago, to send for 2 yd. of green velvet proper for a pulpit cushing with fring and tossels for it or half a pd. of Green Sewing Silk. He would have sent the Money, but I refused it, because I knew it would give you pleasure to make this little present to our Church. You will be so good as to order it put up by the next conveyance. The Fire Brand is not yet arrived. We are under apprehension for her. We have a large French Fleet in our Harbour, yet are daily insulted by British cruizers. There are several officers who belong to the Fleet who hire rooms in the Town, some of them Men of learning and Character. Several of them have got introduced to me. I treat them with civility, but rather avoid a large acquaintance. I have been on Board one 84 Gun ship by the particular invitation of the Captain. Col. Quincy and family accompanied me. This afternoon a Sweed in the French service made me a second visit. He speaks english, is a Man of Learning and is second in command of the America; which is given by Congress in lieu of the Ship which was lost in comeing into the Harbour. These Gentry take a good deal of pains to get an introduction here; seem to consider an acquaintance of much more importance to them, than the people who call themselves geenteel, and who compose our Beau Mond, but who have chiefly risen into Notice since you left the Country. As I have not sought their acquaintance, nor ever appeard in publick since your absence, I have not the *Honour* to be known to many of them—concequently am forgotten or unnoticed by them in all their publick entertainments. Our Allies however recollect that the only Gentleman who is employed abroad in publick service from this state May probably have a Lady and daughter, and it may be proper to notice them out of Regard to the Gentlemans publick Character; and accordingly send out their invitations which I decline and send the daughter. This has been repeatedly the case. I care not a stiver as it respects my own country. Mrs. D[an]a is treated in the same Manner, but people who are accustomed to politeness and good manners notice it. The Manners of our Country are so intirely changed from what they were in those days of simplicity when you knew it, that it has nothing of a Republick but the Name—unless you can keep a publick table and Equipage you are but of very small consideration.

What would You have thought 15 years ago, for young practicioners at the Bar to be setting up their Chariots, to be purchasing—not paying for—their country seats. P. M——n,

B——n, H——n, riding in their Chariots who were clerks in offices when we removed from Town. Hogarth may exhibit his world topsa turva. I am sure I have seen it realized.

Your daughter has been writing to you. Indeed my dear Sir you would be proud of her. Not [that] she is like her *Mamma*. She has a Stat[l]iness in her manners which some misconstrue into pride and haughtyness, but which rather results from a too great reserve; she wants more affability, but she has prudence and discretion beyond her years. She is in her person tall, large and Majestick, Mammas partialiaty allows her to be a good figure. Her sensibility is not yet sufficiently a wakend to give her Manners that pleasing softness which attracts whilst it is attracted. Her Manners rather forbid all kinds of Intimacy; and awe whilst they command.

Indeed she is not like her Mamma. Had not her Mamma at her age too much sensibility, to be *very prudent*. It however won a Heart of as much sensibility—but how my pen runs. I never can write you a short Letter.—My Charles and Tommy are fine Boys. My absent one is not forgotten. How does he. I do not hear from him.—Adieu my dear Friend. How much happier should I be to fold you to my Bosom, than to bid you this Languid adieu, with a whole ocean between us. Yet whilst I recall to your mind tender Scenes of happier days, I would add a supplication that the day May not be far distant, that shall again renew them to your Ever Ever affectionate   PORTIA

AA to JA

December 23. 1782

MY DEAREST FRIEND

I have omited writing by the last opportunity to Holland; because I had but small Faith in the designs of the owners or passengers. The vessel sails from Nantucket, Dr. Winship is a passenger, a Mr. Gray and some others, and I had just written you so largely by a vessel bound to France, the General Galvaye that I had nothing New to say. There are few occurences in this Northen climate at this Season of the year to divert or

entertain you—and in the domestick way, should I draw you
the picture of my Heart, it would be what I hope you still
would Love; tho it contain nothing New; the early possession
you obtained there, and the absolute power you have ever main-
taind over it, leaves not the smallest space unoccupied. I look
back to the early days of our acquaintance, and Friendship, as
to the days of Love and Innocence; and with an undiscribable
pleasure I have seen near a score of years roll over our Heads,
with an affection heightned and improved by time—nor have
the dreary years of absence in the smallest degree effaced from
my mind the Image of the dear untittled Man to whom I gave
my Heart. I cannot sometimes refrain considering the Honours
with which he is invested as badges of my unhappiness. The
unbounded confidence I have in your attachment to me, and
the dear pledges of our affection, has soothed the solitary hour,
and renderd your absence more supportable; for had I [not]
loved you with the same affection it must have been misiry to
have doubted. Yet a cruel world too often injures my feelings,
by wondering how a person possesst of domestick attachments
can sacrifice them by absenting himself *for years*.

If you had known said a person to me the other day, that Mr.
A[dam]s would have remained so long abroad, would you have
consented that he should have gone? I recollected myself a moment, and then spoke the real dictates of my Heart. If I had
known Sir that Mr. A. could have affected what he has done, I
would not only have submitted to the absence I have endured,
painfull as it has been; but I would not have opposed it, even tho
3 years more should be added to the Number, which Heaven
avert! I feel a pleasure in being able to sacrifice my selfish passions to the general good, and in imitating the example which
has taught me to consider myself and family, but as the small
dust of the balance when compaired with the great community.

Your Daughter most sincerely regreets your absence, she sees
me support it, yet thinks she could not imitate either parent in
the disinterested motives which actuate them. She has had a
strong desire to encounter the dangers of the Sea to visit you. I
however am not without a suspicion that she may loose her
realish for a voyage by Spring. The tranquility of mine and my

dear sisters family is in a great measure restored to us, since the recovery of our worthy Friend and Brother. We had a most melancholy Summer. The young folks of the two families together with those of Col. Q[uinc]ys and General W[arre]n preserve a great Intimacy, and as they wish for but few connections in the Beau Mond, it is not to be wonderd at that they are fond of each others company. We have an agreable young Gentleman by the Name of Robbins who keeps our little School, Son to the Revd. Mr. Robbins of Plimouth, and we have in the little circle an other gentleman who has opend an office in Town, for about nine months past, and boarded in Mr. Cranch['s] family. His Father you knew. His Name is Tyler, he studied law upon his comeing out of colledge with Mr. Dana, but when Mr. Dana went to Congress he finished his studies with Mr. Ang[i]er. Loosing his Father young and having a very pretty patrimony left him, possessing a sprightly fancy, a warm imagination and an agreable person, he was rather negligent in persueing his buisness in the way of his profession; and dissipated two or 3 years of his Life and too much of his fortune for to reflect upon with pleasure; all of which he now laments but cannot recall. At 23 the time when he took the resolution of comeing to B[osto]n and withdrawing from a too numerous acquaintance, he resolved to persue his studies, and his Buisness, and save his remaining fortune which sufferd much more from the paper currency than any other cause; so that out of 17 thousand pounds which fell to his share, he cannot now realize more than half that sum, as he told me a few days past. His Mamma is in possession of a large Estate and he is a very favorite child. When he proposed comeing to settle here he met with but little encouragement, but he was determined upon the trial. He has succeeded beyond expectation, he has popular talants, and as his behaviour has been unexceptionable since his residence in Town, in concequence of which his Buisness daily increases, he cannot fail making a distinguished figure in his profession if he steadily persues it. I am not acquainted with any young Gentleman whose attainments in literature are equal to his, who judges with greater accuracy or discovers a more delicate and refined taste. I have frequently looked upon him with the Idea that you would have taken much pleasure in such a pupil. I wish I was as well assured that you would be equally pleased with him in an other character, for such I apprehend are his distant hopes. I early saw that he was possest with powerfull attractions, and as he obtaind and deservd, I believe the character of a gay, tho not a criminal youth, I thought it prudent to keep as great a reserve as possible. In this I was seconded by the discreet conduct of a daughter, who is happy in not possessing all her Mothers Sensibility. Yet I see a growing attachment in him stimulated by that very reserve. I feel the want of your presence and advise. I think I know your Sentiments so well that the merit of a Gentleman will be your first consideration, and I have made every inquiry which I could with decency, and without discloseing my motives. Even in his most dissipated state he always applied his mornings to study, by which means he has stored his mind with a fund of usefull knowledge. I know not a young fellow upon the stage whose language is so pure, or whose natural disposition is more agreable. His days are devoted to his office, his Evenings of late to my fire side. His attachment is too obvious to escape notice. I do not think the Lady wholy indifferent; yet her reserve and apparent coldness is such that I know he is in misirable doubt. Some conversation one Evening of late took place which led me to write him a Billet and tell him, that at least it admitted a possibility that I might quit this country in the Spring; that I never would go abroad without my daughter, and if I did go, I wished to carry her with a mind unattached, besides I could have but one voice; and for that I held myself accountable to you; that he was not yet Established in Buisness sufficient to think of a connection with any one;—to which I received this answer—

Madam

I have made an exertion to answer your Billet. I can only say that the second impulse in my Breast is my Love and respect for you; and it is the foible of my nature to be the machine of those I Love and venerate. Do with me as seemeth good unto thee. I can safely trust my dearest fondest wishes and persuits in the hands of a Friend that can feel, that knows my situation and her designs. If reason pleads against me, you will do well to hesitate. If Friendship and reason unite I shall be happy. Only say I shall be happy when I *deserve;* and it shall be my every exertion to augment my merit, and this you may be assured of, whether I am blessed in my wishes or not, I will endeavour to be a character that you shall not Blush once to have entertaind an Esteem for. Yours respectfully &c.

What ought I say? I feel too powerful a pleader within my own heart and too well recollect the Love I bore to the object of my early affections to forbid him to hope. I feel a regard for him upon an account you will smile at, I fancy I see in him Sentiments, opinions and actions which endeared to me the best of Friends. Suffer me to draw you from the depths of politicks to endearing family Scenes. I know you cannot fail being peculiarly interested in the present. I inclose you a little paper which tho trifling in itself, may serve to shew you the truth of my observations. The other day the gentleman I have been speaking of, had a difficult writ to draw. He requested the favour of looking into your Book of forms, which I readily granted; in the Evening when he returned me the key he put in to my hands a paper which I could not tell what to make of, untill he exclamed "O! Madam Madam, I have now hopes that I shall one day become worthy your regard. What a picture have I caught of my own Heart, my resolutions, my designs! I could not refrain breaking out into a Rhapsody. I found this coppy of a Letter in a pamphlet with observations upon the Study of the Law and many excellent remarks; you will I hope forgive the theft, when I deliver the paper to you, and you find how much benifit I shall derive from it."

I daily see that he will win the affections of a fine majestick Girl who has as much dignity as a princess. She is handsome, but not Beautifull. No air of levity ever accompanies either her words or actions. Should she be caught by a tender passion, sufficient to remove a little of her natural reserve and soften her form and manners, she will be a still more pleasing character. Her mind is daily improveing, and she gathers new taste for literature perhaps for its appearing in a more pleasing form to her.—If I can procure a little ode which accompanied an ice Heart I will inclose it to you.

It is now my dear Friend a long long time since I had a line from you, the Fate of Gibralter leads me to fear that a peace is far distant, and that I shall not see you—God only knows when. I shall say little about my former request, not that my desire is less, but before this can reach you tis probable I may receive your opinion. If in favour of my comeing to you, I shall have no occasion to urge it further—if against it, I would not embarrass you, by again requesting it. I will endeavour to set down, and consider it as the portion alloted me. My dear Sons are well, their application and improvements go hand in hand. Our Friends all desire to be rememberd. The Fleet of our allies expect to sail daily but where destined we know not; a great harmony has subsisted between them and the Americans ever since their residence here. I wish to write to Mr. T[haxte]r but fear I shall not have time. Mrs. D[an]a and children are well. The judge has been very sick of a fever but I believe is better. This Letter is to go by the Iris which sails with the Fleet. I hope it will reach you in safety. If it should fall into the hands of an Enemy, I hope they will be kind enough to distroy it; as I would not wish to see such a family picture in print; adieu my dear Friend. Why is it that I hear so seldom from my dear John; but one Letter have I ever received from him since he arrived in Petersburgh? I wrote him by the last opportunity. Ever remember me as I do you; with all the tenderness which it is possible for one object to feel for an other; which no time can obliterate, no distance alter, but which is always the same in the Bosom of   PORTIA

JA to AA

Paris Jan. 22. 1783

MY DEAREST FRIEND

The Preliminaries of Peace and an Armistice, were signed at Versailles on the 20 and on the 21. We went again to pay our Respects to the King and Royal Family upon the Occasion. Mr. Jay was gone upon a little Excursion to Normandie and Mr. Laurens was gone to Bath, both for their health, so that the signature was made by Mr. Franklin and me.—I want an Excursion too.

Thus drops the Curtain upon this mighty Trajedy, it has unravelled itself happily for Us—and Heaven be praised. Some of our dearest Interests have been saved, thro many dangers. I have no News from my son, since the 8th. December, when he was at Stockholm, but hope every hour to hear of his Arrival at the Hague.

I hope to receive the Acceptance of my Resignation so as to come home in the Spring Ships.

I had written thus far when yours of 23 decr. was brought in. Its Contents have awakened all my sensibility, and shew in a stronger Light than ever the Necessity of my coming home. I confess I dont like the Subject at all. My Child is too young for such Thoughts, and I dont like your Word "Dissipation" at all. I dont know what it means—it may mean every Thing. There is not Modesty and Diffidence enough in the Traits you send me. My Child is a Model, as you represent her and as I know her, and is not to be the Prize, I hope of any, even reformed Rake. A Lawyer would be my Choice, but it must be a Lawyer who spends his Midnights as well as Evenings at his Age over his Books not at any Ladys Fire Side. I should have thought you had seen enough to be more upon your Guard than to write Billets upon such a subject to such a youth. A Youth who has been giddy enough to spend his Fortune or half his Fortune in Gaieties, is not the Youth for me, Let his Person, Family, Connections and Taste for Poetry be what they will. I am not looking out for a Poet, nor a Professor of belle Letters.

In the Name of all that is tender dont criticise Your Daughter for those qualities which are her greatest Glory, her Reserve, and her Prudence which I am amazed to hear you call Want of Sensibility. The more Silent She is in Company, the better for me in exact Proportion and I would have this observed as a Rule by the Mother as well as the Daughter.

You know moreover or ought to know my utter Inability to do any Thing for my Children, and you know the long dependence of young Gentlemen of the most promising Talents and obstinate Industry, at the Bar. My Children will have nothing but their Liberty and the Right to catch Fish, on the Banks of Newfoundland. This is all the Fortune that I have been able to make for myself or them.

I know not however, enough of this subject to decide any Thing.—Is he a Speaker at the Bar? If not he will never be any Thing. But above all I positively forbid any Connection between my Daughter and any Youth upon Earth, who does not totally eradicate every Taste for Gaiety and Expence. I never knew one who had it and indulged it, but what was made a Rascall by it, sooner or later.

This Youth has had a Brother in Europe, and a detestible Specimen he exhibited. Their Father had not all those nice sentiments which I wish, although an Honourable Man.

I think he and you have both advanced too fast, and I should advise both to retreat. Your Family as well as mine have had too much Cause to rue the Qualities which by your own Account have been in him. And if they were ever in him they are not yet out.

This is too serious a subject to equivocate about. I dont like this method of Courting Mothers. There is something too fantastical and affected in all this Business for me. It is not nature, modest, virtuous, noble nature. The Simplicity of Nature is the best Rule with me to judge of every Thing, in Love as well as State and War.

This is all between you and me.

I would give the World to be with you Tomorrow. But there is a vast Ocean.—No Ennemies.—But I have not yet Leave from my Masters. I dont love to go home in a Miff, Pet or Passion nor with an ill Grace, but I hope soon to have leave. I can never stay in Holland—the Air of that Country chills every drop of Blood in my Veins. If I were to stay in Europe another Year I would insist upon your coming with your daughter but this is not to be and I will come home to you.

Adieu ah ah Adieu.

FROM ABIGAIL ADAMS 2D'S DIARY

London, Aug. 7th, 1784.

At 12, returned to our own apartments; when I entered, I saw upon the table a hat with two books in it; every thing around appeared altered, without my knowing in what particular. I went into my own room, the things were moved; I looked around—"Has mamma received letters, that have determined her departure?—When does she go?—Why are these things moved?" All in a breath to Esther.[4]

"No, ma'm, she has recieved no letter, but goes to-morrow morning."

"Why is all this appearance of strangeness?—Whose hat is that in the other room?—Whose trunk is this?—Whose sword and cane?—It is my father's," said I. "Where is he?"

"In the room above."

Up I flew, and to his chamber, where he was lying down, he raised himself upon my knocking softly at the door, and received me with all the tenderness of an affectionate parent after so long an absence. Sure I am, I never felt more agitation of spirits in my life; it will not do to describe.

EARLIEST WRITINGS[1]

Adams's first two published writings, "On Private Revenge" and "On Self-Delusion," derived from a controversial legal dispute and were published in the Boston Gazette in 1763. The issue involved the appointment of Lieutenant Governor Thomas Hutchinson to the Massachusetts Supreme Court, which aroused the ire of James Otis, Jr., who believed the position had been promised to his father. Adams regarded his essays as "trifles of mine," but they demonstrated his keen sense of the psychology of emotions and the way people regard their own behavior as virtuous and that of their antagonists as vicious.

ON PRIVATE REVENGE.

No. I.*

Man is distinguished from other animals, his fellow inhabitants of this planet, by a capacity of acquiring knowledge and civility, more than by any excellency, corporeal, or mental, with which mere nature has furnished his species. His erect figure and sublime countenance would give him but little elevation above the bear or the tiger; nay, notwithstanding those advantages, he would hold an inferior rank in the scale of being, and would have a worse prospect of happiness than those crea-

*From the Boston Gazette, No. 435, 1 August, 1763.

tures, were it not for the capacity of uniting with others, and availing himself of arts and inventions in social life. As he comes originally from the hands of his Creator, self-love or self-preservation is the only spring that moves within him; he might crop the leaves or berries with which his Creator had surrounded him, to satisfy his hunger; he might sip at the lake or rivulet to slake his thirst; he might screen himself behind a rock or mountain from the bleakest of the winds; or he might fly from the jaws of voracious beasts to preserve himself from immediate destruction. But would such an existence be worth preserving? Would not the first precipice or the first beast of prey that could put a period to the wants, the frights, and horrors of such a wretched being, be a friendly object and a real blessing?

When we take one remove from this forlorn condition, and find the species propagated, the banks of clams and oysters discovered, the bow and arrow invented, and the skins of beasts or the bark of trees employed for covering,—although the human creature has a little less anxiety and misery than before, yet each individual is independent of all others. There is no intercourse of friendship; no communication of food or clothing; no conversation or connection, unless the conjunction of sexes, prompted by instinct, like that of hares and foxes, may be called so. The ties of parent, son, and brother, are of little obligation. The relations of master and servant, the distinction of magistrate and subject, are totally unknown. Each individual is his own sovereign, accountable to no other upon earth, and punishable by none. In this savage state, courage, hardiness, activity, and strength, the virtues of their brother brutes, are the only excellencies to which men can aspire. The man who can run with the most celerity, or send the arrow with the greatest force, is the best qualified to procure a subsistence. Hence, to chase a deer over the most rugged mountain, or to pierce him at the greatest distance, will be held, of all accomplishments, in the highest estimation. Emulations and competitions for superiority in such qualities, will soon commence; and any action which may be taken for an insult, will be considered as a pretension to such superiority; it will raise resentment in proportion, and shame and grief will prompt the savage to claim satisfaction or to take revenge. To request the interposition of a third person to arbitrate between the contending parties, would be considered as an implicit acknowledgment of deficiency in those qualifications, without which, none in such a barbarous condition would choose to live. Each one, then, must be his own avenger. The offended parties must fall to fighting. Their teeth, their nails, their feet, or fists, or, perhaps, the first club or stone that can be grasped, must decide the contest, by finishing the life of one. The father, the brother, or the friend, begins then to espouse the cause of the deceased; not, indeed, so much from any love he bore him living, or from any grief he suffers for him dead, as from a principle of bravery and honor, to show himself able and willing to encounter the man who had just before vanquished another. Hence arises the idea of an avenger of blood, and thus the notions of revenge, and the appetite for it grow apace. Every one must avenge his own wrongs when living, or else lose his reputation, and his near relation must avenge them for him after he is dead, or forfeit his. Indeed, nature has implanted in the human heart a disposition to resent an injury when offered; and this disposition is so strong, that even the horse trading by accident on a gouty toe, or a brickbat falling on the shoulders, in the first twinges of pain, seems to excite the angry passions, and we feel an inclination to kill the horse and to break the brickbat. Consideration, however, that the horse and brick were without design, will cool us; whereas the thought that any mischief has been done on purpose to abuse, raises revenge in all its strength and terrors; and the man feels the sweetest, highest gratification, when he inflicts the punishment himself. From this source arises the ardent desire in men to judge for themselves, when, and to what degree they are injured, and to carve out their own remedies for themselves. From the same source arises that obstinate disposition in barbarous nations to continue barbarous, and the extreme difficulty of introducing civility and Christianity among them. For the great distinction between savage nations and polite ones, lies in this,—that among the former every individual is his own judge and his own executioner; but among the latter all pretensions to judgment and punishment are resigned to tribunals erected by the public; a resignation which savages are not, without infinite difficulty, persuaded to make, as it is of a right and privilege extremely dear and tender to an uncultivated nature.

To exterminate from among mankind such revengeful sentiments and tempers, is one of the highest and most important strains of civil and humane policy. Yet the qualities which contribute most to inspire and support them may, under certain regulations, be indulged and encouraged. Wrestling, running, leaping, lifting, and other exercises of strength, hardiness, courage, and activity, may be promoted among private soldiers, common sailors, laborers, manufacturers, and husbandmen, among whom they are most wanted, provided sufficient precautions are taken that no romantic, cavalier-like principles of honor intermix with them, and render a resignation of the right of judging, and the power of executing, to the public, shameful. But whenever such notions spread so inimical to the peace of society, that boxing, clubs, swords, or firearms, are resorted to for deciding every quarrel, about a girl, a game at cards, or any little accident that wine or folly or jealousy may suspect to be an affront,—the whole power of the government should be exerted to suppress them.

If a time should ever come when such notions shall prevail in this Province to a degree, that no privileges shall be able to exempt men from indignities and personal attacks, not the privilege of a counsellor, nor the privilege of a House of Representatives of "speaking freely in that assembly, without impeachment or question in any court or place," out of the General Court—when whole armed mobs shall assault a member of the House, when violent attacks shall be made upon counsellors, when no place shall be sacred, not the very walls of legislation, when no personages shall overawe, not the whole General Court added to all the other gentlemen on 'Change, when the broad noon-day shall be chosen to display before the world such high, heroic sentiments of gallantry and spirit, when such assailants shall live unexpelled from the legislature, when slight censures and no punishments shall be inflicted,—there will really be danger of our becoming universally ferocious, barbarous, and brutal, worse than our Gothic ancestors before the Christian era.

The doctrine, that the person assaulted "should act with spirit," "should defend himself by drawing his sword and killing, or by wringing noses, and boxing it out with the offender," is the tenet of a coxcomb and the sentiment of a brute. The fowl upon the dunghill, to be sure, feels a most gallant and heroic spirit at the crowing of another, and instantly spreads his cloak, and prepares for combat. The bull's wrath enkindles into a noble rage, and the stallion's immortal spirit can never forgive the pawings, neighings, and defiances of his rival. But are cocks and bulls and horses the proper exemplars for the imitation of men, especially of men of sense, and even of the highest personages in the government!

Such ideas of gallantry have been said to be derived from the army. But it was injuriously said, because not truly. For every gentleman, every man of sense and breeding in the army, has a more delicate and manly way of thinking, and from his heart despises all such little, narrow, sordid notions. It is true that a competition, and a mutual affectation of contempt, is apt to arise among the lower, more ignorant, and despicable, of every rank and order in society. This sort of man, (and some few such there are in every profession,) among divines, lawyers, physicians, as well as husbandmen, manufacturers, and laborers, are prone, from a certain littleness of mind, to imagine that their labors alone are of any consequence to the world, and to affect a contempt for all others. It is not unlikely, then, that the lowest and most despised sort of soldiers may have expressed a contempt for all other orders of mankind, may have indulged a disrespect to every personage in a civil character, and have acted upon such principles of revenge, rusticity, barbarity, and brutality, as have been above described. And, indeed, it has been observed by the great Montesquieu, that "From a manner of thinking that prevails among mankind," (the most ignorant and despicable of mankind, he means,) "they set a higher value upon courage than timorousness, on activity than prudence, on strength than counsel. Hence, the army will ever despise a senate, and respect their own officers; they will naturally slight the orders sent them by a body of men whom they look upon as cowards, and therefore unworthy to command them." This respect to their own officers, which produces a contempt of senates and councils, and of all laws, orders, and constitutions, but those of the army and their superior officers, though it may have prevailed among some soldiers of the illiberal character above described, is far from being universal. It is not found in one gentleman of sense and breeding in the whole service. All of this character know that the common law of England is superior to all other laws, martial or common, in every English government, and has often asserted triumphantly its own preëminence against the insults and encroachments of a giddy and unruly soldiery. They know, too, that civil officers in England hold a great superiority to military officers, and that a frightful despotism would be the speedy consequence of the least alteration in these particulars. And, knowing this, these gentlemen, who have so often exposed their lives in defence of the religion, the liberties, and rights of men and Englishmen, would feel the utmost indignation at the doctrine which should make the civil power give place to the military, which should make a respect to their superior officers destroy or diminish their obedience to civil magistrates, or which should give any man a right in conscience, honor, or even in punctilio and delicacy, to neglect the institutions of the public, and seek his own remedy for wrongs and injuries of any kind.

ON SELF-DELUSION.

No. II.

TO THE PRINTERS.*

My worthy and ingenious friend, Mr. J., having strutted his hour upon the stage, and acquired as well as deserved a good reputation, as a man of sense and learning, some time since made his exit, and now is heard no more.

Soon after Mr. J.'s departure, your present correspondent

*From the Boston Gazette, No. 439, 29 August, 1763.

made his appearance, but has not yet executed his intended plan. Mr. J. enlisted himself under the banners of a faction, and employed his agreeable pen in the propagation of the principles and prejudices of a party, and for this purpose he found himself obliged to exalt some characters, and depress others, equally beyond the truth. The greatest and best of all mankind deserve less admiration, and even the worst and vilest deserve more candor, than the world in general is willing to allow them. The favorites of parties, although they have always some virtues, have always many imperfections. Many of the ablest tongues and pens have, in every age, been employed in the foolish, deluded, and pernicious flattery of one set of partisans, and in furious, prostitute invectives against another; but such kinds of oratory never had any charms for me; and if I must do one or the other, I would quarrel with both parties and with every individual of each, before I would subjugate my understanding, or prostitute my tongue or pen to either.

To divert men's minds from subjects of vain curiosity, or unprofitable science, to the useful, as well as entertaining speculations of agriculture; to eradicate the Gothic and pernicious principles of private revenge that have been lately spread among my countrymen, to the debasement of their character, and to the frequent violation of the public peace, and to recommend a careful attention to political measures, and a candid manner of reasoning about them, instead of abusive insolence or uncharitable imputations upon men and characters, has, since I first undertook the employment of entertaining the public, been my constant and invariable view. The difficulty or impracticability of succeeding in my enterprise, has often been objected to me by my friends; but even this has not wholly disheartened me. I own it would be easier to depopulate a province, or subvert a monarchy, to transplant a nation, or enkindle a new war; and that I should have a fairer prospect of success in such designs as those. But my consolation is this,—that if I am unable by my writings to effect any good purpose, I never will subserve a bad one. If engagements to a party are necessary to make a fortune, I had rather make none at all; and spend the remainder of my days like my favorite author, that ancient and immortal husband-

man, philosopher, politician, and general, Xenophon, in his retreat, considering kings and princes as shepherds, and their
people and subjects like flocks and herds, or as mere objects of
contemplation and parts of a curious machine in which I had no
interest, than to wound my own mind by engaging in any party,
and spreading prejudices, vices, or follies. Notwithstanding this,
I remember the monkish maxim,—*fac officium taliter qualiter,
sed sta bene cum priore;* and it is impossible to stand well with
the abbot without fighting for his cause through *fas* and *nefas*.

Please to insert the foregoing and following, which is the last
deviation I purpose to make from my principal and favorite
views of writing on husbandry and mechanic arts.

There is nothing in the science of human nature more curious,
or that deserves a critical attention from every order of men so
much, as that principle which moral writers have distinguished
by the name of self-deceit. This principle is the spurious off-
spring of self-love; and is, perhaps, the source of far the greatest and worst part of the vices and calamities among mankind.

The most abandoned minds are ingenious in contriving ex-
cuses for their crimes, from constraint, necessity, the strength or
suddenness of temptation, or the violence of passion, which
serve to soften the remordings of their own consciences, and to
render them by degrees insensible equally to the charms of
virtue and the turpitude of vice. What multitudes in older countries discover, even while they are suffering deservedly the most
infamous and terrible of civil punishments, a tranquillity and
even a magnanimity like that which we may suppose in a real
patriot dying to preserve his country! Happy would it be for the
world if the fruits of this pernicious principle were confined to
such profligates. But, if we look abroad, shall we not see the
most modest, sensible, and virtuous of the common people, almost every hour of their lives, warped and blinded by the same
disposition to flatter and deceive themselves? When they think
themselves injured by any foible or vice in others, is not this injury always seen through the magnifying end of the perspective?
When reminded of any such imperfection in themselves, by
which their neighbors or fellow-citizens are sufferers, is not the

perspective instantly reversed? Insensible of the beams in our own eyes, are we not quick in discerning motes in those of others? Nay, however melancholy it may be, and how humbling soever to the pride of the human heart, even the few favorites of nature, who have received from her clearer understandings and more happy tempers than other men, who seem designed, under Providence, to be the great conductors of the art and science, the war and peace, the laws and religion of this lower world, are often snared by this unhappy disposition in their minds, to their own destruction, and the injury, nay, often to the utter desolation of millions of their fellow-men. Since truth and virtue, as the means of present and future happiness, are confessed to be the only objects that deserve to be pursued, to what imperfection in our nature, or unaccountable folly in our conduct, excepting this of which we have been speaking, can mankind impute the multiplied diversity of opinions, customs, laws, and religions that have prevailed, and are still triumphant, in direct opposition to both? From what other source can such fierce disputations arise concerning the two things which seem the most consonant to the entire frame of human nature?

Indeed, it must be confessed, and it ought to be with much contrition lamented, that those eyes, which have been given us to see, are willingly suffered by us to be obscured, and those consciences, which by the commission of God Almighty have a rightful authority over us, to be deposed by prejudices, appetites, and passions, which ought to hold a much inferior rank in the intellectual and moral system. Such swarms of passions, avarice and ambition, servility and adulation, hopes, fears, jealousies, envy, revenge, malice, and cruelty, are continually buzzing in the world, and we are so extremely prone to mistake the impulses of these for the dictates of our consciences,—that the greatest genius, united to the best disposition, will find it hard to hearken to the voice of reason, or even to be certain of the purity of his own intentions.

From this true, but deplorable condition of mankind, it happens that no improvements in science or literature, no reformation in religion or morals, nor any rectification of mistaken measures in government, can be made without opposition from numbers, who, flattering themselves that their own intentions are pure, (how sinister soever they may be in fact) will reproach impure designs to others, or, fearing a detriment to their interest or a mortification to their passions from the innovation, will even think it lawful directly and knowingly to falsify the motives and characters of the innocent.

Vain ambition and other vicious motives were charged by the sacred congregation upon Galileo, as the causes of his hypothesis concerning the motion of the earth, and charged so often and with so many terms, as to render the old man at last suspicious, if not satisfied, that the charge was true, though he had been led to this hypothesis by the light of a great genius and deep researches into astronomy. Sedition, rebellion, pedantry, desire of fame, turbulence, and malice, were always reproached to the great reformers, who delivered us from the worst chains that were ever forged by monks or devils for the human mind. Zosimus and Julian could easily discover or invent anecdotes to dishonor the conversion of Constantine, and his establishment of Christianity in the empire.

For these reasons we can never be secure in a resignation of understandings, or in confiding enormous power either to the bramble or the cedar; no, nor to any mortal, however great or good; and for the same reasons we should always be upon our guard against the epithets and reflections of writers and declaimers, whose constant art it is to falsify and blacken the characters and measures they are determined to discredit.

These reflections have been occasioned by the late controversies in our newspapers about certain measures in the political world.* Controversies that have this in common with others of much greater figure and importance, and, indeed, with all others, (in which numbers have been concerned,) from the first invention of letters to the present hour; that more pains have

---

*Hutchinson mentions the year 1763, as the time when parties in Massachusetts began to take their form. "Men took sides in New England upon mere speculative points in government, when there was nothing in practice which could give any grounds for forming parties." The next paragraph, however, be-

been employed in charging desire of popularity, restless turbulence of spirit, ambitious views, envy, revenge, malice, and jealousy on one side; and servility, adulation, tyranny, principles of arbitrary power, lust of dominion, avarice, desires of civil or military commissions on the other; or, in fewer words, in attempts to blacken and discredit the motives of the disputants on both sides, than in rational inquiries into the merits of the cause, the truth, and rectitude of the measures contested.

Let not writers nor statesmen deceive themselves. The springs of their own conduct and opinions are not always so clear and pure, nor are those of their antagonists in politics always so polluted and corrupted, as they believe, and would have the world believe too. Mere readers and private persons can see virtues and talents on each side; and to their sorrow they have not yet seen any side altogether free from atrocious vices, extreme ignorance, and most lamentable folly. Nor will mere readers and private persons be less excusable if they should suffer themselves to be imposed on by others, who first impose upon themselves. Every step in the public administration of government concerns us nearly. Life and fortune, our own and those of our posterity, are not trifles to be neglected or totally entrusted to other hands; and these, in the vicissitudes of human things, may be rendered in a few years either totally uncertain, or as secure as fixed laws and the British constitution well administered can make them, in consequence of measures that seem at present but trifles, and to many scarcely worth attention. Let us not be bubbled then out of our reverence and obedience to government on one hand; nor out of our right to think and act for ourselves in our own department on the other. The steady management of a good government is the most anxious, arduous, and hazardous vocation on this side the grave. Let us not encumber those, therefore, who have spirit

---

trays his sense of the connection these speculative points had with grounds for forming parties which all instinctively felt to be about to be furnished by the mother country. It was the ripple on the face of the still water, indicative of the storm that was soon to follow. *History of Massachusetts*, vol. iii. pp. 103–105.

enough to embark in such an enterprise, with any kind of opposition that the preservation or perfection of our mild, our happy, our most excellent constitution, does not soberly demand.

But, on the other hand, as we know that ignorance, vanity, excessive ambition and venality, will, in spite of all human precautions, creep into government, and will ever be aspiring at extravagant and unconstitutional emoluments to individuals, let us never relax our attention, or our resolution, to keep these unhappy imperfections in human nature, out of which material, frail as it is, all our rulers must be compounded, under a strict inspection and a just control. We electors have an important constitutional power placed in our hands; we have a check upon two branches of the legislature, as each branch has upon the other two; the power I mean of electing, at stated periods, one branch, which branch has the power of electing another. It becomes necessary to every subject then, to be in some degree a statesman, and to examine and judge for himself of the tendency of political principles and measures. Let us examine, then, with a sober, a manly, a British, and a Christian spirit; let us neglect all party virulence and advert to facts; let us believe no man to be infallible or impeccable in government, any more than in religion; take no man's word against evidence, nor implicitly adopt the sentiments of others, who may be deceived themselves, or may be interested in deceiving us.

ON PRIVATE REVENGE.

No. III.

Impiger, iracundus, inexorabilis, acer,
Jura neget sibi nata, nihil non arroget armis.[2]

HOR.

Rebuke the spearmen, and the troops
Of bulls that mighty be.

NOVANG.

TO THE PRINTERS.*

It seems to be necessary for me, (notwithstanding the declaration in my last) once more to digress from the road of agriculture and mechanic arts, and to enter the list of disputation with
a brace of writers in the Evening Post, one of whom has subscribed himself X, and the other W. I shall agree with the first
of these gentlemen, that "to preach up non-resistance with the
zeal of a fanatic," would be as extraordinary as to employ a
bastile in support of the freedom of speech or the press, or an
inquisition in favor of liberty of conscience; but if he will leave
his own imagination, and recur to what I have written, he will
not find a syllable against resistance. Resistance to sudden violence, for the preservation not only of my person, my limbs and
life, but of my property, is an indisputable right of nature
which I never surrendered to the public by the compact of society, and which, perhaps, I could not surrender if I would. Nor
is there any thing in the common law of England, (for which
Mr. X supposes I have so great a fondness,) inconsistent with
that right. On the contrary, the dogmas of Plato, the maxims of
the law, and the precepts of Christianity, are precisely coinci-
dent in relation to this subject.

Plato taught that revenge was unlawful, although he allowed
of self-defence. The divine Author of our religion has taught us
that trivial provocations are to be overlooked; and that if a
man should offer you an insult, by boxing one ear, rather than
indulge a furious passion and return blow for blow, you ought
even to turn the other also. This expression, however, though it
inculcates strongly the duty of moderation and self-government
upon sudden provocations, imports nothing against the right
of resistance or of self-defence. The sense of it seems to be no
more than this: that little injuries and insults ought to be borne
patiently for the present, rather than run the risk of violent
consequences by retaliation.

Now, the common law seems to me to be founded on the
same great principle of philosophy and religion. It will allow of

*From the Boston Gazette, 5 September, 1763.

nothing as a justification of blows, but blows; nor will it justify a furious beating, bruising, and wounding, upon the provocation of a fillip of the finger, or a kick upon the shins; but if I am assaulted, I can justify nothing but laying my hands lightly upon the aggressor for my own defence; nothing but what was absolutely necessary for my preservation. I may parry or ward off any blow; but a blow received is no sufficient provocation for fifty times so severe a blow in return. When life, which is one of the three favorites of the law, comes into consideration, we find a wise and humane provision is made for its preservation. If I am assaulted by another, sword in hand, and if I am even certain of his intention to murder me, the common law will not suffer me to defend myself, by killing him, if I can avoid it. Nay, my behavior must absolutely be what would be called cowardice, perhaps, by Mr. X and W, though it would be thought the truest bravery, not only by the greatest philosophers and legislators, but by the best generals of the world; I must run away from such an assailant, and avoid him if I have room, rather than stand my ground and defend myself; but if I have no room to escape, or if I run and am pursued to the wall or into a corner where I cannot elude his fury, and have no other way to preserve my own life from his violence, but by taking his there, I have an indisputable right to do it, and should be justified in wading through the blood of a whole army, if I had power to shed it and had no other way to make my escape.

What is said by Mr. W, that "if a gentleman should be hurried by his passions so far as to take the life of another, the common law will not adjudge it murder or manslaughter, but justifiable homicide only,"—by which he must mean, if in truth he had any meaning at all, that killing upon a sudden provocation is justifiable homicide,—is a position in comparison of which the observations of the grave-digger upon the death of the young lady, in Shakespeare's Hamlet, ought to be ranked among the *responsa prudentium*.

Every catechumen in law, nay, every common man, and even every porter upon the dock, that ever attended a trial for murder, knows that a sudden provocation raising a violent passion, where there is no precedent malice, is, in consideration of human frailty, allowed to soften killing from murder down to manslaughter; but manslaughter is a heinous crime, and subjected to heavy punishments.

Such is the wisdom and humanity of English law; upon so thorough a knowledge of human nature is it founded, and so well is it calculated to preserve the lives and limbs of men and the interior tranquillity of societies! I shall not dispute with Mr. X my affection for this law, in preference to all other systems of law that have ever appeared in the world. I have no connection with parishioners, nor patients, nor clients, nor any dependence upon either for business or bread; I study law as I do divinity and physic; and all of them as I do husbandry and mechanic arts, or the motions and revolutions of the heavenly bodies; or as I do magistracy and legislation; namely, as means and instruments of human happiness. It has been my amusement for many years past, as far as I have had leisure, to examine the systems of all the legislators, ancient and modern, fantastical and real, and to trace their effects in history upon the felicity of mankind; and the result of this long examination is a settled opinion that the liberty, the unalienable, indefeasible rights of men, the honor and dignity of human nature, the grandeur and glory of the public, and the universal happiness of individuals, were never so skilfully and successfully consulted as in that most excellent monument of human art, the common law of England; a law that maintains a great superiority, not only to every other system of laws, martial or canon, or civil and military, even to majesty itself; it has a never-sleeping jealousy of the canon law, which in many countries, Spain in particular, has subjected all officers and orders, civil and military, to the avarice and ambition, the caprice and cruelty of a clergy; and it is not less watchful over the martial law, which in many cases and in many countries, France in particular, is able to rescue men from the injustice of the municipal laws of the kingdom; and I will own, that to revive in the minds of my countrymen a reverence for this law, and to prevent the growth of sentiments that seemed to me to be in their tendency destructive of it, especially to revive a jealousy of martial laws and cavalier-like tempers, was the turn which I designed to serve for myself and my friends in that piece which had given offence to X and W.

A certain set of sentiments have been lately so fashionable, that you could go into few companies without hearing such smart sayings as these,—"If a man should insult me, by kicking my shins, and I had a sword by my side I would make the sun shine through him;"—"if any man, let him be as big as Golia[t—ED.]h, should take me by the nose, I would let his bowels out with my sword, if I had one, and if I had none, I would beat his brains out with the first club I could find." And such tempers have been animated by some inadvertent expressions that have fallen from persons of higher rank and better sentiments. Some of these have been heard to say, that "should a man offer a sudden insult to them, they could not answer for themselves, but they should lay him prostrate at their feet in his own blood." Such expressions as these, which are to be supposed but modest expressions of the speaker's diffidence of his own presence of mind, and government of his passions, when suddenly assaulted, have been taken for a justification of such returns to an insult, and a determination to practise them upon occasion. But such persons as are watching the lips of others for wise speeches, in order to utter them afterwards as their own sentiments, have generally as little of understanding as they have of spirit, and most miserably spoil, in reporting, a good reflection. Now, what I have written upon this subject was intended to show the inhumanity of taking away the life of a man, only for pulling my nose or boxing my ear; and the folly of it too, because I should be guilty of a high crime, that of manslaughter at least, and forfeit all my goods, besides receiving a brand of infamy.

But I have not yet finished my history of sentiments. It has been said by others that "no man ought to receive a blow without returning it;" "a man ought to be despised that receives a cuff without giving another in return." This I have heard declared for a sober opinion by some men of figure and office and importance. But I beg leave to repeat it,—this is the tenet of a coxcomb and the sentiment of a brute; and the horse, the bull, and the cock, that I mentioned before, daily discover precisely the same temper and the same sense of honor and decency. If, in walking the streets of this town, I should be met by a negro, and that negro should lay me over the head with his cudgel, should I think myself bound in honor or regard to reputation to return the blow with another cudgel? to put myself on a level with that negro, and join with him in a competition which was most expert and skilful at cudgels? If a mad dog should meet me and bite me, should I think myself bound in honor, (I mean before the poison had worked upon me enough to make me as mad as the dog himself,) to fall upon that dog and bite him again? It is not possible for me to express that depth of contempt that I feel for such sentiments, and for every mortal that entertains them; and I should choose to be "the butt, the jest, and contempt" of all companies that entertain such opinions, rather than to be in their admiration or esteem. I would take some other way to preserve myself and other men from such insolence and violence for the future; but I would never place myself upon a level with such an animal for the present.

Far from aiming at a reputation for such qualities and accomplishments as those of boxing or cuffing, a man of sense would hold even the true martial qualities, courage, strength, and skill in war, in a much lower estimation than the attributes of wisdom and virtue, skill in arts and sciences, and a true taste to what is right, what is fit, what is true, generous, manly, and noble, in civil life. The competition between Ajax and Ulysses is well known.

> "Tu vires sine mente geris, mihi cura futuri,
> Tu pugnare potes:
> Tu tantum corpore prodes,
> Nos animo;
> Pectora sunt potiora manu. Vigor omnis in illis." *3

And we know in whose favor the prize was decreed.

I shall not be at the pains of remarking upon all the rodomontade in the two pieces under consideration, and Mr. X and

---

*From the speech of Ulysses, in *Ovid. Metamorphos.* lib. iii. 1. 363–368.

Mr. W, and the whole alphabet of writers may scribble as many volumes as the twenty-four [*sic*—ED.] letters are capable of variations, without the least further notice from me, unless more reasoning and merit appear in proportion to the quantity of lines than is to be found in those two pieces. But since I have made some remarks upon them, it will, perhaps, before I conclude, be worth my while to mention one thing more in each. Mr. X tells us "that cases frequently occur where a man's person or reputation suffer to the greatest degree, and yet it is impossible for the law to make him any satisfaction."

This is not strictly true; such cases but seldom occur, though it must be confessed they sometimes do; but it seldom happens, very seldom indeed, where you know the man who has done you the injury, that you can get no satisfaction by law; and if such a case should happen, nothing can be clearer than that you ought to sit down and bear it; and for this plain reason, because it is necessary, and you cannot get satisfaction in any way. The law, by the supposition, cannot redress you; and you cannot, if you consider it, by any means redress yourself. A flagellation in the dark would be no reparation of the injury, no example to others, nor have any tendency to reform the subject of it, but rather a provocation to him to contrive some other way to injure you again; and of consequence would be no satisfaction at all to a man even of that false honor and delicacy of which I have been speaking, unless he will avow an appetite for mere revenge, which is not only worse than brutal, but the attribute of devils; and to take satisfaction by a flagellation in public would be only, in other words, taking a severe revenge upon yourself; for this would be a trespass and a violation of the peace, for which you would expose yourself to the resentment of the magistrate and the action of the party, and would be like running your sword through your own body to revenge yourself on another for boxing your ears; or like the behavior of the rattle-snake that will snap and leap and bite at every stick that you put near him, and at last when provoked beyond all honorable bearing, will fix his sharp and poisonous teeth into his own body.

I have nothing more to add, excepting one word of advice to

Mr. W and all his readers, to have a care how they believe or practise his rule about "passion and killing," lest the halter and the gibbet should become their portion; for a killing that should happen by the hurry of passion would be much more likely to be adjudged murder than justifiable homicide only. Let me conclude, by advising all men to look into their own hearts, which they will find to be deceitful above all things and desperately wicked. Let them consider how extremely addicted they are to magnify and exaggerate the injuries that are offered to themselves, and to diminish and extenuate the wrongs that they offer to others. They ought, therefore, to be too modest and diffident of their own judgment, when their own passions and prejudices and interests are concerned, to desire to judge for themselves in their own causes, and to take their own satisfactions for wrongs and injuries of any kind.

4

A DISSERTATION ON CANON AND FEUDAL LAW[1]

The Dissertation *was published in 1765 in response to the Stamp Act passed by the British Parliament, which would not only tax colonists without their consent but extend British juridical authority into the colonial court system. Adams sought to educate the colonists to appreciate the ways in which their settlements had escaped the "ecclesiastical authority" and "civil tyranny" of the Old World, the unopposed power of church and state that kept people in a condition of fear and obedience. He argued that Roman Catholicism and absolute monarchism were indifferent to the principle of natural rights derived from the social contract formed to bring humankind out of the state of nature. The Stamp Act had to be resisted, for resistance to unlawful authority is the meaning of liberty.*

Following close upon his Dissertation *was Adams's "Instructions of the Town of Braintree," a legal brief in defense of the town meeting's noncompliance with the Stamp Act. Braintree's representative was Ebenezer Thayer, and Adams told him how to present the case of resistance to the general court in the strongest possible terms, declaring that as long as the colonists were guided by liberal philosophy and Divine Providence, "we can never be slaves."*

"Ignorance and inconsideration are the two great causes of the ruin of mankind." This is an observation of Dr. Tillotson,[2] with relation to the interest of his fellow men in a future and immortal state. But it is of equal truth and importance if applied to the happiness of men in society, on this side the grave. In the earliest ages of the world, absolute monarchy seems to have been the universal form of government. Kings, and a few of their great counsellors and captains, exercised a cruel tyranny over the people, who held a rank in the scale of intelligence, in those days, but little higher than the camels and elephants that carried them and their engines to war.

By what causes it was brought to pass, that the people in the middle ages became more intelligent in general, would not, perhaps, be possible in these days to discover. But the fact is certain; and wherever a general knowledge and sensibility have prevailed among the people, arbitrary government and every kind of oppression have lessened and disappeared in proportion. Man has certainly an exalted soul; and the same principle in human nature,—that aspiring, noble principle founded in benevolence, and cherished by knowledge; I mean the love of power, which has been so often the cause of slavery,—has, whenever freedom has existed, been the cause of freedom. If it is this principle that has always prompted the princes and nobles of the earth, by every species of fraud and violence to shake off all the limitations of their power, it is the same that has always stimulated the common people to aspire at independency, and to endeavor at confining the power of the great within the limits of equity and reason.

The poor people, it is true, have been much less successful than the great. They have seldom found either leisure or opportunity to form a union and exert their strength; ignorant as they were of arts and letters, they have seldom been able to frame and support a regular opposition. This, however, has been known by the great to be the temper of mankind; and they have accordingly labored, in all ages, to wrest from the populace, as they are contemptuously called, the knowledge of their rights and wrongs, and the power to assert the former or redress the latter. I say RIGHTS, for such they have, undoubtedly, antecedent to all earthly government,—*Rights,* that cannot be repealed or restrained by human laws—*Rights,* derived from the great Legislator of the universe.

Since the promulgation of Christianity, the two greatest systems of tyranny that have sprung from this original, are the canon and the feudal law. The desire of dominion, that great principle by which we have attempted to account for so much good and so much evil, is, when properly restrained, a very useful and noble movement in the human mind. But when such restraints are taken off, it becomes an encroaching, grasping, restless, and ungovernable power. Numberless have been the systems of iniquity contrived by the great for the gratification of this passion in themselves; but in none of them were they ever more successful than in the invention and establishment of the canon and the feudal law.

By the former of these, the most refined, sublime, extensive, and astonishing constitution of policy that ever was conceived by the mind of man was framed by the Romish clergy for the aggrandisement of their own order. All the epithets I have here given to the Romish policy are just, and will be allowed to be so when it is considered, that they even persuaded mankind to believe, faithfully and undoubtingly, that God Almighty had entrusted them with the keys of heaven, whose gates they might open and close at pleasure; with a power of dispensation over all the rules and obligations of morality; with authority to license all sorts of sins and crimes; with a power of deposing princes and absolving subjects from allegiance; with a power of procuring or withholding the rain of heaven and the beams of the sun; with the management of earthquakes, pestilence, and famine; nay, with the mysterious, awful, incomprehensible power of creating out of bread and wine the flesh and blood of God himself. All these opinions they were enabled to spread and rivet among the people by reducing their minds to a state of sordid ignorance and staring timidity, and by infusing into them a religious horror of letters and knowledge. Thus was human nature chained fast for ages in a cruel, shameful, and deplorable servitude to him, and his subordinate tyrants, who, it was foretold, would exalt himself above all that was called God, and that was worshipped.

In the latter we find another system, similar in many respects to the former;* which, although it was originally formed, perhaps, for the necessary defence of a barbarous people against the inroads and invasions of her neighboring nations, yet for the same purposes of tyranny, cruelty, and lust, which had dictated the canon law, it was soon adopted by almost all the princes of Europe, and wrought into the constitutions of their government. It was originally a code of laws for a vast army in a perpetual encampment. The general was invested with the sovereign propriety of all the lands within the territory. Of him, as his servants and vassals, the first rank of his great officers held the lands; and in the same manner the other subordinate officers held of them; and all ranks and degrees held their lands by a variety of duties and services, all tending to bind the chains the faster on every order of mankind. In this manner the common people were held together in herds and clans in a state of servile dependence on their lords, bound, even by the tenure of their lands, to follow them, whenever they commanded, to their wars, and in a state of total ignorance of every thing divine and human, excepting the use of arms and the culture of their lands.

But another event still more calamitous to human liberty, was a wicked confederacy between the two systems of tyranny above described. It seems to have been even stipulated between them, that the temporal grandees should contribute every thing in their power to maintain the ascendency of the priesthood, and that the spiritual grandees in their turn, should employ their ascendency over the consciences of the people, in impressing on their minds a blind, implicit obedience to civil magistracy.

Thus, as long as this confederacy lasted, and the people were held in ignorance, liberty, and with her, knowledge and virtue too, seem to have deserted the earth, and one age of darkness succeeded another, till God in his benign providence raised up the champions who began and conducted the Reformation. From the time of the Reformation to the first settlement of America, knowledge gradually spread in Europe, but especially

*Rob. Hist. ch. v. pp. 178–9, &c.

in England; and in proportion as that increased and spread among the people, ecclesiastical and civil tyranny, which I use as synonymous expressions for the canon and feudal laws, seem to have lost their strength and weight. The people grew more and more sensible of the wrong that was done them by these systems, more and more impatient under it, and determined at all hazards to rid themselves of it; till at last, under the execrable race of the Stuarts, the struggle between the people and the confederacy aforesaid of temporal and spiritual tyranny, became formidable, violent, and bloody.

It was this great struggle that peopled America. It was not religion alone, as is commonly supposed; but it was a love of universal liberty, and a hatred, a dread, a horror, of the infernal confederacy before described, that projected, conducted, and accomplished the settlement of America.

It was a resolution formed by a sensible people,—I mean the Puritans,—almost in despair. They had become intelligent in general, and many of them learned. For this fact, I have the testimony of Archbishop King himself, who observed of that people, that they were more intelligent and better read than even the members of the church, whom he censures warmly for that reason. This people had been so vexed and tortured by the powers of those days, for no other crime than their knowledge and their freedom of inquiry and examination, and they had so much reason to despair of deliverance from those miseries on that side the ocean, that they at last resolved to fly to the wilderness for refuge from the temporal and spiritual principalities and powers, and plagues and scourges of their native country.

After their arrival here, they began their settlement, and formed their plan, both of ecclesiastical and civil government, in direct opposition to the canon and the feudal systems. The leading men among them, both of the clergy and the laity, were men of sense and learning. To many of them the historians, orators, poets, and philosophers of Greece and Rome were quite familiar; and some of them have left libraries that are still in being, consisting chiefly of volumes in which the wisdom of the most enlightened ages and nations is deposited,—written, however, in languages which their great-grandsons, though educated in European universities, can scarcely read.*

Thus accomplished were many of the first planters in these colonies. It may be thought polite and fashionable by many modern fine gentlemen, perhaps, to deride the characters of these persons, as enthusiastical, superstitious, and republican. But such ridicule is founded in nothing but foppery and affectation, and is grossly injurious and false. Religious to some degree of enthusiasm it may be admitted they were; but this can be no peculiar derogation from their character; because it was at that time almost the universal character not only of England, but of Christendom. Had this, however, been otherwise, their enthusiasm, considering the principles on which it was founded and the ends to which it was directed, far from being a reproach to them, was greatly to their honor; for I believe it will be found universally true, that no great enterprise for the honor or happiness of mankind was ever achieved without a large mixture of that noble infirmity. Whatever imperfections may be justly ascribed to them, which, however, are as few as any mortals have discovered, their judgment in framing their policy was founded in wise, humane, and benevolent principles. It was founded in revelation and in reason too. It was consistent with the principles of the best and greatest and wisest legislators of antiquity. Tyranny in every form, shape, and appearance was their disdain and abhorrence; no fear of punishment, nor even of death itself in exquisite tortures, had been sufficient to conquer that steady, manly, pertinacious spirit with which they had opposed the tyrants of those days in church and state. They were very far from being enemies to monarchy; and they knew as well as any men, the just regard and honor that is due to the character of a dispenser of the mysteries of the gospel of grace. But they saw clearly, that popular powers must be placed as a guard, a control, a balance, to the powers of the monarch and

---

* "I always consider the settlement of America with reverence and wonder, as the opening of a grand scene and design in Providence for the illumination of the ignorant, and the emancipation of the slavish part of mankind all over the earth."

the priest, in every government, or else it would soon become the man of sin, the whore of Babylon, the mystery of iniquity, a great and detestable system of fraud, violence, and usurpation. Their greatest concern seems to have been to establish a government of the church more consistent with the Scriptures, and a government of the state more agreeable to the dignity of human nature, than any they had seen in Europe, and to transmit such a government down to their posterity, with the means of securing and preserving it forever. To render the popular power in their new government as great and wise as their principles of theory, that is, as human nature and the Christian religion require it should be, they endeavored to remove from it as many of the feudal inequalities and dependencies as could be spared, consistently with the preservation of a mild limited monarchy. And in this they discovered the depth of their wisdom and the warmth of their friendship to human nature. But the first place is due to religion. They saw clearly, that of all the nonsense and delusion which had ever passed through the mind of man, none had ever been more extravagant than the notions of absolutions, indelible characters, uninterrupted successions, and the rest of those fantastical ideas, derived from the canon law, which had thrown such a glare of mystery, sanctity, reverence, and right reverend eminence and holiness, around the idea of a priest, as no mortal could deserve, and as always must, from the constitution of human nature, be dangerous in society. For this reason, they demolished the whole system of diocesan episcopacy; and, deriding, as all reasonable and impartial men must do, the ridiculous fancies of sanctified effluvia from episcopal fingers, they established sacerdotal ordination on the foundation of the Bible and common sense. This conduct at once imposed an obligation on the whole body of the clergy to industry, virtue, piety, and learning, and rendered that whole body infinitely more independent on the civil powers, in all respects, than they could be where they were formed into a scale of subordination, from a pope down to priests and friars and confessors,—necessarily and essentially a sordid, stupid, and wretched herd,—or than they could be in any other country, where an archbishop held the place of a universal bishop, and the vicars and curates that of the ignorant, dependent, miserable rabble aforesaid,—and infinitely more sensible and learned than they could be in either. This subject has been seen in the same light by many illustrious patriots, who have lived in America since the days of our forefathers, and who have adored their memory for the same reason. And methinks there has not appeared in New England a stronger veneration for their memory, a more penetrating insight into the grounds and principles and spirit of their policy, nor a more earnest desire of perpetuating the blessings of it to posterity, than that fine institution of the late Chief Justice Dudley, of a lecture against popery, and on the validity of presbyterian ordination. This was certainly intended by that wise and excellent man, as an eternal memento of the wisdom and goodness of the very principles that settled America. But I must again return to the feudal law. The adventurers so often mentioned, had an utter contempt of all that dark ribaldry of hereditary, indefeasible right,—the Lord's anointed,—and the divine, miraculous original of government, with which the priesthood had enveloped the feudal monarch in clouds and mysteries, and from whence they had deduced the most mischievous of all doctrines, that of passive obedience and non-resistance. They knew that government was a plain, simple, intelligible thing, founded in nature and reason, and quite comprehensible by common sense. They detested all the base services and servile dependencies of the feudal system. They knew that no such unworthy dependencies took place in the ancient seats of liberty, the republics of Greece and Rome; and they thought all such slavish subordinations were equally inconsistent with the constitution of human nature and that religious liberty with which Jesus had made them free. This was certainly the opinion they had formed; and they were far from being singular or extravagant in thinking so. Many celebrated modern writers in Europe have espoused the same sentiments. Lord Kames, a Scottish writer of great reputation, whose authority in this case ought to have the more weight as his countrymen have not the most worthy ideas of liberty, speaking of the feudal law, says,—"A constitution so contradictory to all the principles which govern mankind can never be brought about, one should imagine, but by foreign conquest or native usurpations."* Rousseau, speaking of the same system, calls it,—"That most iniquitous and absurd form of government by which human nature was so shamefully degraded."† It would be easy to multiply authorities, but it must be needless; because, as the original of this form of government was among savages, as the spirit of it is military and despotic, every writer who would allow the people to have any right to life or property or freedom more than the beasts of the field, and who was not hired or enlisted under arbitrary, lawless power, has been always willing to admit the feudal system to be inconsistent with liberty and the rights of mankind.

To have holden their lands allodially, or for every man to have been the sovereign lord and proprietor of the ground he occupied, would have constituted a government too nearly like a commonwealth. They were contented, therefore, to hold their lands of their king, as their sovereign lord; and to him they were willing to render homage, but to no mesne or subordinate lords; nor were they willing to submit to any of the baser services. In all this they were so strenuous, that they have even transmitted to their posterity a very general contempt and detestation of holdings by quitrents, as they have also a hereditary ardor for liberty and thirst for knowledge.

They were convinced, by their knowledge of human nature, derived from history and their own experience, that nothing could preserve their posterity from the encroachments of the two systems of tyranny, in opposition to which, as has been observed already, they erected their government in church and state, but knowledge diffused generally through the whole body of the people. Their civil and religious principles, therefore, conspired to prompt them to use every measure and take every precaution in their power to propagate and perpetuate knowledge. For this purpose they laid very early the foundations of colleges, and invested them with ample privileges and emoluments; and it is remarkable that they have left among

*Brit. Ant. p. 2.
†Social Compact, page 164.

their posterity so universal an affection and veneration for those seminaries, and for liberal education, that the meanest of the people contribute cheerfully to the support and maintenance of them every year, and that nothing is more generally popular than projections for the honor, reputation, and advantage of those seats of learning. But the wisdom and benevolence of our fathers rested not here. They made an early provision by law, that every town consisting of so many families, should be always furnished with a grammar school. They made it a crime for such a town to be destitute of a grammar schoolmaster for a few months, and subjected it to a heavy penalty. So that the education of all ranks of people was made the care and expense of the public, in a manner that I believe has been unknown to any other people ancient or modern.

The consequences of these establishments we see and feel every day. A native of America who cannot read and write is as rare an appearance as a Jacobite or a Roman Catholic, that is, as rare as a comet or an earthquake. It has been observed, that we are all of us lawyers, divines, politicians, and philosophers. And I have good authorities to say, that all candid foreigners who have passed through this country, and conversed freely with all sorts of people here, will allow, that they have never seen so much knowledge and civility among the common people in any part of the world. It is true, there has been among us a party for some years, consisting chiefly not of the descendants of the first settlers of this country, but of high churchmen and high statesmen imported since, who affect to censure this provision for the education of our youth as a needless expense, and an imposition upon the rich in favor of the poor, and as an institution productive of idleness and vain speculation among the people, whose time and attention, it is said, ought to be devoted to labor, and not to public affairs, or to examination into the conduct of their superiors. And certain officers of the crown, and certain other missionaries of ignorance, foppery, servility, and slavery, have been most inclined to countenance and increase the same party. Be it remembered, however, that liberty must at all hazards be supported. We have a right to it, derived from our Maker. But if we had not, our fathers have earned and bought it for us, at the expense of their ease, their estates, their pleasure, and their blood. And liberty cannot be preserved without a general knowledge among the people, who have a right, from the frame of their nature, to knowledge, as their great Creator, who does nothing in vain, has given them understandings, and a desire to know; but besides this, they have a right, an indisputable, unalienable, indefeasible, divine right to that most dreaded and envied kind of knowledge, I mean, of the characters and conduct of their rulers. Rulers are no more than attorneys, agents, and trustees, for the people; and if the cause, the interest and trust, is insidiously betrayed, or wantonly trifled away, the people have a right to revoke the authority that they themselves have deputed, and to constitute abler and better agents, attorneys, and trustees. And the preservation of the means of knowledge among the lowest ranks, is of more importance to the public than all the property of all the rich men in the country. It is even of more consequence to the rich themselves, and to their posterity. The only question is, whether it is a public emolument; and if it is, the rich ought undoubtedly to contribute, in the same proportion as to all other public burdens,—that is, in proportion to their wealth, which is secured by public expenses. But none of the means of information are more sacred, or have been cherished with more tenderness and care by the settlers of America, than the press. Care has been taken that the art of printing should be encouraged, and that it should be easy and cheap and safe for any person to communicate his thoughts to the public. And you, Messieurs printers,* whatever the tyrants of the earth may say of your paper, have done important service to your country by your readiness and freedom in publishing the speculations of the curious. The stale, impudent insinuations of slander and sedition, with which the gormandizers of power have endeavored to discredit your paper, are so much the more to your honor; for the jaws of power are always opened to devour, and her arm is always stretched out, if possible, to destroy the freedom of thinking, speaking, and writing. And if the public in-

*Edes and Gill, printers of the Boston Gazette.

terest, liberty, and happiness have been in danger from the ambition or avarice of any great man, whatever may be his politeness, address, learning, ingenuity, and, in other respects, integrity and humanity, you have done yourselves honor and your country service by publishing and pointing out that avarice and ambition. These vices are so much the more dangerous and pernicious for the virtues with which they may be accompanied in the same character, and with so much the more watchful jealousy to be guarded against.

"Curse on such virtues, they've undone their country."

Be not intimidated, therefore, by any terrors, from publishing with the utmost freedom, whatever can be warranted by the laws of your country; nor suffer yourselves to be wheedled out of your liberty by any pretences of politeness, delicacy, or decency. These, as they are often used, are but three different names for hypocrisy, chicanery, and cowardice. Much less, I presume, will you be discouraged by any pretences that malignants on this side the water will represent your paper as factious and seditious, or that the great on the other side the water will take offence at them. This dread of representation has had for a long time, in this province, effects very similar to what the physicians call a hydropho, or dread of water. It has made us delirious; and we have rushed headlong into the water, till we are almost drowned, out of simple or phrensical fear of it. Believe me, the character of this country has suffered more in Britain by the pusillanimity with which we have borne many insults and indignities from the creatures of power at home and the creatures of those creatures here, than it ever did or ever will by the freedom and spirit that has been or will be discovered in writing or action. Believe me, my countrymen, they have imbibed an opinion on the other side the water, that we are an ignorant, a timid, and a stupid people; nay, their tools on this side have often impudence to dispute your bravery. But I hope in God the time is near at hand when they will be fully convinced of your understanding, integrity, and courage. But can any thing be more ridiculous, were it not too provoking to be laughed at, than to pretend that offence should be taken at home for writings here? Pray, let them look at home. Is not the human understanding exhausted there? Are not reason, imagination, wit, passion, senses, and all, tortured to find out satire and invective against the characters of the vile and futile fellows who sometimes get into place and power? The most exceptionable paper that ever I saw here is perfect prudence and modesty in comparison of multitudes of their applauded writings. Yet the high regard they have for the freedom of the press, indulges all. I must and will repeat it, your paper deserves the patronage of every friend to his country. And whether the defamers of it are arrayed in robes of scarlet or sable, whether they lurk and skulk in an insurance office, whether they assume the venerable character of a priest, the sly one of a scrivener, or the dirty, infamous, abandoned one of an informer, they are all the creatures and tools of the lust of domination.

The true source of our sufferings has been our timidity.

We have been afraid to think. We have felt a reluctance to examining into the grounds of our privileges, and the extent in which we have an indisputable right to demand them, against all the power and authority on earth. And many who have not scrupled to examine for themselves, have yet for certain prudent reasons been cautious and diffident of declaring the result of their inquiries.

The cause of this timidity is perhaps hereditary, and to be traced back in history as far as the cruel treatment the first settlers of this country received, before their embarkation for America, from the government at home. Everybody knows how dangerous it was to speak or write in favor of any thing, in those days, but the triumphant system of religion and politics. And our fathers were particularly the objects of the persecutions and proscriptions of the times. It is not unlikely, therefore, that although they were inflexibly steady in refusing their positive assent to any thing against their principles, they might have contracted habits of reserve, and a cautious diffidence of asserting their opinions publicly. These habits they probably brought with them to America, and have transmitted down to us. Or we may possibly account for this appearance by the great affection and veneration Americans have always entertained for the country from whence they sprang; or by the quiet temper for which they have been remarkable, no country having been less disposed to discontent than this; or by a sense they have that it is their duty to acquiesce under the administration of government, even when in many smaller matters grievous to them, and until the essentials of the great compact are destroyed or invaded. These peculiar causes might operate upon them; but without these, we all know that human nature itself, from indolence, modesty, humanity, or fear, has always too much reluctance to a manly assertion of its rights. Hence, perhaps, it has happened, that nine tenths of the species are groaning and gasping in misery and servitude.

But whatever the cause has been, the fact is certain, we have been excessively cautious of giving offence by complaining of grievances. And it is as certain, that American governors, and their friends, and all the crown officers, have availed themselves of this disposition in the people. They have prevailed on us to consent to many things which were grossly injurious to us, and to surrender many others, with voluntary tameness, to which we had the clearest right. Have we not been treated, formerly, with abominable insolence, by officers of the navy? I mean no insinuation against any gentleman now on this station, having heard no complaint of any one of them to his dishonor. Have not some generals from England treated us like servants, nay, more like slaves than like Britons? Have we not been under the most ignominious contribution, the most abject submission, the most supercilious insults, of some custom-house officers? Have we not been trifled with, brow-beaten, and trampled on, by former governors, in a manner which no king of England since James the Second has dared to indulge towards his subjects? Have we not raised up one family, in them placed an unlimited confidence, and been soothed and flattered and intimidated by their influence, into a great part of this infamous tameness and submission? "These are serious and alarming questions, and deserve a dispassionate consideration."

This disposition has been the great wheel and the mainspring in the American machine of court politics. We have been told that "the word *rights* is an offensive expression;" "that the king, his ministry, and parliament, will not endure to hear Americans talk of their *rights;*" "that Britain is the mother and we the children, that a filial duty and submission is due from us to her," and that "we ought to doubt our own judgment, and presume that she is right, even when she seems to us to shake the foundations of government;" that "Britain is immensely rich and great and powerful, has fleets and armies at her command which have been the dread and terror of the universe, and that she will force her own judgment into execution, right or wrong." But let me entreat you, sir, to pause. Do you consider yourself as a missionary of loyalty or of rebellion? Are you not representing your king, his ministry, and parliament, as tyrants,—imperious, unrelenting tyrants,—by such reasoning as this? Is not this representing your most gracious sovereign as endeavoring to destroy the foundations of his own throne? Are you not representing every member of parliament as renouncing the transactions at Runing Mede, (the meadow, near Windsor, where Magna Charta was signed;) and as repealing in effect the bill of rights, when the Lords and Commons asserted and vindicated the rights of the people and their own rights, and insisted on the king's assent to that assertion and vindication? Do you not represent them as forgetting that the prince of Orange was created King William, by the people, on purpose that their rights might be eternal and inviolable? Is there not something extremely fallacious in the common-place images of mother country and children colonies? Are we the children of Great Britain any more than the cities of London, Exeter, and Bath? Are we not brethren and fellow subjects with those in Britain, only under a somewhat different method of legislation, and a totally different method of taxation? But admitting we are children, have not children a right to complain when their parents are attempting to break their limbs, to administer poison, or to sell them to enemies for slaves? Let me entreat you to consider, will the mother be pleased when you represent her as deaf to the cries of her children,—when you compare her to the infamous miscreant who lately stood on the gallows for starv-

ing her child,—when you resemble her to Lady Macbeth in
Shakespeare, (I cannot think of it without horror,) who

> "Had given suck, and knew
> How tender 'twas to love the babe that milked her,"

but yet, who could

> "Even while 't smiling in her face,
> Have plucked her nipple from the boneless gums,
> And dashed the brains out."

Let us banish for ever from our minds, my countrymen, all
such unworthy ideas of the king, his ministry, and parliament.
Let us not suppose that all are become luxurious, effeminate,
and unreasonable, on the other side the water, as many design-
ing persons would insinuate. Let us presume, what is in fact
true, that the spirit of liberty is as ardent as ever among the
body of the nation, though a few individuals may be corrupted.
Let us take it for granted, that the same great spirit which once
gave Cæsar so warm a reception, which denounced hostilities
against John till Magna Charta was signed, which severed the
head of Charles the First from his body, and drove James the
Second from his kingdom, the same great spirit (may heaven
preserve it till the earth shall be no more) which first seated the
great grandfather of his present most gracious majesty on the
throne of Britain,—is still alive and active and warm in England; and that the same spirit in America, instead of provoking the inhabitants of that country, will endear us to them for
ever, and secure their good-will.

This spirit, however, without knowledge, would be little better than a brutal rage. Let us tenderly and kindly cherish, therefore, the means of knowledge. Let us dare to read, think, speak,
and write. Let every order and degree among the people rouse
their attention and animate their resolution. Let them all become attentive to the grounds and principles of government,
ecclesiastical and civil. Let us study the law of nature; search
into the spirit of the British constitution; read the histories of

ancient ages; contemplate the great examples of Greece and Rome; set before us the conduct of our own British ancestors, who have defended for us the inherent rights of mankind against foreign and domestic tyrants and usurpers, against arbitrary kings and cruel priests, in short, against the gates of earth and hell. Let us read and recollect and impress upon our souls the views and ends of our own more immediate forefathers, in exchanging their native country for a dreary, inhospitable wilderness. Let us examine into the nature of that power, and the cruelty of that oppression, which drove them from their homes. Recollect their amazing fortitude, their bitter sufferings,—the hunger, the nakedness, the cold, which they patiently endured,—the severe labors of clearing their grounds, building their houses, raising their provisions, amidst dangers from wild beasts and savage men, before they had time or money or materials for commerce. Recollect the civil and religious principles and hopes and expectations which constantly supported and carried them through all hardships with patience and resignation. Let us recollect it was liberty, the hope of liberty for themselves and us and ours, which conquered all discouragements, dangers, and trials. In such researches as these, let us all in our several departments cheerfully engage,— but especially the proper patrons and supporters of law, learning, and religion!

Let the pulpit resound with the doctrines and sentiments of religious liberty. Let us hear the danger of thraldom to our consciences from ignorance, extreme poverty, and dependence, in short, from civil and political slavery. Let us see delineated before us the true map of man. Let us hear the dignity of his nature, and the noble rank he holds among the works of God,—that consenting to slavery is a sacrilegious breach of trust, as offensive in the sight of God as it is derogatory from our own honor or interest or happiness,—and that God Almighty has promulgated from heaven, liberty, peace, and good-will to man!

Let the bar proclaim, "the laws, the rights, the generous plan of power" delivered down from remote antiquity,—inform the world of the mighty struggles and numberless sacrifices made by our ancestors in defence of freedom. Let it be known, that British liberties are not the grants of princes or parliaments, but original rights, conditions of original contracts, coequal with prerogative, and coeval with government; that many of our rights are inherent and essential, agreed on as maxims, and established as preliminaries, even before a parliament existed. Let them search for the foundations of British laws and government in the frame of human nature, in the constitution of the intellectual and moral world. There let us see that truth, liberty, justice, and benevolence, are its everlasting basis; and if these could be removed, the superstructure is overthrown of course.

Let the colleges join their harmony in the same delightful concert. Let every declamation turn upon the beauty of liberty and virtue, and the deformity, turpitude, and malignity, of slavery and vice. Let the public disputations become researches into the grounds and nature and ends of government, and the means of preserving the good and demolishing the evil. Let the dialogues, and all the exercises, become the instruments of impressing on the tender mind, and of spreading and distributing far and wide, the ideas of right and the sensations of freedom.

In a word, let every sluice of knowledge be opened and set a-flowing. The encroachments upon liberty in the reigns of the first James and the first Charles, by turning the general attention of learned men to government, are said to have produced the greatest number of consummate statesmen which has ever been seen in any age or nation. The Brookes, Hampdens, Vanes, Seldens, Miltons, Nedhams, Harringtons, Nevilles, Sidneys, Lockes, are all said to have owed their eminence in political knowledge to the tyrannies of those reigns. The prospect now before us in America, ought in the same manner to engage the attention of every man of learning, to matters of power and of right, that we may be neither led nor driven blindfolded to irretrievable destruction. Nothing less than this seems to have been meditated for us, by somebody or other in Great Britain. There seems to be a direct and formal design on foot, to enslave all America. This, however, must be done by degrees. The first step that is intended, seems to be an entire subversion of the whole system of our fathers, by the introduction of the canon and feudal law into America. The canon and feudal systems, though greatly mutilated in England, are not yet destroyed. Like the temples and palaces in which the great contrivers of them once worshipped and inhabited, they exist in ruins; and much of the domineering spirit of them still remains. The designs and labors of a certain society, to introduce the former of them into America, have been well exposed to the public by a writer of great abilities;* and the further attempts to the same purpose, that may be made by that society, or by the ministry or parliament, I leave to the conjectures of the thoughtful. But it seems very manifest from the Stamp Act itself, that a design is formed to strip us in a great measure of the means of knowledge, by loading the press, the colleges, and even an almanack and a newspaper, with restraints and duties; and to introduce the inequalities and dependencies of the feudal system, by taking from the poorer sort of people all their little subsistence, and conferring it on a set of stamp officers, distributors, and their deputies. But I must proceed no further at present. The sequel, whenever I shall find health and leisure to pursue it, will be a "disquisition of the policy of the stamp act." In the mean time, however, let me add,—These are not the vapors of a melancholy mind, nor the effusions of envy, disappointed ambition, nor of a spirit of opposition to government, but the emanations of a heart that burns for its country's welfare. No one of any feeling, born and educated in this once happy country, can consider the numerous distresses, the gross indignities, the barbarous ignorance, the haughty usurpations, that we have reason to fear are meditating for ourselves, our children, our neighbors, in short, for all our countrymen and all their posterity, without the utmost agonies of heart and many tears.

*The late Rev. Dr. Mayhew.

INSTRUCTIONS OF
THE TOWN OF BRAINTREE

TO THEIR REPRESENTATIVE, 1765.

Boston, 14 October [1765].*
We hear from Braintree, that the freeholders and
other inhabitants of that town, legally assembled,
on Tuesday, the twenty-fourth of September last,
unanimously voted, that instructions should be
given their representative for his conduct in General
Assembly on this great occasion. The substance of
these instructions is as follows:—

To Ebenezer Thayer, Esq.

Sir,—In all the calamities which have ever befallen this country,
we have never felt so great a concern, or such alarming apprehensions, as on this occasion. Such is our loyalty to the King,
our veneration for both houses of Parliament, and our affection for all our fellow-subjects in Britain, that measures which
discover any unkindness in that country towards us are the
more sensibly and intimately felt. And we can no longer forbear complaining, that many of the measures of the late ministry, and some of the late acts of Parliament, have a tendency in
our apprehension, to divest us of our most essential rights and
liberties. We shall confine ourselves, however, chiefly to the act
of Parliament, commonly called the Stamp Act, by which a
very burthensome, and, in our opinion, unconstitutional tax,
is to be laid upon us all; and we subjected to numerous and
enormous penalties, to be prosecuted, sued for, and recovered,
at the option of an informer, in a court of admiralty, without a
jury.

*Printed from the Boston Gazette, of Monday, 14 October, 1765.

We have called this a burthensome tax, because the duties are so numerous and so high, and the embarrassments to business in this infant, sparsely-settled country so great, that it would be totally impossible for the people to subsist under it, if we had no controversy at all about the right and authority of imposing it. Considering the present scarcity of money, we have reason to think, the execution of that act for a short space of time would drain the country of its cash, strip multitudes of all their property, and reduce them to absolute beggary. And what the consequence would be to the peace of the province, from so sudden a shock and such a convulsive change in the whole course of our business and subsistence, we tremble to consider. We further apprehend this tax to be unconstitutional. We have always understood it to be a grand and fundamental principle of the constitution, that no freeman should be subject to any tax to which he has not given his own consent, in person or by proxy. And the maxims of the law, as we have constantly received them, are to the same effect, that no freeman can be separated from his property but by his own act or fault. We take it clearly, therefore, to be inconsistent with the spirit of the common law, and of the essential fundamental principles of the British constitution, that we should be subject to any tax imposed by the British Parliament; because we are not represented in that assembly in any sense, unless it be by a fiction of law, as insensible in theory as it would be injurious in practice, if such a taxation should be grounded on it.

But the most grievous innovation of all, is the alarming extension of the power of courts of admiralty. In these courts, one judge presides alone! No juries have any concern there! The law and the fact are both to be decided by the same single judge, whose commission is only during pleasure, and with whom, as we are told, the most mischievous of all customs has become established, that of taking commissions on all condemnations; so that he is under a pecuniary temptation always against the subject. Now, if the wisdom of the mother country has thought the independency of the judges so essential to an impartial administration of justice, as to render them independent of every power on earth,—independent of the King, the Lords, the Commons, the people, nay, independent in hope and expectation of the heir-apparent, by continuing their commissions after a demise of the crown, what justice and impartiality are we, at three thousand miles distance from the fountain, to expect from such a judge of admiralty? We have all along thought the acts of trade in this respect a grievance; but the Stamp Act has opened a vast number of sources of new crimes, which may be committed by any man, and cannot but be committed by multitudes, and prodigious penalties are annexed, and all these are to be tried by such a judge of such a court! What can be wanting, after this, but a weak or wicked man for a judge, to render us the most sordid and forlorn of slaves?—we mean the slaves of a slave of the servants of a minister of state. We cannot help asserting, therefore, that this part of the act will make an essential change in the constitution of juries, and it is directly repugnant to the Great Charter itself; for, by that charter, "no americiament shall be assessed, but by the oath of honest and lawful men of the vicinage;" and, "no freeman shall be taken, or imprisoned, or disseized of his freehold, or liberties of free customs, nor passed upon, nor condemned, but by lawful judgment of his peers, or by the law of the land." So that this act will "make such a distinction, and create such a difference between" the subjects in Great Britain and those in America, as we could not have expected from the guardians of liberty in "both."

As these, sir, are our sentiments of this act, we, the freeholders and other inhabitants, legally assembled for this purpose, must enjoin it upon you, to comply with no measures or proposals for countenancing the same, or assisting in the execution of it, but by all lawful means, consistent with our allegiance to the King, and relation to Great Britain, to oppose the execution of it, till we can hear the success of the cries and petitions of America for relief.

We further recommend the most clear and explicit assertion and vindication of our rights and liberties to be entered on the public records, that the world may know, in the present and all future generations, that we have a clear knowledge and a just sense of them, and, with submission to Divine Providence, that we never can be slaves.*

Nor can we think it advisable to agree to any steps for the protection of stamped papers or stamp-officers. Good and wholesome laws we have already for the preservation of the peace; and we apprehend there is no further danger of tumult and disorder, to which we have a well-grounded aversion; and that any extraordinary and expensive exertions would tend to exasperate the people and endanger the public tranquillity, rather than the contrary. Indeed, we cannot too often inculcate upon you our desires, that all extraordinary grants and expensive measures may, upon all occasions, as much as possible, be avoided. The public money of this country is the toil and labor of the people, who are under many uncommon difficulties and distresses at this time, so that all reasonable frugality ought to be observed. And we would recommend particularly, the strictest care and the utmost firmness to prevent all unconstitutional draughts upon the public treasury.

---

*A Cambridge correspondent of the Evening Post, in October, 1765, enters into a comparison of these instructions with some of an opposite nature, coming from Marblehead, and published at the same time, and picks out this paragraph, as "worthy to be wrote in letters of gold."

5
"THOUGHTS ON GOVERNMENT"[1]

Adams's essay was a response to Thomas Paine's Common Sense, *a powerful polemic that convinced America that it should declare its independence from Britain. Adams believed, as he told Abigail, that Paine was more interested in tearing down government than in giving any thought to reconstituting it. Adams's statement appeared in 1776, a time when America was breaking with England and the various colonies were considering framing their own state constitutions.*

My dear Sir,—If I was equal to the task of forming a plan for the government of a colony, I should be flattered with your request, and very happy to comply with it; because, as the divine science of politics is the science of social happiness, and the blessings of society depend entirely on the constitutions of government, which are generally institutions that last for many generations, there can be no employment more agreeable to a benevolent mind than a research after the best.

Pope flattered tyrants too much when he said,

> "For forms of government let fools contest,
> That which is best administered is best."

Nothing can be more fallacious than this. But poets read history to collect flowers, not fruits; they attend to fanciful images, not the effects of social institutions. Nothing is more certain from the history of nations and nature of man, than that some forms of government are better fitted for being well administered than others.

We ought to consider what is the end of government, before we determine which is the best form. Upon this point all speculative politicians will agree, that the happiness of society is the end of government, as all divines and moral philosophers will agree that the happiness of the individual is the end of man. From this principle it will follow, that the form of government which communicates ease, comfort, security, or, in one word, happiness, to the greatest number of persons, and in the greatest degree, is the best.

All sober inquirers after truth, ancient and modern, pagan and Christian, have declared that the happiness of man, as well as his dignity, consists in virtue. Confucius, Zoroaster, Socrates, Mahomet, not to mention authorities really sacred, have agreed in this.

If there is a form of government, then, whose principle and foundation is virtue, will not every sober man acknowledge it better calculated to promote the general happiness than any other form?

Fear is the foundation of most governments; but it is so sordid and brutal a passion, and renders men in whose breasts it predominates so stupid and miserable, that Americans will not be likely to approve of any political institution which is founded on it.

Honor is truly sacred, but holds a lower rank in the scale of moral excellence than virtue. Indeed, the former is but a part of the latter, and consequently has not equal pretensions to support a frame of government productive of human happiness.

The foundation of every government is some principle or passion in the minds of the people. The noblest principles and most generous affections in our nature, then, have the fairest chance to support the noblest and most generous models of government.

A man must be indifferent to the sneers of modern Englishmen, to mention in their company the names of Sidney, Harrington, Locke, Milton, Nedham, Neville, Burnet, and

Hoadly. No small fortitude is necessary to confess that one has read them. The wretched condition of this country, however, for ten or fifteen years past, has frequently reminded me of their principles and reasonings. They will convince any candid mind, that there is no good government but what is republican. That the only valuable part of the British constitution is so; because the very definition of a republic is "an empire of laws, and not of men." That, as a republic is the best of governments, so that particular arrangement of the powers of society, or, in other words, that form of government which is best contrived to secure an impartial and exact execution of the laws, is the best of republics.

Of republics there is an inexhaustible variety, because the possible combinations of the powers of society are capable of innumerable variations.

As good government is an empire of laws, how shall your laws be made? In a large society, inhabiting an extensive country, it is impossible that the whole should assemble to make laws. The first necessary step, then, is to depute power from the many to a few of the most wise and good. But by what rules shall you choose your representatives? Agree upon the number and qualifications of persons who shall have the benefit of choosing, or annex this privilege to the inhabitants of a certain extent of ground.

The principal difficulty lies, and the greatest care should be employed, in constituting this representative assembly. It should be in miniature an exact portrait of the people at large. It should think, feel, reason, and act like them. That it may be the interest of this assembly to do strict justice at all times, it should be an equal representation, or, in other words, equal interests among the people should have equal interests in it. Great care should be taken to effect this, and to prevent unfair, partial, and corrupt elections. Such regulations, however, may be better made in times of greater tranquillity than the present; and they will spring up themselves naturally, when all the powers of government come to be in the hands of the people's friends. At present, it will be safest to proceed in all established modes, to which the people have been familiarized by habit.

all power cannot be in one place

A representation of the people in one assembly being obtained, a question arises, whether all the powers of government, legislative, executive, and judicial, shall be left in this body? ⌈I think a people cannot be long free, nor ever happy, whose government is in one assembly.⌉ My reasons for this opinion are as follow:—

1. A single assembly is liable to all the vices, follies, and frailties of an individual; subject to fits of humor, starts of passion, flights of enthusiasm, partialities, or prejudice, and consequently productive of hasty results and absurd judgments. And all these errors ought to be corrected and defects supplied by some controlling power.

2. A single assembly is apt to be avaricious, and in time will not scruple to exempt itself from burdens, which it will lay, without compunction, on its constituents.

3. A single assembly is apt to grow ambitious, and after a time will not hesitate to vote itself perpetual. This was one fault of the Long Parliament; but more remarkably of Holland, whose assembly first voted themselves from annual to septennial, then for life, and after a course of years, that all vacancies happening by death or otherwise, should be filled by themselves, without any application to constituents at all.

4. A representative assembly, although extremely well qualified, and absolutely necessary, as a branch of the legislative, is unfit to exercise the executive power, for want of two essential properties, secrecy and despatch.

5. A representative assembly is still less qualified for the judicial power, because it is too numerous, too slow, and too little skilled in the laws.

6. Because a single assembly, possessed of all the powers of government, would make arbitrary laws for their own interest, execute all laws arbitrarily for their own interest, and adjudge all controversies in their own favor.

But shall the whole power of legislation rest in one assembly? Most of the foregoing reasons apply equally to prove that the legislative power ought to be more complex; to which we may add, that if the legislative power is wholly in one assembly, and the executive in another, or in a single person, these two powers will oppose and encroach upon each other, until the contest shall end in war, and the whole power, legislative and executive, be usurped by the strongest.

The judicial power, in such case, could not mediate, or hold the balance between the two contending powers, because the legislative would undermine it. And this shows the necessity, too, of giving the executive power a negative upon the legislative, otherwise this will be continually encroaching upon that.

[To avoid these dangers, let a distinct assembly be constituted, as a mediator between the two extreme branches of the legislature, that which represents the people, and that which is vested with the executive power.]

Let the representative assembly then elect by ballot, from among themselves or their constituents, or both, a distinct assembly, which, for the sake of perspicuity, we will call a council. It may consist of any number you please, say twenty or thirty, and should have a free and independent exercise of its judgment, and consequently a negative voice in the legislature.

[These two bodies, thus constituted, and made integral parts of the legislature, let them unite, and by joint ballot choose a governor,] who, after being stripped of most of those badges of domination, called prerogatives, [should have a free and independent exercise of his judgment, and be made also an integral part of the legislature.] This, I know, is liable to objections; and, if you please, you may make him only president of the council, as in Connecticut. But as the governor is to be invested with the executive power, with consent of council, I think he ought to have a negative upon the legislative. If he is annually elective, as he ought to be, he will always have so much reverence and affection for the people, their representatives and counsellors, that, although you give him an independent exercise of his judgment, he will seldom use it in opposition to the two houses, except in cases the public utility of which would be conspicuous; and some such cases would happen.

In the present exigency of American affairs, when, by an act of Parliament, we are put out of the royal protection, and con-

legislature & executive

sequently discharged from our allegiance, and it has become
necessary to assume government for our immediate security,
the governor, lieutenant-governor, secretary, treasurer, commis-
sary, attorney-general, should be chosen by joint ballot of both
houses. And these and all other elections, especially of representatives and counsellors, should be annual, there not being in
the whole circle of the sciences a maxim more infallible than
this, "where annual elections end, there slavery begins."

These great men, in this respect, should be, once a year,

> "Like bubbles on the sea of matter borne,
> They rise, they break, and to that sea return."

This will teach them the great political virtues of humility, patience, and moderation, without which every man in power becomes a ravenous beast of prey.

This mode of constituting the great offices of state will answer very well for the present; but if by experiment it should be
found inconvenient, the legislature may, at its leisure, devise
other methods of creating them, by elections of the people at
large, as in Connecticut, or it may enlarge the term for which
they shall be chosen to seven years, or three years, or for life, or
make any other alterations which the society shall find productive of its ease, its safety, its freedom, or, in one word, its happiness.

A rotation of all offices, as well as of representatives and
counsellors, has many advocates, and is contended for with
many plausible arguments. It would be attended, no doubt,
with many advantages; and if the society has a sufficient number of suitable characters to supply the great number of vacancies which would be made by such a rotation, I can see no
objection to it. These persons may be allowed to serve for three
years, and then be excluded three years, or for any longer or
shorter term.

Any seven or nine of the legislative council may be made a
quorum, for doing business as a privy council, to advise the
governor in the exercise of the executive branch of power, and
in all acts of state.

The governor should have the command of the militia and of all your armies. The power of pardons should be with the governor and council.

Judges, justices, and all other officers, civil and military, should be nominated and appointed by the governor, with the advice and consent of council, unless you choose to have a government more popular; if you do, all officers, civil and military, may be chosen by joint ballot of both houses; or, in order to preserve the independence and importance of each house, by ballot of one house, concurred in by the other. Sheriffs should be chosen by the freeholders of counties; so should registers of deeds and clerks of counties.

All officers should have commissions, under the hand of the governor and seal of the colony.

The dignity and stability of government in all its branches, the morals of the people, and every blessing of society depend so much upon an upright and skilful administration of justice, that the judicial power ought to be distinct from both the legislative and executive, and independent upon both, that so it may be a check upon both, as both should be checks upon that. The judges, therefore, should be always men of learning and experience in the laws, of exemplary morals, great patience, calmness, coolness, and attention. Their minds should not be distracted with jarring interests; they should not be dependent upon any man, or body of men. To these ends, they should hold estates for life in their offices; or, in other words, their commissions should be during good behavior, and their salaries ascertained and established by law. For misbehavior, the grand inquest of the colony, the house of representatives, should impeach them before the governor and council, where they should have time and opportunity to make their defence; but, if convicted, should be removed from their offices, and subjected to such other punishment as shall be thought proper.

A militia law, requiring all men, or with very few exceptions besides cases of conscience, to be provided with arms and ammunition, to be trained at certain seasons; and requiring counties, towns, or other small districts, to be provided with public stocks of ammunition and intrenching utensils, and with some settled plans for transporting provisions after the militia, when marched to defend their country against sudden invasions; and requiring certain districts to be provided with field-pieces, companies of matrosses, and perhaps some regiments of light-horse, is always a wise institution, and, in the present circumstances of our country, indispensable.

Laws for the liberal education of youth, especially of the lower class of people, are so extremely wise and useful, that, to a humane and generous mind, no expense for this purpose would be thought extravagant.

The very mention of sumptuary laws will excite a smile. Whether our countrymen have wisdom and virtue enough to submit to them, I know not; but the happiness of the people might be greatly promoted by them, and a revenue saved sufficient to carry on this war forever. Frugality is a great revenue, besides curing us of vanities, levities, and fopperies, which are real antidotes to all great, manly, and warlike virtues.

But must not all commissions run in the name of a king? No. Why may they not as well run thus, "The colony of   to A. B. greeting," and be tested by the governor?

Why may not writs, instead of running in the name of the king, run thus, "The colony of   to the sheriff," &c., and be tested by the chief justice?

Why may not indictments conclude, "against the peace of the colony of   and the dignity of the same?"

A constitution founded on these principles introduces knowledge among the people, and inspires them with a conscious dignity becoming freemen; a general emulation takes place, which causes good humor, sociability, good manners, and good morals to be general. That elevation of sentiment inspired by such a government, makes the common people brave and enterprising. That ambition which is inspired by it makes them sober, industrious, and frugal. You will find among them some elegance, perhaps, but more solidity; a little pleasure, but a great deal of business; some politeness, but more civility. If you compare such a country with the regions of domination, whether monarchical or aristocratical, you will fancy yourself in Arcadia or Elysium.

If the colonies should assume governments separately, they should be left entirely to their own choice of the forms; and if a continental constitution should be formed, it should be a congress, containing a fair and adequate representation of the colonies, and its authority should sacredly be confined to these cases, namely, war, trade, disputes between colony and colony, the post-office, and the unappropriated lands of the crown, as they used to be called.

These colonies, under such forms of government, and in such a union, would be unconquerable by all the monarchies of Europe.

You and I, my dear friend, have been sent into life at a time when the greatest lawgivers of antiquity would have wished to live. How few of the human race have ever enjoyed an opportunity of making an election of government, more than of air, soil, or climate, for themselves or their children! When, before the present epocha, had three millions of people full power and a fair opportunity to form and establish the wisest and happiest government that human wisdom can contrive? I hope you will avail yourself and your country of that extensive learning and indefatigable industry which you possess, to assist her in the formation of the happiest governments and the best character of a great people. For myself, I must beg you to keep my name out of sight; for this feeble attempt, if it should be known to be mine, would oblige me to apply to myself those lines of the immortal John Milton, in one of his sonnets:—

> "I did but prompt the age to quit their clogs
>   By the known rules of ancient liberty,
>   When straight a barbarous noise environs me
>   Of owls and cuckoos, asses, apes, and dogs."

6

NOVANGLUS[1]

Novanglus comprised a series of essays beginning in the Boston Gazette in 1774 and continuing to the outbreak of the Revolution in 1775. Adams was responding to the writings of the pseudonymous "Massachusettensis," who turned out to be the loyalist Daniel Leonard. About a third of the colonists, according to Adams's estimate, believed that America had no right to resist or rebel. Leonard tried to convince the colonists that they remained subjects of England and that the authority of the crown and Parliament extended to America, as it did to Ireland and every other place that England claimed as its rightful dominion. Adams could agree that Britain and America had co-existed in certain legal and commercial arrangements, but he denied that the colonists had ever acknowledged the supreme, unlimited authority of Parliament. Britain could not rule over that which it had no means of representing and had no wish to represent.

ADDRESSED TO THE INHABITANTS OF THE COLONY OF MASSACHUSETTS BAY.

No. I.

My Friends,—A writer, under the signature of *Massachusettensis*, has addressed you, in a series of papers, on the great national subject of the present quarrel between the British

administration and the Colonies. As I have not in my possession more than one of his essays, and that is in the Gazette of
December 26, I will take the liberty, in the spirit of candor and
decency, to bespeak your attention upon the same subject.

There may be occasion to say very severe things, before I
shall have finished what I propose, in opposition to this writer,
but there ought to be no reviling. *Rem ipsam dic, mitte male lo-
qui,* which may be justly translated, speak out the whole truth
boldly, but use no bad language.

It is not very material to inquire, as others have done, who is
the author of the speculations in question. If he is a disinterested writer, and has nothing to gain or to lose, to hope or to
fear, for himself more than other individuals of your community; but engages in this controversy from the purest principles,
the noblest motives of benevolence to men, and of love to his
country, he ought to have no influence with you, further than
truth and justice will support his argument. On the other hand,
if he hopes to acquire or preserve a lucrative employment, to
screen himself from the just detestation of his countrymen, or
whatever other sinister inducement he may have, so far as the
truth of facts and the weight of argument are in his favor, he
ought to be duly regarded.

He tells you, "that the temporal salvation of this province
depends upon an entire and speedy change of measures, which
must depend upon a change of sentiment respecting our own
conduct and the justice of the British nation."*

The task of effecting these great changes, this courageous
writer has undertaken in a course of publications in a newspa-

---

* "Were I not fully convinced, upon the most mature deliberation that I am capable of, that the temporal salvation of this province depends upon an entire
and speedy change of measures, which must depend upon a change of sentiment respecting our own conduct and the justice of the British nation, I never
should have obtruded myself on the public. I repeat my promise, to avoid personal reflection, as much as the nature of the task will admit of; but will continue faithfully to expose the wretched policy of the whigs, though I may be
obliged to penetrate the arcana, and discover such things as, were there not a
necessity for it, I should be infinitely happier in drawing a veil over, or covering with a mantle." *Massachusettensis.*

per. *Nil desperandum* is a good motto, and *nil admirari* is another. He is welcome to the first, and I hope will be willing that I should assume the last. The public, if they are not mistaken in their conjecture, have been so long acquainted with this gentleman, and have seen him so often disappointed, that if they were not habituated to strange things, they would wonder at his hopes, at this time, to accomplish the most unpromising project of his whole life. In the character of *Philanthrop,* he attempted to reconcile you to Mr. Bernard. But the only fruit of his labor was, to expose his client to more general examination, and consequently to more general resentment and aversion. In the character of *Philalethes,* he essayed to prove Mr. Hutchinson a patriot, and his letters not only innocent but meritorious. But the more you read and considered, the more you were convinced of the ambition and avarice, the simulation and dissimulation, the hypocrisy and perfidy of that destroying angel.

This ill-fated and unsuccessful, though persevering writer, still hopes to change your sentiments and conduct, by which it is supposed that he means to convince you, that the system of colony administration which has been pursued for these ten or twelve years past is a wise, righteous, and humane plan; that Sir Francis Bernard and Mr. Hutchinson, with their connections, who have been the principal instruments of it, are your best friends; and that those gentlemen, in this province, and in all the other colonies, who have been in opposition to it, are, from ignorance, error, or from worse and baser causes, your worst enemies.

This is certainly an inquiry that is worthy of you; and I promise to accompany this writer in his ingenious labors to assist you in it. And I earnestly entreat you, as the result of all shall be, to change your sentiments or persevere in them, as the evidence shall appear to you, upon the most dispassionate and impartial consideration, without regard to his opinion or mine.

He promises to avoid personal reflections, but to "penetrate the arcana" and "expose the wretched policy of the whigs." The cause of the whigs is not conducted by intrigues at a distant court, but by constant appeals to a sensible and virtuous people; it depends entirely on their good-will, and cannot be pursued a single step without their concurrence, to obtain which, all their designs, measures, and means, are constantly published to the collective body. The whigs, therefore, can have no arcana; but if they had, I dare say they were never so left, as to communicate them to this writer; you will therefore be disappointed, if you expect from him any thing which is true, but what has been as public as records and newspapers could make it.

I, on my part, may, perhaps, in a course of papers, penetrate arcana too; show the wicked policy of the tories; trace their plan from its first rude sketches to its present complete draught; show that it has been much longer in contemplation than is generally known,—who were the first in it—their views, motives, and secret springs of action, and the means they have employed. This will necessarily bring before your eyes many characters, living and dead. From such a research and detail of facts, it will clearly appear, who were the aggressors, and who have acted on the defensive from first to last; who are still struggling, at the expense of their ease, health, peace, wealth, and preferment, against the encroachments of the tories on their country, and who are determined to continue struggling, at much greater hazards still, and, like the Prince of Orange, are resolved never to see its entire subjection to arbitrary power, but rather to die fighting against it in the last ditch.

It is true, as this writer observes, "that the bulk of the people are generally but little versed in the affairs of state;" that they "rest the affairs of government in the hands where accident has placed them." If this had not been true, the designs of the tories had been many years ago entirely defeated. It was clearly seen by a few, more than ten years since, that they were planning and pursuing the very measures we now see executing. The people were informed of it, and warned of their danger; but they had been accustomed to confide in certain persons, and could never be persuaded to believe, until prophecy became history. Now, they see and feel that the horrible calamities are come upon them, which were foretold so many years ago, and they now sufficiently execrate the men who have brought these things upon them. Now, alas! when perhaps it is too late. If they had withdrawn their confidence from them in season, they would have wholly disarmed them.

"The same game, with the same success, has been played in all ages and countries," as Massachusettensis observes. When a favorable conjuncture has presented, some of the most intriguing and powerful citizens have conceived the design of enslaving their country, and building their own greatness on its ruins. Philip and Alexander are examples of this in Greece; Cæsar in Rome; Charles V. in Spain; Louis XII. in France; and ten thousand others.

"There is a latent spark in the breasts of the people, capable of being kindled into a flame, and to do this has always been the employment of the disaffected." What is this latent spark? The love of liberty. *A Deo hominis est indita naturæ.* Human nature itself is evermore an advocate for liberty. There is also in human nature a resentment of injury and indignation against wrong; a love of truth, and a veneration for virtue. These amiable passions are the "latent spark" to which those whom this writer calls the "disaffected" apply. If the people are capable of understanding, seeing, and feeling the difference between true and false, right and wrong, virtue and vice, to what better principle can the friends and mankind apply, than to the sense of this difference? Is it better to apply, as this writer and his friends do, to the basest passions in the human breast—to their fear, their vanity, their avarice, ambition, and every kind of corruption? I appeal to all experience, and to universal history, if it has ever been in the power of popular leaders, uninvested with other authority than what is conferred by the popular suffrage, to persuade a large people, for any length of time together, to think themselves wronged, injured, and oppressed, unless they really were, and saw and felt it to be so.

"They," the popular leaders, "begin by reminding the people of the elevated rank they hold in the universe, as men; that all men by nature are equal; that kings are but the ministers of the people; that their authority is delegated to them by the people, for their good, and they have a right to resume it, and place it in other hands, or keep it themselves, whenever it is made use of to oppress them. Doubtless, there have been instances when these principles have been inculcated to obtain a redress of real grievances; but they have been much oftener perverted to the worst of purposes."

These are what are called revolution principles. They are the principles of Aristotle and Plato, of Livy and Cicero, and Sidney, Harrington, and Locke; the principles of nature and eternal reason; the principles on which the whole government over us now stands. It is therefore astonishing, if any thing can be so, that writers, who call themselves friends of government, should in this age and country be so inconsistent with themselves, so indiscreet, so immodest, as to insinuate a doubt concerning them.

Yet we find that these principles stand in the way of Massachusettensis and all the writers of his class. The Veteran, in his letter to the officers of the army, allows them to be noble and true; but says the application of them to particular cases is wild and utopian.* How they can be in general true, and not applicable to particular cases, I cannot comprehend. I thought their being true in general, was because they were applicable in most particular cases.

Gravity is a principle in nature. Why? Because all particular bodies are found to gravitate. How would it sound to say, that bodies in general are heavy; yet to apply this to particular bodies, and say, that a guinea or a ball is heavy, is wild? "Adopted in private life," says the honest amiable veteran, "they would introduce perpetual discord." This I deny; and I think it plain, that there never was a happy private family where they were not adopted. "In the state, perpetual discord." This I deny; and affirm, that order, concord, and stability in this state, never was nor can be preserved without them. "The least failure in the re-

---

*This refers to a well-written pamphlet, entitled "A Letter from a Veteran to the Officers of the Army, encamped at Boston," and printed without date or place, in 1774. The purport of it is to deprecate excessive harshness in the punishment about to be inflicted on the rebellious colonists.

To a thorough understanding of the American Revolution by future generations, a general history of the mass of pamphlets which it occasioned is becoming very essential.

ciprocal duties of worship and obedience in the matrimonial contract would justify a divorce." This is no consequence from these principles. A total departure from the ends and designs of the contract, it is true, as elopement and adultery, would by these principles justify a divorce; but not the least failure, or many smaller failures in the reciprocal duties, &c. "In the political compact, the smallest defect in the prince, a revolution." By no means; but a manifest design in the prince, to annul the contract on his part, will annul it on the part of the people. A settled plan to deprive the people of all the benefits, blessings, and ends of the contract, to subvert the fundamentals of the constitution, to deprive them of all share in making and executing laws, will justify a revolution.

The author of a "Friendly Address to all reasonable Americans"* discovers his rancor against these principles in a more explicit manner; and makes no scruples to advance the principles of Hobbes and Filmer boldly, and to pronounce damnation, *ore rotundo,* on all who do not practise implicit, passive obedience to an established government, of whatever character it may be. It is not reviling, it is not bad language, it is strictly decent to say, that this angry bigot, this ignorant dogmatist, this foul-mouthed scold, deserves no other answer than silent contempt. Massachusettensis and the Veteran—I admire the first for his art, the last for his honesty.

Massachusettensis is more discreet than any of the others; sensible that these principles would be very troublesome to him, yet conscious of their truth, he has neither admitted nor denied them. But we have a right to his opinion of them, before we dispute with him. He finds fault with the application of them. They have been invariably applied, in support of the revolution and the present establishment, against the Stuarts, the Charleses, and the Jameses, in support of the Reformation and

---

*This is the title of a pamphlet published anonymously, and without date or place, in the year 1774. It is supposed to have been the work of Dr. Myles Cooper, President of King's College, New York, a gentleman who came from the mother country to fill that post, and whose political principles inclined towards the absolute school. The drift of the pamphlet seems to be to rouse the jealousy of the English church against the puritan republicanism of New England.

the Protestant religion; and against the worst tyranny that the genius of toryism has ever yet invented; I mean the Roman superstition. Does this writer rank the revolution and present establishment, the Reformation and Protestant religion, among his worst purposes? What "worse purpose" is there than established tyranny? Were these principles ever inculcated in favor of such tyranny? Have they not always been used against such tyrannies, when the people have had knowledge enough to be apprized of them, and courage to assert them? Do not those who aim at depriving the people of their liberties, always inculcate opposite principles, or discredit these?

"A small mistake in point of policy," says he, "often furnishes a pretence to libel government, and persuade[s—ED.] the people that their rulers are tyrants, and the whole government a system of oppression." This is not only untrue, but inconsistent with what he said before. The people are in their nature so gentle, that there never was a government yet in which thousands of mistakes were not overlooked. The most sensible and jealous people are so little attentive to government, that there are no instances of resistance, until repeated, multiplied oppressions have placed it beyond a doubt, that their rulers had formed settled plans to deprive them of their liberties; not to oppress an individual or a few, but to break down the fences of a free constitution, and deprive the people at large of all share in the government, and all the checks by which it is limited. Even Machiavel himself allows, that, not ingratitude to their rulers, but much love, is the constant fault of the people.

This writer is equally mistaken, when he says, the people are sure to be losers in the end. They can hardly be losers if unsuccessful; because, if they live, they can but be slaves, after an unfortunate effort, and slaves they would have been, if they had not resisted. So that nothing is lost. If they die, they cannot be said to lose, for death is better than slavery. If they succeed, their gains are immense. They preserve their liberties. The instances in antiquity which this writer alludes to are not mentioned, and therefore cannot be answered; but that in the country from whence we are derived, is the most unfortunate for his purpose that could have been chosen. No doubt he means, the resistance to Charles I. and the case of Cromwell. But the people of England, and the cause of liberty, truth, virtue, and humanity, gained infinite advantages by that resistance. In all human probability, liberty, civil and religious, not only in England, but in all Europe, would have been lost. Charles would undoubtedly have established the Romish religion, and a despotism as wild as any in the world. And as England has been a principal bulwark, from that period to this, of civil liberty and the Protestant religion in all Europe, if Charles's schemes had succeeded, there is great reason to apprehend that the light of science would have been extinguished, and mankind drawn back to a state of darkness and misery like that which prevailed from the fourth to the fourteenth century. It is true, and to be lamented, that Cromwell did not establish a government as free as he might and ought; but his government was infinitely more glorious and happy to the people than Charles's. Did not the people gain by the resistance to James II.? Did not the Romans gain by the resistance to Tarquin? Without that resistance, and the liberty that was restored by it, would the great Roman orators, poets, and historians, the great teachers of humanity and politeness, the pride of human nature, and the delight and glory of mankind for seventeen hundred years, ever have existed? Did not the Romans gain by resistance to the Decemvirs? Did not the English gain by resistance to John, when *Magna Charta* was obtained? Did not the Seven United Provinces gain by resistance to Philip, Alva, and Granvelle? Did not the Swiss Cantons, the Genevans, and Grisons gain by resistance to Albert and Gessler? . . .

No. IV.

Massachusettensis, whose pen can wheedle with the tongue of King Richard III., in his first paper, threatens you with the vengeance of Great Britain; and assures you, that if she had no authority over you, yet she would support her claims by her fleets and armies, Canadians and Indians. In his next, he alters his tone, and soothes you with the generosity, justice, and humanity of the nation.

I shall leave him to show how a nation can claim an authority which they have not by right, and support it by fire and sword, and yet be generous and just. The nation, I believe, is not vindictive, but the minister has discovered himself to be so in a degree that would disgrace a warrior of a savage tribe.

The wily Massachusettensis thinks our present calamity is to be attributed to the bad policy of a popular party, whose measures, whatever their intentions were, have been opposite to their profession, the public good. The present calamity seems to be nothing more nor less than reviving the plans of Mr. Bernard and the junto, and Mr. Grenville and his friends, in 1764. Surely this party are, and have been, rather unpopular. The popular party did not write Bernard's letters, who so long ago pressed for the demolition of all the charters upon the continent, and a parliamentary taxation to support government and the administration of justice in America. The popular party did not write Oliver's letters, who enforces Bernard's plans; nor Hutchinson's, who pleads with all his eloquence and pathos for parliamentary penalties, ministerial vengeance, and an abridgment of English liberties.

There is not in human nature a more wonderful phenomenon, nor in the whole theory of it a more intricate speculation, than the *shiftings, turnings, windings,* and *evasions* of a guilty conscience. Such is our unalterable moral constitution, that an internal inclination to do wrong is criminal; and a wicked thought stains the mind with guilt, and makes it tingle with pain. Hence it comes to pass, that the guilty mind can never bear to think that its guilt is known to God or man, no, nor to itself.

> ———"Cur tamen hos tu
> Evasisse putes, quos diri conscia facti
> Mens habet attonitos, et surdo verbere cædit
> Occultum quatiente animo tortore flagellum?
> Pœna autem vehemens ac multo sævior illis,
> Quas et Cæditius gravis invenit aut Rhadamanthus,
> Nocte dieque suum gestare in pectore testem."[2]

*Juv. Sat. xiii. 192.

difference is a tax upon us for the good of the empire. We submit to this cheerfully; but insist that we ought to have credit for it in the account of the expenses of the empire, because it is really a tax upon us.

Another thing; I will venture a bold assertion,—let Massachusettensis or any other friend of the minister confute me,—the three million Americans, by the tax aforesaid, upon what they are obliged to export to Great Britain only, what they are obliged to import from Great Britain only, and the quantities of British manufactures which, in these climates, they are obliged to consume more than the like number of people in any part of the three kingdoms, ultimately pay more of the taxes and duties that are apparently paid in Great Britain, than any three million subjects in the three kingdoms. All this may be computed and reduced to stubborn figures by the minister, if he pleases. We cannot do it; we have not the accounts, records, &c. Now let this account be fairly stated, and I will engage for America, upon any penalty, that she will pay the overplus, if any, in her own constitutional way, provided it is to be applied for national purposes, as paying off the national debt, maintaining the fleet, &c., not to the support of a standing army in time of peace, placemen, pensioners, &c.

Besides, every farthing of expense which has been incurred, on pretence of protecting, defending, and securing America, since the last war, has been worse than thrown away; it has been applied to do mischief. Keeping an army in America has been nothing but a public nuisance.

Furthermore, we see that all the public money that is raised here, and have reason to believe all that will or can be raised, will be applied, not for public purposes, national or provincial, but merely to corrupt the sons of America, and create a faction to destroy its interest and happiness.

There are scarcely three sentences together, in all the voluminous productions of this plausible writer, which do not convey some error in fact or principle, tinged with a coloring to make it pass for truth. He says, "the idea that the stamps were a tax, not only exceeding our proportion, but beyond our utmost ability to pay, united the colonies generally in opposing it." That we thought it beyond our proportion and ability is true; but it was not this thought which united the colonies in opposing it. When he says that at first, we did not dream of denying the authority of parliament to tax us, much less to legislate for us, he discovers plainly either a total inattention to the sentiments of America, at that time, or a disregard of what he affirms.

The truth is, the authority of parliament was never generally acknowledged in America. . . .

No. V.

We are at length arrived at the paper on which I made a few strictures some weeks ago; these I shall not repeat, but proceed to consider the other part of it.

We are told: "It is a universal truth, that he that would excite a rebellion, is at heart as great a tyrant as ever wielded the iron rod of oppression." Be it so. We are not exciting a rebellion. Opposition, nay, open, avowed resistance by arms, against usurpation and lawless violence, is not rebellion by the law of God or the land. Resistance to lawful authority makes rebellion. Hampden, Russell, Sidney, Somers, Holt, Tillotson, Burnet, Hoadly, &c. were no tyrants nor rebels, although some of them were in arms, and the others undoubtedly excited resistance against the tories. Do not beg the question, Mr. Massachusettensis, and then give yourself airs of triumph. Remember the frank Veteran acknowledges, that "the word rebel is a convertible term."*

This writer next attempts to trace the spirit of opposition through the general court and the courts of common law. "It was the policy of the whigs, to have their questions upon high

---

* "That they are rebels cannot be denied; would to God that it could! It is well for them that they are in the hands of a man of approved gentleness, humanity, and justice. But even rebel (in war at least) is a convertible term which knave was never."
Letter from a Veteran to the Officers of the Army encamped at Boston.

matters determined by yea and nay votes, which were published in the gazettes." And ought not great questions to be so
determined? In many other assemblies, New York particularly,
they always are. What better can be devised to discover the true
sense of the people? It is extremely provoking to courtiers, that
they cannot vote as the cabinet direct them, against their consciences, the known sense of their constituents, and the obvious
good of the community, without being detected. Generally, perhaps universally, no unpopular measure in a free government,
particularly the English, ought ever to pass. Why have the
people a share in the legislature, but to prevent such measures
from passing, I mean such as are disapproved by the people at
large? But did not these yea and nay votes expose the whigs, as
well as tories, to the impartial judgment of the public? If the
votes of the former were given for measures injurious to the
community, had not the latter an equal opportunity of improving them to the disadvantage of their adversaries in the next
election? Besides, were not those few persons in the house, who
generally voted for unpopular measures, near the governor, in
possession of his confidence? Had they not the absolute disposal in their towns and counties of the favor of government?
Were not all the judges, justices, sheriffs, coroners, and military
officers in their towns made upon their recommendation? Did
not this give them a prodigious weight and influence? Had the
whigs any such advantage? And does not the influence of these
yea and nay votes, consequently, prove to a demonstration the
unanimity of the people against the measures of the court?

As to what is said of "severe strictures, illiberal invectives,
abuse, and scurrility, upon the dissentients," there was quite as
much of all these published against the leading whigs. In truth,
the strictures, &c. against the tories were generally nothing
more than hints at the particular place or office, which was
known to be the temptation to vote against the country. That
"the dissentient was in danger of losing his bread and involving
his family in ruin," is equally injurious. Not an instance can be
produced of a member losing his bread or injuring his business
by voting for unpopular measures. On the contrary, such vot-

ers never failed to obtain some lucrative employment, title, or honorary office, as a reward from the court.

If "one set of members in committee had always prepared the resolves,"* &c., which they did not, what would this prove, but that this set was thought by the house the fittest for the purpose? Can it ever be otherwise? Will any popular assembly choose its worst members for the best services? Will an assembly of patriots choose courtiers to prepare votes against the court? No resolves against the claims of parliament or administration, or the measures of the governor, (excepting those against the Stamp Act, and perhaps the answers to Governor Hutchinson's speeches upon the supremacy of parliament,) ever passed through the house without meeting an obstacle. The governor had, to the last hour of the house's existence, always some seekers and expectants in the house, who never failed to oppose, and offer the best arguments they could, and were always patiently heard. That "the lips of the dissentients were sealed up;" that "they sat in silence, and beheld with regret measures they dared not oppose," are groundless suggestions, and gross reflections upon the honor and courage of those members. The debates of this house were public, and every man who has attended the gallery, knows there never was more freedom of debate in any assembly.

Massachusettensis, in the next place, conducts us to the agent, and tells us "there cannot be a provincial agent without an appointment by the three branches of the assembly. The whigs soon found that they could not have such services rendered them from a provincial agent as would answer their purposes."

The treatment this province has received respecting the agency, since Mr. Hutchinson's administration commenced, is a flagrant example of injustice. There is no law which requires the province to maintain any agent in England; much less is there

---

* "One particular set of members, in committee, always prepared the resolves and other spirited measures. At first, they were canvassed freely; at length would slide through the house without meeting an obstacle. The lips of the dissentients were sealed up. They sat in silence, and beheld with infinite regret the measures they durst not oppose." *Massachusettensis.*

any reason which necessarily requires that the three branches should join in the appointment. In ordinary times, indeed, when a harmony prevails among the branches, it is well enough to have an agent constituted by all. But in times when the foundations of the constitution are disputed, and certainly attacked by one branch or the other, to pretend that the house ought to join the governor in the choice, is a palpable absurdity. It is equivalent to saying, that the people shall have no agent at all; that all communication shall be cut off; and that there shall be no channel through which complaints and petitions may be conveyed to the royal ear. Because a governor will not concur in an agent whose sentiments are not like his; nor will an agent of the governor's appointment be likely to urge accusations against him with any diligence or zeal, if the people have occasion to complain against him.

Every private citizen, much more, every representative body, has an undoubted right to petition the king, to convey such petition by an agent, and to pay him for his service. Mr. Bernard, to do him justice, had so much regard to these principles, as to consent to the payment of the people's agents while he staid; but Mr. Hutchinson was scarcely seated in the chair, as lieutenant-governor, before we had intelligence from England, that my Lord Hillsborough told Dr. Franklin, he had received a letter from Governor Hutchinson against consenting to the salary of the agent. Such an instruction was accordingly soon sent, and no agent for the board or house has received a farthing for services since that time, though Dr. Franklin and Mr. Bollan have taken much pains, and one of them expended considerable sums of money. There is a meanness in this play that would disgrace a gambler,—a manifest fear that the truth should be known to the sovereign or the people. Many persons have thought that the province ought to have dismissed all agents from that time, as useless and nugatory; this behavior amounting to a declaration, that we had no chance or hopes of justice from a minister.

But this province, at least as meritorious as any, has been long accustomed to indignities and injustice, and to bear both with unparalleled patience. Others have pursued the same method before and since; but we have never heard that their agents are unpaid. They would scarcely have borne it with so much resignation.

It is great assurance to blame the house for this, which was both their right and duty; but it is a stain in the character of his patron which will not be soon worn out. Indeed this passage seems to have been brought in chiefly for the sake of a stroke or two, addressed to the lowest and meanest of the people; I mean the insinuation, that the two agents doubled the *expense,* which is as groundless as it is contracted; and that the ostensible agent for the province was only agent for a few individuals that had got the art of wielding the house; and that several hundred sterling a year, for attending levees and writing letters, were worth preserving. We, my friends, know that no members have the art of wielding us or our house, but by concurring in our principles, and assisting us in our designs. Numbers in both houses have turned about, and expected to wield us round with them, but they have been disappointed, and ever will be. Such apostates have never yet failed of our utter contempt, whatever titles, places, or pensions they might obtain.

The agent has never echoed back, or transmitted to America, any sentiments which he did not give in substance to Governor Shirley, twenty years ago; and, therefore, this insinuation is but another slander.* The remainder of what is said of the agency is levelled at Dr. Franklin, and is but a dull appendix to Wedderburn's ribaldry, having all his malice, without any of his wit or spirit. Nero murdered Seneca, that he might pull up virtue by the roots; and the same maxim governs the scribblers and speechifiers on the side of the minister. It is sufficient to discover that any man has abilities and integrity, a love of virtue

---

* "The person appointed by the house was the ostensible agent of the province; though, in fact, he was only the agent of a few individuals that had got the art of managing the house at their pleasure. He knew his continuing in office depended upon them. An office that yielded several hundred pounds sterling annually, the business of which consisted in little more than attending the levees of the great, and writing letters to America, was worth preserving. Thus, he was under a strong temptation to sacrifice the province to a party; and echoed back the sentiments of his patrons." *Massachusettensis.*

and liberty, he must be run down at all events. Witness Pitt, Franklin, and too many others.

My design in pursuing this malicious slanderer, concealed as he is under so soft and oily an appearance, through all the doublings of his tedious course, is to vindicate this colony from his base aspersions; that strangers now among us, and the impartial public, may see the wicked arts, which are still employed against us. After the vilest abuse upon the agent of the province, and the house that appointed him, we are brought to his majesty's council, and are told that the "whigs reminded them of their mortality. If any one opposed the violent measures, he lost his election the next May. Half the whole number, mostly men of the first families, note, and abilities, attached to their native country, wealthy, and independent, were tumbled from their seats in disgrace. Thus the board lost its weight, and the political balance was destroyed."

It is impossible for any man acquainted with this subject to read this zealous rant without smiling, until he attends to the wickedness of it, which will provoke his utmost indignation. Let us, however, consider it soberly.

From the date of our charter to the time of the Stamp Act, and indeed since that time, (notwithstanding the misrepresentations of our charter constitution, as too popular and republican,) the council of this province have been generally on the side of the governor and the prerogative. For the truth of this, I appeal to our whole history and experience. The art and power of governors, and especially the negative, have been a stronger motive on the one hand, than the annual election of the two houses on the other. In disputes between the governor and the house, the council have generally adhered to the former, and in many cases have complied with his humor, when scarcely any council by mandamus, upon this continent, would have done it.

But in the time of the Stamp Act, it was found productive of many mischiefs and dangers, to have officers of the crown, who were dependent on the ministry, and judges of the superior court, whose offices were thought incompatible with a voice in the legislature, members of council.

In May, 1765, Lieutenant-Governor Hutchinson, Secretary Oliver, and Mr. Belcher, officers of the crown, the judges of the superior court, and some other gentlemen, who held commissions under the governor, were members of council. Mr. Hutchinson was chief justice, and a judge of probate for the first county, as well as lieutenant-governor, and a counsellor; too many offices for the greatest and best man in the world to hold, too much business for any man to do; besides, that these offices were frequently clashing and interfering with each other. Two other justices of the superior court were counsellors, and nearly and closely connected with him by family alliances. One other justice was judge of admiralty during pleasure. Such a jumble of offices never got together before in any English government. It was found, in short, that the famous triumvirate, Bernard, Hutchinson, and Oliver, the ever-memorable, secret, confidential letter-writers, whom I call the junto, had, by degrees, and before the people were aware of it, erected a tyranny in the province. Bernard had all the executive, and a negative on the legislative; Hutchinson and Oliver, by their popular arts and secret intrigues, had elevated to the board such a collection of crown-officers and their own relations, as to have too much influence there; and they had three of a family on the superior bench, which is the supreme tribunal in all causes, civil and criminal, vested with all the powers of the king's bench, common pleas, and exchequer, which gave them power over every act of this court. This junto, therefore, had the legislative and executive in their control, and more natural influence over the judicial than is ever to be trusted to any set of men in the world. The public, accordingly, found all these springs and wheels in the constitution set in motion to promote submission to the Stamp Act, and to discountenance resistance to it; and they thought they had a violent presumption, that they would forever be employed to encourage a compliance with all ministerial measures and parliamentary claims, of whatever character they might be. . . .

Suffer me to introduce here a little history. In 1764, when the system of taxing and new-modelling the colonies was first apprehended, Lieutenant-Governor Hutchinson's friends strug-

gled, in several successive sessions of the general court, to get
him chosen agent for the province at the court of Great Britain.
At this time, he declared freely, *that he was of the same sentiment with the people, that parliament had no right to tax them;
but differed from the country party only in his opinion of the
policy of denying that right in their petitions,* &c. I would not
injure him; I was told this by three gentlemen, who were of the
committee of both houses, to prepare that petition, that he
made this declaration explicitly before that committee. I have
been told by other gentlemen, that he made the same declaration to them. It is possible that he might make use of expressions studied for the purpose, which would not strictly bear
this construction. But it is certain that they understood him so,
and that this was the general opinion of his sentiments until he
came to the chair.

The country party saw that this aspiring genius aimed at
keeping fair with the ministry, by supporting their measures,
and with the people, by pretending to be of our principles, and
between both, to trim himself up to the chair. The only reason
why he did not obtain an election at one time, and was excused
from the service at another, after he had been chosen by a small
majority, was because the members knew he would not openly
deny the right, and assure his majesty, the parliament, and ministry, that the people never would submit to it. For the same reason he was left out of council. But he continued to cultivate his
popularity, and to maintain a general opinion among the people
that he denied the right in his private judgment, and this idea
preserved most of those who continued their esteem for him.

But upon Bernard's removal, and his taking the chair as
lieutenant-governor, he had no further expectations from the
people, nor complaisance for their opinions. In one of his first
speeches he took care to advance the supreme authority of parliament. This astonished many of his friends. They were heard
to say, we have been deceived. We thought he had been abused,
but we now find what has been said of him is true. He is determined to join in the designs against this country. After his promotion to the government, finding that the people had little
confidence in him, and knowing that he had no interest at home

to support him, but what he had acquired by joining with Bernard in kicking up a dust, he determined to strike a bold stroke, and, in a formal speech to both houses, became a champion for the unbounded authority of parliament over the colonies. This, he thought, would lay the ministry under obligation to support him in the government, or else to provide for him out of it, not considering that starting that question before that assembly, and calling upon them, as he did, to dispute with him upon it, was scattering firebrands, arrows, and death in sport. The arguments he then advanced were inconclusive indeed; but they shall be considered, when I come to the feeble attempt of Massachusettensis to give a color to the same position.

The house, thus called upon either to acknowledge the unlimited authority of parliament, or confute his arguments, were bound, by their duty to God, their country, and posterity, to give him a full and explicit answer. They proved incontestably that he was out in his facts, inconsistent with himself, and in every principle of his law he had committed a blunder. Thus the fowler was caught in his own snare; and although this country has suffered severe temporary calamities in consequence of this speech, yet I hope they will not be durable; but his ruin was certainly in part owing to it. Nothing ever opened the eyes of the people so much, as to his designs, excepting his letters. Thus it is the fate of Massachusettensis to praise this gentleman for those things which the wise part of mankind condemn in him, as the most insidious and mischievous of actions. If it was out of his power to do us any more injuries, I should wish to forget the past; but, as there is reason to fear he is still to continue his malevolent labors against this country, although he is out of our sight, he ought not to be out of our minds. This country has every thing to fear, in the present state of the British court, while the lords Bute, Mansfield, and North have the principal conduct of affairs, from the deep intrigues of that artful man.

To proceed to his successor, whom Massachusettensis has been pleased to compliment with the epithet of "amiable." I have no inclination to detract from this praise; but have no panegyrics or invectives for any man, much less for any governor, until satisfied of his character and designs. This gentleman's conduct, although he came here to support the systems of his two predecessors, and contracted to throw himself into the arms of their connections, when he has acted himself, and not been teased by others much less amiable and judicious than himself, into measures which his own inclination would have avoided, has been in general as unexceptionable as could be expected, in his very delicate, intricate, and difficult situation.

We are then told, "that disaffection to Great Britain was infused into the body of the people." The leading whigs have ever, systematically and upon principle, endeavored to preserve the people from all disaffection to the king, on the one hand, and the body of the people of England, on the other; but to lay the blame, where it is justly due, on the ministry and their instruments.

We are next conducted into the superior court, and informed "that the judges were dependent on the annual grants of the general court; that their salaries were small, in proportion to the salaries of other officers of less importance; that they often petitioned the assembly to enlarge them, without success, and were reminded of their dependence; that they remained unshaken amid the raging tempests, which is to be attributed rather to their firmness than situation."

That the salaries were small must be allowed; but not smaller in proportion than those of other officers. All salaries in this province have been and are small. It has been the policy of the country to keep them so; not so much from a spirit of parsimony, as an opinion, that the service of the public ought to be an honorary, rather than a lucrative employment; and that the great men ought to be obliged to set examples of simplicity and frugality before the people.

But, if we consider things maturely, and make allowance for all circumstances, I think the country may be vindicated. This province, during the last war, had such overbearing burdens upon it, that it was necessitated to use economy in every thing. At the peace she was half a million sterling in debt, nearly. She thought it the best policy to get out of debt before she raised the wages of her servants; and if Great Britain had thought as wisely, she would not now have had one hundred and forty millions to pay; and she would never have thought of taxing America. Low as the wages were, it was found that, whenever a vacancy happened, the place was solicited with much more anxiety and zeal than the kingdom of heaven.

Another cause which had its effect was this. The judges of that court had almost always enjoyed some other office. At the time of the Stamp Act the chief justice was lieutenant-governor, which yielded him a profit; and a judge of probate for the county of Suffolk, which yielded him another profit; and a counselor, which, if it was not very profitable, gave him an opportunity of promoting his family and friends to other profitable offices, an opportunity which the country saw he most religiously improved. Another justice of this court was a judge of admiralty, and another was judge of probate for the county of Plymouth. The people thought, therefore, that as their time was not wholly taken up by their offices, as judges of the superior court, there was no reason why they should be paid as much as if it had been.

Another reason was this. Those justices had not been bred to the bar, but taken from merchandise, husbandry, and other occupations; had been at no great expense for education or libraries, and therefore, the people thought that equity did not demand large salaries.

It must be confessed that another motive had its weight. The people were growing jealous of the chief justice, and two other justices at least, and therefore thought it imprudent to enlarge their salaries, and, by that means, their influence.

Whether all these arguments were sufficient to vindicate the people for not enlarging their salaries, I shall leave to you, my friends, whose right it is to judge. But that the judges petitioned "often" to the assembly I do not remember. I knew it was suspected by many, and confidently affirmed by some, that Judge Russell carried home with him, in 1766, a petition to his majesty, subscribed by himself and Chief Justice Hutchinson at least, praying his majesty to take the payment of the judges into his own hands; and that this petition, together with the solicitations of Governor Bernard and others, had the success to procure the act of parliament, to enable his majesty to appropriate the revenue to the support of the administration of justice, &c., from whence a great part of the present calamities of America have flowed.

That the high whigs took *care* to get themselves chosen of the grand juries, I do not believe.* Nine tenths of the people were high whigs; and therefore it was not easy to get a grand jury without nine whigs in ten, in it. And the matter would not be much mended by the new act of parliament. The sheriff must return the same set of jurors, court after court, or else his juries would be, nine tenths of them, high whigs still. Indeed the tories are so envenomed now with malice, envy, revenge and disappointed ambition, that they would be willing, for what I know, to be jurors for life, in order to give verdicts against the whigs. And many of them would readily do it, I doubt not, without any other law or evidence than what they found in their own breasts. The suggestion of legerdemain, in drawing the names of petit jurors out of the box, is scandalous. Human wisdom cannot devise a method of obtaining petit jurors more fairly, and better secured against a possibility of corruption of any kind, than that established by our provincial law. They were drawn by chance out of a box in open town meeting, to which the tories went, or might have gone, as well as the whigs, and have seen with their own eyes, that nothing unfair ever did or could take place. If the jurors consisted of whigs, it was because the freeholders were whigs, that is honest men. . . .

"†It is in vain to seek a government in all points free from a possibility of civil wars, tumults, and seditions; that is a blessing denied to this life, and reserved to complete the felicity of the next. Seditions, tumults, and wars do arise from mistake or from malice; from just occasions or unjust. . . . Seditions proceeding from malice are seldom or never seen in popular governments; for they are hurtful to the people, and none have ever willingly and knowingly hurt themselves. There may be, and of-

---

* "It is difficult to account for so many of the first rate whigs being returned to serve on the petit jury at the term next after extraordinary insurrections, without supposing some legerdemain in drawing their names out of the box." *Massachusettensis.*

†Sidney's *Discourses upon Government*, c. 2, § 24. The extracts quoted here are not, in the original, continuous passages.

ten is, malice in those who excite them; but the people is ever deceived, and whatever is thereupon done, ought to be imputed to error, &c. But in absolute monarchies, almost all the troubles that arise proceed from malice; they cannot be reformed; the extinction of them is exceeding difficult, if they have continued long enough to corrupt the people; and those who appear against them seek only to set up themselves or their friends. The mischiefs designed are often dissembled or denied, till they are past all possibility of being cured by any other way than force; and such as are by necessity driven to use that remedy, know they must perfect their work or perish. He that draws his sword against the prince, say the French, ought to throw away the scabbard; for though the design be never so just, yet the authors are sure to be ruined if it miscarry. Peace is seldom made, and never kept, unless the subject retain such a power in his hands as may oblige the prince to stand to what is agreed; and, in time, some trick is found to deprive him of that benefit.

"It may seem strange to some that I mention seditions, tumults, and wars, upon just occasions; but I can find no reason to retract the terms. God, intending that men should live justly with one another, does certainly intend that he or they, who do no wrong, should suffer none; and the law that forbids injuries were of no use if no penalty might be inflicted on those that will not obey it. If injustice, therefore, be evil, and injuries be forbidden, they are also to be punished; and the law instituted for their prevention must necessarily intend the avenging of such as cannot be prevented. The work of the magistracy is to execute this law; the sword of justice is put into their hands to restrain the fury of those within the society who will not be a law to themselves; and the sword of war to protect the people against the violence of foreigners. This is without exception, and would be in vain if it were not. But the magistrate who is to protect the people from injury, may, and is often known not to have done it; he renders his office sometimes *useless by neglecting to do justice,* sometimes *mischievous by overthrowing it.* This strikes at the root of God's general ordinance, that there should be laws; and the particular ordinances of all societies, that appoint such as seem best to them. *The magistrate, therefore, is comprehended under both, and subject to both, as well as private men.*

"The ways of preventing or punishing injuries, are judicial or extrajudicial. Judicial proceedings are of force against those who submit, or may be brought to trial, but are of no effect against those who resist, and are of such power that they cannot be constrained. It were absurd to cite a man to appear before a tribunal, *who can awe the judges, or has armies to defend him;* and impious to think that he who has added treachery to his other crimes, and usurped a power above the law, should be protected by the enormity of his wickedness. Legal proceedings therefore, are to be used when the delinquent submits to the law; *and all are just, when he will not be kept in order by the legal.*

"The word *sedition* is generally applied to all numerous assemblies without or against the authority of the magistrate, or of those who assume that power. Athaliah and Jezebel were more ready to cry out treason than David, &c. Tumult is from the disorderly manner of those assemblies, where things can seldom be done regularly; and war is that '*decertatio per vim,*' or trial by force, to which men come when other ways are ineffectual.

"If the laws of God and men are therefore of no effect when the magistracy is left at liberty to break them, and if the lusts of those who are too strong for the tribunals of justice, cannot be otherwise restrained than by sedition, tumults, and war; those seditions, tumults, and wars, are justified by the laws of God and man.

"I will not take upon me to enumerate all the cases in which this may be done; but content myself with three, which have most frequently given occasion for proceedings of this kind. The first is, when one or more men take upon them the power and name of a magistracy to which they are not justly called. The second, when one or more, being justly called, continue in their magistracy longer than the laws by which they are called do prescribe. And the third, when he, or they, who are rightly called, do assume a power, though within the time prescribed, that the law does not give, or turn that which the law does give, to an end different and contrary to that which is intended by it.

"The same course is justly used against a legal magistrate who takes upon him to exercise a power which the law does not give; for in that respect he is a private man . . . and may be restrained as well as any other; because he is not set up to do what he lists, but what the law appoints for the good of the people; and as he has no other power than what the law allows, so the same law limits and directs the exercise of that which he has."

"*When we speak of a tyrant that may lawfully be dethroned by the people, we do not mean by the word *people,* the vile populace or rabble of the country, nor the cabal of a small number of factious persons, but the greater and more judicious part of the subject, of all ranks. Besides, the tyranny must be so notorious, and evidently clear, as to leave nobody any room to doubt of it, &c. Now, a prince may easily avoid making himself so universally suspected and odious to his subjects; for, as Mr. Locke says in his Treatise of Civil Government, c. 18, § 209,—'It is as impossible for a governor, if he really means the good of the people, and the preservation of them and the laws together, not to make them see and feel it, as it is for the father of a family not to let his children see he loves and takes care of them.' And therefore the general insurrection of a whole nation does not deserve the name of a rebellion. We may see what Mr. Sidney says upon this subject in his Discourse concerning Government:—'Neither are subjects bound to stay till the prince has entirely finished the chains which he is preparing for them, and put it out of their power to oppose. It is sufficient that all the advances which he makes are manifestly tending to their oppression, that he is marching boldly on to the ruin of the State.' In such a case, says Mr. Locke, admirably well,— 'How can a man any more hinder himself from believing, in his own mind, which way things are going, or from casting about to save himself, than he could from believing the captain of the

*Pufendorf's *Law of Nature and Nations,* 1. vii. c. viii. § 5, 6. Barbeyrac's note on section 6.

ship he was in was carrying him and the rest of his company to Algiers, when he found him always steering that course, though cross winds, leaks in his ship, and want of men and provisions, did often force him to turn his course another way for some time, which he steadily returned to again, as soon as the winds, weather, and other circumstances would let him?' This chiefly takes place with respect to kings, whose power is limited by fundamental laws.

"If it is objected that the people, being ignorant and always discontented, to lay the foundation of government in the unsteady opinion and the uncertain humor of the people, is to expose it to certain ruin; the same author will answer you, that 'on the contrary, people are not so easily got out of their old forms as some are apt to suggest. England, for instance, notwithstanding the many revolutions that have been seen in that kingdom, has always kept to its old legislative of king, lords, and commons; and whatever provocations have made the crown to be taken from some of their princes' heads, they never carried the people so far as to place it in another line.' But it will be said, this hypothesis lays a ferment for frequent rebellion. 'No more,' says Mr. Locke, 'than any other hypothesis. For when the people are made miserable, and find themselves exposed to the ill usage of arbitrary power, cry up their governors as you will for sons of Jupiter; let them be sacred and divine, descended or authorized from heaven; give them out for whom or what you please, the same will happen. The people generally ill treated, and contrary to right, will be ready upon any occasion to ease themselves of a burden that sits heavy upon them. 2. Such revolutions happen not upon every little mismanagement in public affairs. Great mistakes in the ruling part, many wrong and inconvenient laws, and all the slips of human frailty will be borne by the people without mutiny and murmur. 3. This power in the people of providing for their safety anew by a legislative, when their legislators have acted contrary to their trust by invading their property, is the best fence against rebellion, and the probablest means to hinder it; for rebellion being an opposition, not to persons, but authority, which is founded only in the constitutions and laws of the government; those, whoever they be, *who by force break through, and by force justify the violation of them, are truly and properly rebels.* For when men, by entering into society and civil government, have excluded force, and introduced laws for the preservation of property, peace, and unity, among themselves; those who set up force again, in opposition to the laws, do *rebellare,* that is, do bring back again the state of war, and are properly, rebels,' as the author shows. In the last place, he demonstrates that there are also greater inconveniences in allowing all to those that govern, than in granting something to the people. But it will be said, that ill affected and factious men may spread among the people, and make them believe that the prince or legislative act contrary to their trust, when they only make use of their due prerogative. To this Mr. Locke answers, that the people, however, is to judge of all that; because nobody can better judge whether his trustee or deputy acts well, and according to the trust reposed in him, than he who deputed him. 'He might make the like query,' (says Mr. Le Clerc, from whom this extract is taken) 'and ask, whether the people being oppressed by an authority which they set up, but for their own good, it is just that those who are vested with this authority, and of which they are complaining, should themselves be judges of the complaints made against them. The greatest flatterers of kings dare not say, that the people are obliged to suffer absolutely all their humors, how irregular soever they be; and therefore must confess, that when no regard is had to their complaints, the very foundations of society are destroyed; the prince and people are in a state of war with each other, like two independent states, that are doing themselves justice, and acknowledge no person upon earth, who, in a sovereign manner, can determine the disputes between them," &c.

If there is any thing in these quotations, which is applicable to the destruction of the tea, or any other branch of our subject, it is not my fault; I did not make it. Surely Grotius, Pufendorf, Barbeyrac, Locke, Sidney, and Le Clerc, are writers of sufficient weight to put in the scale against the mercenary scribblers in New York and Boston, who have the unexampled impudence and folly, to call these, which are revolution principles, in question, and to ground their arguments upon passive obedience as a corner stone. What an opinion must these writers have of the principles of their patrons . . . when they hope to recommend themselves by reviving that stupid doctrine, which has been infamous so many years. . . .

"The best writers upon the law of nations tell us, that when a nation takes possession of a distant country, and settles there, that country, though separated from the principal establishment, or mother country, naturally becomes a part of the state, equal with its ancient possessions." We are not told who these "best writers" are. I think we ought to be introduced to them. But their meaning may be no more, than that it is best they should be incorporated with the ancient establishment by contract, or by some new law and institution, by which the new country shall have equal right, powers, and privileges, as well as equal protection, and be under equal obligations of obedience, with the old. Has there been any such contract between Britain and the colonies? Is America incorporated into the realm? Is it a part of the realm? Is it a part of the kingdom? Has it any share in the legislative of the realm? The constitution requires that every foot of land should be represented in the third estate, the democratical branch of the constitution. How many millions of acres in America, how many thousands of wealthy landholders, have no representatives there?

But let these "best writers" say what they will, there is nothing in the law of nations, which is only the law of right reason applied to the conduct of nations, that requires that emigrants from a state should continue, or be made, a part of the state.

The practice of nations has been different. The Greeks planted colonies, and neither demanded nor pretended any authority over them; but they became distinct, independent commonwealths. The Romans continued their colonies under the jurisdiction of the mother commonwealth; but, nevertheless, they allowed them the privileges of cities. Indeed, that sagacious city seems to have been aware of difficulties similar to those under which Great Britain is now laboring. She seems to have been sensible of the impossibility of keeping colonies planted at great distances, under the absolute control of her *senatus-consulta.*

Harrington tells us, that "the commonwealth of Rome, by planting colonies of its citizens within the bounds of Italy, took the best way of propagating itself and naturalizing the country; whereas, if it had planted such colonies without the bounds of Italy, it would have alienated the citizens, and given a root to liberty abroad, that might have sprung up foreign, or savage, and hostile to her; *wherefore it never made any such dispersion of itself and its strength* till it was under the yoke of the emperors, who, disburdening themselves of the people, as having less apprehension of what they could do abroad than at home, took a contrary course."* But these Italian cities, although established by decrees of the senate of Rome, to which the colonist was always party, either as a Roman citizen about to emigrate, or as a conquered enemy treating upon terms, were always allowed all the rights of Roman citizens, and were governed by senates of their own. It was the policy of Rome to conciliate her colonies by allowing them equal liberties with her citizens. Witness the example of the Privernates. This people had been conquered, and, complaining of oppression, revolted. At last they sent ambassadors to Rome to treat of peace. The senate was divided in opinion. Some were for violent, others for lenient measures. In the course of the debate, a senator, whose opinion was for *bringing them to his feet,* proudly asked one of the ambassadors what punishment he thought his countrymen deserved. *"Eam, inquit, quam merentur, qui se libertate dignos censent."* That punishment which those deserve who think themselves worthy of liberty. Another senator, seeing that the *ministerial members* were exasperated with the honest answer, in order to divert their anger, asks another question:—What if we remit all punishment? What kind of a peace may we hope for with you? *"Si bonam dederitis, inquit, et fidam et perpetuam; si malam, haud diuturnam."* If you give us a just peace, it will be faithfully observed, and perpetually; but if a bad one, it will not last long. The *ministerial* senators all on fire at this answer, cried out sedition and rebellion; but the wiser majority decreed,—

*Oceana, p. 43.

"*Viri et liberi, vocem auditam; an credi posse ullum populum, aut hominem denique, in ea conditione, cujus eum pœniteat, diutius quam necesse sit mansurum? Ibi pacem esse fidam, ubi voluntarii pacati sint; neque eo loco, ubi servitutem esse velint, fidem sperandam esse.*" That they had heard the voice of a man, and a son of liberty; that it was not natural or credible that any people, or any man, would continue longer than necessity should compel him in a condition that grieved and displeased him. A faithful peace was to be expected from men whose affections were conciliated; nor was any kind of fidelity to be expected from slaves. The consul exclaimed,—"*Eos demum, qui nihil prœterquam de libertate cogitent, dignos esse qui Romani fiant.*" That they who regarded nothing so much as their liberty, deserved to be Romans. "*Itaque et in senatu causam obtinuere; et ex auctoritate patrum, latum ad populum est, ut Privernatibus civitas daretur.*" Therefore the Privernates obtained their cause in the senate; and it was, by the authority of those fathers, recommended to the people, that the privileges of a city should be granted them. The practice of free nations only can be adduced, as precedents of what the law of nature has been thought to dictate upon this subject of colonies. Their practice is different. The senate and people of Rome did not interfere commonly by making laws for their colonies, but left them to be ruled by governors and senates. Can Massachusettensis produce from the whole history of Rome, or from the Digest, one example of a *senatus-consultum*, or a *plebiscitum*, laying taxes on the colony?

Having mentioned the wisdom of the Romans, for not planting colonies out of Italy, and their reasons for it, I cannot help recollecting an observation of Harrington:—"For the colonies in the Indies," says he, "they are yet babes, that cannot live without sucking the breasts of their mother cities, but such as I mistake, if, when they come of age, they do not wean themselves, which causes me to wonder at princes that delight to be exhausted in that way." This was written one hundred and twenty years ago; the colonies are now nearer manhood than ever Harrington foresaw they would arrive in such a period of time. Is it not astonishing, then, that any British minister should ever have considered this subject so little as to believe it possible for him to new-model all our governments, to tax us by an authority that never taxed us before, and subdue us to an implicit obedience to a legislature that millions of us scarcely ever thought any thing about?

I have said, that the practice of free governments alone can be quoted with propriety to show the sense of nations. But the sense and practice of nations is not enough. Their practice must be reasonable, just, and right, or it will not govern Americans.

Absolute monarchies, whatever their practice may be, are nothing to us; for, as Harrington observes, "Absolute monarchy, as that of the Turks, neither plants its people at home nor abroad, otherwise than as tenants for life or at will; wherefore, its national and provincial government is all one."

I deny, therefore, that the practice of free nations, or the opinions of the best writers upon the law of nations, will warrant the position of Massachusettensis,* that, "when a nation takes possession of a distant territory, that becomes a part of the state equally with its ancient possessions." The practice of free nations and the opinions of the best writers are in general on the contrary.

I agree, that "two supreme and independent authorities cannot exist in the same state," any more than two supreme beings

---

*"The colonies are a part of the British empire. The best writers upon the law of nations tell us, that when a nation takes possession of a distant country, and settles there, that country, though separated from the principal establishment, or mother country, naturally becomes a part of the state, equal with its ancient possessions. Two supreme or independent authorities cannot exist in the same state. It would be what is called *imperium in imperio,* the height of political absurdity. The analogy between the political and human body is great. Two independent authorities in a state would be like two distinct principles of volition and action in the human body, dissenting, opposing, and destroying each other. If, then, we are a part of the British empire, we must be subject to the supreme power of the state, which is vested in the estates of parliament, notwithstanding each of the colonies have legislative and executive powers of their own, delegated or granted to them, for the purposes of regulating their own internal police, which are subordinate to, and must necessarily be subject to the checks, control, and regulation of the supreme authority."   *Massachusettensis.*

in one universe; and, therefore, I contend, that our provincial legislatures are the only supreme authorities in our colonies. . . .

No. VIII.

It has often been observed by me, and it cannot be too often repeated, that *colonization* is *casus omissus* at common law. There is no such title known in that law. By common law, I mean that system of customs written and unwritten, which was known and in force in England in the time of King Richard I. This continued to be the case down to the reign of Elizabeth and King James I. In all that time, the laws of England were confined to the realm, and within the four seas. There was no provision made in this law for governing colonies beyond the Atlantic, or beyond the four seas, by authority of parliament; no, nor for the king to grant charters to subjects to settle in foreign countries. It was the king's prerogative to prohibit the emigration of any of his subjects, by issuing his writ *ne exeat regno*.[3] And, therefore, it was in the king's power to permit his subjects to leave the kingdom. "It is a high crime to disobey the king's lawful commands or prohibitions, as not returning from beyond sea upon the king's letters to that purpose; for which the offender's lands shall be seized until he return; and when he does return, he shall be fined, &c.; or going beyond sea against the king's will, expressly signified, either by the writ *ne exeat regno,* or under the great or privy seal, or signet, or by proclamation."* When a subject left the kingdom by the king's permission, and if the nation did not remonstrate against it, by the nation's permission too, at least connivance, he carried with him, as a man, all the rights of nature. His allegiance bound him to the king, and entitled him to protection. But how? Not in France; the King of England was not bound to protect him in France. Nor in America. Nor in the dominions of Louis. Nor of Sassacus, or Massachusetts. He had a right to protection and the liberties of England, upon his return there, not otherwise. How, then, do we New Englandmen derive our laws? I say, not

*Hawkins' *Pleas of the Crown,* c. xxii. § 4.

from parliament, not from common law, but from the law of nature, and the compact made with the king in our charters. Our ancestors were entitled to the common law of England when they emigrated, that is, to just so much of it as they pleased to adopt, and no more. They were not bound or obliged to submit to it, unless they chose it. By a positive principle of the common law they were bound, let them be in what part of the world they would, to do nothing against the allegiance of the king. But no kind of provision was ever made by common law for punishing or trying any man, even for treason committed out of the realm. He must be tried in some county of the realm by that law, the county where the overt act was done, or he could not be tried at all. Nor was any provision ever made, until the reign of Henry VIII., for trying treasons committed abroad, and the acts of that reign were made on purpose to catch Cardinal Pole.

So that our ancestors, when they emigrated, having obtained permission of the king to come here, and being never commanded to return into the realm, had a clear right to have erected in this wilderness a British constitution, or a perfect democracy, or any other form of government they saw fit. They, indeed, while they lived, could not have taken arms against the King of England, without violating their allegiance; but their children would not have been born within the king's allegiance, would not have been natural subjects, and consequently not entitled to protection, or bound to the king.

Massachusettensis seems possessed of these ideas, and attempts in the most awkward manner to get rid of them. He is conscious that America must be a part of the realm, before it can be bound by the authority of parliament; and, therefore, is obliged to suggest that we are annexed to the realm, and to endeavor to confuse himself and his readers, by confounding the realm with the empire and dominions.

But will any man soberly contend, that America was ever annexed to the realm? to what realm? When New England was settled, there was a realm of England, a realm of Scotland, and a realm of Ireland. To which of these three realms was New England annexed? To the realm of England, it will be said. But by what law? No territory could be annexed to the realm of England but by an act of parliament. Acts of parliament have been passed to annex Wales, &c. &c. to the realm; but none ever passed to annex America. But if New England was annexed to the realm of England, how came she annexed to the realm of, or kingdom of Great Britain? The two realms of England and Scotland were, by the act of union, incorporated into one kingdom, by the name of Great Britain; but there is not one word about America in that act.

Besides, if America was annexed to the realm, or a part of the kingdom, every act of parliament that is made would extend to it, named or not named. But everybody knows, that every act of parliament, and every other record, constantly distinguishes between this kingdom and his majesty's other dominions. Will it be said that Ireland is annexed to the realm, or a part of the kingdom of Great Britain? Ireland is a distinct kingdom, or realm, by itself, notwithstanding British parliament claims a right of binding it in all cases, and exercises it in some. And even so, the Massachusetts is a realm, New York is a realm, Pennsylvania another realm, to all intents and purposes, as much as Ireland is, or England or Scotland ever were. The King of Great Britain is the sovereign of all these realms.

This writer says, "that in denying that the colonies are annexed to the realm, and subject to the authority of parliament, individuals and bodies of men subvert the fundamentals of government, deprive us of British liberties, and build up absolute monarchy in the colonies."

This is the first time that I ever heard or read that the colonies are annexed to the realm. It is utterly denied that they are, and that it is possible they should be, without an act of parliament and acts of the colonies. Such an act of parliament cannot be produced, nor any such law of any one colony. Therefore, as the writer builds the whole authority of parliament upon this fact, namely,—that the colonies are annexed to the realm, and as it is certain they never were so annexed, the consequence is, that his whole superstructure falls.

When he says, that they subvert the fundamentals of government, he begs the question. We say, that the contrary doctrines subvert the fundamentals of government. When he says, that they deprive us of British liberties, he begs the question again. We say, that the contrary doctrine deprives us of English liberties; as to British liberties, we scarcely know what they are, as the liberties of England and Scotland are not precisely the same to this day. English liberties are but certain rights of nature, reserved to the citizen by the English constitution, which rights cleaved to our ancestors when they crossed the Atlantic, and would have inhered in them if, instead of coming to New England, they had gone to Otaheite or Patagonia, even although they had taken no patent or charter from the king at all. These rights did not adhere to them the less, for their purchasing patents and charters, in which the king expressly stipulates with them, that they and their posterity should forever enjoy all those rights and liberties.

The human mind is not naturally the clearest atmosphere; but the clouds and vapors which have been raised in it by the artifices of temporal and spiritual tyrants, have made it impossible to see objects in it distinctly. Scarcely any thing is involved in more systematical obscurity than the rights of our ancestors, when they arrived in America. How, in common sense, came the dominions of King Philip, King Massachusetts, and twenty other sovereigns, independent princes here, to be within the allegiance of the Kings of England, James and Charles? America was no more within the allegiance of those princes, by the common law of England, or by the law of nature, than France and Spain were. Discovery, if that was incontestable, could give no title to the English king, by common law, or by the law of nature, to the lands, tenements, and hereditaments of the native Indians here. Our ancestors were sensible of this, and, therefore, honestly purchased their lands of the natives. They might have bought them to hold allodially, if they would.

But there were two ideas, which confused them, and have continued to confuse their posterity; one derived from the feudal, the other from the canon law. By the former of these systems, the prince, the general, was supposed to be sovereign lord of all the lands conquered by the soldiers in his army; and upon this principle, the King of England was considered in law as sovereign lord of all the land within the realm. If he had sent an army here to conquer King Massachusetts, and it had succeeded, he would have been sovereign lord of the land here upon these principles; but there was no rule of the common law that made the discovery of the country by a subject a title to that country in the prince. But conquest would not have annexed the country to the realm, nor have given any authority to the parliament. But there was another mist cast before the eyes of the English nation from another source. The pope claimed a sovereign propriety in, as well as authority over, the whole earth. As head of the Christian church, and vicar of God, he claimed this authority over all Christendom; and, in the same character, he claimed a right to all the countries and possessions of heathens and infidels; a right divine to exterminate and destroy them at his discretion, in order to propagate the Catholic faith. When King Henry VIII. and his parliament threw off the authority of the pope, stripped his holiness of his supremacy, and invested it in himself by an act of parliament, he and his courtiers seemed to think that all the rights of the holy see were transferred to him; and it was a union of these two, (the most impertinent and fantastical ideas that ever got into a human pericranium, namely,—that, as feudal sovereign and supreme head of the church together, a king of England had a right to all the land his subjects could find, not possessed by any Christian state or prince, though possessed by heathen or infidel nations,) which seems to have deluded the nation about the time of the settlement of the colonies. But none of these ideas gave or inferred any right in parliament, over the new countries conquered or discovered; and, therefore, denying that the colonies are a part of the realm, and that as such they are subject to parliament, by no means deprives us of English liberties. Nor does it "build up absolute monarchy in the colonies." For, admitting these notions of the common and feudal law to have been in full force, and that the king was absolute in America, when it was settled; yet he had a right to enter into a contract with his subjects, and stipulate that they should enjoy all the rights and liberties of Englishmen forever, in consideration of their undertaking to clear the wilderness, propagate Christianity, pay a fifth part of ore, &c. Such a contract as this has been made with all the colonies, royal governments, as well as charter ones. For the commissions to the governors contain the plan of the government, and the contract between the king and subject in the former, as much as the charters in the latter.

Indeed, this was the reasoning, and upon these feudal and *catholic* principles, in the time of some of the predecessors of Massachusettensis. This was the meaning of Dudley, when he asked, "Do you think that English liberties will follow you to the ends of the earth?" His meaning was, that English liberties were confined to the realm, and, out of that, the king was absolute. But this was not true; for an English king had no right to be absolute over Englishmen out of the realm, any more than in it; and they were released from their allegiance, as soon as he deprived them of their liberties.

But "our charters suppose regal authority in the grantor." True, they suppose it, whether there was any or not. "If that authority be derived from the British (he should have said English) crown, it presupposes this territory to have been a part of the British (he should have said English) dominion, and as such subject to the imperial sovereign." How can this writer show this authority to be derived from the English crown, including in the idea of it lords and commons? Is there the least color for such an authority, but in the popish and feudal ideas before mentioned? And do these popish and feudal ideas include parliament? Was parliament, were lords and commons, parts of the head of the church; or was parliament, that is, lords and commons, part of the sovereign feudatory? Never. But why was this authority derived from the English, any more than the Scottish or Irish crown? It is true, the land was to be held in socage, like the manor of East Greenwich; but this was compact, and it might have been as well to hold, as they held in Glasgow or Dublin.

But, says this writer, "if that authority was vested in the person of the king in a different capacity, the British constitution and laws are out of the question, and the king must be absolute as to us, as his prerogatives have never been limited." Not the prerogatives limited in our charters, when in every one of them all the rights of Englishmen are secured to us? Are not the rights of Englishmen sufficiently known? and are not the prerogatives of the king among those rights?

As to those colonies which are destitute of charters, the commissions to their governors have ever been considered as equivalent securities, both for property, jurisdiction, and privileges, with charters; and as to the power of the crown being absolute in those colonies, it is absolute nowhere. There is no fundamental or other law that makes a king of England absolute anywhere, except in conquered countries; and an attempt to assume such a power, by the fundamental laws, forfeits the prince's right even to the limited crown.

As to "the charter governments reverting to absolute monarchy, as their charters may happen to be forfeited by the grantees not fulfilling the conditions of them," I answer, if they could be forfeited, and were actually forfeited, the only consequence would be, that the king would have no power over them at all. He would not be bound to protect the people, nor, that I can see, would the people here, who were born here, be, by any principle of common law, bound even to allegiance to the king. The connection would be broken between the crown and the natives of the country.

It has been a great dispute, whether charters granted within the realm can be forfeited at all. It was a question debated with infinite learning, in the case of the charter of London. It was adjudged forfeited in an arbitrary reign; but afterwards, after the revolution, it was declared in parliament not forfeited, and by an act of parliament made incapable of forfeiture. The charter of Massachusetts was declared forfeited too. So were other American charters. The Massachusetts alone were tame enough to give it up. But no American charter will ever be decreed forfeited again; or if any should, the decree will be regarded no more than a vote of the lower house of the Robinhood society. The court of chancery has no authority without the realm; by common law, surely it has none in America. What! the privileges of millions of Americans depend on the discretion of a lord chancellor? God forbid! The passivity of this colony in receiving the present charter in lieu of the first, is, in the opinion of some, the deepest stain upon its character. There is less to be said in excuse for it than the witchcraft, or hanging the Quakers. A vast party in the province were against it at the time, and thought themselves betrayed by their agent. It has been a warning to their posterity, and one principal motive with the people never to trust any agent with power to concede away their privileges again. It may as well be pretended that the people of Great Britain can forfeit their privileges, as the people of this province. If the contract of state is broken, the people and king of England must recur to nature. It is the same in this province. We shall never more submit to decrees in chancery, or acts of parliament, annihilating charters, or abridging English liberties.

Whether Massachusettensis was born, as a politician, in the year 1764, I know not; but he often writes as if he knew nothing of that period. In his attempt to trace the denial of the supreme authority of the parliament, he commits such mistakes as a man of age at that time ought to blush at.* He says, that "when the Stamp Act was made, the authority of parliament to impose external taxes, or, in other words, to lay duties upon goods and merchandise, was admitted," and that when the Tea Act was made, "a new distinction was set up, that parliament had a right to lay duties upon merchandise for the purpose of

---

* "It is curious, indeed, to trace the denial and oppugnation to the supreme authority of the state. When the Stamp Act was made, the authority of parliament to impose internal taxes was denied; but their right to impose external ones, or, in other words, to lay duties upon goods and merchandise, was admitted. When the act was made, imposing duties upon tea, &c., a new distinction was set up, that the parliament had a right to lay duties upon merchandise for the purpose of regulating trade, but not for the purpose of raising a revenue; that is, the parliament had good right, and lawful authority, to lay the former duty of a shilling on the pound, but had none to lay the present duty of threepence. Having got thus far safe, it was only taking one step more to extricate ourselves entirely from their fangs, and become independent states; that our patriots most heroically resolved upon, and flatly denied that parliament had a right to make any laws whatever, that should be binding upon the colonies." *Massachusettensis.*

regulating trade, but not for the purpose of raising a revenue." This is a total misapprehension of the declared opinions of people at those times. The authority of parliament to lay taxes for a revenue has been always generally denied. And their right to lay duties to regulate trade has been denied by many, who have ever contended that trade should be regulated only by prohibitions. . . .

This writer sneers at the distinction between a right to lay the former duty of a shilling on the pound of tea, and the right to lay the threepence. But is there not a real difference between laying a duty to be paid in England upon exportation, and to be paid in America upon importation? Is there not a difference between parliament's laying on duties within their own realm, where they have undoubted jurisdiction, and laying them out of their realm, nay, laying them on in our realm, where we say they have no jurisdiction? Let them lay on what duties they please in England, we have nothing to say against that.

"Our patriots most heroically resolved to become independent states, and flatly denied that parliament had a right to make any laws whatever, that should be binding upon the colonies."

Our scribbler, more heroically still, is determined to show the world, that he has courage superior to all regard to modesty, justice, or truth. Our patriots have never determined or desired to be independent states, if a voluntary cession of a right to regulate their trade can make them dependent even on parliament; though they are clear in theory that, by the common law and the English constitution, parliament has no authority over them. None of the patriots of this province, of the present age, have ever denied that parliament has a right, from our voluntary cession, to make laws which shall bind the colonies, so far as their commerce extends.

"There is no possible medium between absolute independence and subjection to the authority of parliament." If this is true, it may be depended upon, that all North America are as fully convinced of their independence, their absolute independence, as they are of their own existence; and as fully determined to defend it at all hazards, as Great Britain is to defend her independence against foreign nations. But it is not true. An absolute independence on parliament, in all internal concerns and cases of taxation, is very compatible with an absolute dependence on it, in all cases of external commerce.

"He must be blind indeed, that cannot see our dearest interest in the latter, (that is, in an absolute subjection to the authority of parliament,) notwithstanding many pant after the former," (that is, absolute independence.) The man who is capable of writing, in cool blood, that our interest lies in an absolute subjection to parliament, is capable of writing or saying any thing for the sake of his pension. A legislature that has so often discovered a want of information concerning us and our country; a legislature interested to lay burdens upon us; a legislature, two branches of which, I mean the lords and commons, neither love nor fear us! Every American of fortune and common sense, must look upon his property to be sunk downright one half of its value, the moment such an absolute subjection to parliament is established.

That there are any who pant after "independence," (meaning by this word a new plan of government over all America, unconnected with the crown of England, or meaning by it an exemption from the power of parliament to regulate trade,) is as great a slander upon the province as ever was committed to writing. The patriots of this province desire nothing new; they wish only to keep their old privileges. They were, for one hundred and fifty years, allowed to tax themselves, and govern their internal concerns as they thought best. Parliament governed their trade as they thought fit. This plan they wish may continue forever. But it is honestly confessed, rather than become subject to the absolute authority of parliament in all cases of taxation and internal polity, they will be driven to throw off that of regulating trade.

"To deny the supreme authority of the state, is a high misdemeanor; to oppose it by force, an overt act of treason." True; and therefore Massachusettensis, who denies the king represented by his governor, his majesty's council by charter, and house of representatives, to be the supreme authority of this

province, has been guilty of a high misdemeanor; and those
ministers, governors, and their instruments, who have brought
a military force here, and employed it against that supreme authority, are guilty of——, and ought to be punished with——.
I will be more mannerly than Massachusettensis. . . .

7

A DEFENCE OF
THE CONSTITUTIONS OF
THE UNITED STATES
OF AMERICA[1]

The *three-volume* Defence *was written in London
when Adams was serving as a diplomat in Europe after the Revolution. Begun in 1786, it was finished in
1789, just as the new U.S. Constitution had been rat-
ified and the French Revolution was about to break
out. A few members of the Constitutional Convention at Philadelphia read the first volumes and found
them impressive, but their remarks were so vague it is
difficult to say if Adams's writings influenced the proceedings.*

*Adams was responding to French critics of Amer-
ica's constitutional schemes, some of whom, like
A.-R.-J. Turgot and M.-J.-A.-N. de Câritat, the Marquis de Condorcet, had once been his friends while
he was in Paris.* The French thinkers, as well as the
seventeenth-century British writer Marchamont Nedham, all were advocates of the centralization of
power. The assumption was that if authority remains
divided among branches of government, the old order
will continue its aristocratic hegemony, whereas lo-
cating all authority in one central place would make it
responsible to the democratic people. But Adams believed that power could not be democratized, for it
was in the nature of power to move away from the
people. *If democracy expanded and incorporated,*

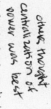

other thought
centralization of
power was best

power contracted and excluded. Power must be dis-
persed, and the establishment of a strong executive
would assure that power would be balanced among
the countervailing mechanisms of checks and con-
trols.

Adams scoured the annals of ancient and modern
history to demonstrate why republics failed to sur-
vive, why the concept of virtue might be a delusion,
why certain authors like Machiavelli shirked from
telling the truth about human nature, why religion
could not be readily relied upon in constructing an
American republic, and why the coming of commer-
cial society could not be avoided.

As Hannah Arendt pointed out in On Revolution,
while other figures of the Enlightenment saw them-
selves as advocates of liberty, equality, and fraternity
or as revolutionists who believed that people were
sovereign and democracy was sacred, Adams alone
was a constitutionalist who believed a revolution had
no means of enduring without the rule of law. Today
the critique of the Enlightenment offered by post-
modernist thinkers insists that the philosophes placed
too much trust in reason and saw knowledge rising to
counter the menace of power. Adams believed that
the only answer to power was the balance of counter-
vailing powers.

Adams's vast survey of the history of republics
from ancient to modern times was intended to ex-
plain why they had proved incapable of sustaining
themselves. The American Republic formed in 1788–
1789 was meant to represent a break from the past
based on what the Federalist *authors called the "new*
science of politics." Republicanism, a theory of gov-
ernment that proposed to do without a monarchy,
seemed to have a long record of failure. The framers
of the American Constitution were also unsure if the
American Republic would last. Adams was convinced
that unless the country's political institutions were

properly constructed, with a sufficient role for a strong executive office—that is, a presidency—America was destined to go the way of all republics and sooner or later experience a decline and fall. However, his case for a strong executive had to struggle against the conventions of an American people who had just fought a war against the king of England. At the Constitutional Convention in 1787 the executive branch of government was attacked as the "foetus of monarchy." Adams had his work cut out for him.

ITALIAN REPUBLICS
OF THE MIDDLE AGE.

Florence.

There is no example of a government simply democratical; yet there are many of forms nearly or remotely resembling what are understood by "All Authority in one Centre." There once existed a cluster of governments, now generally known by the name of the Italian Republics of the Middle Age, which deserve the attention of Americans, and will further illustrate and confirm the principles we have endeavored to maintain. If it appears, from the history of all the ancient republics of Greece, Italy, and Asia Minor, as well as from those that still remain in Switzerland, Italy, and elsewhere, that caprice, instability, turbulence, revolutions, and the alternate prevalence of those two plagues and scourges of mankind, tyranny and anarchy, were the effects of governments without three orders and a balance, the same important truth will appear, in a still clearer light, in the republics of Italy. The sketches to be given of these cannot be introduced with more propriety than by the sentiments of a late writer, because they coincide with every thing that has been before observed.

Limited monarchies were the ancient governments; the jealousies and errors of the nobles, or the oppressions they suf-

fered, stimulated them to render monarchy unpopular, and
erect aristocracies. . . . But . . . let us descend to particulars,
and, quitting the ancient republics of Italy, descend to those of
the middle age, among which Florence is the most illustrious.
As the history of that noble city and magnanimous people has
been written by two authors, among a multitude of others,
who may be compared to any of the historians of Greece or
Rome, we have here an example more fully delineated, an experiment more perfectly made and more accurately described,
than any we have examined before. We shall not, therefore,
find it tedious to consider minutely the affairs of a brave and
enlightened people, to whom the world is indebted for a
Machiavel, a Guicciardini, and an Americus Vespucius; in a
great degree for the resurrection of letters, and a second civilization of mankind. Next to Athens and Rome, there has not
existed a more interesting city. The history is full of lessons of
wisdom, extremely to our purpose.

We have all along contended, that the predominant passion
of all men in power, whether kings, nobles, or plebeians, is the
same; that tyranny will be the effect, whoever are the governors, whether the one, the few, or the many, if uncontrolled by
equal laws, made by common consent, and supported, protected, and enforced by three different orders of men *in equi-
librio*. In Florence, where the administration was, by turns, in
the nobles, the grandees, the commons, the plebeians, the mob,
the ruling passion of each was the same; and the government of
each immediately degenerated into a tyranny so insupportable
as to produce a fresh revolution. We have all along contended,
that a simple government, in a single assembly, whether aristocratical or democratical, must of necessity divide into two parties, each of which will be headed by some one illustrious
family, and will proceed from debate and controversy to sedition and war. In Florence, the first dissension was among the
nobility; the second between the nobles and commons; and the
third between the commons and plebeians. In each of which
contests, as soon as one party got uppermost, it split into two;
and executions, confiscations, banishments, assassinations,
and dispersions of families, were the fruit of every division,

even with more atrocious aggravations than in those of Greece. Having no third order to appeal to for decision, no contest could be decided but by the sword.

It will enable us the better to understand Machiavel, whose history will be abridged and commented on, if we premise from Nardi,* that "the city of Florence had, like all other cities, its people consisting of three genera of inhabitants, that is to say, the nobility, the people of property, and the common people.† Although some too diligently divided the nobility into three sorts, calling the first, nobles, the second, grandees, and the third, families; meaning to signify, that some of the inhabitants had come into the city and become citizens, having been deprived of their own proper country by conquest, while they were attempting to enlarge and extend their territories; others, originally of this country, had become abundant in riches and powerful in dependents, either by their own industry or the favor of fortune; and others, having been foreigners, had come in like manner to inhabit the city, but, from their primitive condition, they still retained the distinctions of lord and vassal, by habit and by fraud, both in the city and the country. And all this mixture were indifferently called nobles, grandees, and families; and they were equally hated, contradicted, and opposed, in the government of the republic, and in all their actions, by that party which was called the substantial people, *il popolo grasso*. The lower class of people, the plebeians, *il popolo minuto*, never intervened in government at all, excepting on one single occasion, when, with violence, they usurped it, as in its proper place will be related. Some persons made still another division of the plebeians, and not without reason; for those who possessed real estate in the city or country, and were recorded in the public books of taxes and tributes of the city, and were called the Enregistered,‡ esteemed themselves, and were considered by their fellow-citizens, as holding a middle station. The remainder of the lower class, who possessed no

---

*Le Istorie della Città di Firenze, p. 1.
†Il popolo grasso, e il popolo minuto.
‡Descritti.

kind of property, were held of no account. Nevertheless, all this undistinguished aggregate were called the people of Florence; and the expression is still in use, as the people of Athens, or the people of Rome, anciently comprehended the whole body of the inhabitants of those cities; to which confused, and, in its nature, pernicious aggregate, as that of the head and tail always is, the body of middling citizens will always remain extremely useful, and proportioned to the constitution of a perfect republic."

[As Machiavel is the most favorable to a popular government, and is even suspected of sometimes disguising the truth to conceal or mollify its defects, the substance of this sketch will be taken from him, referring at the same time to other authors;] so that those young Americans who wish to be masters of the subject, may be at no loss for information.

"The most useful erudition for republicans is that* which exposes the causes of discord; by which they may learn wisdom and unanimity from the examples of others. The factions in Florence are the most remarkable of any. Most other commonwealths have been divided into two; that city was distracted into many. In Rome, the contest between patricians and plebeians, which arose after the expulsion of kings, continued to the dissolution of the republic. The same happened in Athens, and all the other commonwealths of Greece, Italy, and Asia Minor. Such was the patriotism or good fortune of Florence, that she seems to have gathered fresh vigor, and risen stronger for her factions. Some, who escaped in the struggles, contributed more by their courage and constancy to the exaltation of themselves and their country, than the malignity of faction had done to distress them. And if such orders and balances had been established in their form of government as would have kept the citizens united after they had shaken off the yoke of the empire, it might have equalled any republic, ancient or modern, in military power and the arts of peace."

*Istorie Fiorentine di Nic. Macchiavelli, Proemio dell'Autore. The substance of this work is here given by the author, who now and then translates a passage literally, when he desires to comment on it.

[Handwritten margin note: Machiavel most favorable to popular gov't]

"The city of Florence was begun by the inhabitants of Fiesole, who, situated on the top of a hill, marked out a plot of ground upon the plain between the hill and the river Arno, for the conveniency of merchants, who first built stores there for their goods. When the Romans had secured Italy by the destruction of Carthage, this place multiplied exceedingly, and became a city by the name of Villa Arnina. Sylla was the first, and, after him, the three Roman citizens who revenged the death and divided the empire of Cæsar, who sent colonies to Fiesole, that settled in the plain, not far from the town already begun; and the place became so full of buildings and inhabitants, and such provisions were made for a civil government, that it might well be reckoned among the cities of Italy.

"Whence it took the name of Florence is not so well known. Tacitus calls the town Florentia, and the people Florentines. It was founded under the Roman empire; but when that was overrun by barbarians, Totila, King of the Ostrogoths, took and demolished it. Two hundred and fifty years afterwards, it was rebuilt by Charlemagne, from whose time, till 1215, it followed the fortune of those who successively ruled in Italy; for, during that period, it was governed first by the posterity of Charlemagne, then by the Berengarii, and last of all by the German emperors. In 1010 the Florentines took and destroyed Fiesole. When the popes assumed greater authority in Italy, and the power of the German emperors was upon the wane, all the towns of that province began to govern themselves. In 1080 Italy was divided between Henry III. and the church. Until 1215, the Florentines always submitted to the strongest, having no other ambition than to preserve themselves. But as, in our bodies, the later diseases come, the more dangerous they are, so, the longer Florence put off taking a part in the troubles of Italy, the more fatal these proved.

"The cause of its first division is well known. The most powerful families in Florence, in 1215, were the Buondelmonti and the Uberti, and next to them the Amidei and Donati. A quarrel happened about a lady, a Messer Buondelmonte was killed. This murder divided the whole city, one part of it siding with the Buondelmonti, and the other with the Uberti; and as both of the families were powerful in alliances, castles, and adherents, the quarrel continued many years, till the reign of the Emperor Frederick II., who, being likewise King of Naples, and desirous to strengthen himself against the church, and establish his interest more securely in Tuscany, joined the Uberti, who by his assistance drove the Buondelmonti out of Florence; and thus that city became divided, as all the rest of Italy was before, into the two factions of Guelphs and Ghibellines.* The Guelphs, thus driven out of the city, retired into the valley, which lies higher up the Arno, where their strong places and dependencies lay, and defended themselves as well as they could; but when Frederick died, the neutral people in the city endeavored to reunite it, and prevailed upon the Guelphs to forget the wrongs they had suffered, and return, and the Ghibellines to dismiss their jealousies, and receive them.

After they were reunited, they divided the city into six parts, and chose twelve citizens, two to govern each ward, with the ti-

---

*The former of which denominated the adherents of the pope, and the latter those of the emperor; Guelph being the name of the general of the first army for the church in this controversy, and Ghibelline that of the place of birth of the general who commanded for the emperor, about 1139.

Danina, *Rivoluzioni d'Italia.* "There flourished in Germany two principal families, the one called the Henries of Ghibilinga, and the other the Guelphs of Altdorp, which, by the marriage of Azzo d'Este with Cunegund, daughter of Guelph III., engrafted itself into the house of Este, called afterwards, for that reason, Guelfa Estense, from which are descended the Dukes of Modena, and those of Brunswick and Hanover. From the first of which families, namely, the Ghibellines, have arisen many kings and emperors, as the third, fourth, and fifth Henry. Of the other, namely, the Guelphs, there had been for many years famous dukes, who, contending for power and for credit with the emperors, had very often disturbed the tranquillity of the state. Under the reign of Henry V. these two families happily united in alliance, because Frederic, Duke of Suabia, married Judith, daughter of Henry, Duke of Bavaria, and sister of Guelph VI., who was at that time the head of the house of Altdorp."

Commentari de'fatti civili occorsi dentro Firenze. Scritto dal Senatore Filippo de Nerli, p. 2.

Historia Fiorentina di M. Piero Buoninsegni, Gentilhuomo Fiorentino, p. 35.
Annali d'Italia, da Muratori, tom. vii. pp. 150, 151, anno 1215.
Istoria civile del Regno di Napoli, di Pietro Giannone, tom. iii. p. 83.
Muratori, *Dissertazioni,* tom. iii. p. 130.
Muratori, *Antichità Estensi,* parte prima, c. xxxi. p. 305.

tle of Anziani, but to be changed every year. To prevent any
feuds or discontents that might arise from the determination of
judicial matters, they constituted two judges that were not
Florentines, one of whom was styled the captain of the people,
and the other the podestà, to administer justice to the people,
in all causes civil and criminal; and since laws are but of little
authority and short duration, where there is not sufficient
power to support and enforce them, they raised twenty bands
or companies in the city, and seventy-six more in the rest of
their territories, in which all the youth were enlisted, and
obliged to be ready armed under their respective colors, whenever they were required so to be by the captain or the anziani.
Their standard-bearers were changed every year with great formality."

This is the very short description of their constitution. The
twelve anziani appear to have had the legislative and executive
authority, and to have been annually eligible—a form of government as near that of M. Turgot, and March[a—ED.]mont
Nedham, as any to be found;—yet the judicial power is here
separated, and the people could so little trust themselves or the
anziani with this power, that it was given to foreigners.

["By such discipline in their civil and military affairs, the
Florentines laid the foundation of their liberty; and it is hardly
to be conceived, how much strength and authority they acquired in a very short time; for their city not only became the
capital of Tuscany, but was reckoned among the principal in
Italy; and, indeed, there is no degree of grandeur to which it
might not have attained, *if it had not been obstructed by new
and frequent factions.*"]

After this pompous preamble, one can scarce read without
smiling the words that follow: "For the space of ten years they
lived under this form of government;" especially when it appears
that, during all these ten years, they were constantly employed in
wars abroad, as appears by the following words: "During which
time they forced the states of Pistoia, Arezzo, and Siena, to enter
into a confederacy with them; and in their return with their army
from the last city, they took Volterra, demolished several castles,
and brought the inhabitants to Florence."

The United States of America calculated their governments for a duration of more than ten years. There is little doubt to be made, that they might have existed under the government of state congresses for ten years, while they were constantly at war, and all the active and idle were in council or in arms; but we have seen, that a state which could be governed by a provincial congress, and, indeed, that could carry on a war without any government at all, while danger pressed, has lately, in time of profound peace, and under a good government, broken out in seditions.*

This democratical government in Florence could last no longer; "For in all these expeditions," says Machiavel, "the Guelphs had the chief direction and command, as they were much more popular than the Ghibellines, who had behaved themselves so imperiously in the reign of Frederick, when they had the upper hand, that they were become very odious to the people; and because the party of the church was generally thought to favor their attempts to preserve their liberty, whilst that of the emperor endeavored to deprive them of it.

"The Ghibellines, in the mean time, finding their authority so dwindled, were not a little discontented, and only waited for a proper opportunity to seize upon the government again. They entered into correspondence with Manfred, the son of Frederick, King of Naples, in hopes of his assistance; but, for want of due secrecy in these practices, they were discovered by the anziani, who thereupon summoned the family of the Uberti to appear before them; but, instead of obeying, they took up arms, and fortified themselves in their houses; at which the people were so incensed, that they likewise ran to arms, and, by the help of the Guelphs, obliged the whole party of the Ghibellines to quit Florence, and transport themselves to Siena. There they sued to Manfred for aid, who granted it; and the Guelphs were defeated upon the banks of the river Arbia, with such slaughter, by the king's forces under the conduct of Farinata de gli Uberti, that those who escaped from it, giving up their city for lost, fled directly to Lucca. Manfred had given the

---

*This alludes to the state of things existing in Massachusetts in 1786, and to the insurrection of Shays and others.

command of the auxiliaries, which he sent to the Ghibellines, to Count Giordano, a soldier of no small reputation in those times. This Giordano, after his victory, immediately advanced with the Ghibellines to Florence, and not only forced the city to acknowledge Manfred for its sovereign, but deposed the magistrates, and either entirely abrogated or altered all laws and customs that might look like remains of their former liberty; which being executed with great rigor and insolence, inflamed the people to such a degree, that if they did not love the Ghibellines before, they now became their inveterate and implacable enemies; which aversion continually increasing, at last proved their utter destruction."

There is an admirable example of patriotism at this period of the Florentine history, in Farinata Uberti, who successfully and decidedly opposed a plan of his own party of Ghibellines and their allies, for the demolition of the city. He preserved it, however, only for his enemies the Guelphs, who, driven out of Lucca, went to Parma, and joined their friends the Guelphs in that city, drove out the Ghibellines, and had their confiscated estates for their reward. They then joined the pope against Manfred, who was defeated and slain.

"In consequence of this victory, the Guelphs of Florence grew daily bolder and more vigorous, and the party of the Ghibellines weaker and weaker; upon which Count Guido Novello, and those that were left in commission with him to govern Florence, resolved to try, by lenity and gentler treatment, to recover the affections of the people, whom they found they had exasperated to the last degree by their oppressive and violent manner of proceeding. To cajole and ingratiate themselves with the people, they chose six-and-thirty citizens out of the people of Florence, and two gentlemen of higher rank from among their friends at Bologna, to whom they gave a commission to reform the state. These delegates divided the city into distinct arts or trades, over which they constituted a magistrate, who was to administer justice to all who were in his department; and to every art a separate banner was assigned, under which they might assemble in arms, whenever the safety of the public required it.

"But Count Guido must have a tax to maintain his soldiers.

The citizens would not pay it. He attempted to take back the new privilege of magistrates to each trade. The people rose in arms, chose Giovanni Soldanieri for their leader, fought the Count and his Ghibellines, and drove them out of the city. The people, having thus got the upper hand, resolved to unite the city, if possible, and recall all such citizens as had been forced to leave their homes, whether Guelphs or Ghibellines. The Guelphs returned, after six years' banishment; the late attempt of the Ghibellines was pardoned, and they were suffered to come back again; but they still continued very odious both to the Guelphs and the people, the former not being able to forgive the disgrace and hardships of their long exile, nor the latter to forget their insolence and tyranny when they had the government in their hands; so that their ancient animosities were not yet entirely extinguished, either on one side or the other."

The wrangle soon came to a crisis, and the Ghibellines fled out of the city, upon the interposition of a foreign force from Charles, King of Naples, in favor of the Guelphs.

["After the departure of the Ghibellines, the Florentines new-modelled their government, and chose twelve principal magistrates, who were to continue in authority no longer than two months, under the title of buoni homini. Next in power under them they appointed a council of eighty citizens, which they called the Credenza. After this, a hundred and eighty more were elected out of the people, thirty to serve for each sixth, who, together with the credenza and the twelve buoni homini, were called the General Council. Besides which, they instituted another council, consisting of a hundred and twenty members, equally chosen out of the nobility, citizens, and commonalty, which was to confirm whatsoever had been resolved upon by the others, and to act jointly with them in disposing of the public honors and offices of the commonwealth."]

The first government of the anziani was as near a simple democracy as there is any example of; we found it, accordingly, ineffectual. The next, of buoni homini, was no better; and that could not support itself. Now we come to a new plan, which discovers, in the authors of it, a sense of the imperfection of the former two, and an attempt to obviate its inconveniences and dangers; but instead of a judicious plan, founded in the natural divisions of the people, it is a jumble which common sense would see, at this day, must fall to pieces. The buoni homini, the credenza, and the thirty of the hundred and eighty, wore an appearance of three orders; but, instead of being kept separate, they are all huddled together in the general council. Another council still, of a hundred and twenty, equally chosen out of the nobility, citizens, and commonalty, was to confirm whatever was resolved on by the others. Here are two branches, with each a negative. But the mistake was, that the aristocratical and democratical parts of the community were mixed in each of them; which shows, at first blush, that there never could be harmony in either, both being naturally and necessarily split into two factions. But a greater defect, if possible, than even this, was giving the executive power, the power of disposing of public honors and offices, to a joint assemblage of buoni homini, credenza, and the two other assemblies, all in one. The consequence must be, that although every one of these four orders must be divided at once into factions for the loaves and fishes, yet the nobility, by their superior influence in elections, would have the whole power.

Unhappy Florence! thou art destined from this moment to never-ending factions, seditions, and civil wars! Accordingly, we read in the next page, what any one might have foreseen from this sketch of their constitution, "that the government of Florence was fallen into great disorder and misrule; for the Guelph nobility, being the majority, were grown so insolent, and stood in so little awe of the magistracy," (and how could they stand in awe of magistrates whom they had created, and who were ever at their devotion?) "that though many murders, and other violences, were daily committed, yet the criminals generally escaped with impunity, through favor of one or other of the nobles."

"In order to restrain these enormities, instead of twelve governors, they resolved to have fourteen, seven of each party, who should be nominated by the pope, and remain in office one year. Under this form of government, in which they had been obliged in reality to submit to a foreign master, they continued for two years, when the rage of faction again blazed out. They rose in arms, and put the city under a new regulation. This was in 1282, when the companies of arts and trades ordained, that instead of fourteen citizens, three only should govern, and that for two months, who were to be chosen indifferently out of the nobility or commons, provided they were merchants, or professed any art or occupation; and these were called priori. Afterwards, the chief magistracy was vested in six persons, one for each ward, under which regulation the city continued till the year 1342."

But the course of events for these sixty years should be carefully traced, in order to see the operation of such a form of government, even in a single city. This institution, as might be expected, occasioned the ruin of the nobility, who, upon divers provocations, were excluded, and entirely suppressed by the people. The nobility, indeed, were divided among themselves; and by endeavoring to supplant each other, and aspiring to the sole government of the commonwealth, they quite lost all share in it. The priori were afterwards distinguished by the name of signori.

"There remained some sparks of animosity betwixt the nobility and commonalty, which are incident to all republics; for one side being naturally jealous of any encroachment upon their liberty and legal rights, and the other ambitious to rule and control the laws, it is not possible they should ever long agree together. This humor, however, did not show itself in the nobility while they were overawed by the Ghibellines; but when the latter were depressed, it began to appear, and the people were daily injured and abused in such a manner, that neither the laws nor the magistracy had authority enough to relieve them; as every nobleman supported himself in his insolence by the number of his friends and relations, both against the power of the signori and the captain of the people. The heads of the arts, wishing to remedy so great an evil, provided that every signory should appoint a standard-bearer of justice, out of the people, with a thousand men divided into twenty companies, under him, who should be always ready with their standard and arms whenever ordered by the magistracy. This establishment met little opposition, on account of the jealousy and emulation that reigned among the nobility, who were not in the least aware that it was levelled at them, till they felt the smart of it. Then, indeed, they were not a little awed by it for some time; but in a while they returned to the commission of their former outrages; for as some of them always found means to insinuate themselves into the signory, they had it in their power to prevent the standard-bearer from executing his office. Besides, as witnesses were always required upon any accusation, the plaintiff could hardly ever find any one that durst give evidence against the nobility; so that in a short time Florence was involved in its former distractions, and the people exposed to violence and oppression; as justice was grown dilatory, and sentence, though passed, seldom or never executed.

"The people not knowing what course to take, Giano della Bella, a strenuous patriot, though of a very noble family, encouraged the heads of the arts once more to reform the city. By his advice it was enacted, that the gonfalonier should always reside with the signori, and have four thousand armed men under his command. They also entirely excluded the nobility out of that council of the signori, and made a law that all accessaries or abettors should be liable to the same punishment with those that were principals in any crime, and that common fame should be sufficient evidence to convict them. By these laws, which were called Li Ordinamenti della Giustizia,"* (but which were in reality as tyrannical as the edicts of any despot could be,) "the people regained great weight and authority. But Giano being looked upon by the nobility as the author of these laws to bridle their power, became very odious, not only to them, but to the richest of the commonalty."

As well he might, for laws more oppressive and destructive of liberty could not have been made. Tyrannical as they were, however, they were not enough so for the people. "For upon the trial of Corso Donati, a nobleman, for a murder, although he was acquitted even under these new laws, the people were enraged, and ran to arms, and demolished the magistrate's

*Sismondi, *Républiques Italiennes,* vol. iv. pp. 63, 64.

house, instead of applying to the signori. The whole city exceedingly resented this outrage upon all law and government; the blame of it was laid upon Giano, and he was accused before the magistrates as an encourager of insurrection. While his cause was depending, the people took arms to defend him against the signori. Giano went voluntarily into banishment, to appease this tumult.

"The nobility then petitioned the signori, that the severity of the laws against them might be mitigated. As soon as this petition was publicly known, the commons, apprehending the signori would comply with it, immediately rose in a tumultuous manner; so that ambition on one side, and jealousy on the other, at last occasioned an open rupture between them, and both sides were prepared for battle; but by the interposition and mediation of some prudent men, whose arguments with both parties were very judicious, the people at last consented that no accusation should be admitted against a nobleman, without sufficient evidence to support it.

"Both parties laid down their arms, but retained their jealousies, and began soon to raise forces, and fortify themselves as fast as they could. The people thought fit to new-model the government, and reduce the number of the signori, as they suspected some of that body to be too favorably inclined to the nobility.

"A momentary tranquillity succeeded; but the sparks of jealousy and envy still remained betwixt the nobility and people, which soon broke out, on occasion of a quarrel between two families, the Cerchi and Donati, both considerable for their riches, nobility, and dependents. The signori were under no small apprehensions that the whole city would become engaged in the dispute, and hourly expected the two parties would openly attack each other, as soon afterwards happened, and a skirmish ensued, in which many were wounded on both sides. The whole city, commons as well as nobility, divided upon it; nor did the contagion confine itself to the city alone, but infected all the country. So ineffectual was this contemptible government of the signori to the suppression of this animosity, that the pope was applied to. He sent his nuncio to no purpose, and then put the city under an interdict; but this answered no end but to increase the confusion; and frequent battles took place, till the whole city took arms, neither the power of the magistracy, nor the authority of the laws, being able to restrain the fury of the multitude. The wisest and best of the citizens were in great terror; and the Donati, being the weaker party, not a little doubtful of their safety."

Such is the effect of a government of all authority in one centre. Here all was concentrated in the signori, chosen by the people frequently enough; yet although the nobility were arbitrarily excluded from that council, those who were chosen were indebted for their elections, probably to those very nobles, and chiefly to the Donati and Cerchi.

"The Donati were the minority, upon the whole, and therefore had great reason to be doubtful of their safety. It was agreed, at a meeting betwixt Corso Donati, the heads of the Neri family, and the captains of the arts,* to solicit the pope to send some person of royal extraction to reform the city." Here nature breaks out, in spite of all attempts to stifle it. A royal dignity is the most obvious thought, to extinguish animosities between nobles and commons. In this case, the captains of the arts, that is, the people, perceived it, as well as Corso and the Neri, the contending nobles. This meeting, and the result of it,

---

*This is an error in translation by the author, growing out of a misconception of the office referred to. The words in the original are "Capitani *di parte*." "They were the elective heads of the Guelph party, three in number." *Italian Republics*—Lardner's *Cabinet Cyclopædia*, p. 135, note.

Lord Brougham describes them as the heads of a "complete party government within the government of the state. The Guelphs chose every two months their consuls, called *party captains,* who had their secret council of fourteen members, their general council of sixty, three priors, a treasurer, and a prosecutor of Ghibellines. There never certainly was an instance of any party feud being in any country so disciplined and so wielded. The vigorous administration, not only of its own affairs, but those of the republic which it governed, was the result. Had the Jacobin club at Paris been a more regular body, and continued to govern in quiet times, it would have formed a second instance of the same sort." *Political Philosophy,* part 2, p. 346.

It is not difficult to perceive the elements of an organization in many respects not unlike this, at some time or other, in the United States, the concentration of which has been thus far counteracted only by the increasing territorial surface of the country.

was notified to the signori by the other party, who represented it as a conspiracy against the public liberty. Both sides, however, were in arms again, and Dante, who was one of the signori, had the courage to advise the sovereign assembly to arm the people; and they, being joined by great numbers out of the country, found themselves able to force the chiefs of each party to lay down their arms. They assumed an appearance of dignity, banished Corso and the Neri, and, to show their impartiality, several of the Bianchi. . . .

"New disturbances arising, the pope was advised by his legate to summon to Rome twelve of the principal malcontents of Florence. They readily obeyed the summons, and among them was Corso Donati. As soon as they were set out upon their journey, the legate acquainted the exiles that now was their time to return to Florence, as the city was then clear of the only men that had authority enough to oppose their entrance. Drawing together what forces they could, they immediately marched and entered the city; but those very citizens, who but a little before, when they petitioned in the most humble and submissive manner to be admitted, had exerted themselves in the most strenuous manner for their return, now they saw them approach in a hostile manner, were the first that took up arms against them, and joined with the people to drive them back."

One is, however, astonished at the reflection of Machiavel,— "Such was the spirit of patriotism amongst them in those days that they cheerfully gave up their private interests for the public good,"—when every page of his history shows that the public good was sacrificed every day by all parties to their private interest, friendships, and enmities.

"After the exiles were repulsed, the citizens relapsed into their former distractions; and after much violence the governors of the commonwealth reëstablished the companies of the people, and restored the colors under which the arts had formerly been used to assemble. Their captains were called standard-bearers of the companies and colleagues of the signori, and were directed not only to assist the signori in times of peace with their counsel, but to support and defend them by dint of arms in all exigencies and commotions. To assist the two judges who had been constituted in the beginning of their state, they appointed an officer called *il esecutore* or sheriff, who was to act in conjunction with the standard-bearers and see their orders carried into execution, whenever the nobility should be guilty of any enormity or act of oppression.

"The pope died, the eleven citizens returned with Corso, whose restless ambition occasioned such troubles. In order to make himself popular, he constantly opposed the nobility in all their schemes, and which way soever he observed the people to incline, he turned all his authority to support them in it and gain their affection; so that in all contests and divisions, or when they had any extraordinary point to carry, they always resorted to him and put themselves under his directions."

Machiavel indeed observes, "that all might now have lived in peace, if the restless ambition of Corso had not occasioned fresh troubles." But in this Machiavel is mistaken; if Corso had not existed, the people would have found some other leader and confidant. When the people feel that the government is unable or unwilling to protect them against the oppressions of the nobles, they always seek out a Cassius, Mælius, Manlius, or Corso, to assist the old or to erect a new government that will be able and willing to protect them. It is the defect in the government and the wants of the people, that excite and inspirit the ambition of private men. To be sure, the man of any distinction who listens to the complaints of the people in such cases, whether from ambition or humanity, always creates for himself much hatred and envy among the most considerable citizens.

In this instance, these passions increased to such a degree that the faction of the Neri divided and quarrelled among themselves. To alienate the affections of the people from Corso, they gave out, as the aristocracy always does in such cases, that he secretly designed to seize upon the government and make himself king; and his magnificent manner of living, and marriage into the family of Faggivola, head of the Bianchi and Ghibellines, made it easily believed.

"Encouraged by this, his enemies took up arms against him, and the greater part of the people, instead of appearing in his defence, forsook him and joined his adversaries. He was impeached, refused to obey the summons, and was declared a contumacious rebel. Between the accusation and the sentence there was not the interval of more than two hours. A civil war ensued; many were killed on both sides. After a furious defence Corso threw himself from his horse and was killed. Such was the unfortunate end* of Corso Donati, to whom his country and the Neri owed much both of their good and bad fortune, one of the most eminent men that Florence ever produced."

But Machiavel should have laid the blame upon the constitution, not upon the restless disposition or turbulent spirit of Corso; because it is impossible for a man of Corso's genius, valor, and activity, in such a government, not to be restless and turbulent; he is never safe himself, and large bodies of people are continually flattering and soliciting him, while others are threatening and persecuting him. No nation has a right to blame such a citizen until it has established a form of government that is capable of protecting him on one side, and the people against him on the other. This flimsy sovereignty of the signori was inadequate to either purpose.

After the death of Corso the exiles from Florence excited Henry† the emperor to a war against that city for their restoration; the magistrates applied to Robert, King of Naples, and gave him the government of the city for five years to defend it and protect them. This storm, after raging some time, blew over by the death of the emperor.‡ The Ghibellines then, under the command of Faggivola, renewed the war by making themselves masters of Pisa and committing depredations on the Florentine territories. The Florentines fought him and were totally defeated. They then applied to King Robert§ for another general; he sent them the Count di Andria, whose bad conduct, "added," says Machiavel, "to the impatient temper of the Florentines, which is soon tired with any form of government, and ready to fall into factions upon every accident," occasioned the city to divide again. Machiavel's severity ought, however, to

*Nerli, p. 9.
†Nerli, p. 10.
‡Nerli, p. 10.
§Nerli, p. 10. Muratori, Annal. tom. viii. p. 40.

have been applied to the form of government, not to the temper of the people, the latter being but the natural and necessary
effect of the former. In such a government the people have no
protection or security; they are continually oppressed, vexed,
and irritated by one faction or another, one ally or enemy, or
another, one aspiring citizen or family, or another, against
whose usurpations, as the constitution affords no redress, they
are obliged to recur to arms and a change of government. . . .

. . . What ideas of the rights of mankind must these people
have entertained! The commons had been deprived of the government, and they had no idea that the nobility or artisans had
any rights; the nobility were not restored to the government,
which was all they wanted; and the artisans had lost their business; but none of these orders could communicate with the others. Assassination of the Duke seems to have been all the object
in view, as if that would remedy all the evils. The plots, however,
were too freely communicated, and at last were told to the Duke.

In 1343 the city was all in a tumult, and "liberty, liberty!" was
the cry. A war was carried on in the city, and each party changed
sides several times; but, after long distractions, and much blood-
shed and devastation, the Duke was blocked up in the palace,
and the citizens assembled to reform the government.

Fourteen persons, one half of them of the nobility, and the
other commoners, with the archbishop, had full power given
them to new-model the state. The judicial department was
committed to six magistrates, who were to administer justice
till the arrival of the person who should be chosen to fill that
office. "Greater, certainly," says Machiavel, "and more cruel, is
the resentment of the people when they have recovered their
liberty, than when they are acting in defence of it; and an instance of brutal ferocity happened here that is a disgrace to human nature. The people insisted upon some persons being
delivered up to them, and among them a father and son; when
these were brought out and delivered up to thousands of their
enemies; and though the son was not eighteen, yet neither his
youth or innocence, nor the gracefulness of his person, was sufficient to protect him from the rage of the multitude. Many
who could not get near enough to reach them whilst they were

alive, thrust their swords into them after they were dead; and
not content with this, they tore their carcasses to pieces with
their nails and teeth, that so all their senses might be glutted
with revenge; and after they had feasted their ears with their
groans, their eyes with their wounds, and their touch with tearing the flesh off their bones, as if all this was not enough, the
taste likewise must have its share and be gratified."*

This is Machiavel's description of this savage barbarity; and
his words are here preserved, that it may be seen and considered
that human nature is the same in a mob as upon a throne, and
that unbridled passions are at least as brutal and diabolical, and
unlimited power as tyrannical, in a mob, as in a monarch or
senate; they are worse, for there is always a number among
them who are under less restraints of shame and decency.

"When the people were thus satisfied with blood, the Duke
and his friends were suffered to withdraw with their effects un-
molested out of Florence. After some disputes between the nobility and people, it was agreed that one third of the signori,
and one half of the other magistrates and other officers of state,
should consist of the nobility. The city was divided into six
parts, each of which chose one of the signori; and though it
sometimes happened that their number was increased to twelve
or thirteen, yet they were afterwards again reduced to six. But
as these six parts were not duly proportioned, and they designed to give more power and authority to the nobility, it was
necessary to make a new regulation in this point, and to increase the number of signori. They divided the city, therefore,
into quarters, and chose three of the signori out of each. The
standard-bearer of justice, and those of the several companies,
were laid aside; and instead of the twelve buoni homini, they
created eight counsellors, four of each quality.

---

*It is but just to add that this was Guglielmo da Scesi, the most odious of the
Duke's instruments of tyranny, and the judge who had lent himself to all his
acts of cruelty. The son was scarcely fourteen years old, but he had made himself detested by the interest manifested in the execution of the harsh sentences
against offenders. The example of the powerful is seldom copied with more
clearness by those whom they oppress, than in the indulgence of their vindic-
tiveness whenever it comes their turn.

"The commonwealth," says Machiavel, "being settled upon this bottom, might have continued quiet and happy, if the nobility could have been content to confine themselves within the bounds of that moderation which is requisite in all republican governments."

It is impossible to read these grave reflections of Machiavel and Nedham, so often repeated, with patience. It would be as wise to say, that the nation might be quiet and happy under a despot or monarch, if the despot or monarch, and his ministers and minions, could be content and moderate; or that the commonwealth might be happy under an oligarchy or simple aristocracy, if all concerned in government could be content and moderate. When we know human nature to be utterly incapable of this content, why should we suppose it? Human nature is querulous and discontented wherever it appears, and almost all the happiness it is capable of arises from this discontented humor. It is action, not rest, that constitutes our pleasure. All we have to do is to guard and provide against this quality; we cannot eradicate it.

"But the behavior of the nobility was quite the contrary," says Machiavel; "for, as they always disdained the thoughts of equality, even when they lived a private life, so, now they were in the magistracy, they thought to domineer over the whole city, and every day produced fresh instances of their pride and arrogance, which exceedingly galled the people, when they saw they had deposed one tyrant, only to make room for a thousand."

All this, one may safely believe to be exactly true; but what then? Why, they ought to have separated the nobles from the commons, and made each independent on the other. Mixed together in equal halves, the nobles will forever tyrannize. The insolence of one side, and the indignation and impatience of the other, at last increased to such a height, that both sides flew to arms, and the people, being most numerous, carried their point, and deprived the nobles in the signory of their authority; the four counsellors of their order were also turned out of their offices, and the remaining number increased to twelve, which consisted of commoners only. Besides which, the eight who remained in the signory not only made a new standard-bearer of justice, and sixteen other standard-bearers over the companies of the people, [but modelled all the councils in such a manner, that the government was now entirely in the hands of the people; and we shall soon see how well it operated.]

gov't in hand of the people did not work

"There happened a great dearth in Florence, so that there were grievous discontents both among the nobility and common people; the former repining at the loss of their authority, and the latter murmuring for want of bread. Andrea Strozzi sold corn as cheap as Mælius did in Rome. This drew such numbers to his house that he boldly mounted his horse one morning, and putting himself at the head of them, called upon all the rest of the people to take up arms, by which means he got together above four thousand men in less than an hour, and conducting them to the palace of the signori, demanded the doors to be thrown open to him. This attempt was too bold and rash to succeed; yet it gave the nobility fresh hopes of recovering their power, now they saw *the inferior sort of people* so incensed *against the commons*. They resolved to take arms and make use of all manner of allies to regain that by force which they conceived had been taken from them with so much injustice; and to insure success they provided themselves with arms, fortified their houses, and sent to their friends in Lombardy for supplies. The commons and the signori, on the other hand, were no less busy in arming themselves, and sent to the Sienese and Perugians to desire their assistance; so that when the auxiliaries on each side arrived, the whole city was soon in arms."

We ought to pause here and remark a combination of parties that is perfectly natural, though it has seldom occurred in the history of any nation so distinctly as to be descanted on by historians or politicians. Here is as distinct a division between the commons and the lower class as there ever was between nobles and commons. By the commons in this place are meant those citizens who in every nation of the world are commonly denominated *the middling people,* who, it must be confessed, have been in all ages and countries the most industrious and frugal, and every way the most virtuous part of the community. In all countries they have some influence, in many they have had some share in the government; but no other instance than this is at present recollected where they have ever had a sovereignty in their hands, exclusive both of the highest and lowest classes of citizens. As if it had been the intention of Providence to exhibit to mankind a demonstration that power has the same effects upon all minds, we find in this instance the Florentine commons discovering the same disposition to tyrannize over all above and all below them, as clearly as ever kings, nobles, or mobs discovered it when they had the power. The nobility drew up in three divisions. The commons assembled under the standard of justice and the colors of their respective companies, and under the command of the Medici immediately attacked one of the divisions of the nobility. At this time the Medici were only commoners; we shall hereafter see that they became nobles and sovereigns, and placed sons and daughters on some of the thrones of Europe.

The factions between the nobility and the commons, which ended in the utter ruin of the former, have been already related; but peace was not obtained. All authority was in one centre, the commons; and there were other orders of citizens who were not satisfied; the same contest therefore continued under a new form and new names. They now happened between the commons and plebeians, which were only new names in reality for a new nobility and commons; the commons now took the place of the nobility, and the plebeians that of the commons. Machiavel is as clear and full for a mixed government as any writer; but the noble invention of the negative of an executive upon a legislature in two branches, which is the only remedy in contests between nobles and commons, seems never to have entered his thoughts; and nothing is more entertaining than that mist which is perpetually before eyes so piercing, so capable of looking far through the hearts and deeds of men as his, for want of that thought. "There seemed to be no seeds of future dissensions left in Florence." No seeds! Not one seed had been eradicated; all the seeds that ever existed remained in full vigor. The seeds were in the human heart, and were as ready to shoot in commons and plebeians as they had been in nobles. "But the evil destiny of our city and want of good conduct occasioned a new emulation between the families of the Albizzi and the

Ricci, which produced as fatal divisions as those between the Buondelmonti and Uberti, and the other between the Cerchi and Donati had done before."

It was no evil destiny peculiar to Florence; it is common to every city, nation, village, and club. The evil destiny is in human nature. And if the plebeians had prevailed over the commons as these had done over the nobility, some two plebeian families would have appeared upon the stage with all the emulation of the Albizzi and Ricci, to occasion divisions and dissensions, seditions and rebellions, confiscations and banishments, assassinations, conflagrations, and massacres, and all other such good things as appear forever to recommend a simple government in every form.* When it is found in experience, and appears probable in theory, that so simple an invention as a separate executive, with power to defend itself, is a full remedy against the fatal effects of dissensions between nobles and commons, why should we still finally hope that simple governments, or mixtures of two ingredients only, will produce effects which they never did and we know never can? Why should the people be still deceived with insinuations that those evils arose from the destiny of a particular city, when we know that destiny is common to all mankind? ...

"It seems the will of Heaven that certain families should spring up in all commonwealths to be the pest and ruin of them. Our city owes its miseries and distractions not merely to one or two, but to several of those families; first to the Buondelmonti and Uberti, next to the Donati and Cerchi, and now, to our shame be it spoken, to the Ricci and Albizzi. Why may not this commonwealth, in spite of former examples to the contrary, not only be united, but reformed and improved by new laws and constitutions? *You must not impute the factions*

---

* "Similar revolutions broke out at the same time in the other Italian republics. In every one the same progress was to be distinguished. The party which in all had risen to power, as democratic, no sooner felt themselves in possession of it than they turned towards aristocracy. The leaders of the rising generation presented themselves as hereditary tribunes of the people at the same time that they impugned hereditary rights." Lardner's *Cabinet Cyclopædia—History of the Italian Republics*, p. 187.

of our ancestors to the nature of the men, but to the iniquity of the times, which being now altered, afford this city fair hopes of better fortune; and our disorders may be corrected by the institution of wholesome laws, by a prudent restraint of ambition, by prohibiting such customs as tend to nourish and propagate faction, and by substituting others, that may conduce to maintain liberty and good civil government."

This speech, although upon the whole it is excellent, has several essential mistakes. That certain families will spring up in every simple government, and in every injudicious mixture of aristocracy and democracy, to be the pest and ruin of them, is most certain. It is the will of Heaven that the happiness of nations, as well as that of individuals, should depend upon the use of their reason; they must therefore provide for themselves constitutions which will restrain the ambition of families. Without the restraint, the ambition cannot be prevented; nature has planted it in every human heart. The factions of their ancestors ought not to have been imputed to the iniquity of the times, for all times and places are so iniquitous. Those factions grew out of the nature of men under such forms of government; and the new form ought to have been so contrived as to produce a remedy for the evil. This might have been done; for there is a way of making the laws more powerful than any particular persons or families. . . .

The period from 1371 to 1434, is that which is boasted of by Machiavel as the prosperous one, but the prosperity of which he attributes to the virtues and abilities of Maso. Pisa, Cortona, Arezzo, Leghorn, and Monte Pulciano, were added to the dominion.

"All republics, especially such as are not well constituted, undergo frequent changes in their laws and manner of government. And this is not owing to the nature either of liberty or subjection in general, as many think, but to downright oppression on one hand, or unbridled licentiousness on the other." *

---

*Lib. iv. Non mediante la libertà e la servitù, come molti credono, ma mediante la servitù e la licenza. "Not through liberty and servitude, as many think, but through servitude and licentiousness." The idea is somewhat obscurely expressed, and needs the aid of the following sentence which is found translated below.

(margin note: republics must be well constituted)

It is very true that most republics have undergone frequent changes in their laws; but this has been merely because very few republics have been well constituted. It is very true also, that there is nothing in the nature of liberty, or of obedience, which tends to produce such changes; on the contrary, real liberty and true obedience rather tend to preserve constancy in government. It is, indeed, oppression and license that occasion changes; but where the constitution is good, the laws govern, and prevent oppression as well as license.

"The name of liberty is often nothing more than a specious pretence,* made use of both by the instruments of licentiousness, who for the most part are commoners, and by promoters of slavery, who generally are the nobles, each side being equally impatient of restraint and control."

This is a truth, which is proved as well as illustrated by every page of the foregoing history, as well as by the history of almost all other republics, ancient and modern; and the next paragraph shows that Machiavel had an accurate idea of the evil, though a confused one of the remedy.

"When if fortunately happens, which indeed is very seldom, that some wise, good, and powerful citizen, has sufficient authority in the commonwealth to make such laws as may extinguish all jealousies betwixt the nobility and the people, or at least, so to moderate and restrain them, that they shall not be able to produce any bad effect, then that state may properly be called free, and its constitution looked upon as firm and permanent; for being once established upon good laws and institutions, it has no further occasion, like other states, for the virtue of any particular man to support it."

(margin note: an executive)

One would be apt to conjecture from this, that Machiavel was about to propose a first magistrate, armed by the constitution with sufficient authority to mediate, at all times, between the nobles and commons. Such a magistrate, possessed of the whole executive power, with a negative to defend it, has always authority to intervene between the nobles and commons, and

---

*Perchè della libertà solamente il nome é celebrato. "For the name only of liberty is commended by," &c.

to preserve the energy of the laws to restrain both; and whether this executive magistrate is wise and good or not, if the commons have the negative upon the purse and the laws, and the inquest of grievances, abuses, and state crimes, that executive power can hardly be ill used.

"On such laws and principles many of those ancient commonwealths, which so long subsisted, were formerly constituted."

Rome and Sparta were, in some degree, constituted upon these principles, and in proportion as they conformed to them, they were free and happy; but neither was perfectly conformed to them.

"For want of them, others have often varied their form of government from tyranny to license, and from license to tyranny;" and for want of them, such will ever be the vibration. "For as each of those states always has powerful enemies to contend with, it neither is, nor can be possible they should be of any long duration;" and while they last, the liberty and happiness of the citizens are constantly sacrificed. "All good and wise men must of necessity be disgusted at them." So much so, that if it were not for the chance and hope of obtaining a better constitution after all the changes, any man of that character would prefer a simple monarchy at once. "Since much evil may very easily be done in the former and hardly any good in the latter; the insolent having too much authority in one, and the ignorant and inexperienced in the other." These characters of simple aristocracies and simple democracies, which succeed each other so rapidly where the third power is not introduced to control and moderate both the nobles and people, are very just; and Machiavel says what is near the truth, "both must be upheld by the spirit and fortune of one man alone, who yet may either be suddenly taken off by death or overpowered by adversity." It is a pity he had not said, parties must be upheld together by the constitutional, legal authority of one man alone, possessed of the whole executive power of the state, and then, if he is taken off by death, another will succeed; if he be overpowered by adversity, the whole state must be overpowered with him; and no form of government can be devised to warrant states against pestilence, earthquake, and famine, the inevitable and irresistible judgments of heaven. . . .

Cosimo is very tenderly treated by Machiavel; yet he has impartiality enough to record the tragical story of Neri and Baldaccio.

"Among* those who had the chief authority in the government, Neri was one, of whose reputation Cosimo was more jealous than of that of any other person; as he had not only very great credit in the city, but was exceedingly beloved by the soldiery, whose affections he had gained by his bravery, humanity, and good conduct, when he commanded the troops of the republic, as he had done upon several occasions; besides which, the remembrance of the victories that had been gained by him and his father, one of whom had taken Pisa, and the other defeated Piccinino at the battle of Anghiari, made him respected by many and feared by others, who did not desire any more associates in the government.

"But of all their generals, Baldaccio d'Anghiari was certainly the most eminent; nor was there any man at that time in Italy, who surpassed him either in courage, or military skill, or bodily accomplishments; and having always commanded the infantry, they had such an opinion of him, that it was generally believed he could influence them to execute any purpose, and that they would follow him in any undertaking whatsoever. This Baldaccio was very intimate with Neri, for whom he had the highest esteem, on account of his valor and other good qualities, of which he had long been a witness; but it was a connection that excited infinite jealousy among the rest of the principal citizens, who, thinking it dangerous to let him enjoy his liberty, and still more so to imprison him, resolved to have him despatched; in which fortune seemed to second their design."

It is very provoking to read these continual imputations to fortune, made by Machiavel, of events which he knew very well were the effects of secret intrigue; for there is no doubt it had been previously concerted to get Bartolomeo Orlandini appointed standard-bearer of justice, who, having been sent to defend the pass of Marradi, when Piccinino invaded Tuscany, had shamefully deserted it, and abandoned all that country, from the nature of its situation of itself almost inaccessible, to

*Lib. vi.

the fury of the enemy. So flagrant a piece of cowardice provoked Baldaccio to such a degree, that he could not help expressing his contempt of him, both in public conversation and in letters which he wrote to his friends, in terms that not only excited Orlandini's resentment, but made him thirst for revenge, and flatter himself that he should extinguish the infamy of the fact by the death of his accuser. To this resolution some other citizens (the Medici) were privy; who encouraged him in it, and said, that by so doing he would sufficiently revenge the injuries which he had suffered himself, and at the same time deliver the government from the fear of a man whom it was dangerous to employ, and might be their ruin to dismiss. . . .

Machiavel's introduction to his seventh book, according to his custom, is full of grave reflections.

"Those are much mistaken, who think any republican government can continue long united."

So are they who think that any despotical or monarchical government can continue long united; it is as easy to form and preserve the union of a republican as of a monarchical government, and more easy. A constitution formed upon the nature of man, and providing against his discontented temper, instead of trusting to what is not in him (his moderation and contentment in power) may preserve union, harmony, and tranquillity, better than any despotism. Republics that trust the content of one assembly or two assemblies, are as credulous, ignorant, and servile, as nations that trust the moderation of a single man. And it is as true of one as the other, *ubi solitudinem faciunt, pacem appellant.*

"Differences and divisions, for the most part, are prejudicial to republics; and yet it is certain there are some that are of service to them."

The same is true of despotisms and monarchies. Divisions are hurtful for the most part, yet some are beneficial.

"Those, indeed, are hurtful that are attended with parties and factions; but when that is not the case, they tend to the benefit of the commonwealth. As it is impossible, therefore, for any legislator or founder of a republic entirely to prevent feuds and animosities in it, it ought to be his chief care to provide against their growing up into factions."

This is easily done, by distinct and independent legislative, executive, and judicial powers, and by two councils in the legislature. Factions may be infinitely better managed in such a republic, than in a despotism or monarchy.

"It must be considered then, that there are two roads to popularity in such states, the one through public stations, the other through private life. In the former, it is acquired by gaining some signal victory, by the prudent and careful discharge of an embassy, or by giving wise and successful advice in council; in the latter, by beneficence to one's fellow citizens, by screening them from the magistrates, by supplying them with money, by promoting them to honors and employments even when they do not deserve them, by entertaining the people with plays and spectacles, and by distributing largesses among them. This manner of proceeding procures followers and partisans; and as popularity thus obtained is dangerous to the state, because it is commonly applied to serve private and self-interested views; so the reputation that is acquired the other way is of credit and advantage to it, when not made a tool to party and faction, because it conduces to the good of the whole. And though emulation and envy will always spring up, even among citizens of the latter sort, yet, as they have no partisans that follow them for their own private ends, they cannot hurt the commonwealth; on the contrary, they must of necessity be of service to it, for this very emulation will naturally excite their utmost endeavors to excel each other in their merits towards their country, and make them *keep so strict a watch over one another's actions, that none of them will have it in their power to transgress the bounds of good citizens.* But the divisions in Florence constantly ended in factions, and therefore were always pernicious to the republic; nor did any one of those factions continue united any longer than it had subdued the adverse party; for when once that was done, and consequently all fear and restraint were at an end, it immediately subdivided, and split itself into others."

In truth, it is impossible that divisions, in any form of simple government, should ever end in the public good, or in any thing but faction. The government itself is a faction, and an absolute power in a party, which, being without fear and restraint, is as giddy in one of these forms as in any other. "De l'absolu pouvoir, vous ignorez l' ivresse." It must, therefore, divide, if it is not restrained by another faction; when that is the case, as soon as the other faction prevails, they divide, and so on; but when the three natural orders in society, the high, the middle, and the low, are all represented in the government, and constitutionally placed to watch each other, and restrain each other mutually by the laws, it is then only, that an emulation takes place for the public good, and divisions turn to the advantage of the nation. . . .

Let the reader now run over again in his own mind this whole story of Florence, and ask himself whether it does not appear like a satire, written with the express and only purpose of exposing to contempt, ridicule, and indignation, the idea of "a government in one centre," and the "right constitution of a commonwealth." If he suspects that this mean sketch is in any degree varied by prejudice from the truth, let him read over any historian of Florence, as Machiavel, Guicciardini, Nerli, Nardi, Varchi, Villani, or Ammirato, and then say, whether it is not a libel upon Turgot and Nedham. From the beginning to the end, it is one continued struggle between monarchy and aristocracy; a continued succession of combinations of two or three parties of noble, rich, or conspicuous families, to depress the people on the one hand, and prevent an oligarchy or a monarchy from arising up among themselves on the other. Neither the first family, nor any of the others their rivals, made any account of the people, excepting now and then for a moment, for the purposes of violence, sedition, and rebellion.

Instead of devising any regular method for calling the people together, with a reasonable notification beforehand of the time, place, and subject of deliberation, a little junto of principal citizens concert a plan in secret among themselves, give notice previously to such as they please, their own dependents and partisans, order the bells to be rung, and a little flock of their own creatures assemble in the piazza. There the junto nominate a dozen or a score of persons for a balìa, to reform the state at their pleasure; no reasonable method of voting for them, no instructions given them; the people huzza, and all is over. What ideas are here of the rights of mankind? what equality is here among the citizens? what principle of national liberty is here respected? what method is this to obtain the national sense, the public voice? Can this be called the voice of God?

When the balìa is appointed, what is the question before them? Is there any inquiry how the government can be made a fair, equal, and constant representation of the nation, and a sure instrument for collecting the public wisdom? The imborsations are made, and eight hundred names are put in the purses. These alone are citizens; all the rest are to have no vote. These appoint the signori, a small council, for the ordinary administration, and the gonfalonier, who has no more power than a doge of Venice, nor so much dignity. The great council is the centre in which all authority is collected, and he who had most influence in it governed in reality, whoever were the signori or the gonfalonier; consequently, the council and signori too were always divided into parties, at the head of whom were always two of the most noted families; and the only question really was, which should be first. As the waves and winds determined, sometimes one and sometimes another prevailed, and took vengeance of their opponents by banishments and confiscations. The executive power was sometimes managed by the signori, and sometimes by the grand council; the judicial power was always the tool of the prevailing faction. Was there one year, one moment, in the whole history, when the citizens could be truly said to enjoy the blessings of liberty, equality, safety, and good order? . . .

Machiavel, from his long experience of the miseries of Florence in his own times, and his knowledge of their history, perceived many of the defects in every plan of a constitution they had ever attempted. His sagacity, too, perceived the necessity of three powers; but he did not see an equal necessity for the separation of the executive power from the legislative. . . .

Pistoia.

. . . And here ends another most splendid example of the blessings and felicities of a republic without three orders forming a mutual balance! It is quite unnecessary to excite the resentment, or flatter the vanity, of any individuals or families in America, by mentioning their names; but if you begin at New Hampshire, and proceed through all the States to Georgia, you will at once be able to fix your thoughts upon some five or six families in each state, some two of whom will, in the course of fifty years, perhaps of five (unless they are restrained by an independent executive power, three independent branches in the legislature, and an independent judicial department,) be able to divide the state into two parties, one generally at the head of the gentlemen, the other of the simplemen, tear one another to pieces, and rend the vitals of their country with as ferocious animosity, as unrelenting rancor and cruelty, as ever actuated the Cancellieri and the Panciatichi in Pistoia. And it will not be the fault of these individuals or families; they will not be able to avoid it, let their talents or virtues be what they may; their friends, connections, and dependents, will stimulate and urge them forward, by every provocation of flattery, ridicule, and menaces, until they plunge them into an abyss, out of which they can never rise. It will be entirely the fault of the constitution, and of the people who will not now adopt a good one; it will be the misfortune of those individuals and families as much as of the public; for what consolation can it be to a man, to think that his whole life, and that of his son and grandson, must be spent in unceasing misery and warfare, for the sake only of a possibility that his great grandson may become a despot!*

*It is scarcely necessary to point out the mistake which has been here committed by the author as to the probable course of things in the United States. Neither does the escape from the danger here referred to seem to have been so much due to the establishment of the form which he advocates, as to that radical equality of condition which the law and custom of equal distribution of inheritances everywhere establishes. Sixty years have passed away, and such a thing as family influence has not as yet produced the smallest perceptible effect upon the political movements of state or nation

A highly plausible, if not entirely sound view of the progress of government, making the regard for family one of the intermediate stages of civilization, is given by Dr. Arnold in the appendix to the first volume of his edition of Thucydides.

A further elucidation of the author's views on this point will be found in his letters to John Taylor of Caroline, now for the first time published, at the end of this work.

Cremona.

... The city was, in 1246, divided between the two factions; but the Ghibellines had the majority, and obtained the appointment of a podestà. This year the Emperor Frederic was excommunicated by the pope and council at Lyons, in France, and Henry Duke of Thuringia was elected.

The two factions daily increased in violence. The old city, that is the gentlemen, were favorers of the Ghibellines, and adherents of Frederic, the schismatical emperor; and the new city, that is the common people, were partisans of the Guelphs, who adhered to the holy see. The bloody wars occasioned by this division, between Frederic and Innocent, and their respective followers, can be read at leisure, and may cause a laugh at the terrible disgrace of Cremona in the loss of their triumphal chariot,* an infamy which none but the gentlemen could obliterate. The Marquis Uberto Pallavicino, a most powerful man, and of great reputation, but a zealous Ghibelline and old-cityman, was appointed podestà; he fought a memorable battle, made two thousand prisoners, retook the *carroccio,* and returned in triumph to Cremona."

Campo begins his third book in the manner of Machiavel, with deep, grave, and formal reflections, as if a diversity of sentiments, contradictory principles, inconsistent interests, and opposite passions among the citizens, could be reconciled and united by declamations against discord and panegyrics upon unanimity, without a balance, in a government possessed of sufficient force.

According to him, "disunion of the citizens is, indeed, the worst evil in a city; for what mortal pestilence can bring upon them greater damage than discord? This not only precipitates noble and illustrious families to ruin, but exterminates powerful and famous cities; nor is there any principality or kingdom so stable or well founded that it may not be torn up by factions."

If this is true, it is still an argument against constituting a city in such a manner that it must necessarily be destroyed by factions.

"All things are maintained and increased by concord, and go

---

* *"Carroccio."*

to ruin by disunion; union brings victory, and discord defeat; enemies are easily resisted when you agree among yourselves; when members are disunited from the body, the person loses both strength and beauty. When Cyrus divided the Euphrates into three hundred rivulets, a child might ford the largest of them, though his favorite had been drowned in attempting the united water. Italy, the lady and the queen of the world, after infinite conflagrations, sacks, slaughters, pillages, subversions, and ruins, has finally been degraded, by the discord of her sons, into a servant and a handmaid."

All this may be true; but how long will republicans be the dupes of their own simplicity! how long will they depend upon sermons, prayers, orations, declamations, in honor of brotherly love, and against discords, when they know that, without human means, it is but tempting and insulting Providence, to depend upon them for the happiness of life, or the liberty of society! . . .

Padua.

The elements and definitions in most of the arts and sciences are understood alike, by men of education, in all the nations of Europe; but in the science of legislation, which is not one of the least importance to be understood, there is a confusion of languages, as if men were but lately come from Babel. Scarcely any two writers, much less nations, agree in using words in the same sense. Such a latitude, it is true, allows a scope for politicians to speculate, like merchants with false weights, artificial credit, or base money, and to deceive the people, by making the same word adored by one party, and execrated by another. The union of the people, in any principle, rule, or system, is thus rendered impossible; because superstition, prejudice, habit, and passions, are so differently attached to words, that you can scarcely make any nation understand itself. The words monarchy, aristocracy, democracy, king, prince, lords, commons, nobles, patricians, plebeians, if carefully attended to, will be found to be used in different senses, perpetually, by different nations, by different writers in the same nation, and even by the same writers in different pages.

The word *king,* for example. As a Frenchman, What is a king? His answer will be, A man with a crown and sceptre, throne and footstool, anointed at Rheims, who has the making, executing, and interpreting of all laws. Ask an Englishman. His idea will comprehend the throne, footstool, crown, sceptre, and anointing, with one third of the legislative power and the whole of the executive, with an estate in his office to him and his heirs. Ask a Pole; and he tells you, It is a magistrate chosen for life, with scarcely any power at all. Ask an inhabitant of Liege; and he tells you, It is a bishop, and his office is only for life. The word *prince* is another remarkable instance. In Venice, it means the senate, and sometimes, by courtesy, the doge, whom some of the Italian writers call a mere *testa di legno* [wooden head—ED.]. In France, the eldest sons of dukes are princes, as well as the descendants of the blood royal; in Germany, even the rhingraves are princes; and in Russia, several families, not descended from nor allied to royal blood, anciently obtained, by grant of the sovereign, the title of prince, descendible to all their posterity; the consequence of which has been, that the number of princes in that country is at this day prodigious; and the philosopher of Geneva, in imitation of the Venetians, professedly calls the executive power, wherever lodged, the Prince. How is it possible that whole nations should be made to comprehend the principles and rules of government, until they shall learn to understand one another's meaning by words?

But of all the words in all languages, perhaps there has been none so much abused in this way as the words *republic, commonwealth,* and *popular state.* In the *Rerum-Publicarum Collectio,* of which there are fifty and odd volumes, and many of them very incorrect, France, Spain, and Portugal, the four great empires, the Babylonian, Persian, Greek, and Roman, and even the Ottoman, are all denominated republics. If, indeed, a republic signifies nothing but public affairs, it is equally applicable to all nations; and every kind of government, despotisms, monarchies, aristocracies, democracies, and every possible or imaginable composition of them are all republics. There is, no doubt, a public good and evil, a commonwealth and a common impoverishment in all of them. Others define a republic to be a government of more than one. This will exclude only the despotisms; for a monarchy administered by laws, requires at least magistrates to register them, and consequently more than one person in the government. Some comprehend under the term only aristocracies and democracies, and mixtures of these, without any distinct executive power. Others, again, more rationally, define a republic to signify only a government, in which all men, rich and poor, magistrates and subjects, officers and people, masters and servants, the first citizen and the last, are equally subject to the laws. This, indeed, appears to be the true and only true definition of a republic. The word *res,* every one knows, signified in the Roman language wealth, riches, property; the word *publicus,* quasi populicus, and per syncope pôplicus, signified public, common, belonging to the people; *res publica,* therefore, was publica res, the wealth, riches, or property of the people.* *Res populi,* and the original meaning of the word *republic* could be no other than a government in which the property of the people predominated and governed; and it had more relation to property than liberty. It signified a government, in which the property of the public, or people, and of every one of them, was secured and protected by law. This idea, indeed, implies liberty; because property cannot be secure unless the man be at liberty to acquire, use, or part with it, at his discretion, and unless he have his personal liberty of life and limb, motion and rest, for that purpose. It implies, moreover, that the property and liberty of all men, not merely of a majority, should be safe; for the people, or public, comprehends more than a majority, it comprehends all and every individual; and the property of every citizen is a part of the public property, as each citizen is a part of the public, people, or community. The property, therefore, of every man has a share in government, and is more powerful than any citizen, or party of citizens; it is governed only by the law. There is, however, a peculiar sense in which the words, *republic, commonwealth, popular state,* are used by English and French writers; who mean by them a democracy, or rather a representative democracy; a "government in one centre, and that

---

*See any of the common dictionaries, Soranus, Stephens, Ainsworth.

centre the nation;" that is to say, that centre a single assembly, chosen at stated periods by the people, and invested with the whole sovereignty; the whole legislative, executive, and judicial power, to be exercised in a body, or by committees, as they shall think proper. This is the sense in which it was used by Marchamont Nedham, and in this sense it has been constantly used from his time to ours, even by writers of the most mathematical precision, the most classical purity, and extensive learning. What other authority there may be for this use of those words is not known; none has been found, except in the following observations of Portenari, in which there are several other inaccuracies; but they are here inserted, chiefly because they employ the words *republic, commonwealth,* and *popular state,* in the same sense with the English and French writers.

"We* may say with the philosopher,[†] that six things are so necessary to a city, that without them it cannot stand. 1. The first is provisions, without which its inhabitants cannot live. 2. The second is clothes, habitations, houses, and other things, which depend upon the arts, without which civil and political life cannot subsist. 3. The third is arms, which are necessary to defend the city from its enemies, and to repress the boldness of those who rebel against the laws. 4. The fourth is money, most necessary to a city in peace and in war. 5. The fifth is the care of divine worship. 6. The sixth is the administration of justice, and the government of the people. For the first are necessary, cultivators of the land; for the second, artificers; for the third, soldiers; for the fourth, merchants and capitalists; for the fifth, priests; for the sixth, judges and magistrates. Seven sorts of men, therefore, are necessary to a city: husbandmen, artificers, soldiers, merchants, rich men, priests, and judges.

"But, according to the same philosopher,[‡] as in the body natural not all those things, without which it is never found,

---

Della Felicità di Padova, di Angelo Portenari, Padovano Agostino, libre nove, in Padova per Pietro Paolo Tozzi, 1623, p. 115.
[†]Aristot. *Polit.* b. 7, c. 8.
[‡]Arist. *Polit.* lib. vii. c. 9.

are parts of it, but only instruments subservient to some uses, as in animals, the horns, the nails, the hair, so not all those seven sorts of men are parts of the city; but some of them, namely, the husbandmen, the artificers, and the merchants, are only instruments useful to civil life, as is thus demonstrated. A city is constituted for felicity, as to its ultimate end; and human felicity, here below, is reposed, according to the same philosopher, in the operations of virtue, and chiefly in the exertions of wisdom and prudence; those men, therefore, are not parts of a city, the operations of whom are not directed to those virtues; such are the husbandmen who are occupied, not in wisdom and prudence, but in laboring the earth; such are the artisans, who fatigue themselves night and day to gain a livelihood for themselves and their poor families; such, finally, are the merchants, who watch and labor continually, not in wisdom and prudence, but in the acquisition of gold. It is therefore clear, that neither husbandmen, artificers, nor merchants, are parts of a city, nor ought to be numbered among the citizens, but only as instruments which subserve certain uses and conveniences of the city."

We must pause here and admire! The foregoing are not only the grave sentiments of Portenari and of Aristotle, but form the doctrine almost of the whole earth, and of all mankind; not only every despotism, empire, and monarchy, in Asia, Africa, and Europe, but every aristocratical republic, has adopted it in all its latitude. There are only two or three of the smallest cantons in Switzerland, besides England, who allow husbandmen, artificers, and merchants, to be citizens, or to have any voice or share in the government of the state, or in the choice or appointment of any who have. There is no doctrine, and no fact, which goes so far as this towards forfeiting to the human species the character of rational creatures. Is it not amazing, that nations should have thus tamely surrendered themselves, like so many flocks of sheep, into the hands of shepherds, whose great solicitude to devour the lambs, the wool, and the flesh, scarcely leave them time to provide water or pasture for the animals, or even shelter against the weather and the wolves?

It is, indeed, impossible that the several descriptions of men, last enumerated, should, in a great nation and extensive territory, ever assemble in a body to act in concert; and the ancient method of taking the sense of an assembly of citizens in the capital, as in Rome for example, for the sense of all the citizens of a whole republic, or a large empire, was very imperfect, and extremely exposed to corruption; but, since the invention of representative assemblies, much of that objection is removed, though even that was no sufficient reason for excluding farmers, merchants, and artificers, from the rights of citizens. At present a husbandman, merchant, or artificer, provided he has any small property, by which he may be supposed to have a judgment and will of his own, instead of depending for his daily bread on some patron or master, is a sufficient judge of the qualifications of a person to represent him in the legislature. A representative assembly, fairly constituted, and made an integral part of the sovereignty, has power forever to control the rich and illustrious in another assembly, and a court and king, where there is a king. This, too, is the only instrument by which the body of the people can act; the only way in which their opinions can be known and collected; the only means by which their wills can be united, and their strength exerted, according to any principle or continued system.

It is sometimes said, that mobs are a good mode of expressing the sense, the resentments, and feelings of the people. Whig mobs to be sure are meant! But if the principle is once admitted, liberty and the rights of mankind will infallibly be betrayed; for it is giving liberty to tories and courtiers to excite mobs as well as to patriots; and all history and experience shows, that mobs are more easily excited by courtiers and princes, than by more virtuous men, and more honest friends of liberty.

It is often said, too, that farmers, merchants, and mechanics, are too inattentive to public affairs, and too patient under oppression. This is undoubtedly true, and will forever be so; and, what is worse, the most sober, industrious, and peaceable of them, will forever be the least attentive, and the least disposed to exert themselves in hazardous and disagreeable efforts of resistance. The only practicable method, therefore, of giving to farmers, &c. the equal right of citizens, and their proper weight and influence in society, is by elections, frequently repeated, of a house of commons, an assembly which shall be an essential part of the sovereignty. The meanest understanding is equal to the duty of saying who is the man in his neighborhood whom he most esteems, and loves best, for his knowledge, integrity, and benevolence. The understandings, however, of husbandmen, merchants, and mechanics, are not always the meanest; they arise, in the course of human life, many among them of the most splendid geniuses, the most active and benevolent dispositions, and most undaunted bravery. The moral equality that nature has unalterably established among men, gives these an undoubted right to have every road opened to them for advancement in life and in power that is open to any others. These are the characters which will be discovered in popular elections, and brought forward upon the stage, where they may exert all their faculties, and enjoy all the honors, offices, and commands, both in peace and war, of which they are capable. The dogma of Aristotle, and the practice of the world, is the most unphilosophical, the most inhuman and cruel that can be conceived. Until this wicked position, which is worse than the slavery of the ancient republics, or modern West Indies, shall be help up to the derision and contempt, the execration and horror, of mankind, it will be to little purpose to talk or write about liberty. This doctrine of Aristotle is the more extraordinary, as it seems to be inconsistent with his great and common principles,* "that a happy life must arise from a course of virtue; that virtue consists in a medium; and that the middle life is the happiest.

"In every city the people are divided into three sorts, the very rich, the very poor, and the middle sort. If it is admitted that the medium is the best, it follows that, even in point of fortune, a mediocrity is preferable. The middle state is most compliant to reason. Those who are very beautiful, or strong, or noble, or rich, or, on the contrary, those who are very poor, weak, or

*Aristot. *Pol.* lib. iv. c. 11.

mean, with difficulty obey reason. The former are capricious*
and flagitious; the latter, rascally and mean; the crimes of each
arising from their different excesses. Those who excel in riches,
friends, and influence, are not willing to submit to command or
law; this begins at home, where they are brought up too deli-
cately, when boys, to obey their preceptors. The constant want
of what the rich enjoy makes the poor too mean; the poor
know not how to command, but are in the habit of being commanded, too often as slaves. The rich know not how to submit
to any command; nor do they know how to rule over freemen,
or to command others, but despotically. A city composed only
of the rich and the poor, consists but of masters and slaves, not
freemen; where one party despise, and the other hate; where
there is no possibility of friendship, or political community,
which supposes affection. It is the genius of a free city to be
composed, as much as possible, of equals; and equality will be
best preserved when the greatest part of the inhabitants are in
the middle state. These will be best assured of safety as well as
equality; they will not covet nor steal, as the poor do, what belongs to the rich; nor will what they have be coveted or stolen;
without plotting against any one, or having any one plot
against them, they will live free from danger. For which reason,
Phocylides† wisely wishes for the middle state, as being most
productive of happiness. It is plain then that the most perfect
community must be among those who are in the middle rank;
and those states are best instituted wherein these are a larger
and more respectable part, if possible, than both the other; or,
if that cannot be, at least than either of them separate; so that,
being thrown into the balance, it may prevent either scale from
preponderating. It is, therefore, the greatest happiness which
the citizen can enjoy, to possess a moderate and convenient fortune. When some possess too much, and others nothing at all,
the government must either be in the hands of the meanest rab-

---

*ὑβρισταὶ, in the original, "insolent."
†Πολλὰ μέσοισιν ἄριστα· μέσος θέλω ἐν πόλει εἶναι. Which Dr. Gillies interprets
thus:

> "How happy is the middle walk of life,
> O! may it be my portion in the state!"

ble, or else a pure oligarchy. The middle state is best, as being least liable to those seditions and insurrections which disturb the community; and for the same reason extensive governments are least liable to these inconveniences; for there those in the middle state are very numerous; whereas, in small ones, it is easy to pass to the two extremes, so as hardly to have any medium remaining, but the one half rich, and the other poor. We ought to consider, as a proof of this, that the best lawgivers were those in the middle rank of life, among whom was Solon, as is evident from his poems, and Lycurgus, for he was not a king; and Charondas, and, indeed, most others. Hence, so many free states have changed either to democracies or oligarchies; for whenever the number of those in the middle state has been too small, those who were the more numerous, whether the rich or the poor, always overpowered them, and assumed to themselves the administration. When, in consequence of their disputes and quarrels with each other, either the rich get the better of the poor, or the poor of the rich, neither of them will establish a free state, but, as a record of their victory, will form one which inclines to their own principles, either a democracy or an oligarchy. It is, indeed, an established custom of cities, not to desire an equality, but either to aspire to govern, or, when they are conquered, to submit."

These are some of the wisest sentiments of Aristotle; but can you reconcile them with his other arbitrary doctrine, and tyrannical exclusion of husbandmen, merchants, and tradesmen, from the rank and rights of citizens? These, or at least, those of them who have acquired property enough to be exempt from daily dependence on others, are the real middling people, and generally as honest and independent as any; these, however, it must be confessed, are too inattentive to public and national affairs, and too apt to submit to oppression. When they have been provoked beyond all bearing, they have aimed at demolishing the government, and when they have done that, they have sunk into their usual inattention, and left others to erect a new one as rude and ill-modelled as the former. A representative assembly, elected by them, is the only way in which they can act in concert; but they have always allowed themselves to be cheated by false, imperfect, partial, and inadequate representations of themselves, and have never had their full and proper share of power in a state. . . .

"Such, then, was the government of Padua, from the year 1194 to the tyranny of Ezzelino, mixed of monarchy and a republic, and this constitution was restored after the delivery of the city from that fierce and cruel oppression, and lasted happily for fifty years, with a remarkable increase of the city in riches and power; and it would have lasted much longer, if the cursed factions of Ghibellines and Guelphs had not disturbed the peace of the citizens, which afterwards, by little and little, after the fashion of poison, creeping in their hearts, afflicted the city to such a degree that, at last, in the year 1318, it took away their vital spirits, depriving them of their beloved liberty.

"The parties of Ghibellines and Guelphs, under the names of the Empire and the Church, sown in the hearts of men by the enemy of the human race, had poisoned Italy, and distempered the city of Padua."

So says the historian; and, without denying to the devil his share in the instigation of all such party distinctions and animosities, it must be still insisted on, that the essential defect in the constitution of every Italian republic was the greatest cause, and the instrument with which the infernal agent wrought. The parties of rich and poor, of gentlemen and simplemen, unbalanced by some third power, will always look out for foreign aid, and never be at a loss for names, pretexts, and distinctions. Whig and Tory, Constitutionalist and Republican, Anglomane and Francomane, Athenian and Spartan, will serve the purpose as well as Guelph and Ghibelline. The great desideratum in a government is a distinct executive power, of sufficient strength and weight to compel both these parties, in turn, to submit to the laws. . . .

Such, as has been related, were the vicissitudes of the government of the city of Padua after the tyranny of Ezzelino, which may be recapitulated thus. According to the historian, at first, it was a mixture of monarchy and a republic; afterwards it was changed into a democracy, for such he denominates the tribuneship of the plebeians, in which the people attempted the abasement and annihilation of the grandees; and, finally, it terminated in a government mixed of monarchy and aristocracy, having the senate of the optimates, and creating the podestà annually; for the major part of the time, from 1081 to 1318, it was governed by one or other of the two best species of mixed government, as our historian thought, which are composed of monarchy and aristocracy, and of monarchy and a republic.

This sovereignty of Padua was, for the most part, in one assembly; for, although a check was aimed at by the law, that nothing should be done in the great council, which had not been previously debated in the little council, yet, when any thing was proposed by the latter to the former, they sat together and voted as one assembly. At some times the sovereignty was clearly in one assembly of optimates or patricians; at another, in one assembly of plebeians, as that of the tribunes was. At last, two assemblies were formed, with each a negative; but there being no third power to mediate between them, no balance could be formed or maintained between them. At no time had the monarchical power, either under the consuls, anziani, or podestàs, a negative; for, though the podestà was an office of great dignity and splendor, he never had the whole executive power, nor a negative on the legislative. The nobles and commons were mixed together in both councils; and the executive power, the appointment of officers, &c. was always in one or other of the assemblies; and the consequence was instability to the laws, insecurity to life, liberty, and property, constant rivalry between the principal families, particularly the Scaligeri and Carrari, which ended in conquest and subjection to Venice. . . .

8

DISCOURSES ON DAVILA[1]

In some ways a sequel to the Defence, *Adams's Discourses was published in 1790 in response to the French Revolution and its claims that it would rid the world of power, hierarchy, class distinctions, oppression and exploitation, and everything that stood in the way of the heavenly world of Rousseau and the Paris philosophes. The* Discourses *had appeared a year earlier as a series of essays in the* Gazette of the United States. *Although Adams addressed French writers in general, the specific text he had in mind was that by the Italian Enrico Caterino Davila,* Historia delle guerre civili de Francia. *Davila was popular at the time for writing about centuries-old civil wars in France, but he has since fallen into neglect.*

Adams was critical of the Italian for making the same error as the French and looking to the centralization of all authority in one body. But Adams also believed that Davila thought about government in ways that confined his analysis to politics alone, whereas the true object of study is society in all its intense rivalries and emotions of pride and envy. Adams drew directly on Adam Smith to develop a theory of emulation and the need for approbation. Davila *is as much a book in social psychology as political theory. Like Denis Diderot in* Rameau's Nephew, *Adams gives us a description of the human condition in which people may be too alienated to experience their own alienation.*

*This dull, heavy volume, still excites the wonder of
its author,—first, that he could find, amidst the
constant scenes of business and dissipation in
which he was enveloped, time to write it; secondly,
that he had the courage to oppose and publish his
own opinions to the universal opinion of America,
and, indeed, of all mankind. Not one man in America then believed him. He knew not one and has
not heard of one since who then believed him. The
work, however, powerfully operated to destroy his
popularity. It was urged as full proof, that he was
an advocate for monarchy, and laboring to introduce a hereditary president in America.*

J.A. 1812.

I.

Felix, quem faciunt aliena pericula cautum.[2]. . .

Before we proceed in our discourses on Davila, it will assist
us, in comprehending his narration, as well as in making many
useful reflections in morals and policy, to turn our thoughts for
a few moments to the constitution of the human mind. This we
shall endeavor to do in our next essay.

II.

*C'est là le propre de l'esprit humain, que les exem-
ples ne corrigent personne; les sottises des pères
sont perdues pour leurs enfans; il faut que chaque
génération fasse les siennes.* *[3]

Men, in their primitive conditions, however savage, were undoubtedly gregarious; and they continue to be social, not only

*Frederick borrowed this from Fontenelle. J.A. 1812.

in every stage of civilization, but in every possible situation in which they can be placed. As nature intended them for society, she has furnished them with passions, appetites, and propensities, as well as a variety of faculties, calculated both for their individual enjoyment, and to render them useful to each other in their social connections. There is none among them more essential or remarkable, than the *passion for distinction.* A desire to be observed, considered, esteemed, praised, beloved, and admired by his fellows, is one of the earliest, as well as keenest dispositions discovered in the heart of man. If any one should doubt the existence of this propensity, let him go and attentively observe the journeymen and apprentices in the first workshop, or the oarsmen in a cockboat, a family or a neighborhood, the inhabitants of a house or the crew of a ship, a school or a college, a city or a village, a savage or civilized people, a hospital or a church, the bar or the exchange, a camp or a court. Wherever men, women, or children, are to be found, whether they be old or young, rich or poor, high or low, wise or foolish, ignorant or learned, every individual is seen to be strongly actuated by a desire to be seen, heard, talked of, approved and respected, by the people about him, and within his knowledge.

Moral writers have, by immemorial usage, a right to make a free use of the poets.

> The love of praise, howe'er conceal'd by art,
> Reigns, more or less, and glows, in every heart;
> The proud, to gain it, toils on toils endure,
> The modest shun it, but to make it sure.
> O'er globes and sceptres, now on thrones it swells,
> Now, trims the midnight lamp in college cells.
> 'T is tory, whig—it plots, prays, preaches, pleads,
> Harangues in Senates, squeaks in masquerades.
> It aids the dancer's heel, the writer's head,
> And heaps the plain with mountains of the dead;
> Nor ends with life; but nods in sable plumes,
> Adorns our hearse, and flatters on our tombs.

A regard to the sentiments of mankind concerning him, and to their dispositions towards him, every man feels within himself; and if he has reflected, and tried experiments, he has found, that no exertion of his reason, no effort of his will, can wholly divest him of it. In proportion to our affection for the notice of others is our aversion to their neglect; the stronger the desire of the esteem of the public, the more powerful the aversion to their disapprobation; the more exalted the wish for admiration, the more invincible the abhorrence of contempt. Every man not only desires the consideration of others, but he frequently compares himself with others, his friends or his enemies; and in proportion as he exults when he perceives that he has more of it than they, he feels a keener affliction when he sees that one or more of them, are more respected than himself.

This passion, while it is simply a desire to excel another, by fair industry in the search of truth, and the practice of virtue, is properly called *Emulation*. When it aims at power, as a means of distinction, it is *Ambition*. When it is in a situation to suggest the sentiments of fear and apprehension, that another, who is now inferior, will become superior, it is denominated *Jealousy*. When it is in a state of mortification, at the superiority of another, and desires to bring him down to our level, or to depress him below us, it is properly called *Envy*. When it deceives a man into a belief of false professions of esteem or admiration, or into a false opinion of his importance in the judgment of the world, it is *Vanity*. These observations alone would be sufficient to show, that this propensity, in all its branches, is a principal source of the virtues and vices, the happiness and misery of human life; and the history of mankind is little more than a simple narration of its operation and effects.

There is in human nature, it is true, simple *Benevolence,* or an affection for the good of others; but alone it is not a balance for the selfish affections. Nature then has kindly added to benevolence, the desire of reputation, in order to make us good members of society. *Spectemur agendo* expresses the great principle of activity for the good of others. Nature has sanctioned the law of self-preservation by rewards and punishments. The rewards of selfish activity are life and health; the punishments of negligence and indolence are want, disease, and death. Each individual, it is true, should consider, that nature has enjoined the same law on his neighbor, and therefore a respect for the authority of nature would oblige him to respect the rights of others as much as his own. But reasoning as abstruse, though as simple as this, would not occur to all men. The same nature therefore has imposed another law, that of promoting the good, as well as respecting the rights of mankind, and has sanctioned it by other rewards and punishments. The rewards in this case, in this life, are *esteem* and *admiration* of others; the punishments are *neglect* and *contempt;* nor may any one imagine that these are not as real as the others. The desire of the esteem of others is as real a want of nature as hunger; and the neglect and contempt of the world as severe a pain as the gout or stone. It sooner and oftener produces despair, and a detestation of existence; of equal importance to individuals, to families, and to nations. It is a principal end of government to regulate this passion, which in its turn becomes a principal means of government. It is the only adequate instrument of order and subordination in society, and alone commands effectual obedience to laws, since without it neither human reason, nor standing armies, would ever produce that great effect. Every personal quality, and every blessing of fortune, is cherished in proportion to its capacity of gratifying this universal affection for the esteem, the sympathy, admiration and congratulations of the public. Beauty in the face, elegance of figure, grace of attitude and motion, riches, honors, every thing is weighed in the scale, and desired, not so much for the pleasure they afford, as the attention they command. As this is a point of great importance, it may be pardonable to expatiate a little upon these particulars.

Why are the personal accomplishments of beauty, elegance, and grace, held in such high estimation by mankind? Is it merely for the pleasure which is received from the sight of these attributes? By no means. The taste for such delicacies is not universal; in those who feel the most lively sense of them, it is but a slight sensation, and of shortest continuance; but those attractions command the notice and attention of the public;

they draw the eyes of spectators. This is the charm that makes them irresistible. Is it for such fading perfections that a husband or a wife is chosen? Alas, it is well known, that a very short familiarity totally destroys all sense and attention to such properties; and on the contrary, a very little time and habit destroy all the aversion to ugliness and deformity, when unattended with disease or ill temper. [Yet beauty and address are courted and admired, very often, more than discretion, wit, sense, and many other accomplishments and virtues, of infinitely more importance to the happiness of private life, as well as to the utility and ornament of society.] Is it for the momentous purpose of dancing and drawing, painting and music, riding or fencing, that men or women are destined in this life or any other? [Yet those who have the best means of education, bestow more attention and expense on those, than on more solid acquisitions. Why? Because they attract more forcibly the attention of the world, and procure a better advancement in life.] Notwithstanding all this, as soon as an establishment in life is made, they are found to have answered their end, are neglected and laid aside.

Is there any thing in birth, however illustrious or splendid, which should make a difference between one man and another? If, from a common ancestor, the whole human race is descended, they are all of the same family. How then can they distinguish families into the more or less ancient? What advantage is there in an illustration of an hundred or a thousand years? Of what avail are all these histories, pedigrees, traditions? What foundation has the whole science of genealogy and heraldry? Are there differences in the breeds of men, as there are in those of horses? If there are not, these sciences have no foundation in reason; in prejudice they have a very solid one. All that philosophy can say is, that there is a general presumption, that a man has had some advantages of education, if he is of a family of note. But this advantage must be derived from his father and mother chiefly, if not wholly; of what importance is it then, in this view, whether the family is twenty generations upon record, or only two?

The mighty secret lies in this:—An illustrious descent attracts the notice of mankind. A single drop of royal blood, however illegitimately scattered, will make any man or woman proud or vain. Why? Because, although it excites the indignation of many, and the envy of more, it still attracts the *attention* of the world. Noble blood, whether the nobility be hereditary or elective, and, indeed, more in republican governments than in monarchies, least of all in despotisms, is held in estimation for the same reason. It is a name and a race that a nation has been interested in, and is in the habit of respecting. Benevolence, sympathy, congratulation, have been so long associated to those names in the minds of the people, that they are become national habits. National gratitude descends from the father to the son, and is often stronger to the latter than the former. It is often excited by remorse, upon reflection on the ingratitude and injustice with which the former has been treated. When the names of a certain family are read in all the gazettes, chronicles, records, and histories of a country for five hundred years, they become known, respected, and delighted in by every body. A youth, a child of this extraction, and bearing this name, attracts the eyes and ears of all companies long before it is known or inquired whether he be a wise man or a fool. His name is often a greater distinction than a title, a star, or a garter. This it is which makes so many men proud, and so many others envious of illustrious descent. The pride is as irrational and contemptible as the pride of riches, and no more. A wise man will lament that any other distinction than that of merit should be made. A good man will neither be proud nor vain of his birth, but will earnestly improve every advantage he has for the public good. A cunning man will carefully conceal his pride; but will indulge it in secret the more effectually, and improve his advantage to greater profit. But was any man ever known so wise, or so good, as really to despise birth or wealth? Did you ever read of a man rising to public notice, from obscure beginnings, who was not reflected on? Although, with every liberal mind, it is an honor and a proof of merit, yet it is a disgrace with mankind in general. What a load of sordid obloquy and envy has every such man to carry! The contempt that is thrown upon obscurity of ancestry, augments the eagerness for the stupid adoration that is paid to its illustration.

This desire of the consideration of our fellow-men, and their congratulations in our joys, is not less invincible than the desire of their sympathy in our sorrows. It is a determination of our nature, that lies at the foundation of our whole moral system in this world, and may be connected essentially with our destination in a future state.

III.

O fureur de se distinguer, que ne pouvez vous point![4]

                                         VOLTAIRE.

Why do men pursue riches? What is the end of avarice?

The labor and anxiety, the enterprises and adventures, that are voluntarily undertaken in pursuit of gain, are out of all proportion to the utility, convenience, or pleasure of riches. A competence to satisfy the wants of nature, food and clothes, a shelter from the seasons, and the comforts of a family, may be had for very little. The daily toil of the million, and of millions of millions, is adequate to a complete supply of these necessities and conveniences. With such accommodations, thus obtained, the appetite is keener, the digestion more easy and perfect, and repose is more refreshing, than among the most abundant superfluities and the rarest luxuries. For what reason, then, are any mortals averse to the situation of the farmer, mechanic, or laborer? Why do we tempt the seas and encompass the globe? Why do any men affront heaven and earth to accumulate wealth, which will forever be useless to them? Why do we make an ostentatious display of riches? Why should any man be proud of his purse, houses, lands, or gardens? or, in better words, why should the rich man glory in his riches? What connection can there be between wealth and pride?

The answer to all these questions is, *because riches attract the attention, consideration, and congratulations of mankind*; it is not because the rich have really more of ease or pleasure than the poor. Riches force the opinion on a man that he is the object of the congratulations of others, and he feels that they attract the complaisance of the public. His senses all inform him, that his neighbors have a natural disposition to harmonize with all those pleasing emotions and agreeable sensations, which the elegant accommodations around him are supposed to excite.

His imagination expands, and his heart dilates at these charming illusions. His attachment to his possessions increases as fast as his desire to accumulate more; not for the purposes of beneficence or utility, but from the desire of illustration.

Why, on the other hand, should any man be ashamed to make known his poverty? Why should those who have been rich, or educated in the houses of the rich, entertain such an aversion, or be agitated with such terror, at the prospect of losing their property? or of being reduced to live at a humbler table? in a meaner house? to walk, instead of riding? or to ride without their accustomed equipage or retinue? Why do we hear of madness, melancholy, and suicides, upon bankruptcy, loss of ships, or any other sudden fall from opulence to indigence, or mediocrity? Ask your reason, what disgrace there can be in poverty? What moral sentiment of approbation, praise, or honor can there be in a palace? What dishonor in a cottage? What glory in a coach? What shame in a wagon? Is not the sense of propriety and sense of merit as much connected with an empty purse as a full one? May not a man be as estimable, amiable, and respectable, attended by his faithful dog, as if preceded and followed by a train of horses and servants? All these questions may be very wise, and the stoical philosophy has her answers ready. But if you ask the same questions of nature, experience, and mankind, the answers will be directly opposite to those of *Epictetus,* namely,—that there is more respectability, in the eyes of the greater part of mankind, in the gaudy trappings of wealth, than there is in genius or learning, wisdom or virtue.

The poor man's conscience is clear; yet he is ashamed. His character is irreproachable; yet he is neglected and despised. He feels himself out of the sight of others, groping in the dark.

Mankind take no notice of him. He rambles and wanders unheeded. In the midst of a crowd, at church, in the market, at a
play, at an execution, or coronation, he is in as much obscurity
as he would be in a garret or a cellar. He is not disapproved,
censured, or reproached; *he is only not seen.* This total inattention is to him mortifying, painful, and cruel. He suffers a
misery from this consideration, which is sharpened by the
consciousness that others have no fellow-feeling with him in
this distress. If you follow these persons, however, into their
scenes of life, you will find that there is a kind of figure which
the meanest of them all endeavors to make; a kind of little
grandeur and respect, which the most insignificant study and
labor to procure in the small circle of their acquaintances. Not
only the poorest mechanic, but the man who lives upon common charity, nay, the common beggars in the streets; and not
only those who may be all innocent, but even those who have
abandoned themselves to common infamy, as pirates, highway-
men, and common thieves, court a set of admirers, and plume
themselves upon that superiority which they have, or fancy
they have, over some others. There must be one, indeed, who is
the last and lowest of the human species. But there is no risk in
asserting, that there is no one who believes and will acknowledge himself to be the man. To be wholly overlooked, and to
know it, are intolerable. Instances of this are not uncommon.
When a wretch could no longer attract the notice of a man,
woman, or child, he must be respectable in the eyes of his dog.
"Who will love me then?" was the pathetic reply of one, who
starved himself to feed his mastiff, to a charitable passenger,
who advised him to kill or sell the animal. In this *"who will
love me then?"* there is a key to the human heart; to the history
of human life and manners; and to the rise and fall of empires.
To feel ourselves unheeded, chills the most pleasing hope,
damps the most fond desire, checks the most agreeable wish,
disappoints the most ardent expectations of human nature.

Is there in science and letters a reward for the labor they require? Scholars learn the dead languages of antiquity, as well as
the living tongues of modern nations; those of the east, as well

as the west. They puzzle themselves and others with metaphysics and mathematics. They renounce their pleasures, neglect their exercises, and destroy their health, for what? Is curiosity so strong? Is the pleasure that accompanies the pursuit and acquisition of knowledge so exquisite? If *Crusoe,* on his island, had the library of *Alexandria,* and a certainty that he should never again see the face of man, would he ever open a volume? Perhaps he might; but it is very probable he would read but little. A sense of duty; a love of truth; a desire to alleviate the anxieties of ignorance, may, no doubt, have an influence on some minds. But the universal object and idol of men of letters is *reputation.* It is the *notoriety,* the *celebration,* which constitutes the charm that is to compensate the loss of appetite and sleep, and sometimes of riches and honors.

The same ardent desire of the *congratulations* of others in our joys, is the great incentive to the pursuit of honors. This might be exemplified in the career of civil and political life. That we may not be too tedious, let us instance in military glory.

Is it to be supposed that the regular standing armies of Europe engage in the service from pure motives of patriotism? Are their officers men of contemplation and devotion, who expect their reward in a future life? Is it from a sense of moral or religious duty that they risk their lives and reconcile themselves to wounds? Instances of all these kinds may be found. But if any one supposes that all or the greater part of these heroes are actuated by such principles, he will only prove that he is unacquainted with them. Can their pay be considered as an adequate encouragement? This, which is no more than a very simple and moderate subsistence, would never be a temptation to renounce the chances of fortune in other pursuits, together with the pleasures of domestic life, and submit to this most difficult and dangerous employment. No, it is the consideration and the chances of laurels which they acquire by the service.

The soldier compares himself with his fellows, and contends for promotion to be a corporal. The corporals vie with each other to be sergeants. The sergeants will mount breaches to be ensigns. And thus every man in an army is constantly aspiring to be something higher, as every citizen in the commonwealth is constantly struggling for a better rank, that he may draw the observation of more eyes.

all unother rank

IV.

Such bribes the rapid Greek o'er Asia hurled;
For such, the steady Romans shook the world.

In a city or a village, little employments and trifling distinctions are contended for with equal eagerness, as honors and offices in commonwealths and kingdoms.

What is it that bewitches mankind to marks and signs? A ribbon? a garter? a star? a golden key? a marshal's staff? or a white hickory stick? Though there is in such frivolities as these neither profit nor pleasure, nor any thing amiable, estimable, or respectable, yet experience teaches us, in every country of the world, they attract the attention of mankind more than parts of learning, virtue or religion. They are, therefore, sought with ardor, very often, by men possessed in the most eminent degree, of all the more solid advantages of birth and fortune, merit and services, with the best faculties of the head, and the most engaging recommendations of the heart.

Fame

Fame has been divided into three species. *Glory,* which attends the great actions of lawgivers and heroes, and the management of the great commands and first offices of state. *Reputation,* which is cherished by every gentleman. And *Credit,* which is supported by merchants and tradesmen. But even this division is incomplete, because the desire and the object of it, though it may be considered in various lights and under different modifications, is not confined to gentlemen nor merchants, but is common to every human being. There are no men who

ambition

are not ambitious of distinguishing themselves and growing considerable among those with whom they converse. This ambition is natural to the human soul. And as, when it receives a happy turn, it is the source of private felicity and public prosperity, and when it errs, produces private uneasiness and public calamities; it is the business and duty of private prudence, of private and public education, and of national policy, to direct it to right objects. For this purpose it should be considered, that to every man who is capable of a worthy conduct, the pleasure from the approbation of worthy men is exquisite and inexpressible.

It is curious to consider the final causes of things, when the physical are wholly unknown. The intellectual and moral qualities are most within our power, and undoubtedly the most essential to our happiness. The personal qualities of health, strength, and agility, are next in importance. Yet the qualities of fortune such as birth, riches, and honors, though a man has less reason to esteem himself for these than for those of his mind or body, are everywhere acknowledged to glitter with the brightest lustre in the eyes of the world.

the qualities of fortune

As virtue is the only rational source and eternal foundation of honor, the wisdom of nations, in the titles they have established as the marks of order and subordination, has generally given an intimation, not of personal qualities, nor of the qualities of fortune; but of some particular virtues, more especially becoming men in the high stations they possess. Reverence is attributed to the clergy; veneration to magistrates; honor to senators; serenity, clemency, or mildness of disposition to princes. The sovereign authority and supreme executive have commonly titles that designate power as well as virtue—as *majesty* to kings; *magnificent, most honored,* and *sovereign lords* to the government of Geneva; *noble mightinesses* to the States of Friesland; *noble and mighty lords* to the States of Guelderland; *noble, great, and venerable lords* to the regency of Leyden; *noble and grand mightinesses* to the States of Holland; *noble, great and venerable lords,* the regency of Amsterdam; *noble mightinesses,* the States of Utrecht; and *high mightinesses,* the States General.

A death bed, it is said, shows the emptiness of titles. That may be. But does it not equally show the futility of riches, power, liberty, and all earthly things? "The cloud-capt towers, the gorgeous palaces, the solemn temples, the great globe itself," appear "the baseless fabric of a vision," and "life itself, a tale, told by an idiot, full of sound and fury, signifying noth-

death

ing." Shall it be inferred from this, that fame, liberty, property, and life, shall be always despised and neglected? Shall laws and government, which regulate sublunary things, be neglected because they appear baubles at the hour of death?

The wisdom and virtue of all nations have endeavored to regulate the passion for respect and distinction, and to reduce it to some order in society, by titles marking the gradations of magistracy, to prevent, as far as human power and policy can prevent, collisions among the passions of many pursuing the same objects, and the rivalries, animosities, envy, jealousy, and vengeance which always result from them.

Has there ever been a nation who understood the human heart better than the Romans, or made a better use of the passion for consideration, congratulation, and distinction? They considered that, as reason is the guide of life, the senses, the imagination and the affections are the springs of activity. Reason holds the helm, but passions are the gales. And as the direct road to these is through the senses, the language of signs was employed by Roman wisdom to excite the emulation and active virtue of the citizens. *Distinctions* of *conditions,* as well as of ages, were made by difference of clothing. The laticlave or large flowing robe, studded with broad spots of purple, the ancient distinction of their kings, was, after the establishment of the consulate, worn by the senators through the whole period of the republic and the empire. The tribunes of the people were, after their institution, admitted to wear the same venerable signal of sanctity and authority. The angusticlave, or the smaller robe, with narrower studs of purple, was the distinguishing habit of Roman knights. The golden ring was also peculiar to senators and knights, and was not permitted to be worn by any other citizens. The prætext, or long white robe, reaching down to the ancles, bordered with purple, which was worn by the principal magistrates, such as consuls, prætors, censors, and sometimes on solemn festivals by senators. The chairs of ivory; the lictors; the rods; the axes; the crowns of gold; of ivory; of flowers; of herbs; of laurel branches; and of oak leaves; the civil and the mural crowns; their ovations; and their triumphs; every thing in religion, government, and common life, among the Romans, was parade, representation, and ceremony. Every thing was addressed to the emulation of the citizens, and every thing was calculated to attract the attention, to allure the consideration and excite the congratulations of the people; to attach their hearts to individual citizens according to their merit; and to their lawgivers, magistrates, and judges, according to their rank, station, and importance in the state. And this was in the true spirit of republics, in which form of government there is no other consistent method of preserving order, or procuring submission to the laws. To such means as these, or to force and a standing army, recourse must be had for the guardianship of laws and the protection of the people. It is universally true, that in all the republics now remaining in Europe, there is, as there ever has been, a more constant and anxious attention to such forms and marks of distinctions than there is in the monarchies.*

The policy of Rome was exhibited in its highest perfection, in the triumph of Paulus Æmilius over Perseus. It was a striking exemplification of congratulation and sympathy, contrasted with each other. Congratulation with the conqueror; sympathy with the captive; both suddenly changed into sympathy with the conqueror. The description of this triumph is written with a pomp of language correspondent to its dazzling magnificence. The representation of the king and his children must excite the pity of every reader who is not animated with the ferocious sentiments of Roman insolence and pride. Never was there a more moving lesson of the melancholy lot of humanity, than the contrasted fortunes of the Macedonian and the Roman. The one divested of his crown and throne, led in chains, with his children before his chariot; the other, blazing in gold and purple, to the capitol. This instructive lesson is given us by the victor himself in a speech to the people. "My triumph, Romans, as if it had been in derision of all human felicity, has been interposed between the funerals of my children, and both have been exhibited as spectacles before you. Perseus, who himself a

---

*Our mock funerals of Washington, Hamilton, and Ames, our processions, escorts, public dinners, balls, &c., are more expensive, more troublesome, and infinitely less ingenious. J.A. 1812.

captive, saw his children led with him in captivity, now enjoys
them in safety. I, who triumphed over him, having ascended the
capitol, from the funeral chariot of one of my sons, descended
from that capitol to see another expire. In the house of Paulus
none remains but himself.* But your felicity, Romans, and the
prosperous fortune of the public, is a consolation to me under
this destruction of my family."

It is easy to see how such a scene must operate on the hearts of
a nation; how it must affect the passion for distinction; and how
it must excite the ardor and virtuous emulation of the citizens.

V.

The senate's thanks, the Gazette's pompous tale,
With force resistless o'er the brave prevail.
This power has praise, that virtue scarce can warm,
Till fame supplies the universal charm.

                                                                JOHNSON.

The result of the preceding discourses is, that avarice and
ambition, vanity and pride, jealousy and envy, hatred and revenge, as well as the love of knowledge and desire of fame, are
very often nothing more than various modifications of that desire of the attention, consideration, and congratulations of our
fellow men, which is the great spring of social activity; that all
men compare themselves with others, especially those with
whom they most frequently converse, those who, by their employments or amusements, professions or offices, present themselves most frequently at the same time to the view and
thoughts of that public, little or great, to which every man is
known; that emulations and rivalries naturally and necessarily
are excited by such comparisons; that the most heroic actions
in war, the sublimest virtues in peace, and the most useful industry in agriculture, arts, manufactures, and commerce, proceed from such emulations on the one hand, and jealousies,

---

*Logan. Not one drop of Logan's blood remains. *Jefferson's Notes.*

envy, enmity, hatred, revenge, quarrels, factions, seditions, and wars on the other. The final cause of this constitution of things is easy to discover. Nature has ordained it, as a constant incentive to activity and industry, that, to acquire the attention and complacency, the approbation and admiration of their fellows, men might be urged to constant exertions of beneficence. By this destination of their natures, men of all sorts, even those who have the least of reason, virtue or benevolence, are chained down to an incessant servitude to their fellow creatures: laboring without intermission to produce something which shall contribute to the comfort, convenience, pleasure, profit, or utility of some or other of the species, they are really thus constituted by their own vanity, slaves to mankind. Slaves, I say again. For what a folly is it! On a selfish system, what are the thoughts, passions, and sentiments of mankind to us?

"What's fame? A fancied life in others' breath."

What is it to us what shall be said of us after we are dead? Or in Asia, Africa, or Europe, while we live? There is no greater possible or imaginable delusion. Yet the impulse is irresistible. The language of nature to man in this constitution is this—"I have given you reason, conscience, and benevolence; and thereby made you accountable for your actions, and capable of virtue, in which you will find your highest felicity. But I have not confided wholly in your laudable improvement of these divine gifts. To them I have superadded in your bosoms a passion for the notice and regard of your fellow mortals, which, if you perversely violate your duty, and wholly neglect the part assigned you in the system of the world and the society of mankind, shall torture you from the cradle to the grave."

Nature has taken effectual care of her own work. She has wrought the passions into the texture and essence of the soul, and has not left it in the power of art to destroy them. To regulate and not to eradicate them is the province of policy. It is of the highest importance to education, to life, and to society, not only that they should not be destroyed, but that they should be gratified, encouraged, and arranged on the side of virtue. To

confine our observations at present to the great leading passion
of the soul, which has been so long under our consideration.
What discouragement, distress, and despair, have not been occasioned by its disappointment? To consider one instance, among
many, which happen continually in schools and colleges. Put a
supposition of a pair of twin brothers who have been nourished
by the same nurse, equally encouraged by their parents and preceptors, with equal genius, health, and strength, pursuing their
studies with equal ardor and success. One is at length overtaken
by some sickness, and in a few days the other, who escapes the
influenza, is advanced some pages before him. This alone will
make the studies of the unfortunate child, when he recovers his
health, disgustful. As soon as he loses the animating hope of
preëminence, and is constrained to acknowledge a few others of
his form or class, his superiors, he becomes incapable of industrious application. Even the fear of the ferule or the rod, will
after this be ineffectual. The terror of punishment, by forcing attention, may compel a child to perform a task, but can never
infuse that ardor for study, which alone can arrive at great attainments. Emulation really seems to produce genius, and the desire
of superiority to create talents. Either this, or the reverse of it,
must be true; and genius produces emulation, and natural talents,
the desire of superiority; for they are always found together, and
what God and nature have united, let no audacious legislator presume to put asunder.

When the love of glory enkindles in the heart, and influences
the whole soul, then, and only then, may we depend on a rapid
progression of the intellectual faculties. The awful feeling of
a mortified emulation, is not peculiar to children. In an army,
or a navy, sometimes the interest of the service requires, and
oftener perhaps private interest and partial favor prevail, to
promote officers over their superiors or seniors. But the consequence is, that those officers can never serve again together.
They must be distributed in different corps, or sent on different
commands. Nor is this the worst effect. It almost universally
happens, that the superseded officer feels his heart broken by
his disgrace. His mind is enfeebled by grief, or disturbed by re-

sentment; and the instances have been very rare, of any brilliant action performed by such an officer. What a monument to this character of human nature is the long list of yellow admirals in the British service! Consider the effects of similiar disappointments in civil affairs. Ministers of state are frequently displaced in all countries; and what is the consequence? Are they seen happy in a calm resignation to their fate? Do they turn their thoughts from their former employments, to private studies or business? Are they men of pleasant humor, and engaging conversation? Are their hearts at ease? Or is their conversation a constant effusion of complaints and murmurs, and their breast the residence of resentment and indignation, of grief and sorrow, of malice and revenge? Is it common to see a man get the better of his ambition, and despise the honors he once possessed; or is he commonly employed in projects upon projects, intrigues after intrigues, and manœuvres on manœuvres to recover them? So sweet and delightful to the human heart is that complacency and admiration, which attends public offices, whether they are conferred by the favor of a prince, derived from hereditary descent, or obtained by election of the people, that a mind must be sunk below the feelings of humanity, or exalted by religion or philosophy far above the common character of men, to be insensible, or to conquer its sensibility. Pretensions to such conquests are not uncommon; but the sincerity of such pretenders is often rendered suspicious, by their constant conversation and conduct, and even by their countenances. The people are so sensible of this, that a man in this predicament is always on the compassionate list, and, except in cases of great resentment against him for some very unpopular principles or behavior, they are found to be always studying some other office for a disappointed man, to console him in his affliction. In short, the theory of education, and the science of government, may be reduced to the same simple principle, and be all comprehended in the knowledge of the means of actively conducting, controlling, and regulating the emulation and ambition of the citizens.

VI.

"Haud facile emergunt, quorum virtutibus obstat
Res angusta domi."[5]

JUVENAL.

"This mournful truth is everywhere confess'd,
Slow rises Worth, by Poverty depressed."

JOHNSON.

If we attempt to analyze our ideas still further upon this subject, we shall find, that the expressions we have hitherto used, *attention, consideration,* and *congratulation,* comprehend with sufficient accuracy the general object of the passion for distinction, in the greater part of mankind. There are not a few—from him who burned a temple, to the multitudes who plunge into low debauchery—who deliberately seek it by crimes and vices. The greater number, however, search for it, neither by vices nor virtues; but by the means which common sense and every day's experience show, are most sure to obtain it; by riches, by family records, by play, and other frivolous personal accomplishments. But there are a few, and God knows, but a few, who aim at something more. They aim at approbation as well as attention; at esteem as well as consideration; and at admiration and gratitude, as well as congratulation. Admiration is, indeed, the complete idea of approbation, congratulation, and wonder, united. This last description of persons is the tribe out of which proceed your patriots and heroes, and most of the great benefactors to mankind. But for our humiliation, we must still remember, that even in these esteemed, beloved, and adored characters, the passion, although refined by the purest moral sentiments, and intended to be governed by the best principles, is a passion still; and therefore, like all other human desires, unlimited and insatiable. No man was ever contented with any given share of his human adoration. When Cæsar declared that he had lived enough to glory, Cæsar might deceive himself, but he did not deceive the world, who saw his declaration contradicted by every action of his subsequent life. Man constantly craves for more, even when he has no rival. But when he sees another possessed of more, or drawing away from himself a part of what he had, he feels a mortification, arising from the loss of a good he thought his own. His desire is disappointed; the pain of a want unsatisfied, is increased by a resentment of an injustice, as he thinks it. He accuses his rival of a theft or robbery, and the public of taking away what was his property, and giving it to another. These feelings and resentments are but other names for jealousy and envy; and altogether, they produce some of the keenest and most tormenting of all sentiments. These fermentations of the passions are so common and so well known, that the people generally presume, that a person in such circumstances, is deprived of his judgment, if not of his veracity and reason. It is too generally a sufficient answer to any complaint, to any fact alleged, or argument advanced, to say that it comes from a disappointed man.

There is a voice within us, which seems to intimate, that real merit should govern the world; and that men ought to be respected only in proportion to their talents, virtues, and services. But the question always has been, how can this arrangement be accomplished? How shall the men of merit be discovered? How shall the proportions of merit be ascertained and graduated? Who shall be the judge? When the government of a great nation is in question, shall the whole nation choose? Will such a choice be better than chance? Shall the whole nation vote for senators? Thirty millions of votes, for example, for each senator in France! It is obvious that this would be a lottery of millions of blanks to one prize, and that the chance of having wisdom and integrity in a senator by hereditary descent would be far better. There is no individual personally known to an hundredth part of the nation. The voters, then, must be exposed to deception, from intrigues and manœuvres without number, that is to say, from all the chicanery, impostures, and falsehoods imaginable, with scarce a possibility of preferring real merit. Will you divide the nation into districts, and let each district choose a senator? This is giving up the idea of national merit, and annexing the honor and the trust to an accident, that of living on a particular spot. A hundred or a thousand men of the first merit in a nation, may live in one city, and none at all of this description in several whole provinces. Real merit is so remote from the knowledge of whole nations, that were magistrates to be chosen by that criterion alone, and by a universal suffrage, dissensions and venality would be endless. The difficulties, arising from this source, are so obvious and universal, that nations have tried all sorts of experiments to avoid them.

As no appetite in human nature is more universal than that for honor, and real merit is confined to a very few, the numbers who thirst for respect, are out of all proportion to those who seek it only by merit. The great majority trouble themselves little about merit, but apply themselves to seek for honor, by means which they see will more easily and certainly obtain it, by displaying their taste and address, their wealth and magnificence, their ancient parchments, pictures, and statues, and the virtues of their ancestors; and if these fail, as they seldom have done, they have recourse to artifice, dissimulation, hypocrisy, flattery, imposture, empiricism, quackery, and bribery. What chance has humble, modest, obscure, and poor merit in such a scramble? Nations, perceiving that the still small voice of merit was drowned in the insolent roar of such dupes of impudence and knavery in national elections, without a possibility of a remedy, have sought for something more permanent than the popular voice to designate honor. Many nations have attempted to annex it to land, presuming that a good estate would at least furnish means of a good education; and have resolved that those who should possess certain territories, should have certain legislative, executive, and judicial powers over the people. Other nations have endeavored to connect honor with offices; and the names and ideas at least of certain moral virtues and intellectual qualities have been by law annexed to certain offices, as veneration, grace, excellence, honor, serenity, majesty. Other nations have attempted to annex honor to families, without regard to lands or offices. The Romans allowed none, but those who had possessed curule offices, to have statues or portraits. He who had images or pictures of his ancestors, was called noble. He who had no statue or pictures but his own, was called a new man. Those who had none at all, were ignoble. Other nations have united all those institutions; connected lands, offices, and families; made them all descend together, and honor, public attention, consideration, and congratulation, along with them.

This has been the policy of Europe; and it is to this institution she owes her superiority in war and peace, in legislation and commerce, in agriculture, navigation, arts, sciences, and manufactures, to Asia and Africa.* These families, thus distinguished by property, honors, and privileges, by defending themselves, have been obliged to defend the people against the encroachments of despotism. They have been a civil and political militia, constantly watching the designs of the standing armies, and courts; and by defending their own rights, liberties, properties, and privileges, they have been obliged, in some degree, to defend those of the people, by making a common cause with them. But there were several essential defects in this policy; one was, that the people took no rational measures to defend themselves, either against these great families, or the courts. They had no adequate representation of themselves in the sovereignty. Another was, that it never was determined where the sovereignty resided. Generally it was claimed by kings; but not admitted by the nobles. Sometimes every baron pretended to be sovereign in his own territory; at other times, the sovereignty was claimed by an assembly of nobles, under the name of States or Cortes. Sometimes the united authority of the king and states was called the sovereignty. The common people had no adequate and independent share in the legislatures, and found themselves harassed to discover who was the sovereign, and whom they ought to obey, as much as they ever had been or could be to determine who had the most merit. A thousand years of barons' wars, causing universal darkness, ignorance, and barbarity, ended at last in simple monarchy, not by express stipulation, but by tacit acquiescence, in almost all of Europe; the people preferring a certain sovereignty in a single person, to endless disputes, about merit and sovereignty, which never did and never will produce any thing

*This is a truth; but by no means a justification of the system of nobility in France, nor in other parts of Europe. Not even in England without a more equitable representation of the Commons in the legislature. J.A. 1812.

but aristocratical anarchy; and the nobles contenting themselves with a security of their property and privileges, by a government of fixed laws, registered and interpreted by a judicial power, which they called sovereign tribunals, though the legislation and execution were in a single person.

In this system to control the nobles, the church joined the kings and common people. The progress of reason, letters, and science, has weakened the church and strengthened the common people; who, if they are honestly and prudently conducted by those who have their confidence, will most infallibly obtain a share in every legislature. But if the common people are advised to aim at collecting the whole sovereignty in single national assemblies, as they are by the Duke de la *Rochefoucauld* and the Marquis of *Condorcet;* or at the abolition of the regal executive authority; or at a division of the executive power, as they are by a posthumous publication of the Abbé de *Mably,** they will fail of their desired liberty, as certainly as emulation and rivalry are founded in human nature, and inseparable from civil affairs. It is not to flatter the passions of the people, to be sure, nor is it the way to obtain a present enthusiastic popularity, to tell them that in a single assembly they will act as arbitrarily and tyrannically as any despot, but it is a sacred truth, and as demonstrable as any proposition whatever, that a sovereignty in a single assembly must necessarily, and will certainly be exercised by a majority, as tyrannically as any sovereignty was ever exercised by kings or nobles. And if a balance of passions and interests is not scientifically concerted, the present struggle in Europe will be little beneficial to mankind,† and produce nothing but another thousand years of feudal fanaticism, under new and strange names.

---

*Witness the quintuple directory and the triumvirate consulate. J.A.
†Witness France and Europe in 1813. J.A.

VII.

'Tis from high life high characters are drawn,
A saint in crape is twice a saint in lawn.

POPE.

Providence, which has placed one thing over against another, in the moral as well as physical world, has surprisingly accommodated the qualities of men to answer one another. There is a remarkable disposition in mankind to congratulate with others in their joys and prosperity, more than to sympathize with them in their sorrows and adversity. We may appeal to experience. There is less disposition to congratulation with genius, talents, or virtue, than there is with beauty, strength, and elegance of person; and less with these than with the gifts of fortune and birth, wealth and fame. The homage of the world is devoted to these last in a remarkable manner. Experience concurs with religion in pronouncing, most decisively, that this world is not the region of virtue or happiness; both are here at school, and their struggles with ambition, avarice, and the desire of fame, appear to be their discipline and exercise. The gifts of fortune are more level to the capacities, and more obvious to the notice of mankind in general; and congratulation with the happiness or fancied happiness of others is agreeable; sympathy with their misery is disagreeable. From the former sources we derive pleasure, from the latter pain. The sorrow of the company at a funeral may be more profitable to moral purposes, by suggesting useful reflections, than the mirth at a wedding; but it is not so vivid nor so sincere. The acclamations of the populace, at an ovation or triumph, at a coronation or installation, are from the heart, and their joy unfeigned. Their grief at a public execution is less violent at least. If their feelings at such spectacles were very distressing they would be less eager to attend them. What is the motive of that ardent curiosity to see sights and shows of exultation; the processions of princes; the ostentation of wealth; the magnificence of equipage, retinue, furniture, buildings, and entertainment? There is no other answer to be given to these questions than the gayety of heart, the joyous feelings of congratulation with such appearances of felicity. And for the vindication of the ways of God to man, and the perpetual consolation of the many who are spectators, it is certainly true that their pleasure is always as great, and commonly much greater, than that of the few who are the actors.

National passions and habits are unwieldy, unmanageable, and formidable things. The number of persons in any country who are known even by name or reputation to all the inhabitants is, and ever must be, very small. Those whose characters have attracted the affections, as well as the attention of a whole people, acquire an influence and ascendancy that it is difficult to resist. In proportion as men rise higher in the world, whether by election, descent, or appointment, and are exposed to the observation of greater numbers of people, the effects of their own passions and of the affections of others for them become more serious, interesting, and dangerous. In elective governments, where first magistrates and senators are at stated intervals to be chosen, these, if there are no parties, become at every fresh election more known, considered, and beloved by the whole nation. But if the nation is divided into two parties, those who vote for a man, become the more attached to him for the opposition that is made by his enemies. This national attachment to an elective first magistrate, where there is no competition, is very great. But where there is a competition, the passions of his party are inflamed by it into a more ardent enthusiasm. If there are two candidates, each at the head of a party, the nation becomes divided into two nations, each of which is, in fact, a moral person, as much as any community can be so, and are soon bitterly enraged against each other.

It has been already said, that in proportion as men rise higher in the world, and are exposed to the observation of greater numbers, the effects of these passions are more serious and alarming. Impressions on the feelings of the individual are deeper; and larger portions of mankind become interested in them. When you rise to the first ranks and consider the first men,—a nobility who are known and respected at least, perhaps habitually esteemed and beloved by a nation; princes and kings, on whom the eyes of all men are fixed, and whose every motion is regarded,— the consequences of wounding their feelings are dreadful, because the feelings of a whole nation, and sometimes of many nations, are wounded at the same time. If the smallest variation is made in their situation, relatively to each other; if one who was inferior is raised to be superior, unless it be by fixed laws, whose evident policy and necessity may take away disgrace, nothing but war, carnage, and vengeance has ever been the usual consequence of it. In the examples of the houses, Valois and Bourbon, Guise and Montmorenci, Guise and Bourbon, and Guise and Valois, we shall see very grave effects of these feelings; and the history of a hundred years, which followed, is nothing but a detail of other, and more tragical effects of similar causes.

To any one who has never considered the force of *national attention, consideration, and congratulation,* and the causes, natural and artificial, by which they have been excited, it will be curious to read, in Plato's *Alcibiades,* the manner in which these national attachments to their kings were created by the ancient Persians. The policy of the modern monarchies of Europe seems to be an exact imitation of that of the Persian court, as it is explained by the Grecian philosopher. In France, for example, the pregnancy of the queen is announced with great solemnity to the whole nation. Her majesty is scarcely afflicted with a pain which is not formally communicated to the public. To this embryo the minds of the whole nation are turned; and they follow him, day by day, in their thoughts, till he is born. The whole people have a right to be present at his birth; and as many as the chamber will hold, crowd in, till the queen and prince are almost suffocated with the loyal curiosity and affectionate solicitude of their subjects. In the cradle, the principal personages of the kingdom, as well as all the ambassadors, are from time to time presented to the royal infant. To thousands who press to see him, he is daily shown from the nursery. Of every step in his education, and of every gradation of his youthful growth, in body and mind, the public is informed in the gazettes. Not a stroke of wit, not a sprightly sally, not a trait of generous affection, can escape him, but the world is told of it, and, very often, pretty fictions are contrived for the same purpose, where the truth will not furnish materials. Thus it becomes the national fashion, it is the *tone* of the city and the court, to think and converse daily about the dauphin. When he accedes to the throne, the same attention is continued till he dies.

In elective governments, something very like this always takes place towards the first character. His person, countenance, character, and actions, are made the daily contemplation and conversation of the whole people. Hence arises the danger of a division of this attention. Where there are rivals for the first place, the national attention and passions are divided, and thwart each other; the collision enkindles fires; the conflicting passions interest all ranks; they produce slanders and libels first, mobs and seditions next, and civil war, with all her hissing snakes, burning torches, and haggard horrors at last.

This is the true reason, why all civilized free nations have found, by experience, the necessity of separating from the body of the people, and even from the legislature, the distribution of honors, and conferring it on the executive authority of government. When the emulation of all the citizens looks up to one point, like the rays of a circle from all parts of the circumference, meeting and uniting in the centre, you may hope for uniformity, consistency, and subordination; but when they look up to different individuals, or assemblies, or councils, you may expect all the deformities, eccentricities, and confusion, of the Polemic system.

VIII.

Wise, if a minister, but if a king,
More wise, more learn'd, more just, more every thing.
POPE.

There is scarcely any truth more certain, or more evident, than that the *noblesse* of Europe are, in general, less happy than the common people. There is one irrefragable proof of it, which is, that they do not maintain their own population. Families, like stars or candles, which you will, are going out continually; and without fresh recruits from the plebeians, the nobility would in time be extinct. If you make allowances for the state, which they are condemned by themselves and the world to support, they are poorer than the poor; deeply in debt; and tributary to usurious capitalists, as greedy as the Jews. The kings of Europe, in the sight of a philosopher, are the greatest slaves on earth, how often soever we may call them despots, tyrants, and other rude names, in which our pride and vanity take a wonderful delight; they have the least exercise of their inclinations, the least personal liberty, and the least free indulgence of their passions, of any men alive. Yet how rare are the instances of resignations, and how universal is the ambition to be noble, and the wish to be royal.

Experience and philosophy are lost upon mankind. The attention of the world has a charm in it, which few minds can withstand. The people consider the condition of the great in all those delusive colors, in which imagination can paint and gild it, and reason can make little resistance to this impetuous propensity. To better their condition, to advance their fortunes, without limits, is the object of their constant desire, the employment of all their thoughts by day and night. They feel a peculiar sympathy with that pleasure, which they presume those enjoy, who are already powerful, celebrated, and rich. "We favor," says a great writer [Adam Smith—ED.], "all their inclinations, and forward all their wishes. What pity, we think, that any thing should spoil and corrupt so agreeable a situation; we could even wish them immortal; and it seems hard to us, that death should at last put an end to such perfect enjoyment. It is cruel, we think, in nature to compel them from their exalted stations to that humble, but hospitable home, which she has provided for all her children. Great king, live forever! is the compliment, which, after the manner of eastern adulation, we should readily make them, if experience did not teach us its absurdity. Every calamity that befalls them, every injury that is done them, excites in the breast of the spectator ten times more compassion and resentment than he would have felt, had the same things happened to other men. It is the misfortunes of kings only, which afford the proper subjects for tragedy; they resemble, in this respect, the misfortunes of lovers. Those two

situations are the chief which interest us upon the theatre; because, in spite of all that reason and experience can tell us to
the contrary, the prejudices of the imagination attach to these
two states a happiness superior to any other. To disturb or to
put an end to such perfect enjoyment, seems to be the most
atrocious of all injuries. [The traitor who conspires against the
life of his monarch, is thought a greater monster than any other
murderer.] All the innocent blood that was shed in the civil
wars, provoked less indignation than the death of Charles I. A
stranger to human nature, who saw the indifference of men
about the misery of their inferiors, and the regret and indignation which they feel for the misfortunes and sufferings of those
above them, would be apt to imagine, that pain must be more
agonizing, and the convulsions of death more terrible, to persons of higher rank than to those of meaner stations.]

"Upon this disposition of mankind, to go along with all the
passions of the rich and the powerful, is founded the distinction
of ranks, and the order of society. Our obsequiousness to our
superiors more frequently arises from our admiration for the
advantages of their situation, than from any private expectations of benefit from their good will. [Their benefits can extend
but to a few; but their fortunes interest almost everybody. We
are eager to assist them in completing a system of happiness that
approaches so near to perfection; and we desire to serve them
for their own sake, without any other recompense but the vanity or the honor of obliging them.] Neither is our deference to
their inclinations founded chiefly, or altogether, upon a regard
to the utility of such submission, and to the order of society,
which is best supported by it. [Even when the order of society
seems to require that we should oppose them, we can hardly
bring ourselves to do it.] That kings are the servants of the
people, to be obeyed, resisted, deposed, or punished, as the public conveniency may require, is the doctrine of reason and philosophy; but it is not the doctrine of nature. Nature would teach
us to submit to them, for their own sake, to tremble and bow
down before their exalted station, to regard their smile as a reward sufficient to compensate any services, and to dread their
displeasure, though no other evil were to follow from it, as the

severest of all mortifications. To treat them in any respect as men, to reason and dispute with them upon ordinary occasions, requires such resolution, that there are few men whose magnanimity can support them in it, unless they are likewise assisted by familiarity and acquaintance. The strongest motives, the most furious passions, fear, hatred, and resentment, are scarce sufficient to balance this natural disposition to respect them; and their conduct must, either justly or unjustly, have excited the highest degree of all those passions, before the bulk of the people can be brought to oppose them with violence, or desire to see them either punished or deposed. Even when the people have been brought to this length, they are apt to relent every moment, and easily relapse into their habitual state of deference. They cannot stand the mortification of their monarch. Compassion soon takes the place of resentment, they forget all past provocations, their old principles of loyalty revive, and they run to reestablish the ruined authority of their old masters, with the same violence with which they had opposed it. The death of Charles I. brought about the restoration of the royal family. Compassion for James II., when he was seized by the populace in making his escape on shipboard, had almost prevented the revolution, and made it go on more heavily than before.

"Do the great seem insensible of the easy price at which they may acquire the public admiration; or do they seem to imagine that to them, as to other men, it must be the purchase either of sweat or of blood? By what important accomplishments is the young nobleman instructed to support the dignity of his rank, and to render himself worthy of that superiority over his fellow-citizens, to which the virtue of his ancestors had raised them? Is it by knowledge, by industry, by patience, by self-denial, or by virtue of any kind? As all his words, as all his motions are attended to, he learns an habitual regard to every circumstance of ordinary behavior, and studies to perform all those small duties, with the most exact propriety. As he is conscious how much he is observed, and how much mankind are disposed to favor all his inclinations, he acts, upon the most indifferent occasions, with that freedom and elegance which the thought of this naturally inspires. His air, his manner, his deportment, all mark that elegant and graceful sense of his own superiority, which those who are born to inferior stations can hardly ever arrive at. These are the arts, by which he proposes to make mankind more easily submit to his authority, and to govern their inclinations according to his own pleasure; and in this he is seldom disappointed. These arts, supported by rank and preëminence, are upon ordinary occasions, sufficient to govern the world. . . ."

IX.

Heroes, proceed! What bounds your pride shall hold?
What check restrain your thirst of power and gold?
JOHNSON.

The answer to the question in the motto can be none other than this, that, as nature has established in the bosoms of heroes no limits to those passions; and as the world, instead of restraining, encourages them, the check must be in the form of government.

The world encourages ambition and avarice, by taking the most decided part in their favor. The Roman world approved of the ambition of Cæsar; and, notwithstanding all the pains that have been taken, with so much reason, by moral and political writers to disgrace it, the world has approved it these seventeen hundred years, and still esteems his name an honor to the first empire in Europe. Consider the story of the ambition and the fall of Cardinal Wolsey and Archbishop Laud; the indignation of the world against their tyranny has been very faint; the sympathy with their fall has been very strong. Consider all the examples in history of successful ambition, you will find none generally condemned by mankind; on the other hand, think of the instances of ambition unsuccessful and disappointed, or of falls from great heights; you find the sympathy of the world universally affected. Cruelty and tyranny of the blackest kind must accompany the story, to destroy or sensibly diminish this pity. That world, for the regulation of whose prejudices, passions, imaginations, and interests, governments are instituted, is so unjust, that neither religion, natural nor revealed, nor any thing, but a well-ordered and well-balanced government, has ever been able to correct it, and that but imperfectly. It is true, in modern London, as it was in ancient Rome, that the sympathy of the world is less excited by the destruction of the house of a man of merit in obscurity, or even in middle life, though it be by the unjust violence of men, than by the same calamity befalling a rich man, by the righteous indignation of Heaven.

[margin annotation: sympathy for rich]

> Nil habuit Codrus: quis enim negat? et tamen illud
> Perdidit infelix totum nihil: ultimus autem
> Ærumnæ cumulus, quod nudum et frusta rogantem
> Nemo cibo, nemo hospitio tectoque juvabit.
> Si magna Asturii cecidit domus, horrida mater,
> Pullati proceres, differt vadimonia Prætor.
> Tunc geminus casus urbis, tunc odimus ignem.
> Ardet adhuc, et jam occurrit, qui marmora donet,
> Conferat impensas. Hic nuda et candida signa,
> Hic aliquid præclarum Euphranoris et Polycleti,
> Hæc Asianorum vetera ornamenta Deorum,
> Hic libros dabit et forulos mediamque Minervam,
> Hic modium argenti. Meliora et plura reponit
> Persicus orborum lautissimus, ut merito jam
> Suspectus, tanquam ipse suas incenderit ædes.[6]

> But, hark! th' affrighted crowd's tumultuous cries
> Roll through the streets, and thunder to the skies;
> Rais'd from some pleasing dream of wealth and power,
> Some pompous palace, or some blissful bower,
> Aghast you start, and scarce, with aching sight,
> Sustain the approaching fire's tremendous light;
> Swift from pursuing horrors take your way,
> And leave your little all to flames a prey;
> Then thro' the world a wretched vagrant roam,
> For where can starving merit find a home?
> In vain your mournful narrative disclose,
> While all neglect, and most insult your woes.

But,

> Should Heavn's just bolts Orgilio's wealth confound,
> And spread his flaming palace on the ground,
> Swift o'er the land the dismal rumor flies,
> And public mournings pacify the skies;
> The laureat tribe in venal verse relate,
> How virtue wars with persecuting fate;
> With well-feign'd gratitude, the pension'd band
> Refund the plunder of the beggar'd land.
> See! while he builds, the gaudy vassals come,
> And crowd with sudden wealth the rising dome;
> The price of boroughs and of souls restore;
> And raise his treasures higher than before.
> Now bless'd with all the baubles of the great,
> The polish'd marble, and the shining plate,
> Orgilio sees the golden pile aspire,
> And hopes from angry Heav'n another fire.

Although the verse, both of the Roman and Briton, is satire, its keenest severity consists in its truth.

X.

> *Order is Heaven's first law; and, this confess'd,*
> *Some are, and must be, greater than the rest;*
> *More rich, more wise; but who infers from hence,*
> *That such are happier, shocks all common sense.*
>   POPE.

The world is sensible of the necessity of supporting their favorites under the first onsets of misfortunes, lest the fall should be dreadful and irrecoverable; for, according to the great Master of Nature,

> 'Tis certain, greatness, once fallen out with fortune,
> Must fall out with men too. What the declin'd is,
> He shall as soon read in the eyes of others,
> As feel in his own fall; for men, like butterflies,

Show not their mealy wings but to the summer;
And not a man, for being simply man,
Hath any honor; but 's honor'd for those honors
That are without him,—as place, riches, favor,
Prizes of accident as oft as merit.

Mankind are so sensible of these things, that, by a kind of instinct or intuition, they generally follow the advice of the same author:—

Take the instant way,
For honor travels in a strait so narrow,
Where one but goes abreast. Keep, then, the path,
For emulation hath a thousand sons,
That one by one pursue; if you give way,
Or hedge aside from the direct forth-right,
Like to an enter'd tide, they all rush by,
And leave you hindmost;
Or like a gallant horse fall'n in first rank,
Lie there for pavement to the abject rear,
O'errun and trampled on.

The inference, from all the contemplations and experiments which have been made, by all nations, upon these dispositions to imitation, emulation, and rivalry, is expressed by the same great teacher of morality and politics:—

Degree being vizarded,
Th' unworthiest shows as fairly in the mask.
The heavens themselves, the planets, and this centre,
Observe degree, priority, and place,
Insisture, course, proportion, season, form,
Office, and custom, in all line of order;
And, therefore, is the glorious planet Sol,
In noble eminence, enthron'd and spher'd
Amidst the other; whose med'cinable eye
Corrects the ill aspects of planets evil,
And posts, like the commandment of a king,

Sans check, to good and bad; but when the planets
In evil mixture, to disorder wander,
What plagues and what portents! what mutiny!
What raging of the sea! Shaking of earth!
Commotion in the winds! Frights, changes, horrors,
Divert and crack, rend and deracinate,
The unity and married calm of states,
Quite from their fixture? O, when Degree is shak'd,
Which is the ladder to all high designs,
The enterprise is sick! How could communities,
Degrees in schools, and brotherhoods in cities,
The primogenitive and due of birth,
Prerogative of age, crowns, sceptres, laurels,
But by Degree, stand in authentic place?
Take but Degree away; untune that string
And hark! what discord follows! each thing meets
In mere oppugnancy. The bounded waters
Should lift their bosoms higher than the shores,
And make a sop of all this solid globe.
Strength should be lord of imbecility,
And the rude son should strike his father dead.
Force should be right; or rather, right and wrong
Should lose their names, and so should justice too.
Then every thing includes itself in power,
Power into will, will into appetite;
And appetite an universal wolf,
Must make perforce an universal prey,
And, last, eat up himself.
This chaos, when Degree is suffocate,
Follows the choking.
      The General's disdain'd,
By him one step below. He, by the next;
That next, by him beneath. So every step,
Exampled by the first pace that is sick
Of his superior, grows to an envious fever
Of pale and bloodless emulation.
Troy in our weakness stands, not in her strength.

Most wisely hath Ulysses here discovered
The Fever whereof all our power is sick. *

XI.

Think we, like some weak prince, th' eternal cause
Prone, for his fav'rites, to reverse his laws?

POPE.

Emulation, which is imitation and something more—a desire
not only to equal or resemble, but to excel, is so natural a
movement of the human heart, that, wherever men are to be
found, and in whatever manner associated or connected, we
see its effects. They are not more affected by it, as individuals,
than they are in communities. There are rivalries between every
little society in the same city; between families and all the connections by consanguinity and affinity; between trades, faculties, and professions; between congregations, parishes, and
churches; between schools, colleges, and universities; between
districts, villages, cities, provinces, and nations.

National rivalries are more frequently the cause of wars than
the ambition of ministers, or the pride of kings. As long as
there is patriotism, there will be national emulation, vanity, and
pride. It is national pride which commonly stimulates kings
and ministers. National fear, apprehension of danger, and the
necessity of self-defence, is added to such rivalries for wealth,
consideration, and power. The safety, independence, and existence of a nation, depend upon keeping up a high sense of its own
honor, dignity, and power, in the hearts of its individuals, and
a lively jealousy of the growing power and aspiring ambition
of a neighboring state. This is well illustrated in the Political
Geography, published in our newspapers from London, within a

*The style in these quotations from Shakspeare has little of the fluency, and
less of that purity, which sometimes appear in his writings; but the sense is as
immortal as human nature. J.A. 1813.

few weeks. "The jealousies and enmities, the alliances and friend-ships, or rather the combinations of different states and princes, might almost be learned from a map, without attention to what has passed, or is now passing in the world. Next neighbors are political enemies. States between which a common neighbor, and, therefore, a common enemy intervenes, are good friends. In this respect, Europe may be compared to a chess-board marked with the black and white spots of political discord and concord. Be-fore the union between England and Scotland, a friendship and alliance subsisted for centuries between the latter of these king-doms and France, because they were both inimical to England. For a like reason, before a Prince of Bourbon, in the beginning of the present century, was raised to the Spanish throne, a good understanding subsisted for the most part between England and Spain; and before the late alliance, there was peace and kind-ness, with little interruption, for the space of centuries, between England and the Emperor. An alliance has long subsisted be-tween the French and the Turks, on account of the intervening dominion of the Austrians. . . ."

The writer of this paragraph might have added the alliance between England and Portugal, and that between the United States of America and France. The principle of all of these ex-amples is as natural as emulation, and as infallible as the sin-cerity of interest. On it turns the whole system of human affairs. The Congress of 1776 were fully aware of it. With no small degree of vehemence was it urged as an argument for the declaration of independence.* With confidence and firmness was it foretold that France could not avoid accepting the propositions that should be made to her; that the Court of Ver-sailles could not answer it to her own subjects, and that all Eu-rope would pronounce her blind, lost, and undone, if she rejected so fair an opportunity of disembarrassing herself from the danger of so powerful and hostile a rival, whose naval su-periority held all her foreign dominions, her maritime power, and commercial interest at mercy.†

---

*By John Adams.
†France has thrown away all advantages by her want of wisdom.

But why all this of emulation and rivalry? Because, as the whole history of the civil wars of France, given us by Davila, is no more than a relation of rivalries succeeding each other in a rapid series, the reflections we have made will assist us, both to understand that noble historian, and to form a right judgment of the state of affairs in France at the present moment. They will suggest also to Americans, especially to those who have been unfriendly, and may be now lukewarm to their national constitution,* some useful inquiries, such as these, for example: Whether there are not emulations of a serious complexion among ourselves? between cities and universities? between north and south? the middle and the north? the middle and the south? between one state and another? between the governments of states and the national government? and between individual patriots and heroes in all these? What is the natural remedy against the inconveniences and dangers of these rivalries? Whether a well-balanced constitution, such as that of our Union purports to be, ought not to be cordially supported by every good citizen, as our only hope of peace and our ark of safety, till its defects, if it has any, can be corrected? But it must be left to the contemplations of our state physicians to discover the causes and the remedy of that *"fever, whereof our power is sick."* One question only shall be respectfully insinuated: Whether equal laws, the result only of a balanced government, can ever be obtained and preserved without some signs or other of distinction and degree?

We are told that our friends, the National Assembly of France, have abolished all distinctions. But be not deceived, my dear countrymen. Impossibilities cannot be performed. Have they levelled all fortunes and equally divided all property? Have they made all men and women equally wise, elegant, and beautiful? Have they annihilated the names of Bourbon and Montmorenci, Rochefoucauld and Noailles, Lafayette and La Moignon, Necker and De Calonne, Mirabeau and Bailly? Have they committed to the flames all the records, annals, and histories of the nation? All the copies of Mezerai, Daniel, De Thou, Velly, and a thousand others? Have they burned all their pic-

cannot abolish distinction

*The anti-federalists. J.A. 1813.

tures, and broken all their statues? Have they blotted out of all memories, the names, places of abode, and illustrious actions of all their ancestors? Have they not still princes of the first and second order, nobles and knights? Have they no record nor memory who are the men who compose the present national assembly? Do they wish to have that distinction forgotten? Have the French officers who served in America melted their eagles and torn their ribbons?*

XII.

'Tis with our judgments as our watches—none
Go just alike, yet each believes his own.

POPE.

All the miracles enumerated in our last number, must be performed in France, before all distinctions can be annihilated, and distinctions in abundance would be found, after all, for French gentlemen, in the history of England, Holland, Spain, Germany, Italy, America, and all other countries on the globe.

The wisdom of nations has remarked the universal consideration paid to wealth; and that the passion of avarice excited by it, produced treachery, cowardice, and a selfish, unsocial meanness, but had no tendency to produce those virtues of patience, courage, fortitude, honor, or patriotism, which the service of the public required in their citizens in peace and war.

The wisdom of nations has observed that the general attention paid to birth produced a different kind of sentiments,—those of pride in the maxims and principles of religion, morals, and government, as well as in the talents and virtues, which first produced illustration to ancestors.

As the pride of wealth produced nothing but meanness of sentiment and a sordid scramble for money; and the pride of birth produced some degree of emulation in knowledge and virtue;

*How are distinctions abolished now in 1813? J.A.

[margin, handwritten: pride of birth to counter pride of wealth] the wisdom of nations has endeavored to employ one prejudice to counteract another; the prejudice in favor of birth, to moderate, correct, and restrain the prejudice in favor of wealth.

The national assembly of France is too enlightened a body to overlook the inquiry: What effect on the moral character of the nation would be produced, by destroying, if that were possible, all attention to families, and setting all the passions on the pursuit of gain? Whether universal venality and an incorrigible corruption in elections would not be the necessary consequence? It may be relied on, however, that the intentions of that august and magnanimous assembly are misunderstood and misrepresented. Time will develop their designs, will show them to be more judicious than to attempt impossibilities so obvious as that of the abolition of all distinctions.

Alphonsus X., the astronomical king of Castile, has been accused of impiety, for saying that "if, at the time of the creation, he had been called to the councils of the Divinity, he could have given some useful advice concerning the motions of the stars." It is not probable, that any thing was intended by him, more than a humorous sarcasm or a sneer of contempt at the Ptolemaic system, a projection of which he had before him. But if the national assembly should have seriously in contemplation, and should resolve in earnest the total abolition of all distinctions and orders, it would be much more difficult to vindicate them from an accusation of impiety. God, in the constitution of nature, has ordained that every man shall have a disposition to emulation, as well as imitation, and consequently a passion for distinction; and that all men shall not have equal means and opportunities of gratifying it. Shall we believe the national assembly capable of resolving that no man shall have any desire of distinction; or that all men shall have equal means of gratifying it? Or that no man shall have any means of gratifying it? What would this be better than saying, "if we had been called to the councils of the celestials, we could have given better advice in the constitution of human nature?" If nature and that assembly could be thus at variance, which however is not credible, the world would soon see which is the most powerful.

That there is already a scission in the national assembly, like all others, past, present, and to come, is most certain. There is an aristocratical party, an armed neutrality, and most probably a monarchical party; besides another division, who must finally prevail, or liberty will be lost; I mean a set of members, who are equal friends to monarchy, aristocracy, and democracy, and wish for an equal, independent mixture of all three in their constitution. Each of these parties has its chief, and these chiefs are, or will be, rivals. Religion will be both the object and the pretext of some; liberty, of others; submission and obedience of others; and levelling, downright levelling, of not a few. But the attention, consideration, and congratulations of the public will be the object of all. Situation and office will be aimed at by some of all parties. Contests and dissensions will arise between these runners in the same race. The natural and usual progress is, from debate in the assembly to discussions in print; from the search of truth and public utility in both, to sophistry and the spirit of party; evils so greatly dreaded by the ingenuous "Citizens of New Haven," to whom we have now the honor of paying our first respects, hoping that, hereafter, we may find an opportunity to make him our more particular compliments.* From sophistry and party spirit, the transition is quick and easy to falsehood, imposture, and every species of artificial evolution and criminal intrigue. As unbalanced parties of every description can never tolerate a free inquiry of any kind, when employed against themselves, the license, and even the most temperate freedom of the press, soon excite resentment and revenge. A writer, unpopular with an opposite party, because he is too formidable in wit or argument, may first be burnt in effigy; or a printer may have his office assaulted. Cuffs and kicks, boxes and cudgels, are heard of among plebeian statesmen;

---

*Condorcet. It was then my intention to have examined those letters at large; but the rage and fury of the Jacobinical journals against these discourses, increased as they proceeded, intimidated the printer, John Fenno, and convinced me, that to proceed would do more hurt than good. I therefore broke off abruptly. J.A. 1813.

(Condorcet's four letters are printed at the end of the first volume of M. Mazzei's *Recherches historiques et politiques sur les États Unis de l'Amérique septentrionale*.)

challenges and single combats among the aristocratic legislators. Riots and seditions at length break men's bones, or flay off
their skins. Lives are lost; and, when blood is once drawn, men,
like other animals, become outrageous. If one party has not a
superiority over the other, clear enough to decide every thing at
its pleasure, a civil war ensues. When the nation arrives at this
period of the progression, every leader, at the head of his
votaries, even if you admit him to have the best intentions in
the world, will find himself compelled to form them into some
military arrangement, both for offence and defence; to build
castles and fortify eminences, like the feudal barons. For aristocratical rivalries, and democratical rivalries too, when unbalanced against each other by some third mediating power,
naturally and unfailingly produce a feudal system. If this should
be the course in France, the poor, deluded, and devoted partisans would soon be fond enough of decorating their leaders
with the old titles of dukes, marquises and counts, or doing any
thing else to increase the power of their commander over themselves, to unite their wills and forces for their own safety and
defence, or to give him weight with their enemies.*

The men of letters in France are wisely reforming one feudal
system; but may they not, unwisely, lay the foundation of another? A legislature, in one assembly, can have no other termination than in civil dissension, feudal anarchy, or simple
monarchy. The best apology which can be made for their fresh
attempt of a sovereignty in one assembly, an idea at least as ancient in France as *Stephen Boethius,* is, that it is only intended
to be momentary. If a senate had been proposed, it must have
been formed, most probably, of princes of the blood, cardinals,
archbishops, dukes, and marquises; and all these together
would have obstructed the progress of the reformation in religion and government, and procured an abortion to the regeneration of France. Pennsylvania established her single assembly,
in 1776, upon the same principle. An apprehension, that the

---

*See Napoleon's speech, 20 December, 1812, at the close of these discourses.

He still proceeds to exemplify the effects and consequences of rivalries, in
1813. J.A.

Proprietary and Quaker interests would prevail, to the election
of characters disaffected to the American cause, finally preponderated against two legislative councils. Pennsylvania, and
Georgia, who followed her example, have found by experience
the necessity of a change; and France, by the same infallible
progress of reasoning, will discover the same necessity; happy,
indeed, if the experiment shall not cost her more dear. That the
subject is considered in this light by the best friends of liberty in
Europe, appears by the words of Dr. Price, lately published in
this paper:—"Had not the aristocratical and clerical orders,"
says that sage and amiable writer, "been obliged to throw
themselves into one chamber with the commons, no reformation could have taken place, and the regeneration of the kingdom would have been impossible. And in future legislatures,
were these two orders to make distinct and independent states,
all that has been done would probably be soon undone. Hereafter, perhaps, when the new constitution, as now formed, has
acquired strength by time, the national assembly may find it
practicable, as well as expedient, to establish, by means of a
third estate, such a check as now takes place in the American
government, and is indispensable in the British government."*

XIII.

First follow nature; and your judgment frame
By her just standard, which is still the same.

POPE.

The world grows more enlightened. Knowledge is more
equally diffused. Newspapers, magazines, and circulating libraries have made mankind wiser. Titles and distinctions, ranks

---

*Oh! that Dr. Price and Dr. Franklin had lived to read the addresses and an-
swers, of 20 December, 1812, at the end of this volume. Jefferson has lived to
see it. J.A. 1813.

and orders, parade and ceremony, are all going out of fashion.
This is roundly and frequently asserted in the streets, and
sometimes on theatres of higher *rank*.* Some truth is in it; and
if the opportunity were temperately improved, to the reformation of abuses, the rectification of errors, and the dissipation of
pernicious prejudices, a great advantage it might be. But, on
the other hand, false inferences may be drawn from it, which
may make mankind wish for the age of dragons, giants, and
fairies. If all decorum, discipline, and subordination are to be
destroyed, and universal Pyrrhonism, anarchy, and insecurity
of property are to be introduced, nations will soon wish their
books in ashes, seek for darkness and ignorance, superstition
and fanaticism, as blessings, and follow the standard of the first
mad despot, who, with the enthusiasm of another Mahomet,[†]
will endeavor to obtain them.

Are riches, honors, and beauty going out of fashion? Is not the
rage for them, on the contrary, increased faster than improvement in knowledge? As long as either of these are in vogue, will
there not be emulations and rivalries? Does not the increase of
knowledge in any man increase his emulation; and the diffusion
of knowledge among men multiply rivalries? Has the progress of
science, arts, and letters yet discovered that there are no passions
in human nature? no ambition, avarice, or desire of fame? Are
these passions cooled, diminished, or extinguished? Is the rage
for admiration less ardent in men or women? Have these propensities less a tendency to divisions, controversies, seditions, mu-
tinies, and civil wars than formerly? On the contrary, the more
knowledge is diffused, the more the passions are extended, and
the more furious they grow. Had Cicero less vanity, or Cæsar
less ambition, for their vast erudition? Had the King of Prussia
less of one than the other? There is no connection in the mind
between science and passion, by which the former can extinguish or diminish the latter. It, on the contrary, sometimes increases them, by giving them exercise. Were the passions of the

*Read the history of the world, from 1790 to 1813, as a comment.
[†]Napoleon is not all this. J.A. 1813.

Romans less vivid in the age of Pompey than in the time of
Mummius. Are those of the Britons more moderate at this hour
than in the reigns of the Tudors? Are the passions of monks the
weaker for all their learning? Are not jealousy, envy, hatred,
malice, and revenge, as well as emulation and ambition, as rancorous in the cells of Carmelites as in the courts of princes? Go
to the Royal Society of London. Is there less emulation for the
chair of Sir Isaac Newton than there was, and commonly will be,
for all elective presidencies? Is there less animosity and rancor,
arising from mutual emulations in the region of science, than
there is among the most ignorant of mankind? Go to Paris. How
do you find the men of letters? united, friendly, harmonious,
meek, humble, modest, charitable? prompt to mutual forbear-
ance? unassuming? ready to acknowledge superior merit? zealous to encourage the first symptoms of genius? Ask Voltaire and
Rousseau, Marmontel and De Mably.

The increase and dissemination of knowledge, instead of
rendering unnecessary the checks of emulation and the balances of rivalry in the orders of society and constitution of government, augment the necessity of both. It becomes the more
indispensable that every man should know his place, and be
made to keep it. Bad men increase in knowledge as fast as good
men; and science, arts, taste, sense, and letters, are employed
for the purposes of injustice and tyranny, as well as those of
law and liberty; for corruption, as well as for virtue.

Frenchmen! Act and think like yourselves! confessing human
nature, be magnanimous and wise. Acknowledging and boasting yourselves to be men, avow the feelings of men. The affectation of being exempted from passions is inhuman. The grave
pretension to such singularity is solemn hypocrisy. Both are unworthy of your frank and generous natures. Consider that the
government is intended to set bounds to passions which nature
has not limited; and to assist reason, conscience, justice, and
truth, in controlling interests, which, without it, would be as
unjust as uncontrollable.*

Americans! Rejoice, that from experience you have learned

---

*Frenchmen neither saw, heard, nor felt or understood this. J.A. 1813.

wisdom; and instead of whimsical and fantastical projects, you have adopted a promising essay towards a well-ordered government. Instead of following any foreign example, to return to *the legislation of confusion*, contemplate the means of restoring decency, honesty, and order in society, by preserving and completing, if any thing should be found necessary to complete the balance of your government. In a well-balanced government, reason, conscience, truth, and virtue, must be respected by all parties, and exerted for the public good.* Advert to the principles on which you commenced that glorious self-defence, which, if you behave with steadiness and consistency, may ultimately loosen the chains of all mankind. If you will take the trouble to read over the memorable proceedings of the town of Boston, on the twenty-eighth day of October, 1772, when the Committee of Correspondence of twenty-one persons was appointed to state the rights of the colonists as men, as Christians, and as subjects, and to publish them to the world, with the infringements and violations of them,† you will find the great principles of civil and religious liberty for which you have contended so successfully, and which the world is contending for after your example. I could transcribe with pleasure the whole of this immortal pamphlet, which is a real picture of the sun of liberty rising on the human race; but shall select only a few words more directly to the present purpose.

"The first fundamental, positive law of all commonwealths or states is the establishment of the legislative power." Page 9.

"It is absolutely necessary in a mixed government like that of this province, that a *due proportion* or *balance* of power should be established among the several branches of the legislative. Our ancestors received from King William and Queen Mary a charter, by which it was understood by both parties in the contract, that such a <u>proportion or balance was fixed;</u> and therefore, every thing which renders any one branch of the leg-

---

*Americans paid no attention or regard to this. And a blind, mad rivalry between the north and the south is destroying all morality and sound policy. God grant that division, civil war, murders, assassination, and massacres may not soon grow out of these rivalries of states, families, and individuals.

†This Boston pamphlet was drawn by the great James Otis. J.A. 1813.

islative more independent of the other two than it was originally designed, is an alteration of the constitution."

Americans! in your Congress at Philadelphia, on Friday, the
fourteenth day of October, 1774, you laid down, the fundamental principles for which you were about to contend, and
from which it is to be hoped you will never depart. For asserting and vindicating your rights and liberties, you declared, "That,
by the immutable laws of nature, the principles of the English
constitution and your several charters or compacts, you were
entitled to life, liberty, and property; that your ancestors were
entitled to all the rights, liberties, and immunities of free and
natural born subjects in England; that you, their descendants,
were entitled to the exercise and enjoyment of all such of them
as your local and other circumstances enabled you to exercise
and enjoy. That the foundation of English liberty and of all free
governments, is a right in the people to participate in their legislative council. That you were entitled to the common law of
England, and more especially to the great and inestimable privilege of being tried by your peers of the vicinage, according to
the course of that law. *That it is indispensably necessary to
good government, and rendered essential by the English constitution, that the constituent branches of the legislature be
independent of each other."* These among others you then
claimed, demanded, and insisted on, as your indubitable rights
and liberties. These are the principles on which you first united
and associated, and if you steadily and consistently maintain
them, they will not only secure freedom and happiness to yourselves and your posterity, but your example will be imitated by
all Europe, and in time, perhaps, by all mankind. The nations are
in travail, and great events must have birth.

"The minds of men are in movement from the Boristhenes to

---

*The declaration of independence of 4 July, 1776, contained nothing but the
Boston declaration of 1772 and the congress declaration of 1774. Such are the
caprices of fortune. This declaration of rights was drawn by the little John
Adams. The mighty Jefferson, by the declaration of independence of 4 July
1776, carried away the glory of the great and the little. J.A. 1813.

See for the congress declaration of 1774, vol. ii. pp. 375–377, and Appendix, C.

the Atlantic. Agitated with new and strong emotions, they swell and heave beneath oppression, as the seas within the polar circle, at the approach of spring. The genius of philosophy, with the touch of Ithuriel's spear, is trying the establishments of the earth. The various forms of prejudice, superstition, and servility, start up in their true shapes, which had long imposed upon the world, under the revered semblances of honor, faith, and loyalty. Whatever is loose must be shaken; whatever is corrupted must be lopped away; whatever is not built on the broad basis of public utility must be thrown to the ground. Obscure murmurs gather and swell into a tempest; the spirit of inquiry, like a severe and searching wind, penetrates every part of the great body politic; and whatever is unsound, whatever is infirm, shrinks at the visitation. Liberty, led by philosophy, diffuses her blessings to every class of men; and even extends a smile of hope and promise to the poor African, the victim of hard, impenetrable avarice. Man, as man, becomes an object of respect. Tenets are transferred from theory to practice. The glowing sentiment, the lofty speculation, no longer serve 'but to adorn the pages of a book.' They are brought home to men's business and bosoms; and what, some centuries ago, it was daring but to think, and dangerous to express, is now realized and carried into effect. Systems are analyzed into their first principles, and principles are fairly pursued to their legitimate consequences."*

This is all enchanting. But amidst our enthusiasm, there is great reason to pause and preserve our sobriety. It is true that the first empire of the world is breaking the fetters of human reason and exerting the energies of redeemed liberty. In the glowing ardor of her zeal, she condescends, Americans, to pay the most scrupulous attention to your maxims, principles, and example. There is reason to fear she has copied from you errors which have cost you very dear. Assist her, by your example, to rectify them before they involve her in calamities as much greater than yours, as her population is more unwieldy, and her

*This was a summary of the language of the world in 1790, in newspapers, pamphlets, and conversation. In 1813 we can judge of it, as the author of these discourses judged of it then, to the destruction of all his popularity.

situation more exposed to the baleful influence of rival neighbors. Amidst all their exultations, Americans and Frenchmen should remember that the perfectibility of man is only human and terrestrial perfectibility. Cold will still freeze, and fire will never cease to burn; disease and vice will continue to disorder, and death to terrify mankind. Emulation next to self-preservation will forever be the great spring of human actions, and the balance of a well-ordered government will alone be able to prevent that emulation from degenerating into dangerous ambition, irregular rivalries, destructive factions, wasting seditions, and bloody, civil wars.*

The great question will forever remain, *who shall work?* Our species cannot all be idle. Leisure for study must ever be the portion of a few. The number employed in government must forever be very small. Food, raiment, and habitations, the indispensable wants of all, are not to be obtained without the continual toil of ninety-nine in a hundred of mankind. As rest is rapture to the weary man, those who labor little will always be envied by those who labor much, though the latter in reality be probably the most enviable. With all the encouragements, public and private, which can ever be given to general education, and it is scarcely possible they should be too many or too great, the laboring part of the people can never be learned. The controversy between the rich and the poor, the laborious and the idle, the learned and the ignorant, distinctions as old as the creation, and as extensive as the globe, distinctions which no art of policy, no degree of virtue or philosophy can ever wholly destroy, will continue, and rivalries will spring out of them. These parties will be represented in the legislature, and must be balanced, or one will oppress the other. There will never probably be found any other mode of establishing such an equilibrium, than by constituting the representation of each an independent branch of the legislature, and an independent executive authority, such as that in our government, to be a third branch and a mediator or an arbitrator between them. Property must be se-

*View France, Europe, and America, in 1813, and compare the state of them all with this paragraph written twenty-three years ago! J.A.

cured, or liberty cannot exist. But if unlimited or unbalanced power of disposing property, be put into the hands of those who have no property, France will find, as we have found, the lamb committed to the custody of the wolf. In such a case, all the pathetic exhortations and addresses of the national assembly to the people, to respect property, will be regarded no more than the warbles of the songsters of the forest. The great art of law-giving consists in balancing the poor against the rich in the legislature, and in constituting the legislative a perfect balance against the executive power, at the same time that no individual or party can become its rival. The essence of a free government consists in an effectual control of rivalries. The executive and the legislative powers are natural rivals; and if each has not an effectual control over the other, the weaker will ever be the lamb in the paws of the wolf. The nation which will not adopt an equilibrium of power must adopt a despotism. There is no other alternative. Rivalries must be controlled, or they will throw all things into confusion; and there is nothing but despotism or a balance of power which can control them. Even in the simple monarchies, the nobility and the judicatures constitute a balance, though a very imperfect one, against the royalties.

Let us conclude with one reflection more which shall barely be hinted at, as delicacy, if not prudence, may require, in this place, some degree of reserve. Is there a possibility that the government of nations may fall into the hands of men who teach the most disconsolate of all creeds, that men are but fireflies, and that this *all* is without a father? Is this the way to make man, as man, an object of respect? Or is it to make murder itself as indifferent as shooting a plover, and the extermination of the Rohilla nation as innocent as the swallowing of mites on a morsel of cheese? If such a case should happen, would not one of these, the most credulous of all believers, have reason to pray to his eternal nature or his almighty chance (the more absurdity there is in this address the more in character) *give us again the gods of the Greeks; give us again the more intelligible as well as more comfortable systems of Athanasius and Calvin; nay, give us again our popes and hierarchies, Benedictines and Jesuits, with all their superstition and fanaticism, impostures* *and tyranny.* A certain duchess of venerable years and masculine understanding,* said of some of the philosophers of the eighteenth century, admirably well,—"On ne croit pas dans le Christianisme, mais on croit toutes les sottises possibles."[7] . . .

XV.

. . . With a view of vindicating republics, commonwealths, and free states from unmerited reproaches, we have detailed these anecdotes from the history of France. With equal propriety, we might have resorted to the history of England, which is full of contests and dissensions of the same sort. There is a morsel of that history, the life and actions of the Protector, Somerset, so remarkably apposite, that it would be worth while to relate it. For the present, however, it must be waived. It is too fashionable with writers to impute such contentions to republican governments, as if they were peculiar to them; whereas, nothing is further from reality. Republican writers themselves have been as often guilty of this mistake, in whom it is an indiscretion, as monarchical writers, in whom it may be thought policy; in both, however, it is an error. We shall mention only two, Machiavel and De Lolme.

In Machiavel's History of Florence, we read: "It is given from above, that in all republics there should be fatal families, who are born for the ruin of them; to the end that in human affairs nothing should be perpetual or quiet."[†]

If, indeed, this were acknowledged to be the will of Heaven, as Machiavel seems to assert, why should we entertain resentments against such families? They are but instruments, and they cannot but answer their end. If they are commissioned from above to be destroying angels, why should we oppose or resist them? As to "the end," there are other causes enough, which will forever prevent perpetuity or tranquillity, in any

---

*The Duchess d'Enville, the mother of the Duc de la Rochefoucauld. The author heard those words from that lady's own lips; with many other striking effusions of the strong and large mind of a great and excellent female character. J.A.
†Lib. 3.

great degree, in human affairs. Animal life is a chemical process, and is carried on by unceasing motion. Our bodies and minds, like the heavens, the earth, and the sea, like all animal, vegetable, and mineral nature, like the elements of earth, air, fire, and water, are continually changing. The mutability and mutations of matter, and much more of the intellectual and moral world, are the consequence of laws of nature, not less without our power than beyond our comprehension. While we are thus assured that, in one sense, nothing in human affairs will be perpetual or at rest, we ought to remember, at the same time, that the duration of our lives, the security of our property, the existence of our conveniences, comforts, and pleasures, the repose of private life, and the tranquillity of society, are placed in very great degrees in human power. Equal laws may be ordained and executed; great families, as well as little ones, may be restrained. And that policy is not less pernicious, than that philosophy is false, which represents such families as sent by Heaven to be judgments. It is not true in fact. On the contrary, they are sent to be blessings; and they are blessings, until, by our own obstinate ignorance and imprudence, in refusing to establish such institutions as will make them always blessings, we turn them into curses.

There are evils, it is true, which attend them as well as other human blessings, even government, liberty, virtue, and religion. It is the province of philosophy and policy to increase the good and lessen the evil that attends them as much as possible. But it is not surely the way, either to increase the good or lessen the evil which accompanies such families, to represent them to the people as machines, as rods, as scourges, as blind and mechanical instruments in the hands of divine vengeance, unmixed with benevolence. Nor has it any good tendency or effect, to endeavor to render them unpopular; to make them objects of hatred, malice, jealousy, envy, or revenge to the common people. The way of wisdom to happiness is to make mankind more friendly to each other. The existence of such men or families is not their fault. They created not themselves. We, the plebeians, find them the workmanship of God and nature, like ourselves. The constitution of nature, and the course of Provi-

don't hate the families

dence, has produced them as well as us; and they and we must live together; it depends on ourselves, indeed, whether it shall be in peace, love, and friendship, or in war or hatred. Nor are they reasonably the objects of censure or aversion, of resentment, envy, or hatred, for the gifts of fortune, any more than for those of nature. Conspicuous birth is no more in a man's power to avoid than to obtain. Hereditary riches are no more a reproach than they are a merit. A paternal estate is neither a virtue nor a fault. He must, nevertheless, be a novice in this world, who does not know that these gifts of fortune are advantages in society and life, which confer influence, popularity, and power. The distinction that is made between the gifts of nature and those of fortune appears to be not well founded. It is fortune which confers beauty and strength, which are called qualities of nature, as much as birth and hereditary wealth, which are called accidents of fortune; and, on the other hand, it is nature which confers these favors as really as stature and agility.

Narrow and illiberal sentiments are not peculiar to the rich or the poor. If the vulgar have found a Machiavel to give countenance to their malignity, by his contracted and illiberal exclamations against illustrious families as the curse of Heaven, the rich and the noble have not unfrequently produced sordid instances of individuals among themselves, who have adopted and propagated an opinion, that God hates the poor, and that poverty and misery on earth are inflicted by Providence in its wrath and displeasure. This noble philosophy is surely as shallow and as execrable as the other plebeian philosophy of Machiavel; but it is countenanced by at least as many of the phenomena of the world. Let both be discarded, as the reproach of human understanding, and a disgrace to human nature. Let the rich and the poor unite in the bands of mutual affection, be mutually sensible of each other's ignorance, weakness, and error, and unite in concerting measures for their mutual defence against each other's vices and follies, by supporting an impartial mediator.

That ingenious Genevan, to whom the English nation is indebted for a more intelligible explanation of their own constitution, than any that has been ever published by their own Acherly of Bacon, Bolingbroke or Blackstone, has quoted this passage of Machiavel, and applied it, like him, to the dishonor of republican governments. De Lolme says: "I cannot avoid transcribing a part of the speech which a citizen of Florence addressed once to the senate. The reader will find in it a kind of abridged story of all republics."* He then quotes the passage before cited from Machiavel.

Why should so grave an accusation be brought against republics? If it were well founded, it would be a very serious argument, not only against such forms of government, but against human nature. Families and competitions are the unavoidable consequence of that emulation, which God and nature have implanted in the human heart for the wisest and best purposes, and which the public good, instead of cooling or extinguishing, requires to be directed to honor and virtue, and then nourished, cherished, and cultivated. If such contentions appeared only in republican governments, there would be some color for charging them as a reproach to these forms; but they appear as frequent and as violent in despotisms and monarchies as they do in commonwealths. In all the despotisms of Asia and Africa, in all the monarchies of Europe, there are constant successions of emulation and rivalry, and consequently of contests and dissensions, among families. Despotism, which crushes and decapitates, sometimes interrupts their progress, and prevents some of their tragical effects. Monarchies, with their spies, *lettres de cachet,* dungeons, and inquisitions, may do almost as well. But the balance of a free government is more effectual than either, without any of their injustice, caprice, or cruelty. The foregoing examples from the history of France, and a thousand others equally striking which might be added, show that Bourbons and Montmorencis, Guises and Colignis, were as fatal families in that kingdom as the Buondelmonti and Alberti, the Donati and Cerchi, the Ricci and Albizzi, or Medici at Florence.

Instead of throwing false imputations on republican governments; instead of exciting or fomenting a vulgar malignity against the most respectable men and families, let us draw the proper inferences from history and experience; let us lay it down

*On the Constitution of England, book ii. c. 1.

for a certain fact,⌈first, that emulation between individuals, and rivalries among families never can be prevented.⌉ Second, let us adopt it as a certain principle, that they ought not to be prevented, but directed to virtue, and them stimulated and encouraged by generous applause and honorable rewards. And from these premises let the conclusion be, as it ought to be, that an effectual control be provided in the constitution, to check their excesses and balance their weights.⌉ If this conclusion is not drawn, another will follow of itself; the people will be the dupes, and the leaders will worry each other and the people too, till both are weary and ashamed, and from feeling, not from reasoning, set up a master and a despot for a protector. What kind of a protector he will be, may be learned hereafter from Stephen Boetius.*

POSTSCRIPT.

If any one wish to see more of the spirit of rivalry, without reading the great historians of France, he may consult L'Esprit de la Ligue, L'Esprit de la Fronde, and the Memoirs of De Retz and his contemporaries. The history of England is more familiar to Americans; but, without reading many volumes, he may find enough of rivalries in those chapters of Henry's History of Great Britain, which treat of civil and military affairs. If even this study be too grave, he may find in Shakspeare's Historical Plays, especially Henry IV., V., and VI., and Richard III., enough to satisfy him. If the gayety of Falstaff and his associates excite not so much of his laughter as to divert his attention from all serious reflections, he will find, in the efforts of ambition and avarice to obtain their objects, enough of the everlasting pretexts of religion, liberty, love of country, and public good, to disguise them. The unblushing applications to foreign powers, to France, Germany, the Pope, Holland, Scotland, Wales, and Jack

---

*And better still in 1813, from the history of Napoleon, not forgetting Lafayette, Dumouriez, Pichegru; nor Marat, Robespierre, Sieyes, and Talleyrand. Nor should our own country be forgotten. J.A.

Cade, to increase their parties and assist their strength, will excite his indignation, while the blood of the poor cheated people, flowing in torrents on all sides, will afflict his humanity.

The English constitution in that period was not formed. The house of commons was not settled; the authority of the peers was not defined; the prerogatives of the crown were not limited. Magna Charta, with all its confirmations and solemnities, was violated at pleasure by kings, nobles, and commons too. The judges held their offices at pleasure. The *habeas corpus* was unknown; and that balance of passions and interests, which alone can give authority to reason, from which results all the security to liberty and the rights of man, was not yet wrought into the English constitution, nor much better understood in England than in France. The unity of the executive power was not established. The national force, in men and money, was not in the king, but in the landholders, with whom the kings were obliged to make alliances, in order to form their armies and fight their enemies, foreign and domestic. Their enemies were generally able to procure an equal number of powerful landholders, with their forces, to assist them, so that all depended on the chance of war.

It has been said, that it is extremely difficult to preserve a balance. This is no more than to say that it is extremely difficult to preserve liberty. To this truth all ages and nations attest. It is so difficult, that the very appearance of it is lost over the whole earth, excepting one island and North America. How long it will be before she returns to her native skies, and leaves the whole human race in slavery, will depend on the intelligence and virtue of the people. A balance, with all its difficulty, must be preserved, or liberty is lost forever. Perhaps a perfect balance, if it ever existed, has not been long maintained in its perfection; yet, such a balance as has been sufficient to liberty, has been supported in some nations for many centuries together; and we must come as near as we can to a perfect equilibrium, or all is lost. When it is once widely departed from, the departure increases rapidly, till the whole is lost. If the people have not understanding and public virtue enough, and will not be persuaded of the

[marginalia, handwritten: must have balance of power to have liberty]

necessity of supporting an independent executive authority, an independent senate, and an independent judiciary power, as well as an independent house of representatives, all pretentions to a balance are lost, and with them all hopes of security to our dearest interests, all hopes of liberty.

9

CORRESPONDENCE WITH ROGER SHERMAN AND JOHN TAYLOR[1]

Roger Sherman, one of the framers at the Constitutional Convention, stood for the decentralization of power and a government with sovereignty located in the legislative branch. He was one of many who saw Adams's political writings as making the case for monarchy in the guise of the executive branch. To Adams sovereignty had to be divided among the various branches to prevent the ineluctable tendency of power to consolidate, dominate, and exclude. Here and elsewhere Adams predicted that the American presidency would become the most powerful branch of government.

John Taylor of Caroline, a county in Virginia, was an important political philosopher and Adams's leading antagonist. He followed Adams's early writings for twenty years and finally in 1814 wrote a rebuttal, titled An Inquiry into the Principles and Policy of the Government of the United States. It was a direct reply to Adams's Defence as well as to Alexander Hamilton and James Madison's Federalist Papers. By 1814 Hamilton was only a memory, having been shot to death in a duel with Aaron Burr in 1804, and Madison had recanted much of the Federalist and become a Jeffersonian Virginian as the fourth president of the United States. So it seemed that American political philosophy turned on the provocative dialogue between Adams and Taylor. The exchange between the two *thinkers afforded Adams the opportunity to clarify and refine the thoughts that had appeared in the* De- fence *as dense and almost impenetrable.*

THREE LETTERS TO ROGER SHERMAN, ON THE CONSTITUTION OF THE UNITED STATES

I.

Richmond Hill, (New York,) 17 July, 1789.

DEAR SIR,—I read over, with pleasure, your observations on the new federal constitution, and am glad to find an opportunity to communicate to you my opinion on some parts of them. It is by a free and amicable intercourse of sentiments, that the friends of our country may hope for such a unanimity of opinion and such a concert of exertions, as may sooner or later produce the blessings of good government.

You say, "it is by some objected that the executive is blended with the legislature, and that those powers ought to be entirely distinct and unconnected. But is not that a gross error in politics? The united wisdom and various interests of a nation should be combined in framing the laws by which all are to be governed and protected, though it should not be convenient to have them executed by the whole legislature. The supreme executive in Great Britain is one branch of the legislature, and has a negative on all the laws; perhaps that is an extreme not to be imitated by a republic; but the negative vested in the president by the new constitution on the acts of congress, and the consequent revision, may be very useful to prevent laws being passed without mature deliberation, and to preserve stability in the administration of government; and the concurrence of the senate in the appointment to office will strengthen the hands of the executive, and secure the confidence of the people much better than a select council, and will be less expensive."

[margin handwritten note: Adams does not think the executive should be separate]

Is it, then, "an extreme not to be imitated by a republic," to make the supreme executive a branch of the legislature, and give it a negative on all the laws? If you please, we will examine this position, and see whether it is well founded. In the first place, what is your definition of a republic? Mine is this: *A government whose sovereignty is vested in more than one person.* Governments are divided into *despotisms, monarchies,* and *republics.* A despotism is a government in which the three divisions of power, the legislative, executive and judicial, are all vested in one man. A monarchy is a government where the legislative and executive are vested in one man, but the judicial in other men. In all governments the sovereignty is vested in that man or body of men who have the legislative power. In despotisms and monarchies, therefore, the legislative authority being in one man, the sovereignty is in one man. In republics, as the sovereignty, that is, the legislative, is always vested in more than one, it may be vested in as many more as you please. In the United States it might be vested in two persons, or in three millions, or in any other intermediate number; and in every such supposable case the government would be a republic. In conformity to these ideas, republics have been divided into three species, monarchical, aristocratical, and democratical republics. England is a republic, a monarchical republic it is true, but a republic still; because the sovereignty, which is the legislative power, is vested in more than one man; it is equally divided, indeed, between the one, the few, and the many, or in other words, between the natural division of mankind in society,—the monarchical, the aristocratical, and democratical. It is essential to a monarchical republic, that the supreme executive should be a branch of the legislature, and have a negative on all the laws. I say essential, because if monarchy were not an essential part of the sovereignty, the government would not be a monarchical republic. Your position is therefore clearly and certainly an error, because the practice of Great Britain in making the supreme executive a branch of the legislature, and giving it a negative on all the laws, must be imitated by every monarchical republic

I will pause here, if you please; but if you will give me leave, I will write another letter or two upon this subject. Meantime I am, with unalterable friendship, yours.

II.

DEAR SIR,—In my letter of yesterday I think it was demonstrated that the English government is a republic, and that the regal negative upon the laws is essential to that republic. Because, without it, that government would not be what it is, a monarchical republic; and, consequently, could not preserve the balance of power between the executive and legislative powers, nor that other balance which is in the legislature,—between the one, the few, and the many; in which two balances the excellence of that form of government must consist.

Let us now inquire, whether the new constitution of the United States is or is not a monarchical republic, like that of Great Britain. The monarchical and the aristocratical power in our constitution, it is true, are not hereditary; but this makes no difference in the nature of the power, in the nature of the balance, or in the name of the species of government. It would make no difference in the power of a judge or justice, or general or admiral, whether his commission were for life or years. His authority during the time it lasted, would be the same whether it were for one year or twenty, or for life, or descendible to his eldest son. The people, the nation, in whom all power resides originally, may delegate their power for one year or for ten years; for years, or for life; or may delegate it in fee simple or fee tail, if I may so express myself; or during good behavior, or at will, or till further orders.

A nation might unanimously create a dictator or a despot, for one year or more, or for life, or for perpetuity with hereditary descent. In such a case, the dictator for one year would as really be a dictator for the time his power lasted, as the other would be whose power was perpetual and descendible. A nation in the same manner might create a simple monarchy for years, life, or perpetuity, and in either case the creature would be equally a simple monarch during the continuance of his power. So the people of England might create king, lords, and commons, for a year, or for several years, or for life, and in any of these cases, their government would be a monarchical republic, or, if you will, a limited monarchy, during its continuance, as much as it is now, when the king and nobles are hereditary. They might make their house of commons hereditary too. What the consequence of this would be it is easy to foresee; but it would not in the first moment make any change in the legal power, nor in the name of the government.

Let us now consider what our constitution is, and see whether any other name can with propriety be given it, than that of a monarchical republic, or if you will, a limited monarchy. The duration of our president is neither perpetual nor for life; it is only for four years; but his power during those four years is much greater than that of an avoyer, a consul, a podestà, a doge, a stadtholder; nay, than a king of Poland; nay, than a king of Sparta. I know of no first magistrate in any republican government, excepting England and Neuchatel, who possesses a constitutional dignity, authority, and power comparable to his. The power of sending and receiving ambassadors, or raising and commanding armies and navies, of nominating and appointing and commissioning all officers, of managing the treasures, the internal and external affairs of the nation; nay, the whole executive power, coextensive with the legislative power, is vested in him, and he has the right, and his is the duty, to take care that the laws be faithfully executed. These rights and duties, these prerogatives and dignities, are so transcendent that they must naturally and necessarily excite in the nation all the jealousy, envy, fears, apprehensions, and opposition, that are so constantly observed in England against the crown.*

That these powers are necessary, I readily admit. That the laws cannot be executed without them; that the lives, liberties, properties and characters of the citizens cannot be secure with-

---

*M. de Tocqueville has taken a similar view of the President's powers:—

"Le président des États-Unis possède des prérogatives presque royales, dont il n'a pas l'occasion de se servir; et les droits don't jusqu'à présent il peut user sont très circonscrits; *les lois lui permettent d'être fort, les circonstances le maintiennent foible.*"[2] *De la Démocratie en Amérique*, vol. i. chap. 8.

out their protection, is most clear. But it is equally certain, I think, that they ought to have been still greater, or much less. The limitations upon them in the cases of war, treaties, and appointments to office, and especially the limitation on the president's independence as a branch of the legislative, will be the destruction of this constitution, and involve us in anarchy, if not amended. I shall pass over all particulars for the present, except the last; because that is now the point in dispute between you and me. Longitude, and the philosopher's stone, have not been sought with more earnestness by philosophers than a guardian of the laws has been studied by legislators from Plato to Montesquieu; but every project has been found to be no better than committing the lamb to the custody of the wolf, except that one which is called a *balance of power*. A simple sovereignty in one, a few, or many, has no balance, and therefore no laws. A divided sovereignty without a balance, or in other words, where the division is unequal, is always at war, and consequently has no laws. In our constitution the sovereignty,—that is, the legislative power,—is divided into three branches. The house and senate are equal, but the third branch, though essential, is not equal. The president must pass judgment upon every law; but in some cases his judgment may be overruled. These cases will be such as attack his constitutional power; it is, therefore, certain he has not equal power to defend himself, or the constitution, or the judicial power, as the senate and house have.

Power naturally grows. Why? Because human passions are insatiable. But that power alone can grow which already is too great; that which is unchecked; that which has no equal power to control it. The legislative power, in our constitution, is greater than the executive; it will, therefore, encroach, because both aristocratical and democratical passions are insatiable. The legislative power will increase, the executive will diminish. In the legislature, the monarchical power is not equal either to the aristocratical or democratical; it will, therefore, decrease, while the other will increase. Indeed, I think the aristocratical power is greater than either the monarchical or democratical. That will, therefore, swallow up the other two.

In my letter of yesterday, I think it was proved, that a republic might make the supreme executive an integral part of the legislature. In this, it is equally demonstrated, as I think, that our constitution ought to be amended by a decisive adoption of that expedient. If you do not forbid me, I shall write to you again.

III.

DEAR SIR,—There is a sense and degree in which the executive, in our constitution, is blended with the legislature. The president has the power of suspending a law; of giving the two houses an opportunity to pause, to think, to collect themselves, to reconsider a rash step of a majority. He has a right to urge all his reasons against it, by speech or message; which, becoming public, is an appeal to the nation. But the rational objection here is, not that the executive is blended with the legislature, but that it is not enough blended; that it is not incorporated with it, and made an essential part of it. If it were an integral part of it, it might negative a law without much noise, speculation, or confusion among the people. But as it now stands, I beg you to consider it is almost impossible, that a president should ever have the courage to make use of his partial negative. What a situation would a president be in to maintain a controversy against a majority of both houses before a tribunal of the public? To put a stop to a law that more than half the senate and house, and consequently, we may suppose more than half the nation, have set their hearts upon?* It is, moreover, possible, that more than two thirds of the nation, the senate, and house, may, in times of calamity, distress, misfortune, and ill success of the measures of government, from the momentary passion and enthusiasm, demand a law which will wholly subvert the constitution. The constitution of Athens was overturned in such a manner by Aristides himself. The constitution should guard

the executive needs to be blended into the legislature better

---

*Thus far, this has not been found so difficult as was here predicted. But it must be admitted that the occasions in which the negative has been exercised, were not of a kind in which the popular passions are greatly excited.

against a possibility of its subversion; but we may take stronger ground, and assert that it is probable such cases will happen, and that the constitution will, in fact, be subverted in this way. Nay, I go further, and say, that from the constitution of human nature, and the constant course of human affairs, it is certain that our constitution will be subverted, if not amended, and that in a very short time, merely for want of a decisive negative in the executive.

There is another sense and another degree in which the executive is blended with the legislature, which is liable to great and just objection; which excites alarms, jealousies, and apprehensions, in a very great degree. I mean, 1st, the negative of the senate upon appointments to office; 2d. the negative of the senate upon treaties; and 3d. the negative of the two houses upon war. I shall confine myself, at present, to the first. The negative of the senate upon appointments is liable to the following objections:—

1. It takes away, or, at least, it lessens the responsibility of the executive. Our constitution obliges me to say, that it lessens the responsibility of the president. The blame of an injudicious, weak, or wicked appointment, is shared so much between him and the senate, that his part of it will be too small. Who can censure him, without censuring the senate, and the legislatures who appoint them? All their friends will be interested to vindicate the president, in order to screen them from censure. Besides, if an impeachment against an officer is brought before them, are they not interested to acquit him, lest some part of the odium of his guilt should fall upon them, who advised to his appointment?

2. It turns the minds and attention of the people to the senate, a branch of the legislature, in executive matters. It interests another branch of the legislature in the management of the executive. It divides the people between the executive and the senate; whereas, all the people ought to be united to watch the executive, to oppose its encroachments, and resist its ambition. Senators and representatives, and their constituents, in short, the aristocratical and democratical divisions of society ought to be united on all occasions to oppose the executive or the

monarchical branch, when it attempts to overleap its limits. But how can this union be effected, when the aristocratical branch has pledged its reputation to the executive, by consenting to the appointment?

3. It has a natural tendency to excite ambition in the senate. An active, ardent spirit, who is rich and able, and has a great reputation and influence, will be solicited by candidates for office. Not to introduce the idea of bribery, because, though it certainly would force itself in, in other countries, and will probably here, when we grow populous and rich, it is not yet to be dreaded, I hope, ambition must come in already. A senator of great influence will be naturally ambitious and desirous of increasing his influence. Will he not be under a temptation to use his influence with the president as well as his brother senators, to appoint persons to office in the several states, who will exert themselves in elections, to get out his enemies or opposers, both in senate and house of representatives, and to get in his friends, perhaps his instruments? Suppose a senator to aim at the treasury office for himself, his brother, father, or son. Suppose him to aim at the president's chair, or vice-president's, at the next election, or at the office of war, foreign, or domestic affairs. Will he not naturally be tempted to make use of his whole patronage, his whole influence, in advising to appointments, both with president and senators, to get such persons nominated as will exert themselves in elections of president, vice-president, senators, and house of representatives, to increase his interest and promote his views? In this point of view, I am very apprehensive that this defect in our constitution will have an unhappy tendency to introduce corruption of the grossest kinds, both of ambition and avarice, into all our elections, and this will be the worst of poisons to our constitution. It will not only destroy the present form of government, but render it almost impossible to substitute in its place any free government, even a better limited-monarchy, or any other than a despotism or a simple monarchy.

4. To avoid the evil under the last head, it will be in danger of dividing the continent into two or three nations, a case that presents no prospect but of perpetual war.

5. This negative on appointments is in danger of involving the senate in reproach, censure, obloquy, and suspicion, without doing any good. Will the senate use their negative or not? If not, why should they have it? Many will censure them for not using it; many will ridicule them, and call them servile, &c. If they do use it, the very first instance of it will expose the senators to resentment of not only the disappointed candidate and all his friends, but of the president and all his friends, and these will be most of the officers of government, through the nation.

6. We shall very soon have parties formed; a court and country party, and these parties will have names given them. One party in the house of representatives will support the president and his measures and ministers; the other will oppose them. A similar party will be in the senate; these parties will study with all their arts, perhaps with intrigue, perhaps with corruption, at every election to increase their own friends and diminish their opposers. Suppose such parties formed in the senate, and then consider what factious divisions we shall have there upon every nomination.

7. The senate have not time. The convention and Indian treaties.*

You are of opinion "that the concurrence of the senate in the appointments to office, will strengthen the hands of the executive, and secure the confidence of the people, much better than a select council, and will be less expensive."

But in every one of these ideas, I have the misfortune to differ from you.

It will weaken the hands of the executive, by lessening the obligation, gratitude, and attachment of the candidate to the president, by dividing his attachment between the executive and legislative, which are natural enemies. Officers of government, instead of having a single eye and undivided attachment to the executive branch, as they ought to have, consistent with law and the constitution, will be constantly tempted to be fac-

---

*This seems to be an imperfect sentence. The sense is explained at the close of the letter.

tious with their factious patrons in the senate. The president's own officers, in a thousand instances, will oppose his just and constitutional exertions, and screen themselves under the wings of their patrons and party in the legislature.* Nor will it secure the confidence of the people. The people will have more confidence in the executive, in executive matters, than in the senate. The people will be constantly jealous of factious schemes in the senators to unduly influence the executive, to serve each other's private views. The people will also be jealous that the influence of the senate will be employed to conceal, connive at, and defend guilt in executive officers, instead of being a guard and watch upon them, and a terror to them. A council, selected by the president himself, at his pleasure, from among the senators, representatives, and nation at large, would be purely responsible. In that case, the senate would be a terror to privy counsellors; its honor would never be pledged to support any measure or instrument of the executive beyond justice, law, and the constitution. Nor would a privy council be more expensive. The whole senate must now deliberate on every appointment, and if they ever find time for it, you will find that a great deal of time will be required and consumed in this service. Then, the president might have a constant executive council; now, he has none.

I said, under the seventh head, that the senate would not have time. You will find that the whole business of this government will be infinitely delayed by this negative of the senate on treaties and appointments. Indian treaties and consular conventions have been already waiting for months, and the senate have not been able to find a moment of time to attend to them; and this evil must constantly increase. So that the senate must be constantly sitting, and must be paid as long as they sit . . .

But I have tried your patience. Is there any truth in these broken hints and crude surmises, or not? To me they appear well founded and very important.

I am, with usual affection, yours,   JOHN ADAMS.

---

*A singular prediction of what actually happened, afterwards, to himself.

LETTERS.

To John Taylor.
I.

Quincy, 15 April, 1814.

Sir,—I have received your *Inquiry* in a large volume neatly bound. Though I have not read it in course, yet, upon an application to it of the *Sortes Virgilianæ*, scarce a page has been found in which my name is not mentioned, and some public sentiment or expression of mine examined. Revived as these subjects are, in this manner, in the recollection of the public, after an oblivion of so many years, by a gentleman of your high rank, ample fortune, learned education, and powerful connections, I flatter myself it will not be thought improper in me to solicit your attention to a few explanations and justifications of a book that has been misunderstood, misrepresented, and abused, more than any other, except the Bible, that I have ever read.

In the first words of the first section, you say, "Mr. Adams's political system deduces government from a *natural* fate; the policy of the United States deduces it from *moral* liberty."

This sentence, I must acknowledge, passes all my understanding. I know not what is meant by fate, nor what distinction there is, or may be made or conceived, between a natural and artificial, or unnatural fate. Nor do I well know what *"moral liberty"* signifies. I have read a great deal about the words *fate* and *chance;* but though I close my eyes to abstract my meditations, I never could conceive any idea of either. When an action or event happens or occurs without a cause, some say it happens by chance. This is equivalent to saying that chance is not cause at all; it is nothing. Fate, too, is no cause, no agent, no power; it has neither understanding, will, affections, liberty, nor choice; it has no existence; it is not even a figment of imagination; it is a mere invention of a word without a meaning; it is a nonentity; it is nothing. Mr. Adams most certainly never deduced any system from chance or fate, natural, artificial, or unnatural.

Liberty, according to my metaphysics, is an intellectual quality; an attribute that belongs not to fate nor chance. Neither possesses it, neither is capable of it. There is nothing moral or immoral in the idea of it. The definition of it is a self-determining power in an intellectual agent. It implies thought and choice and power; it can elect between objects, indifferent in point of morality, neither morally good nor morally evil. If the substance in which this quality, attribute, adjective, call it what you will, exists, has a moral sense, a conscience, a moral faculty; if it can distinguish between moral good and moral evil, and has power to choose the former and refuse the latter, it can, if it will, choose the evil and reject the good, as we see in experience it very often does.

"Mr. Adams's system," and "the policy of the United States," are drawn from the same sources, deduced from the same principles, wrought into the same frame; indeed, they are the same, and ought never to have been divided or separated; much less set in opposition to each other, as they have been.

That we may more clearly see how these hints apply, certain technical terms must be defined.

1. DESPOTISM. A sovereignty unlimited, that is,—the *suprema lex,* the *summa potestatis* in one. This has rarely, if ever, existed but in theory.

2. MONARCHY. Sovereignty in one, variously limited.

3. ARISTOCRACY. Sovereignty in a few.

4. DEMOCRACY. Sovereignty in the many, that is, in the whole nation, the whole body, assemblage, congregation, or if you are an Episcopalian, you may call it, if you please, *church,* of the whole people. This sovereignty must, in all cases, be exerted or exercised by the whole people assembled together. This form of government has seldom, if ever, existed but in theory; as rarely, at least, as an unlimited despotism in one individual.

5. The infinite variety of mixed governments are all so many different combinations, modifications, and intermixtures of the second, third, and fourth species or division.

Now, every one of these sovereigns possesses intellectual liberty to act for the public good or not. Being men, they have all what Dr. Rush calls a *moral faculty;* Dr. Hutcheson, a *moral sense;* and the Bible and the generality of the world, *a con-*

science. They are all, therefore, under moral obligations to do to others as they would have others *do to them;* to consider themselves born, authorized, empowered for the good of society as well as their own good. Despots, monarchs, aristocrats, democrats, holding such high trusts, are under the most solemn and the most sacred moral obligations, to consider their trusts and their power to be instituted for the benefit and happiness of their nations, not their nations as servants to them or their friends or parties. In other words, to exert all their intellectual liberty to employ all their faculties, talents, and power for the public, general, universal good of their nations, not for their own separate good, or the interest of any party.

In this point of view, there is no difference in forms of government. All of them, and all men concerned in them,—all are under equal moral obligations. The intellectual liberty of aristocracies and democracies can be exerted only by votes, and ascertained only by ayes and noes. The sovereign judgment and will can be determined, known, and declared, only by majorities. This will, this decision, is sometimes determined by a single vote; often by two or three; very rarely by a large majority; scarcely ever by a unanimous suffrage. And from the impossibility of keeping together at all times the same number of voters, the majorities are apt to waver from day to day, and swing like a pendulum from side to side.

Nevertheless, the minorities have, in all cases, the same intellectual liberty, and are under the same moral obligations as the majorities.

In what manner these theoretical, intellectual liberties have been exercised, and these moral obligations fulfilled, by despots, monarchs, aristocrats, and democrats, is obvious enough in history and in experience. They have all in general conducted themselves alike.

But this investigation is not at present before us.

II.

It is unnecessary to discuss the nice distinctions, which follow in the first page of your respectable volume, between mind, body, and morals. The essence and substance of mind and body, of soul and body, of spirit and matter, are wholly withheld as yet from our knowledge; from the penetration of our sharpest faculties; from the keenest of our incision knives, the most amplifying of our microscopes. With some of the attributes or qualities of each and of both we are well acquainted. We cannot pretend to improve the essence of either, till we know it. Mr. Adams has never thought "of limiting the improvements or amelioration" of the properties or qualities of either. The definition of matter is,—a dead, inactive, inert substance. That of spirit is,—a living, active substance, sometimes, if not always, intelligent. Morals are no qualities of matter; nor, as far as we know, of simple spirit or simple intelligence. Morals are attributes of spirits *only* when those spirits are *free* as well as intelligent agents, and have consciences or a moral sense, a faculty of discrimination not only between right and wrong, but between good and evil, happiness and misery, pleasure and pain. This freedom of choice and action, united with conscience, necessarily implies a responsibility to a lawgiver and to a law, and has a necessary relation to right and wrong, to happiness and misery.

It is unnecessary for Mr. Adams to allow or disallow the distinctions in this first page to be applicable to his theory. But if he speaks of natural political systems, he certainly comprehends not only all the intellectual and physical powers and qualities of man, but all his moral powers and faculties, all his duties and obligations as a man and a citizen of this world, as well as of the state in which he lives, and every interest, thing, or concern that belongs to him, from his cradle to his grave. This comprehension of all the perfections and imperfections, all the powers and wants of man, is certainly not for the purpose of *"circumscribing the powers of mind."* But it is to enlarge them, to give them free scope to run, expand, and be glorified.

If you should speak of a natural system of geography, would you not comprehend the whole globe, and even its relations to the sun, moon, and stars? of astronomy, all that the telescope has discovered? of chemistry or natural history, all that the microscope has found? of architecture, every thing that can make a building commodious, useful, elegant, graceful, and ornamental?

In the second page, Mr. Adams is totally misunderstood or misrepresented. He has never said, written, or thought, *"that the human mind is able to circumscribe its own powers."* Nor has he ever asserted or believed that, *"man can ascertain his own moral capacity."* Nor has he ever *"deduced any consequences from such postulata, or erected any scheme of government"* upon them or either of them.

If mankind have not "agreed upon any form of government," does it follow that there is no natural form of government? and that all forms are equally natural? It might as well be contended that all are equally good, and that the constitution of the Ottoman Empire is as natural, as free, and as good, as that of the United States. If men have not agreed in any system of architecture, will you infer that there are no natural principles of that noble art? If some prefer the Gothic, and others the Grecian models, will you say that both are equally natural, convenient, and elegant? If some prefer the Doric, and others the Corinthian pillars, are the five orders equally beautiful? If "human nature has been perpetually escaping from all forms," will it be inferred that all forms are equally natural? equal for the preservation of liberty?

There is no necessity of "confronting Mr. Adams's opinion, that aristocracy is natural, and therefore unavoidable, with the other, that it is artificial or factitious, and therefore avoidable," because the opinions are both true and perfectly consistent with each other.

By *natural aristocracy*, in general, may be understood those superiorities of influence in society which grow out of the constitution of human nature. By *artificial aristocracy*, those inequalities of weight and superiorities of influence which are created and established by civil laws. Terms must be defined before we can reason. By aristocracy, I understand all those men who can command, influence, or procure more than an average of votes; by an aristocrat, every man who can and will influence one man to vote besides himself. Few men will deny that there is a natural aristocracy of virtues and talents in every nation and in every party, in every city and village. Inequalities are a part of the natural history of man.

III.

I believe that none but Helvetius will affirm, that all children are born with equal genius.

None will pretend, that all are born of dispositions exactly alike,—of equal weight; equal strength; equal length; equal delicacy of nerves; equal elasticity of muscles; equal complexions; equal figure, grace, or beauty.

I have seen, in the Hospital of Foundlings, the *"Enfans Trouvés,"* at Paris, fifty babes in one room;—all under four days old; all in cradles alike; all nursed and attended alike; all dressed alike; all equally neat. I went from one end to the other of the whole row, and attentively observed all their countenances. And I never saw a greater variety, or more striking inequalities, in the streets of Paris or London. Some had every sign of grief, sorrow, and despair; others had joy and gayety in their faces. Some were sinking in the arms of death; others looked as if they might live to fourscore. Some were as ugly and others as beautiful, as children or adults ever are; these were stupid; those sensible. These were all born to equal rights, but to very different fortunes; to very different success and influence in life.

The world would not contain the books, if one should produce all the examples that reading and experience would furnish. One or two permit me to hint.

Will any man say, would Helvetius say, that all men are born equal in strength? Was Hercules no stronger than his neighbors? How many nations, for how many ages, have been governed by his strength, and by the reputation and renown of it by his posterity? If you have lately read Hume, Robertson or the Scottish Chiefs, let me ask you, if Sir William Wallace was no more than equal in strength to the average Scotchmen? and whether Wallace could have done what he did without that extraordinary strength?

Will Helvetius or Rousseau say that all men and women are born equal in beauty? Will any philosopher say, that beauty has no influence in human society? If he does, let him read the histories of Eve, Judith, Helen, the fair Gabrielle, Diana of Poitiers, Pompadour, Du Barry, Susanna, Abigail, Lady Hamilton, Mrs. Clark, and a million others. Are not despots, monarchs, aristocrats, and democrats, equally liable to be seduced by beauty to confer favors and influence suffrages?

Socrates calls beauty a short-lived tyranny; Plato, *the privilege of nature;* Theophrastus, a mute eloquence; Diogenes, the best letter of recommendation; Carneades, a queen without soldiers; Theocritus, a serpent covered with flowers; Bion, a good that does not belong to the possessor, because it is impossible to give ourselves beauty, or to preserve it. Madame du Barry expressed the philosophy of Carneades in more laconic language, when she said, *"La véritable royauté, c'est la beauté,"*—the genuine royalty is beauty. And she might have said with equal truth, that it is genuine aristocracy; for it has as much influence in one form of government as in any other; and produces aristocracy in the deepest democracy that ever was known or imagined, as infallibly as in any other form of government. What shall we say to all these philosophers, male and female? Is not beauty a privilege granted by nature, according to Plato and to truth, often more influential in society, and even upon laws and government, than stars, garters, crosses, eagles, golden fleeces, or any hereditary titles or other distinctions? The grave elders were not proof against the charms of Susanna. The Grecian sages wondered not at the Trojan war when they saw Helen. Holofernes's guards, when they saw Judith, said, "one such woman let go would deceive the whole earth."

Can you believe, Mr. Taylor, that the brother of such a sister, the father of such a daughter, the husband of such a wife, or even the gallant of such a mistress, would have but one vote in your moral republic? Ingenious,—but not historical, philosophical, or political,—learned, classical, poetical Barlow! I mourn over thy life and thy death. Had truth, instead of popularity and party, been thy object, your pamphlet on privileged orders would have been a very different thing!

That all men are born to equal rights is true. Every being has a right to his own, as clear, as moral, as sacred, as any other being has. This is as indubitable as a moral government in the universe. But to teach that all men are born with equal powers and faculties, to equal influence in society, to equal property and advantages through life, is as gross a fraud, as glaring an imposition on the credulity of the people, as ever was practised by monks, by Druids, by Brahmins, by priests of the immortal Lama, or by the self-styled philosophers of the French revolution. For honor's sake, Mr. Taylor, for truth and virtue's sake, let American philosophers and politicians despise it.

Mr. Adams leaves to Homer and Virgil, to Tacitus and Quintilian, to Mahomet and Calvin, to Edwards and Priestly, or, if you will, to Milton's angels reasoning high in pandemonium, all their acute speculations about fate, destiny, foreknowledge absolute, necessity, and predestination. He thinks it problematical, whether there is, or ever will be, more than one Being capable of understanding this vast subject. In his principles of legislation, he has nothing to do with these interminable controversies. He considers men as free, moral, and accountable agents; and he takes men as God has made them. And will Mr. Taylor deny, that God has made some men deaf and some blind, or will he affirm that these will infallibly have as much influence in society, and be able to procure as many votes as any who can see and hear?

Honor the day,* and believe me no enemy.

IV.

That aristocracies, both ancient and modern, have been "variable and artificial," as well as natural and unchangeable, Mr. Adams knows as well as Mr. Taylor, and has never denied or doubted. That "they have all proceeded from moral causes," is not so clear, since many of them appear to proceed from physical causes, many from immoral causes, many from pharisaical, jesuitical, and Machiavelian villany; many from sacerdotal and despotic fraud, and as many as all the rest, from democratical dupery, credulity, adulation, corruption, adoration, superstition, and enthusiasm. If all these cannot be regu-

---

* 19 April. The anniversary of the action at Lexington.

men not born equal

lated by political laws, and controlled, checked, or balanced by constitutional energies, I am willing Mr. Taylor should say of them what Bishop Burnet said of the hierarchy, or the severest things he can express or imagine.

That nature makes king-bees or queen-bees, I have heard and read. But I never read in any philosopher or political writer, as I remember, that nature makes state-kings and lords of state. Though even this, for aught I know, might be sometimes pretended. I have read of hereditary rights from Adam to Noah; and the divine right of nobility derived from the Dukes of Edom; but those divine rights did not make kings, till holy oil was poured upon their heads from the vial brought down from heaven in her beak, by the Holy Ghost in the person of a dove. If we consult books, Mr. Taylor, we shall find that nonsense, absurdity, and impiety are infinite. Whether "the policy of the United States" has been wisdom or folly, is not the question at present. But it is confidently asserted, without fear of contradiction, that every page and every line Mr. Adams has ever written, was intended to illustrate, to prove, to exhibit, and to demonstrate its wisdom.

The association of "Mr. Adams with Filmer" in the third page, may excite a smile! I give you full credit, Mr. Taylor, for the wit and shrewdness of this remark. It is droll and good-humored. But if ever policy was in diametrical opposition to Filmer, it is that of the United States. If ever writings were opposed to his principles, Mr. Adams's are so opposed. They are as much so as those of Sidney or Locke.

Mr. Adams thanks Mr. Taylor for proposing in the third page to analyze and ascertain the ideas intended to be expressed by the word "aristocracy." This is one of those words which have been abused. It has been employed to signify any thing, every thing and nothing. Mr. Taylor has read Mr. Locke's chapter "on the abuse of words," which, though it contains nothing but what daily experience exhibits to all mankind, ought, nevertheless, if he had never written any thing else, to secure him immortal gratitude and renown. Without the learning of Luzac, Vanderkemp, Jefferson, or Parsons, Mr. Adams recollects enough of Greek, to remember that "aristocracy" originally signified "the government of the best men."

But who are to be judges of the best men? Who is to make the selection of the best men from the second best? and the third? and the fourth? and so on *ad infinitum?* For good and bad are infinitely divisible, like matter. Ay! there's the rub! Despots, monarchs, aristocrats, and democrats have, in all ages hit, at times, upon the best men, in the best sense of the word. But, at other times, and much more frequently, they have all chosen the very worst men; the men who have the most devotedly and the most slavishly flattered their vanity, gratified their most extravagant passions, and promoted their selfish and private views. Without searching volumes, Mr. Taylor, I will tell you in a few words what I mean by an aristocrat, and, consequently, what I mean by aristocracy. By an aristocrat, I mean every man who can command or influence TWO VOTES; ONE BESIDES HIS OWN.

Take the first hundred men you meet in the streets of a city, or on a turnpike road in the country, and constitute them a democratical republic. In my next, you may have some conjectures of what will appear in your new democracy.

V.

When your new democratical republic meets, you will find half a dozen men of independent fortunes; half a dozen, of more eloquence; half a dozen, with more learning; half a dozen, with eloquence, learning, and fortune.

Let me see. We have now four-and-twenty; to these we may add six more, who will have more art, cunning, and intrigue, than learning, eloquence, or fortune. These will infallibly soon unite with the twenty-four. Thus we make thirty. The remaining seventy are composed of farmers, shopkeepers, merchants, tradesmen, and laborers. Now, if each of these thirty can, by any means, influence one vote besides his own, the whole thirty can carry sixty votes,—a decided and uncontrolled majority of the hundred. These thirty I mean by aristocrats; and they will instantly convert your democracy of ONE HUNDRED into an aristocracy of THIRTY.

Take at random, or select with your utmost prudence, one hundred of your most faithful and capable domestics from your own numerous plantations, and make them a democratical republic. You will immediately perceive the same inequalities, and the same democratical republic, in a very few of the first sessions, transformed into an aristocratical republic; as complete and perfect an aristocracy as the senate of Rome, and much more so. Some will be beloved and followed, others hated and avoided by their fellows.

It would be easy to quote Greek and Latin, to produce a hundred authorities to show the original signification of the word *aristocracy* and its infinite variations and application in the history of ages. But this would be all waste water. Once for all, I give you notice, that whenever I use the word *aristocrat*, I mean a citizen who can command or govern two votes or more in society, whether by his virtues, his talents, his learning, his loquacity, his taciturnity, his frankness, his reserve, his face, figure, eloquence, grace, air, attitude, movements, wealth, birth, art, address, intrigue, good fellowship, drunkenness, debauchery, fraud, perjury, violence, treachery, pyrrhonism, deism, or atheism; for by every one of these instruments have votes been obtained and will be obtained. You seem to think aristocracy consists altogether in artificial titles, tinsel decorations of stars, garters, ribbons, golden eagles and golden fleeces, crosses and roses and lilies, exclusive privileges, hereditary descents, established by kings or by positive laws of society. No such thing! Aristocracy was, from the beginning, now is, and ever will be, world without end, independent of all these artificial regulations, as really and as efficaciously as with them!

Let me say a word more. Your democratical republic picked in the streets, and your democratical African republic, or your domestic republic, call it which you will, in its first session, will become an aristocratical republic. In the second session it will become an oligarchical republic; because the seventy-four democrats and the twenty-six aristocrats will, by this time, discover that thirteen of the aristocrats can command four votes each; these thirteen will now command the majority, and, consequently, will be sovereign. The thirteen will then be an oli-

garchy. In the third session, it will be found that among these
thirteen oligarchs there are seven, each of whom can command
eight votes, equal in all to fifty-six, a decided majority. In the
fourth session, it will be found that there are among these seven
oligarchs four who can command thirteen votes apiece. The republic then becomes an oligarchy, whose sovereignty is in four
individuals. In the fifth session, it will be discovered that two of
the four can command six-and-twenty votes each. Then two
will have the command of the sovereign oligarchy. In the sixth
session, there will be a sharp contention between the two which
shall have the command of the fifty-two votes. Here will commence the squabble of Danton and Robespierre, of Julius and
Pompey, of Anthony and Augustus, of the white rose and the
red rose, of Jefferson and Adams, of Burr and Jefferson, of Clinton and Madison, or, if you will, of Napoleon and Alexander.

This, my dear sir, is the history of mankind, past, present,
and to come.

VI.

In the third page of your "Inquiry," is an assertion which
Mr. Adams has a right to regret, as a gross and egregious misrepresentation. He cannot believe it to have been intentional.
He imputes it to haste; to ardor of temper; to defect of memory; to any thing rather than design. It is in these words,—"Mr.
Adams asserts, 'that every society naturally produces an order
of men, which it is impossible to confine to an equality of
RIGHTS.'" This pretended quotation, marked as it is by in-
verted commas, is totally and absolutely unfounded. No such
expression ever fell from his lips; no such language was ever
written by his pen; no such principle was ever approved or
credited by his understanding, no such sentiment was ever felt
without abhorrence in his heart. On the contrary, he has
through life asserted the moral equality of all mankind. His
system of government, which is the system of Massachusetts,
as well as the system of the United States, which are the same
as much as an original and a copy are the same, was calculated
and framed for the express purpose of securing to all men equal
laws and equal rights. Physical inequalities are proclaimed

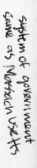

system of government
same as Massachusetts

equal rights

aloud by God Almighty through all his works. Mr. Adams must have been destitute of senses, not to have perceived them in men from their births to their deaths; and, at the same time, not to have perceived that they were incurable and inevitable, by human wisdom, goodness, or power. All that men can do, is to modify, organize, and arrange the powers of human society, that is to say, the physical strength and force of men, in the best manner to protect, secure, and cherish the moral, which are all the natural rights of mankind.

The French are very fond of the phrase "social order." The English commonly hear it, or read it with a broad grin. I am not Englishman enough to join in this ridicule. A "social order" there must be, unless we would return to the forests, and assert individual independence in a more absolute sense than Tartars or Arabs, African negroes, or North American Indians, or Samoyedes, or Hottentots have ever conceived.

A beggar said at my father's house, full seventy years ago, "The world is very unequally divided. But I do not wonder at it, nor think much of it. Because I know, that if it were equally divided to-day, in one month there would be as great odds as ever." The beggar's proverb contained as certain and as important truths as any that was ever uttered by the wise men of Greece.

Will Mr. Taylor profess himself a downright leveller? Will he vote for a community of property? or an equal division of property? and a community of wives and women? He must introduce and establish both, before he can reduce all men to an equality of influence. It is, indeed, questionable, whether such laws would not produce greater inequalities than ever were seen in the world. These are not new projects, Mr. Taylor. They are not original inventions, or discoveries of philosophers of the eighteenth century. They were as familiar to Plato as they were to Helvetius or Condorcet. If I were a young man, I should like to write a romance, and send a hero upon his travels through such a levelling community of wives and wealth. It would be very edifying to record his observations on the opinions, principles, customs, institutions, and manners of this democratical republic and such a virtuous and happy age. But a gentleman whose mind is so active, studious, and contemplative as Mr. Taylor's, must easily foresee, that some men must take care of the property of others, or it must perish with its owners, and that some men would have as many wives as Solomon, and others none at all.

See, what is no uncommon sight, a family of six sons. Four of them are prudent, discreet, frugal, and industrious men; the other two are idle and profligate. The father leaves equal portions of his estate to all the six. How long will it be before the two will request the four to purchase their shares? and how long before the purchase money will be spent in sports, gambled away at race, or cards, or dice, or billiards, or dissipated at taverns or worse houses? When the two are thus reduced to beggars, will they have as much influence in society as any one of the four?

VII.

Suppose another case, which is not without examples,—a family of six daughters. Four of them are not only beautiful, but serious and discreet women. Two of them are not only ugly, but ill tempered and immodest. Will either of the two have an equal chance with any one of the four to attract the attention of a suitor, and obtain a husband of worth, respectability, and consideration in the world?

Such, and many other natural and acquired and habitual inequalities are visible, and palpable, and audible, every day, in every village, and in every family, in the whole world. The imagination, therefore, of a government, of a democratical republic, in which every man and every woman shall have an equal weight in society, is a chimera. They have all equal rights; but cannot, and ought not to have equal power.

Unhappily, the cases before stated are too often reversed, and four or five out of six sons, are unwise, and only one or two praiseworthy; and four or five out of six daughters, are mere triflers, and only one or two whose "price is above rubies." And may I not ask, whether there are no instances, in which the whole of six sons and daughters are found wanting; and instead of maintaining their single vote, and their independence, become all dependent on others? Nay, there are examples of whole families wasted and totally lost by vice and folly. Can these, while any of them existed, have maintained an equality of consideration in Society, with other families of equal numbers, but of virtuous and considerate characters?

matrimony another source of natural aristocracy

Matrimony, then, Mr. Taylor, I have a right to consider as another source of natural aristocracy.

Will you give me leave to ask you, Mr. Taylor, why you employ the phrase, "political power" in this third page, instead of sovereign power,—the *summa potestatis,* the supreme power, the legislative power, the power from which there is no appeal, but to Heaven, and the *ratio ultima regum et rerum-publicarum?* This language would be understood by readers, by scientific people, and by the vulgar. But "political power" is so indefinite, that it belongs to every man who has a vote, and every woman who has a charm. What, Mr. Taylor, is the resemblance of a president or a governor to a monarch? It is the resemblance of Mount Vernon to the Andes; of the Tiber at Washington to the Ganges or Mississippi. A president has the executive power only, and that under severe restrictions, jealous restrictions; and as I am too old to court popularity, I will venture to say, in my opinion, very pernicious restrictions; restrictions that will destroy this constitution before its time. A president has no legislative power; a monarch has it all.

What resemblance has an American senate to a hereditary order? It has a negative upon the laws. In this, it resembles the house of lords in England; but in nothing else. It has no resemblance to any hereditary order. It has no resemblance even to the hereditary descent of lands, tenements, and hereditaments. There is nothing hereditary in it.

hereditary

And here, Mr. Taylor, permit me to ask you, whether the descent of lands and goods and chattels does not constitute a hereditary order as decidedly as the descent of stars and garters? I will be still bolder. Has not this law of descents constituted the Honorable John Randolph one of a hereditary order, for a time, as clearly as any Montmorenci or Howard, any Julius, any of the Heraclides, or any of the blood of Mahomet, or any of his connections by marriage?

You must allow me twenty years to answer a book that cost you twenty years of meditation to compose.

You must allow me also to ask you a question still nearer home. You had the honor and felicity to marry the only child of my honest and sincere friend, the Honorable John Penn, of North Carolina. From this marriage, you derived, with an amiable consort, a handsome fortune.

If you complain that this is personal, I confess it, and intend it should be personal, that it might be more striking to you, and to all others who may ever see or hear of our controversy. In return, I give you full leave to ask me any questions relative to myself, my ancestors, my posterity, my natural or political friends. I will answer every question you can ask with the same frankness, candor, and sincerity.

I will be bolder still, Mr. Taylor. Would Washington have ever been commander of the revolutionary army or president of the United States, if he had not married the rich widow of Mr. Custis? Would Jefferson ever have been president of the United States if he had not married the daughter of Mr. Wales?

I am weary and so are you. Ceremonies avaunt. . . .

XV.

In this fourth page you say, that "Mr. Adams's system tells us that the art of government can never change." I have said no such thing, Mr. Taylor! I know the art of government has changed, and probably will change as often as the arts of architecture, painting, sculpture, music, poetry, agriculture, horticulture, medicine; and that is to say, almost as often as the weather or the fashion in dress.

But all these arts are founded in certain general principles of nature, which have never been known to change; and it is the duty of philosophers, legislators, and artists to study these principles; and the nearer they approach to them, the greater perfection will they attain in their arts. There may be principles in nature, not yet observed, that will improve all these arts; and nothing hinders any man from making experiments and pursuing researches, to investigate such principles and make such improvements. But America has made no discoveries of principles of government that have not been long known. Morality and liberty, and "moral liberty," too, whatever it may mean, have been known from the creation. Cain knew it when he killed Abel, and knew that he violated it.

You say, sir, that I have gravely counted up several victims "of popular rage, as proofs that democracy is more pernicious than monarchy or aristocracy." This is not my doctrine, Mr. Taylor. My opinion is, and always has been, that absolute power intoxicates alike despots, monarchs, aristocrats, and democrats, and jacobins, and *sans culottes*. I cannot say that democracy has been more pernicious, on the whole, than any of the others. Its atrocities have been more transient; those of the others have been more permanent. The history of all ages shows that the caprice, cruelties, and horrors of democracy have soon disgusted, alarmed, and terrified themselves. They soon cry, "this will not do; we have gone too far! We are all in the wrong! We are none of us safe! We must unite in some clever fellow, who can protect us all,—Cæsar, Bonaparte, who you will! Though we distrust, hate, and abhor them all; yet we must submit to one or another of them, stand by him, cry him up to the skies, and swear that he is the greatest, best, and finest man that ever lived!"

It has been my fortune, good or bad, to live in Europe ten years, from 1778 to 1788, in a public character. This destiny, singular in America, forced upon my attention the course of events in France, Holland, Geneva, and Switzerland, among many other nations; and this has irresistibly attracted my thoughts more than has been for my interest. The subject cannot have escaped you. What has been the conduct of the democratic parties in all those nations? How horribly bloody in some! Has it been steady, consistent, uniform, in any? Has it not leaped from democracy to aristocracy, to oligarchy, to military despotism, and back again to monarchy, as often, and as easily, as the birds fly to the lower, the middle, or the upper limbs of a tree, or leap from branch to branch, or hop from spray to spray? Democracy, nevertheless, must not be disgraced; democracy must not be despised. Democracy must be respected; democracy must be honored; democracy must be cherished; democracy must be an essential, an integral part of the sovereignty, and have a control over the whole government, or moral liberty cannot exist, or any other liberty. I have been always grieved by the gross abuses of this respectable word. One party speak of it as the most amiable, venerable, indeed, as the sole object of its adoration; the other, as the sole object of its scorn, abhorrence, and execration. Neither party, in my opinion, know what they say. Some of them care not what they say, provided they can accomplish their own selfish purposes. These ought not to be forgiven.

You triumphantly demand: "What motives of preference between forms of government remain?" Is there no difference between a government of laws and a government of men? Between a government according to fixed laws, concerted by three branches of the legislature, composed of the most experienced men of a nation, established, recorded, promulgated to every individual, as the rule of his conduct, and a government according to the will of one man, or to a vote of a few men, or to a vote of a single assembly, whether of a nation or its representatives?

It is not Mr. Adams's system which can "arrest our efforts or appall our hopes in pursuit of political good." Other causes have obstructed and still embarrass the progress of the science of legislation.

XVI.

In this number I have to hint at some causes which impede the course of investigation in civil and political knowledge. Religion, however, has been so universally associated with government, that it is impossible to separate them in this inquiry.

And where shall I begin, and where end? Shall I begin with the library at Alexandria, and finish with that at Washington, the latter Saracens more ferocious than the former, in proportion as they lived in a more civilized age? Where are the languages of antiquity? all the dialects of the Chaldean tongue? Where is Aristotle's history of eighteen hundred republics, that had existed before his time? Where are Cicero's writings upon government? What havoc has been made of books through every century of the Christian era? Where are fifty gospels, condemned as spurious by the bull of Pope Gelasius? Where are the forty wagon-loads of Hebrew manuscripts burned in France, by order of another pope, because suspected of heresy? Remember the *index expurgatorius,* the inquisition, the stake, the axe, the halter, and the guillotine; and, oh! horrible, the rack! This is as bad, if not worse, than a slow fire. Nor should the Lion's Mouth be forgotten.

Have you considered that system of holy lies and pious frauds that has raged and triumphed for fifteen hundred years; and which Chateaubriand appears at this day to believe as sincerely as St. Austin did? Upon this system depend the royalty, loyalty, and allegiance of Europe. The vial of holy oil, with which the Kings of France and England are anointed, is one of the most splendid and important events in all the legends. Do you think that Mr. Adams's system "arrests our efforts and appalls our hopes in pursuit of political good"? His maxim is, study government as you do astronomy, by facts, observations, and experiments; not by the dogmas of lying priests or knavish politicians.

The causes that impede political knowledge would fill a hundred volumes. How can I crowd a few hints at them in a single volume, much less, in a single letter?

Give me leave to select one attempt to improve civil, political, and ecclesiastical knowledge; or, at least, to arrest and retard the progress of ignorance, hypocrisy, and knavery; and the reception it met in the world, tending to "arrest our efforts and appall our hopes." Can you believe that Jesuits conceived this design? Yet true it is.

About the year 1643, Bollandus, a Jesuit, began the great work, the *"Acta Sanctorum."* Even Jesuits were convinced that impositions upon mankind had gone too far. Henschenius, another Jesuit, assisted him and Papebrock in the labor. The design was to give the lives of the saints, and to distinguish the miracles into the true, the false, and the dubious. They produced fortyseven volumes, in folio, an immense work, which, I believe, has never appeared in America. It was not, I am confident, in the library consumed by Ross, the savage, damned to everlasting fame,* and I fear it is not in the noble collection of Mr. Jefferson. I wish it was. This was a great effort in favor of truth, and to arrest imposture, though made by Jesuits. But what was their reward? Among the miracles, pronounced by these able men to be true, there are probably millions which you and I should believe no more than we do those related by Paulinus, Athanasius, Basil, Jerome, or Chrysostom, as of their own knowledge.

Now, let us see how this generous effort in favor of truth was received and rewarded. Libels in abundance were printed against it. The authors were cited before the Inquisition in Spain, and the Pope in Italy, as authors of gross errors. The Inquisition pronounced its anathema in 1695. All Europe was in anxious suspense. The Pope, himself, was embarrassed by the interminable controversies excited, and, without deciding any thing, had no way to escape but by prohibiting all writings on the subject.

And what were the errors? They were only doubts.

1. Is it certain that the face of Jesus Christ was painted on the handkerchief of Saint Veronica?

2. Had the Carmelites the prophet Elias for their founder?

These questions set Europe in a flame, and might have roasted Papebrock at an *auto-da-fé*, had he been in Spain.

Such dangers as these might "arrest efforts and appall hopes of political good;" but Mr. Adams's system cannot. That gaping, timid animal, man, dares not read or think. The prejudices, passions, habits, associations, and interests of his fellow-creatures surround him on every side; and if his reading or his thoughts interfere with any of these, he dares not acknowledge it. If he is hardy enough to venture even a hint, persecution, in some form or other, is his certain portion. *Party spirit,—l'esprit du corps,—* sects, factions, which threaten our existence in America at this moment, both in church and state, have "arrested all efforts, and appalled all hopes of political good." Have the Protestants accomplished a thorough reformation? Is there a nation in Europe whose government is purified from monkish knavery? Even in England, is not the vial of holy oil still shown to travellers? How

---

*The commander of the British troops, when the public buildings at Washington were burned.

long will it be before the head of the Prince Regent, or the head of his daughter, will be anointed with this oil, and the right of impressing seamen from American ships deduced from it?

XVII.

Mr. Adams's system is that of Pope, in his Essay on Criticism:—

> "First follow Nature, and your judgment frame
> By her just standard, which is still the same."

This rule, surely, cannot "arrest our efforts or appall our hopes." Study government as you build ships or construct steam-engines. The steam frigate will not defend New York, if Nature has not been studied, and her principles regarded. And how is the nature of man, and of society, and of government, to be studied or known, but in the history and by the experience of human nature in its terrestrial existence?

But to come nearer home, in search of causes which "arrest our efforts." Here I am, like the woodcutter on Mount Ida, who could not see wood for trees. Mariana wrote a book, *De Regno*, in which he had the temerity to insinuate that kings were instituted for good, and might be deposed if they did nothing but evil. Of course, the book was prohibited, and the writer prosecuted. Harrington wrote his *Oceana*, and other learned and ingenious works, for which he was committed to prison, where he became delirious and died. Sidney wrote discourses on government, for which he was beheaded, though they were only in manuscript, and robbed from his desk. Montesquieu was obliged to fly his country, and wander about Europe for many years; was compelled by the Sorbonne, after his return, to sign a recantation, as humiliating and as sincere as that of Galileo.*

---

*It is related of Montesquieu, that he suppressed some passages of his Persian Letters in a new edition, because they had been made by the king an obstacle to his admission to the French Academy. But he answered the Sorbonne without recanting; neither did he travel except from inclination. Voltaire says of him: "Montesquieu fut compté parmi les hommes les plus illustres du dix-huitième siècle, et cependant il ne fut pas persécuté, il ne fut qu'un pue molesté pour ses *Lettres Persanes*."[3]

The chagrin produced by the criticisms and misrepresentations of his writings, and the persecutions he suffered, destroyed his health, and he died in 1755.

These instances, among others without number, are the discouragements which "arrest our efforts and appall our hopes." Nor are these all. Mankind do not love to read any thing upon any theory of government. Very few read any thing but libels. Theoretical books upon government will not sell. Booksellers and printers, far from purchasing the manuscript, will not accept it as a gift. For example, no printer would publish these remarks at his own risk; and if I should print them at mine, they would fall dead from the press. I should never sell ten copies of them. I cannot learn that your Inquiry has had a rapid sale. I fear that you or your printer will be a loser, which I shall regret, because I really wish it could be read by every one who can read. To you, who are rich, this loss is of little moment; but to me, who am poor, such losses would be a dangerous "arrest of efforts," and a melancholy "appall of hopes." Writers, in general, are poor and hungry. Few write for fame. Even the great religionist, moralist, and literator, Johnson, could not compose a sermon for a priest from simple charity. He must have the pleasing hope, the animating contemplation of a guinea, before he could write. By all that I can learn, few rich men ever wrote any thing, from the beginning of the world to this day. You, sir, are a *rara avis in terris,* much to your honor.

But I have not yet enumerated all the discouragements which "arrest our efforts and appall our hopes."

I already feel all the ridicule of hinting at my poor four volumes of "Defence and Discourses on Davila," after quoting Mariana, Harrington, Sidney, and Montesquieu. But I must submit to the imputation of vanity, arrogance, presumption, dotage, or insanity, or what you will. How have my feeble "efforts been arrested, and faint hopes appalled"? Look back upon the pamphlets, the newspapers, the handbills, and above all, upon the circular letters of members of congress to their constituents for four-and-twenty years past, and consider in what manner my writings and myself have been treated. Has it not been enough to "arrest efforts and appall hopes"?

Is it not a damper to any ardor in search of truth, to read the absurd criticism, the stupid observations, the jesuitical subtleties, the studied lies that have been printed concerning my writings, in this my dear, native country, for five-and-twenty years? To read the ribaldry of Markoe and Brown, Paine and Callender, four vagabonds from Great Britain? and to see their most profligate effusions applauded and sanctioned by a nation?

In fine, is it not humiliating to see a volume of six or seven hundred pages written by a gentleman of your rank, fortune, learning, genius, and eloquence, in which my system, my sentiments, and my writings, from beginning to end, are totally misunderstood and misrepresented?

After all, I am not dead, like Harrington and Secondat. I have read in a Frenchman, "Je n'ai jamais trop bien compris ce que c'était que de mourir de chagrin." And I can say as confidently as he did, "I have never yet very well understood what it was to die of chagrin." Yet I am daily not out of danger of griefs that might put an end to me in a few hours! Nevertheless, I will wait, if I can, for distempers,—the messenger of NATURE, because I have still much curiosity to see what turn will be taken by public affairs in this country and others. Where can we rationally look for the theory or practice of government, but to nature and experiment, unless you appeal to revelation? If you do, I am ready and willing to follow you to that tribunal. I find nothing there inconsistent with my system.

XVIII.

In your fifth page, you say, "Mr. Adams calls our attention to hundreds of wise and virtuous patricians, mangled and bleeding victims of popular fury, and gravely counts up several victims of democratic rage, as proofs that democracy is more pernicious than monarchy or aristocracy."

Is this fair, sir? Do you deny any one of my facts? I do not say that democracy has been more pernicious on the whole, and in the long run, than monarchy or aristocracy. Democracy has never been and never can be so durable as aristocracy or monarchy; but while it lasts, it is more bloody than either. I beseech you, sir, to recollect the time when my three volumes of

"Defence" were written and printed, in 1786, 1787, and 1788. The history of the universe had not then furnished me with a document I have since seen,—an Alphabetical Dictionary of the Names and Qualities of Persons, "Mangled and Bleeding Victims of Democratic Rage and Popular Fury" in France, during the Despotism of Democracy in that Country, which Napoleon ought to be immortalized for calling IDEOLOGY. This work is in two printed volumes, in octavo, as large as Johnson's Dictionary, and is in the library of our late and excellent Vice-President, Elbridge Gerry, where I hope it will be preserved with anxious care. An edition of it ought to be printed in America; otherwise it will be forever suppressed. France will never dare look at it. The democrats themselves could not bear the sight of it; they prohibited and suppressed it as far as they could. It contains an immense number of as great and good men as France ever produced. We curse the Inquisition and the Jesuits, and yet the Inquisition and the Jesuits are restored. We curse religiously the memory of Mary, for burning good men in Smithfield, when, if England had then been democratical, she would have burned many more, and we murder many more by the guillotine in the latter years of the eighteenth century. We curse Guy Fawkes for thinking of blowing up Westminster Hall; yet Ross blows up the capitol, the palace, and the library at Washington, and would have done it with the same *sang froid* had congress and the president's family been within the walls. O! my soul! I am weary of these dismal contemplations! When will mankind listen to reason, to *nature,* or to revelation?

You say, I "might have exhibited millions of plebeians sacrificed to the pride, folly, and ambition of monarchy and aristocracy." This is very true. And I might have exhibited as many millions of plebeians sacrificed by the pride, folly, and ambition of their fellow-plebeians and their own, in proportion to the extent and duration of their power. Remember, democracy never lasts long. It soon wastes, exhausts, and murders itself. There never was a democracy yet that did not commit suicide. It is in vain to say that democracy is less vain, less proud, less selfish, less ambitious, or less avaricious than aristocracy or *all form of gov't produce same effect*

monarchy. It is not true, in fact, and nowhere appears in history. Those passions are the same in all men, under all forms of simple government, and when unchecked, produce the same effects of fraud, violence, and cruelty. When clear prospects are opened before vanity, pride, avarice, or ambition, for their easy gratification, it is hard for the most considerate philosophers and the most conscientious moralists to resist the temptation. Individuals have conquered themselves. Nations and large bodies of men, never.

When Solon's balance was destroyed by Aristides, and the preponderance given to the multitude, for which he was rewarded with the title of JUST, when he ought to have been punished with the ostracism, the Athenians grew more and more democratic. I need not enumerate to you the foolish wars into which the people forced their wisest men and ablest generals against their own judgments, by which the state was finally ruined, and Philip and Alexander became their masters.

In proportion as the balance, imperfect and unskilful as it was originally, here as in Athens, inclined more and more to the *dominatio plebis,* the Carthaginians became more and more restless, impatient, enterprising, ambitious, avaricious, and rash, till Hannibal swore eternal hostility to the Romans, and the Romans were compelled to pronounce *delenda est Carthago.*

What can I say of the democracy of France? I dare not write what I think and what I know. Were Brissot, Condorcet, Danton, Robespierre, and Monseigneur Egalité less ambitious than Cæsar, Alexander, or Napoleon? Were Dumouriez, Pichegru, Moreau, less generals, less conquerors, or, in the end, less fortunate than the last was? What was the ambition of this democracy? Nothing less than to propagate itself, its principles, its system, through the world; to decapitate all the kings, destroy all the nobles and priests in Europe. And who were the instruments employed by the mountebanks behind the scene, to accomplish these sublime purposes? The firewomen, the badauds, the stage players, the atheists, the deists, the scribblers for any cause at three livres a day, the Jews, and oh! that I could erase from my memory the learned divines,—profound students in the prophecies,—real philosophers and sincere Christians, in amazing numbers, over all Europe and America, who were hurried away by the torrent of contagious enthusiasm. Democracy is chargeable with all the blood that has been spilled for five-and-twenty years.

Napoleon and all his generals were but creatures of democracy, as really as Rienzi, Theodore, Massaniello, Jack Cade, or Wat Tyler. This democratical hurricane, inundation, earthquake, pestilence, call it which you will, at last aroused and alarmed all the world, and produced a combination unexampled, to prevent its further progress.

XIX.

I hope my last convinced you that democracy is as restless, as ambitious, as warlike and bloody, as aristocracy or monarchy.

You proceed to say, that I "ought to have placed right before us the effects of these three principles, namely,—democracy, aristocracy, and monarchy, commixed in the wars, rebellions, persecutions, and oppressions of the English form."

Pray, sir, what was the object of my book? I was not writing a history of England, nor of the world. Inattention to this circumstance has been the cause of all the *honest* misapprehensions, misconstructions, and misrepresentations of the whole work. To see at one glance the design of the three volumes, you need only to look at the first page. M. Turgot "was not satisfied with the constitutions which had been formed for the different states of America. By most of them, the customs of England were imitated, without any particular motive. Instead of collecting all authority into one centre, that of the nation, they have established different bodies,—a body of representatives, a council, and a governor,—because there is in England a house of commons, a house of lords, and a king; they endeavor to balance these different powers."

This solemn opinion of M. Turgot, is the object of the whole of the three volumes. M. Turgot had seen only the constitutions of New York, Massachusetts, and Maryland, and the first constitution of Pennsylvania. His principal intention was to censure the three former. From these three the constitution of the United States was afterwards almost entirely drawn.

The drift of my whole work was, to vindicate these three

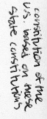

constitutions against the reproaches of that great statesman, philosopher, and really excellent man, whom I well knew, and to defend them against his attacks, and only upon those points on which he had assaulted them. If this fact had been considered, it would have prevented a thousand witticisms and criticisms about the "misnomer," &c.

The points I had to illustrate and to prove, were,—

1. That the people of Massachusetts, New York, and Maryland were not to blame for instituting governors, councils, (or senates) and houses of representatives.

2. That they were not reprehensible for endeavoring to balance those different powers.

3. That they were to be applauded, not reproached, for not "collecting all authority into one centre, that of the nation," in whatever sense those dark, obscure, and incomprehensible words could be understood.

4. Construing these phrases, as it is believed they were intended, to recommend a sovereignty in a single assembly of representatives, that is, a representative of democracy, it was my duty to show that democracy was as unsteady, equally envious, ambitious, avaricious, vain, proud, cruel, and bloody, as aristocracy or monarchy.

5. That an equilibrium of those "different powers" was indispensably necessary to guard and defend the rights, liberties, and happiness of the people against the deleterious, contagious, and pestilential effects of those passions of vanity, pride, ambition, envy, rage, lust, and cruelty, which domineer more or less in every government that has no BALANCE or an imperfect BALANCE.

6. That it was not an affected imitation of the English government, so much as an attachment to their old colonial forms, in every one of which there had been three branches,—a governor, a council, and a house of representatives,—which, added to the eternal reason and unalterable nature of things, induced the legislators of those three states to adopt their new constitutions.

The design of the three volumes, pursued from the first page of the first to the last page of the last, was to illustrate, elucidate, and demonstrate those six important truths. To illustrate and prove these truths, or to show them to be falsehoods, where can we look but into the heart of man and the history of his heart? In the heart were found those appetites, passions, prejudices, and selfish interests, which ought always to be controlled by reason, conscience, and social affections; but which are never perfectly so controlled, even by any individual, still less by nations and large bodies of men, and less and less, as communities grow larger and larger, more populous, more commercial . . .

When, where, have I said that men were always morally the same?

Never, in word or writing. I have said,—

1. There is an inequality of wealth.

2. There is an inequality of birth.

3. There are great inequalities of merit, talents, virtues, services, and reputations.

4. There are a few in whom all these advantages of birth, fortune, and fame, are united.

[I then go on to say, "these sources of inequality, common to every people, founded in the constitution of nature a natural aristocracy, &c. &c."]

Now, sir, let me modestly and civilly request of you a direct and simple answer to the three foregoing questions. Ay or no; yea or nay. You and I have been so drilled to such answers that we can have as little difficulty in promising them as in understanding them; at last, unless we have become greater proficients in pyrrhonism, than we were when we lived together. When I shall be honored with your yea or nay to those three questions, I hope I shall know the real questions between us, and be enabled to confess my error, express my doubts, or state my replication.

[But, sir, let me ask you why you direct your artillery at me alone? at me, a simple individual *"in town obscure, of humble parents born"?*] I had fortified myself behind the intrenchments of Aristotle, Livy, Sidney, Harrington, Dr. Price, Machiavel, Montesquieu, Swift, &c. You should have battered down these strong outworks before you could demolish me.

The word *"crown,"* which you have quoted from me in your eighth page, was used merely to signify *the executive authority.* You, sir, who are a lawyer, know that this figure signifies nothing more nor less. "The prince" is used by J. J. Rousseau, and by other writers on the social compact, for the same thing. Had I been blessed with time to revise a work which is full of errors of the press, I should have noted this as an erratum, especially if I had thought of guarding against malevolent criticism in America. I now request a formal erratum; page 117, at the bottom, dele "crown," and insert "executive authority."

In your eighth page, you begin to consider my natural causes of aristocracy.

1. "Superior abilities." Let us keep to nature and experience. Is there no such thing as genius? Had Raphael no more genius than the common sign-post painters? Had Newton no more genius than even his great master, that learned, profound, and most excellent man, Dr. Barrow? Had Alexander no more genius than Darius? Had Cæsar no more than Catiline, or even than Pompey? Had Napoleon no more than Santerre? Has the Honorable John Randolph no more than Nimrod Hughes and Christopher Macpherson? Has every clerk in a counting-house as great a genius for numbers as Zerah Colburne, who, at six years of age, demonstrated faculties which Sanderson and Newton never possessed in their ripest days? Is there in the world a father of a family who has no perceived diversities in the natural capacities of his children?

These questions deserve direct answers. If you allow that there are natural inequalities of abilities, consider the effects that the genius of Alexander produced! They are visible to this day. And what effect has the genius of Napoleon produced? They will be felt for three thousand years to come. What effect have the genius of Washington and Franklin produced? Had these men no more influence in society than the ordinary average of other men? Genius is sometimes long lived; and it has accumulated fame, wealth, and power, greater than can be commanded by millions of ordinary citizens. These advantages are sometimes applied to good purposes, and sometimes to bad.

XXII.

When superior genius gives greater influence in society than is possessed by inferior genius, or a mediocrity of genius, that is, than by the ordinary level of men, this superior influence I call <u>natural aristocracy.</u> This cause, you say, is "fluctuating." What then? it is aristocracy still, while it exists. And is not democracy "fluctuating" too? Are the waves of the sea, or the winds of the air, or the gossamer that idles in the wanton summer air, more fluctuating than democracy? While I admit the existence of democracy, notwithstanding its instability, you must acknowledge the existence of natural aristocracy, notwithstanding its fluctuations.

I find it difficult to understand you, when you say that "knowledge and ignorance are fluctuating." Knowledge is unchangeable; and ignorance cannot change, because it is nothing. It is a nonentity. Truth is one, uniform and eternal; knowledge of it cannot fluctuate any more than itself. Ignorance of truth, being a nonentity, cannot, surely, become entity and fluctuate and change like Proteus, or wind, or water. You sport away so merrily upon this topic, that I will have the pleasure of transcribing you. You say, "the aristocracy of superior abilities will be regulated by the extent of the space between knowledge and ignorance; as the space contracts or widens, it will be diminished or increased; and if aristocracy may be thus diminished, it follows that it may be thus destroyed."

What is the amount of this argument? Ignorance may be destroyed and knowledge increased *ad infinitum*. And do you expect that all men are to become omniscient, like the almighty and omniscient Hindoo, perfect Brahmins? Are your hopes founded upon an expectation that knowledge will one day be equally divided? Will women have as much knowledge as men? Will children have as much as their parents? If the time will never come when all men will have equal knowledge, it *seems* to follow, that some will know more than others; and that those who know most will have more influence than those who know least, or than those who know half way between the two ex-

(margin notes:) genius = natural aristocracy

knowledge + ignorance

some know more

tremes; and consequently will be aristocrats. "Superior abilities," comprehend abilities acquired by education and study, as
well as genius and natural parts; and what a source of inequality and aristocracy is here! Suffer me to dilate a little in this
place. Massachusetts has probably educated as many sons to
letters, in proportion to her numbers, as any State in the Union,
perhaps as any nation, ancient or modern. What proportion do
the scholars bear to the whole number of people? I wish I had a
catalogue of our Harvard University, that I might state exact
numbers. Say that, in almost two hundred years, there have
been three or four thousand educated, from perhaps two or
three millions of people. Are not these aristocrats? or, in other
words, have they not had more influence than any equal number of uneducated men? In fact, these men governed the
province from its first settlement; these men have governed, and
still govern, the state. These men, in schools, academies, colleges, and universities; these men, in the shape of ministers,
lawyers, and physicians; these men, in academies of arts and sciences, in agricultural societies, in historical societies, in medical
societies and in antiquarian societies, in banking institutions
and in Washington benevolent societies, govern the state, at this
twenty-sixth of December, 1814. The more you educate, without a balance in the government, the more aristocratical will the
people and the government be. There never can be, in any nation, more than one fifth—no, not one tenth of the men, regularly educated to science and letters. I hope, then, you will
acknowledge, that "abilities" form a DISTINCTION and confer
a privilege, in fact, though they give no peculiar rights in society.

2. You appear, sir, to have overlooked or forgotten one great
source of natural aristocracy, mentioned by me in my Apology,
and dilated on in subsequent pages, I mean BIRTH. I should be
obliged to you for your candid sentiments upon this important
subject. Exceptions have been taken to the phrase *well born;*
but I can see no more impropriety in it than in the epithets *well
bred, well educated, well brought up, well taught, well informed,
well read, well to live, well dressed, well fed, well clothed, well
armed, well accoutred, well furnished, well made, well fought,
well aimed, well meant, well mounted, well fortified, well tem-*

pered, well fatted, well spoken, well argued, well reasoned, well decked, well ducked, well trimmed, well wrought, or any other *well* in common parlance.

And here, sir, permit me, by way of digression, to remark another discouragement to honest political literature, and the progress of real political science. If a *well-meant* publication appears, it is instantly searched for an unpopular word, or one that can be made so by misconstruction, misrepresentation, or by any credible and imposing deception. Some ambitious, popular demagogue gives the alarm,—"heresy"? Holy, democratical church has decreed that word to be "heresy"! Down with him! And, if there was no check to their passions, and no balance to their government, they would say, *à la lanterne! à la guillotine! roast him! bake him! boil him! fry him!* The Inquisition in Spain would not celebrate more joyfully an *auto-da-fé.*

Some years ago, more than forty, a writer unfortunately made use of the term *better sort.* Instantly, a popular clamor was raised, and an odium excited, which remains to this day, to such a degree, that no man dares to employ the expression at the bar, in conversation, in a newspaper, or pamphlet, no, nor in the pulpit; though the "baser sort" are sufficiently marked and distinguished in the New Testament, to prove that there is no wrong in believing a "better sort." And if there is any difference between virtue and vice, there is a "better sort" and a worse sort in every human society.

With sincere reverence, let me here quote one of the most profound philosophical, moral, and religious sentiments that ever was expressed:—"*We know not what spirit we are of.*"

XXIII.

I have not yet finished what the poets call an episode, and prose-men a digression. Can you account for a caprice in the public opinion? Burke's *"swinish multitude"* has not been half so unpopular, nor excited half the irritation, odium, resentment, or indignation as that "WELL BORN" and "better sort" have produced. Burke's phrase, nevertheless, must be allowed to be infinitely more unphilosophical, immoral, irreligious, uncivil, impolitic, inhuman, and insolent than either, or both the other. Impudent libeller of your species! Whom do you mean by your "multitude"? The multitude, in your country, means the people of England, Scotland, and Ireland, and all the rest of your dominions. The multitude, in this country, means the people of the United States. The multitude means mankind. Make your exceptions, and then say, after an attention, whether they are not, upon an average, as swinish as the rest. All the delicacy of your classical criticism, all the subtilty of your metaphysical discrimination, cannot devise a justifiable limitation of your words.

But, to return from this digression, till I meet another. Our present subject is BIRTH. It is acknowledged that we are all children of the same benevolent parent; all born under the same moral law of our nature; all equally free; and all entitled to the same equal rights. Thus far, I hope, we are agreed. But, not to repeat the physical inequalities and the intellectual inequalities of capacity, before enumerated, and perhaps more than once, is there not a distinction made in society between children of different parents? and is it not produced by natural causes? If you deny that such distinctions are made in fact and practice, how shall I prove it?

1. The general sense, and still more, the universal consent of mankind, is allowed to be a strong argument to prove the truth of any fact, or any opinion. Is there any practice, custom, or sentiment, in which mankind have more universally agreed, than in making distinctions of nativity, and manifesting more respect for the children of some parents than for those of others? Not only all civilized, cultivated, and polished societies, but all pastoral nations and savage hordes, the negroes of Africa and our Indian tribes, all concur in this usage. If, in all your reading, conversation, or experience, you have found an exception, I pray you to communicate it to me. I know none.

2. Look over our States, (which, I pray, may be sometime or other truly called United). Is no distinction made here? It might be thought invidious to mention names, and indeed it would be endless. But are there not NAMES almost as much revered as those of patriarchs, prophets, or apostles? Have names no influence in governing men? Had the word "Gueux" no influence

in the Dutch Revolution? Had the word *"sans culotte"* none in the French? Have the words "Jacobin," "democrat," no influence? Have the words "federalist" and "republican" no effect? If these transient, momentary, cant words of faction, or at best of party, have such effects, what must be the more permanent influence of names that have been revered for ages, and never heard but like music?

3. In this argument, I have a right to state cases as strong as any that occur in human life. Suppose ten thousand people assembled to see the execution of a man for burglary, robbery, arson, fratricide, patricide, or the meanest, most treacherous, perfidious, and cruel crime that can be committed or imagined. Suppose, the next day, the same ten thousand people should attend the funeral obsequies of Washington, Hamilton, or Ames. Is it possible that these ten thousand people should have the same feelings for the children of the criminal that they have for the hero and the sages?

4. Is there not a presumption in favor of some children? At least a probable presumption, if not a violent presumption? Here, again, I have a right to put strong cases. Here are two families in the same neighborhood; the parents in one are ignorant, intemperate, idle, thievish, lying, and, consequently, destitute; in the other, they are sober, prudent, honest, decent, frugal, industrious, possessed of comfortable property, studious, inquisitive, well informed, and, if you will, literary and scientific. Is there not a violent presumption in favor of the children of the latter family, and against those of the former? Exceptions there are; but exceptions prove the general rule.

5. Is there not a prejudice in favor of some children, and against others? Prejudices, associations, habits, customs, usages, manners, must, in some cases and in some degree, be studied, respected, and indulged by legislators, even the most wise, virtuous, pious, learned, and profound. Here, sir, I will appeal to yourself. A young man appears. You ask of the bystanders who he is? The answer is, "I do not know." "No matter; let him go." Another appears,—"Who is he?" The answer is, "The son of A. B." "I do not know A. B." A third appears,— "Who is this?" "The son of C. D." "C. D.! my friend! He has

been dead these fifty years; but I love his memory, and should be glad to be acquainted with any of his posterity. Please to walk in, sir, and favor me with your company for a few weeks or months; you will be always welcome to my house, and will always oblige me with your company."

6. Theognis, a Greek poet, twenty-four hundred years ago, complains that, although mankind were very anxious to purchase stallions, bulls, and rams of the best breed; yet, in some instances, men would marry wives of mean extraction for the sake of their fortunes, and ladies of high birth would marry men of low descent because they were rich. And I believe there has not been a poet, orator, historian, or philosopher, from his age to this, who has not in his writings expressed or implied some distinction of nativities; nor has there been one of either sex who, in choosing a companion for life, between two rivals of equal youth, beauty, fortune, talents, and accomplishments, would not prefer the one of respectable parentage to the other of meaner and lower original.

XXIV.

I am still upon birth, and my seventh argument is,—

7. It was a custom among the Greeks and Romans,—probably in all civilized nations,—to give names to the castles, palaces, and mansions of their consuls, dictators, and other magistrates, senators, &c. This practice is still followed in England, France, &c. Among the ancients, the distinctions of extraction were most constantly marked by the spots on which they were born. "Illustri loc natus," "claro loco natus," "clarissimo loco natus," "illustrissimo loco natus," were common expressions of conspicuous origin. On the contrary, "obscuro loco nati," "vili loco nati,"[4] designated low original, base extraction, sordid descent, and were expressions, however unjustly, of odium, or at least contempt. I perceive, sir, that you gentlemen of Virginia, who are good classical scholars, have not suffered this observation to escape you. You have taken the modest name of Hazlewood; my friend Richard Lee, the superb name, Chantilly; Mr. Madison, the beautiful name of Montpelier; and Mr. Jef-

ferson, the lofty name of Monticello; and Mr. Washington, the very humble name of a British sea captain, Mount Vernon; the Hon. John Randolph, that of Roanoke. I would advise the present proprietor of Mount Vernon to change the name to Mount Talbot, Truxton, Decatur, Rodgers, Bainbridge, or Hull. And I would advise our Boston gentlemen, who have given this name of the British sea captain to the most beautiful hill on the globe, to change it to Mount Hancock, or Mount Perry, or Mount Macdonough.

8. I wish I could take a walk with you in all the churchyards and burying grounds in Virginia,—Episcopalian, Presbyterian, Methodist, or what you will. Are there not tombs, monuments, gravestones, and inscriptions, ancient and modern? Is there no distinction made among these memorials? Are they all seen with equal eyes, with equal indifference? Is there no peculiar attachment, no particular veneration for any of them? Are they all beheld by the whole people and by every individual with similar sensations and reflections? [How many hundreds of thousands of men, women, and children have lived and died in Virginia, to whom no monument has been erected, whose posterity know not, and cannot conjecture, where their ancestors were deposited? Do all these cemeteries, which are found all over the world, exhibit no distinctions of names and families and persons?] Are not these distinctions natural? produced by natural and inevitable causes?]

the common people not recognized in death

9. I should be highly honored and vastly delighted to visit with you every great planter in Virginia. I should be pleased to look into their parlors, banqueting rooms, bedchambers, and great halls, as Mr. Jefferson and I once did together the most celebrated of the gentlemen's country seats in England. Should we there see no statues, no busts, no pictures, no portraits of their ancestors? no trinkets, no garments, no pieces of furniture carefully preserved, because they belonged to great grandfathers, and estimated at ten times the value of similar articles of superior quality, that might be bought at any shop or store? [What are ancestors, or their little or great elegance or conveniences, to the present planter, more than those of the fifty-acre

ancestors

man, his neighbor, who perhaps never knew the name of his grandfather or father? Are there no natural feelings, and, consequently, no natural distinctions here?

I think I have been impartial, and have suspected no vanity or weakness in Virginians, which I have not recognized in Massachusettensians; and I could enumerate many more. I will go farther. It seems to be generally agreed and settled among men, that John Adams is a weak and vain man. I fall down under the public opinion, the general sense, and frankly and penitently acknowledge, that I have been all my lifetime, and still am, a weak and vain man. One instance of my vanity and weakness I will distinguish. Within two or three years, I have followed to the tomb the nearest, the dearest, the tenderest connections, relations, and friends of my life, from almost ninety years of age to eighteen months. This has made me contemplate much among the tombs,—a gloomy region to which I had been much a stranger. In this churchyard, I found the monumental stones of my father and mother, my grandfather and grandmother, my great grandfather and great grandmother, and my great great grandfather. My great great grandmother died in England. If you will do me the favor, sir, to come to Quincy and spend a few weeks with me, I will take a walk with you, and show you all these monuments and inscriptions, and will confess to you, I would not exchange this line of ancestors for that of Guelphs, or Bowdoins, or Carters, or Winthrops. Such is my vanity, imbecility, and dotage! And I suspect that you are not a whit wiser than I am in this respect. Open your soul, sir, and disclose your natural feelings, and frankly say, whether you would exchange ancestors with any man living. I believe you would not. Is there a human being who would? If these feelings for ancestors are universal, how shall any legislator prevent the rich, the great, the powerful, the learned, the ingenious, from distinguishing by durable, costly, and permanent memorials, their own ancestors, and, consequently, their children and remote posterity, from the descendants of the vast, the immense majority, who lie mingled with the dust, totally forgotten? And how shall he prevent these names and families from being more noted and respected by nations, as well as small communities, than names never before heard?

XXV.

A word or two more upon birth.

10. Birth is naturally and necessarily and inevitably so connected and blended with property, fame, power, education, genius, strength, beauty, learning, science, taste, figure, air, attitudes, movements, &c. &c. &c., that it is often impossible, and always difficult to separate them. Two children are born on the same day, of equal genius,—one, the son of Mr. Jefferson; the other, of Nimrod Hughes. Which will meet with most favor in the world? Would a child of Anthony Benezet, good creature as he was, have an equal chance in life with a son of Robert Morris, when the wealth of nations was believed to be in his power? Would a son of the good Rutherford, the predecessor of General Morgan, have an equal favor in the world with a son of the great General and President Washington? Would a son of Sir Isaac Newton have no more favor in the sight of the whole human race than a son of Mr. Rittenhouse, the worthy President of the Philosophical Society of Philadelphia? Beau Nash meet no more complaisance than one of the Hercules du Roi, whom I have seen leap at Sadlers, Wells, and turn his heels over his head, at a height of ten or twelve feet, and come down on the other side of the stage erect? I leave, sir, to your fertile genius, ample reading, and long experience, to pursue the inquiries. I could continue to enumerate examples through sheets of paper.

11. Have you not observed in life, and have you not remarked in history, that the common people,—and by *common people,* I here mean all mankind, despots, emperors, kings, princes, nobles, presidents, senators, representatives, lawyers, divines, physicians, merchants, farmers, shopkeepers, mechanics, tradesmen, day laborers, tavern haunters, dram-shop frequenters, mob, rabble, and canaille, that is to say, all human kind,—have you not observed that all these feel more respect, more real respect for birth than even for wealth; may I not say than for genius, fame, talents, or power? Though they follow and hosanna for the loaves and fishes, you will often hear them say, "proud as he is, I knew his father, who was only a black-

smith; his grandfather, who was only a carpenter; or his great grandfather, who was only a shoemaker; he need not be so topping."

12. Has not the experience of six thousand years shown that the common people submit more easily and quietly to birth than to wealth, genius, fame, or any other talents? Whence the prejudices against upstarts, parvenus, &c.? Whence the general respect, reverence, and submission in all ages and nations, of plebeians to patricians, of sieurs to monsieurs, of juffrouws to mevrouws? If a man of high birth is promoted, little or nothing is said by the plebeians. If one of their own level, the son of a tradesman or common farmer is advanced, all the envy and bile of his equals is excited. He is abused and belittled, if not reviled, by all his former equals, as they thought themselves, whatever may have been the superiority of his genius, education, services, experiences, or other talents. There is nothing, Mr. Taylor, to which the vulgar, in general, so quietly and patiently and cordially submit as to birth.

13. What in all ages has been the source of the submission of nobility to royalty? Every nobleman envies his sovereign, and would pull him down, if he could get into his throne and wear his crown. But when nobles and ignobles have torn one another to pieces for years or ages in their eternal squabbles of jealousy, envy, rivalry, hatred, and revenge, and all are convinced that this anarchy will not do, that the world will be depopulated, that a head must be set up, and all the members must be guided by it, then, and not till then, will nobles submit to Kings as of superior birth. What subjects all the nobility of Europe to all the kings of Europe, but birth? though some of them cannot well make out their pretensions; particularly the proudest of them all,—the house of Austria.

14. What has excited a universal insurrection of all Europe against Bonaparte, (if we dive to the bottom of this awful gulf, and recollect the succession of coalitions against him and against republican France,) but because he was *obscuro loco natus*, the son of a simple gentillâtre of Corsica?

15. Such, and so universal are the manifest distinctions of birth in every village and every city, so tremendous are their ef-

fects on nations and governments, that one might almost pronounce them self-evident. I may justly be ridiculed for laboring to demonstrate *in re non dubiâ, testibus non necessariis*. Can you discern no good in this eternal ordinance of nature, the varieties of birth? If you cannot, as the facts are indisputable, you must assert that, so far as you can see, the world is ill made, and that the whole of mankind are miscreants. For there are no two of them born alike in any thing but divine right and moral liberty.

17. [*sic*—ED.]Please to remember that birth confers no right on one more than another! But birth naturally and unavoidably produces more influence in society, in some more than in others; and the superiority of influence in society, in some more than in others; and the superiority of influence is aristocracy.

18. When birth, genius, beauty, strength, wealth, education, fame, services, heroism, experience, unite in an individual, they produce inequality of influence, that is, aristocracy with a witness, so that one can chase a thousand, and two put ten thousand to flight in any political conflict; and without any hereditary descent, or any artificial marks, titles, or decorations, whatever.

XXVI.

In page 10, you say, "Mr. Adams has omitted a cause of aristocracy in the quotation, which he forgets not to urge in other places, namely,—exclusive wealth." This is your omission, sir, not mine. In page 109, vol. i. I expressly enumerated, "inequality of wealth" as one of the causes of aristocracy, and as having a natural and inevitable influence in society. I said nothing about "exclusive" wealth. The word "exclusive," is an interpolation of your own. This you acknowledge to be, "by much the most formidable with which mankind have to contend;" that is, as I understand you, superior wealth is the most formidable cause of aristocracy, or of superior influence in society. There may be some difficulty in determining the question, whether distinctions of birth, or distinctions of property, have the greatest influence in the world? Both have very great influence, much too great, when not restrained by something be-

[margin annotations: wealth has influence; which is more important birth or wealth]

sides the passions or the consciences of the possessors. Were I
required to give an answer to the question, my answer would
be, with some diffidence, that, in my opinion, taking into consideration history and experience, birth has had, and still has,
most power and the greatest effects; because conspicuous birth
is hereditary; it is derived from ancestors, descends to posterity,
and is inalienable. Titles and ribbons, and stars and garters,
and crosses and legal establishments, are by no means essential
or necessary to the preservation of it. The evidences of it are in
history and records, and in the memories and hearts they remain, and it never fails to descend to posterity as long as that
posterity furnishes any one or more whose talents and virtues
can support the reputation of the name. Birth and wealth are
commonly so entangled together, from an emperor down to a
constable or tithing-man, that it is difficult to separate them
so distinctly as to place one in one scale, and the other in an
opposite scale, to ascertain in grains and scruples the preponderance. The complaint of Theognis, that pelf is sometimes
preferred to blood, was, and is true; and it is also true that
beauty, wit, art, disposition, and "winning ways," are more
successful than descent; yet, in general, I believe this prevails
oftener than any of the others. I may be mistaken in this opinion; but of this I am certain; that it always has the same weight,
when it is at all considered. You must recur, Mr. Taylor, to
Plato's republic and the French republic, destroy all marriages,
introduce a perfect community of women, render it impossible
to know, or suspect, or conjecture one's own father or mother,
son or daughter, brother or sister, uncle or aunt, before you can
annihilate all distinctions of birth. I conclude, therefore, that
birth has naturally and necessarily and unavoidably some influence, more or less, in human society. Will you say it has
none? I have a right, sir, to an answer to this question, yea or
nay. You have summoned me before the world and posterity, in
my last hours, by your voluminous criticisms and ratiocina-
tions, which gives me a right to demand fair play. On my part,
I promise to answer any question you can state, by an affirma-
tive, negative, or doubt, without equivocation. Property, wealth,

riches, although you allow them to be a cause of aristocracy in your tenth page, yet you will not permit this cause to be "ascribed to nature." But why not? If, as I have heard, "the shortest road to men's hearts is down their throats," this is surely a natural route. Hunger and thirst are natural wants, and the supplies of them are natural. Nature has settled the point, that wood and stones shall not invigorate and enliven them like wine. Suppose one of your southern gentlemen to have only one hundred thousand acres of land. He settles one thousand tenants with families upon it. If he is a humane, easy, generous landlord, will not his tenants feel an attachment to him? will he not have influence among them? will they not naturally think and vote as he votes? If, on the contrary, he is an austere, griping, racking, rack-renting tyrant, will not his tenants be afraid to offend him? will not some, if not all of them, pretend to think with him, and vote as he would have them, upon the same principle as some nations have worshipped the devil, because they knew not into whose hands they might fall? Now, sir, my argument is this. If either the generous landlord or the selfish landlord can obtain by gratitude or fear only one vote more than his own from his tenants in general, he is an aristocrat, whether his vote and those of his dependents be beneficial or maleficial, salutary or pestilential, or fatal to the community.

I remember the time, Mr. Taylor, when one thousand families depended on Mr. Hancock for their daily bread; perhaps more. All men allowed him to be punctual, humane, generous. How many of the heads of these families would naturally be inclined to vote with and for Mr. Hancock? Could not Mr. Hancock command, or at least influence one vote, besides his own? If he could, he was an aristocrat, according to my definition and conscientious opinion. Let me appeal now to your own experience. Are there not in your own Caroline County, in Virginia, two or three, or four, five or six, eight or ten great planters, who, if united, can carry any point in your elections? These are every one of them aristocrats, and you, who are the first of them, are the most eminent aristocrat of them all.

XXVII.

Give me leave to add a few words on this topic. I remember the time when three gentlemen,—Thomas Hancock, Charles Apthorp, and Thomas Green, the three most opulent merchants in Boston, all honorable, virtuous, and humane men,—if united, could have carried any election almost unanimously in the town of Boston.

Harrington, whom I read forty or fifty years ago, and shall quote from memory, being too old to hunt for books and fumble over the leaves of folios, has been called the Newton in politics, and is supposed to have made a great discovery, namely,—that mankind are governed by the teeth, and that dominion is founded on property in land. Mr. Locke and the French economists countenance this opinion. Landed gentlemen are generally not only aristocrats, but tories. What but commerce, manufactures, navigation, and naval power, supported by a moneyed interest, restrains them from establishing aristocracies or oligarchies, as absolute, arbitrary, oppressive, and cruel, as any monarchy ever was? What has annihilated the astonishing commerce and naval power of Holland, but the influence of the landed gentlemen in the inland provinces, overbearing and outvoting the maritime provinces? What is it that prevents France from reducing and restraining, if not annihilating, the commerce, manufactures, and naval power of Great Britain, but the landed gentry,—the proprietors of lands in France? Who never would suffer commerce, manufactures, or naval power to grow in that kingdom? Who would never permit Colbert or Necker to hold power, or even enjoy popularity, but with the moneyed interest? Yet these gentlemen could never be satisfied with the number of soldiers and land armies. No expense, no exertion to increase the number of officers and soldiers in the army could be too much. What has prevented our beloved country, to the astonishment of all Europe, from having at this hour a naval force amply sufficient to burn, sink, or destroy, or bring captive into our harbors, all the men of war that Britain has sent, or can send to our coasts, but the landed gentlemen, the great and little planters, the yeomen and farmers of the United States? Such it was in the beginning, is now, and, I fear, ever will be, world without end.

All these considerations prove the mighty influence of property in human affairs; they prove the influence of birth too; for landed property is hereditary generally all over the world. Truth, Mr. Taylor, cannot be ridiculed into error. Aristophanes could laugh Socrates out of his life, but not out of his merit or his fame. You seem to admit that "aristocracy is created by wealth," but you seem to think it is "artificially," not "naturally," so created. But if superior genius, birth, strength, and activity, naturally obtain superior wealth, and if superior wealth has naturally influence in society, where is the impropriety in calling the influence of wealth "natural?" I am not, however, bigoted to the epithet *natural;* and you may substitute the epithet "actual" in the place of it, if you think it worth while.

"Alienation," you say, "is the remedy for an aristocracy founded on landed wealth." But alienation only transfers the aristocracy from one hand to another. The aristocracy remains the same. If Brutus transfers to Cassius a villa or a principality purchased by the unrighteous profits of usury, Cassius becomes as influential an aristocrat as Brutus was before. If John Randolph should manumit one of his negroes and alienate to him his plantation, that negro would become as great an aristocrat as John Randolph. And the negro, John Randolph, Brutus, and Cassius, were, and are, and would be aristocrats of a scarlet color and a crimson dye, if they could. Alienation, therefore, is no remedy against an aristocracy founded on landed wealth.

You say, sir, that "inhibitions upon monopoly and incorporation are remedies for aristocracy founded on paper wealth." Here, sir, once for all, let me say, that you can write nothing too severe for me against "paper wealth." You may say, if you please, as Swift says of party, that it is the madness of the many for the profit of the few. You may call a swindler, a pickpocket, a pirate, a thief, or a robber, and I will not contradict you, nor dispute with you. But, sir, how will you obtain your "inhibitions upon monopoly and incorporation," when the few are craving and the many mad for the same thing? When democrats and aristocrats all unite, with perhaps only two or three exceptions, in urging these monopolies and incorporations to the last extremity, and when every man who opposes them is sure to be ruined? Paper wealth has been a source of aristocracy in this country, as well as landed wealth, with a vengeance. Witness the immense fortunes made *per saltum* by aristocratical speculations, both in land and paper. In human affairs, sir, we must consider what is practicable, as well as what is theoretical.

But, sir, land and paper are not the only sources of aristocracy. There are master shipwrights, housewrights, masons, &c. &c., who have each of them from twenty to a hundred families in their employment, and can carry a posse to the polls when they will. These are not only aristocrats, but a species of feudal barons. What are demagogues and popular orators, but aristocrats? John Cade and Wat Tyler were aristocrats. Callender and Paine were aristocrats. Shays and Fries were aristocrats. Mobs never follow any but aristocrats.

XXVIII.

Knowledge, you say, invented alienation, and became the natural enemy of aristocracy. This "invention" of knowledge was not very profound or ingenious. There are hundreds in the patent office more brilliant. The right, power, and authority of alienation are essential to property. If I own a snuffbox, I can burn it in the fire, cast it in a salt pond, crush it in atoms under a wagon wheel, or make a present of it to you,—which last alienation I should prefer to all the others,—or I could sell it to a peddler, or give it to a beggar. But, in either case, of gift or sale, would the aristocratical power of the snuffbox be lessened by alienation? Should a palatinate of Poland, or a prince of Russia, alienate his palatinate or his principality, with all the serfs attached to them, would not the buyer derive all the aristocratical influence from the purchase which the latter alienated by the sale? Should a planter in Virginia sell his *clarissimum et illustrissimum et celeberrimum locum* with his thousand negroes, to a merchant, would not the merchant gain the aristocratical influence which the planter lost by his transfer? Run down, sir, through all the ranks of society, or, if you are shocked at the word *rank*, say all the classes, degrees, the

ladder, the theatrical benches of society, from the first planter
and the first merchant to the hog driver, the whiskey dram-
seller, or the Scottish peddler, and consider, whether the alienation of lands, wharves, stores, houses, funded stock, bank
stock, bridge stock, canal stock, turnpike stock, or even lottery
tickets, does not transfer the aristocracy as well as the property.
When the thirsty soul of a hundred acre man carries him to the
whiskey shop till he has mortgaged all his acres, has he not
transferred his aristocracy with them? I hope these hints, sir,
have convinced you that alienation is not an adequate remedy
against the aristocracy of property. . . .

XXXI.

That the first want of man is his dinner, and the second his
girl, were truths well known to every democrat and aristocrat,
long before the great philosopher Malthus arose, to think he
enlightened the world by the discovery.

It has been equally well known that the second want is frequently so impetuous as to make men and women forget the
first, and rush into rash marriages, leaving both the first and
second wants, their own as well as those of their children and
grandchildren, to the chapter of accidents. The most religious
very often leave the consideration of these wants to him who
supplies the young ravens when they cry.

The natural, necessary, and unavoidable consequence of all
this is, that the multiplication of the population so far transcends
the multiplication of the means of subsistence, that the constant
labor of nine tenths of our species will forever be necessary to
prevent all of them from starving with hunger, cold, and pestilence. Make all men Newtons, or, if you will, Jeffersons, or Taylors, or Randolphs, and they would all perish in a heap!

Knowledge, therefore, sir, can never be equally divided
among mankind, any more than property, real or personal, any
more than wives or women.

> In pride, in reasoning pride, our error lies,
> All quit their sphere, and rush into the skies;
> Pride still is aiming at the blest abodes,

> Men would be angels, angels would be gods,
> Aspiring to be gods, if angels fell,
> Aspiring to be angels, men rebel.

The modern improvers of society,—ameliorators of the condition of mankind, instructors of the human species,—have assumed too much. They have not only condemned all the philosophy and policy of all ages of men, but they have undertaken to build a new universe, to ameliorate the system of eternal wisdom and benevolence. I wish, sir, that you would agree with me and my, and, I hope, your friends, Pope and Horace.

> This vault of air, this congregated ball,
> Self-centred sun, and starts that rise and fall,
> There are, my friend, whose philosophic eyes
> Look through, and trust the Ruler with his skies.

> Hune solem, et stellas, et decedentia certis
> Tempora momentis, sunt qui formidine nullâ
> Imbuti spectent.[5]

Turn our thoughts, in the next place, to the characters of learned men. The priesthood have, in all ancient nations, nearly monopolized learning. Read over again all the accounts we have of Hindoos, Chaldeans, Persians, Greeks, Romans, Celts, Teutons, we shall find that priests had all the knowledge, and really governed all mankind. Examine Mahometanism, trace Christianity from its first promulgation; knowledge has been almost exclusively confined to the clergy. And, even since the Reformation, when or where has existed a Protestant or dissenting sect who would tolerate A FREE INQUIRY? The blackest billingsgate, the most ungentlemanly insolence, the most yahooish brutality is patiently endured, countenanced, propagated, and applauded. But touch a solemn truth in collision with a dogma of a sect, though capable of the clearest proof, and you will soon find you have disturbed a nest, and the hornets will swarm about your legs and hands, and fly into your face and eyes.

When we are weary of looking at religion, we will, if you please, turn our eyes to government. Is there toleration in politics? Where shall we find it, if not in Virginia? The Honorable John Randolph informs us that, in consequence of the independence of his soul, he is on bad terms with the world; that his nerves are of too weak a fibre to bear the questions ordinary and extraordinary from our political inquisitors; talks of the rancorous hatred of the numerous enemies he has made in his course; and says, that the avenue to the public ear is shut against him in Virginia, where the press is under a virtual *imprimatur,* and where it would be easier to force into circulation the treasurer's notes, than opinions militating against the administration, through the press. If these things are so in Virginia, sir, where Callender was applauded, nourished, cherished, and paid; where the great historian, Wood, who wrote and printed the elegant and classical History of the Administration of John Adams, was kindly received and employed; and where the sedition act, the gag law, was so unpopular; where can we look with any prospect or hope of finding a candid freedom of the press? The truth is, party opinions, interests, passions, and prejudices may be as decisive an *imprimatur* as that of a monarch; and the public opinion, which is not always right, until it is too late, is sometimes as arbitrary a prohibition as an *index expurgatorius.* I hope it will be no offence to say, that public opinion is often formed upon imperfect, partial, and false information from the press. Public information cannot keep pace with facts. Knowledge cannot always accompany events. How many days intervene between a victory or a defeat, and the universal knowledge of it? How long do *we* wait for the result of a negotiation? How many erroneous public opinions are formed in the intervals? How long is a law enacted before the proclamation of it can reach the extremities of the nation?

XXXII.

A few words more concerning the characters of literary men. What sort of men have had the conduct of the presses in the United States for the last thirty years? In Germany, in England, in France, in Holland, the presses, even the newspapers, have been under the direction of learned men. How has it been in America? How many presses, how many newspapers have been directed by vagabonds, fugitives from a bailiff, a pillory, or a halter in Europe?

You know it is one of the sublimest and profoundest discoveries of the eighteenth century, that knowledge is corruption; that arts, sciences, and taste have deformed the beauty and destroyed the felicity of human nature, which appears only in perfection in the savage state,—the children of nature. One writer gravely tells us that the first man who fenced a tobacco yard, and said, "this is mine," ought instantly to have been put to death; another as solemnly says, the first man who pronounced the word "dieu," ought to have been despatched on the spot; yet these are advocates of toleration and enemies of the Inquisition.*

I never had enough of the ethereal spirit to rise to these heights. My humble opinion is, that knowledge, upon the whole, promotes virtue and happiness. I therefore hope that you and all other gentlemen of property, education, and reputation will exert your utmost influence in establishing schools, colleges, academies, and universities, and employ every means and opportunity to spread information, even to the lowest dregs of the people, if any such there are, even among your own domestics and John Randolph's serfs. I fear not the propagation and dissemination of knowledge. The conditions of humanity will be improved and ameliorated by its expansion and diffusion in every direction. May every human being,—man, woman, and child,—be as well informed as possible! But, after all, did you ever see a rose without a briar, a convenience without an inconvenience, a good without an evil, in this mingled world? Knowledge is applied to bad purposes as well as to good ones. Knaves and hypocrites can acquire it, as well as honest, candid, and sincere men. It is employed as an engine and a vehicle to propagate error and falsehood, treason and vice, as well as truth, honor, virtue, and patriotism. It composes and pronounces, both panegyrics and philippics, with exquisite

* *Vide* Rousseau and Diderot *passim.*

art, to confound all distinctions in society between right and wrong. And if I admit, as I do, that truth generally prevails, and virtue is, or will be triumphant in the end, you must allow that honesty has a hard struggle, and must prevail by many a well-fought and fortunate battle, and, after all, must often look to another world for justice, if not for pardon.

There is no necessary connection between knowledge and virtue. Simple intelligence has no association with morality. What connection is there between the mechanism of a clock or watch and the feeling of moral good and evil, right or wrong? A faculty or a quality of distinguishing between moral good and evil, as well as physical happiness and misery, that is, pleasure and pain, or, in other words, a CONSCIENCE,—an old word almost out of fashion,—is essential to morality.

Now, how far does simple, theoretical knowledge quicken or sharpen conscience? La Harpe, in some part of his great work, his Course of Literature, has given us an account of a tribe of learned men and elegant writers, who kept a kind of office in Paris for selling at all prices, down to three livres, essays or paragraphs upon any subject, good or evil, for or against any party, any cause, or any person. One of the most conspicuous and popular booksellers in England, both with the courtiers and the citizens, who employed many printers and supported many writers, has said to me, "the men of learning in this country are stark mad. There are in this city a hundred men, gentlemen of liberal education, men of science, classical scholars, fine writers, whom I can hire at any time at a guinea a day, to write for me for or against any man, any party, or any cause." Can we wonder, then, at any thing we read in British journals, magazines, newspapers, or reviews?

Where are, and where have been, the greatest masses of science, of literature, or of taste? Shall we look for them in the church or the state, in the universities or the academies? among Greek or Roman philosophers, Hindoos, Brahmins, Chinese mandarins, Chaldean magi, British druids, Indian prophets, or Christian monks? Has it not been the invariable maxim of them all to deceive the people by any lies, however gross? "Bonus populus vult decipi; ergo decipiatur."

And after all that can be done to disseminate knowledge, you never can equalize it. The number of laborers must, and will forever be so much more multitudinous than that of the students, that there will always be giants as well as pygmies, the former of which will have more influence than the latter; man for man, and head for head; and, therefore, the former will be aristocrats, and the latter democrats, if not Jacobins or *sans culottes.*

These morsels, and a million others analogous to them, which will easily occur to you, if you will be pleased to give them a careful mastication and rumination, must, I think, convince you, that no practicable or possible advancement of learning can ever equalize knowledge among men to such a degree, that some will not have more influence in society than others; and, consequently, that some will always be aristocrats, and others democrats. You may read the history of all the universities, academies, monasteries of the world, and see whether learning extinguishes human passions or corrects human vices. You will find in them as many parties and factions, as much jealousy and envy, hatred and malice, revenge and intrigue, as you will in any legislative assembly or executive council, the most ignorant city or village. Are not the men of letters,— philosophers, divines, physicians, lawyers, orators, and poets— all over the world, at perpetual strife with one another? Knowledge, therefore, as well as genius, strength, activity, industry, beauty, and twenty other things, will forever be a natural cause of aristocracy.

CORRESPONDENCE OF JOHN AND ABIGAIL ADAMS WITH THOMAS JEFFERSON[1]

The correspondence between John Adams and Thomas Jefferson began in 1777, two years into the Revolutionary War with England. The war itself and the momentous Declaration of Independence saw Adams and Jefferson as fellow patriots fighting for a common cause. In the years following the successful outcome of the Revolution, however, the two men had a falling-out because of their differing responses to internal upheavals and class tensions in America, the proposal for the new federal constitution, and the outbreak of revolution in France in 1789. Jefferson suspected Adams of being too enamored of England and even possibly of being a secret monarchist. When Adams was vice president under Washington and likely successor as president of the United States, Jefferson grew even more anxious and hired journalist scandalmongers to spread rumors that Adams would groom his son as his successor and leave America with an inherited monarchy under the hegemony of England. As the letters below indicate, Abigail Adams asked Jefferson to explain his conduct, and President Jefferson, Adams's successor, took time from the duties of office to respond to her. In their later years of retirement, Adams and Jefferson grew close to each other and carried on one of the great exchanges of letters in American history.

ABIGAIL ADAMS TO JEFFERSON

London Janry. 29th. 1787

MY DEAR SIR

I received by Col. Franks your obliging favour and am very sorry to find your wrist still continues lame; I have known very salutary effects produced by the use of British oil upon a spraind joint. I have sent a servant to see if I can procure some. You may rest assured that if it does no good: it will not do any injury.

With regard to the Tumults in my Native state* which you inquire about, I wish I could say that report had exagerated them. It is too true Sir that they have been carried to so allarming a Height as to stop the Courts of justice in several Counties. Ignorant, wrestless desperadoes, without conscience or principals, have led a deluded multitude to follow their standard, under pretence of grievences which have no existance but in their immaginations. Some of them were crying out for a paper currency, some for an equal distribution of property, some were for annihilating all debts, others complaining that the Senate was a useless Branch of Government, that the Court of common pleas was unnecessary, and that the sitting of the General Court in Boston was a grievence. By this list you will see the materials which compose this rebellion, and the necessity there is of the wisest and most vigorus measures to quell and suppress it. Instead of that laudible spirit which you approve, which makes a people watchfull over their Liberties and alert in the defence of them, these mobish insurgents are for sapping the foundation, and distroying the whole fabrick at once.—But as these people make only a small part of the state, when compared to the more sensible and judicious, and altho they create a just allarm and give much trouble and uneasiness, I cannot help flattering myself that they will prove sallutary to the state at large, by leading to an investigation of the causes which have produced these commotions. Luxery and extravagance both in

*Shays's Rebellion.

furniture and dress had pervaded all orders of our Countrymen and women, and was hastning fast to sap their independance by involving every class of citizens in distress, and accumulating debts upon them which they were unable to discharge. Vanity was becoming a more powerfull principal than patriotism. The lower order of the community were prest for taxes, and tho possest of landed property they were unable to answer the demand, whilst those who possest money were fearfull of lending, least the mad cry of the mob should force the Legislature upon a measure very different from the touch of Midas.*

By the papers I send you, you will see the beneficial effects already produced. An act of the Legislature laying duties of 15 per cent upon many articles of British manufacture and totally prohibiting others—a number of Vollunteers Lawyers physicians and Merchants from Boston made up a party of Light horse commanded by Col. Hitchbourn, Leit. Col. Jackson and Higgenson, and went out in persuit of the insurgents and were fortunate enough to take 3 of their principal Leaders, Shattucks Parker and Page. Shattucks defended himself and was wounded in his knee with a broadsword. He is in Jail in Boston and will no doubt be made an example of.

Your request my dear sir with respect to your Daughter shall be punctually attended to, and you may be assured of every attention in my power towards her.

You will be so kind as to present my Love to Miss Jefferson, compliments to the Marquiss and his Lady. I am really conscience smitten that I have never written to that amiable Lady, whose politeness and attention to me deserved my acknowledgment.

The little balance which you stated in a former Letter in my favour, when an opportunity offers I should like to have in Black Lace at about 8 or 9 Livres pr. Ell. Tho late in the Month, I hope it will not be thought out of season to offer my best

---

*In AA's draft of this letter the following paragraph appears at this point: "The disturbances which have taken place have roused from their Lethargy the Supine and the Indolent animated the Brave and taught wisdom to our Rulers." Boyd, XI, 87, n. 7.

wishes for the Health, Long Life and prosperity of yourself and family, or to assure you of the Sincere Esteem and Friendship with which I am Your's etc. etc.,   A. ADAMS

JEFFERSON TO ABIGAIL ADAMS

Paris Feb. 22. 1787.

DEAR MADAM

I am to acknolege the honor of your letter of Jan. 29. and of the papers you were so good as to send me. They were the latest I had seen or have yet seen. They left off too in a critical moment;* just at the point where the Malcontents make their submission on condition of pardon, and before the answer of government was known. I hope they pardoned them. The spirit of resistance to government is so valuable on certain occasions, that I wish it to be always kept alive. It will often be exercised when wrong, but better so than not to be exercised at all. I like a little rebellion now and then. It is like a storm in the Atmosphere. It is wonderful that no letter or paper tells us who is president of Congress, tho' there are letters in Paris to the beginning of January. I suppose I shall hear when I come back from my journey, which will be eight months after he will have been chosen. And yet they complain of us for not giving them intelligence. Our Notables assembled to-day, and I hope before the departure of Mr. Cairnes I shall have heard something of their proceedings worth communicating to Mr. Adams. The more remarkeable effect of this convention as yet is the number of puns and bon mots it has generated. I think were they all collected it would make a more voluminous work than the Encyclopedie. This occasion, more than any thing I have seen, convinces me that this nation is incapable of any serious effort but under the word of command. The people at large view every object only as it may furnish puns and bon mots; and I pronounce that a good punster would disarm the whole nation

*In Shays's Rebellion.

were they ever so seriously disposed to revolt. Indeed, Madam, they are gone. When a measure so capable of doing good as the calling the Notables is treated with so much ridicule, we may conclude the nation desperate, and in charity pray that heaven may send them good kings.—The bridge at the place Louis XV. is begun. The hotel dieu is to be abandoned and new ones to be built. The old houses on the old bridges are in a course of demolition. This is all I know of Paris. We are about to lose the Count d'Aranda, who has desired and obtained his recall. Fernand Nunnez, before destined for London is to come here. The Abbés Arnoux and Chalut are well. The Dutchess Danville somewhat recovered from the loss of her daughter. Mrs. Barrett very homesick, and fancying herself otherwise sick. They will probably remove to Honfleur. This is all our news. I have only to add then that Mr. Cairnes has taken charge of 15. aunes of black lace for you at 9 livres the aune, purchased by Petit and therefore I hope better purchased than some things have been for you; and that I am with sincere esteem Dear Madam your affectionate humble servt.,   TH: JEFFERSON

ADAMS TO JEFFERSON

Grosvenor Square Oct. 9. 1787

DEAR SIR

I sent you a Copy of my second volume by Mr. Barthelemy the French Chargé here now Minister, with a Letter about Money matters. In your favour of Sept. 28. you dont mention the receipt of them.—I have indeed long thought with Anxiety of our Money in the hands of our Friends, whom you mention, and have taken the best Precaution in my Power, against Accidents. I do not consider the Game as up. But a disgrace has happened, which is not easy to get rid of.—Disgrace is not easily washed out, even with blood. Lessons my dear Sir, are never wanting. Life and History are full. The Loss of Paradise, by eating a forbidden apple, has been many Thousand years a Lesson to Mankind; but not much regarded. Moral Reflections, wise

Maxims, religious Terrors, have little Effect upon Nations when they contradict a present Passion, Prejudice, Imagination, Enthusiasm or Caprice. Resolutions never to have an hereditary officer will be kept in America, as religiously as that of the Cincinnati was in the Case of General Greens son.* Resolutions never to let a Citizen ally himself with things will be kept untill an Opportunity presents to violate it. If the Duke of Angoleme, or Burgundy, or especially the Dauphin should demand one of your beautiful and most amiable Daughters in Marriage, all America from Georgia to New Hampshire would find their Vanity and Pride, so agreably flattered by it, that all their Sage Maxims would give way; and even our Sober New England Republicans would keep a day of Thanksgiving for it, in their hearts. If General Washington had a Daughter, I firmly believe, she would be demanded in Marriage by one of the Royal Families of France or England, perhaps by both, or if he had a Son he would be invited to come a courting to Europe.— The Resolution not to call in foreign Nations to settle domestic differences will be kept untill a domestic difference of a serious nature shall break out.—I have long been settled in my own opinion, that neither Philosophy, nor Religion, nor Morality, nor Wisdom, nor Interest, will ever govern nations or Parties, against their Vanity, their Pride, their Resentment or Revenge, or their Avarice or Ambition. Nothing but Force and Power and Strength can restrain them. If Robert Morris should maintain his Fortune to the End, I am convinced that some foreign Families of very high rank will think of Alliances with his Children. If the Pen Family should go to America, and engage in public affairs and obtain the Confidence of the People, you will see Connections courted there. A Troop of Light Horse from Philadelphia meeting Dick Pen in New Jersey, will strike the Imaginations of Princes and Princesses. How few Princes in Eu-

---

*Immediately after General Nathanael Greene's funeral at Savannah, June 20, 1786, members of the Georgia Society of the Cincinnati convened and resolved, out of respect to the late general, that his eldest son, George Washington Greene, be admitted to the Society, to take his seat on reaching the age of eighteen. G. W. Greene, *Life of Nathanael Greene* (N.Y., 1871), III, 535–36.

rope could obtain a Troop of Light Horse to make them a Compliment of Parade. In short, my dear Friend you and I have been indefatigable Labourers through our whole Lives for a Cause which will be thrown away in the next generation, upon the Vanity and Foppery of Persons of whom we do not now know the Names perhaps.—The War that is now breaking out will render our Country, whether she is forced into it, or not, rich, great and powerful in comparison of what she now is, and Riches Grandeur and Power will have the same effect upon American as it has upon European minds. We have seen enough already to be sure of this. A Covent Garden Rake will never be wise enough to take warning from the Claps caught by his Companions. When he comes to be poxed himself he may possibly repent and reform. Yet three out of four of them become even by their own sufferings, more shameless instead of being penitent.

Pardon this freedom. It is not Melancholly: but Experience and believe me without reserve your Friend, O tempora—*oh mores* JOHN ADAMS.

ADAMS TO JEFFERSON

London Decr. 6. 1787

DEAR SIR

The Project of a new Constitution, has Objections against it, to which I find it difficult to reconcile my self, but I am so unfortunate as to differ somewhat from you in the Articles, according to your last kind Letter.

You are afraid of the one—I, of the few. We agree perfectly that the many should have a full fair and perfect Representation.—You are Apprehensive of Monarchy; I, of Aristocracy. I would therefore have given more Power to the President and less to the Senate. The Nomination and Appointment to all offices I would have given to the President, assisted only by a Privy Council of his own Creation, but not a Vote or Voice would I have given to the Senate or any Senator, unless he were of the Privy Council. Faction and Distraction are the sure and certain Consequence of giving to a Senate a vote in the distribution of offices.

You are apprehensive the President when once chosen, will be chosen again and again as long as he lives. So much the better as it appears to me.—You are apprehensive of foreign Interference, Intrigue, Influence. So am I.—But, as often as Elections happen, the danger of foreign Influence recurs. The less frequently they happen the less danger.—And if the Same Man may be chosen again, it is probable he will be, and the danger of foreign Influence will be less. Foreigners, seeing little Prospect will have less Courage for Enterprize.

Elections, my dear sir, Elections to offices which are great objects of Ambition, I look at with terror. Experiments of this kind have been so often tryed, and so universally found productive of Horrors, that there is great Reason to dread them.

Mr. Littlepage who will have the Honour to deliver this will tell you all the News. I am, my dear Sir, with great Regard,

JOHN ADAMS

ADAMS TO JEFFERSON

Braintree July 29. 1791.

DEAR SIR

Yesterday, at Boston, I received your friendly Letter of July 17th. with great pleasure. I give full credit to your relation of the manner in which your note was written and prefixed to the Philadelphia edition of Mr. Paines pamphlet on the rights of Man: but the misconduct of the person, who committed this breach of your confidence, by making it publick, whatever were his intentions, has sown the Seeds of more evils, than he can ever attone for. The Pamphlet, with your name, to so striking a recommendation to it, was not only industriously propogated in New York and Boston; but, that the recommendation might be known to every one, was reprinted with great care in the Newspapers, and was generally considered as a direct and open personal attack upon me, by countenancing the false interpretation of my Writings as favouring the Introduction of hereditary Monarchy and Aristocracy into this Country. The Question every where was, What Heresies are intended by the Secretary of State? The answer in the Newspapers was, The Vice Presidents notions of a Limited Monarchy, an hereditary Government of King and Lords, with only elective commons. Emboldened by these murmurs, soon after appeared the Paragraphs of an unprincipled Libeller in the New Haven Gazette, carefully reprinted in the Papers of New York, Boston and Philadelphia, holding up the Vice President to the ridicule of the World for his meanness, and to their detestation for wishing to subjugate the People to a few Nobles. These were soon followed by a formal Speech of the Lieutenant Governor of Massacuhsetts [sic—ED.] [Samuel Adams] very solemnly holding up the Idea of hereditary Powers, and cautioning the Publick against them, as if they were at that moment in the most imminent danger of them.* These Things were all accompanied with the most marked neglect both of the Governor [John Hancock] and Lieutenant Governor of this State towards me; and alltogether opperated as an Hue and Cry to all my Ennemies and Rivals, to the old constitutional faction of Pensilvania in concert with the late Insurgents of Massachusetts, both of whom consider my Writings as the Cause of their overthrow,† to hunt me down like a hare, if they could. In this State of Things, Publicola, who, I suppose, thought that Mr. Paines Pamphlet was made Use of as an Instrument to destroy a Man, for whom he had a regard, [whom] he thought innocent, and in the present moment [o]f some importance to the Publick, came forward.

You declare very explicitly that you never did, by yourself or by any other, have a Sentence of yours, inserted in a Newspaper

---

*Samuel Adams's speech to the two houses of the Massachusetts legislature had been preceded by correspondence with JA, Sept.–Nov. 1790, in which they argued about the nature of republican government and popular sovereignty versus a mixed government "of three powers, forming a mutual balance." *Works*, VI, 411–26.
†JA had condemned the Pennsylvania Constitution of 1776, which was replaced by a new one in 1790, providing for a more balanced government; and he had strenuously opposed Shays's Rebellion in Massachusetts.

without your name to it. And I, with equal frankness declare that I never did, either by my self or by any other, have a Sentence of mine inserted in any Newspaper since I left Philadelphia. I neither wrote nor corrected Publicola. The Writer in the Composition of his Pieces followed his own Judgment, Information and discretion, without any assistance from me.

You observe "That You and I differ in our Ideas of the best form of Government is well known to us both." But, my dear Sir, you will give me leave to say, that I do not know this. I know not what your Idea is of the best form of Government. You and I have never had a serious conversation together that I can recollect concerning the nature of Government. The very transient hints that have ever passed between Us have been jocular and superficial, without ever coming to any explanation. If You suppose that I have or ever had a design or desire, of attempting to introduce a Government of King, Lords and Commons, or in other Words an hereditary Executive, or an hereditary Senate, either into the Government of the United States or that of any Individual State, in this Country, you are wholly mistaken. There is not such a Thought expressed or intimated in any public writing or private Letter of mine, and I may safely challenge all Mankind to produce such a passage and quote the Chapter and Verse. If you have ever put such a Construction on any Thing of mine, I beg you would mention it to me, and I will undertake to convince you, that it has no such meaning. Upon this occasion I will venture to say that my unpolished Writings, although they have been read by a sufficient Number of Persons to have assisted in crushing the Insurrection of the Massachusetts, in the formation of the new Constitutions of Pennsylvania, Georgia and South Carolina, and in procuring the Assent of all the States to the new national Constitution, yet they have not been read by great Numbers. Of the few who have taken the pains to read them, some have misunderstood them and others have willfully misrepresented them, and these misunderstandings and misrepresentations have been made the pretence for overwhelming me with floods and Whirlwinds of tempestuous Abuse, unexampled in the History of this Country.

It is thought by some, that Mr. Hancock's friends are preparing the Way, by my destruction, for his Election to the Place of Vice President, and that of Mr. Samuel Adams to be Governor of this Commonwealth, and then the Stone House Faction* will be sure of all the Loaves and Fishes, in the national Government and the State Government as they hope. The Opposers of the present Constitution of Pensilvania, the promoters of Shases Rebellion and County Resolves, and many of the Detesters of the present national Government, will undoubtedly aid them. Many People think too that no small Share of foreign Influence, in revenge for certain untractable conduct at the Treaty of Peace, is and will be intermingled. The Janizaries of this goodly Combination, among whom are three or four, who hesitate at no falsehood, have written all the Impudence and Impertinence which have appeared in the Boston Papers upon this memorable Occasion.

I must own to you that the daring Traits of Ambition and Intrigue, and those unbridled Rivalries which have already appeared, are the most melancholly and alarming Symptoms that I have ever seen in this Country: and if they are to be encouraged to proceed in their Course, the sooner I am relieved from the Competition the happier I shall be.

I thank you, Sir very sincerely for writing to me upon this Occasion. It was high time that you and I should come to an explanation with each other. The friendship that has subsisted for fifteen Years between Us without the smallest interruption, and untill this occasion without the slightest Suspicion, ever has been and still is, very dear to my heart. There is no office which I would not resign, rather than give a just occasion to one friend to forsake me. Your motives for writing to me, I have not a doubt were the most pure and the most friendly; and I have no suspicion that you will not receive this explanation from me in the same candid Light.

---

*Hancock's mansion on Beacon Hill was a two-story granite structure. Justin Winsor, ed., *The Memorial History of Boston . . .* (Boston, 1881–86), III, 201–3; Anson E. Morse, *The Federalist Party in Massachusetts to the Year 1800* (Princeton, 1909), 62–66, 140.

I thank You Sir for the foreign Intelligence and beg leave to present You with the friendly compliments of Mrs. Adams, as well as the repeated Assurances of the friendship, Esteem and respect of Dear Sir Your most obedient and most humble Servant

JOHN ADAMS

ABIGAIL ADAMS TO JEFFERSON

Quincy July 1st 1804

SIR

Your Letter of June 13th came duly to hand; if it had contained no other sentiments and opinions than those which my Letter of condolence could have excited, and which are expressed in the first page of your reply, our correspondence would have terminated here: but you have been pleased to enter upon some subjects which call for a reply: and as you observe that you have wished for an opportunity to express your sentiments, I have given to them every weight they claim.

"One act of Mr. Adams's Life, and *one* only, you repeat, ever gave me a moments personal displeasure. I did think his last appointments to office personally unkind. They were from among my most ardent political enemies."

As this act I am certain was not intended to give any personal pain or offence, I think it a duty to explain it so far as I then knew his views and designs. The constitution empowers the president to fill up offices as they become vacant. It was in the exercise of this power that appointments were made, and Characters selected whom Mr. Adams considerd, as men faithfull to the constitution and where he personally knew them, such as were capable of fullfilling their duty to their country. This was done by president Washington equally, in the last days of his administration so that not an office remaind vacant for his successor to fill upon his comeing into the office. No offence was given by it, and no personal unkindness thought of. But the different political opinions which have so unhappily divided our Country, must have given rise to the Idea, that personal unkindness was intended. You will please to recollect Sir, that at the time these appointments were made, there was not any certainty that the presidency would devolve upon you,* which is an other circumstance to prove that personal unkindness was not meant. No person was ever selected by him from such a motive—and so far was Mr. Adams from indulging such a sentiment, that he had no Idea of the intollerance of party spirit at that time, and I know it was his opinion that if the presidency devolved upon you, except in the appointment of Secretaries, no material Changes would be made. I perfectly agree with you in opinion that those should be Gentlemen in whom the president can repose confidence, possessing opinions, and sentiments corresponding with his own, or if differing from him, that they ought rather to resign their office, than cabal against measures which he may think essential to the honour safety and peace of the Country. Much less should they unite, with any bold, and dareingly ambitious Character, to over rule the Cabinet, or betray the Secrets of it to Friends or foes. The two Gentlemen who held the offices of secretaries,† when you became president were not of this Character. They were appointed by your predecessor nearly two years previous to his retirement. They were Gentlemen who had cordially co-opperated with him, and enjoyed the public confidence. Possessing however different political sentiments from those which you were known to have embraced, it was expected that they would, as they did, resign.

I have never felt any enmity towards you Sir for being elected president of the United States. But the instruments made use of, and the means which were practised to effect a change, have my utter abhorrence and detestation, for they were the blackest calumny, and foulest falshoods. I had witnessed enough of the

---

*Since the electoral vote in 1800 was a tie, 73–73, between TJ and Aaron Burr, the election was thrown into the House of Representatives, where on Feb. 17, 1801, on the thirty-sixth ballot TJ was elected president. Cunningham, *Jeffersonian Republicans,* 239, 244. Since JA's appointments were not made until the beginning of March, AA's chronology is in error; therefore her defense of JA fails in part.

†Benjamin Stoddert, secretary of the navy, 1798–1801; Samuel Dexter, secretary of war, 1800, secretary of the treasury, 1801–2.

anxiety, and solicitude, the envy jealousy and reproach attendant upon the office as well as the high responsibility of the
Station, to be perfectly willing to see a transfer of it. And I can
truly say, that at the time of Election, I considerd your pretentions much superior to his [Mr. Burr's], to whom an equal vote
was given. Your experience I venture to affirm has convinced
you that it is not a station to be envy'd. If you feel yourself a
free man, and can act in all cases, according to your own sentiments, opinions and judgment, you can do more than either of
your predecessors could, and are awfully responsible to God
and your Country for the measures of your Administration. I
rely upon the Friendship you still profess for me, and (I am
conscious I have done nothing to forfeit it), to excuse the freedom of this discussion to which you have led with an unreserve, which has taken off the Shackles I should otherways
have found myself embarrassed with.—And now Sir I will
freely disclose to you what has severed the bonds of former
Friendship, and placed you in a light very different from what
I once viewd you in.

One of the first acts of your administration was to liberate a
wretch* who was suffering the just punishment of the Law due
to his crimes for writing and publishing the basest libel, the lowest and vilest Slander, which malice could invent, or calumny
exhibit against the Character and reputation of your predecessor,
of him for whom you profest the highest esteem and Friendship, and whom you certainly knew incapable of such compli-
cated baseness. The remission of Callenders fine was a public
approbation of his conduct. Is not the last restraint of vice, a

---

*James Thomson Callender, Scottish immigrant and pamphleteer, began his
rabid attacks on the Federalist administration in 1797. After a stint in Philadelphia he moved to Virginia and wrote for the Richmond *Examiner,* a Republican paper. In 1800 Callender published *The Prospect before Us,* attacking the
Federalist leaders. For his remarks about JA he was tried under the Sedition
Law, fined $200, and sentenced to nine months' imprisonment by Justice
Samuel Chase in June 1800. President Jefferson pardoned him in 1801 and re-
mitted his fine. James Morton Smith, *Freedom's Fetters: The Alien and Sedition Laws and American Civil Liberties* (Ithaca, 1956), Chap. XV; Dumas
Malone, "Callender, James Thomson," *DAB,* III, 425–26.

sense of shame, renderd abortive, if abandoned Characters do not excite abhorrence.* If the chief Majestrate of a Nation, whose elevated Station places him in a conspicuous light, and renders his every action a concern of general importance, permits his public conduct to be influenced by private resentment, and so far forgets what is due to his Character as to give countanance to a base Calumniater, is he not answerable for the influence which his example has upon the manners and morals of the community?

Untill I read Callenders seventh Letter containing your compliment to him as a writer and your reward of 50 dollars, I could not be made to believe, that such measures could have been resorted to: to stab the fair fame and upright intentions of one, who to use your own Language "was acting from an honest conviction in his own mind that he was right." This Sir I considered as a personal injury. This was the Sword that cut assunder the Gordian knot, which could not be untied by all the efforts of party Spirit, by rivalship by Jealousy or any other malignant fiend.

The serpent you cherished and warmed, bit the hand that nourished him,† and gave you sufficient Specimens of his talents, his gratitude his justice, and his truth. When such vipers are let lose upon Society, all distinction between virtue and vice are levelled, all respect for Character is lost in the overwhelming deluge of calumny—that respect which is a necessary bond in the social union, which gives efficacy to laws, and teaches the subject to obey the Majestrate, and the child to submit to the parent.

There is one other act of your administration which I considerd as personally unkind, and which your own mind will readily suggest to you, but as it neither affected character, or reputation, I forbear to state it.

---

*The most recent article on Callender and TJ is Charles A. Jellison, "That Scoundrel Callender," Va. Mag. of Hist. and Biog., 67 (1959), 295–306.
†Callender soon turned against TJ, attacked the Republican administration with his vitriolic pen, and propagated scandal concerning TJ's private life. He died in 1803. DAB, III, 425–26.

This Letter is written in confidence—no eye but my own has seen what has passed. Faithfull are the wounds of a Friend. Often have I wished to have seen a different course pursued by you. I bear no malice I cherish no enmity. I would not retaliate if I could—nay more in the true spirit of christian Charity, I would forgive, as I hope to be forgiven. And with that disposition of mind and heart, I subscribe the Name of   ABIGAIL ADAMS

JEFFERSON TO ABIGAIL ADAMS

Washington July 22.04.

DEAR MADAM

Your favor of the 1st inst. was duly received, and I would not again have intruded on you but to rectify certain facts which seem not to have been presented to you under their true aspect. My charities to Callendar are considered as rewards for his calumnies. As early, I think, as 1796, I was told in Philadelphia that Callendar, the author of the Political progress of Britain, was in that city, a fugitive from persecution for having written that book, and in distress.* I had read and approved the book: I considered him as a man of genius, unjustly persecuted. I knew nothing of his private character, and immediately expressed my readiness to contribute to his relief, and to serve him. It was a considerable time after, that, on application from a person who thought of him as I did, I contributed to his relief, and afterwards repeated the contribution. Himself I did not see till long after, nor ever more than two or three times. When he first began to write he told some useful truths in his coarse way; but no body sooner disapproved of his writings than I did, or wished more that he would be silent. My charities to him were no more meant as encouragements to his scurrilities than those I give to the beggar at my door are meant as rewards for the

---

*Callender's pamphlet, criticizing the British government, had led to his indictment for sedition in Jan. 1793. He did not answer the court summons and so became a fugitive from justice and fled to the United States. *Ibid.*

vices of his life, and to make them chargeable to myself. In truth they would have been greater to him had he never written a word after the work for which he fled from Britain. With respect to the calumnies and falsehoods which writers and printers at large published against Mr. Adams, I was as far from stooping to any concern or approbation of them as Mr. Adams was respecting those of Porcupine,* Fenno, or Russell, who published volumes against me for every sentence vended by their opponents against Mr. Adams. But I never supposed Mr. Adams had any participation in the atrocities of these editors or their writers. I knew myself incapable of that base warfare, and believed him to be so. On the contrary, whatever I may have thought of the acts of the administration of that day, I have ever borne testimony to Mr. Adams's personal worth, nor was it ever impeached in my presence without a just vindication of it on my part. I never supposed that any person who knew either of us could believe that either meddled in that dirty work.

But another fact is that I 'liberated a wretch who was suffering for a libel against Mr. Adams.' I do not know who was the particular wretch alluded to: but I discharged every person under punishment or prosecution under the Sedition law, because I considered and now consider that law to be a nullity as absolute and as palpable as if Congress had ordered us to fall down and worship a golden image; and that it was as much my duty to arrest it's execution in every stage, as it would have been to have rescued from the fiery furnace those who should have been cast into it for refusing to worship their image. It was accordingly done in every instance, without asking what the offenders had done, or against whom they had offended, but whether the pains they were suffering were inflicted under the pretended Sedition law. It was certainly possible that my motives for contributing to the relief of Callender and liberating sufferers under the Sedition law, might have been to protect, encourage and reward slander: but they may also have

*Porcupine's Gazette was a Federalist newspaper published in Philadelphia, 1797–99, by William Cobbett.

been those which inspire ordinary charities to objects of distress, meritorious or not, or the obligations of an oath to protect the constitution, violated by an unauthorized act of Congress. Which of these were my motives must be decided by a regard to the general tenor of my life. On this I am not afraid to appeal to the nation at large, to posterity, and still less to that being who sees himself our motives, who will judge us from his own knolege of them, and not on the testimony of a Porcupine or Fenno.

You observe there has been one other act of my administration personally unkind, and suppose it will readily suggest itself to me. I declare on my honor, Madam, I have not the least conception what act is alluded to. I never did a single one with an unkind intention.

My sole object in this letter being to place before your attention that the acts imputed to me are either such as are falsely imputed, or as might flow from good as well as bad motives, I shall make no other addition than the assurances of my continued wishes for the health and happiness of yourself and Mr. Adams.   TH: JEFFERSON

ABIGAIL ADAMS TO JEFFERSON

Quincy August 18th 1804

SIR

Your Letter of July 22d was by some mistake in the post office at Boston sent back as far as New York, so that it did not reach me untill the eleventh of this Month. Candour requires of me a reply. Your statement respecting Callender, (who was the wretch referd to) and your motives for liberating him, wear a different aspect as explaind by you, from the impression which they had made, not only upon my mind, but upon the minds of all those, whom I ever heard speak upon the subject. With regard to the act under which he was punished, different persons entertain different opinions respecting it. It lies not with me to decide upon its validity. That I presume devolved upon the supreem Judges of the Nation: but I have understood that the power which makes a Law, is alone competent to the repeal. If a Chief Majestrate can by his will annul a Law, where is the difference between a republican, and a despotic Government? That some restraint should be laid upon the asassin, who stabs reputation, all civilized Nations have assented to. In no Country has calumny falshood, and revileing stalked abroad more licentiously, than in this. No political Character has been secure from its attacks, no reputation so fair, as not to be wounded by it, untill truth and falshood lie in one undistinguished heap. If there are no checks to be resorted to in the Laws of the Land, and no reperation to be made to the injured, will not Man become the judge and avenger of his own wrongs, and as in a late instance, the sword and pistol decide the contest?* All the Christian and social virtues will be banished the Land. All that makes Life desirable, and softens the ferocious passions of Man will assume a savage deportment, and like Cain of old, every Mans hand will be against his Neighbour. Party spirit is blind malevolent uncandid, ungenerous, unjust and unforgiving. It is equally so under federal as under democratic Banners, yet upon both sides are Characters who possess honest views, and act from honorable motives, who disdain to be led blind-fold, and who tho entertaining different opinions, have for their object the public welfare and happiness. These are the Characters, who abhor calumny and evil speaking, and who will never descend to News paper revileing. And you have done Mr. Adams justice in believing him, incapable of such conduct. He has never written a line in any News paper to which his Name has not been affixed, since he was first elected president of the united States. The writers in the public papers, and their employers are alltogether unknown to him.

I have seen and known that much of the conduct of a public ruler, is liable to be misunderstood, and misrepresented. Party hatred by its deadly poison blinds the Eyes and envenoms the

---

*Referring, no doubt, to the duel between Hamilton and Burr, fought on July 11, 1804, in which Hamilton was killed.

heart. It is fatal to the integrity of the moral Character. It sees
not that wisdom dwells with moderation, and that firmness of
conduct is seldom united with outrageous voilence [i.e., vio-
lence] of sentiment. Thus blame is too often liberally bestowed
upon actions, which if fully understood, and candidly judged
would merit praise instead of censure. It is only by the general
issue of measures producing banefull or benificial effects that
they ought to be tested.

You exculpate yourself from any intentional act of unkindness towards any one. I will freely state that which I referd to
in my former Letter, and which I could not avoid considering a
personal resentment. Soon after my eldest son's return from
Europe, he was appointed by the district Judge to an office into
which no political concerns enterd, personally known to you,
and possessing all the qualifications, you yourself being Judge,
which you had designated for office. As soon as congress gave
the appointments to the president you removed him.* This
looked so particularly pointed, that some of your best Friends
in Boston, at that time exprest their regret that you had done
so. I must do him the Justice to say, that I never heard an
expression from him of censure or disrespect towards you in
concequence of it. With pleasure I say that he is not a blind fol-
lower of any party.

I have written to you with the freedom and unreserve of former Friendship to which I would gladly return could all causes
but mere difference of opinion be removed. I wish to lead a
tranquil and retired Life under the administration of the Government, disposed to heal the wounds of contention, to cool
the rageing fury of party animosity: to soften the Rugged Spirit
of resentment, and desirious of seeing my Children and Grand
Children, Heirs to that freedom and independance which you
and your predesessor, united your efforts to obtain. With these
sentiments I reciprocate my sincere wishes for your Health and
happiness.   ABIGAIL ADAMS

---

*In his letter of Sept. 11, 1804, to AA, TJ provided a correct and satisfying an-
swer to her complaint. See Bemis, *John Quincy Adams*, 112.

ADAMS TO JEFFERSON

Quincy Feb. 10 1812

DEAR SIR

I have received with great pleasure your favour of the 23 of January. I suspected that the Sample was left at the Post Office and that you would soon have it. I regret the shabby Condition in which you found it: but it was the only Copy I had, and I thought it scarcely worth while to wait till I could get a Sett properly bound.

The Dissertation on the State of real homespun was a feast to me, who delight in every Information of that kind. In a moral œconomical and political point of View, it ought to be considered by every American Man Woman and child as a most precious Improvement in the Condition and prosperity of our Country.

Although you and I are weary of Politicks, You may be surprised to find me making a Transition to such a Subject as Prophecies. I find that Virginia produces Prophets, as well as the Indiana Territory. There have been lately sent me from Richmond two Volumes, one written by Nimrod Hewes and the other by Christopher Macpherson; both, upon Prophecies, and neither, ill written. I should apprehend that two such Mulattoes might raise the Devil among the Negroes in that Vicinity: for though they are evidently cracked, they are not much more irrational than Dr. Towers who wrote two ponderous Vollumes, near twenty years ago to prove that The French Revolution was the Commencement of the Millenium, and the decapitation of The King of France but the beginning of a Series, immediately to follow, by which all The Monarchies were to be destroyed and succeeded by universal Republicanism over all Europe; nor than Dr. Priestly who told me soberly, cooly and deliberately that though he knew of Nothing in human Nature or in the History of Mankind to justify the Opinion, Yet he fully believed upon the Authority of Prophecy that the French Nation would establish a free Government and that the King of France who had been executed, was the first of the Ten Horns of the great Beast, and that all the other Nine Monarks were soon to fall off after him; nor than The Reverend Mr. Faber who has lately written a very elegant and learned Volume to prove that Napoleon is Antichrist; nor than our worthy Friend Mr. Joseph Wharton of Philadelphia, who in consequence of great Reading and profound Study has long since settled his opinion, that the City of London is or is to be the Head Quarters of Antichrist; Nor than the Prophet of the Wabash [Tenskwatawa], of whom I want to know more than I do, because I learn that the Indians the Sons of the Forrest are as Superstitious as any of the great learned Men aforesaid, and as firm believers in Witchcraft as all Europe and America were in the Seventeenth Century and as frequently punish Witches by splitting their Sculls with the Tomahawk, after a solemn Tryal and Adjudication by the Sachems and Warriours in Council.

The Crusades were commenced by the Prophets and every Age since, when ever any great Turmoil happens in the World, has produced fresh Prophets. The Continual Refutation of all their Prognostications by Time and Experience has no Effect in extinguishing or damping their Ardor.

I think these Prophecies are not only unphilosophical and inconsistent with the political Safety of States and Nations; but that the most sincere and sober Christians in the World ought upon their own Principles to hold them impious, for nothing is clearer from their Scriptures than that Their Prophecies were not intended to make Us Prophets.

Pardon this strange Vagary. I want only to know something more than I do about the Richmond and Wabash Prophets.

Called to Company and to dinner I have only time to repeat the Assurances of the Friendship and Respect of   JOHN ADAMS

ADAMS TO JEFFERSON

Quincy, June 28 1812

DEAR SIR

I know not what, unless it were the Prophet of Tippacanoe [Tenskwatawa], had turned my Curiosity to inquiries after the metaphisical Science of the Indians, their ecclesiastical Establishments and theological Theories: but your Letter, written with all the Accuracy perspicuity and Elegance of your Youth and middle Age, as it has given me great Satisfaction, deserves my best Thanks.

It has given me Satisfaction, because, while it has furnished me with Information *where* all the Knowledge is to be obtained, that Books afford: it has convinced me that I shall never know much more of the Subject than I do now. As I have never aimed at making any Collection of Books upon this Subject I have none of those you have abridged in so concise a manner. Lafitau, Adair and De Bry were known to me only by Name.

The various Ingenuity which has been displayed in Inventions of hypotheses to account for the original Population of America; and the immensity of learning profusely expended to support them, have appeared to me, for a longer time than I can precisely recollect, what the Physicians call the Litteræ nihil Sanantes.* Whether Serpents Teeth were sown here and sprung up Men; whether Men and Women dropped from the Clouds upon this Atlantic Island; whether the Almighty created them here, or whether they immigrated from Europe, are questions of no moment to the present or future happiness of Man. Neither Agriculture, Commerce, Manufactures, Fisheries, Science, Litterature, Taste, Religion, Morals, nor any other good will be promoted, or any Evil averted, by any discoveries that can be made in answer to those questions.

The Opinions of the Indians and their Usages, as they are represented in your obliging letter of the 11. June, appear to me to resemble the Platonizing Philo, or the Philonizing Plato, more than the Genuine System of Judaism.

The philosophy both of Philo and Plato are at least as absurd. It is indeed less intelligible.

Plato borrowed his doctrines from Oriental and Egyptian Philosophers, for he had travelled both in India and Egypt.

The Oriental philosophy, immitated and adopted in part if not the whole by Plato and Philo was

---

* "Writings correcting nothing."

1. One God the good.

2. The Ideas, the thought, the Reason, the Intellect, the Logos, the Ratio, of God.

3. Matter, the Universe, the Production of the Logos, or contemplations of God. This Matter was the Source of Evil.

Perhaps, the three powers of Plato, Philo, the Egyptians and Indians, can not be distinctly made out, from your account of the Indians, but

1. The great Spirit, the good, who is worshiped by the Kings, Sachems and all the great Men in their solem Festivals as the Author, the Parent of Good.

2. The Devil, or the Source of Evil. They are not metaphisicians enough as yet to suppose it, or at least to call it matter, like the Wiseacres of Antiquity, and like Frederic the Great, who has written a very silly Essay on the Origin of Evil, in which he ascribes it all to Matter, as if this was an original discovery of his own.

The Watchmaker has in his head an Idea of the System of a Watch before he makes it. The Mechanician of the Universe had a compleat idea of the Universe before he made it: and this Idea, this Logos, was almighty or at least powerful enough to produce the World, but it must be made of Matter which was eternal. For creation out of Nothing was impossible. And Matter was unmanageable. It would not, and could not be fashioned into any System, without a large mixture of Evil in it; for Matter was essentially evil.

The Indians are not Metaphisicians enough to have discovered This *Idea,* this Logos, this intermediate Power between good and Evil, God and Matter. But of the two Powers The Good and the Evil, they seem to have a full Conviction; and what Son or Daughter of Adam and Eve has not?

This Logos of Plato seems to resemble if it was not the Prototype of the *Ratio and its Progress* of Manilius The Astrologer; of the *Progress of the Mind* of Condorcet; and the Age of Reason of Tom. Payne.

I could make a System too. The seven hundred Thousand Soldiers of Zingis, when the whole or any part of them went to battle, they sett up a howl, which resembled nothing that human Imagination has conceived, unless it be the Supposition that all the Devils in Hell were let loose at once to set up an infernal Scream, which terrified their Ennemies and never failed to obtain them Victory. The Indian Yell resembles this: and therefore America was peopled from Asia.

Another System. The Armies of Zingis, sometimes two or three or four hundred Thousands of them, surrounded a Province in a Circle, and marched towards the Centre, driving all the wild Beasts before them, Lyons, Tigers, Wolves, Bears, and every living thing, terrifying them with their Howls and Yells, their Drums, Trumpetts, etc., till they terrified and tamed enough of them to Victual the whole Army. Therefore the Scotch Highlanders who practice the same thing in miniature, are emigrants from Asia. Therefore the American Indians, who, for anything I know, practice the same custom, are emigrants from Asia or Scotland.

I am weary of contemplating Nations from the lowest and most beastly degradations of human Life, to the highest Refinement of Civilization: I am weary of Philosophers, Theologians, Politicians, and Historians. They are immense Masses of Absurdities, Vices and Lies. Montesquieu had sense enough to say in Jest, that all our Knowledge might be comprehended in twelve Pages in Duodecimo: and, I believe him, in earnest. I could express my Faith in shorter terms. He who loves the Workman and his Work, and does what he can to preserve and improve it, shall be accepted of him.

I also have felt an Interest in the Indians and a Commiseration for them from my Childhood. Aaron Pomham the Priest and Moses Pomham the King of the Punkapaug and Neponsit Tribes, were frequent Visitors at my Fathers house at least seventy Years ago. I have a distinct remembrance of their Forms and Figures. They were very aged, and the tallest and stoutest Indians I have ever seen. The titles of King and Priest, and the names of Moses and Aaron were given them no doubt by our Massachusetts Divines and Statesmen. There was a numerous Family in this Town, whose Wigwam was within a Mile of this

House. This Family were frequently at my Fathers house, and I in my boyish Rambles used to call at their Wigwam, where I never failed to be treated with Whortle Berries, Blackberries, Strawberries or Apples, Plumbs, Peaches, etc., for they had planted a variety of fruit Trees about them. But the Girls went out to Service and the Boys to Sea, till not a Soul is left. We scarcely see an Indian in a year. I remember the Time when Indian Murders, Scalpings, Depredations and conflagrations were as frequent on the Eastern and Northern Frontier of Massachusetts as they are now in Indiana, and spread as much terror. But since the Conquest of Canada, all this has ceased; and I believe with you that another Conquest of Canada will quiet the Indians forever and be as great a Blessing to them as to Us.

The Instance of Aaron Pomham made me suspect that there was an order of Priesthood among them. But according to your Account, the Worship of the good Spirit was performed by the Kings, Sachems, and Warriors, as among the ancient Germans, whose highest Rank of Nobility were Priests. The Worship of the Evil Spirit by the Conjurers, Jongleurs, Praestigiatores.

We have War now in Earnest. I lament the contumacious Spirit that appears about me. But I lament the cause that has given too much Apology for it: the total Neglect and absolute Refusal of all maritime Protection and Defence.

Money, Mariners, and Soldiers would be at the Public Service, if only a few Frigates had been ordered to be built. Without this our Union will be a brittle China Vase, a house of Ice or a Palace of Glass. I am, Sir, with an affectionate Respect, yours.

JOHN ADAMS

ADAMS TO JEFFERSON

Quincy June 30th. 1813

DEAR SIR

Before I proceed to the Order of the day, which is the terrorism of a former day: I beg leave to correct an Idea that some readers may infer from an expression in one of your Letters.

No sentiment or expression in any of my Answers to Addresses were obtruded or insinuated by any Person about me. Every one of them was written with my own hand. I alone am responsable for all the Mistakes and Errors in them. To have called Council to deliberate upon such a Mass of [writings] would have taken all the time; and the Business of the State must have been suspended. It is true, I was sufficiently plagued by Ps. and Ts. and Ss.* These however, were but Puppets danced upon the Wires of two Jugglers behind the Scene: and these Jugglers were Hamilton and Washington. How you stare at the name of Washington! But to return, *for the present* to

"The Sensations excited, in free yet firm Minds by the Terrorism of the day." You say, "none can conceive them who did not witness them, and they were felt by one party only."

Upon this Subject I despair of making myself understood by Posterity, by the present Age, and even by you. To collect and arrange the documents illustrative of it, would require as many Lives as those of a Cat. You never felt the Terrorism of Chaises Rebellion in Massachusetts.† I believe You never felt the Terrorism of Gallatins Insurrection in Pensilvania:‡ You certainly never reallized the Terrorism of Fries's,§ most outragious Riot and Rescue, as I call it, Treason, Rebellion as the World and great Judges and two Juries pronounced it. You certainly never felt the Terrorism, excited by Genet, in 1793, when ten thousand People in the Streets of Philadelphia, day after day, threatened to drag Washington out of his House, and effect a Revolution in the Government, or compell it to declare War in

---

*I.e., "the Pickerings, . . . the Tracys, the Sedgwicks." TJ to JA, June 15, 1813.
†On Shays's Rebellion.
‡As representative in Congress from western Pennsylvania, Albert Gallatin led the opposition to Hamilton's whiskey tax in 1792, but he was also opposed to violence and his peace policy won out in the Whiskey Rebellion of 1794. Henry Adams, *The Life of Albert Gallatin* (Philadelphia, 1880), 88–89, 123–40.
§Fries Rebellion occurred in Bucks and Northampton counties, Pa., in 1799. Farmers, led by John Fries, gave armed resistance to a federal tax on land and houses, and women poured scalding water on the assessors. The rebellion was put down by federal troops; Fries was tried for treason and sentenced to be hanged, but President John Adams pardoned him. W. W. H. Davis, *The Fries Rebellion* (Doylestown, Pa., 1899).

favour of the French Revolution, and against England. The coolest and the firmest Minds, even among the Quakers in Philadelphia, have given their Opinions to me, that nothing but the Yellow fever, which removed Dr. Hutchinson and Jonathan Dickenson Sargent from this World, could have saved the United States from a total Revolution of Government. I have no doubt You was fast asleep in philosophical Tranquility, when ten thousand People, and perhaps many more, were parading the Streets of Philadelphia, on the Evening of my Fast Day;* When even Governor Mifflin himself, thought it his Duty to order a Patrol of Horse And Foot to preserve the peace; when Markett Street was as full as Men could stand by one another, and even before my Door; when some of my Domesticks in Phrenzy, determined to sacrifice their Lives in my defence; when all were ready to make a desperate Salley among the multitude, and others were with difficulty and danger dragged back by the others; when I myself judged it prudent and necessary to order Chests of Arms from the War Office to be brought through bye Lanes and back Doors: determined to defend my House at the Expence of my Life, and the lives of the few, very few Domesticks and Friends within it. What think you of Terrorism, Mr. Jefferson? Shall I investigate the Causes, the Motives, the Incentives to these Terrorisms? Shall I remind you of Phillip Freneau, of Loyd? of Ned Church? of Peter Markoe[?] of Andrew Brown? of Duane? of Callender? of Tom Paine? of Greenleaf, of Cheetham, of Tennison at New York? of Benjamin Austin at Boston?† But above all; shall I request you, to collect the circular Letters from Members of Congress in the middle and southern States to their Constituents? I would give all I am worth for a compleat Collection of all those circular Letters. Please to recollect Edward Livingstones motions and Speeches and those of his Associates in the case of Jonathan Robbins.

---

*President John Adams proclaimed April 25, 1799, as a fast day, that God "would withhold us from unreasonable discontent, from disunion, faction, sedition, and insurrection. . . ." *Works,* IX, 172–74.
†All of the foregoing were Republican writers and editors, vehement in their denunciation of the Federalists.

The real terrors of both Parties have allways been, and now are, The fear that they shall loose the Elections and consequently the Loaves and Fishes; and that their Antagonists will obtain them. Both parties have excited artificial Terrors and if I were summoned as a Witness to say upon Oath, which Party had excited, Machiavillialy, the most terror, and which had really felt the most, I could not give a more sincere Answer, than in the vulgar Style "Put Them in a bagg and shake them, and then see which comes out first."

Where is the Terrorism, now, my Friend? There is now more real Terrorism in New England than there ever was in Virginia. The Terror of a civil War, a La Vendee, a division of the States etc. etc. etc. How shall We conjure down this damnable Rivalry between Virginia, and Massachusetts? Virginia had recourse to Pensilvania and New York, Massachusetts has now recourse to New York. They have almost got New Jersey and Maryland, and they are aiming at Pensilvania.* And all this in the midst of a War with England, when all Europe is in flames.

I will give you a hint or two more, on the Subject of Terrorism. When John Randolph in the House and Stephens Thompson Mason in the Senate were treating me, with the Utmost Contempt, when Ned Livingston was threatening me with Impeachment for the murder of Jonathan Robbins *the native of Danvers in Connecticutt.* When I had certain Information, that the daily Language in an Insurance Office in Boston, was, even from the Mouth of Charles Jarvis, "We must go to Philadelphia, and dragg that John Adams from his Chair."

I tha[n]k God that Terror never Yet seized on my mind. But I have had more excitements to it, from 1761 to this day than any other Man. Name the other if you can. I have been disgraced and degraded and I have a right to complain. But as I always expected it, I have always submitted to it; perhaps often with too much tameness.

---

*In the election of 1808 Pennsylvania and New York went heavily Republican; in 1812 most of New York, New Jersey, and Maryland voted Federalist, as did certain sections of Pennsylvania. By 1816 all these states were back in the Republican ranks. Charles O. Paullin, *Atlas of the Historical Geography of the United States* (Washington, 1932), pl. 102.

The amount of all the Speeches of John Randolph in the House for two or three Years is, that himself and myself, are the only two honest and consistent Men in the United States. Himself, eternally in Opposition to Government, and myself as constantly in favour of it. He is now in Correspondence with his Friend Quincy. What will come of it, let Virginia and Massachusetts Judge. In my next, you may find Something, upon "Correspondencies" Whigg and Tory; Federal and democratic; Virginian and Novanglian; English and French; Jacobinic and despotic, etc.

Mean time, I am as ever Your Friend,   JOHN ADAMS

ADAMS TO JEFFERSON

Quincy July 9 1813

Lord! Lord! What can I do, with so much Greek? When I was of your Age, young Man, i.e. 7 or 8 or 9 Years ago I felt, a kind of pang of Affection, for one of the flames of my Youth, and again paid my Addresses to Isocrates and Dionissius Hallicarnassensis etc. etc. etc. I collected all my Lexicons and Grammers and sat down to περι συνθεσεως ονοματων* etc. In this Way I amused myself for sometime: but I found, that if I looked a Word to day, in less than a Week I had to look it again. It was to little better purpose, than writing Letters on a pail of Water.

Whenever I sett down to write to you, I am precisely in the Situation of the Wood Cutter on Mount Ida: I can not see Wood for Trees. So many Subjects crowd upon me that I know not, with which to begin. But I will begin, at random with Belsham, who is, as I have no doubt, a Man of merit. He had no malice against you, nor any thought of doing mischief: nor has he done any, though he has been imprudent. The Truth is the Dissenters of all Denominations in England and especially the Unitarians, are cowed, as We used to say at Colledge. They

---

* "Concerning the treatment of words." Dion. Hal. wrote a treatise by this name on composition.

are ridiculed, insulted, persecuted. They can scarcely hold their heads above water. They catch at Straws and Shadows to avoid drowning. Priestley sent your Letter to Linsay, and Belsham printed it from the same motive, i.e., to derive some countenance from the Name of Jefferson. Nor has it done harm here. Priestley says to Linsay "You see he is almost one of Us, and He hopes will soon be altogether as such as We are." Even in our New England I have heard a high Federal Divine say, your Letters had increased his respect for you.

"The same political parties which now agitate U.S. have existed through all time." Precisely. And this is precisely the complaint in the preface to the first volume of my defence. While all other Sciences have advanced, that of Government is at a stand; little better understood; little better practiced now than 3 or 4 thousand Years ago. What is the Reason? I say Parties and Factions will not suffer, or permit Improvements to be made. As soon as one Man hints at an improvement his Rival opposes it. No sooner has one Party discovered or invented an Amelioration of the Condition of Man or the order of Society, than the opposite Party, belies it, misconstrues it, misrepresents it, ridicules it, insults it, and persecutes it. Records are destroyed. Histories are annihilated or interpolated, or prohibited sometimes by Popes, sometimes by Emperors, sometimes by Aristocratical and sometimes by democratical Assemblies and sometimes by Mobs.

Aristotle wrote the History and description of Eighteen hundred Republicks, which existed before his time. Cicero wrote two Volumes of discour[s]es on Government, which, perhaps were worth all the rest of his Works. The Works of Livy and Tacitus etc that are lost, would be more interesting than all that remain. Fifty Gospells have been destroyed, and where are St. Lukes World of Books that had been written? If you ask my Opinion, who has committed all the havoc? I will answer you candidly; Ecclesiastical and Imperial Despotism has done it, to conceal their Frauds.

Why are the Histories of all Nations, more ancient than the Chr[is]tian Æra, lost? Who destroyed the Alexandrian Library? I believe that Christian Priests, Jewish Rabbies Grecian

Sages and Roman Emperors had as great a hand in it as Turks and Mahomitans.

Democrats, Rebells and Jacobins, when they possessed a momentary Power, have shewn a disposition, both to destroy and to force Records, as vandalical, as Priests and Despots. Such has been and such is the World We live in.

I recollect, near 30 years ago to have said car[e]lesly to You, that I wished I could find time and means to write something upon Aristocracy. You seized upon the Idea, and encouraged me to do it, with all that friendly warmth that is natural and habitual to you. I soon began, and have been writing Upon that Subject ever since. I have been so unfortunate as never to be able to make myself understood. Your "ἄριστοι ["aristocrats"]" are the most difficult Animals to manage, of anything in the whole Theory and practice of Government. They will not suffer themselves to be governed. They not only exert all their own Subtilty Industry and courage, but they employ the Commonalty, to knock to pieces every Plan and Model that the most honest Architects in Legislation can invent to keep them within bounds. Both Patricians and Plebeians are as furious as the Workmen in England to demolish labour-saving Machinery.

But who are these "ἄριστοι"? Who shall judge? Who shall select these choice Spirits from the rest of the Congregation? Themselves? We must first find out and determine who themselves are. Shall the congregation choose? Ask Xenophon. Perhaps hereafter I may quote you Greek. Too much in a hurry at present, english must suffice. Xenophon says that the ecclesia, always chooses the worst Men they can find, because none others will do their dirty work.* This wicked Motive is worse than Birth or Wealth. Here I want to quote Greek again. But the day before I received your Letter of June 27. I gave the Book to George Washington Adams† going to the Accadamy at Hing-

---

*This statement was attributed to Xenophon in JA's time, but it was later recognized as from the unknown author of *Treatise of the Old Oligarch.*
†JA's grandson, the son of John Quincy Adams, who died in 1829. Bemis, *John Quincy Adams,* 276.

ham. The Title is ΗΘΙΚΗ ΠΟΙΗΣΙΣ a Collection of Moral
Sentences from all the most Ancien[t] Greek Poets.* In one of
the oldest of them I read in greek that I cannot repeat, a couplet
the Sense of which was

"Nobility in Men is worth as much as it is in Horses Asses or
Rams: but the meanest blooded Puppy, in the World, if he gets
a little money, is as good a man as the best of them." Yet Birth
and Wealth together have prevailed over Virtue and Talents
in all ages. The Many, will acknowledge no other "αριστοι."
Your Experience of this Truth, will not much differ from that
of your old Friend   JOHN ADAMS

ADAMS TO JEFFERSON

Quincy July 13th. 1813

DEAR SIR

Let me allude, to one circumstance more, in one of your Letters to me, before I touch upon the Subject of Religion in your
Letters to Priestley.

The first time, that you and I differed in Opinion on any material Question; was after your Arrival from Europe; and that
point was the french Revolution.

You was well persuaded in your own mind that the Nation
would succeed in establishing a free Republican Government: I
was as well persuaded, in mine, that a project of such a Government, over five and twenty millions people, when four and
twenty millions and five hundred thousands of them could neither write nor read: was as unnatural irrational and impracticable; as it would be over the Elephants Lions Tigers Panthers
Wolves and Bears in the Royal Menagerie, at Versailles. Napoleon has lately invented a Word, which perfectly expresses my
Opinion at that time and ever since. He calls the Project Ideology. And John Randolph, tho he was 14 years ago, as wild an
Enthusiast for Equality and Fraternity, as any of them; appears

* "Moralia ex Poetis," compiler unknown.

to be now a regenerated Proselite to Napoleons Opinion and mine, that it was all madness.

The Greeks in their Allegorical Style said that the two Ladies Αριστοκρατια ["Aristocracy"] and δημοκ[ρ]ατια ["democracy"], always in a quarrel, disturbed every neighbourhood with their brawls. It is a fine Observation of yours that "Whig and Torey belong to Natural History." Inequalities of Mind and Body are so established by God Almighty in his constitution of Human Nature that no Art or policy can ever plain them down to a Level. I have never read Reasoning more absurd, Sophistry more gross, in proof of the Athanasian Creed,* or Transubstantiation, than the subtle labours of Helvetius and Rousseau to demonstrate the natural Equality of Mankind. Jus cuique ["Justice for everyone"]; the golden rule; do as you would be done by; is all the Equality that can be supported or defended by reason, or reconciled to common Sense.

It is very true, as you justly observe, I can say nothing new on this or any other Subject of Government. But when La Fayette harrangued You and me, and John Quincy Adams, through a whole evening in your Hotel in the Cul de Sac, at Paris; and develloped the plans then in Operation to reform France: though I was as silent as you was, I then thought I could say something new to him. In plain Truth I was astonished at the Grossness of his Ignorance of Gover[n]ment and History, as I had been for Years before at that of Turgot, Rochefaucault, Condorcet and Franklin. This gross Ideology of them all, first suggested to me the thought and the inclination which I afterwards hinted to you in London, of writing Something upon Aristocracy. I was restrained for years by many fearful considerations. Who and what was I? A Man of no name or consideration in Europe. The manual Exercise of Writing was painful and distressing to me, almost like a blow, on the elbow or the knee; my Style was habitually negligent, unstudied, unpolished; I should make Enemies of all the French Patriots, the Dutch Patriots, the English

---

*The belief in the Trinity, upheld by Athanasius, later Bishop of Alexandria, against Arius at the Council of Nicaea in 325, the first ecumenical council of the Christian Church.

Republicans, Dissenters, Reformers, call them what you will; and what came nearer home to my bosom than all the rest, I knew, I should give offence to many, if not all of my best Friends in America, and very probably destroy all the little Popularity I ever had, in a Country where Popularity had more Omnipotence than the British Parliament assumed. Where should I get the necessary Books? What Printer or Bookseller would undertake to print such hazardous Writings?

But when the French Assembly of Notables met, and I saw that Turgots "Government in one Centre and that Center the Nation" a Sentence as misterious or as contradictory as the Athanasian Creed, was about to take place; and when I saw that Shaises Rebellion was breaking out in Massachusetts, and when I saw that even my obscure Name was often quoted in France as an Advocate for simple Democracy; when I saw that the Sympathies in America had caught the French flame: I was determined to wash my own hands as clean as I could of this foulness. I had then strong forebodings that I was sacrificing all the honours and Emoluments of this Life; and so it has happened: but not in so great a degree as I apprehended.

In Truth my "defence of the Constitutions" and "Discourses on Davila," laid the foundation of that immense Unpopula[ri]ty, which fell like the Tower of Siloam upon me. Your steady defence of democratical Principles, and your invariable favourable Opinion of the french Revolution laid the foundation of your Unbounded Popularity.

Sic transit Gloria Mundi.

Now, I will forfeit my Life, if you can find one Sentence in my Defence of the Constitutions, or the Discourses on Davila, which by a fair construction, can favour the introduction of hereditary Monarchy or Aristocracy into America.

They were all written to support and strengthen the Constitutions of the United States.

The Woodcutter on Ida, though he was puzzled to find a Tree to chop, at first, I presume knew how to leave off, when he was weary; But I never know when to cease, when I begin to write to you   JOHN ADAMS

ADAMS TO JEFFERSON

Quincy. July 18th. 1813

DEAR SIR

I have more to say, on Religion. For more than sixty Years I have been attentive to this great Subject. Controversies, between Calvinists and Arminians, Trinitarians and Uniterians, Deists and Christians, Atheists and both, have attracted my Attention, whenever the singular Life I have lead would admit, to all these questions. The History of this little Village of Quincy, if it were worth recording would explain to you, how this happened. I think, I can now say I have read away Bigotry, if not Enthusiasm.

What does Priestly mean, by an Unbeliever? When he applies it to you? How much did he "unbelieve," himself? Gibbon had him right, when he denominated his Creed, "Scanty." We are to understand, no doubt, that he believed The Resurrection of Jesus, some of his Miracles. His Inspiration, but in what degree? He did not believe in the Inspiration of the Writings that contain his History. Yet he believed in the Apocalyptic Beast, and he believed as much as he pleased in the Writings of Daniel and John. This great, excellent and extraordinary Man, whom I sincerely loved esteemed and respected, was really a Phenomenon; a Comet in the System, like Voltaire Bolingbroke and Hume. Had Bolingbroke or Voltaire taken him in hand, what would they have made of him and his Creed?

I do not believe you have read much of Priestleys "Corruptions of Christianity." His History of early Opinions of Jesus Christ. His Predestination, his No Soul System or his Controversy with Horseley.*

---

*Priestley's best known theological work was *History of the Corruptions of Christianity* (London, 1782). His four-volume *History of Early Opinions Concerning Jesus Christ* (London, 1786), rejecting the doctrine of the infallibility of Christ, "has brought me more antagonists," he wrote, "and I now write a pamphlet annually in defence of the Unitarian doctrine against all my opponents." *Memoirs of the Rev. Joseph Priestley to the Year 1795.* Written by Himself with a Continuation, to the Time of His Decease, by His Son, Joseph Priestley (Reprinted from the American edn.; London, 1809), 88.

I have been a diligent Student for many Years in Books whose Titles you have never seen. In Priestleys and Lindsay Writings; in Farmer, Cappe, in Tuckers or Edwards Searches, Light of Nature pursued; in Edwards and Hopkins, and lately in Ezra Styles Ely; his reverend and learned Panegyrists and his elegant and spirited Opponents. I am not wholly uninformed of the Controversies in Germany and the learned Researches of Universities and Professors; in which the Sanctity of the Bible and the Inspiration of its Authors are taken for granted or waived; or admitted, or not denied. I have also read Condorcets Progress of the human mind.

Now, what is all this to you? No more, than if I should tell you that I read Dr. Clark and Dr. Waterland and Emlyn, and Lelands View or Review of the Deistical Writers more than fifty Years ago, which is a literal Truth.

I blame you not for reading Euclid and Newton, Thucidides and Theocritus: for I believe you will find as much entertainment and Instruction in them as I have found, in my Theological and Ecclesiastical Instructors: Or even as I have found in a profound Investigation of the Life Writings and Doctrines of Erastus, whose Disciples were Milton, Harrington, Selden, St. John, the Chief Justice, Father of Bolingbroke, and others the choicest Spirits of their Age: or in La Harpes History of the Philosophy of the 18th Century, or in Van der Kemps vast Map of the Causes of the Revolutionary Spirit, in the same and preceeding Centuries. These Things are to me, at present, the Marbles and Nine Pins of old Age: I will not say the Beads and Prayer Books.

I Agree with you, as far as you go. Most cordially and I think solidly. How much farther I go, how much more I believe than You, I may explain in a future Letter.

Thus much I will say at present, I have found so many difficulties, that I am not astonished at your stopping where you are. And so far from sentencing you to Perdition, I hope soon to meet you in another Country.   JOHN ADAMS

JEFFERSON TO ADAMS

Monticello Oct. 28. 13.

DEAR SIR

According to the reservation between us, of taking up one of the subjects of our correspondence at a time, I turn to your letters of Aug. 16. and Sep. 2.

The passage you quote from Theognis, I think has an Ethical, rather than a political object. The whole piece is a moral *exhortation,* παραίνεσις, and this passage particularly seems to be a reproof to man, who, while with his domestic animals he is curious to improve the race by employing always the finest male, pays no attention to the improvement of his own race, but intermarries with the vicious, the ugly, or the old, for considerations of wealth or ambition. It is in conformity with the principle adopted afterwards by the Pythagoreans, and expressed by Ocellus in another form. Περι δε τῆς ἐκ τῶν αλληλων ανθρωπων γενεσεως etc.—ουχ ἡδονης ἑνεκα ἡ μιξις. Which, as literally as intelligibility will admit, may be thus translated. "Concerning the interprocreation of men, how, and of whom it shall be, in a perfect manner, and according to the laws of modesty and sanctity, conjointly, this is what I think right. First to lay it down that we do not commix for the sake of pleasure, but of the procreation of children. For the powers, the organs and desires for coition have not been given by god to man for the sake of pleasure, but for the procreation of the race. For as it were incongruous for a mortal born to partake of divine life, the immortality of the race being taken away, god fulfilled the purpose by making the generations uninterrupted and continuous. This therefore we are especially to lay down as a principle, that coition is not for the sake of pleasure." But Nature, not trusting to this moral and abstract motive, seems to have provided more securely for the perpetuation of the species by making it the effect of the oestrum implanted in the constitution of both sexes. And not only has the commerce of love been indulged on this unhallowed impulse, but made subservient also to wealth and ambition by marriages without regard to the beauty, the healthiness, the understanding, or virtue of the subject from which we are to breed. The selecting the best male for a Haram of well chosen females also, which Theognis seems to recommend from the example of our sheep and asses, would doubtless improve the human, as it does the brute animal, and produce a race of veritable αριστοι ["aristocrats"]. For experience proves that the moral and physical qualities of man, whether good or evil, are transmissible in a certain degree from father to son. But I suspect that the equal rights of men will rise up against this privileged Solomon, and oblige us to continue acquiescence under the 'Αμαυρωσις γενεος ἀστων ["the degeneration of the race of men"] which Theognis complains of, and to content ourselves with the accidental aristoi produced by the fortuitous concourse of breeders. For I agree with you that there is a natural aristocracy among men. The grounds of this are virtue and talents. Formerly bodily powers gave place among the aristoi. But since the invention of gunpowder has armed the weak as well as the strong with missile death, bodily strength, like beauty, good humor, politeness and other accomplishments, has become but an auxiliary ground of distinction. There is also an artificial aristocracy founded on wealth and birth, without either virtue or talents; for with these it would belong to the first class. The natural aristocracy I consider as the most precious gift of nature for the instruction, the trusts, and government of society. And indeed it would have been inconsistent in creation to have formed man for the social state, and not to have provided virtue and wisdom enough to manage the concerns of the society. May we not even say that that form of government is the best which provides the most effectually for a pure selection of these natural aristoi into the offices of government? The artificial aristocracy is a mischievous ingredient in government, and provision should be made to prevent it's ascendancy. On the question, What is the best provision, you and I differ; but we differ as rational friends, using the free exercise of our own reason, and mutually indulging it's errors. *You* think it best to put the Pseudo-aristoi into a separate chamber of legislation where they may be hindered from doing mischief by their coordinate branches, and where also they may be a protection to wealth against the Agrarian and plundering enterprises of the Majority of the people. I think that to give them power in order to prevent them from doing mischief, is arming them for it, and increasing instead of remedying the evil. For if the coordinate branches can arrest their action, so may they that of the coordinates. Mischief may be done negatively as well as positively. Of this a cabal in the Senate of the U.S. has furnished many proofs. Nor do I believe them necessary to protect the wealthy; because enough of these will find their way into every branch of the legislation to protect themselves. From 15. to 20. legislatures of our own, in action for 30. years past, have proved that no fears of an equalisation of property are to be apprehended from them.

I think the best remedy is exactly that provided by all our constitutions, to leave to the citizens the free election and separation of the aristoi from the pseudo-aristoi, of the wheat from the chaff. In general they will elect the real good and wise. In some instances, wealth may corrupt, and birth blind them; but not in sufficient degree to endanger the society.*

It is probable that our difference of opinion may in some measure be produced by a difference of character in those among whom we live. From what I have seen of Massachusets and Connecticut myself, and still more from what I have heard, and the character given of the former by yourself, [vol. 1. pa. 111.]† who know them so much better, there seems to be in those two states a traditionary reverence for certain families, which has rendered the offices of the government nearly hereditary in those families. I presume that from an early period of your history, members of these families happening to possess virtue and talents, have honestly exercised them for the good of the people, and by their services have endeared their names to them.

---

*The foregoing is TJ's most explicit statement concerning natural aristocracy. Cf. his "Autobiography," Ford, I, 49–50, 68–69.
†TJ's note, referring to JA's *Defence*.

In coupling Connecticut with you, I mean it politically only, not morally. For having made the Bible the Common law of their land they seem to have modelled their morality on the story of Jacob and Laban. But altho' this hereditary succession to office with you may in some degree be founded in real family merit, yet in a much higher degree it has proceeded from your strict alliance of church and state. These families are canonised in the eyes of the people on the common principle "you tickle me, and I will tickle you." In Virginia we have nothing of this. Our clergy, before the revolution, having been secured against rivalship by fixed salaries, did not give themselves the trouble of acquiring influence over the people. Of wealth, there were great accumulations in particular families, handed down from generation to generation under the English law of entails. But the only object of ambition for the wealthy was a seat in the king's council. All their court then was paid to the crown and it's creatures; and they Philipised in all collisions between the king and people. Hence they were unpopular; and that unpopularity continues attached to their names. A Randolph, a Carter, or a Burwell must have great personal superiority over a common competitor to be elected by the people, even at this day.

At the first session of our legislature after the Declaration of Independence, we passed a law abolishing entails. And this was followed by one abolishing the privilege of Primogeniture, and dividing the lands of intestates equally among all their children, or other representatives. These laws, drawn by myself, laid the axe to the root of Pseudo-aristocracy. And had another which I prepared been adopted by the legislature, our work would have been compleat. It was a Bill for the more general diffusion of learning.* This proposed to divide every county into wards of 5. or 6. miles square, like your townships; to establish in each ward a free school for reading, writing and common arithmetic; to provide for the annual selection of the best subjects from these schools who might recieve at the public expence a

---

* "A Bill for the More General Diffusion of Knowledge," No. 79 in the "Catalogue of Bills Prepared by the Committee of Revisors," Boyd, II, 526–35 and *n*.

higher degree of education at a district school; and from these district schools to select a certain number of the most promising subjects to be compleated at an University, where all the useful sciences should be taught. Worth and genius would thus have been sought out from every condition of life, and compleatly prepared by education for defeating the competition of wealth and birth for public trusts.

My proposition had for a further object to impart to these wards those portions of self-government for which they are best qualified, by confiding to them the care of their poor, their roads, police, elections, the nomination of jurors, administration of justice in small cases, elementary exercises of militia, in short, to have made them little republics, with a Warden at the head of each, for all those concerns which, being under their eye, they would better manage than the larger republics of the county or state. A general call of ward-meetings by their Wardens on the same day thro' the state would at any time produce the genuine sense of the people on any required point, and would enable the state to act in mass, as your people have so often done, and with so much effect, by their town meetings. The law for religious freedom,* which made a part of this system, having put down the aristocracy of the clergy, and restored to the citizen the freedom of the mind, and those of entails and descents nurturing an equality of condition among them, this on Education would have raised the mass of the people to the high ground of moral respectability necessary to their own safety, and to orderly government; and would have compleated the great object of qualifying them to select the veritable aristoi, for the trusts of government, to the exclusion of the Pseudalists: and the same Theognis who has furnished the epigraphs of your two letters assures us that 'ουδεμιαν πω, Κυρν' αγαθοι πολιν ὤλεσαν ἀνδρες ["Curnis, good men have never harmed any city"]'. Altho' this law has not yet been acted on but in a small and inefficient degree, it is still considered as

---

* "An ACT for establishing RELIGIOUS FREEDOM, passed in the Assembly of Virginia in the beginning of the year 1786," in TJ, *Notes on the State of Virginia*, ed. by Peden (1955), 223–25.

before the legislature, with other bills of the revised code, not yet taken up, and I have great hope that some patriotic spirit will, at a favorable moment, call it up, and make it the keystone of the arch of our government.

With respect to Aristocracy, we should further consider that, before the establishment of the American states, nothing was known to History but the Man of the old world, crouded within limits either small or overcharged, and steeped in the vices which that situation generates. A government adapted to such men would be one thing; but a very different one that for the Man of these states. Here every one may have land to labor for himself if he chuses; or, preferring the exercise of any other industry, may exact for it such compensation as not only to afford a comfortable subsistence, but wherewith to provide for a cessation from labor in old age. Every one, by his property, or by his satisfactory situation, is interested in the support of law and order. And such men may safely and advantageously reserve to themselves a wholsome controul over their public affairs, and a degree of freedom, which in the hands of the Canaille of the cities of Europe, would be instantly perverted to the demolition and destruction of every thing public and private. The history of the last 25. years of France, and of the last 40. years in America, nay of it's last 200. years, proves the truth of both parts of this observation.

But even in Europe a change has sensibly taken place in the mind of Man. Science had liberated the idea of those who read and reflect, and the American example had kindled feelings of right in the people. An insurrection has consequently begun, of science, talents and courage against rank and birth, which have fallen into contempt. It has failed in it's first effort, because the mobs of the cities, the instrument used for it's accomplishment, debased by ignorance, poverty and vice, could not be restrained to rational action. But the world will recover from the panic of this first catastrophe. Science is progressive, and talents and enterprize on the alert. Resort may be had to the people of the country, a more governable power from their principles and subordination; and rank, and birth, and tinsel-aristocracy will finally shrink into insignificance, even there. This however we have no right to meddle with. It suffices for us, if the moral and physical condition of our own citizens qualifies them to select the able and good for the direction of their government, with a recurrence of elections at such short periods as will enable them to displace an unfaithful servant before the mischief he meditates may be irremediable.

I have thus stated my opinion on a point on which we differ, not with a view to controversy, for we are both too old to change opinions which are the result of a long life of inquiry and reflection; but on the suggestion of a former letter of yours, that we ought not to die before we have explained ourselves to each other. We acted in perfect harmony thro' a long and perilous contest for our liberty and independance. A constitution has been acquired which, tho neither of us think perfect, yet both consider as competent to render our fellow-citizens the happiest and the securest on whom the sun has ever shone. If we do not think exactly alike as to it's imperfections, it matters little to our country which, after devoting to it long lives of disinterested labor, we have delivered over to our successors in life, who will be able to take care of it, and of themselves.

Of the pamphlet on aristocracy which has been sent to you, or who may be it's author, I have heard nothing but thro' your letter. If the person you suspect* it may be known from the quaint, mystical and hyperbolical ideas, involved in affected, new-fangled and pedantic terms, which stamp his writings. Whatever it be, I hope your quiet is not to be affected at this day by the rudeness of intemperance of scribblers; but that you may continue in tranquility to live and to rejoice in the prosperity of our country until it shall be your own wish to take your seat among the Aristoi who have gone before you. Ever and affectionately yours.   TH: JEFFERSON

P.S. Can you assist my memory on the enquiries of my letter of Aug. 22?

---

*John Taylor of Caroline.

ADAMS TO JEFFERSON

Quincy November 15.13

DEAR SIR

I cannot appease my melancholy commiseration for our Armies in this furious snow storm in any way so well as by studying your Letter of Oct. 28.

We are now explicitly agreed, in one important point, vizt. That "there is a natural Aristocracy among men; the grounds of which are Virtue and Talents."

You very justly indulge a little merriment upon this solemn subject of Aristocracy. I often laugh at it too, for there is nothing in this laughable world more ridiculous than the management of it by almost all the nations of the Earth. But while We smile, Mankind have reason to say to Us, as the froggs said to the Boys, What is Sport to you is Wounds and death to Us. When I consider the weakness, the folly, the Pride, the Vanity, the Selfishness, the Artifice, the low craft and meaning cunning, the want of Principle, the Avarice the unbounded Ambition, the unfeeling Cruelty of a majority of those (in all Nations) who are allowed an aristocratical influence; and on the other hand, the Stupidity with which the more numerous multitude, not only become their Dupes, but even love to be Taken in by their Tricks: I feel a stronger disposition to weep at their destiny, than to laugh at their Folly.

But tho' We have agreed in one point, in Words, it is not yet certain that We are perfectly agreed in Sense. Fashion has introduced an indeterminate Use of the Word "Talents." Education, Wealth, Strength, Beauty, Stature, Birth, Marriage, graceful Attitudes and Motions, Gait, Air, Complexion, Physiognomy, are Talents, as well as Genius and Science and learning. Any one of these Talents, that in fact commands or influences true Votes in Society, gives to the Man who possesses it, the Character of an Aristocrat, in my Sense of the Word.

Pick up, the first 100 men you meet, and make a Republick. Every Man will have an equal Vote. But when deliberations and discussions are opened it will be found that 25, by their Talents, Virtues being equal, will be able to carry 50 Votes. Every one of these 25, is an Aristocrat, in my Sense of the Word; whether he obtains his one Vote in Addition to his own, by his Birth Fortune, Figure, Eloquence, Science, learning, Craft Cunning, or even his Character for good fellowship and a bon vivant.

What gave Sir William Wallace his amazing Aristocratical Superiority? His Strength. What gave Mrs. Clark, her Aristocratical Influence to create Generals Admirals and Bishops? her Beauty. What gave Pompadour and Du Barry the Power of making Cardinals and Popes? their Beauty. You have seen the Palaces of Pompadour and Du Barry: and I have lived for years in the Hotel de Velentinois, with Franklin who had as many Virtues as any of them. In the investigation of the meaning of the Word "Talents" I could write 630 Pages, as pertinent as John Taylors of Hazelwood. But I will select a single Example: for female Aristocrats are nearly as formidable in Society as male.

A daughter of a green Grocer, walks the Streets in London dayly with a baskett of Cabbage, Sprouts, Dandlions and Spinage on her head. She is observed by the Painters to have a beautiful Face, an elegant figure, a graceful Step and a debonair. They hire her to Sitt. She complies, and is painted by forty Artists in a Circle around her. The scientific Sir William Hamilton outbids the Painters, sends her to Schools for genteel Education and Marries her. This Lady not only causes the Tryumphs of the Nile of Copinhagen and Trafalgar, but seperates Naples from France and finally banishes the King and Queen from Sicilly. Such is the Aristocracy of the natural Talent of Beauty. Millions of Examples might be quoted from History sacred and profane, from Eve, Hannah, Deborah Susanna Abigail, Judith, Ruth, down to Hellen Madame de Maintenon and Mrs. Fitcherbert. For mercy's sake do not compell me to look to our chaste States and Territories, to find Women, one of whom lett go, would, in the Words of Holopherne's Guards "deceive the whole Earth."

The Proverbs of Theognis, like those of Solomon, are Observations on human nature, ordinary life, and civil Society, with moral reflections on the facts. I quoted him as a Witness of the Fact, that there was as much difference in the races of Men as in the breeds of Sheep; and as a sharp reprover and censurer of the sordid mercenary practice of disgracing Birth by preferring gold to it. Surely no authority can be more expressly in point to prove the existence of Inequalities, not of rights, but of moral intellectual and physical inequalities in Families, descents and Generations. If a descent from, pious, virtuous, wealthy litterary or scientific Ancestors is a letter of recommendation, or introduction in a Mans his favour, and enables him to influence only one vote in Addition to his own, he is an Aristocrat, for a democrat can have but one Vote. Aaron Burr had 100,000 Votes from the single Circumstance of his descent from President Burr and President Edwards.

Your commentary on the Proverbs of Theognis reminded me of two solemn Charactors, the one resembling John Bunyan, the other Scarron. The one John Torrey: the other Ben. Franklin. Torrey a Poet, an Enthusiast, a superstitious Bigot, once very gravely asked my Brother Cranch, "whether it would not be better for Mankind, if Children were always begotten from religious motives only"? Would not religion, in this sad case, have as little efficacy in encouraging procreation, as it has now in discouraging it? I should apprehend a decrease of population even in our Country where it increases so rapidly. In 1755 Franklin made a morning Visit, at Mrs. Yards to Sam. Adams and John. He was unusually loquacious. "Man, a rational Creature!" said Franklin. "Come, Let Us suppose a rational Man. Strip him of all his Appetites, especially of his hunger and thirst. He is in his Chamber, engaged in making Experiments, or in pursuing some Problem. He is highly entertained. At this moment a Servant Knocks, 'Sir dinner is on Table.' 'Dinner! Pox! Pough! But what have you for dinner?' Ham and Chickens. 'Ham!' 'And must I break the chain of my thoughts, to go down and knaw a morsel of a damn'd Hogs Arse?' 'Put aside your Ham.' 'I will dine tomorrow.'"

Take away Appetite and the present generation would not live a month and no future generation would ever exist. Thus the exalted dignity of human Nature would be annihilated and lost. And in my opinion, the whole loss would be of no more importance, than putting out a Candle, quenching a Torch, or crushing a Firefly, *if in this world only We have hope.*

Your distinction between natural and artificial Aristocracy does not appear to me well founded. Birth and Wealth are conferred on some Men, as imperiously by Nature, as Genius, Strength or Beauty. The Heir is honours and Riches, and power has often no more merit in procuring these Advantages, than he has in obtaining an handsome face or an elegant figure. When Aristocracies, are established by human Laws and honour Wealth and Power are made hereditary by municipal Laws and political Institutions, then I acknowledge artificial Aristocracy to commence: but this never commences, till Corruption in Elections becomes dominant and uncontroulable. But this artificial Aristocracy can never last. The ever-lasting Envys, Jealousies, Rivalries and quarrells among them, their cruel rapacities upon the poor ignorant People their followers, compell these to sett up Caesar, a Demagogue to be a Monarch and Master, pour mettre chacun a sa place ["to put each one in his place"]. Here you have the origin of all artificial Aristocracy, which is the original of all Monarchy. And both artificial Aristocracy, and Monarchy, and civil, military, political and hierarchical Despotism, have all grown out of the natural Aristocracy of "Virtues and Talents." We, to be sure, are far remote from this. Many hundred years must roll away before We shall be corrupted. Our pure, virtuous, public spirited federative Republick will last for ever, govern the Globe and introduce the perfection of Man, his perfectability being already proved by Price Priestly, Condorcet Rousseau Diderot and Godwin.

"Mischief has been done by the Senate of U.S." I have known and felt more of this mischief, than Washington, Jefferson and Madison altoge[the]r. But this has been all caused by the constitutional Power of the Senate in Executive Business, which ought to be immediately, totally and eternally abolished.

Your distinction between the aristoi and pseudo aristoi, will not help the matter. I would trust one as soon as the other with unlimited Power. The Law wisely refuses an Oath as a witness in his own cause to the Saint as well as to the Sinner.

No Romance would be more amusing, than the History of your Virginian and our new England Aristocratical Families. Yet even in Rhode Island, where there has been no Clergy, no Church, and I had almost said, no State, and some People say no religion, there has been a constant respect for certain old Families. 57 or 58 years ago, in company with Col. Counsellor, Judge, John Chandler, whom I have quoted before, a Newspaper was brought in. The old Sage asked me to look for the News from Rhode Island and see how the Elections had gone there. I read the List of Wantons, Watsons, Greens, Whipples, Malbones etc. "I expected as much" said the aged Gentleman, "for I have always been of Opinion, that in the most popular Governments, the Elections will generally go in favour of the most ancient families." To this day when any of these Tribes and We may Add Ellerys, Channings Champlins etc are pleased to fall in with the popular current, they are sure to carry all before them.

You suppose a difference of Opinion between You and me, on the Subject of Aristocracy. I can find none. I dislike and detest hereditary honours, Offices Emoluments established by Law. So do you. I am for ex[c]luding legal hereditary distinctions from the U.S. as long as possible. So are you. I only say that Mankind have not yet discovered any remedy against irresistable Corruption in Elections to Offices of great Power and Profit, but making them hereditary.

But will you say our Elections are pure? Be it so; upon the whole. But do you recollect in history, a more Corrupt Election than that of Aaron Burr to be President, or that of De Witt Clinton last year. By corruption, here I mean a sacrifice of every national Interest and honour, to private and party Objects.

I see the same Spirit in Virginia, that you and I see in Rhode Island and the rest of New England. In New York it is a struggle of Family Feuds. A fewdal Aristocracy. Pensylvania is a contest between German, Irish and old English Families. When Germans and Irish Unite, they give 30,000 majorities. There is virtually a White Rose and a Red Rose a Caesar and a Pompey in every State in this Union and Contests and dissentions will be as lasting. The Rivalry of Bourbons and Noailleses produced the French Revolution, and a similar Competition for Consideration and Influence, exists and prevails in every Village in the World.

Where will terminate the Rabies Agri ["madness for land"]? The Continent will be scattered over with Manors, much larger than Livingstons, Van Ranselaers or Phillips's. Even our Deacon Strong will have a Principality among you Southern Folk. What Inequality of Talents will be produced by these Land Jobbers?

Where tends the Mania for Banks? At my Table in Philadelphia, I once proposed to you to unite in endeavours to obtain an Amendment of the Constitution, prohibiting to the separate States the Power of creating Banks; but giving Congress Authority to establish one Bank, with a branch in each State; the whole limited to Ten Millions of dollars. Whether this Project was wise or unwise, I know not, for I had deliberated little on it then and have never thought it worth thinking much of since. But you spurned the Proposition from you with disdain.

This System of Banks begotten, hatched and brooded by Duer, Robert and Go[u—ED.]verneur Morris, Hamilton and Washington, I have always considered as a System of national Injustice. A Sacrifice of public and private Interest to a few Aristocratical Friends and Favourites. My scheme could have had no such Effect.

Verres plundered Temples and robbed a few rich Men; but he never made such ravages among private property in general, nor swindled so much out of the pocketts of the poor and the middle Class of People as these Banks have done. No people but this would have borne the Imposition so long. The People of Ireland would not bear Woods half pence. What Inequalities of Talent, have been introduced into this Country by these Aristocratical Banks!

Our Winthrops, Winslows, Bradfords, Saltonstalls, Quincys, Chandlers, Leonards Hutchinsons Olivers, Sewalls etc are precisely in the Situation of your Randolphs, Carters and Burwells, and Harrisons. Some of them unpopular for the part they took in the late revolution, but all respected for their names and connections and whenever they fall in with the popular Sentiments, are preferred, cetoris paribus to all others. When I was young, the Summum Bonum in Massachusetts, was to be worth ten thousand pounds Sterling, ride in a Chariot, be Colonel of a Regiment of Militia and hold a seat in his Majesty's Council. No Mans Imagination aspired to any thing higher beneath the Skies. But these Plumbs, Chariots, Colonelships and counsellorships are recorded and will never be forgotten. No great Accumulations of Land were made by our early Settlers. Mr. Bausoin a French Refugee, made the first great Purchases and your General Dearborne, born under a fortunate Starr is now enjoying a large Portion of the Aristocratical sweets of them.

As I have no Amanuenses but females, and there is so much about generation in this letter that I dare not ask any one of them to copy it, and I cannot copy it myself I must beg of you to return it to me, your old Friend   JOHN ADAMS

ADAMS TO JEFFERSON

Quincy July 16. 1814

DEAR SIR

I recd. this morning your favour of the 5th. and as I can never let a Sheet of your's rest I sit down immediately to acknowledge it.

Whenever Mr. Rives, of whom I have heard nothing, shall arrive he shall receive all the cordial Civilities in my power.

I am sometimes afraid that my "Machine" will not "surcease motions" soon enough; for I dread nothing so much as "dying at top" and expiring like Dean Swift "a driveller and a Show" or like Sam. Adams, a Grief and distress to his Family, a weeping helpless Object of Compassion for Years.

I am bold to say that neither you nor I, will live to see the Course which "the Wonders of the Times" will take. Many Years, and perhaps Centuries must pass, before the current will acquire a settled direction. If the Christian Religion as I understand it, or as you understand it, should maintain its Ground as

I believe it will; Yet Platonick Pythagoric, Hindoo, and cabballistical Christianity which is Catholic Christianity, and which has prevailed for 1500 Years, has recd. a mortal Wound of which the Monster must finally die; Yet so strong is his constitution that he may endure for Centuries before he expires. Government has never been much studied by Mankind. But their Attention has been drawn to it, in the latter part of the last Century and the beginning of this, more than at any former Period: and the vast Variety of experiments that have been made of Constitutions in America in France, in Holland, in Geneva in Switzerland, and even in Spain and South America, can never be forgotten. They will be studied, and their immediate and remote Effects, and final Catastrophys noted. The result in time will be Improvements. And I have no doubt that the horrors We have experienced for the last forty Years, will ultimately, terminate in the Advancement of civil and religious Liberty, and Ameliorations, in the condition of Mankind. For I am a Believer, in the probable improvability and Improvement, the Ameliorabi[li]ty and Amelioration in human Affairs: though I never could understand the Doctrine of the Perfectability of the human Mind. This has always appeared to me, like the Phylosophy or Theology of the Gentoos, viz. "that a Brachman by certain Studies for a certain time pursued, and by certain Ceremonies a certain number of times repeated, becomes Omniscient and Almighty."

Our hopes however of sudden tranquility ought not to be too sanguine. Fanaticism and Superstition will still be selfish, subtle, intriguing, and at times furious. Despotism will still struggle for domination; Monarchy will still study to rival nobility in popularity; Aristocracy will continue to envy all above it, and despize and oppress all below it; Democracy will envy all, contend with all, endeavour to pull down all; and when by chance it happens to get the Upper hand for a short time, it will be revengefull bloody and cruel. These and other Elements of Fanaticism and Anarchy will yet for a long time continue a Fermentation, which will excite alarms and require Vigilance.

Napoleon is a Military Fanatic like Achilles, Alexander, Caesar, Mahomet, Zingis Kouli, Charles 12th. etc. The Maxim and

Principle of all of them was the same "Jura negat sibi cata [i.e., nata], nihil non arrogat Armis."*

But is it strict, to call him An Usurper? Was not his Elevation to the Empire of France as legitimate and authentic a national Act as that of William 3d. or the House of Hanover to the throne of the 3 Kingdoms or as the Election of Washington to the command of our Army or to the Chair of the States.

Human Nature, in no form of it, ever could bear Prosperity. That peculiar tribe of Men, called Conquerors, more remarkably than any other have been swelled with Vanity by any Series of Victories. Napoleon won so many mighty Battles in such quick succession and for so long a time, that it was no Wonder his brain became compleatly intoxicated and his enterprises, rash, extravagant and mad.

Though France is humbled, Britain is not. Though Bona is banished a greater Tyrant and wider Usurper still domineers. John Bull is quite as unfeeling, as unprincipled, more powerful, has shed more blood, than Bona. John by his money his Intrigues and Arms, by exciting Coalition after coalition against him made him what he was, and at last, what he is. How shall the Tyrant of Tyrants, be brought low? Aye! there's the rub. I still think Bona great, at least as any of the Conquerors. "The Wonders of his rise and fall," may be seen in the Life of King Theodore, or Pascall Paoli, or Rienzi, or Dyonisius or Mazzionelli, or Jack Cade or Wat Tyler. The only difference is that between miniatures and full length pictures. The Schoolmaster at Corinth, was a greater Man, than the Tyrant of Syracuse; upon the Principle, that he who conquers himself is greater than he who takes a City. Tho' the ferocious Roar of the wounded Lion, may terrify the Hunter with the possibility of another dangerous leap; Bona was shot dead at once, by France. He could no longer roar or struggle, growl or paw, he could only gasp the grin of death. I wish that France may not still regret him. But these are Speculations in

---

* "He denies that laws were made for him; he arrogates everything to himself by force of arms." Horace, *Ars Poetica*, 122.

the Clouds. I agree with you that the Milk of human kindness in the Bourbons is safer for Mankind than the fierce Ambition of Napoleon.

The Autocrator, appears in an imposing Light. Fifty Years ago English Writers, held up terrible Consequences from "thawing out the monstrous northern Snake." If Cossacks and Tartars, and Goths and Vandalls and Hunns and Ripuarians, should get a taste of European Sweets, what may happen? Could Wellingtons or Bonapartes, resist them? The greatest trait of Sagacity, that Alexander has yet exhibited to the World is his Courtship of the United States. But whether this is a mature well digested Policy or only a transient gleam of thought, still remains to be explained and proved by time.

The "refractory Sister" [Massachusetts] will not give up the Fisheries. Not a Man here dares to hint at so base a thought.

I am very glad you have seriously read Plato: and still more rejoiced to find that your reflections upon him so perfectly harmonize with mine. Some thirty Years ago I took upon me the severe task of going through all his Works. With the help of two Latin Translations, and one English and one French Translation and comparing some of the most remarkable passages with the Greek, I laboured through the tedious toil. My disappointment was very great, my Astonishment was greater and my disgust was shocking. Two Things only did I learn from him. 1. that Franklins Ideas of exempting Husbandmen and Mariners etc. from the depredations of War were borrowed from him. 2. that Sneezing is a cure for the Hickups. Accordingly I have cured myself and all my Friends of that provoking disorder, for thirty Years with a Pinch of Snuff.

Some Parts of some of his Dialogues are entertaining, like the Writings of Rousseau: but his Laws and his Republick from which I expected most, disappointed me most. I could scarcely exclude the suspicion that he intended the latter as a bitter Satyre upon all Republican Government, as Xenophon undoubtedly designed by his Essay on Democracy, to ridicule that Species of Republick. In a late letter to the learned and ingenious Mr. Taylor of Hazelwood, I suggested to him the Project of writing a Novel, in which The Hero should be sent upon his travels through Plato's Republick, and all his Adventures, with his Observations on the principles and Opinions, the Arts and Sciences, the manners Customs and habits of the Citizens should be recorded. Nothing can be conceived more destructive of human happiness; more infallibly contrived to transform Men and Women into Brutes, Yahoos, or Dæmons than a Community of Wives and Property. Yet, in what, are the Writings of Rousseau and Helvetius wiser than those of Plato? "The Man who first fenced a Tobacco Yard, and said this is mine ought instantly to have been put to death" says Rousseau. "The Man who first pronounced the barbarous Word "Dieu," ought to have been immediately destroyed," says Diderot. In short Philosophers antient and modern appear to me as Mad as Hindoos, Mahomitans and Christians. No doubt they would all think me mad; and for any thing I know this globe may be, the bedlam, Le Bicatre [i.e., Bicêtre] of the Universe.

After all; as long as Property exists, it will accumulate in Individuals and Families. As long as Marriage exists, Knowledge, Property and Influence will accumulate in Families. Your and our equal Partition of intestate Estates, instead of preventing will in time augment the Evil, if it is one.

The French Revolutionists saw this, and were so far consistent. When they burned Pedigrees and genealogical Trees, they anni[hi]lated, as far as they could, Marriages, knowing that Marriage, among a thousand other things was an infallible Source of Aristocracy. I repeat it, so sure as the Idea and the existence of PROPERTY is admitted and established in Society, Accumulations of it will be made, the Snow ball will grow as it rolls.

Cicero was educated in the Groves of Academus where the Name and Memory of Plato, were idolized to such a degree, that if he had wholly renounced the Prejudices of his Education his Reputation would have been lessened, if not injured and ruined. In his two Volumes of Discourses on Government We may presume, that he fully examined Plato's Laws and Republick as well as Aristotles Writings on Government. But these have been carefully destroyed; not improbably, with the general Consent of Philosophers, Politicians and Priests. The Loss is as much to be regretted as that of any Production of Antiquity.

Nothing seizes the Attention, of the stareing Animal, so surely as Paradox, Riddle, Mystery, Invention, discovery, Mystery, Wonder, Temerity.

Plato and his Disciples, from the fourth Century Christians, to Rousseau and Tom Paine, have been fully sensible of this Weakness in Mankind, and have too successfully grounded upon it their Pretensions to Fame. I might indeed, have mentioned Bolingbroke, Hume, Gibbon Voltaire Turgot Helvetius Diderot, Condorcet, Buffon De La Lande and fifty others; all a little cracked! Be to their faults a little blind; to their Virtues ever kind.

Education! Oh Education! The greatest Grief of my heart, and the greatest Affliction of my Life! To my mortification I must confess, that I have never closely thought, or very deliberately reflected upon the Subject, which never occurs to me now, without producing a deep Sigh, an heavy groan and sometimes Tears. My cruel Destiny separated me from my Children, allmost continually from their Birth to their Manhood. I was compelled to leave them to the ordinary routine of reading writing and Latin School, Accademy and Colledge. John alone was much with me, and he, but occasionally. If I venture to give you any thoughts at all, they must be very crude. I have turned over Locke, Milton, Condilac Rousseau and even Miss. Edgeworth as a bird flies through the Air. The Præcepter,* I have thought a good Book. Grammar, Rhetorick, Logic, Ethicks mathematicks, cannot be neglected; Classicks, in spight of our Friend Rush,† I must think indispensable. Natural History, Mechanicks, and experimental Philosophy, Chymistry etc att least their Rudiments, can not be forgotten. Geography Ast[ron]omy,

---

*[Robert Dodsley], *The Preceptor: Containing a General Course of Education* . . . 2 vols. (5th edn.; London, 1764). Listed in *Catalogue of the John Adams Library in the Public Library of the City of Boston* (Boston, 1917).

†Benjamin Rush advocated dropping Greek and Latin from the school curriculum, except for the few students who would go to college. The vast majority ought to take practical subjects; but he did "not reject modern languages as a part of academical education." Butterfield, ed., *Letters of Rush*, I, 524, 531, 605–7.

and even History and Chronology, tho' I am myself afflicted with a kind of Pyrrhonism in the two latter, I presume cannot be omitted. Theology I would leave to Ray, Derham, Nicuenteyt and Payley, rather than to Luther Zinzindorph, Sweedenborg Westley, or Whitefield, or Thomas Aquinas or Wollebius.* Metaphysics I would leave in the Clouds with the Materialists and Spiritualists, with Leibnits, Berkley Priestley and Edwards, and I might add Hume and Reed, or if permitted to be read, it should be with Romances and Novels. What shall I say of Musick, drawing, fencing, dancing and Gymnastic Exercises? What of Languages Oriental or Occidental? of French Italian German or Russian? of Sanscrit or Chinese?

The Task you have prescribed to me of Grouping these Sciences, or Arts, under Professors, within the Views of an inlightened Economy, is far beyond my forces. Loose indeed and indigested must be all the hints, I can note. Might Gramar, Rhetoric, Logick and Ethicks be under One Professor? Might Mathematicks, Mechanicks, Natural Phylosophy, be under another? Geography and Astro[no]my under a third. Laws and Gover[n]ment, History and Chronology under a fourth. Classicks might require a fifth.

Condelacs course of Study has excellent Parts. Among many Systems of Mathematicks English, French and American, there is none preferable to Besouts Course La Harps Course of Litterature is very valuable.†

But I am ashamed to add any thing more to the broken innuendos except Assurances of the continued Friendship of

JOHN ADAMS

---

*In other words, JA would leave theology to the naturalists rather than to the revealed religionists.
†See JA to TJ, July 18, 1813.

ADAMS TO JEFFERSON

Quincy March 2. 16

DEAR SIR

I cannot be serious! I am about to write You, the most frivolous letter, you ever read.

Would you go back to your Cradle and live over again Your 70 Years? I believe You would return me a New England Answer, by asking me another question "Would you live your 80 Years over again?"

If I am prepared to give you an explicit Answer, the question involves so many considerations of Metaphysicks and Physicks, of Theology and Ethicks of Philosophy and History, of Experience and Romance, of Tragedy Comedy and Farce; that I would not give my Opinion without writing a Volume to justify it.

I have lately lived over again, in part, from 1753, when I was junior Sophister at College till 1769 when I was digging in the Mines, as a Barrister at Law, for Silver and gold, in the Town of Boston; and got as much of the shining dross for my labour as my Utmost Avarice at that time craved.

At the hazard of all the little Vision that is left me, I have read the History of that Period of 16 Years, in the six first Volumes of the Baron de Grimm. In a later Letter to you, I expressed a Wish to see an History of Quarrels and Calamities of Authors in France, like that of D'Israeli in England. I did not expect it so soon: but now I have it in a manner more masterly than I ever hoped to see it. It is not only a Narration of the incessant great Wars between the Ecclesiasticks and the Phylosophers, but of the little Skirmishes and Squabbles of Poets, Musicians, Sculptors Painters Architects Tragedians, Comediens, Opera Singers and Dancers, Chansons, Vaudevilles Epigrams, Madrigals Epitaphs, Anagrams Sonnets etc.

No man is more Sensible than I am, of the Service to Science and Letters, Humanity, Fraternity, and Liberty, that would have been rendered by the Encyclopedists and Œconomists, By Voltaire, Dalembert, Buffon Diderot, Rouseau La Lande, Frederick and Catharine, if they had possessed Common Sense. But they were all totally destitute of it. They all seemed to think that all Christendom was convinced as they were, that all Religion was "Visions Judaicques" and that their effulgent Lights had illuminated all the World. They seemed to believe, that whole Nations and Continents had been changed in their Principles Opinions Habits and Feelings by the Sovereign Grace of their Almighty Philosophy, almost as suddenly as Catholicks and Calving[is]ts believe in instantaneous Conversion. They had not considered the force of early Education on the Millions of Minds who had never heared of their Philosophy.

And what was their Phylosophy? Atheism; pure unadulterated Atheism. Diderot, D'Alembert, Frederick, De Lalande and Grimm were indubitable Atheists. The Univer[s]e was Matter only and eternal; Spirit was a Word Without a meaning; Liberty was a Word Without a Meaning. There was no Liberty in the Universe; Liberty was a Word void of Sense. Every thought Word Passion Sentiment Feeling, all Motion and Action was necessary. All Beings and Attributes were of eternal Necessity. Conscience, Morality were all nothing but Fate.

This was their Creed and this was to perfect human Nature and convert the Earth into a Paradise of Pleasure. Who, and what is this Fate? He must be a sensible Fellow. He must be a Master of Science. He must be Master of spherical Trigonometry and Great Circle sailing. He must calculate Eclipses in his head by Intuition. He must be Master of the Science of Infinitesimal "Le Science des infiniment petits." He must involve and extract all the Roots by Intuition and be familiar with all possible or imaginable Sections of the Cone. He must be a Master of Arts Mechanical and imitative. He must have more Eloquence than Demosthenes, more Wit than Swift or Volltaire, more humour than Butler or Trumbull. And what is more comfortable than all the rest, he must be good natured, for this is upon the whole a good World. There is ten times as much pleasure as pain in it.

Why then should We abhor the Word God, and fall in Love with the Word Fate? We know there exists Energy and Intellect enough to produce such a World as this, which is a sublime and beautiful one, and a very benevolent one, notwithstanding all our snarling, and a happy one, if it is not made otherwise by our own fault.

Ask a Mite, in the Center of your Mammoth Cheese,* what he thinks of the "το παν."†

I should prefer the Philosophy of Tymæus of Locris, before that of Grimm and Diderot, Frederick and D'Alembert. I should even prefer the Shast[r]a of Indostan, or the Chaldean Egyptian, Indian, Greek, Christian Mahometan Tubonic or Celtic Theology.

Timæus and Ocellus taught that three Principles were eternal, God, Matter and Form. God was good, and had Ideas. Matter was Necessity, Fate, dead, without Ideas, without form without Feeling, perverse, untractible, capable however of being cutt into Forms of Spheres Circles, Triangles, Squares cubes Cones etc. The Ideas of the good God laboured upon matter to bring it into Form: but Matter was Fate Necessity, Dulness Obstinacy and would not always conform to the Ideas of the good God who desired to make the best of all possible Worlds but Matter, Fate Necessity resisted and would not let him compleat his Idea. Hence all the Evil and disorder, Paine Misery and Imperfection of the Universe.

We all curse Robespierre and Bonaparte; but were they not both such restless vain extravagant Animals as Diderot and Voltaire? Voltaire was the greatest Litterary Character and Bona the greatest Military Character of the 18 Century. There is all the difference between them. Both equally Heros and equally Cowards.

When You asked my Opinion of a University, it would have been easy to Advise Mathematicks Experimental Phylosophy, Natural History Chemistry and Astronomy Geography and the Fine Arts, to the Exclusion of Ontology Metaphysicks and

---

* "The Mammoth Cheese," made by the citizens of Cheshire, Mass., in honor of TJ and his Republicanism, was presented to him at the executive mansion in Washington on Jan. 1, 1802, by the Reverend John Leland, Baptist elder, former citizen of Virginia. He had lent valuable support toward Virginia's ratification of the Constitution in 1788 and the passage of the Bill of Rights by Congress in 1791. L. H. Butterfield, "Elder John Leland, Jeffersonian Itinerant," American Antiquarian Society, *Proceedings*, 62, pt. 2 (Oct. 1952), 214–29.
† "The all," i.e., "totality."

Theology. But knowing the eager Impatience of the human Mind to search into Eternity and Infinity, the first Cause and last End of all Things I thought best to leave it, its Liberty to inquire till it is convinced as I have been these 50 Years that there is but one Being in the Universe, who comprehends it; and our last Resource is Resignation.

This Grimm must have been in Paris when You was there. Did You know him or hear of him?

I have this moment recd. two Volumes more, but these are from 1777 to 1782, leaving the Chaine broken from 1769 to 1777. I hope hereafter to get the two intervening Volumes. I am your old Friend   JOHN ADAMS

JEFFERSON TO ADAMS

Monticello Oct. 14. 16.

Your letter, dear Sir, of May 6. had already well explained the Uses of grief, that of Sep. 3. with equal truth adduces instances of it's abuse; and when we put into the same scale these abuses, with the afflictions of soul which even the Uses of grief cost us, we may consider it's value in the economy of the human being, as equivocal at least. Those afflictions cloud too great a portion of life to find a counterpoise in any benefits derived from it's uses. For setting aside it's paroxysms on the occasions of special bereavements, all the latter years of aged men are overshadowed with it's gloom. Whither, for instance, can you and I look without seeing the graves of those we have known? And whom can we call up, of our early companions, who has not left us to regret his loss? This indeed may be one of the salutary effects of grief; inasmuch as it prepares us to lose ourselves also without repugnance. Dr. Freeman's instances of female levity cured by grief are certainly to the point, and constitute an item of credit in the account we examine.

I was much mortified by the loss of the Doctor's visit by my absence from home. To have shewn how much I feel indebted to you for making good people known to me would have been one pleasure; and to have enjoyed that of his conversation, and the benefits of his information so favorably reported by my family, would have been another. I returned home on the third day after his departure. The loss of such visits is among the sacrifices which my divided residence costs me.

Your undertaking the 12. volumes of Dupuis is a degree of heroism to which I could not have aspired even in my younger days. I have been contented with the humble atchievement of reading the Analysis of his work by Destutt-Tracy in 200 pages 8vo [octavo]. I believe I should have ventured on his own abridgment of the works in one 8vo. volume, had it ever come to my hands; but the marrow of it in Tracy has satisfied my appetite: and, even in that, the preliminary discourse of the Analyser himself, and his Conclusion, are worth more in my eye than the body of the work. For the object of that seems to be to smother all history under the mantle of allegory. If histories so unlike as those of Hercules and Jesus, can, by a fertile imagination, and Allegorical interpretations, be brought to the same tally, no line of distinction remains between fact and fancy. As this pithy morsel will not overburthen the mail in passing and repassing between Quincy and Monticello, I send it for your perusal. Perhaps it will satisfy you, as it has me; and may save you the labor of reading 24 times it's volume. I have said to you that it was written by Tracy; and I had so entered it on the title-page, as I usually do on Anonymous works whose authors are known to me. But Tracy had requested me not to betray his anonyme, for reasons which may not yet perhaps have ceased to weigh. I am bound then to make the same reserve with you. Destutt-Tracy is, in my judgment, the ablest writer living on intellectual subjects, or the operations of the understanding. His three 8vo. volumes on Ideology,* which constitute the foundation of what he has since written, I have not entirely read; because I am not fond of reading what is merely abstract, and unapplied immediately to some useful science. Bonaparte, with his repeated derisions of Ideologists (squinting at this author) has by this time felt that true wisdom does not lie in mere practice without principle. The next work Tracy wrote was the Commentary on Montesquieu, never published in the original,

*Elements d'ideology . . . , 5 pts. (Paris, 1803–15).

because not safe; but translated and published in Philadelphia [1811], yet without the author's name. He has since permitted his name to be mentioned. Although called a Commentary, it is in truth an elementary work on the principles of government, comprised in about 300. pages 8vo. He has lately published a third work on Political economy, comprising the whole subject within about the same compass; in which all it's principles are demonstrated with the severity of Euclid, and, like him, without ever using a superfluous word. I have procured this to be translated, and have been 4 years endeavoring to get it printed. But as yet, without success.* In the mean time the author has published the original in France, which he thought unsafe while Bonaparte was in power. No printed copy, I believe, has yet reached this country. He has his 4th. and last work now in the press at Paris, closing, as he concieves, the circle of metaphysical sciences. This work which is on Ethics, I have not seen, but suspect I shall differ from it in it's foundation, altho not in it's deductions. I gather from his other works that he adopts the principle of Hobbes, that justice is founded in contract solely, and does not result from the construction of man. I believe, on the contrary, that it is instinct and innate, that the moral sense is as much a part of our constitution as that of feeling, seeing, or hearing; as a wise creator must have seen to be necessary in an animal destined to live in society: that every human mind feels pleasure in doing good to another; that the non-existence of justice is not to be inferred from the fact that the same act is deemed virtuous and right in one society, which is held vicious and wrong in another; because as the circumstances and opinions of different societies vary, so the acts which may do them right or wrong must vary also: for virtue does not consist in the act we do, but in the end it is to effect. If it is to effect the happiness of him to whom it is directed, it is virtuous, while in a society under different circumstances and opinions the same act might produce pain, and would be vicious. The essence of virtue is in doing good to others, while what is good may be one thing

---

*A Treatise on Political Economy . . . By the Count Destutt de Tracy . . . Translated from the unpublished French original (Georgetown, D.C., 1817). The original was not published until five years later (Paris, 1822).

in one society, and it's contrary in another. Yet, however we may differ as to the foundation of morals, (and as many foundations have been assumed as there are writers on the subject nearly) so correct a thinker as Tracy will give us a sound system of morals. And indeed it is remarkable that so many writers, setting out from so many different premises, yet meet, all, in the same conclusions. This looks as if they were guided, unconsciously, by the unerring hand of instinct.

Your history of the Jesuits, by what name of the Author, or other description is it to be enquired for?

What do you think of the present situation of England? Is not this the great and fatal crush of their funding system, which, like death, has been foreseen by all, but it's hour, like that of death, hidden from mortal prescience? It appears to me that all the circumstances now exist which render recovery desperate. The interest of the national debt is now equal to such a portion of the profits of all the land and the labor of the island, as not to leave enough for the subsistence of those who labor. Hence the owners of the land abandon it and retire to other countries, and the laborer has not enough of his earnings left to him to cover his back, and to fill his belly. The local insurrections, now almost general,* are of the hungry and the naked, who cannot be quieted but by food and raiment. But where are the means of feeding and clothing them? The landholder has nothing of his own to give, he is but the fiduciary of those who have lent him money: the lender is so taxed in his meat, drink, and clothing, that he has but a bare subsistence left. The landholder then, must give up his land, or the lender his debt, or they must compromise by giving up each one half. But will either consent *peaceably* to such an abandonment of property? Or must it not be settled by civil conflict? If peaceably compromised, will they agree to risk another ruin under the same government unreformed? I think not; but I would rather know what you think;

---

*They resulted from the new Corn Law of 1815, raising the import duties on grains to the point of excluding them unless prices were very high. Wage earners suffered not only from exorbitant food prices but also from the post-war depression in industry, bringing low wages and unemployment.

because you have lived with John Bull, and know, better than I do the character of his herd. I salute Mrs. Adams and yourself with every sentiment of affectionate cordiality and respect.

TH: JEFFERSON

ADAMS TO JEFFERSON

Montezillo December 21st. 1819

DEAR SIR

I must answer your great question of the 10th. in the words of Dalembert to his Correspondent, who asked him what is Matter—"Je vous avoue que Je n'en scais rien ["I confess that I know nothing about it"]."

In some part of my Life I read a great Work of a Scotchman on the Court of Augustus, in which with much learning, hard Study, and fatiguing labour, he undertook to prove that had Brutus and Cassius been conqueror, they would have restored virtue and liberty to Rome.

Mais Je n'en crois rien ["But I don't believe it"]. Have you ever found in history one single example of a Nation th[o]roughly Corrupted, that was afterwards restored to Virtue, and without Virtue, there can be no political Liberty.

If I were a Calvinest, I might pray that God by a Miracle of Divine Grace would instantaneously convert a whole Contaminated Nation from turpitude to purity, but even in this I should be inconsistent, for the fatalism of Mahometnism Material[i]sts, Atheists, Pantheists and Calvinests, and Church of England Articles, appear to me to render all prayer futile and absurd. The French and the Dutch in our day have attempted reforms and Revolutions. We know the results, and I fear the English reformers will have no better success.

Will you tell me how to prevent riches from becoming the effects of temperance and industry? Will you tell me how to prevent riches from producing luxury? Will you tell me how to prevent luxury from producing effeminacy intoxication extravagance Vice and folly? When you will answer me these questions, I hope I may venture to answer yours. Yet all these ought not to discourage us from exertion, for with my friend Jeb, I believe no effort in favour of Virtue is lost, and all good Men ought to struggle both by their Council and Example.

The Missouri question I hope will follow the other Waves under the Ship and do no harm. I know it is high treason to express a doubt of the perpetual duration of our vast American Empire, and our free Institution[s], and I say as devoutly as Father Paul, estor [i.e., esto] perpetua ["be thou everlasting"], but I am sometimes Cassandra enough to dream that another Hamilton, another Burr might rend this mighty Fabric in twain, or perhaps into a leash, and a few more choice Spirits of the same Stamp, might produce as many Nations in North America as there are in Europe.

To return to the Romans, I never could discover that they possessed much Virtue, or real Liberty there. Patricians were in general griping Usurers and Tyrannical Creditors in all ages. Pride, Strength and Courage were all the Virtues that composed their National Characters. A few of their Nobles effecting simplicity frugality and Piety, perhaps really possessing them, acquired Popularity amongst the Plebeians and extended the power and Dominions of the Republic and advanced in Glory till Riches and Luxury come in, sat like an incubus on the Republic, victamque ulcissitur orbem.*

Our Winter setts in a fortnight earlier than usual, and is pretty severe. I hope you have fairer skyes and Milder Air. Wishing your health, may last as long as your Life, and your Life as long as you desire it, I am dear Sir   Respectfuly and affectionately

JOHN ADAMS

ADAMS TO JEFFERSON

Montezillo June 11th. 1822

DEAR SIR,

Half an hour ago I received, and this moment have heard read for the third or fourth time, the best letter that ever was

---

*"And take vengeance on a conquered world."

written by an Octogenearian, dated June the 1st. It is so excellent that I am almost under an invincible temptation to commit a breach of trust by lending it to a printer. My Son, Thomas Boylston, says it would be worth five hundred dollars to any newspaper in Boston, but I dare not betray your confidence.

I have not sprained my wrist, but both my Arms and hands are so over strained that I cannot write a line. Poor Starke remembered nothing, and talked of nothing, but the Battle of Bennington. Poor Thomson is not quite so reduced. I cannot mount my Horse, but I can walk three miles over a rugged rockey Mountain, and have done it within a Month. Yet I feel when setting in my chair, as if I could not rise out of it, and when risen, as if I could not walk across the room; my sight is very dim; hearing pritty good; memory poor enough.

I answer your question, Is Death an Evil? It is not an Evil. It is a blessing to the individual, and to the world. Yet we ought not to wish for it till life becomes insupportable; we must wait the pleasure and convenience of this great teacher. Winter is as terrible to me, as to you. I am almost reduced in it, to the life of a Bear or a torpid swallow. I cannot read, but my delight is to hear others read, and I tease all my friends most unmercifully and tyrannically, against their consent. The Ass has kicked in vain, all men say the dull animal has missed the mark.

This globe is a Theatre of War, its inhabitants are all heroes. I believe the little Eels in Vinegar and the animalcule in pepper water, I believe are quarrelsome. The Bees are as warlike as Romans, Russians, Britains, or Frenchmen. Ants or Caterpilars and Canker worms are the only tribes amongst whom I have not seen battles. And Heaven itself, if we believe Hindoos, Jews, and Christians, has not always been at peace. We need not trouble ourselves about these things nor fret ourselves because of Evil doers but safely trust the ruler with his skies. Nor need we dread the approach of dotage, let it come if it must. Thomson, it seems, still delights in his four stories. And Starke remembers to the last his Bennington, and exulted in his Glory. The worst of the Evil is that our friends will suffer more by our imbecility than we ourselves.

Diplomatic flickerings, it seemes, have not yet ceased. It seems as if a Council of Ambassadors could never agree.

In wishing for your health and happiness I am very selfish, for I hope for more letters; this is worth more than five hundred dollars to me, for it has already given me, and will continue to give me more pleasure than a thousand. Mr. Jay who is about your age I am told experiences more decay than you do. I am your old friend   JOHN ADAMS

ADAMS TO JEFFERSON

Quincy 22d January 1825

DEAR SIR

Your letter of the 8th has revived me. It is true, that my hearing has been very good, but the last year it has decayed so much, that I am in a worse situation than you are; I cannot hear any of the common conversation of my family, without calling upon them to repeat in a louder tone.

The presidential election has given me less anxiety than I, myself could have imagined. The next administration will be a troublesom one to whomso-ever it falls. And our John has been too much worn to contend much longer with conflicting factions. I call him our John, because when you was at Cul de sac at Paris, he appeared to me to be almost as much your boy as mine. I have often speculated upon the consequences that would have ensued from my takeing your advice, to send him to William and Mary College in Virginia for an Education.

As to the decision of your Author, though I wish to see the Book I look upon it as a mere game at push-pin. Incision knives will never discover the distinction between matter and spirit, or whether there is any or not. That there is an active principle of power in the Universe is apparent, but in what substance that active principle of power resides, is past our investigation. The faculties of our understanding are not adiquate to penetrate the Universe. Let us do our duty which is, to do as we would be done by, and that one would think, could not be difficult, if we honestly aim at it.

Your University is a noble employment in your old Age, and your ardor for its success, does you honour, but I do not approve of your sending to Europe for Tutors, and Professors. I do believe there are sufficent scholars in America to fill your Professorships and Tutorships with more active ingenuity, and independent minds, than you can bring from Europe. The Europeans are all deeply tainted with prejudices both Ecclesiastical, and Temporal which they can never get rid of; they are all infected with Episcopal and Presbyterian Creeds, and confessions of faith, They all believe that great principle, which has produced this boundless Universe. Newtons Universe, and Hershells universe, came down to this little Ball, to be spit-upon by Jews; and untill this awful blasphemy is got rid of, there never will be any liberal science in the world.

I salute your fire side, with best affection, and best wishes for their health, wealth, and prosperity. Ever your friend

JOHN ADAMS

ADAMS TO JEFFERSON

Quincy 23rd. January 1825.

MY DEAR SIR.

We think ourselves possessed or at least we boast that we are so of Liberty of conscience on all subjects and of the right of free inquiry and private judgment, in all cases and yet how far are we from these exalted privileges in fact. There exists I believe throughout the whole Christian world a law which makes it blasphemy to deny or to doubt the divine inspiration of all the books of the old and new Testaments from Genesis to Revelations. In most countries of Europe it is punished by fire at the stake, or the rack or the wheel: in England itself it is punished by boring through the tongue with a red hot poker: in America it is not much better, even in our Massachusetts which I believe upon the whole is as temperate and moderate in religious zeal as most of the States. A law was made in the latter end of the last century repealing the cruel punishments of the former laws but substituting fine and imprisonment upon all those blasphemers upon any book of the old Testament or new. Now what free inquiry when a writer must surely encounter the risk of fine or imprisonment for adducing any argument for investigation into the divine authority of those books? Who would run the risk of translating Volney's Recherches Nouvelles? who would run the risk of translating Dupuis? But I cannot enlarge upon this subject, though I have it much at heart. I think such laws a great embarassment, great obstructions to the improvement of the human mind. Books that cannot bear examination certainly ought not to be established as divine inspiration by penal laws. It is true few persons appear desirous to put such laws in execution and it is also true that some few persons are hardy enough to venture to depart from them; but as long as they continue in force as laws the human mind must make an awkward and clumsy progress in its investigations. I wish they were repealed. The substance and essence of Christianity as I understand it is eternal and unchangeable and will bear examination forever but it has been mixed with extraneous ingredients, which I think will not bear examination and they ought to be separated. Adieu   JOHN ADAMS

JEFFERSON TO ADAMS

Monticello Feb. 15. 25. *

DEAR SIR

The people of Europe seem still to think that America is a mere garden plat, and that whatever is sent to one place is at home as to every other. The volume I forward you by this mail was found on Majr. Cartwright's death, to have in his own handwriting an address for you altho' mistaking your Christian name. His friends having occ[asio]n to write to me on another subject, and supposing we were our next door n[eigh]bors sent this vol. to N.Y. under my address, whence it has travelled post to this place, and must now travel back again and thence to the point to which it o[ugh]t to have gone at first.

*This letter is a draft in TJ's hand, in Jefferson Papers, Lib. Cong. See JA to TJ. April 19, 1825.

I sincerely congratulate you on the high gratific[atio]n which the issue of the late election must have afforded you. It must excite ineffable feelings in the breast of a father to have lived to see a son to whose educ[atio]n and happiness his life has been devoted so eminently distinguished by the voice of his country. Nor do I see any reason to suppose the next adm[inistratio]n will be so difficult as in your favor of Jan. 22. you seemed to expect. So deeply are the principles of order, and of obedience to law impressed on the minds of our citizens generally that I am persuaded there will be as immediate an acquiescence in the will of the majority as if Mr. Adams had been the choice of every man. The scriblers in newspapers may for a while express their disapp[oint]m[en]t in angry squibs; but these will evaporate without influence[in]g the public functionaries, nor will they prevent their harmonising with their associates in the transaction of public affairs. Nights of rest to you and days of tranquility are the wishes I tender you with my affect[iona]te respects   TH: J.

ADAMS TO JEFFERSON

Quincy 25th. Feby. 1825

DEAR SIR

Every line from you exhilarates my spirits and gives me a glow of pleasure, but your kind congratulations are a solid comfort to my heart. The good-natured and good-humoured acquiescence of the friends of all the candidates gives me a comfortable hope that your prediction may be fulfilled, that the ensuing administration will not be so difficult as in a former letter I had apprehended.

Here we have lost Eustace in whom the people appeared to be better united than under any former Governor, but we have a prospect now of a successor in Lincoln, in whom the people promise to be still more united; so that it is probable that this State will not be so troublesome to the National administration as it was some time ago.

I had not heard of the death of Major Cartwright. That gentleman has been an anxious and laborious writer against boroughs and borough-mongers for more than fifty years. He appears to have had an ardent love for liberty but he never understood the system necessary to secure it—One of those ardent spirits whose violent principles defeated all their benevolent purposes, of whom Horne Took was the most eminent and the great Greek scholar another.*

I look back with rapture to those golden days when Virginia and Massachusetts lived and acted together like a band of brothers and I hope it will not be long before they may say redeunt saturnia regna.† . . .   JOHN ADAMS

---

*Probably Richard Bentley (1662–1742), master of Trinity College, Cambridge, who was influential in the restoration of classical learning in Great Britain. *Dict. Nat. Biog.*, IV, 306–14.
†"The golden age is returning."

Editor's Notes

Footnotes within the text appeared in the original sources; the notes below have been added for the Penguin edition. Bracketed material within the text appeared in the original sources, with the exception of most bracketed dates and all bracketed insertions marked "—ED.," which have been added for the Penguin edition.

CHAPTER 1:
DIARY AND AUTOBIOGRAPHY

1. The following excerpts are drawn from *The Life and Works of John Adams,* ed. Charles Francis Adams (Boston: Little, Brown, 1850–56), 10 vols.
2. Jonathan Mayhew, a liberal theologian, who supported the cause of American independence.
3. Arminianism emphasized free will against Calvinist determinism and the teachings of Jesus but not the divinity of Christ.
4. Abigail.
5. "Finistere, End of the Earth, is the most western cape [in Brittany], not only in France and Spain, but even of Europe; the Ancients who knew nothing beyond it, gave it its name, which signified the Extremity of the Earth, or the end of the world. There is a City by the same name."
6. As one sees the waves, raised by the storm,
   Founder on a vessel which defies their rage.
   The wind shivers with its fury in the sails,
   The sea, whitened by the whitecaps, and the far-off groaning air.
   The troubled sailor, whose skill fails him,
   Believes he sees in every wave the death which encircles him.

7. "You have eaten enough, you have sported enough, and have drunk enough; it is time for you to depart" (Horace, *Epistles*, 2.2.214–215).

8. "Alas! All the conductors of Mr. Franklin's had not prevented the lightning from falling on Mademoiselle de Passy."

9. "How charming it was to see Solon and Sophocles embrace."

10. Edmund Burke, the British political philosopher.

11. The lines contain a pun on the name *Ruiter* and the words *terruit* (he terrified) and *ruit* (he rushed or fell to ruin).

> He terrified the Spanish, Ruiter, he who terrified the English
> Rushed three times against the Gauls/French, and he himself,
>   terrified, fell into ruin.

12.   When you are in Rome, live according to the Roman manner;
        When you are elsewhere, live as they do there. (Proverbial.)

13. "You are a celebrated man. Your name is well known here." . . . "Oh no, sir, it is your modesty."

14. "I congratulate you on your success." . . . "Sir, my faithful friend, you have succeeded marvelously well. You have made your independence gain recognition; you have made a treaty; and you have procured money. Here is a perfect success." . . . "You have done marvels in Holland: you defied the governor-general and the English party; you contributed well to the movement, you stirred all the world." . . . "Sir, you are the Washington of the negotiation."

CHAPTER 2:
CORRESPONDENCE OF JOHN AND ABIGAIL ADAMS

1. These excerpts are drawn from *The Book of Abigail and John: Selected Letters of the Adams Family, 1762–1784,* ed. L. H. Butterfield, Marc Friedlaender, and Mary-Jo Kline (Cambridge: Harvard University Press, 1975).

2. December.

3. Passy, a modest neighborhood on the outskirts of Paris.

4. Esther Field, a servant from Braintree.

CHAPTER 3:
EARLIEST WRITINGS

1. The following excerpts are drawn from *The Life and Works of John Adams.*

2. "Indefatigable, wrathful, inexorable, keen, let him deny that laws were made for him, let him claim everything by arms" (Horace, *Ars Poetica*, 121–22).
3. "You show strength without thought; I am mindful of the future. You are able to fight: you display only the body, I the spirit. Minds are stronger than hands—all force is in them."

CHAPTER 4:
A DISSERTATION ON CANON AND FEUDAL LAW

1. The following excerpts are drawn from *The Life and Works of John Adams*.
2. Archbishop John Tillotson, a well-known English theologian.

CHAPTER 5:
"THOUGHTS ON GOVERNMENT"

1. This essay is taken from *The Life and Works of John Adams*.

CHAPTER 6:
NOVANGLUS

1. This excerpt is drawn from *The Life and Works of John Adams*.
2. "Why do you think you have avoided those terrified men whom the mind, aware of awful deeds, has power over, and whom concealed guilt cuts to pieces with a silent whip, after the spirit has been shaken by its torturer? However, the [truly] violent punishment—far more terrible than this—is the one that graven Caeditius or Rhadamanthus met with, to carry his head on his chest, night and day."
3. "He shall not leave the kingdom."

CHAPTER 7:
A DEFENCE OF THE CONSTITUTIONS OF THE UNITED STATES OF AMERICA

1. These excerpts are drawn from *The Life and Works of John Adams*.

CHAPTER 8:
DISCOURSES ON DAVILA

1. The following excerpts are drawn from *The Life and Works of John Adams*.
2. "Fortunate, he whom another's trials make cautious."
3. "It is peculiar to the human mind that examples educate no one; the follies of the fathers are lost to their children; each generation must cope on its own."
4. "Oh, the fury to distinguish yourself that you can do nothing about."
5. "Those whose worth is limited by scant means at home do not easily rise up."
6. "Codrus has nothing: who will deny it? And still he, unlucky, lost this nothing, which was his all. The last trouble in his heap of troubles is this: Though he is naked and begging in vain, no one will help him with food, or with hospitality and a roof. [However], if the grand house of Asturius falls, the matrons shudder, and the great men dress in mourning, and the Praetor postpones the court proceedings. Then we weep at the city's misfortunes, then we disdain its flames. Still the house burns, and already someone arrives with a gift of marble or building materials. Another offers nude and shining statues, a third a distinguished piece of Euphranor's or Polycletus's, this other, old ornaments of Asian gods. Yet others will offer books and bookcases and Minerva in the midst, or an abundance of silver. So Persicus, happiest of childless men, replaces his belongings with better and more plentiful goods, and with good reason is suspected to have set his own house on fire."
7. "We do not believe in Christianity, but believe in all possible follies."

CHAPTER 9:
CORRESPONDENCE WITH ROGER SHERMAN
AND JOHN TAYLOR

1. These excerpts are drawn from *The Life and Works of John Adams*.
2. "The president of the United States possesses almost royal prerogatives, which he has no occasion to use. And until the present the laws he can use are very circumscribed. The laws permit him to be strong; the circumstances keep him weak." This observation by Tocqueville was noted by Charles Francis Adams, who edited the collected works of his grandfather.

3. "Montesquieu was considered among the most illustrious men of the eighteenth century, and while he was not persecuted, he was harassed for his *Persian Letters.*"

4. "Born in a distinguished rank," "born in a renowned rank," "born in a very renowned rank," "born in a very distinguished rank" . . . "born in a mean rank," "born in a lowly rank."

5. "There are those who, imbued with no fear, look upon this sun, and the stars, and the seasons moving on a fixed times" (Horace, *Epistles,* 1.6.3–5).

CHAPTER 10:
CORRESPONDENCE OF JOHN AND ABIGAIL ADAMS WITH THOMAS JEFFERSON

1. These excerpts are drawn from *The Adams-Jefferson Letters: The Complete Correspondence Between Thomas Jefferson and Abigail and John Adams,* ed. Lester J. Cappon (1959; Chapel Hill: University of North Carolina Press, 1988).

CLICK ON A CLASSIC
www.penguinclassics.com

The world's greatest literature at your fingertips

Constantly updated information on more than a thousand titles, from Icelandic sagas to ancient Indian epics, Russian drama to Italian romance, American greats to African masterpieces

•

The latest news on recent additions to the list, updated editions, and specially commissioned translations

•

Original essays by leading writers

•

A wealth of background material, including biographies of every classic author from Aristotle to Zamyatin, plot synopses, readers' and teachers' guides, useful web links

•

Online desk and examination copy assistance for academics

•

Trivia quizzes, competitions, giveaways, news on forthcoming screen adaptations

The Portable Enlightenment Reader
Edited by Isaac Kramnick
This volume brings together the era's classic works from great thinkers such as Kant, Diderot, Voltaire, Newton, Rousseau, Locke, Franklin, Jefferson, and Paine, among others.

ISBN 0-14-024566-9

The Portable Thomas Jefferson
Thomas Jefferson
Edited by Merrill D. Peterson
This volume presents a broad view of Jefferson in the fullness of his thought and imagination, including his famous essays, notes, state papers and addresses, including the Declaration of Independence, and letters to George Washington, James Madison, John Adams, and others.

ISBN 0-14-015090-3

The Portable Abraham Lincoln
Abraham Lincoln
Edited by Andrew Delbanco
The essential Lincoln, including all the great public speeches, along with less familiar letters and memoranda that chart Lincoln's political career. With an indispensable introduction, headnotes, and a chronology of Lincoln's life.

ISBN 0-14-017031-6

The Federalist Papers
James Madison, Alexander Hamilton, and John Jay
Edited with an Introduction by Isaac Kramnick
The definitive exposition of the American Constitution, *The Federalist Papers* were considered by Thomas Jefferson to be the best commentary on the principle of government ever written. This collection of all eighty-five papers contains the complete first-edition text of the collected essays published from 1787 to 1788 in New York by J. A. McLean. Includes the U.S. Constitution.

ISBN 0-14-044495-5

FOR THE BEST IN PAPERBACKS, LOOK FOR THE

In every corner of the world, on every subject under the sun, Penguin represents quality and variety—the very best in publishing today.

For complete information about books available from Penguin—including Penguin Classics, Penguin Compass, and Puffins—and how to order them, write to us at the appropriate address below. Please note that for copyright reasons the selection of books varies from country to country.

In the United States: Please write to *Penguin Group (USA), P.O. Box 12289 Dept. B, Newark, New Jersey 07101-5289* or call 1-800-788-6262.

In the United Kingdom: Please write to *Dept. EP, Penguin Books Ltd, Bath Road, Harmondsworth, West Drayton, Middlesex UB7 0DA.*

In Canada: Please write to *Penguin Books Canada Ltd, 10 Alcorn Avenue, Suite 300, Toronto, Ontario M4V 3B2.*

In Australia: Please write to *Penguin Books Australia Ltd, P.O. Box 257, Ringwood, Victoria 3134.*

In New Zealand: Please write to *Penguin Books (NZ) Ltd, Private Bag 102902, North Shore Mail Centre, Auckland 10.*

In India: Please write to *Penguin Books India Pvt Ltd, 11 Panchsheel Shopping Centre, Panchsheel Park, New Delhi 110 017.*

In the Netherlands: Please write to *Penguin Books Netherlands bv, Postbus 3507, NL-1001 AH Amsterdam.*

In Germany: Please write to *Penguin Books Deutschland GmbH, Metzlerstrasse 26, 60594 Frankfurt am Main.*

In Spain: Please write to *Penguin Books S. A., Bravo Murillo 19, 1° B, 28015 Madrid.*

In Italy: Please write to *Penguin Italia s.r.l., Via Benedetto Croce 2, 20094 Corsico, Milano.*

In France: Please write to *Penguin France, Le Carré Wilson, 62 rue Benjamin Baillaud, 31500 Toulouse.*

In Japan: Please write to *Penguin Books Japan Ltd, Kaneko Building, 2-3-25 Koraku, Bunkyo-Ku, Tokyo 112.*

In South Africa: Please write to *Penguin Books South Africa (Pty) Ltd, Private Bag X14, Parkview, 2122 Johannesburg.*